P9-COO-804

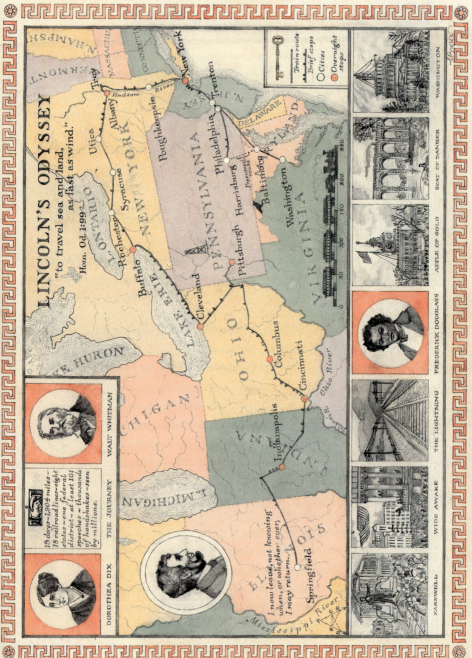

LINCOLN'S ODYSSEY

"to travel sea and land, as fast as wind."

Hom. Od. 1:992

Key
Train route
Brief stops
○ Cities
● Overnight stops

"I now leave, not knowing when, or whether ever, I may return."

WALT WHITMAN — THE JOURNEY

19 days – 1,904 miles – 18 railroad lines – eight states – one federal district – at least 101 speeches – thousands of handshakes – seen by millions.

DOROTHEA DIX

WASHINGTON — SEAT OF DANGER — APPLE OF GOLD — FREDERICK DOUGLASS — THE LIGHTNING — WIDE AWAKE — FAREWELL

ADDITIONAL PRAISE FOR
LINCOLN ON THE VERGE

"Widmer portrays a politician who has a populist touch but exercises this power responsibly, achieving what Frederick Douglass later called 'wonderful success in organizing the loyal American people for the tremendous conflict before them.'"

—*The New Yorker*

"An impressively vivid and intimate portrait of Abraham Lincoln on his historic 1861 train journey from Illinois to Washington, D.C. With a deft blend of textured storytelling and fresh research Widmer recounts the widespread uncertainty and fear that consumed the nation on the eve of the Civil War. Highly recommended!"

—**Douglas Brinkley, CNN Presidential Historian**

"Lincoln's journey by train from Springfield to Washington in February 1861 was full of drama and tension caused by a nation breaking in two. Ted Widmer projects the reader back in time to that fateful journey."

—**James M. McPherson, Pulitzer Prize–winning author of**
Battle Cry of Freedom: The Civil War Era.

"A positively elegiac account of the most consequential pre-inauguration journey—and pre-presidential public relations offensive—in American history. Ted Widmer has successfully undertaken a great task of his own in crafting a stirring account of the politically fraught, emotionally draining, and physically dangerous voyage that brought Illinois' favorite son to the nation's capital in time, and shape, to meet his destiny."

—**Harold Holzer, winner of the Gilder Lehrman Lincoln Prize and**
author of *Lincoln and the Power of the Press*

"With clarity of purpose, command of subject, coherence of narrative and creativity of prose, Widmer paints an extensively researched, richly detailed landscape that depicts the geographic and human aspects of Lincoln's journey into Washington, into history and into the heart of a grateful nation."

—*The Free Lance-Star*

THIRTEEN

DAYS

TO

WASHINGTON

LINCOLN

ON THE

VERGE

TED WIDMER

SIMON & SCHUSTER PAPERBACKS

NEW YORK LONDON TORONTO SYDNEY NEW DELHI

For FRW

γλυκερὸν φάος

Simon & Schuster Paperbacks
An Imprint of Simon & Schuster, Inc.
1230 Avenue of the Americas
New York, NY 10020

First Simon & Schuster trade paperback edition December 2020

SIMON & SCHUSTER PAPERBACKS and colophon are
registered trademarks of Simon & Schuster, Inc.

For information about special discounts for bulk purchases, please contact Simon &
Schuster Special Sales at 1-866-506-1949 or business@simonandschuster.com.

The Simon & Schuster Speakers Bureau can bring authors to your live event. For
more information or to book an event, contact the Simon & Schuster Speakers
Bureau at 1-866-248-3049 or visit our website at www.simonspeakers.com.

Interior design by Ruth Lee-Mui

Endpapers by Connie Brown of Redstone Studios

Manufactured in the United States of America

5   7   9   10   8   6   4

Library of Congress Cataloging-in-Publication Data is available.

ISBN 978-1-4767-3943-4
ISBN 978-1-4767-3944-1 (pbk)
ISBN 978-1-4767-3945-8 (ebook)

"I have reached this city of Washington under circumstances considerably differing from those under which any other man has ever reached it."

—Abraham Lincoln, Response to a Serenade, February 28, 1861

Invitation to join President-Elect Abraham Lincoln aboard the *Presidential Special*[1]

CONTENTS

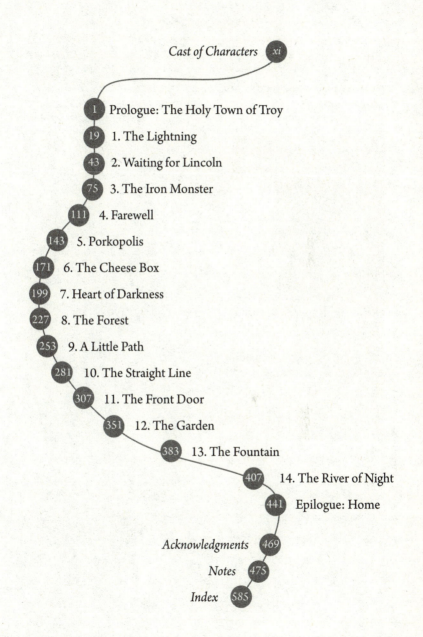

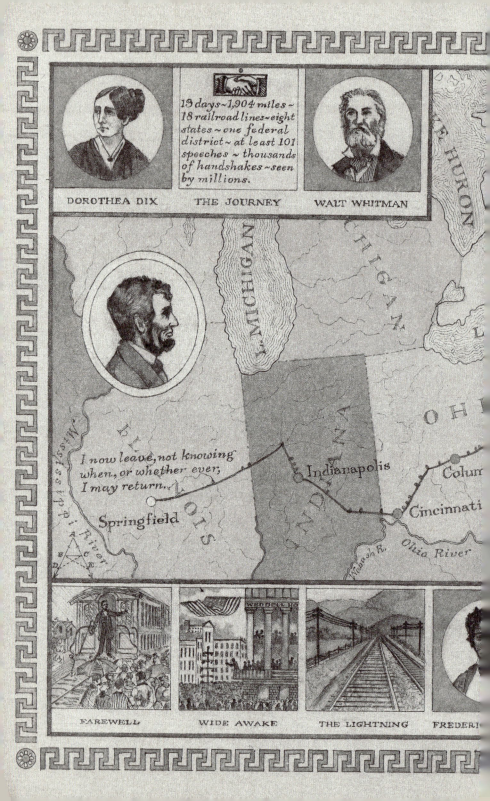

DOROTHEA DIX

THE JOURNEY

13 days ~ 1,904 miles ~ 18 railroad lines ~ eight states ~ one federal district ~ at least 101 speeches ~ thousands of handshakes ~ seen by millions.

WALT WHITMAN

L. HURON

L. MICHIGAN

MICHIGAN

OHIO

Mississippi River

ILLINOIS

INDIANA

I now leave, not knowing when, or whether ever, I may return.

Springfield

Indianapolis

Colum

Cincinnati

Wabash R.

Ohio River

FAREWELL

WIDE AWAKE

THE LIGHTNING

FREDERI

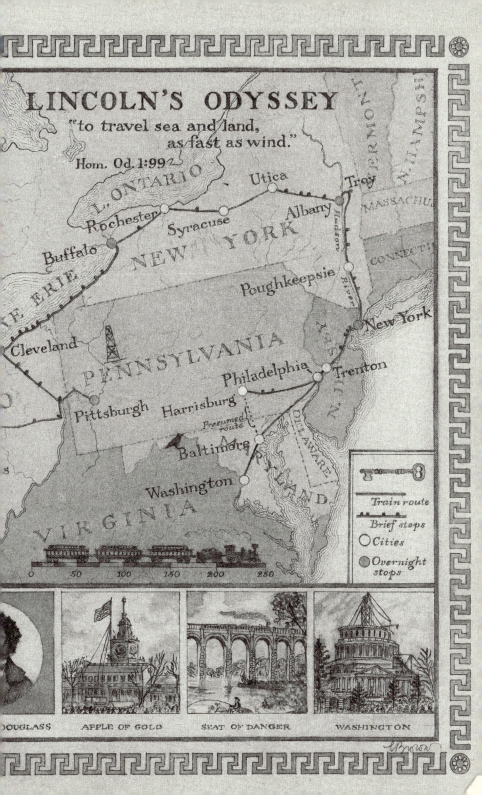

LINCOLN'S ODYSSEY

*"to travel sea and land,
as fast as wind."*

Hom. Od. 1:99

L. ONTARIO

Rochester
Syracuse
Utica
Troy
Albany

NEW YORK

VERMONT
N. HMPSH
MASSACHU
CONNECTI

Buffalo

LAKE ERIE

Poughkeepsie

Hudson River

New York

Cleveland

PENNSYLVANIA

N.JERSEY

Pittsburgh

Philadelphia
Trenton

Harrisburg

Presumed route

Baltimore

DELAWARE

Washington

MARYLAND

VIRGINIA

Key

Train route
Brief stops
○ Cities
● Overnight stops

0   50   100   150   200   250

DOUGLASS | APPLE OF GOLD | SEAT OF DANGER | WASHINGTON

CAST OF CHARACTERS

HENRY ADAMS: historian and observer, son of Representative Charles F. Adams (Sr.) of Massachusetts

JOHN WILKES BOOTH: successful actor with Southern sympathies

JAMES BUCHANAN: fifteenth president of the United States

ANDREW CARNEGIE: assistant to Thomas Scott of the Pennsylvania Railroad

LUCIUS CHITTENDEN: Vermont delegate to Washington Peace Conference

JEFFERSON DAVIS: president-elect of the Confederate States of America

DOROTHEA DIX: mental-health advocate with extensive political connections in the South

FREDERICK DOUGLASS: antislavery advocate, author

ELMER ELLSWORTH: organizer of Zouave militias

SAMUEL FELTON: president of the Philadelphia, Wilmington and Baltimore Railroad

CYPRIANO FERRANDINI: Corsican immigrant and barber in Baltimore

MILLARD FILLMORE: thirteenth president of the United States

HANNIBAL HAMLIN: vice president-elect of the United States

JOHN HAY: assistant secretary to Abraham Lincoln

GEORGE W. HAZZARD: captain in the United States Army

JOSEPH HOWARD, JR.: New York Times correspondent

WILLIAM DEAN HOWELLS: Ohio writer

DAVID HUNTER: major in the United States Army

WILLIAM JOHNSON: African-American barber and valet to Abraham Lincoln

NORMAN JUDD: Chicago-based friend to Lincoln, liaison to detectives

WARD HILL LAMON: friend and bodyguard to Abraham Lincoln

MARY ANN CUSTIS LEE: great-granddaughter of Martha Washington, and wife of Robert E. Lee

ROBERT E. LEE: lieutenant colonel in the United States Army

ABRAHAM LINCOLN: president-elect of the United States

MARY TODD LINCOLN: wife of Abraham Lincoln

ROBERT TODD LINCOLN: eldest son of Abraham Lincoln

TAD LINCOLN: son of Abraham Lincoln

WILLIE LINCOLN: son of Abraham Lincoln

JOHN NICOLAY: secretary to Abraham Lincoln

ALLAN PINKERTON: detective

JOHN POPE: captain in the United States Army

THOMAS SCOTT: Pennsylvania Railroad official

WINFIELD SCOTT: commanding general of the United States Army

FREDERICK SEWARD: son of and assistant to William Henry Seward

WILLIAM HENRY SEWARD: New York senator and future secretary of state

ALEXANDER STEPHENS: vice president-elect of the Confederate States of America

CHARLES P. STONE: aide to Winfield Scott and colonel in the United States Army

GEORGE TEMPLETON STRONG: New York lawyer and diarist

JOHN TYLER: tenth president of the United States

EDWIN SUMNER: colonel in the United States Army

HENRY VILLARD: German immigrant, *New York Herald* correspondent

KATE WARNE: detective

ELIHU WASHBURNE: friend to Abraham Lincoln, Illinois member of the House of Representatives

THURLOW WEED: New York political boss

WALT WHITMAN: itinerant carpenter and poet from Brooklyn

FERNANDO WOOD: Mayor of New York City

WILLIAM WOOD: trip organizer

LINCOLN
ON THE
VERGE

Troy, Kansas

THE HOLY TOWN
OF TROY

Tell me about a complicated man.
Muse, tell me how he wandered and was lost
when he had wrecked the holy town of Troy,
and where he went, and who he met, the pain
he suffered in the storms at sea, and how
he worked to save his life and bring his men
back home. . . .
Tell the old story for our modern times.
Find the beginning.

—Homer, *The Odyssey*, book 1, lines 1–11[1]

The wind whips across the prairie in late November, hinting at the wrath of winter to come. In 1859 a German immigrant, Henry Villard, was fighting the cold as he drove his wagon east from Colorado, where he had been living among gold prospectors. Villard had a long way to go—650 miles in all—snaking along the Platte River, through Nebraska and Kansas, as he made his way back toward the Missouri River, and civilization. He survived by constantly gathering buffalo chips, or dried dung, which he burned to stay warm and cook his meals. At night, he slept outdoors, covered with buffalo pelts. "The prairie traveler is not particular about toilette," noted an English traveler after meeting a rough specimen in the same parts, who unsheathed a long knife he called his "Arkansas toothpick."[2] One night it snowed eighteen inches, but Villard kept going, desperate to reach his destination before more storms came through.

Thirty miles west of Saint Joseph, Missouri, Villard saw a distant speck on the immense horizon, growing larger, kicking up dust. As it came closer, the speck grew into a horse and buggy, with two occupants. Surprisingly, Villard recognized one of the passengers. He had been in Illinois a year earlier, during the excitement of the Lincoln-Douglas debates, and as the carriage approached, he began to make out the ungainly form of Abraham Lincoln himself, four hundred miles west of where he normally could be found.[3]

Lincoln laughed when he realized that Villard had transformed himself into a full-fledged pioneer. A year earlier, Lincoln had known him as a clean-shaven reporter for the German-American press. Now he was almost unrecognizable beneath a luxuriant beard and all those buffalo pelts. For his part, Villard was amazed to encounter Lincoln, still smooth-faced, with nothing to protect him from the prairie wind except a short overcoat and no covering for his long legs. To make matters worse, he was heading directly into the rough weather Villard had put behind him.

It was a frigid morning, and the wind blew in from the Northwest—"cuttingly," as Villard put it. Not far away, in Leavenworth, the Missouri River was beginning to freeze as the thermometer plunged toward zero. Lincoln was already shivering in his exposed buggy, with no roof and a great distance still to go. But he was determined to continue, for he had a speaking engagement, and there could be no rest in the struggle to prevent the spread of slavery into these wide-open spaces. Villard offered one of his buffalo robes, which Lincoln accepted gratefully.

After a short chat, they separated, two ships passing in opposite directions. Travelers often compared the prairie to a vast inland ocean—Herman Melville thought it looked like "the bed of a dried-up sea," with its undulating grassy billows resembling waves.[4] In his prairie schooner, Lincoln kept sailing into the cold.

A different account picks up the thread soon after. A young writer, Albert Richardson, was crossing the prairie along a different vector that same day. His destination was a small cluster of wooden structures ambitiously called Troy. The tiny Kansas settlement (population 131) aspired to be a city someday, but "save a shabby frame courthouse, a tavern, and a few shanties, its urban glories were visible only to the eye of faith." In the piercing cold, it looked even worse than usual. Richardson wrote, "The sweeping prairie wind rocked the crazy buildings, and cut the faces of travelers like a knife."

The English traveler, Richard Burton, was even harsher. He recorded, "Passing through a few wretched shanties called Troy," the very name of which was an "insult to the memory" of the ancient citadel described by Homer. Burton had been through the desert wastes of the Arabian Peninsula and the jungles of Africa, but he considered these prairie landscapes among the most desolate he had ever seen, and likened them to "the ends of the earth."[5]

Troy was Lincoln's destination as well. He had been invited to talk about slavery, in the heart of the Kansas Territory that had seen so much bloodletting. The small town with the crazy buildings was not much more than a smudge on the map. But it was on the front lines of an argument that had raged across Kansas for five years, pitting slavery's critics and defenders against one another. In small towns like this, from door to door, the great question of America's future was being settled. Would this country be free, in keeping with the Declaration of Independence and its hymn to human rights? Or would it would be a permanent slave society, with no rights of any kind for the wrong sort of humans?

As Lincoln had noted a year earlier, it could not be both at the same time. Did all people have rights, as the Declaration claimed? Or was that an elaborate deception—a bit of pretty writing designed to obscure a harsher reality, like the Corinthian columns that they thrust in front of their courthouses and penitentiaries?

Was democracy a sham? Did the words mean anything at all?

It was hard to draw confidence from Washington, D.C., where there were plenty of words, most of which meant nothing. As the year was ending, the president of the United States, James Buchanan, was finishing his third annual message to Congress. It was a remarkable document, full of the contortions that were necessary to believe that America stood proudly for both slavery and freedom. Buchanan praised a recent Supreme Court decision, in the case of Dred Scott, a slave who argued that he had become free after years of living in Northern states. The Court denied his petition, and went on to rule that African-Americans held no rights of any kind. The president tried to claim this as a humane act, one that would enshrine slavery as a national institution, radiating "kindness and humanity."

Then Buchanan tacked in the opposite direction and piously celebrated the end of the African slave trade, an atrocity could never be permitted in "a Christian and moral nation." Except that it was permitted *all the time*. The slave trade had *never* been suppressed, despite its apparent end five decades earlier. Slavers routinely plied the waters off Africa, flaunting the American flag, as if they, and not their critics, were carrying out the true purpose of the nation.

As Buchanan was writing, a huge ship, the *Clotilda*, was in Mobile, Alabama, being fitted out for a journey to capture slaves from Africa. Its owner had wagered that he could easily avoid any punishment from a federal government too weak to notice and too corrupt to care. It would set sail on March 4, 1860, exactly a year before the next president would be inaugurated.[6]

For all of these reasons, Lincoln had shivered his way across the prairie. He understood that these insults would simply *never* end unless Americans restored meaning to the words and began the long journey of reclaiming their republic.

As he came into Troy, Lincoln may have found the hamlet underwhelming. If so, the townsfolk were all too happy to say the same thing about him. When he arrived, they noticed that the awkward visitor was turning "blue with cold," despite the buffalo robes.

That night, forty people came out to hear him speak inside the barewalled courthouse. It was not a large crowd, but out here, every vote counted. Without knowing his political future—he had not held office for more than a decade—Lincoln was pulled toward these places, not yet defined, where he could argue for a better America. He had been reading the words of the founders, looking for references to slavery, like a doctor seeking to isolate a bacillus. Here on the front lines, he wanted to share what he knew.[7]

Albert Richardson had vaguely heard of Lincoln and was curious to hear him. As he began his remarks, Richardson was surprised that Lincoln had ever run for *anything*. Even before the first words came out, his physical awkwardness was evident, as he struggled to appear dignified at the podium. Audiences expecting immaculately clad politicians were invariably disappointed when Lincoln arrived in his rumpled suit, and his strange body language made things worse. He seemed shy at first, as if he would rather be anywhere else. He spoke with few gestures and none of the operatic drama that audiences expected from their orators—the verbal crescendos, the quavering accusations, the pointed fingers and arched eyebrows. He simply conversed with them, like a farmer from the next county, sprinkling his remarks with pungent, rustic stories.

If the Illinoisans considered this a great man, Richardson wondered, their ideas must be "very peculiar." But slowly Lincoln drew him in, then overwhelmed him with the clarity of his logic, the depth of his research, and the growing force of his argument against slavery. Richardson said that it felt like watching a blacksmith forge a chain, link by link. It was irresistible.

Lincoln spoke to the small gathering for an hour and three-quarters. When it was over, the audience turned to a prominent local slave owner, from Kentucky, for his rebuttal. He stood up and said that he could never agree with the doctrines that had just been argued, but that it was "the most able—the most logical—speech I ever listened to."[8]

That same evening, John Brown was enjoying his last few hours on earth. The antislavery crusader had been captured after his raid on Harper's Ferry, and condemned to death. The next morning, he was executed. Before the sentence was carried out, he wrote, "I, John Brown, am now quite certain that the crimes of this guilty land will never be purged away but with blood."[9] Among the people watching him die were Robert E. Lee, Stonewall Jackson, and John Wilkes Booth.[10]

The next morning, Lincoln was asked to speak again, in Leavenworth. There he made a startling prediction, speaking aloud to the South. "If constitutionally we elect a president," he began, and in response, "you undertake to destroy the Union," then "it will be our duty to deal with you as old John Brown has been dealt with."[11] It was as if he could already see the future. Somehow he knew that the South would secede if it lost its stranglehold on the presidency. It would pull out of the Union, not because it had been invaded, or coerced, but simply because it did not like the result of an election.

In fact, that very morning, a remarkable blueprint of the future was offered to the reading public. As Lincoln was turning blue on the prairie, an article in the *New York Herald* described a secret plan already hatching. With grim precision, it explained how the South's political masters were preparing for the possibility that a "black Republican" would win the upcoming presidential election. If that happened, they would be ready, on short notice, to declare an "independent Southern confederacy." One by one, the Southern states would secede, while taking care to leave a quorum of Southern politicians behind in Washington—just enough to immobilize the federal government. During the long four-month interregnum between the election and the inauguration, they would organize a new country around a resurgent Slave Power. A civil war would soon follow—the article used the phrase—which the South would win.[12]

The South *always* won. Southerners had won most of the presidential elections, they controlled the lion's share of the patronage, and they dominated the Southern city where the government resided. They were adroit political insiders, skilled at getting their way. To start a new country in 1860 was almost an afterthought for these cynical operatives; they could do it simply for "the fun of the thing," as a Washington newspaper put it, after reviewing news of the secret plan.

Southerners had threatened to walk out before, and the author of the article wondered if this was another example of the "Southern scarecrow"—more bluster than reality. But scarecrows could be plenty terrifying. A witness to John Brown's execution thought that he resembled a "corn-field scarecrow" as he dangled from his noose, with his body twisting and his coat skirts fluttering in a light breeze.[13]

As he came through Troy, Lincoln was a distant long shot for higher office. He had lost his bid for the Senate a year earlier, and he would be left off all the lists of possible presidential candidates prepared at the end of 1859. But as travelers noted, the wind could shift quickly in the West. A year earlier, Lincoln's friend Elihu Washburne, an Illinois Congressman, had noticed the strong gusts "sweeping down the prairies" as he came into Freeport, Illinois, to hear a momentous debate between Lincoln and Stephen Douglas, whose sparkling career had always seemed so impressive next to Lincoln's.[14] Thousands of years earlier, the Greeks had named the western wind *Zephyrus*. They considered it a harbinger of change.

Less than a year later, Lincoln would be elected president of the United States. He had encountered many rivals, of much greater sophistication. They had access to more money than he did; superior political networks; greater national stature. He had destroyed all of them.

It was not merely the blacksmith's chain of unassailable logic or the way he looked—awkward, yet *American*. It was also his willingness to go the extra mile for a cause he believed in. That was no figure of speech: Lincoln was traveling in an ever-widening circumference as he argued for the nation's soul. To press his case, he raced across the continent's great distances, to meet the people in all of the neighborhoods where they lived—in Troy and a hundred other places.

Each locality deepened him and bolstered him for the longer journey to come. He went to Cincinnati to meet with German immigrants and to Wisconsin to speak to farmers. As he made his way across Kansas in late 1859, a newspaper reported that Lincoln's legs were so gangly that his knees "stood up like the hind joints of a grasshopper's legs."[15] Gangly, but strong from leaping from one prairie town to the next.

Soon he would jump all the way to New York, where he would give his biggest speech yet, in February 1860, at the Cooper Union, before an audience of urban sophisticates. It was chock-full of all the ideas that he was testing out before these frigid Kansas audiences. Troy was little more than a tiny settlement at the edge of the map, but all of these places mattered. Here at the western fringe, the country's future was being determined. Against the backdrop of a vast sky and a horizon that stretched as far as the eye could see, Lincoln pleaded for a better version of the United States.

As it turned out, this trip marked the farthest west he ever came.[16] The next day, he visited a few more small towns, then returned to Springfield, ready for a new year to begin, full of promise. He had important work to do. Eighteen days after his visit to Troy, Lincoln sent an autobiographical sketch to a friend. In it, he remembered how far he had come since he, too, lived on a frontier. His schooling had been sketchy in southern Indiana, where teachers were hard to come by. If someone wandered into the settlement with a rudimentary knowledge of Latin or Greek, he was looked upon as a kind of "wizzard"—a word Lincoln spelled with two z's, as if to stress the point.[17]

But Lincoln had overcome these obstacles the way he overcame so many others: by simply walking in search of what he needed. Locomotion had never failed him. As a youth, he gathered knowledge in all the ways he could, reading voraciously in the meager private libraries that he could find. Stories abound of long walks Lincoln took to find books, many miles from home. In these simple journeys, he grew, and as he read, he grew more, as if one kind of journey led to the other. Many of his cherished books described long quests. *Robinson Crusoe* was an early favorite; he likely read *Don Quixote* as well. An old neighbor later recalled that a dog-eared copy of Homer was passed around from settlement to settlement.[18] Even after thousands of years, the strange stories of the *Iliad* and the *Odyssey* had lost none of their power to bewitch listeners.

Perhaps no book inflamed Lincoln's imagination more than John Bunyan's *The Pilgrim's Progress*, and its story of an epic voyage through a sinful nation. Although written in seventeenth-century England, the book was widely read by Americans, and, in some ways, its geography seemed to fit the United States. The object of the pilgrimage was a shimmering Celestial City, which, like Washington, was perched upon a hill. Its resplendent buildings could be glimpsed from a great distance, but the actual approach was treacherous, thanks to a River of Death that ran adjacent.

To even get close, a traveler had to cross interminable swamps and bogs, all too familiar to Americans used to terrible road conditions. Even worse were all the sinkholes of sin, tempting pilgrims away from the straight and narrow path. Bunyan described a wicked city called Vanity Fair, which resembled New York in uncanny ways, with citizens who obsessed over their luxuries, and realtors who were unapologetically in league with Beelzebub.

With his imagination fired by his reading, a teenage Lincoln went out into the world; tentatively at first, but then further, almost as if an unseen hand were guiding him forward. He was often described as slow moving and slow thinking when he was younger, but a raw energy coursed below those deceptive surfaces. As a flatboat pilot, he earned his first few coins ferrying people across the Ohio River, an apprenticeship inside the very boundary that separated the North from the South. Then he earned his independence with longer trips downriver, toward New Orleans. It was there, according to family lore, that he saw slavery in its ugliest form, with a young woman for sale on an auction block, and rival bidders probing her to determine how high they would bid. His "heart bled" at these scenes, and he resolved that if he ever had a chance to strike back at slavery, he would "hit it hard."[19]

He continued to move, overcoming obstacles and clearing them so that others might follow. Lincoln was a natural leveler, with a talent for smoothing away snags and hazards. A student of rivers, he invented a flotation device to help lift a boat over a sandbar if it ran aground. In his legal work, he helped to remove obstacles for the railroads that were bringing so many families into the West. All of that fit his vision of a flat society, welcoming to all. It was a vision of a moral universe, in which hardship existed, but people could eventually make their way, on life's journey, toward a safe haven. The arc of that journey might be long, but it ultimately bent toward Troy, and a thousand other hamlets where people were hard at work, tilling the earth and building new lives.

Slavery had no place in such a vision. It made democracy look absurd. It violated every one of the rights proclaimed by the Declaration—not just life, liberty, and the pursuit of happiness, but the general idea that a government derives legitimacy from consent. It could not be legislated away from the Southern states where it had always existed, but it could be kept out of great spaces of the West. Here at the edge, it was possible to find a better path.

Alexander Gardner, *On the Great Plains, in Kansas, Near Monument, 385 Miles West of the Missouri River,* 1867[20]

But to hit slavery hard, he would need to complete a difficult journey of his own. Sometimes the journey was literal, as in late 1859, when Henry Villard encountered him, turning blue with cold, on his way to Troy. At other times, it was a reader's journey, as he sorted through the writings of the founders, seeking reliable landmarks to steer by. Sharp observers noted how much the words meant to him; he became even taller as he straightened himself to read the Declaration of Independence.

Yet as Lincoln entered the labyrinth of their writings, he often encountered impediments they had left behind. It was not merely that the founders contradicted one another—and themselves—changing their stories as they aged.[21] In other ways, as well, they made it difficult for anyone to alter the edifice that they had built. One was the decision to locate the edifice in a Southern place, at a sleepy bend in the Potomac River. Somehow, Washington was a part of the problem. On the morning that John Brown was executed, a New York newspaper noted that the noose and a sixteen-foot rope of cotton had been "carefully knit" in neighboring Alexandria.[22]

It had always been like that: the thread always led back to Washington. Just when it seemed like slavery might be on its way toward extinction, a toxic exhalation would belch from a gaseous air pocket near the Potomac, to protect it for another generation. In his reading, Lincoln had found many instances when the nation's architects expressed a private hope that the peculiar institution might, someday, expire. But there was always the problem of this capital, chosen by the founders, which had turned into a citadel for the very institution that they claimed to despise.

To hit at slavery, it would be necessary to somehow penetrate the citadel's defenses. That would require a great deal of cunning. To begin, it was not easy to reach, even for a river pilot who could get his flatboat around just about any obstacle. The capital had been at Washington since 1800, after a deal that was brokered over a mysterious dinner party at Thomas Jefferson's rented dwelling in Lower Manhattan around June 20, 1790. It is remarkable how many of the details remain shrouded in secrecy, from what may have been the most important bit of horse trading in American history.

We know that Alexander Hamilton and James Madison were there, and we have other details, adding flavor. The meal was prepared by James Hemings, an enslaved chef, who had spent years in Paris, along with his younger sister, Sally, serving Jefferson's complicated needs. On a windowsill, Jefferson was growing seedlings, "luxuriantly," as part of a project to diversify Southern agriculture. These included a sample of East Indian mountain rice gathered on the Pacific island of Timor by British Royal Navy captain William Bligh, who a year earlier had endured a mutiny on his ship, the HMS *Bounty*, and a 3,600-mile ride in a twenty-three-foot launch. It is possible that a few grains of that heroic rice enhanced the dinner.[23]

There are no transcripts of the conversation that evening. But soon after, Hamilton's economic program was funded by a Congress that had been opposed to it. Coincidentally, the Southern dream of moving the capital to a permanent location along the Potomac was approved around the same time. In all likelihood, a deal was struck.

Yet it was a curious location for many reasons, far less accessible than its promoters had boasted. They had predicted that a great city would spring into existence with no labor at all, and an immense traffic would simply flow down the Potomac from the interior. Jefferson promised that the river would "pour into our lap the whole commerce of the Western World."[24]

Unfortunately, they had taken some liberties with the truth. Above Washington, the Potomac was impassable, because of waterfalls and dangerous rocks that Lincoln's flotation device could never get over.[25] Below, the river meandered inconclusively for more than 160 miles before reaching Chesapeake Bay, ensuring that it would never be an important artery. Not that it was entirely useless: George Washington noted that the Potomac held "an inexhaustible fund of manure." That would help local farmers, but a shallow, brackish river was less ideal for a sparkling new seat of government.[26]

Yet if Washington was ill-suited for commerce or industry, it compensated with a remarkable ability to talk about itself as if no other place existed. This may be the only city that *lobbied* itself into existence. An early indigenous name for the region was *Cohongarooton,* or Honking Geese, and loud claims of self-importance were audible from the start.[27] The boosters promised that the new city would be larger than London within a decade. It would soon be the greatest city *of all time,* so virtuous that its mere existence would bring comfort to people around the world, including "sufferers in the wilds of Siberia."[28] The "children of future ages" would someday regard it with "rapture" as "the only imperial city ever yet founded on the immutable and eternal principles of liberty and reason."[29]

Still, doubts lingered. "Liberty and reason" seemed a stretch for a capital that openly embraced human servitude and exploded into a rage as soon as anyone noted the fact. Enslaved African-Americans were ubiquitous in Washington, performing the labor that kept legislators comfortable in the sweltering Southern city. By locating their capital here, the founders conceded an enormous advantage to the Slave Power at the birth of the republic. Since then, politicians had come and gone, promising that slavery would disappear someday. But it had only grown stronger, thanks to the machinations of insiders and lobbyists, growing like weeds in this congenial habitat.

For Northerners, it was a challenge to even get to Washington. The roads south of the Mason-Dixon Line were treacherous, as a New Yorker, Gouverneur Morris, found on his way to Thomas Jefferson's inauguration in 1801. It took him ten hours to travel the twenty-five miles from Annapolis, Maryland, after his carriage became stuck in the mud. Facetiously, he wrote, "This is the best city of the world to live in—in the future."[30]

For Westerners it was even harder, especially as the frontier kept moving across the continent, and the distances grew longer. Predictably, presidents began to arrive from the newer states. But the trip was nearly as punishing as the job itself. Indeed, the hardship of the journey may have killed William Henry Harrison, coming in from the far West of his day. In 1841 Harrison took fifteen days to travel from Cincinnati to Washington (where he arrived in a snowstorm on his sixty-eighth birthday). His progress was impeded when his steamboat hit a rock at Pittsburgh, and by a constant stream of local receptions, which weakened him well before he arrived. He died a month into his presidency.[31]

Eight years later, it took Zachary Taylor a full month to get from Baton Rouge, Louisiana, to Washington. Along the way, the presidential party was detained over and over again. A rudder accident stopped his progress on the Mississippi, near Memphis. They went aground again near Marietta, Ohio. In Madison, Indiana, he was injured by a falling trunk. Near Moundsville, in what is now West Virginia, he and his entourage were reduced to trudging through snow. The endless journey seemed like a grueling foretaste of the presidency itself, a kind of death march toward a city that barely existed.[32]

These continuing problems raised existential doubts about democracy, nagging at Americans despite their voracious appetite for more territory. Was the country simply too big to govern itself? Were the regions too far apart? These were legitimate questions, going back to the founding of the republic, when many wondered if smaller republics would work better. Could the people's representatives work together over a great distance? Had the founders not complained vociferously against England's King George

III, in the Declaration of Independence, for summoning legislators to inconvenient locations?

One of the two guests at Thomas Jefferson's dinner party, James Madison, had pondered these questions as he and Jefferson's other guest, Alexander Hamilton, wrote most of the *Federalist Papers*, the essays that explained the new form of government they were creating. In Federalist 14, Madison argued that distance was not a problem. As long as the elected representatives could get to one spot, all would be fine, and in theory, "a republic may be extended over a large region." How large, exactly, would depend on how often they had to meet, and how good the roads were. Madison tried to be exact: "The natural limit of a republic is that distance from the centre which will barely allow the representatives to meet as often as may be necessary for the administration of public affairs."

But how often was "barely" enough?[33] And how far could the line be drawn? Across the Mississippi? The Rockies? To the North Pole? To the equator? Could a president someday be born halfway across the Pacific—say, in the Sandwich Islands, as Hawaii was then known? That seemed unlikely, but American sea captains were already girdling the earth.

The decision to move the capital to a sleepy, shallow river with poor roads did not solve these riddles. This was "the centre"? Madison put the best face he could on the situation by promising that Americans would spend the money necessary to build roads from one distant part of their huge territory to another.[34] But that was hardly a foregone conclusion in a country that had recently completed a revolution over excessive tax measures and was simmering with resentment over new levies to support the federal structure coming into existence. By placing their capital in such an inaccessible place, the founders increased the burden of proof. There might come a time when the simple act of getting to Washington would become so difficult for a president-elect that it would place the entire experiment in jeopardy.

What if all the difficulties anticipated in the *Federalist Papers*—regional tensions, unscrupulous leaders, and a dysfunctional Congress—happened at precisely the same moment? What if the person elected to solve them was forced to travel over the greatest distance yet, only to arrive at a capital filled with people who wanted to kill him? What if his election was the cause of shattering the Union that the founders had built with a jeweler's precision? What if these turbulent emotions stemmed from slavery, the deepest problem of them all, so rarely mentioned by the founders in their visionary pronouncements, but so enmeshed within the edifice?

Surely these difficulties would give reason to believe, as so many foreign observers did, that the United States of America was at best a forlorn aspiration. Was it not doomed to end like so many of the other imperfect republics cited by the *Federalist Papers*—Carthage, Rome, and Venice—in a pile of toppled Corinthian columns, broken under the weight of their ambition? In fact, that is what Washington looked like as the United States entered the greatest crisis in its history. Its buildings were as crazy as Troy's, half finished, built too far apart, at strange angles. To the untrained eye, it was unclear if this city of ruins was on the way up or down. Perhaps the glorified people were simply not up the challenge? In Federalist 39, Madison argued for "the capacity of mankind for self-government." But he seemed unsure, and who could blame him? As he admitted, no genuine republic had ever been created.

In such a situation, the journey to the White House would become something more perilous—it would become a quest to save the very form of government that the founders, with all their imperfections, had bequeathed. It would become an odyssey to save democracy, as it were, from itself.

Much depended on the outcome. Democracy was in retreat around the world, and the failures of the French Revolution and the revolutions of 1848 had not exactly increased confidence in the people. But if Americans could conquer their demons, they might show the world a better way. A daring claim for human dignity had been proclaimed, along with independence, at the beginning of the experiment. The two aspirations reinforced each other, like architectural counterweights, bearing the mass of a cathedral. Government of the people depended, in theory, upon a decent respect for *all* people.

But it was not clear that democracy would survive, especially if the United States broke apart. It had failed so many times, John Adams seemed to expect it. In 1814 he wrote, "Democracy never lasts long. It soon wastes exhausts and murders itself. There never was a Democracy Yet, that did not commit suicide."[35]

Within a year of Lincoln's visit to Troy, that prophecy seemed to be fulfilling itself. The very act of selecting a leader had nearly destroyed the people's government. It was not simply that the Southern states were seceding; they were also spreading contempt for the basic assumptions of democracy. Hostility to the Declaration of Independence, with its soaring claim of human rights, was as fundamental to the Confederacy as Lincoln's embrace of the Declaration was to the Union. It was, in short, a race between two competing philosophies. That race would become literal in February 1861, as Lincoln tried to reach Washington, while his rival, Jefferson Davis, hurried toward his own inauguration in Montgomery, Alabama.

The stakes could not have been higher. If Lincoln succeeded, the United States would endure a bit longer and perhaps inspire others around the world to seek freedom in their own ways. If he failed, the country would splinter into at least two fragments, and probably more, after the logic of secession sheared off Texas, Utah, and California. But the time had come to decide, once and for all, what kind of country this was.

Later, Lincoln's admirers would seek to explain his achievement in almost mythological language. His secretary, John Hay, called him "an earthgiant, like autumnus," who "always gains strength by contact with his mother earth." Ralph Waldo Emerson eulogized him as a "native, aboriginal man," "an acorn from the oak," as if he had grown out of the western mud. That description might have fit on the day he arrived in Troy, clad in a heavy buffalo skin. But Lincoln was *not* an earth-giant, or a tree. He was simply a clear thinker who studied his country's past, charted the best course he could, and stayed true to it. His moral compass worked.

That gave him a remarkable assurance as he endured setbacks that would have overwhelmed most. He was canny, he was lucky, and he was stubborn. As America's problems mounted, in the summer of 1860 he wrote to a young man, disappointed by a rejection, "You can not fail, if you reasonably determine, that you will not."[36]

From Troy, Lincoln came back to fulfill his destiny. But even after winning the presidency, he faced a great challenge. He would need to complete an odyssey of his own, simply to reach the Southern city where he would be inaugurated. The 1900-mile journey through a divided country would be as arduous as any quest he had read about in his childhood. He survived by the slenderest of threads, thanks to a voice that reached him from a most unlikely source: a specialist in mental health, working overtime during America's descent into madness. His survival ensured that of the republic.

The next five years imposed a terrible cost—John Hay called it "our *Iliad*."[37] In many ways, we are still paying for it. But Lincoln's success at reaching his destination saved his country, and ours. It made his presidency possible, and all of our subsequent history.

Lincoln in Chicago, October 4, 1859,
seven weeks before his trip to Troy[38]

Two days after the Republican nomination, May 20, 1860[1]

1

THE LIGHTNING

he drilled
through every plank and fitted them together,
fixing it firm with pegs and fastenings.
As wide as when a man who knows his trade
Marks out the curving hull to build a ship . . .

—Homer, *The Odyssey*, book 5, lines 246–250[2]

NOVEMBER 6, 1860

Abraham Lincoln was in the headquarters of the Illinois & Mississippi Telegraph Company, on the north side of Springfield's public square, when he received the news that he was likely to win New York, and with it, the presidency.[3] It began with a sound—the *click-clack* of the telegraph key, springing to life as the information raced toward him. A reporter for the *New-York Tribune* heard the returns begin to "tap in," audibly, with the first "fragments of intelligence."[4] Then, a flood, as more returns came in from around the country, bringing news as electric as the devices clattering around the room.

All wires led to Springfield that evening, or so it felt to John Hay, who wrote that Lincoln's room was "the ear of the nation and the hub of the solar system."[5] As dispatchers danced around the suite, Lincoln sat languidly on a sofa, like a spider at the center of an enormous web. That word had already been used to describe the invisible strands connecting Americans through the telegraph.[6] Every few minutes, the web twitched again, as an electromagnetic impulse, transmitted from a distant polling station, was transcribed onto a piece of thin paper, like an onion skin, and handed to him.[7] Not long after ten, one of these scraps was rushed into his hands. The hastily scribbled message read, "The city of New York will more than meet your expectations."[8]

Immediately after, he crossed the square to meet his rapturous supporters, when he was handed another telegram, from Philadelphia. He read it aloud: "The city and state for Lincoln by a decisive majority." Then he added his all-important commentary: "I think that settles it." Bedlam ensued.[9]

Lincoln elected!

It was the headline of the century, and Americans sent it all night long, tapping out the Morse code for Lincoln as quickly as possible: the single long dash, for *L*, beginning the word that would be repeated endlessly through American history from that night forward. It was already so familiar that many just compressed his name to a single letter, especially when paying to send a telegram. "*L* and *H* were elected," James A. Garfield noted into his diary, omitting needless letters (the *H* stood for Hannibal Hamlin of Maine, Lincoln's running mate). "God be praised!!" he wrote when he finally heard the news, wrested from the wires, in a rural Ohio telegraph station. The future president had driven his horse and carriage fifteen miles in the middle of the night, just to be connected.[10]

In newspaper offices, editors struggled to find type sizes big and bold enough to match the import of what they were hearing. Across the country, crowds stayed up late, hoping to glean new scraps of intelligence from the wires that thrummed with the sensational news. In New Haven, Connecticut, people flat-out screamed for a full ten minutes when the result was announced.[11] In Port Huron, Michigan, a thirteen-year-old boy, Thomas Alva Edison, was so eager to get the news that he put his tongue on a wire to receive its electric impulse directly. In Galena, Illinois, young Republicans held a spontaneous "jollification" inside a leather shop, where they were served oysters by the owner's son, Ulysses Grant. Despite the fact that he leaned toward Democrat Stephen Douglas, the younger Grant seemed "gratified."[12]

In Springfield, it seemed like the entire town was out in the streets, as a crowd described as "10,000 crazy people" descended upon the square, "shouting, throwing up their hats, slapping and kicking one another." The last stragglers went home around dawn, after yelling themselves hoarse.[13]

But the news did not go to sleep; it traveled all night along the wires that stretched across the oceanic expanse of the United States. The word *telegraph* derived from Greek, to connote "far writing," an accurate description of an American grid extending from the frigid wastes of northern Maine to tropical Florida. No one built them more quickly: not far from Troy, Kansas, an English traveler was astonished to see new lines racing across the prairie, six miles closer to the Pacific each day.[14]

Not everyone had welcomed the clunky overhead lines when they were first introduced; New York City had briefly refused, for fear that "the Lightning," as the telegraph was called, would attract real lightning.[15] The wires were not always reliable in the early years; the news might vanish along the way, due to storms or atmospheric disturbances. A year earlier, at the end of August 1859, an intense solar flare known as the Carrington Event wreaked havoc on the grid, causing flames to shoot out, and machines to turn on and off, as if operated by witches. In a small Pennsylvania town—Gettysburg—a minister recorded his observation of "a mass of streamers," red and orange, streaking across the sky."[16]

In the years leading up to the election, the Lightning had become a part of the republic's bloodstream. Readers thrilled to the "telegraphic intelligence" that filled newspaper columns, with hard information about stock prices, ship arrivals, and the movements of armies around the world. They also enjoyed news that was not quite news, describing royal birthdays in Europe or the arrival of visiting "celebrities"—to use a term that was coming into vogue to describe people who were known simply for being known.[17]

But even if the Lightning could race across great distances, it could not bring Americans closer together. Some worried that it was actually driving them apart. In 1858, three days after the first Atlantic Cable connected New York and London, the *New York Times* asked if the news would become "too fast for the truth?"[18] Two years later, as Lincoln ran for the presidency, hateful innuendoes were streaking from one end of the country to another, accelerated by the Lightning.[19] Many observed that the first word in the country's name—*United*—had become a glaring misnomer. Things got so bad that the Architect of the Capitol, Benjamin Brown French, began to put quotation marks around it.[20]

Every day, the news made one side or the other angry. In the North, law-abiding citizens were sickened by the never-ending degradation of African-Americans, as the Slave Power stretched its tentacles into the other sections.[21] It was one thing to ignore slavery, as many Northerners were perfectly content to do. But when the federal government sent U.S. marshals into free states to find runaways, readers in the free states wondered what had happened to the moral purpose of the republic.[22] Southern politicians never stopped asking for *more*: more slave states, more *empire*, to encircle the Gulf of Mexico and the Caribbean. In their conclaves, they began to fantasize about a new kind of realm, modeled on the ancient Mediterranean, to be funded by the open plunder of Mexican silver and an inexhaustible supply of Africans.[23] That did not sound much like the United States of America.[24]

But Southerners were no less wary of the news, particularly when they heard about John Brown's bloody raid on Harpers Ferry or simply read the 1860 census returns that were already coming in. Since 1850, the population of just one state, Lincoln's Illinois, had shot up more than the *combined* increase of South Carolina, North Carolina, Georgia, Florida, Alabama, Mississippi, and Virginia. Who *were* all these people? Were they even American?

Could these two versions of the same country be reconciled? No one would ever expect a thoughtful answer from the White House. It almost seemed as if Buchanan's regime was leasing the country's name, as his friends enriched themselves and presided over a machinery of government that was lubricated with bribery, brandy, and insider deals. In New York, a lawyer, George Templeton Strong, wrote in his diary that he felt like he was reliving "the Roman Empire in its day of rotting."[25]

Younger Americans, especially, felt estranged. A few years earlier, in Brooklyn, a carpenter had poured out his feelings of rage in a language quite unlike the curious poems he sometimes published at his own expense. Walt Whitman brimmed with anger as he wrote of the "crawling, serpentine men" who held office in Washington, "gaudy outside with gold chains made from the people's money."[26] The Capitol had turned into a hiding place for nocturnal creatures ("bats and night-dogs") and swamp-dwellers ("lobbyers, sponges"). Instead of reporting on corruption, the administration's pet journalists were "spaniels well trained to carry and fetch." Supplying much of the money was the largest lobby of all, the Slave Power, the "freedom sellers of the earth." So pervasive was the culture of fear and intimidation that Whitman found an unusual word to describe it: *terrorist*.[27]

It was not merely that slavery seemed unstoppable; even more insulting was the fact that the Slave Power now claimed to be the genuine voice of America. It was almost as if the other parts of the story were being erased, as the ink faded a little more from the Declaration of Independence every year. Whitman complained, "Slavery is adopted as an American institution, superior, national, constitutional, right in itself, and under no circumstances to take any less than freedom takes." The country was being run by "blusterers" and "braggarts," "screaming in falsetto." "Where is the real America?" he wondered.[28]

But even as he despaired, Whitman had a vision of the kind of leader he longed for. In his mind, he imagined a westerner, bearded, speaking words as straight as the prairie grass. Whitman could see him as clearly as if he were already standing before him:

"I would be much pleased to see some heroic, shrewd, full-informed, healthy-bodied, middle-aged, beard-faced American blacksmith or boatman come down from the West across the Alleghanies [sic], and walk into the Presidency, dressed in a clean suit of working attire, and with the tan all over his face, breast, and arms; I would certainly vote for that sort of man."[29]

Remarkably, Whitman's daydream grew real in the spring of 1860, as a new candidate stepped into view. Lincoln did not yet have a beard, but the former boatman fit the poet's description in almost all other ways. To many easterners, he seemed to have sprung out of the western clay fully formed, with barely any known history. He was unlike anyone who had ever run for president. But could such a strange candidate actually win? Whitman spoke for many: "No man knows what will happen next, but all know that some such things are to happen as mark the greatest moral convulsions of the earth."[30]

Even the heavens seemed to portend great change. A little before ten o'clock on the evening of July 20, Americans were astonished to see the skies light up, as a meteor procession flew over the country before exploding in a shower of sparks. The meteors were followed by a long tail, which one observer described as "a great glowing train in the sky." Another stunned eyewitness called it a "train of fire." To many, it was a sign of Lincoln's impending victory, since the meteors originated in the upper Midwest before sweeping over the East.[31]

On November 6 the Lightning struck quickly. Only four years earlier, it had taken up to ten days for some remote sections of the United States to learn the result of the presidential election. In 1860 Lincoln's triumph was absorbed in one night. But as the news spread, a second wave of false stories followed closely. The *New-York Tribune* reported that "gigantic" rumors were spreading like a prairie fire through Lincoln's Springfield, already fearful for its native son. It was whispered that Washington, D.C., had been set ablaze; slaves were rebelling in Virginia; Jefferson Davis had declared independence for Mississippi; James Buchanan had resigned the presidency; blood was running down the gutters of New York City.[32] None of it was true, but the rumors conveyed as well as any fact that democracy had reached a breaking point.[33] "God help me, God help me," Lincoln sighed, as the news finally settled in.[34]

As he trudged home to his family, with celebrants firing off guns behind him, the president-elect had a great deal to ponder. No doubt a change was coming: he saw two shooting stars on his way home, as if nature, too, wanted to join in the fireworks. The people had spoken, but in so many voices that it would take some time to process what they had said.

The phrase *e pluribus unum* had been adopted by the founders for the Great Seal of the United States, suggesting a whole greater than the sum of its parts. It rang true when the poet Virgil wrote it, centuries earlier, to describe a pesto he was assembling from cheese, garlic, and parsnips.[35] But what if the people proved to be less compatible? In New York, George

Templeton Strong confided to his diary that the country would need to change its motto to *"e pluribus duo."*[36]

The lessons of history were hard to ignore. Every democracy ever known had failed, beginning with the Greeks twenty-four centuries earlier. They had succumbed, one by one, to all the well-known vices of the people: corruption, greed, lust, ethnic hatred, distractibility, or simply a fatal indifference.

On his walk home, Lincoln passed a Greek Revival capitol, a Greek Revival courthouse, and a Greek Revival insurance building.[37] The persistence of the ancient forms may have offered a momentary comfort—a reminder of the power of an idea to endure. But no underwriter could offer the slightest assurance that government of the people would survive. Even before the night was over, great forces were arrayed against this solitary figure making his way home in the dark.

THE REVOLUTION OF 1860

Far from Springfield, the Lightning continued to do its work. By the time the news sparks had traveled down the wires to the South, they might as

Two days after Lincoln's election, the citizens of Savannah held a rally around a bonfire with a flag that read "Don't Tread on Me"[38]

well have been a lit fuse. Seven hundred miles away, one of Lincoln's rivals, Stephen Douglas, was in Mobile, Alabama, where he too heard the results as they tapped into a telegraph key, clacking inside a newspaper office. On the last day of the campaign, he had come down the Alabama River from Selma, after a bruising tour through the South. Douglas was injured in a dockside mishap, taunted by crowds, and targeted by "a shower of eggs." In a suspicious accident, his train was nearly derailed.[39]

It was a lonely crusade for the Illinois Senator, whose friendliness toward the South had once seemed likely to propel him to the White House. As joy was spreading above the Ohio River, rage was fanning out below it, as fast as the Lightning could carry the news. In fact, the Lightning seemed to be part of the problem, as far as Southerners were concerned.[40] For many, the speed of modern life was yet another reason to hate the North. It was all *too fast*—too much information, coming too quickly, from too many people. The *New Orleans Bee* editorialized, "The election of Abraham Lincoln is a fixed fact. The telegraph made known the disastrous result almost before the expiration of the day on which the contest took place."[41] Another Southern editor harrumphed, "Newspapers and Telegraphs have ruined the country."[42] That was a curious view for a newspaper editor, but Southern opinion shapers had painted Lincoln in such lurid colors before the election that they became unhinged as the result crackled through the wires.

Inside their hothouse, Lincoln was a monster, a tyrant, a would-be dictator—that is, when he was not a weak and vacillating politician, the creature of others. No rumor was too extreme: the Republicans were Communists, they wanted to redistribute wealth, they even shared their wives. Lincoln's running mate, Hannibal Hamlin, was falsely described as a mulatto; it was said that he "looked, acted, and thought so much like a Negro" that he could be sold as a field hand. A sexual hysteria simmered close to the surface, as Republicans were accused of embracing "free love, free lands, and free Negroes." Northern newspapers were not above hysteria, either: the *New York Herald* warned that "hundreds of thousands" of fugitive slaves would come north if Lincoln won, specifically to consummate "African amalgamation with the fair daughters of the Anglo Saxon, Celtic, and Teutonic races."[43]

But the worst fear of all was that four million slaves would rise up and slit the throats of their masters if Lincoln won.[44] All summer, as the election drew nearer, observers had noticed a rising independence among African-Americans, merely because of the possibility that he might win. In addition to the underground railroad, there was also an underground telegraph—an informal network of gossip, spread from one plantation to the next, by African-Americans eager for any scrap of information about the election. As November 6 approached, they were awakening to the possibility of a Day of Jubilee. Booker T. Washington was a four-year-old child in southwestern Virginia, enslaved and illiterate. But he recalled later, "The slaves on our far-off plantation, miles from any railroad or large city or daily newspaper, knew what the issues involved were."[45]

Slave owners did their best to distort the news. To their slaves, they told lurid tales of a monstrous Lincoln, a cannibal, "with tails and horns," who would "devour every one of the African race." Unafraid, African-Americans began to tell stories of a Lincoln who was larger than life, coming soon "on the train" to liberate them.[46]

After the result came through, a wave of terror swept over the Southland. In the early hours, it was difficult to separate what was real from what was feared, as rumors swept from one plantation to the next. In Texas, the wells were thought to be poisoned. In Virginia, slave owners claimed to have uncovered an insurrection. In Alabama, plantation owners prepared for fires—in part because of a drought that seemed to be punishing the South at the same time that weather conditions had favored the North with a historic harvest. In rural Georgia, a group of sixty slaves wandered from their plantation, believing that they had been set free.[47] Not far away, in Augusta, a four-year-old boy named Tommy overheard a stranger pass by his house, speaking with "intense tones," saying "Mr. Lincoln was elected and there was to be war." Decades later, Woodrow Wilson would identify this searing moment as his earliest memory.[48]

In Florida, Mary Chesnut was traveling by train to see her mother, when the Lightning brought the news. Immediately, the car was in an uproar. She called it an "earthquake," shattering all known reality. "The excitement was very great," she wrote. "Everybody was talking at the same time."

She resolved to keep a new journal, as if conscious that a new age had begun. "From to-day forward, I will tell the story in my own way," she explained to herself. It would become one of the great documents of the war.[49]

Another train was carrying Edmund Ruffin, one of the South's so-called fire-eaters. All night long, as he traveled from Virginia toward South Carolina, he saw people gathered around the stations, eager for any scrap of information. "It is good news for me," he wrote triumphantly in his diary, so ready to leave the United States that he could barely write the name. Emotions were running high, and in Charleston, angry citizens borrowed the language of the Boston Tea Party, even as they rushed to separate from Boston and everything associated with the North. A local paper wrote, "The tea has been thrown overboard—the revolution of 1860 has been initiated![50] Each district of the state soon had a branch of "Minute Men," and they were quickly arming themselves. Volunteers gave "a pledge of honor to provide a rifle and revolver to march at a minute's notice to Washington for the purpose of preventing Lincoln's inauguration."[51]

Other secret societies sprang up as well, particularly in Maryland. Baltimore was the largest slaveholding city in the country, and proud of it. In saloons and back alleys, angry young men fueled by alcohol, money, and a blind fury against Lincoln were enlisting in furtive organizations. One secret society, the Knights of the Golden Circle, had originally formed to promote Southern expansion into Mexico and the Caribbean. But the election results transformed it into a more extremist group, with the specific purpose of preventing Lincoln from arriving in Washington. John Wilkes Booth was likely a member.[52]

Many Southerners simply rejected the news as unacceptable. In Charlottesville, Virginia, a newspaper tried to argue that Lincoln's supporters were guilty of undermining democracy by daring to outnumber Southern voters, an offense the paper tried to pass off as "numerical tyranny." In Washington, after hearing the results, a group of Democrats stormed the Republican headquarters, firing pistols, throwing rocks through its windows, and destroying its furniture, flags, and printing type, as if to prevent any more news from flowing.[53]

Could the news of Lincoln's election be turned back as if it were a piece of mail delivered to the wrong address? Many Southerners thought so. To them, Lincoln was not only unlikable, he was *unthinkable*. A New Orleans newspaper reported soberly to its readers that they could relax because he would never become president—it was not possible to conceive.[54] The paper urged its readers to continue going on as before, as if no election had taken place at all.

Even many Northerners found the news difficult to believe. Nathaniel Hawthorne was a specialist in fantasy, and yet his creative powers simply shut down when he tried to imagine a Lincoln presidency. It was the "strangest" thing, Hawthorne wrote, and a true measure of "the jumble" of the times, that Lincoln, "out of so many millions," had prevailed. He was "unlooked for," "unselected by any intelligible process," and "unknown" even to "those who chose him." How could such a nonentity have found a way "to fling his lank personality into the chair of state?"[55]

STAR OF THE NORTH, OR THE COMET OF 1861.

Lincoln as a comet; envelope image, 1861[56]

SECESSIA

The morning after the election, Lincoln surveyed the new political landscape from his parlor, where the chair of state was likely in need of uphol-
stering. He was undeniably the president-elect, but of what? A very hard
road lay ahead, beginning with the challenge of persuading his fellow Americans that he had actually been elected. That would take some doing, given
the modesty of his victory and the intensity of the South's emotions.

It was not simply that Lincoln threatened slavery's expansion. He also
struck at its vitals, because a new party could offer jobs and contracts to
supporters, in the time-honored tradition, and chip away at all the protections that Southern politicians had so carefully built into the architecture
of power. That would send the lobbyists scurrying—and the Slave Power
had many, eager to do its bidding. Controlling the War Department meant
abundant jobs to give out in the shipyards of New York and Philadelphia,
and all the advantages in presidential elections that stemmed from that. The
New-York Tribune believed that Southern politicians were more interested
in protecting "the spoils" than in anything else. Or, as a Washington insider
put it, more graphically, they would secede simply because they could not
"have all the old sow's teats to suck."[57]

Since the beginning of the United States, the South had controlled the
lion's share of the patronage. Its politicians were skilled at deploying the language of states' rights whenever slavery was threatened, but, in fact, the
South had a far more sophisticated understanding of federal power than the
North did. The future vice president of the Confederacy, Alexander Stephens, admitted as much when he urged Georgia not to secede, saying,
"We have always had the control of it." In the first sixty-one years of the
government, slaveholders held the presidency for fifty years, the Speaker
of the House's chair for forty-one years, and the chairmanship of the House
Ways and Means Committee for fifty-two years. Eighteen of thirty-one Supreme Court justices hailed from the South, even though four-fifths of the
actual business of the court came from the North. No Northern president
had been reelected. Most of the attorneys general and military officers had

been Southerners, along with a vast majority of the officers of the Senate and House: the doorkeepers, pages, and sergeants at arms.[58] In the executive branch, two-thirds of the collectors and clerks came from the South, even though the North earned three-quarters of the revenue.[59] That was now going to change, with the most far-reaching consequences.[60]

With this new reality dawning, the two sides began to separate. Well before Lincoln's inauguration, the tectonic plates were shifting, out of view, heralding the earthquake to come. More than ever, it felt as if there were two alternative versions of the same country. Southern papers began to report news from the North under a heading for "the Foreign Press."[61]

But what would this new geography look like? Where would one America end and the other begin? Which version did Washington, D.C., belong to? All around the slaveholding section, including the capital, young men wore cockades and ribbons signaling their sympathy for the Palmetto Republic, as South Carolina was beginning to describe itself. A flag was designed and soon fluttered on South Carolina's vessels, even in Northern harbors. Step by step, the protocountry grew. Nathaniel Hawthorne would later call the Confederate states "Secessia"—as good a name as any for a place that often seemed to be a state of mind as much as a working government.[62]

Secessia became more real six weeks later, on December 20, 1860, when South Carolina became the first state to withdraw from the Union. It was followed by Mississippi (January 9, 1861), Florida (January 10), Alabama (January 11), Georgia (January 19), Louisiana (January 26), and Texas (February 1).[63] That brought some clarity, but much remained to be determined, as the two Americas coexisted uneasily in the weeks after the election. *Secessia* was not entirely its own country—many Southern buildings remained in federal control, including the forts guarding the entrances to Charleston and other Southern cities.[64]

But the United States was not entirely its own country, either, as Southern officials still working inside the Buchanan administration did all they could to subvert federal authority. So many future Confederate leaders were sprinkled throughout the Cabinet and Congress, it was as if a parasite were occupying the organism it sought to displace, eating away at its host.

Oddly, Washington acted like the capital of *both* Americas. From the Capitol, Southern senators spoke ramblingly about their intention to start a new country centered around slavery, and began to resign. But they lingered in their farewell speeches, as if they did not want to leave, and continued to attack Lincoln as the root of all evil. A senior Cabinet official, Treasury Secretary Howell Cobb, called the president-elect "an enemy of the human race." [65]

Northerners, too, were restless. In an essay titled "*E Pluribus Unum*," the writer James Russell Lowell wondered if the stars on the flag represented "a grand and peaceful constellation" or something far less ordered, with no gravitational pull of any kind—a chaos of "jostling and splintering stars," more like the universe we know. [66]

One thing was certain: the antidote to secession was *succession*—a normal transfer of power. It would require meticulous planning to assemble a new government and to determine a safe route to Washington, nestled so uncomfortably between two slave states. With the world watching, it was essential to preserve continuity between the regimes. If Lincoln failed to arrive, it would signal to the world that democracy was little more than a pretty daydream—an idealistic footnote, from ancient Greece, like one of Plato's airy dialogues—but no blueprint for a working government.

All eyes now turned to the agent who had precipitated the crisis. To solve the gravest challenge in American history, the people—all 31,443,321 of them—began to wait for the unlikely victor of the presidential contest. Abraham Lincoln had not won an election since 1846, when he became a U.S. congressman for a grand total of two years. Since then, he had failed in two attempts to become a senator, after indifferently pursuing a few other offices earlier. He had never been the executive of *anything*. Yet somehow, from this litany of underachievement, he had assembled the victory that had eluded so many better-known politicians. All knew that a giant was needed to solve the immense problems looming over the republic; but to most Americans, the incoming president seemed to be more of a "tall dwarf," as even a supporter, Carl Schurz, admitted. [67]

Could anyone live up to these expectations? George Templeton Strong

Lincoln made of rails; a cartoon by Frank Bellew, 1860[68]

wrote in his diary that Lincoln's election was "an experiment that tests our Boiler."[69]

THE RAIL CANDIDATE

As the results were tabulated over the next few days, it was evident that Lincoln's victory concealed some anemic numbers. A huge percentage of voters, 81.2 percent, had gone to the polls to choose one of four candidates in the most charged political contest Americans had ever seen. The Democratic Party had split into Northern and Southern wings, led by Stephen Douglas and the current vice president, John Breckinridge, respectively. A new party named after "Constitutional Union," whatever that was, had divided the country further, peeling off Virginia, Kentucky, and Tennessee from the rest of the South behind its candidate, John Bell.

Those fissures had helped Lincoln but did not build confidence in his mandate. In fact, he won only 39 percent of the vote; the lowest margin any victor has ever received, except John Quincy Adams in 1824. He won almost no votes in the South, even in the five states where he was on the ballot, and most of that came from German-Americans in Saint Louis. In Virginia, where he was on the ballot, he received a pitiful 1 percent of the state's total. In his native Kentucky, he received less than that.[70] He won California by only 734 votes. In Illinois, he won by only 12,000 out of 350,000 cast, and he lost his home county, Sangamon, though he won his hometown, Springfield, by a whisker: 73 votes.[71]

A strategy of silence had worked during the campaign, when Lincoln avoided campaigning and let the Republican platform speak for him. Though moderate in many ways, it was firm on an essential point: that slavery must not be extended out of the states where it already existed.[72] That was the rock that now loomed before the ship of state.

As president-elect, Lincoln needed to reassure an anxious people that all was well. Yet there were few tools available to him, and his strengths in the campaign turned into liabilities as soon as the result was known. Lincoln's distance from Washington—attractive in a candidate—now made it difficult to coordinate policy with his allies. The newness of the Republican apparatus—founded only six years earlier—added to his weakness. Not yet grand or old, the party remained a work in progress, organized state by state, and woefully unprepared for the national crisis that came with victory.

For all their foresight, the founders had never anticipated a threat as fundamental as the one that began the day after Lincoln's election. His victory made the outgoing president, James Buchanan, seem even more irrelevant, but it did not bring Lincoln any real power. Through a long interregnum, stretching from November 6 until March 4, the government would be rudderless at exactly the moment leadership was most needed. In such a vacuum, it was far easier to secede than to hold the country together. Stuck in Springfield, Lincoln could do precious little to slow the momentum of disunion. To his secretary, John Nicolay, the soon-to-be sixteenth president worried aloud about his predicament. Surely any government had the authority to maintain its integrity; but in a democracy, the people were supposed to come together voluntarily. Ominously, he added, "The ugly point of the matter is the necessity of keeping the government together by force, as ours should be a government of fraternity."[73]

Foreign observers had marveled at the chaotic way in which Americans elected their presidents. The French writer, Alexis de Tocqueville, saw it as a quadrennial "crisis," like a recurring fever in an otherwise healthy patient. "Artificial passions" could be easily stoked, he wrote, raising the temperature. A self-absorbed president, catering to the "worst caprices" of his supporters, could easily distract their attention from plodding matters of governance, and whip their enthusiasms into a frenzy, especially if he divided his supporters and his critics into "hostile camps." With the cooperation of the press, all conversation would turn to the present rather than the future, until the nation would begin to "glow" with its "feverish" obsessions.

All of these symptoms would be bad enough in normal cycles; but Tocqueville warned that America's hatreds could become "perilous" if left unchecked. He used a vivid metaphor, that of a river dangerously overflowing its banks. After an election, he expected that the river would recede back to its usual level. But still, the potential for lasting damage was always lurking.[74]

Tocqueville knew something about surging rivers. He had seen many of them during his travels in the interior, in 1831 and 1832, and had gone a considerable length of the Ohio and Mississippi Rivers—the very rivers that Lincoln was navigating when Tocqueville arrived. It is hard to imagine what they would have said to each other if the diminutive Frenchman had encountered the towering youth. Lincoln later described himself at this time as "a strange, friendless, uneducated, penniless boy working on a flatboat—at ten dollars per month."[75]

How did that strange and friendless boy transform himself into a mighty instrument of change? There were glimmers of a special destiny—presentiments among friends and neighbors, frontier people who often consulted oracles and soothsayers. An early acquaintance, remembering Lincoln's mother, recalled the day when she arrived in their Kentucky settlement, pregnant with the future president, or as he put it, "enceint [sic] with Abe Lincoln the man of destiny yet unborn."[76]

But the man of destiny took a long time to prove himself. Already, artists were complaining that there was something difficult to capture about Lincoln. Despite the fact that all eyes were upon him, they noted certain features that were nearly impossible to get right: the quick mood changes, the dreamy look in his gray eyes, the melancholy that "dripped from him as he walked," in the words of his law partner, William Herndon.[77] With the advantage of hindsight, it seems fitting that our most bipolar president arrived at the moment the country was splitting in two.

A few months earlier, the mere possibility of Lincoln's election would have struck most Republican insiders as inconceivable. Near the end of 1859, a New York publisher had printed a list of *Twenty-one Prominent Candidates for the Presidency in 1860*, and Lincoln's name was not among them.[78] While attending early meetings of Republicans to plan the 1860 campaign, he had to put his own name forward as a possibility, because the thought had not occurred to anyone else.[79] There had been other dark horses, but few whose fortunes changed as dramatically in so short a time.

As he himself furnished the details, in the various autobiographies that he provided for the 1860 campaign, it was clear that he came from an unusual background: the poverty deeper, the setbacks more severe, and the upward thrust more surprising than that of the first fifteen presidents. Lincoln remembered arresting moments from his long obscurity. At age ten, "He was kicked by a horse, and apparently killed for a time." At nineteen, he took a flatboat to New Orleans, and below Baton Rouge, he was "attacked by seven negroes with intent to kill."[80] Any one of these brushes with mortality could have quietly removed him from consideration.

The nearness of death was a fact of life on the frontier, but Lincoln retained his fatalism to an unusual degree for a working politician. He wrote odd poems about trees that were shedding dewdrop tears, and described the sound of a funeral dirge that followed him, which only he could hear, "as if I dreamed." In fact, Lincoln did dream, intensely, and his verses also spoke of a "midway world" that he liked to visit, where he could be a "companion of the dead." It was a well-known political trick to register the names of deceased voters; but Lincoln seemed to be *actually* conversing with them. In his poem, he was "living in the tombs."[81]

In 1860 he emerged from these shadows quickly, and the fact that he was so unlikely began to turn into an advantage. A westerner was appealing, and a nonincumbent even more so, as Washington sank deeper into the swamp of its dysfunction. Lincoln also benefited dramatically from a decision to stage the Republican Convention in Chicago. That had been arranged only a few months earlier, at a conclave held at New York City's Astor House, on December 21, 1859, only weeks after his visit to Troy. As a gesture to Chicago's surging importance, it was chosen over Saint Louis by a single ballot.[82] Without that vote, Lincoln might never have been nominated.

In other ways as well, the doors seemed to open at just the right moment. Before the Chicago convention, a meeting of Illinois Republicans was held in Decatur, the same town where Lincoln had arrived from Indiana, thirty years earlier. His friend Richard Oglesby was seeking to lift him and, with a flash of insight, came up with the perfect lever. With a relative of Lincoln's, he visited a nearby field and liberated two old fence rails that had possibly been split by Lincoln as a young man. At a dramatic moment, they carried them into the crowded convention hall, with a banner that proclaimed Lincoln as "The Rail Candidate." According to the *Weekly Illinois State Journal*, "the effect was electrical."[83]

A future House Speaker, Joseph Cannon, was a young man at the time and never forgot the moment. To Cannon, it was almost as if Lincoln had walked out of an enchanted forest to save his country. He used the word *forest* often as he remembered the frame Lincoln walked through, "with posts cut from the forest, stringers cut from the forest, and covered with boughs cut from the forest."[84]

The rail was the perfect symbol for the lanky nominee, straight and true, easily drawn by the caricaturists of the newspapers. They showed Lincoln handling rails in every imaginable context: sitting on a fence, playing the newly popular game of baseball, or, as tensions heightened in the fall, wielding a sharpened wooden stake that looked decidedly lethal.

The "rail enterprize," as Lincoln called it, worked on many levels.[85] Rails spoke of honest labor, self-sufficiency, and well-marked boundaries, all relevant to the argument over slavery.[86] There was something rough-hewn about Lincoln, too.[87] Henry Villard, the same pioneer whom Lincoln had met on the prairie a year earlier, described him as "lean, lank," and "indescribably gawky." Villard was horrified by a glimpse of democracy up close, when two young farmers carried the Rail Candidate on their shoulders, a "grotesque figure," with "his legs dangling from their shoulders, and his pantaloons pulled up so as to expose his underwear almost to his knees."[88]

That kind of indignity did Lincoln no harm in the West and advertised to people that this was a new kind of politician. He did not speak with the formal gestures that so many politicians still used: neoclassical poses, stiff gestures, hortatory words delivered formally. Instead, he spoke to Americans in their own language, with an exquisite moral clarity. When talking about human dignity, he could transport himself—and his audience—into a higher realm. A journalist listening to him in 1856 wrote, "At times Lincoln seemed to reach up into the clouds and take out the thunderbolts."[89]

Even in New York, Lincoln's homespun style won over the sophisticates, although one of them recalled that the first impression was "wild and wooly."[90] When the Westerner came to speak at the Cooper Union, a reporter commented on his disheveled clothes ("ill-fitting, badly wrinkled"), and a body that seemed out of place in the East: "His bushy head, with the stiff black hair thrown back, was balanced on a long and lean stock, and when he raised his hands in an opening gesture, I noticed that they were very large." A snide comment followed: "Old fellow, you won't do. It is all very well for the wild west, but this will never go down in New York." By the end of the speech, the writer himself had been westernized: "Forgetting myself, I was on my feet with the rest, yelling like a wild Indian."[91]

Over the course of a frantic year, "the Rail Candidate" evolved into "the Rail-Splitter." Rails seemed to be everywhere, carried by Lincoln supporters in cities and towns throughout New England, New York, and the Northwest. Lincoln stayed at home in Springfield, where he kept a home that was quite far from frontier conditions. In fact, most of his political career had been dedicated to eliminating those conditions, as Springfield grew into a modern state capital with well-appointed hotels and elegant homes on "Aristocracy Hill."[92]

But if wooden rails were hard to find in Springfield, iron ones were never far away. Railroads brought thousands of Lincoln partisans to Chicago during the Republican Convention, held in a huge barn called the Wigwam.[93] It was a marvel of light and speed, brilliantly illuminated, and wired with telegraph lines to get its result out to a nation hanging on its deliberations.[94] On the third ballot, a reporter felt the weather change and described a leveling gust that seemed to come straight off the prairie—a "great wind" clearing everything before it. As he put it, "There was a silence for a moment, and the next instant there was a noise in the Wigwam like the rush of a great wind in the van of a storm." In another breath, he continued, "the storm was there," and "thousands were cheering with the energy of insanity."[95]

That noise, "the Lincoln yawp," soon swept across the entire United States.[96] As quickly as the Lightning could carry the news, a huge noise followed, with church bells tolling, factory whistles shrieking, locomotives blasting their horns, and cannon fire.[97] Within minutes, in Springfield, Lincoln was notified by a small boy, running from the telegraph office.

From relative obscurity, Lincoln went quickly to the opposite extreme. The information economy demanded fuel, and his supporters supplied it with prints, speeches, and human interest stories. One paper wrote, "Mr. Lincoln's admiring friends will be delighted to hear that he eats, sleeps, coughs, sneezes, and obeys the *other calls of nature* regularly."[98] Another paper wrote that Lincoln had received fifty-two applications to write his biography. He joked that he was being besieged with "attempts on my life."[99]

Unfortunately, that was all too true. In the toxic climate of 1860, there was a long list of people ready to stop Lincoln's bandwagon. Even in the North, the newspapers could be cruel, and they routinely insulted his appearance. A Massachusetts newspaper wondered half-jokingly if it was safe for expectant mothers to purchase his image. The *New York Times* opined that he could split rails simply by looking at them. A Republican newspaper amused many when it misprinted a headline: "Hurrah for Old Ape!"[100] In the South, it was far worse, as Lincoln was hanged in effigy, over and over again.[101] In Baltimore, the Republican headquarters was gutted, and his image shredded.[102]

In the final days of the campaign, the Democrats made a furious push. They were willing to use all tricks at their disposal, including racial taunts, patronage, and rivers of alcohol. Charles Dickens, who happened to be in New York for a campaign event, wrote a lurid account of democracy in America, darker than anything Tocqueville had seen. To the author of *A Christmas Carol*, it felt almost as if he were wandering in his nightshirt through a nightmare. The "Monster Democratic Rally and Ox-Roast" broke down into chaos as soon as the ox and pig carcasses were wheeled out. Thousands of people, squinting through "rowdy eyes," tore down fences to get at them, tearing the meat off in a carnivorous rampage. The strongest and "most brutal" got there first and helped themselves. Nearby, stumbling drunks bumped into one another, and gangs such as the Rough Skins, the Dead Rabbits, and the dreaded Double Pumps of Baltimore looked for trouble. Orators called for Lincoln to be hanged, and the crowd roared its approval, "seething," its angry faces illuminated by torchlight.[103]

But the Republican rallies were equally intense, as Lincoln's partisans rejoiced in the feeling that their moment had come. The candidate hardly spoke a word during the campaign, but it mattered not to his supporters, swept up in the whirlwind. It kept blowing, right up to the day of the election. As Lincoln voted, a reporter wrote that the crowd cheered with an intensity that bordered upon mental derangement. When the Lightning finally brought its tally of "the Republican thunder" rolling in from New York and Pennsylvania, there was a final yawp, and the crowd responded with "a forty-horsepower shout," like a locomotive.[104]

Four decades later, John Hay remembered the force of those winds. In 1902, near the end of his life, he stood up in the Capitol to give the memorial address to another assassinated president, William McKinley, shot in the abdomen by an anarchist in Buffalo the year before. McKinley's murder might have led Hay to conclude that democracy, for all of its good intentions, was too idealistic for a world of such visceral hatred.

Instead, he said something close to the opposite: democracy was worth the struggle to get right. As he looked back on McKinley's career, he found himself remembering the fall of 1860, when so many young people were awakened by the dignity of Lincoln's appeal. It was an awakening as spiritual as it was political, in Hay's retelling. Democracy had been tarnished by corruption, insider deals, and broken promises. It had been degraded, specifically, by the Slave Power, aggressively intensifying its assault on the basic human rights that the republic had been founded upon. With Lincoln's election, the people had drawn a line.

Transporting himself backward in time, Hay recalled vividly the night the Lightning struck, and Lincoln was elected. The atmosphere changed that evening, much as it does when real lightning flashes, in the electric moments that precede a thunderstorm. Hay described it as a landscape painter would, as an excitement that "filled the earth and sky when the long twilight of doubt and uncertainty was ending and the time of action had come." In towns and villages across the North, they had decided: "The country was worth saving; it could be saved only by fire; no sacrifice was too great; the young men of the country were ready for the sacrifice; come weal, come woe, they were ready."[105]

But even with victory in hand, a great ordeal remained. The people had spoken, but no one had ever been elected from so far away, with so small a mandate, in a climate of such hatred. How exactly would Lincoln claim his distant, thankless office? Before his presidency could begin, he would have to travel through the heartland of a country that simmered with resentments along every mile of his route. The *New York Times* quoted a French observer, who said that he had never seen a government trying so hard to end its own existence. America seemed "on the verge of the precipice," in his words, and a step in any direction was dangerous. Lincoln was about to enter a peculiar no-man's-land, the not-quite-president of a disintegrating nation.

To make matters worse, he faced an existential dilemma: Could he even reach his capital? And if he did, would it still be in the United States?[106]

James Buchanan, fading away[1]

2

WAITING FOR LINCOLN

Great Captain,
A fair wind and the honey lights of home
Are all you seek. But anguish lies ahead,
The god who thunders on the land prepares it . . .
—Homer, *The Odyssey*, book 11, lines 112–15[2]

In the days that followed his election, Lincoln tried to maintain the semblance of a normal life; he was observed buying hair tonic at the drugstore on November 10. But he was in the maw of history now. Every act commanded attention as the storm clouds gathered.

In ever-greater numbers, the people came to "Mecca"—Hay's and Nicolay's term for Springfield—in order to gaze at him.[3] Often they brought storm clouds of their own. Henry Villard described the haze of cigar smoke that would begin to envelop Lincoln as he welcomed a constant stream of western visitors. Sitting near the president-elect, "puffing away," they would try to "gorgonize" him with their "silent stares." When satisfied that they had seen enough of him, they would head home, after a brief touch of "the presidential fingers."[4]

In the weeks that followed, Lincoln tried to reach out to Southerners. But few were looking to ease his predicament. Even before the election, Jefferson Davis said it would be a "disgrace" to live under a "Black-Republican."[5] An Atlanta newspaper swore that the South would never permit the "humiliation" of Abraham Lincoln's inauguration, even if it meant that the Potomac would flow crimson with "human gore," and Pennsylvania Avenue would be "paved ten fathoms deep with mangled bodies." In Nashville, the paper predicted "war to the knife."[6]

As these grisly futures were predicted, in lurid detail, the act of waiting for Lincoln became a long agony. It would be four months until his inauguration, and every passing day deepened the darkness the country had plunged into. Over dinner tables and bar counters, all of the Gothic nightmares that haunted the Southern imagination were now brought to life. If Lincoln succeeded in launching his presidency, they feared, the Republicans would soon march into the South and "distribute the white females among the negroes." Then, to further his goal of racial amalgamation, each invader would carry off "an ebony beauty to ornament and grace his home in the North."[7] Week after week, fresh hate mail was delivered to the president-elect's home, explaining all the ways that he would be killed if he dared to come to Washington.

Lincoln must have sensed intuitively that it would help his administration to cohere if he were seen in public, unafraid. He was now liberated from the artificial requirement of staying home, silent, as if unaware of the election. Accordingly, he began to move.

The great journey to the White House began with small steps. Two days after the election, on November 8, he wrote to his running mate, Hannibal Hamlin, asking for a meeting on "as early a day as possible." That day came on November 21, when Lincoln journeyed by train to Chicago to meet his soon-to-be vice president. Mary Todd Lincoln joined him, and the outing yielded a number of healthy effects.[8] Out among the people, Lincoln seemed to breathe more freely. After months of disciplined silence, he gave three short speeches from the train. In one of them, he complained about having been "shut up in Springfield," a sign that he was enjoying himself in the open air.[9] As he and Hamlin toured the federal structures of Chicago—a customhouse, a courthouse, a post office—the idea of a Lincoln presidency began to seem real.

In other ways, too, Lincoln seemed to be in transition. As if girding himself for battle, he had begun to acquire a protective layer. If his features appeared fuzzy to the people as he flew through the Illinois countryside, that's because, upon closer inspection, they *were*. On November 22 an Illinois newspaper reported that "Old Abe" is "commencing to raise a beautiful pair of whiskers."[10] A suggestion to grow them had come from an eleven-year-old girl, Grace Bedell, of Westfield, New York, and that charming story would soon enter the national folklore. Most agreed that the beard improved his appearance—although an Illinois newspaper added this postmortem: "Still, there is no disguising the fact that he is homely." Lincoln joked privately that "apparent hair" was improving the "heir apparent."[11]

To the young, beards spoke wordlessly of generational change, even revolution. Americans had thrilled to the speeches of a bearded freedom fighter from Hungary, Lajos Kossuth, who toured the country in 1851 and 1852, hoping for support from Americans eager to see new democracies sprout in Europe. He was more successful at growing a beard than a government, but his message stirred Lincoln, who offered a resolution in support of the would-be liberator.[12] Walt Whitman, who was suspicious of fresh-faced men ("foofoos"), argued that beards were necessary for orators because they offered "a great sanitary protection to the throat."[13] The absence of beards among the cadaverous Cabinet of James Buchanan was all the more reason to explore this hairy new frontier.[14]

Day after day, Lincoln kept moving. He often went to his improvised office in the state house, where he tolerated the swarms of people trying to get a look at the Rail-Splitter. Many were office seekers, following the crumbs that led to his door, intruding into his shrinking time. With what little remained, the president-elect worked on his inaugural address and did his best to keep up with his correspondence.[15]

But the long wait was frustrating, especially as it became clear that South Carolina would carry out its threat to secede. As it did so, on December 20, it sent a shudder through the entire government of the United States, which appeared to go into shock and then paralysis in the days that followed. From Washington, the messages grew more insistent that Lincoln should come soon.[16]

Still, it was no simple matter. To come too early might seem presumptuous and cause more damage, allowing Southern fire-eaters to argue that a Northern "invasion" was under way. To come too late might mean missing

the opportunity to set things right. So he waited, past the first phase of secession, then past the second, well into the new year. A carefree song from
the campaign, "The Lincoln Quick Step," had suggested a Rail-Splitter who
was light on his feet, but reality was proving otherwise.

The American Capitoline, 1860[17]

DECLINE AND FALL

In Washington, the weather was getting cold, and the days were short, adding to the prevailing gloom. Southern politicians muttered vague threats
about stopping Lincoln, and there were still ways that they might use their
guile to alter the election result. A month after the election, an Ohio congressman wrote to Lincoln from the capital, "The sky is overcast. No one
can foresee clearly what is in the future."[18]

So began "the Great Secession Winter," to use a phrase coined by a
young historian who had just moved to Washington. Henry Adams was only
twenty-two but already steeped in history, thanks to a bookish upbringing

and his pride of descent from two American presidents. He remembered his grandfather, John Quincy Adams, for his library full of documents, pistols, and jars full of caterpillars that never quite turned into butterflies. The other, his great-grandfather, John Adams, had already sailed into the mists of history (in their correspondence, Thomas Jefferson used a nautical term, *Argonaut*, to describe their long journey together). But he was still alive to his descendant, who embraced the family legacy as if anointed to a priestly caste.

The elder Adams had not been invited to the famous dinner party at which Jefferson, Hamilton, and Madison relocated the capital. But he was president when the move actually happened, in 1800, and it was he who gave the order to pack up the government records, load them onto the backs of animals, and haul them to the new Federal City. Given the state of the roads, the caravan's success in finding the Potomac must be counted as a major achievement of the Adams administration. Adams was also the first president to live in the swampy new location, before learning, shortly after his arrival, that he had been voted out of the house he had gone to so much trouble to move into.[19]

The approach to Washington still seemed difficult fifty years later, when Henry Adams first made the trip, as a twelve-year-old boy, visiting his grandmother. Looking out his train window, he noticed the "raggedness" of the Maryland landscape, as if it were cursed. He sensed a kind of cosmic despair, as he saw pigs, cows, and enslaved children roaming without purpose, dangerously close to an unfenced train track. Toward the end of his life, as he remembered this trip, he realized that he had received his first impression of "what slavery caused."[20] But he loved the South, too: the smell of catalpa trees, the warmth of the sun, and the "softness" of his gentle grandmother, a former first lady, as they lay in bed chatting. Like Lincoln, his bloodlines drew from both sides of the divide.[21]

As the Great Secession Winter came on, Washington's thoroughfares seemed even more forlorn than usual. Adams noted how muddy the deeply rutted streets were. A Jeffersonian slogan had been repeated in happier days: "that government is best which governs least." Now it appeared to be the guiding mantra of a city that ceased to govern at all. It was as if a ruin was forming before his very eyes.

Henry Adams was drawn to ruins. A few months earlier, in May 1860, he had been happy, visiting Rome for the first time. In the same month that Lincoln was nominated, and events began to accelerate, the young historian was trying to slow them down so that he might absorb the centuries. He was especially drawn to the Capitoline, the hill that had administered the Roman Empire. Its ruins had famously inspired one of the greatest works of history ever written. In 1776, as the American empire was rising, the British historian Edward Gibbon began to publish his monumental work on the question of how empires disintegrate.[22]

The History of the Decline and Fall of the Roman Empire began with a vision of barefooted friars chanting Vespers in what remained of the old Temple of Jupiter. The young Adams went to the Capitoline many times to relive the moment and contemplate the moral collapse of Rome in the years before its sacking. It was a capital that had forgotten what its monuments even stood for, with temples "no longer inhabited, either by gods or men," empty libraries, and theaters that sought to excite rather than enlighten the people. The latter-day Romans robbed materials from their older buildings to build new ones, more cheaply, from stolen materials. In so doing, they "demolished, with sacrilegious hands, the labors of their ancestors."[23] It would be hard to find a phrase more resonant for a young Adams.

A half year later, he found himself in Washington, contemplating another Capitoline, dilapidating in real time. He had arrived with his father, Charles Francis Adams, a Massachusetts congressman, as they, like everyone else, awaited Lincoln's arrival and the great unknown that would follow. He was soon joined by his older brother, Charles Francis Adams Jr., another recent graduate of Harvard University. There they had studied the classics with a kindly professor of Greek, Cornelius Felton, now elevated to the university presidency. Felton was a gifted Hellenist who, unlike most, had actually been to Greece.[24] Such was his influence that one of his students, Henry Thoreau, read Homer in the original throughout his idyll at Walden Pond.

But Felton's brother Samuel may have done even more to influence Thoreau's reading time. As a railroad official, he put through the train track that ran a hundred yards from the writer's cabin, noisily intruding into his reverie in the woods. Samuel Felton was far less interested in the Greek gods than his brother was, but the fates would pull him into the story nevertheless. Indeed, he would be instrumental in saving Lincoln's life as he approached the American Capitoline.[25]

The Adams brothers often reverted to classical antiquity as they sought to convey the desolation of a city that feared the invasion of the Northern hordes in the final weeks of the Buchanan administration. Like Gibbon, they saw a decadent capital, dominated by warring tribes, with very little memory of its founding ideals. Thanks to their grandfather, John Quincy Adams, Washington had a scientific institution, the Smithsonian, but its ambition was so modest that it could do little more than measure the decline and fall of the thermometer each day.[26] The great orators had come and gone; now the leading politicians just spoke more loudly, while saying less. Charles Francis Adams Jr. described the House of Representatives as a "national bear-garden," because of the congressmen who liked to stand on their hind legs and roar.[27] Lobbyists were everywhere, like "cormorants," skilled at diving down deep in the muck to feed themselves."[28] Job seekers resembled "vultures," tearing at their carrion "on the very steps of the White House."[29]

But the most depressing problem was the one that struck countless European visitors as the central paradox of American democracy. The ideals of the Declaration were hardly self-evident in a city that still enforced racial subjugation with the constant threat of violence. Slavery was slowly waning in the district, but the South refused to abolish it, and coffles of men continued to shuffle along in chains near the Capitol.[30] Near, but not *too* near: African-Americans were not allowed to desecrate the sanctity of "the Capitol inclosure," unless they were "performing menial duties."[31]

The Adams brothers saw these shortcomings clearly, as they surveyed a city that had not come together as magnificently as its earliest boosters had hoped. Washington was another caterpillar that had failed to become a butterfly. Henry Adams described the capital as a rude colony camped in the forest, littered with "unfinished Greek temples," set apart along pockmarked roads as if they were "in the abandoned gravel-pits of a deserted Syrian city."[32]

That might have been a disservice to the Syrians, who had actually completed their buildings before the centuries did their work. In Washington, it seemed like everything began to decompose as soon as it was commenced. The Washington Monument was a disaster. As any child could see, it was built in the wrong location. Instead of dominating the landscape from the point where it was intended to be—at the axis of the Capitol and White House—it stood a few hundred yards away, up a small hillock, where the ground was less swampy. Then it was abandoned after political disputes interrupted its funding. There it stood, a stump in search of a point.

To many observers, a trip to Washington felt like a journey to a nullity more than a place. When Charles Dickens paid a visit in 1842, he found a city more notable for what was missing than what was there, with "spacious avenues that begin in nothing, and lead nowhere." There was no trade, no

Washington Monument, circa 1860[33]

commerce, and no potable water, thanks to its "dull and sluggish" creeks, which flowed far less freely than the spit Dickens noticed everywhere he looked. He saw so much of it that he called Washington the "head-quarters of tobacco-tinctured saliva."[34]

Congress was an especially bleak house. The House and Senate chambers could quickly become overheated during a debate, and the worst place to be was in the gallery, where visitors had to endure a constantly rising cloud of hot air, emanating not only from the speeches but also from a faulty ventilation system. One horrified visitor described how "the effluvia of human bodies and of tobacco-juice greet the nostrils and afflict the lungs" as soon as one entered the shrine. Ladies, given seats in the front row, sometimes fainted from the privilege.[35]

Even getting there was a challenge. The buildings were too far apart, as Dickens noted, and, in other ways, democracy appeared to be an uphill struggle. To travel from the executive to the legislative branch was not a task for the faint of heart. The city's chief artery, Pennsylvania Avenue, was "full of mud-holes, some of them axle-deep," and its red clay was churned into "thick mortar" by the heavy traffic of horses. John Randolph, a witty Virginian, had called it "the great Serbonian bog," after a lagoon on Egypt's Sinai Peninsula, known for its prolific insect habitats.[36]

That was all too accurate, thanks to a rivulet that brought stagnant water nearby and became even more fetid after its diversion into a canal that did not work. Goose Creek had been renamed the Tiber, after Rome's river, but the resemblance ended there. It was so shallow that it was difficult to tell whether it was actually a river, or simply a wet place for animals to slink off to and die. An observer in 1860 cast an eye on the city's canals and glimpsed "dead cats and all kinds of putridity" in a pool "reeking with pestilential odors."

This public ossuary could not have been better designed to attract mosquitoes, and many legislators, especially Northerners, fell ill as a result. Full of raw sewage, the Tiber's odor was as disturbing as its appearance. As it wound its way toward the Capitoline, it could be smelled all the way into the Senate chamber.[37] To an abolitionist such as William Lloyd Garrison, Washington was a moral swamp as well as a physical one, which "stinks in the nostrils of the world." Sewage backing up into a kitchen may have explained why many guests, including President Buchanan, came away from one of his inaugural dinners stricken with dysentery and diarrhea.[38] Walt Whitman may have been more accurate than he knew when he wrote, "The President eats dirt and excrement for his daily meals, likes it." [39]

The Capitol had fared better than the Washington Monument, but its dome was still not finished, and many wondered if it ever would be. Everything felt temporary atop an incline that had already known many names, dating back to the seventeenth century, when Capitol Hill was part of a manorial estate known as New Troy. Inside the building, the work was never finished; there was an ongoing debate over whether to call the central chamber a rotunda or a "rotundo." The statuary strained to summon imposing attitudes, but as one critic observed, the statue of Peace represented "a matronly dame, somewhat advanced in life and heavy in flesh, who carries an olive branch as if she desired to use it to keep off flies." Around the grounds, visitors could see large blocks of marble and stone carvings that did not quite work, or were simply too heavy to lift into place. There they remained for years. Of the hundred Corinthian columns needed to complete the porticoes, a grand total of three had been set into place.[40]

Seventy years after George Washington laid its cornerstone, the central edifice of American democracy failed to cohere. In so doing, it all too accurately reflected the political realities of late 1860. The Tiber may have been filthy, but it paled in comparison to the rivers of ill-gotten wealth that greased nearly every deal that was conducted inside these gilded chambers. Still, they were not as gilded as they might have been: one reason that it was so difficult to finish the Capitol is that its valuable artifacts were being stripped and sold for private gain by cronies hired to protect the building.[41]

As the Buchanan administration was sinking under the weight of its corruption, the public learned that it had awarded contracts for work on the Capitol to insider friends, who then outsourced the labor and pocketed the profits. Indignant, a prominent senator from Mississippi tried to steer the project back onto the right course. But his attention began to fade on the day that Lincoln was elected—for Jefferson Davis suddenly had a new project to absorb his interest.[42] It was as if this strange city—and by extension, democracy—had been built on a foundation of mud, silt, and sand.

A recently discovered photograph of a column being eased into position at the Capitol on the day Lincoln was elected, November 6, 1860[43]

END DAYS

In the aftermath of Lincoln's election, Washington fell apart a little more. The Adams brothers had front-row seats and wondered if these were the end days of the republic.[44] Every day brought a fresh outrage, as the edifice that their great-grandfather had helped to build began to crumble before their eyes. William Seward was a frequent guest in their household. The "wily old scarecrow," as they called him, always brought the latest gossip, which he distributed like canapés before dinner.[45]

Week after week, the old rituals of civility broke off, like vandalized pieces of statuary. Northerners were jostled and shoved by crowds of angry young men loitering on sidewalks, and pro-Southern militias paraded with their weapons.[46] Henry Adams wrote that there was a feeling of treason in the air, worthy of ancient Rome.[47] When Congress convened in early December, he thought it would be its last session.[48] In a letter to his brother, he wondered if the city would spontaneously combust.[49]

It was difficult to know which part of the government would ignite first. The Supreme Court had plenty of dry kindling: most of its justices were old men born in the previous century. Congress was eternally bickering. And no executive had ever underperformed quite as spectacularly as James Buchanan. As November turned to December, he began to fail. Henry Adams thought that the government's dysfunction was taking place inside his body, as he lost any form of initiative, and contradicted himself on the rare occasions he said anything.[50]

Buchanan had never radiated a great deal of charisma; George Templeton Strong called him an "old mollusk," not quite in the vertebrate class.[51] Many of his photographic likenesses are little more than smudges, suggesting that the camera detected a certain chemical deficiency. But he and his cronies were energetic in one respect. In his inaugural address, the new president had insisted that he intended to avoid "the taint, or even the suspicion of corruption."[52] Soon after, it was reported that "enormous sums of money" had been spent to bribe election officials in Indiana and Pennsylvania. They offered no-bid contracts to their cronies; they rewarded political supporters with no experience; they outsourced government printing contracts for profit; and they participated enthusiastically in the gluttonous feeding that Washington's ecosystem encouraged.[53]

Money had never been all that far from politics, but corruption deepened in the 1850s, with the arrival of a flourishing lobbying culture, centered around gambling houses and other dens of iniquity. One establishment, the Palace of Fortune, was especially lavish. Every night, its parlors filled with cigar smoke, and a great deal of political business was

transacted over the sound of clinking glasses, as African-American wait-
ers kept suitors plied with toddies and whiskey-straights carried on silver
trays. Presidential candidates, senators, Cabinet members, and journalists
all could be found there late into the night. One Democratic appointee
was forced to ask for a loan from the Palace of Fortune after losing a large
stake, in order to make it to China, where he was to be Buchanan's envoy.
The proprietor was a Virginian who easily guided bills through Congress
that favored his business interests. When he died, President Buchanan
attended the funeral.[54]

But Lincoln's election imperiled the subterranean world of influence
peddling. It was impossible to imagine him in a gambling house, and that
was one of the reasons he had won. The voters were exhausted by years of
scandal and fraud.[55] They longed for a president capable of speaking from
the heart, or speaking at all—in four years, Buchanan had given just three
speeches, including his inaugural.[56]

So ingrained were the lobbying habits that many expected them to
survive long after the government had folded. As South Carolina was preparing to secede, it was also trying to negotiate the "most-favored" trading
benefits of equal powers. Accordingly, it did what all great nations do: it
sent a diplomatic representative to its "embassy," a large house on K Street.
A fashionable young man was sent to represent the interests of this new
country. Years later, he was remembered as a young "ambassador" whose
tailoring was better thought through than his mission. With an imperial
mustache, patent leather shoes, and a cane topped by a golden horse head
and tapered into a horse's hoof, he left no doubt that he was "the dude of
the dudes."[57]

That was a long distance from Abraham Lincoln. But as the weeks
went by, it was not at all clear that the old order would give way. Resistance
was concentrated in the Senate and the Cabinet, where people were acting strangely. For some time, Northerners had noticed that three Cabinet
secretaries always seemed to be standing near Buchanan, as if trying to prevent his escape from the White House. They were Howell Cobb of Georgia

(Secretary of the Treasury), John B. Floyd of Virginia (Secretary of War), and Jacob Thompson of Mississippi (Secretary of the Interior). It was said that they wielded an "occult influence" over the president.[58]

All three would serve the Confederacy in high offices. In effect, they already were Confederated, as they conferred with leading Southern senators and intentionally undermined their own departments. Cobb left the Treasury empty before quitting in early December 1860. Thompson crossed the South, drumming up support for secession, which would remove enormous swaths of public land from the United States.[59]

Floyd may have been the worst. As secretary of war, he had sworn to defend the United States against all enemies. Instead, he surreptitiously shipped arms from Northern arsenals to the South. (The Confederacy would later brag about his disloyalty.)[60] If Pittsburgh's citizens had not protested a shipment of heavy guns, the damage would have been even worse.[61] Floyd was also found to have indulged in massive fraud and crooked land deals.[62] One newspaper, disgusted by how much he had stolen, called him "the $6,000,000 Man."[63]

The details of these swindles were coming out the same week that South Carolina seceded, in late December, leading to a crisis of confidence. Floyd was forced to resign—which helped—but it also added to the instability. The Secretary of State, Lewis Cass, had also resigned, leaving the country with no official to shape its foreign policy.[64] The situation deteriorated further in the last week of 1860, as bitter disputes raged over what to do with South Carolina, especially after Major Robert Anderson improved his position by retreating to Fort Sumter in Charleston Harbor. It was later alleged that Interior Secretary Thompson secretly telegraphed the details of Cabinet meetings to South Carolina officials.[65] Buchanan's attempts to please each side exasperated everyone, and after an angry Cabinet meeting on December 29, he more or less ceased to function.[66] The final hours of the year seemed to signal the utter collapse of civility. From the Senate balcony, unruly mobs jeered, "Abe Lincoln will never come here!"[67]

It seemed ever more dangerous to try. A stranger wrote to Lincoln from

Baltimore that day, saying that it would be "madness" to go through the city on his way to Washington, because of the hatred already whipped up against him. The writer added, "I have had my head shaved twice merely for making the remark that I consider you a gentleman."[68] A friend, writing from Washington, said, "We are in a revolution," and urged Lincoln to come "very soon"—but in disguise.[69]

With each passing day, the gloom deepened in the capital, as former friends stopped speaking, and social events turned into a slog. A joke going around town proposed that the government rearrange the letters of its own name, replacing "United" with "Untied." Henry Adams saw signs of brooding violence everywhere as he wandered through grim receptions, with Washington's factions glaring at each other. The young historian thought the great experiment was over, and grew depressed at "the ghost of this murdered republic."[70]

The earliest known photograph of the White House, taken by a Welsh immigrant, John Plumbe Jr., ca. 1846.[71]

COUP D'ÉTAT

Many desperate plans were contemplated during these dark days, as 1860 gave way to 1861, and wild rumors were whispered in the shadows of the Capitol. An ardent secessionist, Senator Louis Wigfall of Texas, was later accused of plotting to kidnap James Buchanan in order to elevate the vice president, John Breckinridge, who had just lost to Lincoln in the election.[72] Northern leaders suspected that Southerners were already negotiating with the British. The British government was said to be rejoicing that the "bubble" of democracy had finally burst.[73]

Another rumor, reported in many diaries and letters, described an imminent invasion of Washington by militias loyal to the South.[74] The capital was vulnerable, not only because it was so close to the Southern states but also because roughly two out of three residents supported the secessionists.[75] A former governor of Virginia, Henry Wise, was openly advocating for an attack. On December 18 the *Richmond Enquirer* urged Virginians to resist Lincoln's inauguration by any means possible.[76] On Christmas, its editors asked, "Can there not be found men bold and brave enough in Maryland to unite with Virginians in seizing the capital?" Newspapers as far away as New York joined in, urging Southerners to "save the republic of Washington from the taint of niggerism" and to physically "expel Lincoln and his free-nigger horde from the federal district." Local conspirators bragged that they could quickly summon a hundred thousand men to surround the Capitol and restore the District to its rightful control by Maryland and Virginia.[77]

A week later, the governor of Maryland, Thomas Hicks, confirmed that dangerous plans were being hatched by conspirators. In an address to the people of Maryland, delivered on January 3, he warned against these violent schemes. In so doing, he gave all the details of the plot: "They have resolved to seize the federal Capitol and the public archives, so that they may be in a position to be acknowledged by foreign governments as the *United States of America*."[78] In other words, they did not intend to secede—they planned on taking over the entire project, including the name. Southern senators taunted that the capital would be in the hands of the South on Inauguration Day.[79]

These fears were corroborated by many others. William Seward heard rumors of an attempted coup d'état.[80] Henry Adams maintained that the planners included Cabinet members. News of the plot reached Springfield as well, where Lincoln's secretary, John Nicolay, noted it with alarm.[81] Many of Lincoln's friends wrote long letters disclosing what they knew of the plan. Lincoln's close ally Elihu Washburne warned of a "powerful conspiracy to seize the Capitol." Government of the people hung by a slender thread.[82]

As the symbol of democracy, the Capitol was an attractive target.[83] It held nearly the entirety of the government: both chambers of the legislative branch, the judicial branch, and most of the archives, going back to the country's earliest documents. No one knew the building better than Jefferson Davis, who had been supervising its renovations. The Mississippi senator was fascinated by national symbols—the last book he checked out from the Library of Congress was a history of the American flag.[84] Davis had his eye on the White House as well; his wife Varina told friends in New York that she hoped they would visit her there after her husband returned to occupy their new home in the spring.[85]

It would have been a simple matter, from a military perspective. The one time Washington had been threatened before, in 1814, it had quickly folded. The American army was still very small, with thirteen thousand men; a tenth the size of Switzerland's.[86] Most of the troops were deployed far away in forts on the western frontier. Nor was the navy in much better shape. There were ninety vessels in the fleet, but only forty-two were in commission. Of the entire navy, only two ships lay at anchor, ready, and one of them had orders to sail for Africa.[87] Fewer than five hundred regular troops were available to defend the capital, with perhaps another five hundred who could be called up—but their loyalty was not certain in a city that was more against Lincoln than for him.[88] The Columbian Armory, where arms were stored, was guarded by a grand total of two men.[89] In the Washington Navy Yard, loyal officers were worried about an amphibious invasion across the Potomac. They knew that it was possible to wade across the river at low tide.[90]

If anti-Lincoln militias had captured the Capitol in late December, the year 1861 would have begun very differently. Instead of organizing a new country, with its capital a thousand miles away in Alabama, the South might have simply held on to the old one. With whatever rump Congress they chose to assemble, they could have expelled the Northern members, welcomed back South Carolina, and abruptly disinvited Lincoln from his own inaugural. In effect, they would have turned back the news of his election.[91]

That would have put the responsibility on the Northern and Western states to organize a new government, shorn of the historical documents that do so much to give the United States its sense of origin. The Declaration of Independence, the Constitution, and the Bill of Rights would have remained in the possession of the South.[92] So would the other badges of legitimacy—all of the seals, treaties, maps, laws, patents, and census reports prepared by earlier generations. In effect, they would have seized American history itself. It would have been a kind of bloodless acquisition; a corporate takeover organized by a powerful minority interest with a strong sense of its right to rule.[93]

One set of records was especially valuable to the conspirators, desperate to make sure that Lincoln's words would never be spoken from the steps of the Capitol. Inside the same building, two boxes held the confirmation that Lincoln had, in fact, been elected. After the election, each state had tabulated its votes and prepared formal certificates, which they sent dutifully to Washington. Remarkably, they were routed to the office of Vice President John Breckinridge, the president of the Senate.[94] He had been the South's candidate in the election, and he was the very person who would gain the most if the boxes were destroyed, or stolen, or simply misplaced. The Capitol had many secret chambers, well suited for the deep storage of idealistic legislation.

Even if Southern militias did not surround the Capitol, there was another way Lincoln's election could be turned back, striking for its simplicity. On February 13 the two boxes would be taken from Breckinridge's office and brought into the House chamber, where they would be opened, and the votes counted. But anything might happen in a city that had effectively ceased to play by any rules. Perhaps the certificates had not been signed and sealed properly? Lincoln's enemies might declare a miscount, throwing the election into the House. In 1824, Congress had denied another Westerner, Andrew Jackson, the presidency after some intense horse trading behind closed doors. Or, leading Southerners might simply ask the vice president to become an "acting president" in light of the collapse in leadership from James Buchanan.[95]

Yet another plan to prevent Lincoln's arrival was even starker. It was simply to kill him, either during his long and exposed journey to Washington or, perhaps, on the very steps of the Capitol as he was about to be inaugurated. As it turned out, Henry Adams was not the only young man obsessed with Rome: according to one account, a cabal of plotters had been reading Shakespeare's *Julius Caesar*. That play offered a blueprint for eliminating a tyrant, killed while entering the Capitoline—one of the plotters was reported to be an actor who would actually declaim from the play in their meetings.[96]

Lincoln had been receiving warnings for months from friends who had heard rumors about these shadowy cabals.[97] Some of the threats even made the papers. In December, the *Chicago Tribune* reported that $40,000 had been raised in New Orleans to hire assassins.[98] In the gambling houses, immense sums were said to be wagered on the result, as if Lincoln's death were a sporting event. To many bettors, it was not all that different; a battle of wits, between a form of prey and his pursuers. They were used to foxhunts, and duck blinds, and steeplechase rides through the countryside. There would be many opportunities to catch this quarry, none better than the final stretch of his approach.[99]

Winfield Scott, 1851[100]

RATS IN A TRAP

Yet a frail hope remained, even in these darkest days of the republic. The simple fact that Lincoln was coming had a galvanic effect on people. After all of the corruption and the constant braying of secession threats, Americans felt encouraged that a transition was imminent. Hay and Nicolay likened it to a barometric change and called it the "first fresh breeze" of a reaction, as if the great prairie wind of the summer were still blowing.[101] In small towns and large cities, citizens began to stand up for their country. They went to public meetings, they talked over fences, and they readied themselves for any hardship. They may not have voted for Lincoln, but they now felt a strong interest in his survival.

They felt it even in the South, where there were brave Americans willing to stand up and risk the anger of the Lincoln haters. The country's leading military figure, Winfield Scott, was a native Virginian but a staunch Unionist. He was older than the capital, and had seen many presidents come and go. Thomas Jefferson had personally interviewed him about his desire to serve, at the beginning of a glorious career. Most felt that career was finished, but on December 12 Scott returned to Washington to do battle once more. Despite his age and girth (he could no longer mount a horse), he knew that a strong hand was needed to save the republic.[102]

Scott soon took charge of a deteriorating situation. He enlisted the aid of a capable officer, Charles P. Stone and, in their first meeting, explained that the situation was so tense, "a dogfight might cause the gutters of the capital to run with blood."[103] Many army officers were actually taking steps to defend Washington against the *North*. Until Scott arrived, guns had been given to pro-Southern militias but not to regular companies willing to fight for the United States.[104]

Stone quickly shored up the defenses of the government buildings.[105] Soon he was drilling new recruits: volunteers he had found among ordinary citizens who had worked hard to build up their city and did not want to see it seized by gaudy secessionists. They included firemen, stonecutters, housepainters, and more than a few immigrants.[106] Stone wrote of these rank-and-file Americans, "Without them, Mr. Lincoln never would have been inaugurated."[107]

The breeze blew in other ways as well. Following the resignation of the disloyal Cabinet members, it became easier to lead the government. James Buchanan remained incapable of action, but the crisis eased as others began to step into the breach. Attorney General Edwin Stanton secretly communicated urgent information to William Seward, the acknowledged head of the Republican Party in Washington. They never met face-to-face at the time, but by cooperating, they were able to keep the government of the United States intact until Lincoln's arrival.[108] "History is being made very rapidly," Henry Adams wrote breathlessly.[109]

The South did not give up easily. On January 5, according to several sources, a secret conclave was held at the Washington home of Jefferson Davis to draft a blueprint for the Confederacy. It decreed that Davis would lead the protocountry, and that Southerners would pretend to negotiate with Northerners, to lull them into complacency. But they would sabotage the incoming administration in every way possible. Then, on the morning of Lincoln's inaugural, they would have cannon ready, and, with help from Virginians, they would take over the capital.[110]

These claims remain conjectural, but many aspects of the plan track with reality, including the efforts of Southerners to offer a bewildering variety of compromises in the weeks leading up to Lincoln's arrival. One of these was a peace conference convened by former president John Tyler, which began to deliberate on February 4 inside the Willard Hotel, a well-known shrine to lobbying (the Willard lobby was said to be where the word originated). There the delegates would be comfortable eating and drinking to their hearts' content.

Throughout January and February, Washington was on pins and needles, waiting for a hostile takeover. On February 3 Lincoln's friend Elihu Washburne wrote him a confidential letter warning that the evidence of a conspiracy to seize the Capitol was "overwhelming" and that he should "prepare for the worst."[111] Henry Adams wrote, "If the news comes to the North some fine morning that the telegraph wires are down, and the railroad interrupted between here and Baltimore, you may take it for granted that the war has begun and that we are shut up here like so many rats in a trap, to work out our own salvation."[112] He was beginning to appreciate a serious flaw in the apparatus that his great-grandfather had helped to design. The wait for an incoming president was simply too long.

Dorothea Dix[113]

CITY OF THE DEAD

As the country's schizophrenia deepened, a specialist in mental health was making her way through the South. Dorothea Dix hailed from New England, but she had forged many Southern friendships during her career advocating for more humane treatment of the mentally ill. In recent months, she had been in Tennessee, Mississippi, and South Carolina, where she had arrived during the frenzy of secession. She called it "insane," not a word she used lightly. From there she found her way north to Washington, reaching the capital just before Christmas. To her practiced eye, it was as if a plague had struck. She described it as a "city of the dead.[114]" But it was not simply that the government was in danger of collapse; she had also heard about a plot to assassinate Lincoln as he approached. In response, Dix made a fateful visit to a railroad executive who operated the only track that connected Washington to the rest of the country.

Samuel Felton was the same civil engineer who had rudely disrupted
Thoreau's solitude at Walden by sending a railroad through his sylvan paradise. He was now the president of the Philadelphia, Wilmington and Baltimore Railroad, where he specialized in solving engineering challenges. His
brother Cornelius, the Greek specialist, wrote, "Sam is a genius for getting
over rivers and difficulties." [115]

Felton waited twenty years to describe her visit; Dix never mentioned
it. They had a long interview, more than an hour, on a Saturday. Felton
noted that it was remarkable, when so many male leaders of the country
were "utterly at sea," that "the keen insight and military decision of mind of
a woman should have lighted on the precise point where the greatest peril
to the nation lay." [116] She had discovered an "extensive" conspiracy "through
the South" to seize Washington, "with its archives and records," and declare
the Southern confederacy "the Government of the United States." That was
identical to the conspiracy that the governor of Maryland and many others
were warning against.

But what distinguished Dix's account was its command of the details.
She had hard knowledge that militias were already drilling along Maryland
train tracks, ready to kill Lincoln as he drew near. The conspiracy's leaders had carefully studied the bridges going in and out of Baltimore. They
would also cut railroad traffic into Washington, effectively sealing it off, and
declare it the capital of a Southern nation called the "United States of America." She used the phrase that others had: *coup d'état.* [117]

With this alarming intelligence, Felton sprang into action and communicated the news to Winfield Scott. The general feared that Lincoln
would have to be inaugurated in Philadelphia. Felton then began his own
intelligence gathering, using all the resources available to a railroad president. With time, he learned more details. According to one source, the
conspirators intended to dress "as negroes" and pour combustible material over a bridge near Baltimore as Lincoln's train was approaching. In
the chaos that ensued, they would kill him with whatever weapons were
handy.

An 1866 watercolor of Kate Warne[118]

Felton knew exactly whom to call in an emergency like this. Allan Pinkerton was a Scottish immigrant who had been active in the Underground Railroad and developed a comfortable practice as a railroad detective, working out of Chicago. On January 19 he came to Philadelphia to meet with Felton. Eight days later, he agreed to accept the assignment of infiltrating the conspiracy and foiling the plot to kill Lincoln. On February 1 he left for Maryland with eight detectives.

Among them was a recent widow, roughly twenty-seven, who had succeeded in convincing Pinkerton that women could be just effective as men, and often more so. Pinkerton later remembered Kate Warne as "a commanding person, with clear-cut, expressive features, and with an ease of manner that was quite captivating at times." She was a "brilliant conversationalist" who could be "quite vivacious" but also understood "that rarer quality: the art of being silent." For all of these reasons, she was a perfect spy. Like Dorothea Dix, Warne would play a large but unsung role in protecting Lincoln.[119]

Felton also organized a force of two hundred men, whom he stationed at the bridges along the route of his railroad. They pretended to whitewash the bridges but secretly were reporting back all observations of suspicious activity.[120] In Washington, Winfield Scott was conducting his own intelligence sweeps. Most of the threats centered around Baltimore. In coordination with Seward, he too hired specialists, including the superintendent of the New York City police, John Kennedy.[121]

Far away in Springfield, Lincoln's mail continued to pile up with disturbing messages. Many tried to be helpful. A Cleveland clairvoyant urged him to drink lots of hot milk after seeing a vision of Lincoln being poisoned.[122] An Iowa supporter offered to build him a "coat of chain mail," as if he were riding a steed into battle.[123] Others were more graphic, sending drawings to his wife that showed him being lynched, or tarred and feathered. He tried to burn much of it.[124]

From Maryland, the warnings were more specific. "A Lady" in Baltimore warned him anonymously of "a league of ten persons, who had sworn that you should never pass through that city alive."[125] An army officer whom he trusted also sent troubling reports, including one that predicted it would take fifty thousand men to get him through Maryland and recommended that he simply go incognito.[126] It was not entirely clear that Maryland would still be in the Union when he came through; a large public meeting would be held there on February 18 about whether to secede.[127]

CLOSE-WALKING

Waiting was as difficult for Lincoln as it was for everyone else. He was eight hundred miles away, powerless to stop the country from sliding into something close to anarchy. On the first day of 1861, he wrote a friend, "Every hour adds to the difficulties I am called upon to meet . . . he [Buchanan] is giving away the case, and I have nothing to say and can't stop him." He

Two days before departure: Lincoln, February 9, 1861[128]

almost thought the case lost, adding, "I only wish I could have got there to lock the door before the horse was stolen."[129]

But in his own way, Lincoln was already fighting to save his country, with his words, as he diligently wrote out his early drafts of an inaugural address. He too valued an archives, and in the library of the Illinois State House, he consulted earlier speeches from American history, slowly jotting down phrases that he liked. Like a jeweler stringing beads along a necklace, Lincoln's lapidary writing technique required patience. He would write fragments on small scraps of paper, often thrust into his pockets; then rework them. After enough scraps had been joined into coherent paragraphs, he had an early draft secretly typeset. The oldest scrap remaining comes from the very first sentence. It began, "In compliance with a custom as old as the government itself . . ."[130] Like the secessionists eying the Capitol, he was reaching into the past in search of a legitimacy of his own. But he differed from them, as he sought his way toward a *grasp* of the founding documents—not merely their possession.

The search for the right language was a good way to prepare for the journey that was looming. The country might be enormous, but it shared a common history. To travel through America's diverse regions was another way of reinforcing the essential doctrine of *e pluribus unum*. But time was running short, and communication was difficult, with the mails and telegraph unsafe. No trip this complicated had ever been planned for an incoming president. The challenges ranged from the vastness of the land itself, to the multiplicity of possible routes, and the constant exposure of a vulnerable human being who had engendered more hatred than anyone in American history.

Certainly he would not be safe in the South, where violence was continually threatened against him. As a candidate, Lincoln had written to a friend in Kentucky, wondering if he would be lynched if he tried to visit his birthplace.[131] To his friends, he shrugged and said, "If they want to kill me, there is nothing to prevent it."[132]

But to save democracy in its hour of darkness, it was essential that Lincoln travel publicly, unafraid, to his inauguration. He never wavered, even if there were flickers of his awareness of the danger. After sending a memo to Winfield Scott urging him to hold the forts, he said, "There can be no doubt that in any event that is good ground to live by and die by."[133] When a visitor mentioned that the secessionists might seize Washington, he answered with heat, promising, "I will suffer death," before giving in to any compromise that made it look like he was "buying the privilege" of the office to which he had been legitimately elected. Since he would never "concede to traitors," he was ready, if need be, for his soul to "go back to God from the wings of the Capitol." On the eve of his journey, he said to an old friend, "I will die before I will depart from any of those things under threats made by traitors and secessionists under arms, defying the government.[134]

Walt Whitman would later use the term "close-walking" to describe the feeling of holding hands with death, as a companion.[135] In his own youthful poetry, Lincoln had expressed a similar thought in his poetry, about the "midway world" where the living and the dead were free to mingle. From the election on, he would never be free from the knowledge that people were trying to kill him as he tried to save the country—that, in fact, his life and the life of democracy were, for a time, running parallel to each other. In a letter to a congressman from Pennsylvania, Lincoln said that he would never give in to the threats: "If we surrender, it is the end of us, and of the government." [136]

But if he survived, a successful trip might answer nagging questions about the country. Traveling through hundreds of villages and cities on his way to Washington was a danger, but it also presented an opportunity to unite Americans and reflect on the deeper purpose of the republic. In many ways, the country remained fissiparous, more *pluribus* than *unum*. It was not merely that North and South were pulling apart; there were countless other Americas as well. The West stretched so far that it included vast expanses with barely any awareness of the United States at all. There were self-governing indigenous peoples, and Mormons in Utah, reluctant to acknowledge any government except their own. California was a universe unto itself. Texas might easily return to its earlier status as an independent republic. Even in the East, there were fragments of states that had belonged to other states, when the ink was not quite dry on the old maps. An alarming report sent to Lincoln by Winfield Scott on the eve of the election expressed the old general's fear that the country would split—not into two but *four* confederacies. [137]

But Lincoln was conversant with James Madison's cheeky assertion in Federalist 14 that republican government could survive as far as people were willing to go. There is evidence that he was reading it at precisely this moment, as he wrote his inaugural address. Madison's "cords of affection" reverberate in Lincoln's "bonds of affection" and "mystic chords of memory." [138] The country desperately needed to feel those cords of affection again.

Many centuries earlier, when the kings of England and France traveled through the countryside, they were believed to possess magical healing powers. If those afflicted with scrofula drew near, they might, if they were lucky, receive the "the royal touch"—a laying on of hands that was widely believed to cure the people's suffering. [139] Of course, not many clung to these old superstitions in a country as modern as the United States of America.

Yet some kind of laying on of hands was needed. In desperation, a woman wrote to Lincoln on the last day of the year, asking him to speak and to give Americans "the inspiration of a new hope."[140]

A well-conceived journey could remind Americans, in this perilous hour, just how much they had in common. It would not only allow millions of citizens to see *him*, but also allow him to see *them*. That education would be useful for an incoming president. Lincoln understood that it would be healthy for the people and their president to have a "closer acquaintance." As his close advisers knew, there was something about "live sympathy" that made democracy work.[141]

But could he win that sympathy, with so many challenges before him? From Washington, the distress signals were getting louder. Henry Adams conveyed the gravity of the situation when he worried that Lincoln's task "was one which might have filled with alarm the greatest statesman that ever lived."[142] Glum, he saw little hope. His brother Charles, even more darkly, saw a ship of state "drifting on the rocks of a lee shore; nothing could save it." It was remotely possible that "the coming change of commanders would alter the whole aspect of the situation," but so many questions remained. Adams asked, "where and what sort of a man was the new commander?" He continued, "Abraham Lincoln was an absolutely unknown quantity; and yet he was the one possible *Deus ex machina*!"[143]

The phrase *deus ex machina* was Latin, but the concept dated back to Greek tragedy, and the machine, usually a crane, that would casually drop an actor onto the stage from an unseen location or help spirit the actor away. In *Medea*, by Euripides, the machine was a chariot, drawn by dragons, that allowed the heroine to leave at a moment when a hasty departure was necessary. Lincoln may have wished such a device was available, to flee the office seekers and a situation that was growing worse by the day.

That prompted the thought that Lincoln would need to leave Springfield soon and that some care should be given to the delicate matter of what sort of *machina* ought to transport him to the capital. It should project a presidential aura, at a time when the presidency had nearly ceased to exist. It should bring him into contact with the people and restore their confidence in democracy. It should show a firm, implacable purpose, to remind his many enemies that he had, in fact, been elected to lead the country. It should have windows, so he could see the people. And it should go fast.

Fortunately, such a machine existed. The railroad had been carrying Lincoln in a widening radius from his home for years. He *knew* railroads; he had studied their gear mechanisms; he had charted their routes. They were the vehicle of choice for huge numbers of new Americans coming out west, swelling the census returns, and adding precious votes into his column. This was the *deus ex machina* he needed to reach his capital. A specially outfitted private car would carry him and his family nearly two thousand miles toward Washington. In effect, this rolling land barge would become the ship of state, for however long it took to get him there. A friend of Lincoln's wrote, "The car which carries him to Washington carries the welfare of a great nation."[144]

As 1861 began, the planning became more serious. On January 3 Lincoln wrote to William Seward that he wanted to arrive after the official counting of the electoral votes on February 13.[145] That provided focus. Soon after, Henry Villard reported that a man with railroad experience, William S. Wood, a "former organizer of pleasure excursions," had arrived to take charge of the trip.[146]

By late January, the route was nearly finished.[147] It was important to visit the governors, as they would be instrumental, especially if soldiers were needed. Accordingly, the route would wind through the capitals of Indiana, Ohio, New York, New Jersey, and Pennsylvania, the states that had elected him. It would be a grueling odyssey, from one Greek Revival state house to the next, until he reached the city of ruins along the Potomac. But that was the only way Lincoln could breathe new life into a republic that had all but given up the ghost.

Just before his inauguration, in 1789, George Washington had written that he felt like "a culprit who is going to the place of his own execution."[148] But his long trip from Mount Vernon to New York had helped to make his presidency real to the people. Now, in order to save the country, Lincoln needed to summon all of his strength for an even longer journey, back to the place Washington had approved as the seat of government. And he needed to get there quickly, while there was a country left to save.

Tioga, May 1848, Philadelphia [1]

3

THE IRON MONSTER

But come now, change thy theme, and sing of the building of the horse . . .
—Homer, *The Odyssey*, book 8, lines 493–94[2]

CROSSING THE RUBICON

As the days dwindled, Lincoln felt his past tugging at him, even as he contemplated the trip about to begin. He was often seen near the train tracks, as if readying himself. In late January he went there three nights in a row to wait in the snow and cold for his wife to come back from a shopping trip to New York.[3] Then, as his time drew short, he set out on a short train journey to the east, like the longer one to come.

Across the country, people were saying good-bye as the new world shaped by secession came into focus. Some said it loudly: two days earlier, on January 28, Senator Alfred Iverson of Georgia had stood in the Senate to say, "The Rubicon is passed, and it shall never, with my consent, be recrossed." The Rubicon was a popular crossing all of a sudden: a week before, five Southern senators had said their farewells to the Senate in a single day. One of them, Jefferson Davis, was unable to leave before reminding his audience, once again, that the Declaration of Independence had never applied to African-Americans.[4]

Others took their leave more quietly, within the family. As Lincoln wrapped up his affairs in Springfield, he realized that he needed to say a special good-bye. On January 3 he received a letter from a kinsman concerning his seventy-two-year-old stepmother, Sarah Bush Lincoln. The letter explained that "she is getting somewhat childish and is very uneasy about you, fearing some of your political opponents will kill you. She is very anxious to see you once more." [5]

Lincoln had bigger problems than the fretting of an elderly widow, but he went. On the morning of January 30, he slipped away and boarded a train in Springfield for the 120-mile journey to a small town called Charleston. By Illinois standards, that was not a great distance, but it was a difficult trek and must have reminded him of the hardships of his youth, when surging freshets could make travel to the next town impossible.

The trip was a comedy of errors, with missed connections and improvised arrangements that did not augur well for the long journey approaching. Lincoln actually rode twelve miles in the caboose of a freight train after having missed a passenger train.[6] He handled it the way he usually did: fellow passengers remembered that he told an endless succession of droll stories, punctuated by his own hearty laughter. He was wearing a "faded" hat and a short coat, like "a sailor's pea jacket." All of his luggage was stuffed into a well-worn carpetbag, "quite collapsed."[7] Finally, the president-elect made it to the farmhouse after fording a river full of ice. For him, the Rubicon was all too real.[8]

But the reunion was worth the effort. The local school released the children for the day, and Lincoln laughed with them. (He told them he'd rather be in their place than his.) Some walked in his shoes, to feel what it was like to "be president." That evening Lincoln spoke about his childhood, before a large crowd. He rarely went into autobiographical territory, so it must have been a special remembrance, but unfortunately his words were not transcribed.[9] To all who listened, he praised the woman who had found him after his mother had died and began to make him and his older sister "more human," in her words.

When she first encountered him, as a young boy of ten, he seemed distinctly less than that: a half-naked boy, starving after living alone in the wilderness with his sister, while his father sought a new wife. Abraham's stomach had grown "leathery" from going so long without food, and he possessed so few clothes that he was "almost nude."[10] Sarah, a widow with three children of her own, fed him, clothed him, and offered access to a small library of books she kept, despite her own illiteracy. She remembered later, "His mind and mine, what little I had, seemed to run together, more in the same channel." [11] Her memories included a young boy's passion for words and his astonishing, almost Homeric facility for memorizing speeches.

Lincoln's final good-bye to his stepmother was described in a letter written by one of her kin, complete with grammatical lapses: "She embraced him when they parted and said she would never be permitted to see him again that she felt his enemies would assassinate him. He replied no Mama (he always called her Mama) they will not do that. Trust in the Lord and all will be well We will see each other again." After Sarah died in 1869, she was buried in a black dress Lincoln had given her on this visit—as if they were already in mourning. [12]

Lincoln may have been tempted to remain in that deep place, beyond the ice floes. But duty called, and after he returned to Springfield, time seemed to speed up. With little more than a week left before his departure, he busied himself with small tasks: the renting of his house, the sale of his furniture, final meetings with friends and advisers. He gave his dog, Fido, a yellowish lab mix, to the family of a carpenter who had done some work for him. In a way, Fido was a casualty of the celebrity that had already come to Lincoln. On the night he was elected, Fido was terrified by the cannon fire announcing victory, and the Lincolns believed that the crush of attention would overwhelm him on the journey to come. [13]

On February 8 Lincoln moved out of his home of sixteen years and into a hotel, Chenery House, a block from the Chicago and Alton Railroad Station. There in his new rooms, he could hear the whistle of the trains and the bells tolling as each hour slipped away. The bells had multiplied with Springfield's journey toward self-importance, and Lincoln's rooms were within easy earshot of several churches. He kept a pew at one of them, the First Presbyterian. Its bell had been purchased after a church supper held by the ladies (including Mrs. Lincoln) raised $1,300 on January 11, 1853, following a lecture on "Power" by Ralph Waldo Emerson. [14]

The word must have seemed remote to Lincoln in 1853, four years removed from his single term as a congressman, with no plan for a political comeback. That night, Emerson wondered aloud if there were any great westerners ready to shape the age. Lincoln was presumably there in the crowd, pondering the imponderables cast out by the Sage of Concord. Emerson asked, "Who shall set a limit to the influence of a human being?" Answering his own question, he argued that there were certain rare men who "by their sympathetic attractions, carry nations with them." If such individuals possessed a "magnetism" strong enough to command "material and elemental powers," they would find that "immense instrumentalities organize around them." He almost seemed to be describing a literal magnetism—a man who would attract other bits of metal to him.

Springfield was impressed by Emerson. Unfortunately, the feeling was not mutual. Emerson wrote, "There is mud such as I never beheld," and cleaned pounds of it off his shoes.[15] But he drew enough people that the bell was duly purchased with the proceeds. Now that bell was across the street, reminding Lincoln, as a church ought to, that he was running out of time.

On Saturday, February 9, an unusually elegant train pulled into Springfield, exciting attention. The Presidential Special was no ordinary conveyance. A Cleveland reporter described every feature, down to the shape of the headrests. Lincoln's private car had leather seat backs and two round tables for meetings. These were covered with red cloth, embroidered with the eagle and shield, and surrounded by yellow stars.[16] Yellow was also the color of a passenger car and baggage car attached to the train. They were pulled by a locomotive, the *L. M. Wiley*, named after a railroad official. Unfortunately, he was a Southern slave owner with extensive property in South Carolina, Georgia, and Alabama, all three of which had seceded.[17]

Yellow and red were an incendiary choice for the national insignia, but the colors matched the moment, and a country that felt like it might burst into flames at any moment. On February 9, the same day that Lincoln's car arrived, delegates met in Montgomery to organize the Confederate States of America. The papers were announcing that Fort Sumter would be attacked any day. Around the world, others were feeling a tension in the air during the first week of February. In some cases, the air itself was the problem. On

February 7 an Irish scientist, John Tyndall, delivered the Bakerian Lecture before the Royal Society in London and warned that "a change of climate" would ultimately harm humanity if too many heat-trapping gases formed "an atmospheric envelope on the temperature of the planet."[18]

To see the tracks stretching toward the horizon was another reminder that the hour of departure was fast approaching. Writers had already likened the railroad to a kind of destiny. At Walden, alongside the right-of-way that Samuel Felton built, Henry Thoreau praised the railroad as "a fate, an Atropos, that never turns aside." Thoreau must have learned the word from his old Greek teacher, Felton's brother Cornelius. Atropos was the eldest of the three Fates, and the one who chose how mortals would die. (*Atropos* means "she who cannot be turned.")

But, in fact, a railroad *can* turn aside when necessary. As Lincoln and his advisers planned the journey, they realized that the most direct route would take them into harm's way. An insider revealed later what Lincoln could not: the president-elect "abandoned the idea of coming to Washington via Wheeling (then in Virginia) in consequence of certain alleged threats of violence from parties in Virginia and Maryland."[19]

Instead, he would choose a roundabout route, adding miles but taking care of important business as he visited the capitals of five essential states— in addition to the great metropolis of New York City—before the final thrust southward. In a stroke of genius, a stop was added at Philadelphia for February 22, which would allow him to visit the high altar of democracy, Independence Hall, on George Washington's birthday.[20] As the engine behind the engine, Lincoln was surely involved in that decision.

The odyssey that was beginning would draw on all of his mental and physical reserves. Over a grueling route that stretched nearly two thousand miles, he would need to conquer the impediments that nature had put before him; the hills and valleys that delighted observers of the picturesque, but vexed civil engineers. He needed to lap the miles, in Emily Dickinson's phrase, moving quickly enough to avoid danger but slowly enough to establish a common purpose with the people he passed in hundreds of small towns along the way. His support was so thin and his challenge so immense that he could not spare a single vote. In effect, he needed to campaign all over again, from a moving platform, to save the republic.

For thirteen days, Abraham Lincoln would travel through his divided country as he made his passage to the White House. It would require Herculean endurance to suffer through the receptions and receiving lines, as the destinations piled up on top of one another, every few miles, each with its host committee, its sprawling buffet, its jostling local politicians, and its relentless scrutiny of the tall stranger. To be endlessly watched was a new kind of ordeal for an awkward westerner, still uncomfortable in the formal parlors of the East.

After months of strategic silence, Lincoln would be expected to speak incessantly on topics both serious and frivolous whenever he arrived at a new destination. While enduring these conditions, he would need to work on the inaugural address that all were waiting to hear once he made his way to the East Front of the Capitol on March 4. There he would be utterly exposed.

Springfield, *Ballou's Pictorial Drawing Room Companion*, November 15, 1856

ACCELERATION

A little more than four years earlier, Springfield had been profiled in *Ballou's Pictorial Drawing-Room Companion*, a fashionable illustrated magazine. In one illustration, a train could be seen in the background, belching smoke into the air, behind hoop-skirted women chatting amiably. The more it belched, the more amiable the people of Springfield became—as the railroad brought more goods, more people, and more magazine profiles.[21]

The snort of locomotives was distinctly audible in the background as Lincoln's career accelerated in the years leading up to his election. He described that sound as an "eloquent music," and it is easy to see why it pleased him.[22] Trains shuttled him to his debates against Stephen Douglas in 1858, and they whisked him in and out of New York when he was still an exotic western specimen. Even though he stayed at home in 1860, his words raced everywhere that trains could take them.

Trains were not only fast, they were *smart*, beaming the latest political intelligence from the telegraphs that could be found inside every depot, and carrying stacks of newspapers up and down a buzzing information corridor. Near the tracks, Americans felt "interlinked," as Whitman phrased it.

Adroit politicians took notice. To many who were used to the long-winded blather of floor speeches in Congress, Lincoln sounded as different as he looked. His speeches were lean and linear. They made points, they went from A to B. A cartoon from the campaign of 1860 showed him in a locomotive about to plough into a wagon stuck on the tracks, representing the Democratic party.[23] For many Southern politicians, that summed up the situation, as they clung desperately to power in a rapidly shifting universe, with Lincoln's train bearing down on them.

Alarmed, some Southern leaders tried to define a strange new kind of freedom—not so much freedom of information as freedom *from* information. The Virginia congressman John Randolph refused to even *look* at a train; they threatened his worldview.[24] But the trains kept coming, carrying the irresistible facts of the nineteenth century along their capillaries. New structures, built of iron and steel, spread like an invasive species; when they could not spread laterally, they simply went up in the air, vertically, as they were beginning to do in New York City, thanks to the newly invented elevator. Steam engines burrowed deep into the earth, as if they were feeding, extracting the minerals they needed to slake their hunger. A French observer wrote, "The Americans have railroads in the water, in the bowels of the earth, and in the air."[25]

Even in the anxious days that followed Lincoln's election, Northern newspapers glowed with announcements of new discoveries. Someday Americans might drive "steam carriages" down paved highways or simply skip the highways and take "flying machines." One article in *Scientific American* tried to calculate the amount of time it would take a locomotive to fly to the sun (five hundred years).[26] To rural Southerners, increasingly wary of this glut of information, they could legitimately ask: *Were Yankees out of their minds?*

They had a reason to fear the Iron Horse, or as some called it, the Iron Monster.[27] From the moment that railroads charged into the landscape, they offered a freedom to move that was inherently threatening to the old land-based order. European aristocrats had noticed that trains undermined the notion that the people should *know their place*. From their turrets, they thundered against a machine that never seemed to stop. The Grand Duke of Hanover was appalled that "any cobbler or tailor could travel as fast as I." King William III of Prussia was annoyed that anyone would see any reason to hurry at all.[28] In the Vatican, the railroad was denounced by Pope Pius IX as "the work of the devil," but eventually he came around and embellished a private car with statues of saints arranged around the perimeter—a rolling cathedral on wheels.[29] In England, until the 1840s, the poor were considered "freight" and forced to sit in the open air, where they would be showered with hot coals, soot, and smoke.[30]

It was different in America. Trains might be uncouth—Charles Dickens was horrified by the jets of tobacco juice that stained the cars[31]—but they revealed a people on the move *together*. An Argentinian was shocked by trains in the United States; people walked between the cars "just for the fun of it and to feel free." To his dismay, he was forced to sit next to a laborer. Confused, he decided that Americans had built their trains "in order to inspire and honor the poor."[32]

This freedom of movement was not spelled out anywhere in the Bill of

Rights. But it was a significant instrument in its way. To be sure, it benefited some more than others. African-Americans faced far more difficulty in seizing it, but even for them, the train could bring liberation. Frederick Douglass escaped slavery by boarding a northbound train as it began to move, in Baltimore. From that moment, "a new world had opened upon me," he wrote.[33] Henry Thoreau was delighted to learn that the Underground Railroad could be an *actual* railroad, and he helped a slave, Henry Williams, escape by rail to Canada.[34] By their very existence, these information corridors undermined slavery.[35]

Once unleashed, the Iron Horse galloped freely across the wide-open spaces of a country that seemed to have been built for it. Locomotives were objects of beauty, with their daring paint schemes and turnip-shaped stacks. But they were also prodigies of strength and precision, built from more than six thousand interlocking parts, carefully calibrated to work together.[36] Watching from his hermitage, Henry Thoreau saw something supernatural in the train's power and was reminded of Pegasus, the winged horse of old. But this "fiery dragon" was anything but ancient; as it charged past him every day, he felt that it was writing "a new Mythology," and it made him feel "as if the earth had got a race now worthy to inhabit it."

A few prescient observers voiced cautionary words about the concentration of power in too few hands; their voices would grow louder in the decades after the Civil War. To later generations, railroad corporations could seem like a law unto themselves, with little empathy for the laborers who built their tracks, or the Native Americans whose lands they crossed. But in the early years, Americans were enraptured by these dragons. Michel Chevalier, a French visitor, had never seen a people who loved their railroads more. He thought Americans and their trains spoke to each other, railroad-whispering. "The one seems to hear and understand the other," he wrote.[37] By 1860, the United States had more than half of the world's train tracks, with only about three percent of its population.[38]

But these rosy statistics concealed a growing disparity between the regions. Between 1850 and 1860, more than two-thirds of the new tracks built were in the North or West, near Lincoln. Thirty years earlier, Alexis de

Tocqueville had predicted trouble if the Southern states, with their slower communication networks, began to "languish by comparison with the rest."[39] The South built trains, too, but less quickly and less well. Its disadvantage deepened during the acceleration of the 1850s, when Americans living north of the Ohio River began to live faster lives in every way.

As the great trunk lines were completed between the cities of the East and Chicago, it became easier for a westerner to run for president.[40] It took a tremendous labor to build these straight Euclidean lines across Pennsylvania and upstate New York. But a generation of talented civil engineers rose to the challenge, concocting bridges that seemed to suspend from the heavens, tunnels that bored through mountains, and tracks that snaked along rivers. Many were German immigrants who did not wish to live in a slave society. It was as if they were responding literally to the Book of Isaiah and its injunction to exalt every valley, lower mountains, and straighten crooked roads.[41]

This leveling impulse fortified Lincoln's argument for union. What had been a metaphysical concept grew stronger as it was bolted together with iron, copper, and steel. To be able to travel fluidly from one state to another weakened the notion that a state boundary was inviolate, and quietly validated a more federal sense of America.

Once the trunk lines were built, the time required to travel from New York to Chicago was reduced from two weeks to three days. No trunks of comparable importance were built in the South, and its cities grew more slowly.[42] That meant diminishing power in Congress. The railroad acted as a giant conveyor belt, moving millions of new Americans into Lincoln's West, to the South's disadvantage. Thousands of new towns sprang up, each requiring self-government, services, and schools at a time when the new Republican Party spoke to those needs.

As Lincoln knew, hearing the train whistles in those final nights before his departure, time was the key to it all. In his childhood, that had been a loose concept, based on the height of the sun in the sky, and it varied from one hilltop to the next. Wisconsin had thirty-eight local times![43] But now, with tracks crisscrossing in places such as Springfield, trains had to be closely correlated by dispatchers relying upon telegraphs and observatories to control arrivals and departures to the second.

Accordingly, time tightened in the North. But in the South, where agricultural rhythms continued as they had for centuries, there was less urgency.[44] By 1860, travelers were commenting that it felt like two different Americas. In the North, information was a precious lifeblood. The words never stopped flying overhead along the telegraph wires that shadowed the tracks. Northerners read more books and sent more mail.[45] They opened more schools, and the children stayed in school longer. All of these enterprises deepened the hunger for more information, and those living near the tracks received it more quickly. From around the country, applications for new inventions flooded the patent office in Washington, a Greek temple to American ingenuity. But they came overwhelmingly from the places touched by the railroad. In the two decades before the Civil War, at most one in ten inventions came from the future states of the Confederacy.[46] But in a town like Springfield, it was the most normal thing in the world to see a lawyer submit a design for a device to improve river navigation. Or for his secretary, a German-American immigrant, to submit several patents of his own, including one for an exercise machine.[47]

With so many ideas flying down the tracks, new words were needed to describe a rapidly changing landscape. To many, the embroidery of wires and tracks suggested something delicate and fine, like a fisherman's nets or a spider's spinning. By 1848, a new word was in use to describe a "net-work like a spider's web." A special census report of 1852 announced that the telegraph system was already the largest in the world, creating "a net-work over the length and breadth of the land."[48]

All Americans knew exactly where to find the capital of this networked nation. At the dawn of telegraphy, in 1844, Samuel Morse had sent his earliest telegrams from Washington, D.C., and specifically from the basement of the Capitol. But since then, New York had commandeered the information economy, thanks to a better location, stronger rail connections to the West, and the constant ingenuity of its news brokers. In lower Manhattan, especially, there was a concentration of newspapers, magazines, and book publishers feeding off one another and desperate for any competitive edge. A large publisher, Harper's, dazzled its competition when it built a new plant with assembly lines that used "little railways" to push a book toward its final form. The conveyor belt was accelerated by "the lifelike actions of the iron fingers" of machines that were acting with increasingly human intelligence.[49]

Iron fingers and Iron Monsters did a great deal of work for Lincoln in the campaign of 1860. He did not speak much; he did not need to. His words were already flying, with wings of their own. More than 850,000 copies of his Cooper Union speech were shipped, and sixteen different biographies of the candidate were issued—nearly as many as for the other three candidates combined. In a very noisy year, more than five million messages were sent through a web that extended nearly fifty thousand miles.[50]

Because it was also a census year, a vivid snapshot of the nation is available, which highlights just how different the North and South had become. The Eighth Census began to be processed on July 1, a little more than a month after Lincoln's nomination. The Republican candidate was reading the returns closely, for they affected the future apportionment of Congress. (South Carolina was going to lose representatives.) Even in September, two months before the election, early news was coming in that confirmed that growth was *stunning* for the North and the West. Since 1850, a single city, New York, had gained more people than the entire white population of South Carolina.[51] Tellingly, Illinois had grown the most quickly of any state, while South Carolina had grown the most slowly.[52] As the census explained, the growth had come from a "vast and connected system" of moving goods and people—"like a web"—that the railroad had made possible.[53]

The census was a wake-up call. It served notice to the South that it was losing the race for America's future.[54] If there was a red-hot center of growth in the United States in 1860, it was Lincoln's Illinois.[55] After the railroad came, Chicago became a huge wheel, with spokes radiating in all directions. That unleashed spectacular development in Wisconsin and Michigan—the fertile crescent of Republicanism.[56] Enormous quantities of corn, lumber, and livestock came through Chicago's yards, and it became the largest wheat depot in the world, a breadbasket for Europe as well as America.[57] Even cotton, the Southern staple, was diverted there, away from New Orleans and the Mississippi River.[58]

This was the nightmare that Thomas Jefferson had dreaded. The railroad had fundamentally shifted the balance of power from South to North. In the *Iliad*, Homer told the story of a new contrivance, the Trojan horse, that altered a power dynamic. Now the Iron Horse had wrought a similar change. Despite winning a Southern location for the capital, and despite decades of parliamentary brilliance, the Southern dream of dominance was now imperiled by these demographic changes. There were just too many people, moving too fast, on too many trains.

The *Best Friend of Charleston*

BEST FRIEND

The South's slowness was not ordained by destiny. The first locomotive in the United States, the *Best Friend of Charleston,* was introduced in South Carolina. When it began to take passengers, in 1830, it thrilled onlookers with its speed, darting forth "like a rocket." By 1833, its route already extended 136 miles northwest from Charleston; it was briefly the longest railroad in the world.[59]

For a time, South Carolina's leaders were keen to keep up the pace. A leading architect, Robert Mills, proposed a "railroad" from Charleston to New Orleans (actually, a horse-drawn monorail). He also talked about steam-powered carriages, and urged a paved highway between South Carolina and Texas a century before the interstate highway system.[60] To the end of his life, Senator John C. Calhoun was pushing for other routes, toward Memphis, the Mississippi, and ultimately, the Pacific.[61]

But these grandiose plans began to sound delusional after the first burst of enthusiasm had waned. The Southern obsession with states' rights made it difficult to build tracks across boundaries. Local traditions also discouraged the financial tactics that were needed to build railroads but were perceived as Northern: forming large combinations to raise money, working with legislatures to incorporate new entities, and levying new taxes.[62]

In other ways as well, state pride slowed down the South. A vexing problem related to gauge, or the width of a railroad track. In the beginning, few railroads took the time to consult others about how their lines would meet. As a result, Americans were forever getting off and on trains to adapt to new gauges. It would be difficult to think of a better argument for a federal approach to solving a problem. But the nightmare of mismatched gauges persisted for decades and was not resolved until well after the Civil War. It was felt in the North, too: only 53 percent of American railways were standard gauge (four feet, eight and a half inches) in 1861.

But the situation was far worse in the South.[63] North Carolina proudly refused to adopt measures that would allow its trains to connect with those coming from South Carolina and Virginia. Mississippi had a gauge unique to itself. All of Florida's railroads except one (near Pensacola) stopped short of its boundary, for fear of treading too delicately on the sensibilities of its neighbors. Huge sections of Georgia, Alabama, and Mississippi had no railroads; Texas was not connected to the South at all.

These problems were evident in leading Southern cities as well. It was hard to travel north from Charleston, as if the city planners disliked going in that direction. Of the six lines coming into Richmond, not one connected to another.[64] But one city was notoriously difficult. For anyone trying to reach Washington from the northern states, Baltimore was a frustrating choke point. The two lines that came in from the north failed to connect with the lines heading south and west, with the result that much time was wasted moving passengers and goods at a snail's pace through the city's clogged streets.[65] Yet there was no other way, even for an incoming president. [66]

Another problem for Southern railroads was that they required large numbers of slaves to build and maintain them. They rented slaves from plantations, and they also owned them outright as corporate property. By 1860, fifteen thousand slaves were working on Southern railroads.[67] Southern defenders argued that slavery and railroads were perfectly compatible, but evidence suggested otherwise. A plentiful supply of free labor allowed the North to build its lines faster, with no need for precautions against runaways. But in the South, as trains spread, they only increased the fear that slaves would escape or receive news from other parts of the country.[68] Slavery required close control of information, and Southern railroads had fewer telegraphs running alongside the tracks (which also impeded the scheduling of the trains). They had fewer mechanics, fewer tools, fewer printers to issue maps and schedules, and fewer schools teaching science and technology.[69] Glass was scarcer, which meant it was harder to build observatories, to synchronize time with the rest of the country.[70]

These differences added up. There were always Northerners willing to do business with Southern slaveholders, and slavery would not have lasted as long as it did without their enthusiastic support. But it was becoming more difficult to justify two different systems, existing awkwardly alongside each other. Emerson wrote, "Slavery does not love the whistle of the railroad."[71] In the North, trains promoted a sense that new worlds of information were opening, as they had for Frederick Douglass.[72] In the South, no one could claim that.

Southerners never gave up: in the 1850s, they added 7,454 miles of track, according to the census of 1860.[73] But they never sewed the kind of iron lacework that northern and western railroads did. They built them quickly and cheaply, often with rails made of inferior metals—or even of wood—and with very few double-tracks.[74] Their trains connected smaller cities, spread farther apart, doing less business. They did not lead to economic diversification, and they tended to concentrate the heavy dependence on cotton. Despite a head start, the railroad failed to become the best friend of Charleston.[75]

In the earliest days of the railroad, promoters had promised that an extensive national system would foster solidarity between the regions. Instead, it did something close to the opposite, bringing an immense power to the North, and connecting it to the West, at the South's expense. It was telling that Lincoln, growing up in the middle of the country, had first gone south in search of opportunity. After the train came to Springfield, he would have no need to go downriver again.

Lincoln later expressed his view that secession would have been inconceivable if there had been more railroads connecting the Ohio Valley to the south. As they lost the battle to keep up, many Southerners began to condemn the trains that they had once embraced. A leading secessionist, Senator Louis Wigfall of Texas, took pride in his lack of interest in new ideas. "We are an agricultural people," he boasted. "We have no cities—we don't want them. We have no literature—we don't need any yet. We have no press—we are glad of it."[76] Not one of those statements was actually true, but his belligerence was shared by many Southerners in 1861. It was the opposite of the way in which Southerners had led the push toward railroads thirty years earlier. Jefferson Davis ranted against "the industrial system of the world." Confusingly, he also bragged that the South would outproduce all of its rivals.[77] In the end, none of his boasts proved true.

As Lincoln was making his final preparations, Davis was also readying himself for a journey. By a strange quirk of fate, he and Lincoln would begin their trips on the same day, as if the gods wanted to see a race. Davis was not a natural spokesman for the railroad, but in the summer of 1860, as he searched for the right image to excite a rally in Washington, he could not help himself. "Our fires are up!" he declared, likening the Southern cause to an express. He added a menacing note: "The cowcatcher is down, let stragglers beware!" The crowd cheered, delighted with the image of Northerners scampering before the pointy prow of his imaginary locomotive.[78]

Then, to their disappointment, the Northerners did *not* scamper, and now Lincoln was boarding a train of his own to take possession of the government. It was true that the president-elect had failed to achieve anything like the sparkling career of his rival. But he was vastly superior in his understanding of the powerful new forces that had been unleashed by "the Railroad Revolution," as some called it.[79]

Lincoln famously called America "a house divided," and from a railroad point of view, it was hard to argue against him. In a country with the world's longest railroads, no one had thought to build a train that ran continuously from North to South. For the Southern senators who were resigning from the Senate, it was far easier to cross the Rubicon, in their speeches, than any river in their own states. There were only four places in the country where it was even possible to connect Northern and Southern rail networks in 1861, and they were flawed, requiring passengers to disembark and get across rivers before finding trains on the other side.[80] One of the crucial places where North and South failed to meet was Washington—trains could not yet cross the Potomac. As he prepared to board his train, Lincoln was essentially going as far south as it was possible to go.

A railroad official and the locomotive *Romulus Saunders*, ca. 1860[81]

THE LEVELER

Lincoln never spoke much about what the railroad meant to him personally. But the evidence suggests that it was far more than a convenience. For a striving young man, the train, with its power to level obstacles, symbolized something of profound importance.

A simple slash—indicating the number 1—had recorded his presence in the 1810 census, when his parents listed him as their one-year-old child, the first time he was acknowledged by the government that he would lead one day. But it was a long, uphill journey after that, as the Lincoln family tried, and mostly failed, to find greener pastures.

The mythology of the West is that the frontier always beckoned. But for the Lincolns, experiencing the underside of the American dream, immobility added to life's burdens. Their crude homes were difficult to reach, on ground that was anything but level. Lincoln was born on a Kentucky farm called Sinking Spring, which, a neighbor explained, was "uneven" and "disagreeable to work for farming."[82] At age two, his family moved to Knob Creek, named after the steep hills called "knobs" that surrounded it, and made the ravine dark and subject to flooding. A cousin called it "knotty-knobby as a piece of land could be."[83] He later remembered that farm as an exercise in abject futility, surrounded by, as he recalled it, a landscape of "high hills and deep gorges." Whenever he was told to plant corn and pumpkin seeds, heavy rains would invariably wash away all of his labor."[84] On occasion, they nearly washed *him* away; he almost drowned one day after he fell in a creek he was trying to cross.[85]

In 1832, when Lincoln first ran for office, he wrote, "I was born and have ever remained in the most humble walks of life." *Walk* was the correct word, for locomotion usually meant travel by foot, behind an ox, as the Lincolns moved from one frontier hollow to another, desperate to try again.[86] The nearness of a great artery of transportation—the Ohio—might have eased some of those challenges. But to Lincoln's father, the river carried more danger than opportunity, and family disasters often took place there. Now and then, Thomas summoned the energy to organize a small boatload of goods to sell farther down the river. Inevitably, his goods were lost. Once, a load was stolen by "a pair of sharpers" who promised to meet him in New Orleans. Lincoln's voice dripped with sarcasm as he recounted that his father expected to make a profit "without labor or inconvenience."[87]

In another instance, when he was nine, the family was moving again, this time from Kentucky to Indiana. As a relative recalled, his father, Thomas Lincoln, traded his homestead for four hundred gallons of whiskey, then loaded the whiskey, his tools, and a chest—all of his worldly wealth—and set out ahead of his family to sell it. Suddenly the boat capsized, and "all he had in it was thrown into the river." Once again, Thomas Lincoln lost everything.[88]

Transportation was always a challenge in these tales of frontier misery. After moving to Indiana, the Lincolns found a dense thicket full of grape-vines, so impenetrable that it took days to go a short distance, cutting away the brush. Their home lot was a mile from the nearest source of fresh water, requiring endless trips for young Lincoln, whose duty it was to fetch it. Years later, after they moved to Illinois, a neighbor recalled that most of the families took their crops to market in a wagon, while Tom Lincoln lugged "a basket or a large tray." It was if he came from another time, before the wheel.[89]

The odds grew longer when Lincoln's mother died in 1818, in part because the nearest doctor was thirty miles away. Lincoln helped his father to build her coffin, a grim apprenticeship in carpentry well before he split any rails.[90] She was buried on an elevation, uphill from the Lincoln homestead, and from that moment, Lincoln's walk grew steeper still.

Many scholars have speculated that Lincoln's dislike of slavery stemmed from his indentured servitude to his father. That form of servitude was sometimes called *thrall*. Years later, Lincoln would use the word *disenthrall* to describe the importance of seeking out new ways to think. "As our case is new, so we must think anew, and act anew," he wrote in his 1862 message to Congress. Then, he added, "We must disenthrall ourselves, and then we shall save our country."

He was already learning that he could disenthrall himself in small ways, through his own form of locomotion. Walking in ever-expanding circles, the young Lincoln was finding his way toward the books that he needed.[91] Inside them, words were already acting as vehicles, transporting him to other worlds.

The river helped, too. When he established himself at New Salem, Illinois, after the so-called Winter of the Deep Snow (1830–31), he described himself as "a sort of floating driftwood on the great freshet produced in the thawing of that snow."[92] But even before that, he had been on the water, disenthralling himself.[93] As a teenager in Indiana, Lincoln found work near the shore, in places where boats were unloaded. Then, as he grew older, he learned how to build the boats that would deliver him from his isolation. They were simple rafts, but they were enough to ease him away from the shore, and eventually to ferry people around the creeks leading to the Ohio, and into the great river itself.

An immense human pageant was passing in front of him as he spent more time at the water's edge, near the tiny community of Troy, Indiana. There the Anderson River entered the Ohio and gave Lincoln a safe haven for his flatboat. He was soon known for "his quick river eye."[94] A good pilot could see the snags below the surface: wrecks of boats, shifting sandbars, jagged rocks. It was an excellent training ground for a future president.

Years later, in the White House, he recounted to his Cabinet the story of a transformative event on the river. Two strangers, late for the steamboat, asked him to ferry them into the middle of the Ohio in order to board the boat. After they transferred, they casually threw two silver half-dollars into his boat. Lincoln was dumbfounded by this capital gain. He remembered, "It was a most important incident in my life," and the beginning of his escape from poverty. He added, "The world seemed wider and fairer before me; I was a more hopeful and thoughtful boy from that time."[95]

The further he went out into that widening world, the more he learned. The Ohio was a busy corridor, attracting visitors from all parts of the country and Europe as well. For thousands of families, it was a major immigration route, and Lincoln would have heard a plethora of languages as the large boats went by. When the Marquis de Lafayette returned to the United States for a triumphant tour in 1824 and 1825, his steamboat sank close to Lincoln, after striking a rocky outcropping near Cannelton, Indiana. Though he lost a treasured snuffbox, Lafayette was able to board the next steamer.[96] To Lincoln, savoring every anecdote of Washington, it must have seemed like a ghost had stepped out of the pages of history and into his river.

The river continued to widen him as he grew older. But as he drifted south with the current, he encountered slavery in disturbing ways. In 1828 Lincoln went all the way to New Orleans with a friend on a flatboat of his own construction. It is likely that he encountered his first glimpse of a slave auction on this trip.[97] It was on this same trip that he was attacked by a group of slaves on the river and hurt in the struggle—he carried a scar above his right eye for the rest of his life. Three years later, he returned and again came away bruised.[98] His cousin compared slavery to a harpoon—"it ran its iron in him then & there."[99] His law partner and biographer, William Herndon, believed that Lincoln had seen the auction of a mulatto girl, forced by the auctioneer to "trot up and down the room like a horse." He left with an "unconquerable hate" for the peculiar institution.[100]

Lincoln would continue to travel on steamboats as he grew into adulthood. They were uniquely valuable to the Southern economy and could pull right up to a large plantation, like that of Jefferson Davis.[101] But the Iron Monster was beginning to smash these cozy relationships. As trains and steamboats competed across the 1850s, Lincoln was a key player in a tug-of-war that pulled Illinoisans in both directions. With rivers that flowed south, and trains that went north, Springfield was at the epicenter of a national debate.

He had lived each side of the question. Herndon later remembered the first time he saw Lincoln, on an exciting day in the short career of New Salem, before the village was abandoned. An opulent steamboat, the *Talisman*, was coming up the Sangamon from Cincinnati, groaning with extravagant wares, but so weighed down that she was having trouble in her final approach.[102] Out of nowhere, Lincoln appeared to clear away low-hanging branches.

The *Talisman* did not survive long—she overstayed her welcome and failed to leave before the waters of the Sangamon receded, leaving her stranded. But Lincoln was just getting started. Obsessed by transportation, he floated a grandiose idea, and wondered if the citizens of New Salem might build a railroad. It was absurd to expect a train to appear magically in the wilds of Illinois, far from any parts suppliers or, for that matter, any cities. The nearest track was roughly eight hundred miles away, just west of Baltimore, where the Baltimore and Ohio line was pressing westward. But there was Lincoln, envisioning a locomotive that did not exist, to pull cars that did not exist, along tracks that did not exist.

It was unlike Lincoln to traffic in speculation. He would later earn respect for the surveyor's exactitude with which he charted every word. But he was all of twenty-three years old, brimming with possibility, and the railroad was a superb vehicle for his unrealized dreams. The way Lincoln wrote about the railroad made it sound almost like a mythical creature ready to fly over the obstacles that made life more level for some than for others.[103]

A year later, he was elected to the state legislature, and supported every improvement he could—bridges, canals, and, finally, an actual railroad, edging closer to Springfield, his new home.[104] It arrived in 1842, a year after the legislature convened there for the first time.[105] What had been a simple frontier settlement (John Hay called it "a city combining the meanness of the North with the barbarism of the South") became something more civilized.[106] Year by year, new connections were established: to Chicago in 1854, to Saint Louis in 1855, and to Indiana in 1856. Property values quadrupled.

By that time, Chicago's great metamorphosis was well under way, and there, too, Lincoln was active, shearing away obstacles. His first speech before a wider audience took place in July 1847, at a large gathering convened to demand federal support for transportation.[107] It marked a turning point for Chicago, and for him. He met hundreds of delegates from neighboring states. They would remember one another when it came time to form a new party, the Republicans, in the 1850s.[108]

It was a coup for Lincoln that he could address so many opinion shapers at an embryonic moment for his own career. Still, his national debut was marred by another comic mishap related to his rustic appearance. His friend Elihu Washburne remembered a baptism by fire: a group of delegates was sitting on a sidewalk when Lincoln appeared, "angular and awkward," strutting down the street, wearing "a short-waisted, thin, swallow-tail coat, a short vest of the same material, thin pantaloons scarcely coming down to his ankles, a straw hat, and a pair of brogans, with woolen socks." "*Just look at Old Abe!*" they clucked, and "Old Abe" became another nickname.[109]

Lincoln survived their ridicule, and, during his single term in Congress, he pressed for more improvements.[110] He also took advantage of his time in Washington to see more of the country. On one of these trips, he was heading back to Illinois by water when his vessel was stranded on a sandbar. Lincoln watched intently as the captain lifted the boat with planks and casks, allowing it to pass over the bar. Captivated, Lincoln worked on an invention of his own: a device "to buoy vessels over shoals."[111] In Springfield, he asked a local mechanic to help him build a wooden model, and Lincoln even did some of the whittling.[112] After returning to Washington, he finished his term and submitted an application for patent number 6469.[113] It was never built, but the model gave more evidence of a mind leveling everything in its path.[114]

As his term was ending, Lincoln returned to the capital briefly in 1849 and stayed up late with friends on the night Zachary Taylor was inaugurated.[115] Taylor's former son-in-law, Jefferson Davis, chaired the committee that planned the inaugural parties, a role that brought him into brief contact with the lame-duck Illinois congressman. Unlike Davis, an up-and-comer, Lincoln seemed to have no future in Washington—he had been passed over for renomination after opposing the Mexican War.

The specific moment of his ignominious departure was recalled later by Elihu Washburne. As they left the inaugural parties at four in the morning, Washburne glimpsed Lincoln trudging toward the Capitol without his hat, which he had lost in the festivities. So ended the political career of "Old Abe"—at least, that is what his friend believed as the long night wound down, with Lincoln walking up another hill.

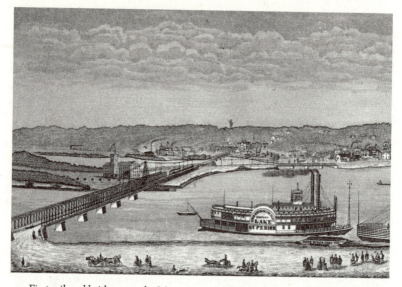

First railroad bridge over the Mississippi, at Rock Island, Illinois, circa 1860[116]

ROCK ISLAND LINE

Lincoln returned to Illinois as an economic surge was beginning, and his leveling instincts were useful.[117] He did some work for the Alton and Sangamon Railroad; then a great deal more for the Illinois Central, smoothing obstacles.[118] He handled forty-seven cases for it, and was likely on a permanent retainer for the firm he called simply "The Co." in his correspondence.[119]

Much of that work was ordinary: a farmer suing because his cow had wandered onto the tracks, or an injured employee. Some landowners were angry that the railroad had come too close; others, that it had not come close at all. During the long acceleration of the 1850s, Lincoln was at every juncture, making the rough places plain. He helped map routes, he calculated taxes, he explained local politics to "the Co."[120] He was not simply an apologist; on occasion, he represented plaintiffs against the railroad, including passengers ejected unfairly from trains, or suppliers who needed to be paid, or mangled workers seeking compensation after coming too close to the Iron Monster.[121] But in all of these ways, he brought clarity.

Lincoln was naturally drawn to this flattening new world. He was valued for his sound common sense, his friendships with Illinois judges, and his powers of persuasion before a jury. He also liked riding the rails. On all of the lines spanning out from Springfield, he became a familiar figure, telling stories, talking politics, and wearing the "chalked hat" of a special guest. These travelers wore a white ticket inside their hatband and were allowed to travel for free. (Some called them "dead heads.") He knew everyone from board members to the train personnel.[122]

Two cases were especially important. The first, argued between 1853 and 1855, related to whether a county (McLean) could tax the railroad. If he had lost, any county might have placed encumbrances upon the great roads that were going through. Once again, he smoothed the way.[123] Another case of transcendent importance was *Hurd v. Rock Island Bridge Company*, in 1857. It grew out of a contest between two mighty interests, the steamboat and the railroad, and the right of the latter to build a bridge across the Mississippi River at Rock Island, 180 miles west of Chicago.[124]

Rock Island has entered American folklore for its own reasons, as a place sung about by Leadbelly and Johnny Cash.[125] But before a "Rock Island Line" could be built, a railroad bridge had to reach the island, and that took some doing. It was the natural place for a bridge across the great river, but if the Iron Monster made it across, it would threaten the steamboat interests of the South. Jefferson Davis, then secretary of war, tried to stop the bridge after it was begun in 1853, insisting that the island was needed for a fort. But that was a difficult argument to make, without any serious military threat for thousands of miles.

The bridge opened for traffic on April 21, 1856; two weeks later, a steamboat, the *Effie Afton*, struck the bridge and disabled it. The trial that followed pitted the steamboats against the rising power of the railroads. But it was much more than that; it was already as if two enormous geographies were in conflict.[126]

As if the rails were carrying him toward his destiny, Lincoln found his way into the heart of this riveting debate. He came from Springfield, midway between Chicago and Saint Louis, the two cities whose interests were clashing in the case. He understood each side, intuitively. He spent days walking around the river embankments, talking to locals and learning about the intricacies of navigation, much as he had as a teenage boy. With his quick river eye, he could read the water currents and the position of the pilings. He also studied the paper trail, including a detailed survey drawn up earlier by an army officer, Robert E. Lee.[127]

Because the case involved interstate commerce, the trial was held in a federal court in Chicago—an advantage. It opened in September 1857, and Lincoln ably mixed his command of the details with sweeping statements relating to the rise of the West and the right of *all* people to travel through it. Then he got to the point and insisted that the right to *bridge* a river was equal to the right to *travel* a river. This was a significant new right. In his own words, "One man had as good a right to cross a river as another had to sail up or down it."[128]

His closing statement read like a manifesto for the West, no longer dependent on the steamboat or the South. According to witnesses, he drew himself "up to his full height," then "delivered a peroration that thrilled the courtroom and, to the minds of most persons, settled the case."[129] "There is a travel from east to west whose demands are not less than that of those of the river," he said. "It is growing larger and larger . . . with a rapidity never before seen in the history of the world."

In these dry exchanges between lawyers, Southerners could hear the death knell of slavery. If a "current of travel" could carry Americans across the Mississippi, on trains, then immigrants would soon arrive in huge numbers. That would weaken the South in Congress. Lincoln's fellow lawyers were amazed at the force of his argument. Once again, the railroad was propelling him forward.[130]

During the Rock Island case, Lincoln lived in Chicago. He met new friends there and enjoyed the hurly-burly of a city already becoming famous for that quality. One of them, Norman Judd, would play a pivotal role in Lincoln's nomination and then again in his journey to Washington, doing all that he could to protect his fellow traveler. One night, during the trial, Judd and his wife, Adeline, hosted Lincoln at their home overlooking Lake Michigan. In the early evening, they took a stroll, as the stars were beginning to peek out, and a brilliant new moon was rising. According to Adeline Judd,

Lincoln was stirred by the scene. In his "mild, pleasant voice," he began to speak of the "poetry and beauty" that the Ancients saw when they looked up at the constellation Orion and the star Arcturus "wheeling" across the heavens, as if their chariots were racing.[131] Then Lincoln offered a spontaneous discourse on science, describing the "computations" of astronomers and scientists ever since, and the "possibilities of knowledge" that the future would bring."[132] They remembered that evening for a long time; it seemed as if a chariot was waiting for him.

By the late 1850s, Lincoln was moving at lightning speed, and it was remarkable to think that any of his rustic neighbors might have once thought of him as slow. To parry the Slave Power and its thrust into the West, he traveled great distances on trains.[133] In 1856 he "traversed the state in every direction" and gave about fifty speeches for the first Republican presidential candidate, John C. Fremont. Then, in 1858, the pace picked up. The seven Lincoln-Douglas debates were a moveable feast, with trains carrying everyone, from the candidates to the crowds, to the location of the day.[134] Like Lincoln, Stephen Douglas had made his career around the railroad, and they each traveled thousands of miles in the campaign.[135] Douglas rode on a special private car; Lincoln more humbly.[136] One day Henry Villard, reporting for a German newspaper, found him at a flag crossing, twenty miles west of Springfield, sitting in an empty freight car while a thunderstorm was passing through. It was there, squatting on the floor, that Lincoln first confessed to Villard his desire to run for the presidency.[137]

On another occasion, during the debates, he was heading toward southern Illinois in the caboose of a freight train when it was unceremoniously diverted to a sidetrack, so that a special train carrying Douglas could go by, with a band playing the audible strains of "Hail to the Chief." Lincoln laughed and said, "Boys, the gentlemen in that car evidently smelt no royalty in our carriage!"[138]

Because they were on trains so often, as they raced from one debate to the next, Lincoln and Douglas were both well known to the train personnel. B. F. Smith, a brakeman on the Illinois Central, recalled that Stephen Douglas offered him a cigar and a shot of liquor from a small bottle. Lincoln, on the other hand, called him over to look at a sunrise over a stretch of uncultivated Illinois prairie, marveling at the beauty of "the sun just rising over those beautiful, undulating hills."[139] That difference spoke volumes.

Another train employee, a retired conductor, said Lincoln was the most "folksy" politician he ever met: "He put on no airs." But, he added, "there was something about him which we plain people couldn't explain that made us stand a little in awe of him. . . . You could get near him in a sort of neighborly way . . . but there was something tremendous between you and him all the same."[140]

As they wrote about him and the destiny that seemed to be carrying him forward, Lincoln's friends often invoked the railroad.[141] Herndon wrote that his partner's ambition was "a little engine that knew no rest," and suggested that Lincoln's body and mind worked "creakingly," as if they needed "oiling."[142] Lincoln himself likened his mind to "a piece of steel, very hard to scratch anything on it and almost impossible after you get it there to rub it out."[143] Once, talking to Herndon, he explained that his apparent slowness concealed a great power, not unlike a locomotive. Herndon remembered his words: "I may not emit ideas as rapidly as others, because I am compelled by nature to speak slowly, but when I do throw off a thought, it seems to me, though it comes with some effort, it has force enough to cut its own way and travel a greater distance."[144]

People who encountered Lincoln on trains in the 1850s invariably remembered him for his storytelling or the simple comedy of his appearance. He often took catnaps, on two seats turned together. ("He could lie down and take an hour's sound refreshing sleep almost anywhere.") Then, unexpectedly, he might wake up and run to make a connection. ("He had something like the speed of a racehorse," a younger companion remembered).[145]

In these rapidly moving offices, Lincoln also met many of the figures who would play roles in the next phase of his journey.[146] A train was the setting for his first encounter with Carl Schurz, a political ally and a leading German-American who had fled his native land after democracy failed there in 1848. Schurz was transfixed by his melancholy eyes and called him the most "grotesque" figure he had ever seen.[147] The rails also led Lincoln to Allan

Pinkerton, who worked as a special agent of the U.S. postal system, protecting the railroads and express companies from interference. In fact, Lincoln drafted the detective's contract with the Illinois Central. They would ride together through a dark night in the final approach to Washington.[148]

In 1860, as he drew near the presidency, it seemed as if each station on Lincoln's journey was made possible by the railroad. Trains delivered him to New York, to raise his profile; then back to Springfield to await nomination.[149] He attended only a single nominal campaign event, but it was a big one: a rally in Springfield on August 8. It nearly ended in disaster, though, after "monster trains" brought fifteen thousand people. After his carriage was trapped by the crowd, Lincoln was barely able to escape, on a fast horse.[150]

Lincoln traveled less in the final weeks of the campaign, but the world kept beating a path to his doorstep. In one remarkable week, both a future king, the Prince of Wales, and William H. Seward came through Springfield on trains of their own, on September 26 and October 1, respectively. It seemed to fulfill Emerson's prediction, only seven years earlier, that a magnetic man would rise in the West and cause the earth to move. Power had come to Springfield.[151]

Lincoln on the verge: February 9, 1861[152]

WHIRLWIND SPEED

In the days before the trip, telegrams were flying up and down the lines, setting up receptions and making sure that the right equipment would be ready in each city as Lincoln came through. Incredibly, at a time when so much depended on close coordination, there were days when the distant president-elect could not communicate with Washington. On January 16 John Nicolay complained that nothing was getting through—because of rain and fog.[153]

On February 9, two days before his departure, a very different presidential election took place among the Confederate delegates meeting in Montgomery, Alabama. Jefferson Davis was easily elected, but it took some time to get the message to him. His plantation, Brierfield, was located along a remote bend of the Mississippi, eighteen miles from the nearest telegraph office. Once the news came in to Vicksburg, it required an effort to find him. (Davis received it while relaxing with his rose cuttings in his garden.) Then more time elapsed before his acceptance could be carried back to Vicksburg and telegraphed to Montgomery.[154] In contrast, Lincoln had known he was elected immediately, thanks to the ever-clacking telegraph key.

On the same day, February 9, Lincoln listed his financial assets in a document that resembled a will.[155] But he also posed for two photographs, full of life. One was a side profile; the other revealed him staring straight at the lens. It showed a beard that had fully come in and a leonine Lincoln, ready to embrace his destiny.

By now, the prospect of a rail journey was nothing new, but this would still be the longest trip of his life. For most of the reporters accompanying him, the story was Lincoln's effect upon the country: his speeches and the way in which the people responded to this unusual politician. But it was fair to wonder, how would the country affect *him*? Would the trip expand him, as his flatboat journeys had? Or would the ordeal wear him down, in the way that earlier presidents had withered? By traveling so far, under such dire circumstances, he was entering unknown territory.

Thirty years earlier, Alexis de Tocqueville had come with one purpose—to scrutinize penitentiaries—and emerged with another. What gave *Democracy in America* such richness was the feeling that a real journey lay underneath; he had grown as he walked through the forests and floated down rivers, studying the invisible physics that held Americans together.

Lincoln's journey would evolve as well. No journey as long as this could go entirely in a straight line. He was still a relatively young man, far younger than William Henry Harrison or Zachary Taylor had been as they submitted to their ordeals. That gave some hope. But the newspaper description of the train's interior, with its cut glass and coverlets, suggested that his high office was already trying to smother him.

Fortunately, the constantly moving panorama outside the windows would offer a form of escape; a private cinema all his own. Writers had tried to capture that effect. In France, Victor Hugo used words that anticipated Impressionist paintings long before they were created. The flowers had become streaks of color; the grain fields were "great shocks of yellow hair," and steeples and trees were performing "a crazy mingling dance on the horizon." [156] Ralph Waldo Emerson thought the scenes flying past looked like the leaves of a dictionary, shuffling quickly. Nathaniel Hawthorne also saw kaleidoscopes outside the window, in a nonsensical sequence . . . an empty solitude . . . followed by a village . . . then everything gone again, "as if swallowed by an earthquake." Meetinghouse spires were "set adrift from their foundations." Everything was "unfixed" and "moving at whirlwind speed." [157]

Whirlwind speed was an apt description for the final days of planning. But at last, the president-elect would be *moving*. By appearing before so many Americans, Lincoln could restore the vigor of the office after a season in which it had nearly vanished. The train offered a mobile stage to speak from, and to stand in the open air was an exciting way to breathe new life into the republic. It was also an act of defiance to those who would hold democracy hostage to the threat of violence.

To survive a train trip was a low bar for success, but so much was up in the air in February 1861 that Lincoln's safe delivery would become, over the next thirteen days, a powerful symbol for the survival of democracy in America. As he traveled his circuitous route, Lincoln carried the aspirations of millions on his shoulders. Around the country, they were waiting for him: the young Lincoln supporters calling themselves "Wide Awakes," parading in Northern cities with capes and torches . . . the veterans of three wars, who had defended the republic in earlier crises . . . the immigrants who had sailed across an ocean to start new lives . . . and the millions of African-Americans who, like a four-year-old Booker T. Washington, already sensed that a different kind of leader was coming, to end their thrall.

To project confidence, Lincoln continued to go about his routines in these final days. But already his friends were treating him differently—not merely because of the enormity of his task, but also because of a premonition that he would not survive his ordeal. Writing in the *New York Herald* on February 9, Henry Villard detected a rising emotion: "His interview with the most intimate of his friends are more frequent and affectionate."[158] One of these old friends was among Springfield's more exotic citizens: William de Fleurville, an African-American business owner known far and wide as "Billy the Barber." As a child, he had escaped Haiti during its long revolution, then made his way west, along with so many other pioneers, before settling in the Illinois capital. He and Lincoln had known each other a long time—they met in New Salem, in 1831, as young men with similarly little to recommend them except a willingness to work. During this final haircut, Billy the Barber felt a strong instinct that he would never see his customer again.[159]

In the South, many were already celebrating the new Confederacy. In Memphis, a newspaper described a riotous parade in favor of secession. Some banners threatened to hang their enemies, or denounced "Negro Equality" or "Negro Socialism." A large transparency ridiculed Lincoln's running mate, Hannibal Hamlin, as secretly African, and placed his image next to "a jolly negro wench."[160] More soberly, the *New York Herald* published an article that explained the security arrangements for Lincoln's train.[161] It already seemed to anticipate trouble.

On his last full day in Springfield, Sunday, February 10, Lincoln spent time with friends and went over his inaugural address.[162] Henry Villard reported that "the close approach of the departure has made him unusually grave and reflecting."[163] The news from the South was bad, as the Confederates continued to set up their government. In many ways, they were ahead of the United States, barely governed at all in the final weeks of the Buchanan administration. Lincoln would need railroad speed to catch up.

Henry Villard noted that the imminent departure "saddens him and directs his thoughts to his cherished past rather than the uncertain future." But he finished his article about Lincoln's last day in Springfield with a statement of resolution that almost certainly came from the main source. Despite all of these "tender feelings," Villard assured readers that "he fully realizes the solemnity of the mission on which he is now to enter and is resolved to fulfill it firmly, fearlessly, and conscientiously."[164]

A neighbor later told the story of seeing Lincoln carrying his "literary bureau": a "well-filled satchel" overflowing with his manuscripts and speeches. He left it with one of his wife's relatives, adding that "if he ever returned to Springfield, he would claim it," but if not, she could dispose of it as she liked. Those two ifs did not convey much confidence. The neighbor added that he spoke these words with "indescribable sadness," as if resigned to a violent fate.

Allan Pinkerton later claimed that the day before the journey was to begin, he received "very decisive information" that Lincoln was to be assassinated in Baltimore. If so, that information was presumably communicated to the president-elect. He had been reading his hate mail again; a neighbor thought that it was weighing on him.[165]

Certainly, Lincoln had thought about death before, on many occasions. For years, his intimate friends had noticed a morbidity that was as keen within Lincoln as his well-chronicled ability to laugh. Herndon reported that in their law office, Lincoln would sometimes say, "I am sure I will meet with some terrible end," adding that this darkness "ran through his being like the thin blue vein through the whitest marble."

As a young man, he memorized a favorite poem, "Mortality," by a lugubrious Scot, William Knox. It seemed to predict the train trip that would follow the telegraphed news of his election:

> Oh! why should the spirit of mortal be proud?
> Like a swift-fleeting meteor, a fast-flying cloud
> A flash of the lightning, a break of the wave
> He passeth from life to his rest in the grave.[166]

Lincoln briefly revealed his own feelings about mortality during his final visit with Herndon, his partner of sixteen years, at their law office. Lincoln "was never in a more cheerful mood," Herndon later recounted. For some moments, Lincoln said nothing, his face toward the ceiling. Then, after a few "ludicrous" stories about their early practice, he grew serious and, with a "significant lowering of his voice," asked his partner not to remove the sign that hung at the foot of the stairway, from rusty hinges, announcing the firm of Lincoln and Herndon. "Let it hang there undisturbed," Lincoln continued, adding, "If I live, I'm coming back sometime, and then we'll go right on practicing law as if nothing had ever happened." More darkly, he whispered that he did not expect to return alive. Then he gathered a bundle of books and papers for his journey the next morning.[167]

The firm's junior member recorded these instructions faithfully, with the three words—"If I live"—lingering in the air. Herndon also revealed another telling detail about this final meeting. Just as he said good-bye, Herndon asked Lincoln "if he expected to give any last words at the Great Western depot the next morning." Lincoln replied "that he did not suppose there would be occasion for any, as only those going would be there." Herndon disagreed; he argued that "there would be many others, and believed there was a general expectation that he would say something about the distracted condition of the country."

Lincoln said nothing. But Herndon, who knew how to read his partner's silences as well as his words, thought that "on leaving him, he gave his mind up to meditation on a farewell speech, and that the thoughts he delivered became shaped before he slept that night; though neither he nor anyone else could be sure of this." [168] As that last sentence indicated, much about the trip was still being improvised, only a few hours before it would begin.

Old State Capitol, Springfield, 1858[1]

4

FAREWELL

Men gladly look to him;
his speech is steady, with calm dignity.
He stands out from his audience, and when
He walks through town, the people look at him
As if he were a god.

—Homer, *The Odyssey*, book 8, lines 170–74[2]

FEBRUARY 11, 1861

A COLD RAIN

The day of departure arrived with a thud. Lincoln's friend Ward Hill Lamon would make the entire journey with him, as an unofficial bodyguard. Later, he remembered how it began, inauspiciously: "It was a gloomy day; heavy clouds floated overhead, and a cold rain was falling."[3]

But there could be no delay. The time had been announced in the newspapers, and a card printed, with Lincoln's schedule, down to the minute. Fate—and railroad efficiency—now pushed him forward, as the seconds ticked down toward eight o'clock. Despite the drizzle, a crowd was forming at the Great Western depot, where the yellow train stood ready to cut through the gloom and mist. The Special was fueled, watered, and ready to go.

For much of the previous year, Lincoln had held his tongue, a silence enforced by the protocols of the campaign. From this moment forward, he was free to speak to the people directly. Never had a president-elect *needed* to speak quite so urgently.

Lincoln had not given a proper speech since April 10, in Bloomington, Illinois—ten months earlier. Exactly a year before, on February 11, 1860, his first serious profile had appeared in an obscure Pennsylvania paper, the *Chester County Times*. Then the floodgates opened, as he became the most famous man in America.[4] Each trap door opened in perfect succession: he secured the nomination, the Democrats split in half, and he won it all on November 6. But some mystery still surrounded him, deepened by his long silence. Even political friends were complaining privately about the "Sphinx of Springfield."[5]

Lincoln may have decided to speak only the night before. But he had been a lawyer on the circuit for more than two decades, and his preparation was legendary for an important case. He might appear to be spontaneous—with consummate timing, he would drop in a homespun anecdote at just the right moment and swing a jury to his side. Yet there was a great deal of forethought involved. Like any artist, he worked to conceal his sculptor's marks.

In fact, an *actual* sculptor was witnessing Lincoln at work that winter as he coaxed the words that he wanted to say to the American people. Thomas D. Jones had been studying Lincoln's face closely while he worked on a bust of the president-elect, but the famous face kept changing as Lincoln's beard grew out. Jones noticed the deep work that was absorbing his subject. Without the distractions of office seekers, Lincoln was free to think, and he used these quiet sessions to incubate his speeches. These included not just the inaugural but also all of the major speeches of the upcoming trip, meticulously labeled and placed in envelopes in advance of departure.[6] Jones even sharpened Lincoln's Faber pencils, one sculptor aiding another, as Lincoln smoothed out the rough edges in his arguments.

Jones had a good eye and watched Lincoln as he wrote, wrestling with the words. It required a balancing act much like the political message he was developing. Lincoln wrote "very deliberately," but also somewhat precariously, with legs involved as well as hands and arms. As Jones sculpted him, he sat "with a small portfolio and paper resting on his knee," and "with a copy of his published speeches lying beside him for reference," scratching out the precious speeches, one word at a time. It is almost possible to hear the sound of the Faber, bearing down. Jones added that Lincoln would "very modestly read it to me" after the labor of writing was done.[7]

Lincoln had reason to concentrate, for each word would be critical in the weeks ahead. To take a hard line would imperil his chances of holding on to the crucial border states, including Maryland, without which he could not make it to Washington. To take a soft line would infuriate Republicans, who had seen Northern presidents wilt as soon as they moved to the hothouse atmosphere of the Southern capital.

Then there was the special challenge of his farewell to Springfield. It was important to make the right kind of statement as he began the journey. Lincoln did not usually betray a great deal of himself in his remarks. Yet his visit to his stepmother a fortnight earlier had opened up something inside him. Now he would say another difficult good-bye, to his friends and neighbors. He would need to choose his words carefully, for Springfield had become the most closely watched political stage in the United States, with a pack of journalists waiting carnivorously for any scrap of news that Lincoln cared to give them.

At the same time, he could not linger. He would have to speak quickly in order to stay on schedule. As soon as the bells of Springfield pealed the hour, he would board the train and go. On that point the time card was insistent. A close reading revealed some anxiety in the italicized sentences.

All other trains must be kept out of the way.

It is very important that this train should pass over the road in safety.

Then, a final warning, even more urgent:

Red is the signal for danger.

CHENERY HOUSE

He did not have to look far to find it. According to one source, Henry Villard, Mary Todd Lincoln chose the moment of departure to throw a tantrum, angry at her husband's refusal to appoint an office seeker who had sent her a diamond necklace. Instead of serenely composing his remarks, Lincoln was trying to put down an unexpected rebellion, close to home.

Chenery House[8]

In the *New York Herald*, Villard reported tersely that Lincoln, "accompanied by his lady and a number of friends, left his hotel at half past seven a.m. and rode up to the Great Western depot." But in the more detailed writings that his sons edited for publication decades later, Villard conveyed much more information. If his later memories were accurate, Lincoln failed to appear at the crucial moment of departure. As the minutes ticked by, a friend, Hermann Kreismann, went to Lincoln's room to see what was causing the delay.[9] When he arrived, he found Lincoln seated in a chair "with his head bowed and a look of the utmost misery." Mary Todd Lincoln was lying on the floor, beside herself. Lincoln explained that "she will not let me go" until he promised an office for one of her friends. In the end, he yielded.[10]

With this difficult business resolved, Lincoln was free to leave. Years later, townspeople would remember every detail—a woman known to

Springfield's children as "the bird lady" recalled that he passed her going down the stairs to breakfast, and asked about her health.[11] The *Springfield Register* reported that he then went to the hotel office, where he put ropes around his trunks, took some of the hotel cards and on the back of them wrote: "A. Lincoln White House Washington, D.C."[12] He signed an autograph for the hotel owner's daughter just before leaving in an omnibus carriage that backed up to the hotel.[13] That carriage was driven by Lincoln's neighbor, Jamieson Jenkins, an African-American who was active in the Underground Railroad. He had delivered many passengers to freedom, but this short journey was not exactly liberating for his passenger. From this moment forward, Lincoln would never be free again.[14]

Great Western depot, Springfield, 1887 (National Park Service)

THE GREAT WESTERN DEPOT

It was a short ride to the depot of Great Western Railroad. Nicolay and Hay dismissed it as a "rather dingy little railroad station." It was not even the largest station in town.[15]

The Presidential Special was there waiting. So was much of Springfield.

Several commentators estimated that a thousand citizens had gathered in the rain.[16] But Henry Villard remembered it as "only about one hundred people," and a young man who was there, Louis Zumbook, gave a deposition in 1916, when he was seventy-six, and said the crowd "numbered perhaps between one and two hundred."[17]

As the farewell began to unfold, there were strikingly different memories of how it actually happened. Some reliable commentators—Nicolay and Hay—wrote that it was snowing. Others called it rain. Emotions were running high. One detail stands out, relating to the racial composition of the crowd. According to one source, writing in 1942, "the old people of Springfield told how nearly every colored person in town lined the streets, stood on boxes, waved and yelled as Lincoln passed by on his way to the station to entrain for Washington."[18]

The Special had backed up onto a stub, to be ready for boarding, but also, as a young man later recalled, "so he could speak to the people."[19] After Lincoln arrived, his baggage was transferred to the Special, including a small satchel, which he gave to his seventeen-year-old son Robert for safekeeping. John Nicolay later remembered it as a "little old-fashioned black oil-cloth carpet-bag."[20] This tiny piece of luggage was precious, for it held the typeset version of his inaugural address, the document that he hoped would keep Americans from going to war.

Lincoln went briefly into a private room, then reemerged with the trip organizer, William Wood. In the weeks before the journey, Wood had traveled the length of the route, inspecting it for signs of danger. But as events would prove, he was as dangerous in his own way. Within weeks, he would be exposed for his attempts to flatter Mary Todd Lincoln with expensive gifts.[21] Lincoln had enemies everywhere he looked, even in the heart of his traveling party.

But on this cold, rainy morning, they were outnumbered by his friends. Ward Hill Lamon, recalled later: "At precisely five minutes before eight, Mr. Lincoln, preceded by Mr. Wood, emerged from a private room in the station, and passed slowly to the car, the people falling back respectfully on either side, and as many as possible shaking his hand."[22]

For a few moments, Lincoln stood there, visibly moved, shaking as many hands as he could.[23] Henry Villard wrote, "His face was pale, and quivered with emotion so deep as to render him almost unable to utter a single word."[24]

One of the most arresting accounts came from Lincoln's sculptor, Thomas D. Jones. He could be expected to be precise with the details of Lincoln's face, and he was:

"The people assembled early to say their last good-bye to the man they loved so much. The railroad office was used as the reception room. Lincoln took a position where his friends and neighbors could file by him in a line. As they came up, each one took his hand in silence. The tearful eye, the tremulous lips and inaudible words was a scene never to be forgotten. When the crowd had passed him, I stepped up to say good-bye. He gave me both his hands—no words after that."[25]

A great noise then burst upon the silence as the train's bells began to clang.[26] In the minutes before departure, it would have been firing its boiler to reach the high heat needed to make enough steam.

It was time for Lincoln to board the Special. Another reporter observed, "as Mr. Lincoln mounted the platform of the car," the people were "deeply affected, and he himself scarcely able to check the emotions of the hour."[27] With operatic timing, Mary Todd Lincoln arrived at precisely this moment, according to Thomas Jones. He claimed that he gave her "my umbrella and arm," then approached Lincoln "as near as we could," and listened to "the last and best speech ever delivered in Springfield."[28]

A few seconds elapsed before the speech could be delivered, and they, too, were important. Lincoln needed time to compose himself. Ward Lamon described how he "drew himself up to his full height" and "stood for several seconds in profound silence." Then, "his eye roved sadly over that sea of upturned faces; and he thought he read in them again the sympathy and friendship which he had often tried, and which he never needed more than he did then. There was an unusual quiver on his lip, and a still more unusual tear on his furrowed cheek. His solemn manner, his long silence, were as full of melancholy eloquence as any words he could have uttered."[29]

Nicolay and Hay added the detail that he raised his hand to command attention. Nearby, the conductor paused, with "his hand lifted to the bell-rope."[30]

Having regained his composure, Lincoln did something unusual. He removed his hat as if he were in church, and asked for silence. Nicolay and Hay added: "the bystanders bared their heads to the falling snowflakes, and standing thus, his neighbors heard his voice for the last time."[31]

Manuscript of farewell address, showing movement from train[32]

THE STRANGE, CHEQUERED PAST

What followed was one of the great speeches in the Lincoln canon, delivered without notes. Lincoln had obviously thought about it since his conversation with Herndon the night before, and an earlier promise, to a claque of reporters, to say nothing of importance.[33] It was only nine sentences long, give or take, and probably took a mere two minutes to say. In a nutshell, he thanked his friends and neighbors for their support, reflected on the daunting challenge before him, and asked for their prayers.

But the speech was much more than that. It is worth studying these two minutes carefully, because they altered the political atmosphere at a critical moment in the history of the United States. Like a sudden downpour at the end of a summer afternoon, Lincoln's remarks cleared the air. They declared his purpose, in a language that any American could understand. He could not have begun his journey more effectively, with an act of statecraft that was more sophisticated than it appeared.

Obviously, he was saying good-bye, but he was also introducing himself to the American people and explaining where he came from. By giving a farewell address, he was in good company. George Washington had made a habit of carefully orchestrated good-byes to his officers and to the nation at large, as Lincoln knew well. In fact, he had been consulting Washington's farewell address as he wrote out his inaugural.[34]

In that speech, Washington used an unusual word to describe his faith in the Union: he called it the *palladium* of America's safety and prosperity. It was a term that dated back to the Trojan War, when ownership of a palladium—a small wooden statue of Athena, the Greek goddess of wisdom—was thought to tip the balance in battle.[35]

Ironically, Washington had become something of a palladium himself. His statues were spread out equally through the North and the South, and either side might have claimed him in the murky early days of the Confederacy. Jefferson Davis was the son of a Revolutionary War veteran and, like Washington, a military officer of distinction. As he launched a train trip of his own toward Montgomery, he too might have draped Washington's laurels around his new government. But he was mute, and Lincoln stole an advantage.[36]

The speech was brief; its words assembled with care. There was nothing extraneous in them; just a lean, lapidary explanation of purpose.

> My friends: No one, not in my situation, can appreciate my feeling of sadness at this parting. To this place, and the kindness of these people, I owe every thing. Here I have been a quarter of a century, and have passed from a young to an old man. Here my children have been born, and one is buried. I now leave, not knowing when, or whether ever, I may return, with a task before me greater than that which rested upon Washington. Without the assistance of the Divine Being who ever attended him, I cannot succeed. With that assistance I cannot fail. Trusting in Him who can go with me, and remain with you and be every where for good, let us confidently hope that all will yet be well. To His care commending you, as I hope in your prayers you will commend me, I bid you an affectionate farewell [37]

Note the absence of a final period in that ultimate sentence—not so much a refusal to say good-bye as a faithful recognition of the way Lincoln wrote it out, a few minutes later, in the closest thing we have to an official manuscript of the speech. Already he was showing the odd cadences that separate his speeches from others: the rhythmic repetition of *here*, the comma pauses, the balance between *with* and *without*.[38] In the days leading up to his departure, he had voiced a few similar thoughts in casual conversation.[39] But in this speech, Lincoln burnished each thought to a gem-like brilliance, especially in the version he wrote out shortly after delivering it.

Yet other versions reveal more.[40] A reporter for the *Illinois State Journal* heard almost a hundred extra words (245 instead of 152), and he heard them in a different sequence.[41] This version contained evocative lines not present in Lincoln's written draft. Strikingly, Lincoln described himself as "an old man" saying good-bye. He never would have used that phrase during the campaign, when images of a strapping Rail-Splitter paraded his vigor before the public. He was on the eve of his fifty-second birthday, the third-youngest man yet elected to the presidency after Franklin Pierce and James Polk. But it softened him to present himself as a wise elder seeking to save his country. He also added a remarkable sentence about memory: "All the strange, chequered past seems to crowd now upon my mind." He was surely feeling that way, as his old friends pressed around him.

Throughout, the crowd was adding its own cheers, giving the speech a call-and-response quality absent from most written versions. A reporter for *Harper's Weekly* magazine added some of this noise into his account. In one place, he inserted the phrase "[Loud applause, and cries of 'We will pray for you!']," then added, "His exhortation to pray elicited choked exclamations of 'We will do it, we will do it!' "[42] This was the electric current of democracy flowing back and forth between an elected leader and the people. It was the spark Lincoln needed to begin his journey.

The *Illinois State Journal* added more commentary the next day, noting how extraordinary these two minutes had been. Even for experienced Lincoln watchers, something special had taken place on the stub track:

"It was a most impressive scene. We have known Mr. Lincoln for many years; we have heard him speak upon a hundred different occasions; but we never saw him so profoundly affected, nor did he ever utter an address, which seemed to us as full of simple and touching eloquence, so exactly adapted to the occasion, so worthy of the man and the hour."[43]

He came close to weeping while delivering it. *Harper's Weekly* reported, "Toward the conclusion of his remarks, himself and audience were moved to tears."[44] A witness, James C. Conkling, wrote to his son the next day, "It was quite affecting. Many eyes were filled to overflowing as Mr. Lincoln uttered those few and simple words which you will see in the papers. His own breast heaved with emotion, and he could scarcely command his feelings sufficiently to commence."[45]

It would have been difficult to conjure a more evocative picture of small-town life, and the "habits of the heart" that Alexis de Tocqueville identified as essential to democracy. Lincoln was speaking as a neighbor, volunteering for a difficult assignment, to serve the entire community.

His words revealed him to be different from the caricature the South had been warned against. Here was a gentle soul who had known tragedy; who loved his home and family; who was leaving with the greatest reluctance. Unusually, for a politician, he did not seem comfortable talking about himself.

In all of these ways, Lincoln made a powerful argument for union before he even stepped onto the train. It was an impressive display of political legerdemain, all the more so for its contrast with the ineffectual sputterings of James Buchanan or the bombastic threats coming from Jefferson Davis. The next day, the *Chicago Tribune* was filled with grim tidings, including the seizure of a federal arsenal by secessionists in Little Rock, Arkansas. With so much depressing news, it helped to have many columns of newsprint devoted to "The Presidential Journey" with all of its "Highly Interesting Details." At the center of the coverage, in every Northern newspaper, was the speech itself, its nine sentences arguing for a simple notion of *home* that all Americans could understand.

But in spite of the conciliatory tone, there was something in the speech that was not modest at all. The bully pulpit was an unknown concept before that drizzly day. Presidents rarely gave speeches; it was even rarer for a president-elect to say something of interest. By speaking, Lincoln had reclaimed the active power that lies at the heart of the presidency. For months, the relationship between citizens and their government had been eroding. Now Lincoln began to reforge the link. With each step, he appeared more presidential and less like the accidental victor of a divided election. It was a masterstroke.

John Hay could always be counted upon to add a little poetry, and he wrote later that Lincoln had struck "the key-note of the journey."[46] *Key-note* was an apt phrase—a musical term for the short humming of a tone before a chorus finds the right key to sing in. That was precisely what Lincoln had found, to the accompaniment of Springfield's bells and whistles.

Lincoln rarely spoke of assassination, but after all the hate mail he had been receiving, he must have wondered if this might be the last time he would ever see his hometown. Nicolay and Hay suggested as much when they wrote of the address that it was "so chaste and pathetic, that it reads as if he already felt the tragic shadow of forecasting fate."[47]

Most leave-takings by presidents-to-be are joyous affairs; this one unleashed a flood of bereavement. It is almost as if, by removing their hats, the people of Springfield were participating in a religious ceremony, one that eerily resembled Lincoln's own eulogy for himself. One of Lincoln's favorite bits of Shakespeare was *Richard the Second*'s morbid meditation on the death of kings, a scene in which the character Death stalks nearby, grinning at the royal pomp. Lincoln would read it aloud, fascinated by the end it portended: a king who approaches ever nearer to Death the more powerful he becomes.[48]

Most accounts of the speech describe its impact upon the audience. But Lincoln's friend Lamon speculated about what it meant to *him*. To the people there, it meant "Good-by for the present." To Lincoln, it was a more permanent farewell—"his last solemn benediction until the resurrection."[49] In other words, Lamon seemed to suggest, he knew that he would not return.

Having delivered the speech, there was nothing left to do but go. Accordingly, the engineer threw a lever, releasing the steam that had been building while Lincoln spoke. As the pistons began to churn, the Special shuddered forward and began to pull Lincoln from his home. A haunting final line concluded the article from *Harper's Weekly* that John Hay pasted into his scrapbook: "As he turned to enter the cars, three cheers were given, and a few seconds afterward the train moved slowly out of the sight of the silent gathering."[50]

He never saw Springfield again.

GREAT WESTERN RAILROAD.

TIME CARD

For a Special Train, Monday, Feb. 11, 1861,

WITH

His Excellency, Abraham Lincoln, President Elect.

Leave	SPRINGFIELD,	8.00 A. M.
"	JAMESTOWN,	8.15 "
"	DAWSON,	8.24 "
"	MECHANICSBURG,	8.30 "
"	LANESVILLE,	8.37 "
"	ILLIOPOLIS,	8.49 "
"	NIANTIC,	8.58 "
"	SUMMIT,	9.07 "
Arrive at	DECATUR,	9.24 "
Leave	DECATUR,	9.29 "
"	OAKLEY,	9.45 "
"	CERRO GORDO,	9.54 "
"	BEMENT,	10.13 "
"	SADORUS,	10.40 "
Arrive at	TOLONO,	10.50 "
Leave	"	10.55 "
"	PHILO,	11.07 "
"	SIDNEY,	11.17 "
"	HOMER,	11.30 "
"	SALINA,	11.45 "
"	CATLIN,	11.59 "
"	BRYANT,	12.07 P. M.
"	DANVILLE,	12.12 "
Arrive at	STATE LINE,	12.30 P. M.

This train will be entitled to the road, *and all other trains must be kept out of the way.*

Trains to be passed and met must be on the side track at least 10 minutes before this train is due.

Agents at all stations between Springfield and State Line must be on duty when this train passes, and examine the switches and know *that all is right before it passes.*

Operators at Telegraph Stations between Springfield and State Line must remain on duty until this train passes, and immediately report its time to Chas. H. Speed, Springfield.

All Foremen and men under their direction must be on the track and know positively that the track is in order.

It is very important that this train should pass over the road in safety, and all employees are expected to render all assistance in their power.

Red is the signal for danger, but any signal apparently intended to indicate alarm or danger must be regarded, the train stopped, and the meaning of it ascertained.

Carefulness is particularly enjoined.

F. W. BOWEN,
Supt.

Time Card, February 11, 1861 (Alfred Whital Stern Collection of Lincolnia, Library of Congress)

ALL ABOARD

Lincoln's "strange, chequered past" vanished quickly, along with Springfield, as the Special got up to speed. For additional safety, a pilot train was running ahead, and guards were posted at every major crossing.

Up-to-the minute information concerning Lincoln's whereabouts was conveyed instantaneously down the line, through telegraph operators in all of the stations and on board the Special itself. His plush new home was also a mobile communications hub, allowing him to send and receive news as he raced across the Illinois prairie. The local papers were agog with the Special's speed and sophistication.[51] As it accelerated, it passed the home of a Springfield minister, who prayed for Lincoln while the cars flew by.[52]

For the first few minutes of the ride, Lincoln seemed disconsolate. As John Hay wrote, "Something of the gloom of parting . . . seemed to rest upon the President," and he needed time alone in his private car, where he could be "abstracted, sad, thoughtful."[53] Henry Villard saw it too. Instead of relishing his triumph at Springfield, the man about to assume the presidency sat by himself, "alone and depressed."[54]

Boldly, Villard approached Lincoln and asked him to write out what he had just said. His normally steady hand wobbled—not from emotion but from the movement of the train. After growing frustrated, he handed the paper to his secretary, John Nicolay, who wrote the next few sentences before returning it. In the act of writing it down, Lincoln began to turn the speech into a more polished document with tighter sentences, fewer adjectives. Like his sculptor friend, Thomas D. Jones, he pared away what was not needed.[55]

Villard took care of the rest and telegraphed the contents of the shaky-looking hand all around the information network. Shorn of extra verbiage, the streamlined version was perfect for the Lightning. Within minutes of transmission, it was clutched by New York's iron fingers and printed in huge numbers, creating an instant Lincoln classic as the trip was getting under way. The next day, it ran on the front page of nearly every Northern newspaper, and it was printed separately as a handbill. As those nine sentences appeared in print, not shaky at all, the farewell address became an immediate rallying cry for the Union. By breakfast time, millions of Americans could digest it, and Lincoln's presidency became more real.

Eventually he emerged from his funk and began to chat with the friends he had invited along for the ride. The guest list had expanded, despite William Wood's efforts to limit it. Lincoln needed his two young secretaries, John Nicolay and John Hay, for help with his daunting paperwork. His son Robert Todd Lincoln added to the feeling of youthful exuberance, along with two friends that he'd brought.[56] There were old friends such as Lamon, and political allies from Illinois, and his brother-in-law, Dr. William S.

Wallace, who also served as the family physician. According to a scrapbook kept by Hay, a young African-American was also aboard. William H. Johnson would act as a barber and messenger for Lincoln. Importantly, he was described as a member of the traveling party and not merely its servant. If only more sources existed to express his perspective as the Special sped through America's changing landscapes.[57]

The train also conveyed a quiet aura of military authority, thanks to four U.S. Army officers who had sounded alarms about threats to disrupt his inauguration or assassinate him on his way to Washington: Colonel Edwin Sumner, Major David Hunter, and Captains George W. Hazzard and John Pope. Hazzard had lived in Baltimore, he knew how dangerous it would be to get through.

Another soldier on board was an irregular officer whom Villard described as "a sort of pet of Mr. Lincoln." Though only twenty-three years old, Elmer Ellsworth had achieved considerable renown, thanks to a genius for military pageantry and drilling. As John Hay later put it, "The central idea of Ellsworth's short life was the thorough reorganization of the militia of the United States." In Chicago, after a chance encounter with a former French soldier, fresh from the wars in Algeria, Ellsworth formed a crack militia of Zouaves, patterned after the elite French units of that name.[58] His new Zouaves thrilled onlookers with their dash, their athleticism, and their exotic North African uniforms. As Hay recounted later, for a brief hour, Ellsworth became "the most talked-of man in the country."[59] Lincoln was so impressed that he invited the young officer to read law with him in Springfield. There Lincoln is said to have found him "the worst law clerk that ever lived," but also "the best executive to handle young men that I ever saw." He performed nobly throughout the campaign, stirring up enthusiasm for Lincoln.

A telegraph superintendent, J. J. S. Wilson, was also on board to make sure messages flowed smoothly through a portable telegraph.[60] The press was out in force as well, comforting and afflicting Lincoln in roughly equal measure. He needed them to portray him in a sympathetic light, at a time when so many Americans doubted his credentials. But they could be critical, too. There were Illinois writers, and correspondents from the large papers in New York, Chicago, and Philadelphia.[61] The Associated Press had a cohort of five writers.[62] *Frank Leslie's Illustrated Newspaper* sent an artist, ready to draw Lincoln during his major appearances.[63]

With every passing mile, Lincoln's mood lightened. Clearly, his fellow travelers were enjoying themselves. Telegrams from every stop reported the group "in fine spirits."[64] The *Chicago Tribune* described the group as "On the Wing," as if they were flying, and noted that the 120 miles from Springfield to the Indiana border were "the fastest of any portion of the route to New York."[65] The mood lightened further as Lamon pulled out his banjo and, according to Villard, "amused us with negro songs."[66]

There were still reasons to worry: the pilot train found a suspicious fence stretched across the track twenty miles out of Springfield, which it cleared.[67] But the Special was gliding along briskly, and Lincoln grew "anecdotal."[68] In his diary, a friend, Orville Browning noted that he and Lincoln spent considerable time talking over politics. ("He is entirely firm and decided in his purpose to maintain the Constitution and the Union.")[69]

To look out the windows was also uplifting, with a never-ending panorama scrolling by. Mile after mile, queues of people lined the tracks, holding flags, cheering for Lincoln and Union. The *Chicago Tribune* wrote: "At every station and crossing and cabin, the people gathered, some of whom came many miles over heavy roads, to see the train and strive to catch a glimpse of one who bears the hopes of so many." From time to time, Lincoln went out and stood on the rear platform, to make it easier for them.[70]

These were Lincoln's kind of people, and he reached out toward them every few miles, waving, or bowing, or shaking hands, or saying a few quick words, sometimes from a train that slowed but did not stop as it labored to keep its appointments down the road. These were meaningful seconds for thousands of Americans—the only time they would ever encounter Abraham Lincoln. Nicolay explained that Lincoln, shy in certain respects, felt otherwise when a crowd was standing nearby. "His personal relationship to the throngs was one of joyous comradeship. A crowd of clamorous, enthusiastic American citizens drew him irresistibly."[71]

Having broken his silence, Lincoln would give roughly a hundred speeches over the next twelve days.[72] Nicolay wrote that it seemed like "one continuous crowd."[73] Thomas Ross, the train's brakeman, commented later with amazement, "I never knew where all the people came from. They were not only in the towns and villages, but many were along the track in the country, just to get a glimpse of the President's train."[74] They were not merely spectators; they were *citizens*, participating in the journey, giving strength to the new president as he raced toward his rendezvous with destiny.[75]

DECATUR

But even as the Special surged, the strange, chequered past followed Lincoln. At 9:24, the Special stopped in Decatur, his earliest home in Illinois. He had come here from Indiana in 1830, when Decatur was little more than a dozen log houses set in a grove of oak trees. There were still old-timers who could remember his earliest speech, when he had called for better river policies (shortly after falling through some ice).[76] As the Special pulled in, an "immense" crowd was ready, headed by Richard J. Oglesby, who had baptized Lincoln as the Rail Candidate only nine months earlier. Lincoln delivered another farewell speech, shook hands "vigorously" with old friends, then climbed back into the train.

To the east were more towns that he knew intimately.[77] Bement, for example, which Lincoln passed through at precisely 10:13. It was a blip out the window but another turning point in his destiny: the hamlet where Stephen Douglas had agreed to debate him only three years earlier. At the time, it was a great coup to get Douglas to even recognize him as an equal, as Lincoln doggedly followed the incumbent senator's regal trains around the state. The Special slowed, so that Lincoln could salute the crowd, but it did not break its momentum. Years later, brakeman Tom Ross recalled a striking memory: "I remember that, after passing Bement, we crossed a trestle, and I was greatly interested to see a man standing there with a shotgun. As the train passed, he presented arms. I have often thought he was there, a volunteer, to see that the president's train got over it in safety."[78]

At 10:50, the Special reached a small town called Tolono, whose name had been concocted by a railroad executive who liked the letter O. Roughly a thousand people came out, in a town of 277, to hear a short speech in which Lincoln expressed his hope that the sun was shining behind the clouds. That tired cliché was ameliorated by the fact that it happened to be true; the day was clearing. But nearly anything Lincoln said would have pleased the crowd, and they responded with "as wild an intensity of delight as if it had been a condensed embodiment of the substance of his inaugural." A national salute was fired, and the train took on water to slake its thirst for the next thrust eastward.[79]

At 11:30 in the morning, the Special passed through the tiny town of Homer, one of many tiny places in the United States named after the Greek poet. Henry Villard claimed later that he wired Lincoln's farewell speech at precisely this time, which would have placed him in this location."[80] Lincoln next made brief remarks at Danville (12:12 p.m.) before the train approached the boundary with Indiana. The crowds were increasing as he sped through villages, towns, and places with no names at all. The *Tribune* noticed people gathering even at the humblest crossroads, and commented on a loud cheer that erupted from "quite a company of farmers on horseback" as the train swept by.[81] The morning had gone well.

But even in Illinois, in the last few minutes that he would be in his home state, Lincoln was not free from danger. About a mile before the border, a railroad employee found something disturbing as he inspected the track. It was reported that "a machine for cars had been fastened upon the rails in such a manner that if a train run at full speed had struck it, the engine and cars must have been thrown off and many persons killed."[82]

THE MIDWAY WORLD

At 12:30, the Special reached State Line, Indiana, and found another "large and enthusiastic crowd," three times the size of the town's population.[84] Crossing from one state into another necessitated a few political changes, as a delegation of Indiana politicians boarded the train, including Schuyler P.

Balloon with mail leaving Lafayette, Indiana, August 17, 1859[85]

Colfax, a future House Speaker and vice president, and Caleb Smith, a former railway official who would become Lincoln's secretary of the interior.
Indiana had been a critical state for Lincoln as he sought the nomination.
(Smith seconded it.) Its delegation screamed loudly when his name was put
into play; then, ballot after ballot, they stayed with him, offering ballast in
the early voting. Indeed, his ability to carry Indiana, one of the crucial swing
states, was a key reason he won.[86]

Reaching the first border seemed a worthy excuse for a celebration, so
the passengers disembarked and ate lunch. Henry Villard joined a long jour-
nalistic tradition, complaining about the food he was served: "a miserable
dinner, for which they were charged one dollar per head, twice the amount
charged to common travelers."[87]

The Special then resumed its journey eastward, easily crossing the
Wabash River, a formidable obstacle when the Lincoln family was moving
west in 1830.[88] Returning to Indiana was never simple for Lincoln; every
mile was freighted with memories, as he revealed in the strange poems

he wrote about being near the graves of his mother and sister Sarah. For Lincoln, Indiana was a midway world in every sense: a dreamscape where he might parley with shades from the underworld, and a step closer to Washington.[89]

The Special reached Lafayette at 2:40 to find a huge crowd, many thousands strong, swarming downtown.[90] Lafayette was a county seat of modest size (population 9,387), but it had global aspirations: eighteen months earlier, on August 17, 1859, the first attempt at air mail had originated from its town square, when a balloonist named John Wise tried to reach New York City. (He landed in Crawfordsville, Indiana, thirty miles distant, and the mail was put on the train.) Wise completed 463 flights during his long career as a balloonist and was last seen, during his 464th, heading north over Lake Michigan.

Lincoln's remarks were longer than his earlier speeches, likely because the Special was changing its locomotive, an operation requiring about ten minutes.[91] Already he was marveling at how far and how fast he had come.[92] Then it was back on the train, speeding south. After thirty miles, the Special found Thorntown, a small town, where Lincoln experienced a comedian's nightmare. From the back platform, he began to tell a story about a slow horse, and just as he was nearing the punch line, the train began to pull away. The crowd, hanging on every word, ran after the train so they could hear how the story turned out. Lincoln could only laugh and wave. When he got to the next town, Lebanon, he finished the joke, which was about an undertaker, worried that his horse was so slow that it was bad for business (because the day of resurrection would arrive before the horse did). Slowness was not a problem for the Special, reaching every station on time as it glided across the midway world.[93]

SPORTING WITH FIREBALLS

In Indianapolis, at five o'clock in the late afternoon, a huge crowd was gathered in and around Union Station, waiting for any sign of the Special. All day, they had been coming in on special trains of their own.[94] Excitement was at such a

The Indiana Capitol, modeled on the Parthenon (Prints and Photographs Division, Library of Congress)

fever pitch that the crowd surged too early—running toward an eight-car train as it pulled in and screaming "Lincoln!" as a confused man descended onto the platform, clutching his carpet sack. Disappointingly, he was not.

So they waited some more. Soon the throng grew to 50,000, in a city of 18,611.[95] Union Station was cavernous, but no one had seen anything like this. It was the first Union Station in America, so called because five different lines united there.[96]

The station was a natural magnet for young people, drawn to the electricity that flowed down the tracks. In 1864 a teenage telegraph operator would be working there when he began to discover a better system for regulating news traffic. It was the first of thousands of inventions that would ultimately be credited to Thomas Edison. Later, he considered this breakthrough in Union Station the beginning of his work toward the phonograph.[97]

As the Special approached, the crowd grew frenzied. One young man there was a rising Republican who, like every other local official, had worked on the plan for Lincoln's reception. Nearly three decades later, Benjamin Harrison would be elected the twenty-third president of the United States,

Thomas Edison at sixteen (Gerry Beals)

a successor to Lincoln, and to his grandfather, William Henry Harrison, the ninth president—whom Lincoln had supported when he was a young man two decades earlier. Benjamin Harrison's voice would be captured on Edison's phonograph, the first time a president was so immortalized. It was as if Lincoln's brief passage through Indianapolis was accelerating particles already in the atmosphere.[98]

As the train pulled into Union Station, the situation quickly turned dangerous. The police could not control the crowd, and the presidential party had to make its way forward, unprotected, through the scrum. According to John Nicolay, many had to "force their way, luggage in hand, as best they could, to their hotel."[99] Even so, they arrived before Lincoln, who made it into a carriage drawn by four white horses but could only inch forward through the mob. Uncovered, he stood, bowing to them.[100]

Eventually he reached his hotel, the Bates House, a gigantic barn that took up a city block. Villard called it a "beehive," and it was buzzing. Villard reported that Lincoln barely made it through the "merciless throngs" and "only got in by wedging himself through."[101]

After settling in, Lincoln was called upon, repeatedly, to address a crowd desperate to hear his thoughts about the future. He had been here before: in September 1859 he gave a folksy speech to his "fellow citizens" of Indiana, as he phrased it. The speech included his childhood memories of a constant battle against "trees and logs and grub," before turning to the more serious subject of slavery.[102]

But as president-elect, he needed to tread carefully through the various traps arrayed all around him.[103] Obviously, he wanted to win Indiana to his cause, but he also needed to bear in mind that the entire nation was listening to words that would fly along the Lightning as soon as they were uttered.[104]

Lincoln survived the evening, but the strain was palpable as the crowd kept asking for more. His first speech came at a crowded reception, in response to a greeting from Governor Oliver P. Morton, a strong supporter.[105] Lincoln responded effectively, with both force and modesty, insisting that he would do all he could to preserve the Union but also reminding them that he was merely one man, fifty-two years of age, "an accidental instrument" of the people's will.[106] Nicolay wrote, "This was not the usual complimentary oratory. It was a blast of cool logic and had in it a ring of authority. Already he was the ruler."[107]

That would have been enough, but having broken his long silence, Lincoln kept going and gave another speech from the balcony. In his first remarks, he used a draft that he had prepared in Springfield.[108] From the balcony, he was less careful. Breezily, he went into sensitive questions, including the relationship of a state to the federal government, and the definition of words such as *coercion* and *invasion*.[109] There was much to admire in the speech, including his linguistic precision and his explanation that it was not "coercion" to "hold" a fort that already belonged to the United States. But Lincoln went further and said a single word of enormous consequence— "retaking"—which implied he would attempt to capture the forts now in possession of the seceding states. Suddenly he was on thin ice.

Then he kept going until there was no ice holding him up at all. As Lincoln continued to speak off the cuff, he tried to please the crowd and compared the South's loose theory of union to "free love" rather than a legitimate marriage. The crowd laughed long and hard at this coarse witticism. On a day that was already tense enough because of politics, Lincoln had introduced sex into the conversation. That was a topic that had never been broached, even remotely, by a president or president-elect—and certainly not in the explosive context of secession.

The crowd's sustained laughter may have come from Indiana's own experience. A settlement at New Harmony had daringly experimented with alternative approaches to marriage, and its leader, Robert Dale Owen, had proposed liberal divorce laws before the Indiana legislature. In 1860 he and the New York editor Horace Greeley had published a short book on divorce in Indiana. Owen had done much good already, securing for widows the right to control their property and generally arguing for women's rights as equal partners in a marriage. But this was unfamiliar terrain for any president-elect to wander into.[110]

Lincoln's temporary hit came at a price, and many newspapers the next day palpitated with shock at his violation of Victorian sensibilities. To doubters, his brief descent into frontier humor awakened fears that the relatively unknown Westerner was not ready for the presidency. For Lincoln, trying to assume the mantle of George Washington, it was a setback he might easily have avoided. John Hay recorded the crowd's enormous pleasure at the impromptu speech: "The applause was deafening, and there were loud exclamations from the crowd, of 'That's the talk,' 'We've got a President now,' &c."[111] But the remarks on free love, made a bit too casually, received intense coverage the next day and showed how easy it would be for Lincoln's journey to go off the rails. A Kentucky newspaper wrote that the president-to-be was "sporting with fireballs in a powder magazine."[112]

A LOST SPEECH

Nor was Lincoln's ordeal over. The crowd, insatiable, tried to get one more speech out of him, from the same balcony, and he politely murmured a few

Lincoln in the cloakroom [113]

more words, his eleventh speech of a long day. At last, Lincoln and his entourage were able to crawl off to bed around midnight. They were not all
happy with the arrangements: Orville Browning complained in his diary
about having to sleep two in a bed. But they had survived the first day, and
the White House was 240 miles closer. [114]

Lincoln had broken his long silence, and then broken it over and over
again, as the train passed through one hamlet after another. All day long,
the people had come out for him. They swarmed the small towns, and they
lined the route in the countryside, bringing entire families down dusty
roads, toward the speeding train, where they could feel the wind of the
Special as it whipped past. As Hay wrote: "There is something inspiring in
the individual presence of the man." [115] In one day, it is safe to estimate that
he had seen more than a hundred thousand people.

But the pace was already taking its toll. The raw energy of the crowds
in Indianapolis left Lincoln's inner circle unsettled. John Nicolay wrote a
letter to his fiancée that night conveying how frightening it was to be at

the epicenter of this confusing new cult of celebrity. "The house is literally jammed full of people," he began. He could hear them, feral, outside the door, as they tried to force their way into Lincoln's suite. "Three or four ladies and as many gentlemen have even invaded the room assigned to Mr. Lincoln; while outside the door, I heard the crowd grumbling and shouting in an almost frantic endeavor to get to another parlor at the door of which Mr. Lincoln stands shaking hands with the multitude." Nicolay concluded, "It is a severe ordeal for us, increased tenfold for him."[116]

A daunting challenge was the act of shaking hands with all of these people. Lincoln shook hands firmly; Herman Melville met Lincoln a month later and wrote his wife that Lincoln "shook hands like a good fellow— working hard at it like a man sawing wood at so much per cord."[117] To look a stranger in the eye and give a firm shake was another act of union, restoring confidence, one clasp at a time. But to multiply it by many thousand times was another Herculean challenge. Lincoln commented privately that shaking so many hands was "harder work than mauling rails."[118] John Hay compared it to ancient forms of torture: the thumb screw, the rack, and the cap of silence.[119]

Benjamin Harrison noted a dark mood as well, despite the surface jubilation: "It seemed to me hardly to be a glad crowd, and he not to be a glad man. . . . The hour was shadowed with forebodings." Though a loyal Republican, he worried about Lincoln's appearance, and thought that the president-elect's "large angular form and face" portrayed "a man and a mind that, while acute and powerful, had not the balance and touch of statecraft that the perilous way before us demanded."[120]

Like Nicolay, John Hay was worried, too. Even in the sober Midwest, the people Hay called "Indianapolitans" were out of control. Men embraced one another "wildly without provocation," and they "smothered" the shorthand reporters taking down every one of Lincoln's precious words, which they rendered in "phonetic characters, resembling flys' legs."[121] They had "too many elbows, too much curiosity, and a perfectly gushing desire to shake hands with somebody—the president, if possible; if not, with somebody who had shaken hands with him." The hotel began to wilt under these pressures, as food orders were confused, or knocked over, or intercepted by a crowd growing "mania-cal." Even Lincoln, "the great elect himself, had to wait at least twenty minutes before his supper was brought him." Then, after "supper," Lincoln was forced to shake hands with "several thousand" more.[122]

Still, that was a mild inconvenience compared to a near catastrophe. For weeks, Lincoln had been composing his inaugural address. The success or failure of that document would settle many questions: whether more Southern states would secede; whether the seceders could be persuaded to come back peacefully; and if not, whether there would be war. Lincoln had privately printed three earlier versions of the address, then a dozen copies of the fourth. These were guarded zealously, under "perfect secrecy," for fear that their contents would leak to the voracious press.[123]

As the journey was beginning, Lincoln entrusted his own copy to his son Robert in the small black bag he gave him to look after. After they all arrived safely in Indianapolis, he turned to Robert for the speech. But the seventeen-year-old was nowhere to be found—he was off with "the boys," having the time of his life. According to Nicolay, Lincoln made "feverish" attempts to find him. Even after his return, Robert replied only with "bored and injured virtue" to his father's frantic questions about the bag. Then he explained nonchalantly that he had left it with a clerk at the hotel desk. Reading between the lines of the newspapers, there is a distinct possibility that the "Prince of Rails" was drunk. (Robert was described as adhering "closely to the refreshments saloon, the gayest of the gay.") This was a disaster of the first magnitude for an indul-gent father seeking to appear as a responsible authority figure.[124]

Nicolay evocatively captured the slapstick scene that followed. Hor-rified at the prospect that his speech might be lost or leaked to the press, Lincoln sprang into action. Normally slow moving, he wasted no time bounding toward the lobby. As Nicolay recounted, a "look of stupefaction" passed over his face, while "visions of that inaugural in all the next morning's newspapers floated through his imagination." In a flash, "without a word," Lincoln was out the door and rushed back into the very crowded hallways that he had just escaped, and made his way toward the hotel office. There he literally sprang into action, jumping across the hotel desk with "one single stride of his long legs." He then "fell upon the small mountain of luggage" that was stored there, including many black bags that looked exactly like his. With a key, Lincoln opened as many as he could, "while bystanders craned their necks, and the horrified clerk stood open-mouthed." The first six yielded nothing but random articles tumbling out. Then, at last, Lincoln found his bag, and his speech, intact. Nicolay noted drily that "Robert had no more porter's duty during the rest of the trip." [125]

Lincoln's friend Ward Hill Lamon also claimed to witness the scene. He wrote, "I had never seen Mr. Lincoln so much annoyed, so much perplexed, and for the time so angry." [126] He added a poignant glimpse of Lincoln's expression or the way he bowed his head for a moment, and whispered "I guess I have lost my certificate of moral character, written by myself." [127] Lincoln was not wrong to feel desperate. At a moment so fraught, with public opinion so volatile, losing his speech might have turned into a larger symbol of a hapless Sucker—slang for Illinoisan—with nothing to say.

Fortunately, Lincoln's moral certificate was safe. But could democracy survive many more days like this? Henry Villard, who had lived through Germany's failed revolution of 1848, wondered. He could be waspish in his comments and often found Lincoln unpresidential, resembling "a country clodhopper appearing in fashionable society." [128] But Villard also saw Lincoln's courage in holding up under the strain of a journey that was going to tax all of "his physical and mental strength."

Even after just one day, it was obvious that Lincoln was walking along a precipice. To shore up democracy, he needed to speak every time that a crowd formed near his train. But at the same time, he was exhausting himself, and worse. By shaking hands with all of the other clodhoppers, he was exposing himself to grave danger. Democracy required that he present himself, unapologetically, before the people. But that meant that anyone could come near him, at exactly the times that the newspapers had announced his arrival. Already, it seemed, someone had tried to throw the train from its track, even before the trip was four hours old. It was reasonable to expect more to come, especially after the journey headed south.

Before the first evening was over, messages were crackling along the

Lightning, among Lincoln's friends, wondering how they could possibly protect him. Thanks to the early warnings of Dorothea Dix, Allan Pinkerton's agents were on the ground in Baltimore, picking up intelligence about assassination plans. Wearing the black-and-white cockade of a Southern sympathizer, Kate Warne brilliantly acted the part of a recently arrived Alabaman, which helped to bring in a rich harvest of gossip from other Southern women in restaurants and hotels. Meanwhile, Pinkerton's other agents frequented the city's saloons, trawling for information.

A great deal had already come in: that evening, as Lincoln was looking for his bag in the crowded hotel baggage area, Allan Pinkerton was trying desperately to send a warning to Lincoln's friend Norman Judd, part of the entourage.[129] Judd was having a busy night, if we can believe an account by Ward Hill Lamon, Lincoln's burly, banjo-playing friend. Near the end of the evening, a group of Lincoln's friends took Lamon aside. As he recalled, they locked him in a room, and said, "We entrust the sacred life of Mr. Lincoln to your keeping; and if you don't protect it, never return to Illinois, for we will murder you on sight."[130] They had every right to use strong language, for Lincoln's safe delivery was now critical to the survival of the "great experiment"—the phrase George Washington had conjured for the cause of American democracy.

By coincidence, another journey had begun earlier the same day, equally freighted with meaning. After organizing his affairs, Jefferson Davis had set out from Brierfield, his Mississippi plantation, on a quixotic voyage of his own.[131] Already the newspapers were presenting the two journeys as a split screen of sorts. In that morning's *New York Times*, readers could read two columns, side by side, describing every act of the two would-be presidents, almost as if they were mirror images of each other.

But as Davis left, there was no speech about preserving the ideals of the founders. Instead, his journey began quietly, as it might have thousands of years earlier, in a rowboat pulled by the labor of slaves. They went three miles down the Mississippi until a packet ship spotted him, picked him up, and brought him to Vicksburg, where he spoke briefly and forgettably. He then transferred to a train for Jackson, where he gave incendiary speeches about bringing war "into the enemy's territory." Davis later denied giving these speeches and blamed "Northern newspapers" for falsely reporting them. But they were reported in Southern papers as well.[132]

Like Lincoln, Davis needed to reach his capital in order to make his presidency real. His destination was far closer than Lincoln's but required an embarrassing detour along a route that zigzagged in four directions. Montgomery was only 250 miles from Jackson, but there was no track between them. To reach his inauguration, Davis had to go an absurd distance, on a roundabout trek that did not bode well for the Confederacy. He would head north, into Tennessee, then east, before turning south into Georgia, and doubling back to the west, into Alabama. That would mean eight hundred hard miles, or three times the actual distance. And Tennessee had not even joined his strange new country. In other words, the only way for Davis to reach his capital was to pass through the country he called his "enemy"—the United States of America.[133]

Of course, as far as Lincoln was concerned, *all* of these places were a part of the United States. But he had no power yet. As he retired for the night, he surely knew the latest news from Washington, thanks to the Lightning. It was sobering. In Congress, an influential congressman from North Carolina, a state that had not yet seceded, offered a resolution that the president of the United States be "required" to acknowledge the independence of the Confederate States of America and receive any ambassadors or commissioners sent.[134] In New Orleans, the collector of customs was refusing to allow goods to travel along the Mississippi River unless the United States recognized Louisiana. That meant that a huge amount of trade, throughout the interior, was being held hostage by a single state. At Fort Sumter, the commanding officer sent a dispatch warning that conflict was imminent.[135]

In Washington, the waiting continued. Lincoln's friends were worried about his "uncertainty of purpose," and Seward complained to Charles Francis Adams that the city was descending into "agony and panic."[136] At long last, the journey had begun, and Lincoln was moving quickly, at railroad speed. But a huge distance stretched ahead, and the country seemed to be falling apart by the hour.

Flag from Lincoln's procession through Cincinnati[1]

5

PORKOPOLIS

Then she struck them,
Using her magic wand, and penned them
In the pigsty.

—Homer, *The Odyssey*, book 10, lines 238–40[2]

FEBRUARY 12, 1861
INDIANAPOLIS TO CINCINNATI

HAPPY BIRTHDAY

Dawn brought clear skies, a favorable omen for Lincoln's fifty-second birthday. In his reporting, Henry Villard praised the sunrise too eagerly, as if this might be added to Lincoln's slender list of accomplishments.[3] But every note of optimism helped, as the trip's moving pictures were sketched before the nation's readers, hanging on every word.

Around the country, millions of Americans were filtering the information of the previous day, and the drama playing out before them, as Abraham Lincoln and Jefferson Davis raced across the country. Throughout the Great Secession Winter, the hapless James Buchanan had subtracted from the presidency each time that he appeared. Now the deficit had turned into a surplus, with two would-be presidents chugging toward their destinations. A Cleveland newspaper described "two hens setting on one nest."

The Republican papers were full of praise for Lincoln's sober statements of the day before, especially his farewell address. But as the words of his evening speech came in, with his unexpected detour into free love, many hostile papers argued that he was unfit for office. The *New York Herald* accused Lincoln of "stupidity and ignorance." The *Cleveland Journal* regretted that he "finally opened his mouth," only to put his foot in it. In South Carolina, the *Charleston Mercury* conveyed utter contempt for Lincoln's "vulgar, slang-whanging" speech and expressed amazement that the country could have elected such an "ill-bred, indecent old man."[4]

Happy birthday!

But a new day was beginning, and as the sun climbed higher, the people were in the streets, streaming toward his hotel, hoping for a glimpse of the man who had brought so much noise into Indiana.[5] John Hay noted that Lincoln had sloughed off much of his "despondency" from the previous day, and was beginning to look and talk "like himself."[6] Yet there were signs that it would be a long day. Lincoln tried to have a breakfast meeting with Governor Oliver Morton, but his fame was growing unmanageable, and everywhere he went, people stood nearby, gawking. Hay wrote that it was difficult for Lincoln's party to make it back to the hotel, because the streets were so crowded.[7]

To be hemmed in by friendly crowds was not the worst problem. But others, more serious, were piling on quickly. At 8:10, Allan Pinkerton sent a message to Norman Judd, with new intelligence about the threat to Lincoln's life.[8] In Baltimore, the plotters were studying bridges and tracks. They knew that Lincoln would find it difficult to resist the temptation to appear in public, to prove that he had nothing to fear. He would be hard to miss during the awkward passage between two stations, standing in a carriage pulled by horses, with occasional deep bows to the crowds. That was a habit he had begun to cultivate the day before, as he came into Indianapolis. It would be hard to imagine an easier target.

William Henry Harrison's tomb, with the Ohio River and Kentucky in background (Prints and Photographs Division, Library of Congress)

TIPPECANOE

Just after ten o'clock, the crowds outside the Bates House began to lose patience, shouting "Old Abe!" and becoming "so violent" that Lincoln came out onto his balcony again. He spoke a few words, then bowed backward into his room. Hay commented that this only "redoubled" the noise of the crowd.[9]

The entourage now turned to the business of leaving the Bates House and getting back to Union Station in order to continue the journey toward Ohio. But first, Lincoln needed to say yet another farewell—to the Illinoisans who were heading back home. A mock ceremony took place in the president-elect's suite, in which his old friends said good-bye, clipped a lock of his hair for safekeeping, and, in the words of Hay, sought to "macadamize" him (a form of road surfacing) with "hydraulic" embraces.[10]

Lincoln also had a more serious consultation with Orville Browning, one of those returning to Springfield.[11] He had nearly lost his inaugural address the night before; he needed to keep working on it, even under unimaginable writing conditions. Lincoln trusted Browning's judgment and asked him to read it.[12] Five days later, Browning wrote Lincoln to say that the speech was "just and true." But he added an important edit: Lincoln had proposed to "reclaim the public property and places which have fallen" and then "hold, occupy, and possess these." Each tiny modulation of meaning within those verbs was sensitive. Browning argued that "reclaim" was too strong; it would sound like an invasion to South Carolina's hotheads and to the critically important border states still in the Union. Lincoln would accept Browning's advice. It was a crucial adjustment, which Nicolay and Hay later called "the most vital change in the document."[13]

At ten thirty, the president-elect and his entourage began to make their way to the train station. Hay observed that "apparently the entire population of Indianapolis" decided to join them. When they arrived, they found a crowd of five thousand in a "fever heat."[14]

The Special looked different today. A new locomotive, the *Samuel Wiggins*, was jubilantly bedecked with flags, evergreens, and portraits of the fifteen previous presidents, with George Washington occupying the place of honor. The Special now had four passenger cars, in addition to a baggage car.[15] Lincoln's car, the last of the four, was ornately decorated with elaborate silk tapestries.[16] The third car carried the press and Ohio's political leaders. But they were not alone: the railroad, ever eager to maximize earnings, had offered every seat in the first two cars to "excursionists"—men and women who simply wanted to go along for the ride. A reporter noted, "There was no privacy for Mr. and Mrs. Lincoln except when they went into their sleeping compartment. Everybody walked in or out; and talked or listened as he pleased."[17]

As that comment suggests, the Lincoln party had expanded; Mary Todd Lincoln had just arrived with their two younger sons, seven-year-old Tad and ten-year-old Willie, only minutes before Lincoln's departure. That added to the frantic excitement, but it surely brought comfort to the president-elect to know that his entire family was now united under one roof—albeit a moving one.[18]

They were ushered into Lincoln's car, where they enjoyed a momentary freedom from the crowds and the Ohio politicians, already welcoming

Lincoln to Cincinnati even before he had left Indianapolis.[19] One of them was a rising star who would make a journey of his own to Washington sixteen years later to become the nineteenth president. Rutherford B. Hayes had been part of the throng the evening before, where, with Benjamin Harrison, he had glimpsed the Republican future. Now he had a more official role, escorting Lincoln to the next station of his journey.

Hayes knew Lincoln slightly from previous encounters and had shown him to his hotel room during an 1859 visit to Cincinnati, when, as Hayes observed, "the presidential bee had already begun to buzz." This time he was able to talk at length with the man of the hour. Fortunately, he described the conversation between presidents in a long letter to his uncle. Hayes wrote: "In private conversation, he was discreet but frank. He believes in a policy of kindness, of delay to give time for passions to cool, but not in a compromise to extend the power and the deadly influence of the slave system." He added, "This gave me great satisfaction. The impression he made was good. He undoubtedly is shrewd, able, and possesses strength in reserve. This will be tested soon."[20]

At eleven o'clock, the train pulled away from Indianapolis, with Lincoln on the back platform, bowing to the throngs. He was now heading below the latitude of Springfield, where the drawls deepened. Eyewitnesses described a festive voyage. Hayes called the entourage "jolly," and in the reporting of Henry Villard, one can distinctly hear the sounds of laughter: "The president was the merriest of the merry and kept those around him in a perpetual roar." Mary was also in a good mood, and Villard commented, "Although very much fatigued by night travel, Mrs. Lincoln kept up a spirited conversation during the entire journey." Willie and Tad, irrepressible, were adding to the merriment. They found it hilarious to go up to strangers and ask, "Do you want to see Old Abe?" Then they would point to someone else.[21]

Once again, the people lined the route. A fragment in Henry Villard's unpublished notes reveal what it felt like to look out the window of the speeding ship of state:

"The train moved at the rate of over thirty miles an hour. Men with Union flags were stationed every half-mile. Every town and village passed was decorated. Hundreds and thousands were assembled at every point shouting and waving flags and handkerchiefs as the train swept by. . . . Flag-men were stationed at every road crossing and every half mile displaying the American flag as a sign of 'all right.' "[22]

As the train continued south, Lincoln spoke repeatedly to what Villard called the "wild multitudes." He reached the Ohio River at Lawrenceburg, Indiana, where an "immense gathering" was waiting.[23] Once again, Lincoln was standing before the great river that had done so much to open up the world to him. His native Kentucky lay on the other side; in fact, it began just a few feet away, near the water's edge. Somewhere in those murky depths ran the line between slavery and freedom.

Lincoln felt a special bond with the state of his birth. His wife and in-laws were Kentuckians, as was one of his closest friends, Joshua Speed. His earliest memories stemmed from the Knob Creek farm where his parents had moved when he was two years old. But in all of Kentucky, he had won only 1,364 votes, or less than 1 percent. Even in a sizeable city, Louisville, he had only won 100 votes.[24]

As the Special eased into the station, the crowd pressed in, expecting a speech. Lincoln could not disappoint them, especially because there were Kentuckians crowded in with the Indianans. It was essential to keep both states in the Union. (He is reported to have said, "I hope to have God on my side, but I must have Kentucky.") Later in 1861, he would repeat the thought to Orville Browning. Losing Kentucky would mean losing "the whole game." Missouri and Maryland would follow, he reasoned, and there would be no alternative except to surrender the Capitol.[25]

Lincoln spoke bravely, answering the questions that were hurled at him. The setting was dramatic, and he used the river as a backdrop in his speech. When he pointed across the Ohio and promised "justice to all," they let out "loud cheering." As Lincoln was looking into Kentucky, according to one newspaper account, a voice in the crowd cried out, "May the rulers be as right as the people!" Lincoln responded deftly, speaking directly to their fears: "Yes; and let me tell you, if the people remain right, your public men can never betray you. If I, in my brief connection with public affairs, shall be wicked or foolish, if you remain true and honest, you cannot be betrayed."[26]

Another version of that transcript recorded his final charge to this audience: "if you, the *people*, are but true to yourselves and to the Constitution, there is but little harm I can do, *thank God!*"[27]

It was an electric exchange and helped Lincoln before the moderates he desperately needed to keep inside his fragile coalition. The old flatboat pilot had navigated the river's currents with skill. Not only had he survived—he had gone where no president had dared to, into a direct conversation with voters, unscripted, with the media standing by. It was impossible to imagine James Buchanan exposing himself to such a volatile set of questions. The result was a more buoyant ship of state, as if Lincoln's patent had suddenly come to life. As this sparkling debate was sent around the wires, readers could feel as if they were there at the water's edge.

Fascinatingly, Lincoln prepared a draft of a speech to Kentuckians, suggesting that he was considering a visit to the other side of the river. In that speech—never given, but found in his notes—he argued that he could not abandon his platform without abandoning his principles.[28] It also offered a glimpse of his fatalistic belief that the world's democratic hopes were riding with him on the train. As a proud Kentuckian—a word he used to describe himself—he promised that he was willing to die in that cause before abandoning it.

After adapting to a new gauge, the Special resumed its speedy progress and soon crossed into Ohio. Snaking along the river's edge, it found the hamlet of North Bend, where the Ohio reached its most northerly point for hundreds of miles in either direction. At the precise spot where the river curved, the train slowed for another brush with Lincoln's past.

There, outside the window, a family could be seen standing by a tomb, waiting for him. They belonged to the ninth president of the United States, William Henry Harrison, whose campaign for the White House had utterly absorbed Lincoln twenty-one years earlier. What a noise! It had been a raucous affair, with uproarious songs about "Tippecanoe," as Harrison was known, and abundant toasts of hard cider. Lincoln had given his all for Tippecanoe, though he struck some as a comical figure, a bit like Don Quixote as he combed the backwoods, a lanky silhouette on a sagging horse, looking for speaking opportunities.[29]

But all the noise ended abruptly with Harrison's death, soon after his own exhausting trek to Washington. There were still westerners who believed that he had been poisoned in the treacherous salons of the capital.[30] As the train went by, Lincoln stood with his hat removed, on the rear platform, in silent communion with the dead.[31] The ghosts of the midway world were trailing behind him, even as he left Indiana.

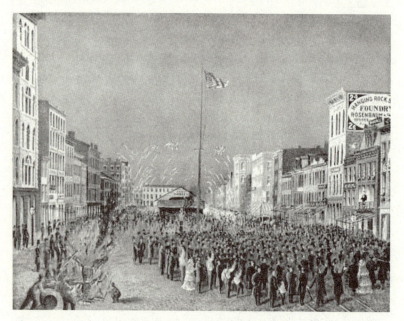

Lincoln in Cincinnati, September 17, 1859[32]

THE QUEEN CITY OF THE WEST

The Special was now hugging the shoreline, keeping the Ohio close, and offering spectacular views as the train entered the outskirts of Cincinnati. Shortly after Lincoln nodded to the Harrisons, a reporter noted that "the spires of the Western Metropolis" were coming into view.[33] There was no shortage of them: Cincinnati boasted 109 churches at midcentury, and 8 synagogues as well.[34] To Jews, it was a special place; a sanctuary from persecution before New York City fully embraced that role. Reform Jewry was active in this free-thinking city, especially after a leading rabbi, Isaac Mayer Wise, settled there in 1854.[35]

In other ways, as well, this middle-American community seemed like an extension of Mitteleuropa. Germans had come in huge numbers, especially after the failed revolutions of 1848, when so many young people transferred their hopes to the United States.[36] Fully a third of the city was German, and in some neighborhoods, such as Over-the-Rhine, the home language was spoken openly. The father of the jurist Louis Brandeis once recalled that he could walk sixty to eighty miles in the Ohio Valley without hearing a word of English.[37] No fewer than *four* newspapers were published in German.[38] A Russian visitor passing through, looking at their signs and their trim houses, wondered if he was in Bavaria.[39]

These immigrants had already turned out for Lincoln when he needed them. Nine months earlier, his nomination came at a climactic moment in the convention, when four Ohio delegates switched their votes, helping him over the top. That released pandemonium inside the Wigwam and set in motion the train of events that now brought Lincoln to the Queen City of the West.

Cincinnati had provided two of those four votes; they came from a local lawyer, Durbin Ward, and Friedrich Hassaurek, another refugee from 1848. Lincoln would appoint him as minister to Ecuador, where he would bring his credentials to a city, Quito, that sits more than nine thousand feet above sea level. (Hassaurek thanked Lincoln for appointing him to the highest position in the United States government.)[40]

If it seemed incongruous to send a German to represent the United States in the Andes, it made perfect sense in Cincinnati, well on its way to becoming one of America's most eclectic cities.[41] When Lincoln was a boy, growing up downriver, it was impossible to ignore the Athens of the West, as Cincinnati styled itself, among other nicknames.[42]

As he grew older, he naturally came to see it for himself, for reasons ranging from medical advice to legal cases.[43] Some of these encounters were bruising, including a difficult encounter with Edwin Stanton, destined to be one of his closest advisers. In 1855 Lincoln was invited to join a legal team preparing for an important trial, *McCormick v. Manny*, that would test Cyrus

McCormick's ownership of the reaper that bears his name. But something went awry when Lincoln tried to assist Stanton, a more established lawyer. According to later reports, Stanton called him a "long, lank creature from Illinois, wearing a dirty linen duster for a coat, on the back of which the perspiration had splotched wide stains that resembled a map of the continent." At other times, Stanton called him a "giraffe" and a "long-armed baboon."[44] Lincoln complained to his partner, William Herndon, that he had been "handled roughly."

For a time after that, he steered a wide berth around Cincinnati and swore never to return.[45] But time healed his bruised pride, and Lincoln's capacity for forgiveness always served him well. In 1859, with his political star on the rise, he came back to support an Ohio Republican running for governor, William Dennison Jr. Cincinnati was kinder this time. Lincoln delivered a rousing outdoor speech from balcony to a crowd that thrilled to his heated attack upon slavery.[46] Local accounts described an explosive evening.[47] A cannon blast even made it into the official transcript, shattering glass nearby and interrupting him.[48] A striking lithograph captures the excitement of the nocturnal rally, with fires burning in the margins, arms upraised, and a tiny figure speaking from a balcony, illuminated by an ethereal light behind him. That speech kept Lincoln's name before Ohio electors in the critical months leading up to 1860.

Now he could thank all of his friends and speak again to the country. Cincinnati was a good place for that. To many, it felt like the "grand centre of the United States," as a guidebook claimed, with something from every region.[49] It was set in a natural amphitheater, surrounded by seven hills, and the amphitheater had filled quickly. Between 1840 and 1860, Cincinnati more than tripled, from 46,338 to 161,094, to become the nation's seventh largest city.

They had come from all directions, and that was important, for the Queen City of the West was a place where Northerners and Southerners could live on equal footing.[50] They commingled freely, living together on every street, strolling in the same lovely parks.[51] Ohio seemed to belong to *all* Americans. When the new state was created in 1803, northern and southern states had both given up old claims. In almost every way, Cincinnati's geography seemed calibrated for balance: the Ohio flowed north, briefly, on its way into the Queen City, before curving again to the south. Even compasses seemed unwilling to point for too long in one direction: scientists had noticed an unusual "magnetic intensity" that sometimes caused them to go haywire.[52]

To be northern, southern, and western all at the same time gave Cincinnati a wide-open quality, as many European visitors noticed. When Alexis de Tocqueville and his traveling companion, Gustave de Beaumont visited, they called it "a town which seems to want to get built too quickly."[53] The English writer Frances Trollope lived there for two years and caught its contradictions nicely. As a river port, Cincinnati had a rough-and-tumble quality—she once heard an obscenity spoken seventeen times in a row; in horror, she deleted the vowels and wrote it down as "g-d d-n."[54] But at the same time, its pretty hills glittered with Greek temples, dedicated to the new gods of banking, insurance, and science.[55]

One of them, an observatory, sat atop Mount Adams, named after John Quincy Adams when he came for the dedication in 1843.[56] Here New Englanders could feel welcome, closer to heaven and to one another. Once again, the railroad helped: a small track built inside the observatory allowed one of the world's largest telescopes to be moved to a more suitable viewing position each night.[57] Nearby, a device could measure time to the thousandth of a second.[58] That was Cincinnati, pointing north.

But the languor of the South was also palpable, in the warm air, and the reliable current of the Ohio, pulling everything toward New Orleans. Lighter clothes could be worn, and the climate was splendid.[59] After a New Jerseyan, Nicholas Longworth, arrived, he started a vineyard on the slopes of one of Cincinnati's hills, where he grew Catawba grapes and dispensed sparkling champagne that delighted visitors.[60] Lincoln himself went to see the famous estate during a break from his trial experience in 1855. He walked around the city extensively and viewed a beautiful cemetery, Spring Grove, where forty Union generals would later come home to rest.[61]

On a good day, it seemed as if Cincinnati could balance its contradictions.

But as the railroad charged into these Edenic landscapes, it tipped the balance to the North. Northerners just kept coming. Salmon P. Chase arrived as a boy from New Hampshire after his father died. From his new home, he forged a glittering legal and political career, which included courageous opposition to slavery.[62] Chase's circle of friends included many other scintillating northern lights. Harriet Beecher Stowe and her father, Lyman Beecher, came from Connecticut when he was offered the presidency of the Lane Theological Seminary. Her husband, Calvin Stowe, a biblical scholar from Massachusetts, taught sacred literature there. They met through the kind of association New Englanders loved: a genteel literary society called the Semi-Colon Club.[63]

"Semi-Colon" would suggest a pause now and then, but these transplanted New Englanders never ceased their relentless improving. They published frantically: a list compiled in 1851 reported no fewer than fifty-three periodicals emanating from Cincinnati, on every possible subject, from dentistry to botanicals.[64] They fancied fine art: a young Vermonter, Hiram Powers, came as a boy and found a niche sculpting Cincinnati's merchants and their wives in suitably Greek and Roman poses. As more Harvard and Yale graduates came looking for work, they brought pastimes of their own, and the beginnings of professional baseball can be traced to their sporting activities around Cincinnati in the late 1850s.[65]

That would eventually lead to red stockings; but Cincinnati's bluestockings were also active. Women were achieving at a high level in the Queen City of the West. Feminist pioneers were drawn to this center of free thinking, including Frances Wright, a Scottish-born activist who dared to speak her views in public. The mere sight of a woman holding the floor was shocking, even to the like-minded. Frances Trollope was amazed by the spectacle of Wright speaking, wearing a garment of plain white muslin, hung around her in folds that "recalled the drapery of a Grecian statue."[66] Harriet Beecher Stowe outperformed all of them, and her *Uncle Tom's Cabin* elevated strong women as resolutely as it attacked slavery and the emotionally withered men who perpetuated it.[67] Its original subtitle was *The Man That Was a Thing.*

As the success of that novel proved, there was one contradiction that Cincinnatians could not quite manage. Slavery was never far away, festering beneath the city's gleaming surfaces. Slave owners were always noticeable in restaurants and taverns, where they spent freely and were described as the city's "best customers." They, too, founded organizations—the ardently pro-Southern Knights of the Golden Circle among them.[68]

For a time, prosperity deflected a full reckoning, but it was inevitable that a clash would come. In 1839 an abolitionist complained about the strangeness of the situation: "Cincinnati is the outpost of the antislavery cause—and more beset by proslavery influence than any other spot in the free states."[69] Frances Trollope saw the hypocrisy everywhere she looked. "I never could get accustomed to the manner in which all Americans talk of the blacks in their presence," she wrote.[70]

By the 1850s, Cincinnati had become a serious flash point over slavery. But the argument was impossible to resolve, because of rising passions and because race itself was a loose construct in a city that boasted every shade imaginable. As the physician Daniel Drake put it, in a study of his hometown, "The streets present as many mulatto, griffe, and quadroon complexions as those of New Orleans," and "the varieties of national physiology are very great."[71] On one occasion, Salmon P. Chase and Nicholas Longworth helped to free a woman named Eliza who was 1/64th African-American, sold at auction in Kentucky.[72]

Because it was so close to the South, Cincinnati became a busy depot on the Underground Railroad. In theory, Ohio's laws freed enslaved African-Americans as soon as they arrived, especially after a ruling by the Ohio Supreme Court in 1841.[73] But the laws were often flouted, and slave catchers routinely came over from Kentucky to round up suspected escapees—often kidnapping the wrong people in the process. In one highly charged case, a former slave named Jackson surfaced in Cincinnati after escaping from his owner, the late vice president William R. King. There were desperate attempts to recapture him, as a point of pride for the South, but he ultimately made it to Cleveland, and freedom.[74]

Not every escape attempt succeeded, though. Sometimes the results were horrific. In January 1856 a U.S. marshal helped a group of slave catchers conduct a raid that led a young African-American mother named Margaret Garner to kill her own two-year-old daughter to prevent the child's capture. In this case, life was imitating fiction, for Stowe had included a similar scene in *Uncle Tom's Cabin*.[75] Even many who did not consider themselves abolitionists were sickened by stories like these, and by the cruel role played by federal agents acting on behalf of one pro-slavery administration after another. They wanted the flag to stand for freedom again.

The South never gave up its claim to Cincinnati, and tried to build rails and canals from Charleston.[76] But their efforts fell short. As Lincoln approached the city, he would have seen a curious monument to that failure. On each side of the Ohio, an enormous stone structure rose out of the mud and silt of the riverbank. These twin towers seemed to be reaching toward each other. They had been built to support a massive bridge between Ohio and Kentucky, but there was no roadway; the project had run into funding problems. Instead, they had become unwitting symbols of a gulf that was growing wider every minute.[77]

But if Lincoln could build bridges of his own, through his speeches, he could do a great deal of good for the cause of Union. He could not falter in a city as important as this one. With Cincinnati enthusiastically behind him, Kentucky was that much less likely to join the South. Still, he would have to tread carefully. That same week, the *New York Times* reported that agents were actively trying to recruit the city into the Confederacy as a kind of city-state on the northern border of the new country. In effect, as Lincoln snaked along the river, he was traveling through a bitterly contested borderland, with passions running high.[78]

"Journey to the Slaughterhouse," Cincinnati[79]

THE METROPOLIS OF PIG

Lincoln was nearly there, but before he could glimpse Cincinnati's splendid Greek temples, he had to go through a different neighborhood, distinctive for its odors as well as its reddish-colored creeks. As he followed the curve of the Ohio into downtown, he could see warehouses lining the waterfront. This was the slaughterhouse district, where a half million pigs a year were processed into meat by-products. It was a ruthlessly efficient operation that began when the animals were led into a door at the top of the hill. In short order, they were slaughtered and carved up by butchers standing near a dis-assembly line of sorts, carrying the carcasses downhill, hanging from large hooks, powered by a grooved metal track in the ceiling. In effect, this was another form of railroad—a gruesome ride, perhaps, but one that was feeding huge numbers of Americans.[80] Cincinnatians boasted that they used every part of the pig "except the squeal." Pork was even used as a local currency.[81] When carmakers began to set up assembly lines in Michigan a half century later, they remembered Cincinnati.

As the Special went past the slaughterhouses, it crossed a rivulet called Deer Creek that often turned pink in the middle of the day from the runoff. A guidebook put it as poetically as possible: "the stream is crimsoned until it mingles with the Ohio." A Russian traveler, trying to be delicate, used the word *opalescent*.[82]

For some, the slaughter was hard to square with Cincinnati's hopes to become a literary mecca, where the best was thought and said. Frances Trollope discovered the contradiction as she sought poetic inspiration in the hills that surrounded the city. Now and then she would try to clear her head with a nature walk "that promised pure air and a fine view." It usually ended badly, with her feet "entangled in pigs' tails and jawbones" or discolored after wading through a brook that was "red with the stream from a pig slaughterhouse." Instead of inhaling "the thyme that loves the green hill's breast," she was greeted by "odours that I will not describe, and which I heartily hope my readers cannot imagine."[83]

But most citizens agreed that the benefits outweighed the costs. They were proud of the city's ten slaughterhouses and the staggering quantities of food they created.[84] The meat-rendering district had given another nickname to Cincinnati, less regal than "the Queen City." To many travelers, Cincinnati was simply "Porkopolis." The Greek suffix -*polis* could be added to just about any word—Lincoln had already come through Indianapolis and a small village in Illinois called Illiopolis. *Polis* originally referred to the small political units that gave life to democracy in Greece. Why not add it, like a pig's tail, to *Pork*? That night, John Hay wrote with a flourish that they had arrived at "the metropolis of Pig."[85] Others simply called it "Hamsterdam."

One of the reasons that Cincinnati grew so quickly was that it was in the perfect place to feed all of the hungry people heading west. This mobile population needed ready-made clothing, inexpensive furniture, and food, in huge quantities.[86] Pig meat could be preserved in many ways: pickled, or cured, or smoked, or converted to sausage and bacon. Then it was a simple matter to ship the processed meat along the tracks.[87] For decades, steamboats had done the bulk of this work, but in 1855, trains began to surpass them.[88]

The pig was also generous to Cincinnati in other ways, for its by-products gave rise to other industries, including soap, candles, grease, and brush bristles. It was remarkable what a little ingenuity could do, as Cincinnatians turned bones into buttons, and blood into paint, and hides and hooves into glue and leather. Two enterprising immigrants, William Procter and James Gamble, became brothers-in-law, then business partners, and profitably repurposed all of the parts of the pig as they built a humble concern in soap and candles into a nationwide business.

Each breakthrough fed the next: a Cincinnati scientist helped find the formula to separate oils and fats from animal tissue in 1841, and the oils became highly prized in the two decades prior to the discovery of petroleum. They lubricated factory machinery, they illuminated the lamps inside miner's helmets, and they lightened the way for the trains themselves, for the front lamps of locomotives used lard oil from Cincinnati pigs. If the Special's headlight was on—a fair assumption on a February afternoon—it was thanks to the oil that had been extracted from a local hog.[89]

These oils also led to beauty products, including a vast proliferation of soaps and perfumes extracted from pig gristle. To disguise their origin, another new science developed, in the form of advertising and marketing. Here, too, Cincinnati led the way. From this mass of entrails, Procter and Gamble would eventually create a product, Ivory soap, that could be advertised as "99 and 44/100 pure."[90]

In short, Porkopolis was thriving. By 1860, it was served by five railroads, all of which pulled Cincinnati toward the North. It built its own locomotives, too, including the one that was powering the Special as it chugged the final miles of its journey.[91]

All of this contrasted painfully with the situation on the opposite side of the Ohio. An Englishwoman, Isabella Bird, was shocked at the contrast between the bustle on one side of the river and the "decay" on the other.[92] Land was worth ten times more on the northern side, but despite the higher cost, immigrants vastly preferred living there because they liked freedom. So Cincinnati kept growing while Kentucky slumbered. An Ohio politician compared the Ohio River to the Styx, separating "the land of darkness, slavery, and oppression" from the "Elysium" of virtue that Cincinnati represented, at least to itself.[93]

A year and a half earlier, when he came to Cincinnati, Lincoln had called himself "one of the old Ohio River boatmen."[94] He was again drawing near the water as his improvised ship of state pulled into the depot, adjacent to the wharves. But the crowds were so thick that the train was forced to stop just short of the station.[95] Once more, the people had come out in force, eager to glimpse the next stage in this accelerating drama. For the train was bringing more than a new administration. They understood intuitively that nothing would ever be the same. Like all Americans, they hoped for peace. But a grimmer fate seemed just as likely as they beheld the sad-eyed stranger, riding his iron horse across a river of blood.

A bridge too far: in 1861, only the towers stood, with no roadway; Cincinnati finally bridged the Ohio in 1867[96]

THE PARADE

Thirty years earlier, Frances Trollope had been in Cincinnati when another president, Andrew Jackson, came through the multitudes. It was a joyous occasion, although she seemed to miss the point as she confessed her disgust at "the brutal familiarity" of democracy. "Why," she exclaimed, "any 'greasy fellow' could go up and talk to him!"[97]

That was nothing compared to the democratic chaos that now enveloped Lincoln as he entered Cincinnati in the fading light. It began with the "distant whistling of the fast-approaching locomotive," audible even before the crowd could see it. Then, pandemonium, as the people screamed his name. The New York Times reported that "Porkopolians" were on "the verge of insanity."[98] After military authorities restored order, the Special crept the last few feet into the station.[99]

Upon arrival, Lincoln encountered a city even more out of control than Indianapolis. John Hay estimated that 150,000 people thronged the streets. (The population was 161,044.)[100] The noise hit a crescendo at the moment he stepped off the train, when the crowd surged toward him.[101] At that moment, a huge number of readers saw Lincoln up close, thanks to a correspondent for the New York Times. Joseph Howard Jr. was studying the new arrival with the attention of a phrenologist: "He has a large head, with a very high shelving forehead; thick, bushy, dark hair; a keen, bright, piercing, indeterminable colored eye; a prominent, thin-nostriled nose; a large, well-bowed mouth; a round, pretty chin; a first crop of darkish whiskers . . ."[102]

After descending from the train, Lincoln found a profusion of people trying to greet him. One banner proclaimed, "The Time Has Come When Demagogues Must Go Under," but it failed to deter the local politicians, who were out in force.[103] Hay described a gaggle of minor officeholders hoping to be seen with the president-elect and, if possible, to hug him. ("He puts up with it gravely, although I think he wishes they wouldn't.")[104] A welcoming ceremony added a bit more noise. Lincoln gave short remarks, then began a long ride through Cincinnati in an open carriage.[105] One observer was reminded of the Russian tarantass, a kind of chariot.[106]

According to Hay, the streets along the route were as "populous as the cities of the Orient. Every window was thronged," he added, and every balcony "fluttered with handkerchiefs." Flags were "laughably profuse," and the noise was earsplitting, thanks to the constant *oom-pah* of all the competing brass bands a Teutonic city could muster.

As the parade wound through the city, it came close to a home belonging to a local lawyer and railroad official, Alphonso Taft, another transplanted New Englander.[107] It is reasonable to assume that his young family came out to see the parade, including Taft's three-year-old son, William Howard, already drawing notice for his girth. If so, the sixteenth president was briefly in the company of the twenty-seventh.

Many in the press were caustic as they regarded these tumultuous scenes. To jaded writers, Lincoln looked too raw to be president, and the

William Howard Taft as a baby (National Park Service)

New York Times complained about "a shockingly bad hat and a very thin old overcoat." A Louisville reporter wrote that Lincoln was "trotting through the free states," hoping to look "like a lion on exhibition," but instead resembled "an ass in lion's skin."[108]

Others were more generous. Rutherford B. Hayes observed this democratic chaos up close and approved of the way Lincoln stood up in the carriage, bowing to the people, unpretentiously. As he reported to his uncle, the reception given to the president-elect was "most impressive."[109] Hayes was privately amused by Lincoln's "awkward look when he bows. It cannot be caricatured . . . his chin rises—his body breaks in two at the hips—there is a bend of the knees at a queer angle."[110] But on the whole, he admired the strength and raw physicality of a man close to the peak of his physical powers: "He is in good health; not a hair gray or gone; in his prime and fit for service, mentally and physically. Great hopes may be felt."[111]

Burnet House, Cincinnati (Prints and Photographs Division, Library of Congress)

BURNET HOUSE

At five o'clock, Lincoln reached the Burnet House, a large downtown hotel with 340 steam-heated rooms. The president-elect almost could not reach the hotel through the crowd, but he finally made it to a platform and gave a serious speech to "good old Cincinnati." Perhaps embarrassed by his journey into free love the night before, Lincoln spoke chastely about his respect for all people on both sides of the Ohio. He promised his Kentucky "brethren"—an evangelical word—that he would treat them well, repeating a line from his speech in Cincinnati two years earlier: "We mean to remember that you are as good as we are."

Lincoln then retired to eat with his family, but it was impossible to escape. The *New York Times* noted that "in passing to his room, those that could rushed at him, throwing their arms around him, patting him on the back, and almost wrenching his arms off."[112]

After the meal, the ordeal continued. At eight, according to Villard, he "repaired to the large dining room of the hotel" and greeted "a steady throng."[113] Lincoln endured it for two more hours, until his hands became sore from handshaking.[114] Each ethnic group wanted a piece of him. The *New York Times* noted: "Germans in battalions, Irishmen in squads, Africans in groups, and Americans in abundance." With dismaying irreverence, they shouted their pet names at him—Old Abe, Old Man, Old Boy, Old Cock—and each passerby "considered it his duty to shake 'Old Abe's' hand as if it were a pump handle." A correspondent tried to count how many times people wished God's blessing on him, and came up with "about six hundred and fifty." When "a big-bellied, fob-chained, high-collared gentleman" tried to absorb too much of Lincoln's time, "the surging crowd behind him, impatient of delay, would give him a boost which would send him irresistibly on, like a wad from a pop-gun."[115]

Lincoln also had one more speech to give, this time to two thousand German-Americans who had marched to the Burnet House, singing and carrying torches. Lincoln had cultivated many German-Americans during his rise.[116] His closest aide, John Nicolay, was born in Essingen, Bavaria. But some Republican leaders were wary of celebrating Germans too overtly, for fear of antagonizing the significant numbers of voters who were skeptical of immigrants. So this innocent evening speech represented a challenge. Again Lincoln struck the right tone, stating, "In regard to the Germans and the foreigners, I esteem them no better than any other people, nor any worse." They applauded him loudly.[117]

With that, he returned to his suite, where security was tighter.[118] Many members of his party stayed up late, excited by the day. John Hay was still scribbling after midnight. He felt proud of "the great arrival" and speculated that "every inhabitant of Cincinnati, with the exception of some fellows who are making a row in the adjoining room, had gone to bed in a state of delirious devotion to republican principles, as embodied in the tall person of 'Old Abe.' "

Hay was right to conflate the person and the cause. Every triumph for Lincoln was a validation of democracy itself, and Cincinnati had given him "a thorough and magnificent success."[119] The secretary's ears were still ringing as he reflected on a day of cannonry, songs, and huzzahs—a noise loud enough to be heard across the river.[120] It was not simply the hilarity of a grand parade. There was a feeling of justice in the air, as Cincinnati's citizens reclaimed their country. The next day's paper argued that the people had felt something more important than "excitement." They had felt their own power and saw in Lincoln the means of delivery from an administration that had brought "treachery, imbecility, and rascality" into their lives. It was time to rescue the republic from "the anarchy which has disgraced this great people in the eyes of the whole world."[121]

The journey was only two days old, but already America's chemistry was changing. The country felt more coherent. Henry Villard wrote, "All honor to the Queen City of the West. A more magnificent ovation than that extended by her this afternoon was never witnessed west of the

Alleghenies." Here was a *polis*, indeed. A crowd of 150,000 people had stood in one place for hours to greet their incoming president. That was almost four times the population of Charleston. It was more people than the entire state of Florida. Even cynical journalists were impressed by "the spontaneous turnout of at least a hundred thousand people, comprising all classes."[122]

But even so, the crush of attention remained oppressive. In the middle of the night, after Lincoln had gone to bed, he put his calfskin boots out in the hallway, perhaps hoping for a shine. Instead, the same press that was so quick to criticize his appearance intervened. A reporter walked right up— revealing how precarious the security arrangements were—and measured the boots so that his readers would know everything they wanted to about "the Lincolnian foot." He verified that it was "as long as a sheet of foolscap paper."[123]

While these asinine articles were being written, the press was largely indifferent to the serious threats Lincoln faced. Hay noted that "a large number of Kentuckians are here," and that some, "dark of aspect," gathered in groups and scowled darkly.[124] When Lincoln arrived at the hotel, the *New York Times* reported, a "queer-looking box" had been left for him under suspicious circumstance, and was later removed by the police.[125]

At the end of a long day, more bad news came in from Baltimore, where Pinkerton's agents were uncovering evidence of a massive plot. They had been busy loitering in saloons and billiard halls, picking up small talk and infiltrating meetings of those seeking to strangle the new administration in its cradle. The conspirators were fixated on Lincoln's train and wanted to know every detail relating to its route into Baltimore. They were also eager to plan a disruption in Washington. One agent, speaking with a bartender, learned of a plan "to blow up the Capitol on the day that the votes were counted," then destroy other government buildings, and "what else he dare not tell." The day the votes would be counted was, in fact, the very next day.[126]

These warnings were rising to a level of such alarm that a young agent named William Scott was trying desperately to reach the Lincoln entourage that evening with a dispatch from Pinkerton. He arrived at the Burnet House at two o'clock in the morning and waited up all night near the rooms of the presidential suite. He had calculated Lincoln's location by simply reading a newspaper.[127]

Around the rest of the country, the news was ominous. The *New York Times* glumly informed its readers that the Southern "Congress" (it put the word in quotations) had adopted a resolution to approve a new design for a flag. Disunion seemed to be traveling faster than Lincoln, as Confederate agents met with leaders of border states, and Texans passed a resolution "favoring the speedy formation of a Southern Confederacy." It was coming together, as Jefferson Davis prepared to board his train for Montgomery and ranted of the South's military supremacy to any who would listen.[128]

In New Orleans, they were laughing riotously at Lincoln. It was the culminating evening of a spirited Mardi Gras, and the city's krewes were out in force with their parade floats, to the delight of huge crowds. Less than a year earlier, Lincoln's unlikely journey to the White House had begun when he was dubbed the Rail Candidate. Now, savage laughter erupted at the sight of a Lincoln impersonator "riding a rail of his own splitting . . . carried by negroes." Another float ridiculed Lincoln's train and showed a dilapidated version of "Old Abe's Express Wagon," limping along too slowly for anyone to care.[129]

In Washington, a different kind of masquerade was playing out. In the evening, capital elites attended a lavish ball at the home of Stephen Douglas. In its own way, it was as ghoulish a midway world as anything Lincoln might have dreamed up, with spectral evidence of earlier administrations drifting through the rooms. Henry Adams was there and described it as a final twitch of the old order, where guests mingled unhappily, drank watered-down champagne, and self-segregated into hostile factions. The tenth president, John Tyler, graced the event, along with an adoring entourage, but he looked so ancient that Adams wondered if he had walked out of his grave to be there. The young Bostonian nearly got into several fights just walking through the crowd.[130] Even the smallest acts of governance seemed too hard, as the departing Southern representatives carried away books from the Library of Congress and thumbed their nose at the city that they had controlled for so long.[131] The Confederacy continued to grow like a malignant tumor, hourly, but President Buchanan was too distracted to intervene. That same day, he submitted a long and boring letter to the Senate about Paraguay.

Overseas, the *Times* of London reported on February 12 that "there was no such thing as loyalty among the American people." British officials gloated that democracy appeared to be failing, after its temporary success in 1776. The "sudden and complete success of a movement of rebellion" had revealed a fatal "inherent weakness," a structural defect that had been there from the start, like the swampy foundation that destabilized so many of Washington's buildings. Already the British were declaring secession a fait accompli. It was as if the history books were being rewritten. Far from being a success, the American Revolution was a gaudy failure. Once again, a people's government was flickering out.

But from his besieged hotel room, Lincoln refused to give his consent. Tomorrow would bring another chance to argue for the republic. He had come a long distance today and claimed the Queen City of the West. He had seen a great many people and established a connection with them as he performed his awkward bow from his carriage. He had issued another brace of speeches, speaking directly to German immigrants and wavering Kentuckians. He had come more than a hundred miles closer to Washington.

Yet there were growing concerns within the privacy of the presidential party. By the end of the day, the *Times* was reporting that Lincoln looked "very pale, very thin, very tired, and very dusty."[132] Up close, Lincoln's friends could see that the brutal pace of the trip was already taking its toll. Ward Lamon wrote later, "After having been en route a day or two, he told me that he had done much hard work in his life, but to make speeches day after day, with the object of speaking and saying nothing, was the hardest work he had ever done. 'I wish,' said he, 'that this thing were through with, and I could find peace and quiet somewhere.' "[133] With more than a thousand miles to go, peace and quiet were unlikely to come anytime soon.

Ohio State House, 1860[1]

6

THE CHEESE BOX

The South Wind hurls it, then the North Wind grabs it,
then East Wind yields and lets the West Wind drive it.
—Homer, *The Odyssey*, book 5, lines 331–32[2]

CINCINNATI TO COLUMBUS
FEBRUARY 13, 1861

BY INCHES

The presidential party rose at 6:15 and ate breakfast at 7:00.[3] But even in the early morning, with the sun rising splendidly, there was an undercurrent of gloom, thanks to the agent who had arrived from Baltimore in the dead of night. Pinkerton's man, William Scott, took a room after failing to find anyone awake. Finally, at eight o'clock, he located Lincoln's friend, Norman Judd. Using a cipher based on Greek mythology, he laid out all of the emerging details of the plot to kill the president-elect.[4]

Lincoln's friends had been anticipating trouble on February 13, but for a different reason. This was the second Wednesday of the month; the day that the electoral votes of the presidential election would finally be counted in the House Chamber of the Capitol.[5]

The vote count was far from a formality. In fact, this was a kind of second election, nearly as fraught as the first. Ever since Lincoln's victory in November, rumors had ricocheted around Washington that the recount offered the South a chance to turn back the election. Its leaders still wielded great power, which increased in the building's labyrinthine corridors and back offices, where the horse trades were settled. Through parliamentary maneuver, or sleight of hand, it might be possible to declare a miscount and throw Lincoln's election back into the cloakrooms. There a more acceptable result could be found.

The House had interfered with the election of a president before, within living memory. In 1824 Lincoln's hero, Henry Clay, had helped to award the prize to John Quincy Adams over Andrew Jackson, in the deal that Jackson denounced as a "Corrupt Bargain." Like Jackson, Lincoln was in a weak position, coming from a greater distance, with a smaller percentage (39.8 percent) of the popular vote than Jackson's in 1824 (41 percent). Once again, a westerner appeared vulnerable to the wiles of Congress.

Could Lincoln be stopped? In theory, it was possible. The state electoral certificates were already in the South's possession; they had been routed into the office of the Vice President, John Breckinridge. Anything might happen as they were carried along a subterranean hallway from the Senate to the House for the count. They might be waylaid, or stolen by the armed militias who were increasingly seen marching around Washington, reporting to no one in particular. During the count, if it got that far, the Southern masters of Congress might declare a certificate unacceptable, simply because it looked wrong. Or they could appoint a committee to investigate voting discrepancies in November. Such a committee might take a very long time to reach a verdict—plenty of time for the Confederacy to establish itself.

Lincoln was not immune to these fears. In early January he had warned William H. Seward, "it seems to me the inauguration is not the most dangerous point for us. Our adversaries have us clearly at disadvantage, on the second Wednesday of February, when the votes should be officially counted. If the two Houses refuse to meet at all, or meet without a quorum of each, where shall we be?"[6] It was a valid question, given the speed with which Southern delegations were walking out of Congress. That made it even more essential that the border states remain in the Union until Lincoln could be inaugurated.[7]

Outside the Burnet House, an eight-carriage procession was ready to take Lincoln to a large depot on the eastern side of Cincinnati. There they would board a new version of the Special, waiting with three cars and approximately a hundred passengers, including a delegation from the Ohio legislature.[8] All along the route, crowds of people were drifting toward the tracks.

Another throng was waiting at the station, but Lincoln managed to escape with a quick set of bows, then boarded the Special in time for its nine o'clock departure.[9] Once again, Joseph Howard Jr. got a close look as he walked past. In his reporting for the *Times*, he saw a frailer specimen than the man he had glimpsed a day earlier. Howard studied him carefully, "as he stood on the platform, with his head bared," and was "startled" by "the careworn, anxious look he wore." He added, "His forehead and face are actually seamed with deep-set furrows and wrinkles, such as no man of his years should have." Howard worried that trip was "wearing the life out of him by inches."[10]

Or maybe by a smaller margin. Just before the train left, an unattended carpetbag was found in Lincoln's car. When it was opened, a "grenade of the most destructive character" was discovered inside, live, and "so arranged that within fifteen minutes it would have exploded, with a force sufficient to have demolished the car and destroyed the lives of all the persons in it."[11]

That remarkable story was reported in the *Syracuse Journal* but omitted from the daily coverage of the New York City and Chicago papers. Was Lincoln nearly blown up on the third day of his journey? To this day, the historic record presents a kaleidoscopic confusion about what, exactly, took place from moment to moment on Lincoln's trip. Clearly no single person, including Lincoln, knew everything that was happening as the Special barreled toward Washington.

But the dramatic claim that a second and more serious assassination attempt had just been attempted at Cincinnati was strengthened four years later when the editor of the *New York Times*, Henry J. Raymond, confirmed it.[12] At the time, the press was reticent to report on the danger that shrouded Lincoln everywhere he went, though there were flickers: in the *Times*, Howard commented on the "poisoned honey and suspicious boxes" that Lincoln was receiving in the mail, and confirmed that "threats of assassination have been definitely ascertained." He added that Lincoln's friends were "prone to be very cautious and to scan carefully every proposed movement of the president-elect."[13] Their security phalanx was tightening around him, by necessity, to protect him from adoring crowds as well as the darker threats.

If a bomb had detonated, the news would have offered a perfect pretext for Congress to take charge of the election. Instead, the suspicious bag was removed from the car, and Lincoln kept going, unharmed. Henry Villard wrote, "The president, although somewhat stiffened in his limbs by his handshaking exertion last night, and suffering from a cold, was in the best of humor all day, and chatted and laughed continually." Mary Todd Lincoln was convivial as well, and their son Bob, despite "liberally" quaffing Cincinnati's Catawba wine the night before, was in full recovery, showing off his "gay, colloquial ways." Villard added that "the two youngest Lincoln sprigs were also exuberant with juvenile delight at the exciting scenes they passed through."[14] It was charming to see the Lincolns enjoying a quiet moment at home—on a speeding train—but it had been a close call.

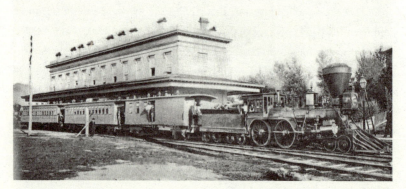

1865 photo of a Cincinnati-built locomotive, the *Dr. Goodale*, pulling a train through Xenia, Ohio[15]

*X*s AND *O*s

A traveler's reference, *The Ohio Railroad Guide*, described all the train routes of 1861; its pages help to re-create the sights outside the window, as Lincoln's train began to move.[16]

The Special began by threading its way to the east, through the industrial outskirts of Cincinnati ("dingy volcanic establishments pouring forth flame and smoke").[17] To have kept going straight would have brought him to Washington far faster. But that route would have taken him into Virginia, a state teetering on secession. So, after six miles, "almost imperceptibly," the cars began to turn north, and the train followed the Little Miami River toward Columbus.[18]

Soon the Special entered a fertile breadbasket of farms and forests. The *Guide* gave the local tree names in English and Latin, including *Aesculus maxima*, the buckeye.[19] Outside of Ohio, it was often called the horse chestnut, a close cousin. Lincoln had a special fondness for the tree, which had once helped him to make a point about the precision of words. In his first debate against Stephen Douglas, as he tried to explain specifically what he thought about slavery, he protested his opponent's "specious and fantastic arrangement of words, by which a man can prove a horse chestnut to be a chestnut horse." That kind of argument, rooted in things that were themselves rooted, went over well among farmers.

The *Guide* noted other sights out the window, almost as if the land were speaking. Nearby were strange hillocks and undulations, shaped like great circles and serpents. These ancient mounds bore witness to the existence of other peoples in these fertile valleys, millennia before any Europeans arrived.[20] But in a few seconds, they were gone, as the Special sped forward, blasting through the centuries. Every so often, the train slowed just "long enough to permit the president-elect to bow, shake hands with a few people, and bid the crowd farewell."[21] Now and then, he offered small remarks, greeting the townsfolk while the train refueled (or as he joked, "while the iron horse stops to water himself").[22]

At one o'clock, the Special pulled into Xenia. It was only a small town, but as Xenians liked to say, it was the largest place in the country that began with the letter X. It was also an important crossroads of several lines—an X in its own right—and the passengers were looking forward to lunch here.

Xenians were proud of their hospitality, and they could plausibly argue that it defined who they were. The name came from an ancient Greek ideal: a code of honor which demanded that a host provide shelter and nourishment to a guest (*xenos*). The story went that in 1803, as the town fathers were struggling to find a name, a scholarly man stepped forward and said, "In view of the kind and hospitable manner in which I have been treated whilst a stranger to most of you, allow me to suggest the name of *Xenia*, taken from the Greek signifying hospitality."[23] Impressed, the townsfolk agreed.

But Xenia was about to confront an identity crisis. On the day Lincoln rolled in, the town forgot its creed. To be sure, elaborate preparations were made in advance of Lincoln's visit. It was not every day that a president-elect came through; and a special reception was organized, with no expense spared, to welcome the great dignitary and his footmen. But as the Special came into view, the crowd of five thousand surged out of control. The *New York Times* wrote, "At Xenia they were really crazy. They jumped upon the car-roof, climbed in at the windows, attempted to force the doors and storm the platform."[24]

The situation deteriorated further as the crowd, overexcited, turned its attention to a large buffet awaiting the presidential party. Specifically, they noticed that "a lunch, varied and extensive in its dainties" had been left on the table in the depot. Unfortunately, they reached it before he could. Like ants at a picnic, they fell upon it and devoured every crumb. Then they demanded a speech! Lincoln, starving, responded with a short address.[25] Sadly, *xenia* was in short supply that day.

The feeling of resentment on the train was conveyed colorfully in the *New York Times,* which reported that the passengers were upset when "the chairman of the gastronomic department" reported that all of the food had been eaten.[26] In frustration, the president's son tried a well-known palliative for hunger, and smoked his pipe until he was encircled by the smoke. "Enclouded in the savoring vapor, he was lost to view," the paper reported.[27]

Following Xenia's underwhelming performance, the Special hurried toward Columbus. This last section of the trip was nearly a straight shot, a fifty-four-mile "air line," in railroad parlance. The Special slowed in the final approach to Ohio's capital, skirting the quarries that had yielded the limestone needed to build the largest State House in the United States. That was Lincoln's destination today, a vivid symbol of Ohio's rough-hewn democracy.[28]

All day the people had been trailing into Columbus. Many were young; they were waiting for the purifying blast of a western wind. By noon, there were five thousand; by two o'clock, it was more than ten times that.[29] Henry Villard wrote that the city's "population must have tripled today."[30]

Just before two, the train drew near. An alert witness described the way it could be "felt" even before it arrived, because of the crowd feeling.[31] The *Times* compared the sound of the cheers to the roar of the ocean. Local militia added the noise of their cannon, which "thundered out a hearty how-are-you."[32]

As the Special came close, it was "at once besieged by hundreds of men wild with enthusiasm." After one or two minutes, Lincoln appeared on the back platform, "with head uncovered and a pleasant smile." At this simple display, "the air was rent with deafening shouts."[33] As usual, he bowed. He had reached another station of the journey.

CIRCLES

Columbus was not a large city (population 18,554), but it wielded significant influence as the capital of a crucial state. Lincoln had narrowly lost Columbus to Douglas, but he had won Ohio—albeit barely, with 51 percent.[34]

Bird's-eye view of Circleville, south of Columbus[35]

Now its support was even more critical. There was no scenario for the preservation of the Union that did not include this central place, in many ways the beating heart of the republic.

According to the 1860 census, the country's mean center of population was now in Ohio, near Chillicothe—the first time it had ever been in a free state, after moving west from Virginia. That shift spoke volumes.[36] Nearly a tenth of the country now lived in Ohio: 2.34 million people, behind only New York (3.88 million) and Pennsylvania (2.9 million). Back in the fall, Lincoln had confessed that he would be as powerless as "a block of buckeye wood" if he went to Washington without a moral principle.[37] The word may well have popped into his head for a more strategic reason. Without the Buckeye State, he had no chance.

Columbus was situated along a river, like most state capitals. The Scioto, a tributary of the Ohio, helped ex-slaves escaping north by water, but Columbus was never much of a port. Instead, it grew into a different kind of city. Its geographical location, in the center of the state, facilitated its role as an administrative hub, governing a domain so large that it was nearly a republic within the republic. Railroads helped, allowing state representatives to travel easily to this central location. Like spokes of a wheel, the lines went in all directions, toward Cleveland, Cincinnati, Dayton, and Toledo. There was a circular logic to the state, and not simply because of the O that formed the first and last letter of its name.[38]

Lincoln had encountered circles during his long immersion in the geometric writings of Euclid, the ancient Greek mathematician. He read Euclid for pleasure, but also to improve his ability to prove a proposition in court. Lincoln's fellow lawyers on the circuit grew used to the sight of him reading late at night in these strange books filled with circles, squares and triangles.[39]

Euclid defined a circle as a shape with a center, from which all lines can be drawn equally.[40] Columbus did its best to live up to that idea, open to all the young strivers who found their way into the gear mechanisms of a busy state capital. A generation later, an ambitious young mechanic named Samuel Bush would rise quickly through the ranks to become a superintendent of motive power for a local railroad, then general manager of the Buckeye Steel Castings Company, which specialized in railroad couplers.[41] Following new lines of energy, his children and grandchildren would move toward Connecticut, then Texas. In the fullness of time, the Bush family would supply the United States with two presidents, the forty-first and the forty-third.

Lincoln needed to speak to all Ohioans, not merely his supporters. Fortunately, a shrine had been built for that purpose. The Ohio State House was no ordinary edifice. It was arguably the most beautiful State House in the country, with immense Doric columns and a cupola that permitted light to flood into the rotunda below.[42] Some found the cupola too small and dubbed the building "the Cheese Box." But most Ohioans admired a structure that seemed wide open, like the state itself. The rotunda covered a round chamber, shaped like the letter O, another one of Ohio's circles.

Lincoln was arriving at a favorable moment: the Cheese Box was finally nearing completion after more than two decades of slow progress.[43] As he walked up its twelve steps, he would have seen a building that spoke eloquently of the people's aspirations to govern themselves.[44] Indeed, if he had looked very carefully at the walls, he might even have seen an older story, one that preceded human beings and their messy problems. Inside those immense columns, and throughout the building, tiny fossils could be seen in the limestone. Swirling shapes—snails, mollusks, cephalopods, trilobites—all seemed to be swimming in a primordial soup, as they had hundreds of millions of years ago. Conservative Republicans were sometimes called "Fossil Whigs" by the more radical Republicans; but in this case, the fossils were real.[45]

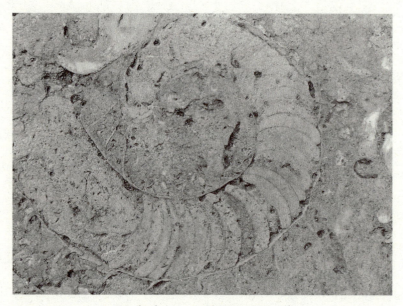

Fossil in limestone, Ohio State House[46]

BRACHIOPODS

Columbus had already helped Lincoln in one way. The need to print the state's legislative business had spun off a modest literary industry of sorts, with publishers nearby ready to print Ohio's official pronouncements. Two years earlier, after Lincoln's debates with Stephen Douglas, an enterprising local publisher, Follett, Foster and Company, issued the debate transcripts as a book. It went on to sell more than a hundred thousand copies, including many that were sent east, raising his profile.[47]

The principal organ of state business was the *Ohio State Journal*, a newspaper which guaranteed a steady stream of income to local printers. Some of that money also trickled into the pockets of local writers, and a tiny literary scene began to grow. At the time of Lincoln's arrival, two young writers were supporting themselves in this way, holding on for dear life, like brachiopods at the bottom of the food chain. Each worked in the State House, and each in his own way had been waiting for him.

William Coggeshall was a prolific contributor to the *Ohio State Journal* who had, by dint of his constant scribbling, secured appointment as Ohio's state librarian.[48] Bearded, Republican, against slavery, he was like so many of the young people who were ready to be carried by the fresh wind blowing in from the prairie. Throughout the fall, he campaigned for Lincoln, caught up in the excitement, much like eight years earlier, when the fiery Hungarian Lajos Kossuth electrified Columbus on a whistle-stop tour of his own. Coggeshall became Kossuth's personal secretary for part of the journey. He had been hoping for someone else to pick up the torch ever since.[49]

Naturally, he was looking to the West. For most of the previous decade, Coggeshall had been scouring the landscape for writers he might include in his anthologies of western literati. Sadly, his readership could be indifferent to the cause of their betterment. When he started his *Monthly Magazine of the West* in 1854, he proclaimed that he was ready "to starve, write & preach all for the glory of the West." The historian David Donald remarked drily that he nearly did all three: his total receipts for 1855 were $1. But Coggeshall kept at it until, at last, he found his desk inside the state library. There he could sound his barbaric yawp to the world—provided he did so in a librarian's whisper.[50]

Another young writer waiting for Lincoln was a sensitive poet, twenty-three years old, in a lather from the books he read each night. "I was reading,

reading, reading," William Dean Howells remembered later, "my veins might well have run ink rather than blood."[51]

Like Coggeshall, Howells had fallen for Kossuth after hearing him speak thrillingly from the steps of the State House. Decades later, Howells could remember every detail of Kossuth's braided Magyar coat and "the hat with an ostrich plume up the side which set a fashion amongst us." Howells bravely wore an ostrich plume of his own for a few days, despite relentless teasing from his peers. As he explained, tersely, "The opinion of boys without plumes in their hats caused me to take the feather out."[52]

Howells had a small desk inside the State House, on the senate floor, where he dutifully transcribed the words he heard around him and dreamed of writing his own someday. Fortunately, the *Ohio State Journal* was willing to publish his small poems. He had begun working there as a mere stripling of fifteen, getting ink on his fingers as a compositor. (His father was the *Journal's* printer.) Now the words were coming more quickly, thanks to Howells's anger at the Slave Power and his hope for the new president.[53]

In fact, the campaign had helped his literary aspirations, when Follett and Foster asked Howells to write a biography of the Rail-Splitter. The resulting *Life of Abraham Lincoln* was the first of 103 works that would appear under his name over a long publishing career; a river of prose that never stopped flowing for the rest of his life.[54]

Yet it was an imperfect launch. To conduct the research, Howells was expected to journey to Springfield and spend time with the candidate. Instead, he hired someone even less qualified, a twenty-year-old law student named James Q. Howard, to grill Lincoln with secondhand questions about his life.[55]

Howells admitted later, "I missed the greatest chance of my life in its kind." But when the raw material of the research came back to him, he did a decent job rendering it readable. He offered vivid descriptions of Lincoln as a young man, reading so much that his neighbors wondered if he was "altogether right in his mind."[56] One suspects Howells put some of himself in that description. It was an attractive vision in a political landscape that had become barren of fresh ideas and struck many as utterly deforested. Language was another field of combat: like many young people, Howells was hungry for words that sounded *real*. He used the word *reality* to describe Lincoln's appeal.

Many older readers were still following "the Southern taste for the classic and the standard in literature," but Howells was going in a different direction, embracing the "modern" wherever he could find it.[57] That included German literature, which Howells loved for its social conscience. He found it easy to practice his German in Columbus, which boasted a flourishing German quarter and restaurants where he could try a tankard of beer "as an expression of my love of German poetry." Unfortunately, it made him sick, but he could always find comfort in the pages of the magazine *Atlantic Monthly*, shipped reliably along the rails from Boston, bringing new waves of realism. It was almost as if the real Atlantic—the ocean—was lapping at the shores of the Scioto.[58]

So, as the train chugged into Columbus, Howells could legitimately feel that Lincoln's journey was connected to his own. The president-elect was exactly what these young writers were looking for: a strong western hero, bearded like Kossuth, fighting to restore freedom as it seeped away in Washington.[59] If Howells introduced a fresh blast of realism into American writing, it was closely tied to the linguistic honesty of a new politician who refused to go along with the lies that were routinely fed to the people. Decades later, when he closed a loving portrait of his friend Mark Twain—the writer above all others whom he championed—Howells ended with the highest tribute he could think of, calling him, simply, "the Lincoln of our Literature."[60]

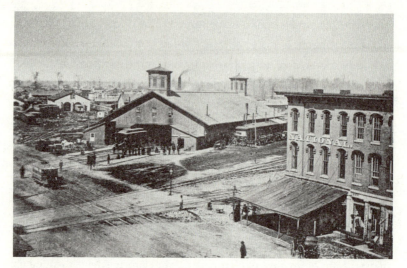

Columbus Union Station in 1864[61]

PICKLES IN A JAR

Once again the arrival was noisy. As in Cincinnati, Lincoln made a triumphal ride through the city, standing upright in a carriage, bowing to the crowds. They were everywhere, in all the windows and on top of the buildings, straining for a view.[62]

The weather helped. Howells remembered odd details later. The warmth of spring was in the air, but the wrong birds were there, having arrived too early from the South, as if they too sensed a change in the wind.[63] Many Ohioans, seeing Lincoln for the first time, felt a premonition that a great change was coming. The state would send 313,180 young men into harm's way over the next four years; 35,475 would never return.[64]

The carriage finally brought Lincoln to the western steps of the State House, where people were "packed as closely as pickles in a jar."[65] A flag raising was cheered, and then people with passes were allowed into the building. Many were women; the *New York Times* described a "beauteous circle" with "vast numbers of smiling ladies," waving their handkerchiefs and showering the visitor with "encouraging smiles and bright, loving glances."[66]

Lincoln had been here in 1859 during his electioneering tour of Ohio, when he gave a spirited speech insisting that the Declaration of Independence applied to all Americans, black and white.[67] He was now taken into the House Chamber, where he was introduced by state officials, who reminded the crowd of the drama unfolding in a different House Chamber, back in Washington, with the counting of the electoral votes.[68]

In his response, Lincoln faltered at first. Henry Villard noted that he was "profoundly moved" by this simple introduction and hardly able to respond. But then Lincoln's earnestness won over the room, and, as Villard wrote, the look on his face spoke even more eloquently than his actual words.[69]

He began by alluding to his own obscurity a year earlier and the extraordinary weight he now carried. Then, for the first time, he acknowledged his long silence during the campaign. Pursuing the thought further, he blundered, stating an unfinished thought that was not perfectly crafted. Lincoln said, "I have not maintained silence from any want of real anxiety. It is a good thing that there is no more than anxiety, for there is nothing going wrong."

Nothing going wrong! Seven states had left the Union, and it was far from certain that he would make it to Washington. With hindsight, it is clear that he was trying to say something calming to his audience: that no war had yet broken out, despite secession. His next sentence explained, "It is a consoling circumstance that when we look out, there is nothing that really hurts anybody."

In the moment, his remarks pleased the room; the applause was "quick and hearty."[70] But the damage had been done, and it deepened as the press corps sent Lincoln's words flying around the nation. Critics pounced, arguing that a man of low intelligence had been elected to the highest office in the land. The *Baltimore Sun* wrote that it was impossible to read Lincoln's remarks without "irresistible bursts of laughter."[71] The *New York Herald* scolded that Lincoln had shown "a most lamentable degree of ignorance" and made "a mess of it," adding, " 'Nothing going wrong'? Why, sir, we may more truly say there is nothing going right."[72] The *Cincinnati Daily Enquirer* seemed to speak for many when it wrote, "Old Abe is a failure as a president. By the time he gets through his tour, his friends will wish they had boxed him up and sent him home."[73] Little did they know how grimly realistic a prospect that was.

Lincoln went out to the western steps of the State House to speak to the people. The *Times* mentioned that "Mr. Lincoln was visibly moved to tears" by the sight of the huge crowd. He gave a short speech, punctuated by pauses, "so that at every sentence, cheer after cheer rent the very air."[74]

That was followed by another punishing ordeal. Resolved to meet as many Ohioans as possible, Lincoln positioned himself in the rotunda of the State House, ready to shake hands with the entire state, if necessary. "Almost immediately," a witness wrote, "the vast rotunda was crowded with eager, turbulent, pushing, crowding, jostling sovereigns, frantic to wrench the hand of the president-elect." Desperate attempts were made to clear lanes and impose order on the situation, and a few "Spartans" deserved special praise for their attempts to hold back the crowd, which "heaved and surged to and fro." But no one could really stop a force like this.[75]

What ensued was nearly as anthropological as it was political. Lincoln stood at the center of the O-shaped room, as thousands of Ohioans approached. Relentlessly they came, pressing closer and closer, revolving around him in ever-smaller circumferences, forming a circle of their own at the center of this terribly important state. Lincoln had arrived at Ohio's innermost ring. To an observer perched in the dome above, this frenzied scene might have resembled a beehive, with crowds of workers pressing up against the larger body of their monarch in search of electric signals.

Lincoln did his best to provide those signals, wordlessly, by simply touching as many as he could. At the center of the scrum, he reached out in all directions, ultimately with his left and right hands simultaneously. An eyewitness wrote, "Every man in the crowd was anxious to wrench the hand of Abraham Lincoln. He finally gave both hands to the work, with great good nature." The witness continued, "People plunged at his arms with frantic enthusiasm, and all the infinite variety of shakes, from the wild and irrepressible pump-handle movement, to the dead grip, was executed upon the devoted dexter and sinister of the president."[76] Another compared Lincoln to an "old-fashioned ship telegraph," vibrating with the intensity of his double-fisted effort.[77] One old-timer came at him with his cane raised— another threat? According to a witness, Lincoln understood: when the elderly man "elevated his cane," Lincoln shook the other end of it, and his "assailant" went away "gratified."[78]

Writing later about what had happened in the rotunda, Lincoln's secretary John Nicolay revealed how much anxiety the presidential party had felt.[79] A note of panic can still be detected in his account, as the crowd surged toward the innermost O. "Before anyone was well aware of the occurrence," he remembered, "there was a concentric jam of the crowd toward the president-elect which threatened to crush him and those about him." The pressure was so intense that it began to push people up into the air, "like a mole hill."[80] Fortunately, Ward Lamon was nearby, "a man of extraordinary size and herculean strength," and was able to stand in front of Lincoln, blocking the rush. By a "formidable exertion," he was able "to hold back the advancing pressure until Mr. Lincoln could be hurried to a more secure place behind the corner of a pilaster."[81] The columns had given Lincoln a way to protect himself from the mob—a virtue of the Greek Revival that no one had anticipated. It had been another close call.[82]

There was something heroic, perhaps even foolhardy, in these efforts to touch as many people as possible. Nicolay was perceptive about Lincoln's need to be near a crowd. He did not love the official receiving lines he was forced to submit to; in fact, the New York Times noticed that his face quickly became bored and listless when surrounded by minor officialdom. But he had an almost physical need to touch the people; a need they reciprocated. Nicolay wrote, "For a time, it seemed as though Mr. Lincoln could not resist." His "sympathy with and for the people" was simply too strong for him to think of his own safety. Time and again, he thrust himself before them. Despite all the obvious reasons for caution, he felt a "fascination." It did not matter how many there were, or where they came from, or whether they were immigrants or not. They were fellow Americans, and "he could not easily wrench himself away."[83]

Nicolay later tried to break down the reasons that these encounters were so effective. It was almost as if an invisible current flowed back and forth, which he compared to electricity. It was a "subtle, psychological" force, spelled out nowhere in the Constitution but essential for the workings of democracy. It began even before he spoke; there was something in his twangy accent and his awkward gestures that worked, paradoxically, in his favor. Nicolay wrote that "his whole bearing, manner, and utterance carried conviction to all beholders that the man was of them as well as for them."[84]

But drawing so close to the crowds was taking a toll. In a letter to his fiancée two days later, Nicolay expressed his fear that Lincoln was being "killed with kindness"—and assured her that he meant the phrase literally.[85] For a time, they tried a different approach, less exhausting, in which the president-to-be would stand and be seen by the crowds filing past but not shake their hands. This proved to be ridiculous: Lincoln felt as if he were part of "an animal show," and they returned to the system of real handshakes. That was where the electricity was—"a cordial grasp of the hand and a fitting word formed an instantaneous circuit of personal communion."[86]

Those few seconds could last a lifetime in the memories of those who were there. For millions, it was the only time they ever saw him. Several young Ohioans left enduring accounts. A teenage schoolboy named Smith Stimmel arrived early and positioned himself perfectly, right where Lincoln descended from the train. ("Everybody knew him when they saw him.") For a few seconds, Lincoln gave them a long look, and hundreds of handkerchiefs fluttered. It was a happy scene, but Stimmel could see "the deep careworn lines in his tired-looking face."[87] Still, those first seconds were important, and, Stimmel explained, "To see Lincoln was to feel closely drawn to him." With his "freedom and good humor" and his raw physicality (Stimmel admired "his big, bony hands"), he persuaded all of those crowds, "instinctively," that he was "a man of the people."[88]

Thousands of others had a second or two of their own that day: a word in passing or a shake of those big hands. James A. Garfield was there, a young state senator with literary interests, drinking in the moment.[89] There was a brief planetary alignment as these two doomed presidents passed near each other. Garfield described the encounter to his wife. Lincoln was "distressingly homely," but in most respects, "he surpassed expectations." Despite "his awkward homeliness, there is a look of transparent, genuine goodness which at once reaches your heart and makes you trust and love him." To a friend, he wrote that Lincoln's western sense and "condensed style of expression" were exactly what was needed to counteract "Buchanan's weakness and cowardly imbecility." All in all, Lincoln's immersion in the people was producing "a fine effect."[90]

Coggeshall and Howells, the two young writers who were waiting so eagerly for Lincoln, were also there, scribbling away. Coggeshall brought his family and underwent an experience so intense that it was like an epiphany. They may have spoken; soon after, Coggeshall sent two copies of his massive survey of western poetry to Lincoln and his wife.[91] Many decades later, Coggeshall's widow poured out her memories to her daughter in a long letter. She had been one step above Lincoln during the tumultuous scene in the rotunda, and she relived what it felt like to be near the epicenter, as thousands filed by the man and his outstretched hands. She also added a story that Lincoln asked her husband to join him for the trip to Washington, and that Coggeshall later saved the president-elect's life by throwing a live grenade out the window of the train. The story strains credulity but suggests the intensity of one family's emotional response to Lincoln. Coggeshall did chronicle Lincoln's journey, and a book he published in 1865 supplied important information.[92]

William Dean Howells had seen Lincoln once before, in 1859, when he stood before a large crowd on the western side of the state house. Howells was at the back, and from his perspective, Lincoln was a tiny speck against the building's white background.[93] But the memory lingered for decades, a chiaroscuro of light and dark: "I have only the vision of his figure against the pale stone, and the black crowd spread vaguely before him."

On the day Lincoln came back, in 1861, Howells got very close. He saw Lincoln shaking the hands of a "never-ending crowd" in the rotunda; a living, breathing president-to-be, laying hands on the people who had elected him. Something in this raw physical contact was healthy and helped to restore "the strange anomaly which called itself the government," but which, under Buchanan, had been "constantly betraying itself." The young Ohioan's literary talents were clear from this attentive passage, realistic down to Lincoln's eyelashes:

The people who pushed upward to seize the great hand held out to everyone looked mostly like the country folk such as he had been of, and the best of him always was, and I could hear their hoarse or cracked voices as they hailed him, oftenest in affectionate joking, sometimes in fervent blessing; but for anything I could make out, he answered nothing. He stood passive, submissive, with the harsh lines of his lower face set immovably, and his thick-lashed eyes sad above them, while he took the hands held up to him one after another and shook them wearily, wearily.[94]

It was impossible to know how many people had grasped Lincoln's swollen hands. As John Nicolay understood better than most, the physical ordeal had been "something fearful."[95] But each small bridge that he built strengthened the Union.

Lincoln's reception (Prints and Photographs Division, Library of Congress)

THE COUNT [96]

As democracy was reviving itself in Columbus, it was undergoing a crucial test in Washington, inside a poorly ventilated chamber, its air thick with resentment. On the floor of the House, the votes were being counted to validate Lincoln's election in November. The House was crowded with anxious spectators from every part of the political spectrum, eager to watch the ritual.

For some time, this had appeared to many as the most vulnerable moment of the transition. Unionists had become more alert since the alarming developments of late December, when it seemed as if the Capitol might be occupied by pro-Southern militias. Still, the *Baltimore Sun* reported that it was "not impossible" that the Capitol would be blown up—police were checking the basement every night for bombs.[97]

Lucius Chittenden was in Washington as a young Vermont delegate to the peace conference. He wrote that the country never escaped a crisis "more alarming" than that of February 13. Very few in Washington "doubted that a conspiracy to seize the government existed," he explained. He described a city seething with anger, made more so by an influx of truculent outsiders spoiling for a fight. From eight in the morning, they were trying to enter the Capitol to cause trouble during the vote.[98]

Winfield Scott was ready for them. He posted armed guards at the building's entrances and refused entry to any but members of Congress and authorized visitors carrying passes. Guns and ammunition were stacked in committee rooms, and a regiment of men was in civilian clothes, mingling with the crowds, ready to restore order.[99] The people outside tried to get into the building with "prayers, bribes, entreaties, oaths, objurgations," but the soldiers stood their ground. Consequently, "the amount of profanity launched forth against the guards would have completely annihilated them if words could kill."[100]

But words did not intimidate Winfield Scott, and he deployed a few of his own, with panache. The indomitable general warned that anyone who tried to interfere with the count of the electoral vote "should be lashed to the muzzle of a twelve-pounder and fired out of the window of the Capitol." Colorfully, he added, "I would manure the hills of Arlington with the fragments of his body"—as if he already knew that it would become a cemetery someday.[101]

These threats only increased the excitement and turned the vote count into a tense spectacle of waiting. No one quite knew if the United States would survive the day. Some fled Washington, fearing the worst.[102] But most stayed, curious. Leading foreign ministers were there, and the galleries were soon "densely crowded."[103] Henry Adams wrote to his brother, "the family have gone up to the Capitol to see the counting of the votes."[104] His father also noted the event in his diary, and voiced a specific fear that Vice President John Breckinridge would be attacked while carrying the boxes of certified votes from the Senate to the House. If the votes were stolen, there would be no way to count them. The theft would be staged—and "not unwelcome" to Breckinridge, since he might then offer himself as the savior of the nation.[105]

Many Southerners were there as well. Chittenden saw them all around him and thought that they constituted "a vast majority." He was amazed at the raw emotion in the room. "To one who knew nothing of the hot treason which was seething beneath the quiet exterior," he wrote, "the exercises would have appeared to be tame and uninteresting."[106] To sophisticated observers, it was anything but. The counting of the vote offered a drama of Shakespearean intensity, with the country's fate hanging in the balance.

Even before it started, there were signs of stress. The House tried to pass a spending bill that would keep the government from imminent default, but it was opposed by a Virginian, Muscoe Garnett, who accused Lincoln of "tyranny" even before he arrived.[107] During a prayer by the chaplain, preceding the counting of the vote, Garnett stormed out, stamping his feet and loudly denouncing the proceedings. The *New York Times* wrote that he resembled the actor Junius Booth in *Richard the Third* as he did so.[108]

Shortly after noon, the House welcomed in the entire Senate. Its presiding officer was Vice President Breckinridge. He was ardently in favor of slavery and would resign to serve the Confederacy as its secretary of war. But on this critical day, he performed his duty. A senator from

Massachusetts, Henry Dawes, wrote later, "We owe much to Mr. Breck-inridge for the dignity and propriety of his conduct, though his heart was so thoroughly with the rebels he was among the earliest to join their army."[109]

Breckinridge gave the boxes with the votes to the "tellers," one of whom was Lincoln's old friend Elihu Washburne, now a congressman from Illinois. After the official count, the vice president duly certified Lincoln's election, reading out the prophetic words: "Abraham Lincoln, of Illinois, having re-ceived a majority of the whole of the electoral votes, is elected president of the United States, for four years, commencing on the fourth of March."[110] The ritual took about two hours.[111]

An enormous tumult ensued, as angry shouts were heard around the chamber. These included taunts to Lincoln, cheers for Jefferson Davis,

William Dean Howells at eighteen

and especially harsh invective directed toward Winfield Scott: "Old dotard!" "Traitor to the state of his birth!" "Free-state pimp!" But after these expressions of Southern vitriol, there were no more outbursts, and the vote was declared official. The *New York Times* wrote, "The public pulse beats freer." [112]

Through the Lightning, the news was sent around the country. The victor was among the first to learn the happy result. At 4:30, he went into the governor's room in the Ohio State House. The general superintendent of the Western Telegraph had been traveling with Lincoln all day for precisely this reason. He handed him a telegram that read: "The votes were counted peaceably. You are elected." Lincoln glanced at the note and put it into his pocket without reading it aloud or displaying any emotion at all. When he saw everyone looking at him, waiting for a response, he said simply, "What a beautiful building you have here," to a round of laughter. [113]

The New York diarist George Templeton Strong wrote, "This was the critical day for the peace of the capital. A foray of Virginia gents . . . could have done infinite mischief by destroying the legal evidence of Lincoln's election." [114] In fact, much malice was still planned. But Lincoln had now survived two assassination attempts and a hard recount, and he was getting closer by the hour.

A TALL DRINK OF WATER

Liberated at last from his public duties, Lincoln dined at the governor's mansion—perhaps his first meal since breakfast. Then Governor William Dennison threw open the doors of his residence for another "thronging multitude." [115] Lincoln returned to the State House, where the public called on him one more time. [116] Then at last, his long day of public events drew to a close, and he went to sleep in the governor's home.

The western wind would continue to blow long after Lincoln's visit to Columbus was a fading memory. It carried one Ohioan especially far. The first time he saw Lincoln speak, in 1859, William Dean Howells described himself as a mere "particle" in the crowd. [117] But Lincoln's election lifted many others as well, and his young biographer would be given a lovely plum: the consulship of Venice.[118] Howells admitted, it was "the beginning of the best luck I have had in the world."

Ohio would never leave him, even after he left Ohio. More than fifty years later, on the eve of World War I, the aging "Dean of American Letters" would experience a powerful surge of remembrance and write out stories of his youth. As he searched for a title, he came back to the domed State House. *In an Old-Time State Capital* appeared in three issues of *Harper's* magazine across the fall of 1914, as another war engulfed Europe.[119] Lincoln's passage through Columbus was the moment it all changed for Howells, as one world ended and a new one began.

Howells recorded one last memory of the laconic human being who had come through his hometown with so much hoopla. It came later, after the trip was over. On the day that Nicolay and Hay invited Howells to the White House to finalize the details for his overseas posting, the president could not have been more vivid. As Howells entered the White House, he first met with the two secretaries and enjoyed "some young men's joking and laughing together in the anteroom where they received me."

Nearby was "the great soul"—Lincoln—"working silently behind a closed door." Suddenly the great soul stirred. Hay and Nicolay asked Howells if he had ever seen Lincoln, and he answered that he had seen him at Columbus from a distance. It seemed as if Lincoln were coming toward him, and Howells hoped to thank him for the honor of representing the United States in the Lombardo-Venetian Kingdom. That was a mouthful, even for a talented wordsmith.

At last, Howells was getting his wish: in the corridor, he stood face-to-face with Lincoln. But the president seemed not to see him. The great soul "looked at the space I was part of with his ineffably melancholy eyes," without knowing that his biographer stood before him. Howells faltered a moment, strongly wanting to speak to him. But then he was overcome by a second thought. Howells decided that anyone who chose *not* to bother Lincoln, or shake his hand, or mumble a few words actually "did him a kindness." Instead, he simply watched, attentively, a much better

biographer than he had been a year earlier. Howells described a remarkably simple act—taking a drink of water—and he described it to perfection. It was *real*.

"He walked up to the water-cooler that stood in the corner and drew
himself a full goblet from it, which he poured down his throat with a backward tilt of his head, and then went wearily within doors. The whole affair,
so simple, has always remained one of a certain pathos in my memory, and I
would rather have seen Lincoln in that unconscious moment than on some
statelier occasion." [120]

Years later, Howells wrote a poem, "From Generation to Generation,"
that seemed to speak to all the souls whose lives hung in the balance on the
brilliant day that Lincoln came through Columbus.

> *The doom is on us, as it is on you,*
> *That nothing can undo;*
> *And all in vain you warn:*
> *As your fate is to die, our fate is to be born.*

As Lincoln was drifting off to sleep, Jefferson Davis was planning the next
phase of his own journey.[121] He would arrive sooner than Lincoln, despite
his serpentine train route. But the peaceful count of the votes in the Capitol
had removed a significant scare. The *New York Times* noticed the relief felt
by the presidential party. After hearing the news that Washington was safe,
"a profound and quieting impression" settled in.

There was much to celebrate. Lincoln had survived a bomb scare and
had heightened his own reality before huge crowds. He had won this critical
state for the Union, forever. He was a hundred miles closer to his destination. War had not broken out yet, despite the appearance of a sensational
news story, earlier in the day, that Fort Sumter had been attacked, with 150
casualties. It turned out to be a false report, seized too eagerly by a New York
newspaper.[122]

Still, there were concerns from those watching him up close. His host,

Governor Dennison, noted privately that Lincoln was "worn out by the fatigues of the journey." He added that the president-elect seemed to be "in trouble" in some way he couldn't specify.[123] In the *Times*, Joseph Howard Jr. made a perceptive point: getting closer to Washington only increased the intensity of the hatred. As he wrote, "It is a terrible ordeal" to pass through, made worse by the knowledge that he was heading toward "a scene of discord, trouble, and possible danger."[124]

J. Milligan, weighmaster, Sligo Iron Works, Pittsburgh [1]

7

HEART OF DARKNESS

The iron takes on its power.

—Homer, *The Odyssey*, book 9, line 393[2]

COLUMBUS TO PITTSBURGH
FEBRUARY 14, 1861

VALENTINES

As Valentine's Day dawned, hearts were fluttering around the country for all of the usual reasons. Some of those hearts belonged to merchants, thrilled to have another reason to move their wares. The holiday was well on its way to becoming a commercial bonanza. The *Chicago Tribune* estimated that fifteen thousand cards were sent to sweethearts in that city alone, including eighty-four sent to one lucky girl, the daughter of "a well-known poultry dealer."[3]

Lincoln's mail was less romantic. On the same day, he received an obscene note that spoke for many in the South:

Sir

Mr Abe Lincoln

if you don't Resign we are going to put a spider in your dumpling and play the Devil with you you god or mighty god dam sunnde of a bith go to hell and

buss my Ass suck my prick and call my Bolics your uncle Dick god dam a fool
and goddam Abe Lincoln who would like you goddam you excuse me for using
such hard words with you but you need it you are nothing but a goddam Black
nigger

yours &c
Mr. A. G. Frick

Tennessee Missouri Kentucky Virginia N. Carolina and Arkansas is going to
secede Glory be to god on high[4]

In Columbus, it was cold and overcast, although that did not deter the
crowds who milled in the streets, hoping to catch a glimpse of the celebrity
in their midst. The Lincolns woke up early, then left at seven o'clock for
Union Station, where they found the Special. Lincoln and his son Robert
boarded without difficulty. But Mary was nearly separated from the party,
along with Tad and Willie. They made the train, barely, after running to
catch it. Nothing would be easy on this long day.[5]

As the Special lurched eastward, the skies darkened. Then the rain
came, "first in drops and then in perfect torrents," according to a passenger.[6]
Lincoln privately expressed his hope that it would keep people from coming
out to hear him—he was beginning to wear down.

That morning's *Chicago Tribune* opened with a welcome headline, "Lincoln Elected," based on the official vote count a day earlier. But there were
uglier stories, too, about a capital that was essentially under siege. The Capitol was under constant surveillance for fear that it would be bombed, and
Cabinet secretaries were sleeping in the White House to "keep out villains
steeped in treason." It added that "all of the hopes of the republic hang" on
Lincoln's successful arrival in Washington.[7]

Other reports from around the country were equally ominous. Tempers were flaring, and each day brought new stories of incivility as the

old order broke down. In Savannah, Georgia, at a time when Southern leaders were assiduously courting the United Kingdom, a British sea captain was tarred and feathered by a mob simply because he had allowed an African-American dockworker to join his crew for a meal. In Virginia, a convention was beginning to consider secession. But that was not fast enough for South Carolina, where secessionists were "expected to secede" a second time, this time from the Confederacy, because the newly elected president, Jefferson Davis, had not yet launched a military assault on Fort Sumter.

To the north, the unraveling continued, one family at a time. In Mound City, Illinois, on the northern shore of the Ohio, a light-skinned former slave was captured by his owner after having escaped from a Mississippi plantation. The case was complicated: he claimed that he had been born to white parents but sold into slavery after he was orphaned at a young age. Yet it was very difficult to tell fact from fiction; anyone could invent a family narrative. In the end, he was reenslaved by his owner, W.C. Falkner—the great-grandfather of William Faulkner. He had run away in November, possibly in response to Lincoln's election.[8]

The president-elect may have wanted to run away, too. Each city brought more welcoming committees, more speeches, and more hands to shake. The new day had begun in darkness, and it would only get darker as he headed toward Pittsburgh, already famous as a place where it was hard to see because of the clouds of black smoke that sat over the city and its factories. In the book he loved as a child, *Pilgrim's Progress*, the path toward the Celestial City wound through the Valley of the Shadow of Death. Now he would descend into a valley of his own, searching for new sources of power.

WHISTLING DIXIE

Despite the weather, the mood began to lighten as the Special devoured the miles, and the presidential party relaxed with what Henry Villard called

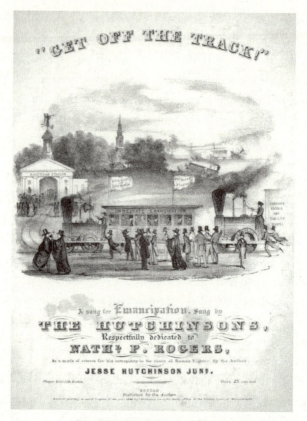

"Get Off the Track!" sheet music[9]

"divers [*sic*] hilarious pastimes."[10] These included a spontaneous musical interlude. In the forward car, some of the delegation's younger members began to sing. Leading them was Robert Lincoln, nursing a broken heart from "a Columbus beauty" he had met the night before. They were joined by Ward Lamon, who brought out his banjo. Thanks to alert reporting, we have the set list.[11]

"Get Off the Track!" was a perfect song for the Special, an antislavery number made famous by the Hutchinson Family Singers that warned bystanders to move aside as a train called "the Liberator" barreled past. "Get out of the way!" the chorus implored, as "Freedom's car" went "through the nation," chasing selfish merchants and other equivocators out of its path.

"None Shall Weep a Tear for Me" was a new song by Pittsburgh's own Stephen Foster, a maudlin ballad about a flower about to die. That, too, might have felt relevant in the final weeks of the old republic. They also sang a new song, "Dixie's Land," written by Ohio's Dan Emmett, a songwriter who composed the tune two years earlier while passing through New York. Despite these Yankee origins, it was irresistibly spreading through the South, where it struck a nerve in a region seeking to define itself. Four days later, it was performed at the inaugural of Jefferson Davis in Montgomery, cementing its reputation as the song of the Confederacy.[12] Lincoln called it "one of the best tunes I ever heard."[13]

To the people gathered by the tracks, it must have been disorienting to hear a fragment of "Dixie" wafting from the Special as it sped by. The *Chicago Tribune* reported that "the Buckeyes were out in force" and "not to be cheated out of their demonstration by a drizzling rain." Henry Villard noted that "immense multitudes" gathered everywhere, under umbrellas, to cheer the Special with shouts, songs, and "the roar of artillery."[14]

As usual, there were stops for fuel, water, and the endless hydration of speeches. At Newark, Lincoln fell back on an old ruse: making fun of his own features, or as he termed it, "my very interesting countenance."[15] Just outside of town, the Special raced past another enormous mound running through the woods. The Great Circle Earthworks had been built more than a millennium earlier, by a people eager to read the moon as it journeyed through the heavens. In the twentieth century, it would be repurposed as a golf hazard.[16]

At Cadiz Junction, Lincoln and his party enjoyed a hearty meal. The president-elect repeated a favorite joke, that if he kept stopping every few miles, he would not get to Washington until well after his inauguration.[17] But he was making progress, and as the Special approached Steubenville, around two in the afternoon, the weather cleared. At that very moment, the Special came around a curve to find an old friend, the Ohio River, narrower than at Cincinnati the morning before.

Kentucky was now an ancient memory. The Special had come so far that Lincoln was looking at Virginia, the state where his mother was born, and four of the first five presidents. Only a little earlier, he had been singing

"Look away, look away, look away, Dixie Land." Now he didn't have to look far, as the South stretched out before him.

What was Virginia doing so far north, above Pittsburgh and Philadelphia? It almost seemed a mapmaker's error, this panhandle thrusting itself nearly as far north as New York City. Clearly, it was no simple matter to separate "North" from "South." Many Virginians would have agreed. They still belonged to the United States; but only a day before, their leaders had begun to deliberate over secession. Lincoln could look across as much as he wanted, but he could not set foot in the commonwealth, for fear of inflaming public opinion at a delicate moment. That was a curious predicament for a candidate who had highlighted his family's Virginian heritage in his campaign materials.

Some of the most sensitive questions in American history had centered upon this stretch of river. The twists and turns of the Ohio were lovely, but they concealed how hard it was to govern a people who did not care for distant administrators. A century earlier, George Washington's early adventures in these parts had helped to trigger the imperial conflict between England and France, which in turn led to the American Revolution. But even after the Americans had won independence, it was not clear that they could control these regions so far from their capital.[18]

Before, during, and after the Revolution, Virginians were floating ideas for notional western entities—Vandalia, or Pittsylvania, or Westsylvania—to be liberated from France, or England, or perhaps even from the United States. It sometimes seemed as if a new nation might be founded in America's rich interior, against the wishes of the tiny government. A renegade former vice president, Aaron Burr, had explored the limits of this idea; his misadventures in the Ohio Valley tapped into a rich vein of antifederal feeling, which deepened, with the river, as it flowed south and west. Such a nation would surely have incorporated slavery into whatever charter it chose to write for itself. But there were always others with a larger vision of the United States, as a nation that would become more free as it spread to the West. George Washington was one of them, a point Lincoln made repeatedly.

As the Special slowed for Steubenville, Edwin Stanton's hometown, there were reminders of just how important this place had once been to the settlement of the free West. The first federal land office was still standing, a tiny building that had been there since 1801. Its ledgers held thousands of land claims, painstakingly entered, as a never-ending stream of families came through.

Sixty years later, Steubenville had more than six thousand souls.[19] Nearly twice that, ten thousand, came out to hear Lincoln's brief remarks. Many Virginians also came across the river to take his measure. As Lincoln took the carpeted stage, the sounds of cannonry boomed down the valley, ricocheting from the Ohio side to Virginia and back again. Lincoln gave a short, graceful speech, insisting that both sides of the river loved the Constitution equally.

Then it was on to the next town, Wellsville, Ohio, just up the river. According to the *Chicago Tribune,* "a brawny Irish miner," struggled to pull himself out of the crowd and clamber onto the stage with Lincoln. (The paper's

The Point of Beginning[20]

spelling of his words suggests that he was drunk.) To the crowd's amusement, he began to engage Lincoln in a very public conversation, saying, "God bless ye, Misther Lincoln! I didn't vote for ye, sure; but I wish ye luck, and I want to shake yer hand." A hearty shake followed, after which Lincoln asked how he had voted. "For Douglas," came the answer, while the crowd roared. Lincoln then asked him to "keep the ship together and right on her course for four years," so that Douglas would have another chance, and to keep the "good ship" from being broken up. "That's so, Misther Lincoln," his new friend responded. "I'm thinkin' meself you'll save the Union sure, and we'll all help ye." The crowd roared again.[21] The old river pilot had navigated another snag.

After passing through East Liverpool, Ohio, the Special came near a narrow stone obelisk, so close that Lincoln might almost have reached out and touched it. This was the fabled Point of Beginning. Here, in 1785, the infant government had laid down a marker. From this point, extending through the Northwest Territory (and eventually across the entire continent, including Alaska and Hawaii), the land would be divided meticulously into a pattern of squares, six miles per side, facilitating the formation of townships. The first geographer of the United States, Thomas Hutchins, had come here to plot what he called the Geographer's Line, heading due west, measured in twenty-two-yard increments by his chain.[22] To this day, anyone flying over the checkerboard pattern of the West can trace a line extending backward to the Point of Beginning.

The name was a simple geographer's term, for the place where Hutchins put a stake in the earth and began to measure out those chain lengths. But in a larger sense, the Point of Beginning also marked the place where Americans tried to build a better country. The original colonies had all belonged, in theory, to the English Crown. But after the Revolution, Americans needed to define the extent of their new realm—and its character as well. Even after they won their independence, it was unclear whether these fissiparous states could work together.

At the Point of Beginning, they began to. The plan was driven by a powerful optimism. The new America that would be built to the west would help to pay for the costs of self-government, through land sales. It would discourage divisions between rich and poor by demanding square townships, divided into equal parts, with money set aside for schools. Crucially, slavery was banned. In these ways, the founders had put their own kind of marker in the ground, hoping to define the more perfect Union that the United States would someday become. This was the story Lincoln kept retelling to a people who had forgotten their own history. The country's ideals could be marked as clearly as its boundaries.

Just past East Liverpool, he entered Pennsylvania. Thomas Jefferson's early followers had called it "the keystone in the federal arch." [23] The phrase fit, both for Jefferson's architectural interests and because Pennsylvania was so central to the federal project. When the capital was relocated to Washington, Pennsylvania Avenue was given the place of honor as the thoroughfare connecting the Capitol and the White House. The street preceded them, as a muddy path between construction sites, before either edifice was built.

To win the nomination, Lincoln had followed an imaginary Pennsylvania Avenue of his own, picking up the support of the state's leaders at crucial moments. But that path went through some more mud, thanks to the promises his advisers had made in return for support. Now he had to negotiate his way through a state whose bosses largely detested one another.

Some of the hardest miles of the journey were now beginning as the Special began to curve sharply, with the river, toward Pittsburgh. At Rochester, Pennsylvania, the most northerly place reached by the Ohio, the Special stopped for some routine maintenance. That meant another obligation to speak, and once again a visitor crashed the stage. This time it was a "tall coal heaver" who stepped onto the platform and said loudly to Lincoln, "I want to shake hands with you; I can lick salt off the top of your head." That signaled a challenge to a height contest. The crowd erupted in laughter, especially after Lincoln straightened to his full six feet four inches and won the contest, barely. [24] It would have been difficult to imagine Jefferson Davis or James Buchanan indulging in similar antics, but these humble encounters, described in the press, humanized Lincoln before a national audience that was still getting to know him.

All the while, the Special continued to follow the bends of the river.

After Rochester, the Special turned south again and reached a small town called Freedom. In theory, Lincoln might have given an expansive speech on that topic. But unfortunately, the Special ground to an ignominious halt. To be stuck in Freedom was not a headline Lincoln wanted.

Despite all the precautions that his trip planners had taken to clear the way, an ordinary freight train had broken down up the line. Until it could be moved, the Special was forced to wait, unable to pass through this narrow aperture. In nearly every way imaginable, it was a public relations nightmare for a president-elect who was still trying to find a path forward between extremists on all sides. A delay of nearly three hours ensued, wrecking all the reception plans for Pittsburgh, only twenty-two miles away. There was nothing to do, and Lincoln had to wait with everyone else until the damaged train could be moved.[25]

Finally, the way was cleared, and the Special resumed its descent. To descend was, in fact, the only way to approach Pittsburgh, nestled at the confluence of its three rivers, surrounded by hills. Charles Dickens had enjoyed the ride because he was able to see into so many people's lives as the train went through their backyards in its final approach to the city. Dickens loved the furtive pleasure of "catching glimpses, through the tree-tops, of scattered cabins, children running to the doors, dogs bursting out to bark, whom we could see without hearing; terrified pigs scampering homewards; families sitting out in their rude gardens; cows gazing upward with a stupid indifference; men in their shirtsleeves, looking on at their unfinished houses, planning out tomorrow's work, and we riding onward, high above them, like a whirlwind."[26]

Lincoln's train was a whirlwind, too, trying to make up for lost time as it sped him toward his destination. But this introduced new elements of danger, for it was dark and raining. To race down a hill under these conditions while heading toward a large crowd was asking for trouble. American railroads excelled at power and speed, but they had found less success with braking, an inexact science at best. Each car had to be stopped individually by brakemen running from one car roof to the next, and it usually required a mile to accomplish properly—with the result that trains often stopped well past the station, and had to either back up or discharge their passengers a hundred yards farther away than expected. When Lincoln had visited his stepmother two weeks earlier, his slow-moving train managed to miss the station, pulling up too short.

Eight years later, on exactly this stretch of track, a young inventor, George Westinghouse, would perfect a new system of air brakes capable of stopping all the cars at the same time thanks to a system of compressed air running through the entire train. The breakthrough would allow trains to grow longer, faster, and safer. Westinghouse would go on to invent a long roster of rail improvements before turning to electricity, alternating current, and the power grids necessary to feed the huge appetites of the new system he was wiring. In the fullness of time, radio and television would stem from these experiments, although that was a long way off as the Special careened down the slick tracks.[27]

Pittsburgh scene, *Ballou's Pictorial Drawing Room Companion,* February 21, 1857[28]

WONDROUS BLACKNESS

It was dark as the Special began to approach Pittsburgh, applying its brakes as it gently slowed. Mercifully, they worked. Lincoln would have seen little out the window.[29] But even in daytime, Pittsburgh was famous for its soot, the residue of an economy built around the constant burning of bituminous coal, buried in the hills that Lincoln was now coming through. Visitors routinely commented on the black clouds that gave the city an otherworldly quality. Its low visibility added to its aura as a place of alchemy, where metallurgists were forging the future.

The haze was already there, in the earliest accounts. In 1790 Pittsburgh was little more than a smudge on the map, but visitors already found it hard to see. The French traveler Michel Chevalier saw heavy "flakes of soot" falling like snow. Anthony Trollope called it the darkest place he had ever seen, full of "filth and wondrous blackness."[30]

Pittsburghers paid them no mind and lived bravely in their version of the Cloud, which they celebrated with their fashion choices (women preferred to wear black) and a dark humor.[31] It was said that "men kiss each other's wives in Pittsburgh," simply because it was so difficult to see, and that mothers wrote out messages to shopkeepers on the faces of their children.[32]

To enter this grimy place was disorienting enough in the daytime. But as the Special came through the darkness, with crowds milling on either side, illuminated by torches and gas jets, the passengers must have wondered if they were entering a station of the underworld. Another traveler who arrived at night saw menacing shapes out the window and "fiery eyes" formed by coke ovens glowering from the hills. He concluded that Pittsburgh was simply another word for "hell with the lid taken off."[33]

In one of his funnier short stories, "The Celestial Railroad," Nathaniel Hawthorne described a train that brought its passengers to an infernal place where the people were all "smoke-begrimed," and even emitted smoke out of their mouths and nostrils. Once the train arrived in this "Dark Valley," there was no way out. That predicament that may have worried Lincoln's advisers as they kept sliding down the tracks toward an unhappy crowd that had been waiting a long time in the cold.

Railroad station at Allegheny City (Pittsburgh)[34]

A MORE PERFECT FIZZLE

Despite a "pelting rain" and the long delay, the crowd was sizeable when Lincoln finally arrived.[35,36] When the four-car train pulled up at eight o'clock amidst the usual explosions of cannonade, they went "wild with excitement."[37] But because of the weather, the reception had to be scrapped.[38] A Cincinnati newspaper carped, "a more perfect fizzle was never witnessed."[39]

It was a hard arrival, Lincoln's first at night, and tensions increased as they tried to make their way through the drenched crowd. Nicolay later wrote an appraisal of that evening, still burned in his memory. There were only a few gas jets working, which did more to "intensify" the darkness than dispel it. The private carriages reserved for Lincoln and his party were held so close to the station that the horses were "seized with a fright" when the Special came in with "its steam whistle going, its bell ringing." The result was "almost a stampede."

In these conditions, with the terrified animals bolting and the crowd pressing in, Lincoln was forced to find his carriage. Nicolay confessed that it was terrifying and nearly spun out of control. He called it "an absolutely uncontrollable mélé [melee] of moving wheels and hoofs, of noise and shouting, in a half-light that confused correct judgment and baffled caution, permitting only the single vivid and realistic impression that chaos had come." *Chaos*—the same word that James Russell Lowell had used as he looked at the stars on the flag and wondered if there was any gravitational force at all holding them together. Lincoln was walking along the edge of an abyss.[40]

Pittsburgh, 1871[41]

WELL SITUATED

After hugging the Ohio for so many miles, Lincoln was now at the source of the great river, where it was formed by the meeting of the Allegheny and the Monongahela. Even in the smoke and darkness, it was obvious that he had reached a special place. Its strategic importance had been perfectly clear to George Washington when he first visited "the Forks of the Ohio" in 1753. He described the location as "extremely well situated."[42]

But even after the French and English had finished fighting over it, Pittsburgh's future remained uncertain. Was it Pennsylvanian or Virginian? The charter claims overlapped and left enough doubt that Virginian mapmakers, such as Jefferson's father, could easily shift the boundaries to include this prize. Pennsylvanians sometimes agreed, especially when they did not want to pay taxes for Pittsburgh's defense.[43]

Not until the American Revolution were the claims resolved, in favor of Pennsylvania.[44] But the old memories lingered. The Ohio could trace its sources both ways, with its waters commingling from north and south. The Allegheny winds down from western New York, and the Monongahela comes up from the western counties of Virginia, in what is now West Virginia. From their confluence, the waters eventually reach the Mississippi, nearly a thousand miles to the west. More than just "well situated," it was vital to the destiny of the United States.

In other words, Lincoln had arrived at a city he absolutely needed for the Union. Yet there were disturbing signs. On the day that he visited Pittsburgh, the papers reported that "a mammoth Palmetto flag," the symbol of South Carolina, was "suspended from the telegraph wire," startling the town of Shippensburg, in central Pennsylvania.[45]

That was not entirely surprising, in a state that had never been easy to govern, despite its role in the founding. Pennsylvania was full of small pockets, several of which Lincoln's ancestors had inhabited during their long shuffle west in the eighteenth century. The trip between Philadelphia and Pittsburgh was famously difficult, and when Tocqueville and Beaumont tried a trip of their own, the latter called it "one of the most arduous I have ever taken," with "detestable" roads, steep impasses, and "a perpetual tornado of snow." It took them three full days.[46]

That distance had made it harder to unite Pennsylvania, and some of the most intense opposition to the Constitution came from the very state where it was written, as if half of the state refused to be governed by the other.[47] During the Whiskey Rebellion of 1794, five thousand men assembled near Pittsburgh to protest a whiskey tax and fight for their liberties against the "aristocratic Money Bags of the East." Ultimately, the first president's immense prestige saved the day. At the time, Virginians mustered to defend the federal idea, and Pennsylvanians—some of them, anyway—to oppose it.[48]

As Lincoln approached, they were lining up differently. In the last week of December 1860, the Virginian secretary of war, John Floyd, tried to transfer more than a hundred pieces of artillery from Pittsburgh's Allegheny Arsenal to Southern military posts.[49] He was thwarted by the action of loyal citizens, who held two mass meetings to block the shipment. But the narrowness of that outcome showed how close Pittsburgh was to the front lines of a struggle that did not yet have a name. By massing in protest, the people of Pittsburgh had taken matters into their hands and revealed deep wellsprings of feeling for the Union.[50]

Wellsprings were important in a city where geology ruled. To the American public, Pennsylvania was a place of probity, where Quakers went about their silent business, and German-speaking farmers tilled the soil. But millions of years earlier, it had been the scene of one violent disruption after the next, as mountains formed and collapsed, and the land buckled and folded upon itself.

Out of these upheavals, a great mineral wealth was born.[51] When the earliest settlers arrived, they were delighted to find iron ore, which helped when they needed cooking implements, farming tools, and, in less Quakerly moments, cannonballs.[52] The land was generous in other ways as well. Plentiful seams of anthracite coal could be found in eastern Pennsylvania, and as the earliest settlers reached Pittsburgh, new beds of bituminous coal seemed almost to be offering themselves, with barely any digging required.[53]

George Washington noticed the coal, and he found other strange properties in the wilds of western Pennsylvania. There were unusual places that seemed almost to spontaneously combust. He recorded one site where "the Indians said is always a fire."[54] Many explorers observed similar phenomena: pools of dark oil floating on river surfaces, or places where bubbling creeks would ignite spontaneously and "blaze like brandy."[55]

At first, these mysterious elements were poorly understood, and local settlers ignored them.[56] But eventually the availability of fossil fuels in Pennsylvania became one of the great economic facts of American history, feeding the industrial economy of the United States at exactly the moment it was beginning to surge. Later, deeper questions would be asked about the cost of this extraction. But those questions were a long way away in 1861, and in the urgency of the crisis, Lincoln needed every source of power he could find.

The same census that was tabulating people in 1860 was also counting natural resources, including all of these combustible materials in the earth. Pennsylvania seemed to have been favored by the gods.[57] More than 80 percent of the nation's coal workers were in Pennsylvania. In every measurable category, the North had more—more iron, more steel—which meant more bridges, more railroads, more factories.[58] The coal regions had become essential to the entire industrial output of the United States, fueling plant operations and the trains that never stopped running. In the late 1850s, coal was replacing wood as the fuel for railroads, with the result that brightly colored trains began giving way to black locomotives and dark cars, to disguise the soot.[59]

Pittsburgh was perfectly situated to take advantage of these developments. Roughly half of America's iron production came from the place where the three rivers met.[60] Coal consumption had doubled since 1850.[61] Everywhere the railroad went, it brought a hunger for raw materials. Pittsburgh's factories just kept rolling iron, burning coal, and belching black clouds into the air, to the delight of onlookers. "Smoke is a blessing," the city's residents murmured contentedly, to anyone who asked.[62]

For generations, politicians had described a mystical union, composed of shared aspirations, and the memory of the Revolution. Now something more literal was being welded from these ores and metals, as engineers connected far-flung Americans with wires, cables, and train tracks. Near Pittsburgh, a German immigrant named John Roebling had begun to weave together iron strands into heavy cables strong enough to build great suspension bridges across rivers. It would be hard to imagine a more literal display of *e pluribus unum*. With its hills and valleys, Pittsburgh was a perfect laboratory for bridge building, and Roebling's spans, made from local iron, gave the city more coherence. Steel, even stronger, began to be made in larger quantities after the Bessemer process was perfected in the 1850s. With time, that would lead to a seemingly limitless business for a country growing rapidly. All roads seemed to lead to this beating industrial heart, glowing with the light of a thousand forges.[63]

Naturally, a place rich in minerals would attract railroads. It required some engineering to cross the Allegheny Mountains, but after the first line opened between Philadelphia and Pittsburgh in 1852, Pittsburgh's growth was explosive. That single line expanded to two in 1858, and in January 1861, a month before Lincoln's arrival, a new line was completed—the Baltimore and Ohio—bringing Baltimore, with all of its secessionist sympathies, into close commercial contact with this reliably Northern city. That strengthened Lincoln's position as he groped his way forward in the darkness.[64]

From the moment that Pittsburgh was yoked, Pennsylvania's internal union fortified the larger Union. It was as if a steel beam had been put in place, joining east and west—a new kind of arch held together by iron trusses instead of keystones. Instead of resisting the republic, as it had under George Washington, Pittsburgh was now girding it. Its gritty reality perfectly grounded the airy promises that the founders had offered at Philadelphia.

In essence, that was the purpose of Lincoln's trip: to make those promises real. He used a hard, metallic word in December when asked to respond to the vague offers of compromise that were endlessly belching out of the swamp. To his old friend Elihu Washburne, Lincoln insisted, "Hold firm, as with a chain of steel."[65]

James Hamilton, *Burning Oil Well at Night, Near Rouseville, Pennsylvania,* 1861 (Smithsonian American Art Museum)

OIL ON THE BRAIN

After the hardship of the arrival, Lincoln was safely escorted into his carriage, and a nocturnal procession began toward his hotel, the Monongahela House. But even this short trip required concentration. The train station was in Allegheny City; to reach the hotel, the entourage had to cross a bridge over the Allegheny River. An ambitious new span had just been completed by John Roebling, yet another connecting link.

Below the bridge, the Allegheny flowed swiftly as it prepared to merge with the Monongahela and form the Ohio. It is unlikely that Lincoln could have seen much of it on a rainy night. But if he had been able to peer into its

Stygian depths, he might have seen flecks of color on the surface, catching the gaslight. This was the residue of a viscous substance that had been found a hundred miles upstream only a year and a half earlier, bringing an economic revolution nearly as profound as the political one that delivered Lincoln.[66]

Since late 1859, the Allegheny had been crowded with barges carrying huge quantities of "rock oil" in forty-two-gallon barrels toward a market that could not get enough of it. In only the past few months, production had surged, roughly quadrupling from 1,200 barrels a day to more than 5,000. Even local journalists were astonished by the speed of this change or the power of the new force spurting out of the derricks north of Pittsburgh. "The earth seems to bleed like a mad ox, wrathfully and violently," wrote an editor in Titusville, one of the main nodes of production.[67]

It had always been there: a reddish-brown liquid, seeping out of the earth, so plentiful that it barely needed to be extracted. The Native Americans had known it well; they skimmed it off the surface and gathered it in blankets, distributing it in small quantities to help with ailments. Even before the Revolutionary War, English mapmakers were adding a strange new word, *petroleum*, to their maps, showing where this substance could be found. A few local entrepreneurs tried to sell it, without much success, arguing that it would cure blotchy skin, or diarrhea, or help the elderly to recover their youth.[68]

But in the years just before Lincoln's arrival, petroleum grew much more valuable. New York investors were eager to find reliable sources of energy, with a decline expected in sperm oil, thanks to the overhunting of whales.[69] Investors wondered if they could extract petroleum in large quantities through drilling underground—a mechanical operation that drew much of its technology from lessons learned from building railroads and tunnels. On August 27, 1859, they hit pay dirt, when drillers struck a gusher near Titusville. After a boom started, the surrounding lands were given exotic new nicknames, like Oildom and Petrolia.[70] Colorful flags flew from the tops of derricks, with "strange mottoes," as if this were a medieval caravansary, full of new principalities who intended to rule themselves. In a lawless climate, that was no exaggeration.[71]

The announcement of the oil strike at Oil Creek sent fibrillations around the country.[72] Soon large numbers of investors and prospectors had "Oil on the Brain," to quote a novelty song penned in the days following the strike.[73] The revolution was felt immediately around Pittsburgh, where the new businesses related to Oildom set up offices.[74] It was a dangerous business: two months after Lincoln's visit, an apocalyptic fire burned for days after a sixty-foot gusher exploded out of the earth.[75] One painter, James Hamilton, was shrewd enough to rush to the scene to capture an eerie interplay of light and darkness that no one had quite beheld before.[76]

But despite the danger, oil extraction was so lucrative that young fortune seekers flooded every aspect of the business. These Petrolians added to Pittsburgh's reputation as a wide-open city, and they must have been in the crowd as Lincoln crossed the oily river to find his hotel.[77] A contemporary account described the way they looked: fierce, bearded, with "toughened constitutions," swarming like bees near the substance they wanted.[78] They were filling Pittsburgh's hotels and bars on their way to the oil fields; or just as often, on their way back, unhappily, without the riches they had come here to acquire. John Wilkes Booth would become one of them after failing to launch a business he called the Dramatic Oil Company.[79]

But there were others who brought a more constructive approach to the challenge of tapping the great force bubbling out of the earth. One enterprising young man had a simple idea; he designed a better wooden vat to hold the oil before shipment down the river. Franklin Tarbell did not make a fortune, but he provided a decent living for his daughter Ida, who was three years old as the Special came through Pennsylvania. She grew up a natural muckraker, having seen so much of the runoff in her childhood. A generation later, she exposed the venality of the Standard Oil Company in a pioneering work of investigative journalism.[80] She also became one of Lincoln's most sensitive biographers, helping new generations to hear the words he was speaking in the desperate days of February 1861.

Andrew Carnegie, right, age sixteen, telegraph messenger

RAILROAD MEN

As in Ohio, many young Pennsylvanians felt the force of the new winds carrying Lincoln from the West. The *Zephyrus* would sweep several brilliant railroaders all the way to Washington. Thomas A. Scott, the vice president of the Pennsylvania Railroad, had cut his way through logistical thickets for eleven years to build a great rail network. In the dark days that were coming, his organizational skills would play a crucial role in guarding Lincoln's life during the final approach to Washington.[81]

Scott was also a shrewd judge of talent, and he kept promoting a young Scottish immigrant with a head for figures. On the day that Lincoln arrived, Andrew Carnegie was more than ready. He had arrived in the United States when he was twelve years old, and rose quickly by staying close to the information corridor that was beginning to reach the city he called, affectionately, "dirty, smoky Pittsburgh."[82] At fifteen, he became a telegraph messenger boy; his ear was so attuned to the clicks of the instruments that he could interpret messages at lightning speed, before they were even finished. Once, when the lines went down between Steubenville and Wheeling, he single-handedly kept communications flowing between the eastern and western halves of the United States, thanks to his transmission speed.[83]

Like Scott, Carnegie became a relentless efficiency expert, eliminating delays as if he were a carpenter with a lathe. His autobiography conveys vividly the attraction of speed, information, and getting to the point. "Iron was the thing," he wrote, in a characteristically terse sentence that brooked no waste.

Although still too young to vote, Carnegie was present when the Republican Party held its first national meeting, in Pittsburgh, on Washington's Birthday in 1856. He was ready for a better country and naturally gravitated toward Lincoln, whose economy of language set him apart from other politicians. Lincoln's body language also set him apart; he was "always alive and in motion," Carnegie wrote admiringly. His autobiography contains several glimpses of the president-elect, who left a deep impression. "I never met a great man who so thoroughly made himself one with all men as Mr. Lincoln," Carnegie remembered.[84] Unifying different elements to forge a stronger compound—that was precisely why Lincoln had come to Pittsburgh.

MONONGAHELA HOUSE

Following the chaotic arrival ceremony in the darkness and the river crossing, an exhausted Lincoln was brought to the Monongahela House, a five-story hotel with two hundred rooms. From its upper stories, a journalist wrote in 1868, a visitor could look out over the panorama of the rivers and see "the Great West" beginning.[85] As usual, huge and insistent crowds were waiting for him, ten thousand strong, blocking the entrance and all doorways to the building.

Monongahela House (1889)[86]

Local militias found a way forward, brandishing their bayonets, but it was another hurdle for the weary delegation.[87] According to the *Chicago Tribune*, "The streets were thronged and the excitement was tremendous." Everyone expected him to speak, both inside and outside the hotel. The huge crowd blocked all avenues and made a tremendous volume of noise. ("They cheered—they vociferated—they made everything ring.") They refused to leave until the man identified by the *Tribune* as "Mr. L" came out to see them.[88]

He complied, speaking from a chair, reluctantly. He began unpromisingly, complaining that he was "inclined to silence," disliked "long speeches," and preferred "a man who can hold his tongue" to one who cannot.[89] But once started, he enjoyed an easy rapport with the crowd. An account in the *Pittsburgh Dispatch* revealed considerable banter back and forth between the president-elect and the people who had come out to see him. After one of Lincoln's sallies, a voice said, "Go on, split another rail," to general laughter, while another shouted, "No railery Abe!"[90]

After concluding that speech, he was prevailed upon to give another, briefly, that did little more than promise to give another one the next morning. But even that did not release him, and he was trapped in a hotel parlor, unable to leave. Finally, his young friend Elmer Ellsworth forced a way through the throng, and with great difficulty, they managed to escape.[91] After another push, his entourage was at last able to clear a way for him to go upstairs to his room. John Nicolay, dismayed, wrote again to his fiancée that Lincoln's life was in constant danger, even from these adoring crowds. Remembering the mob that was "pushing and pulling and yelling all around us," he concluded, "I hope we shall never get into another such."[92]

At last, Valentine's Day was ending for Lincoln, as he and his family found their way to their suite.[93] He had survived another grueling day: coming through the rain, the knot at Freedom, the night arrival, and the crowds that would not give way. Each step of the journey had been harder than the one before, but at the end of a brutal slog, Lincoln could take solace in the fact that he had survived his passage through the dark valley.

By coming to Pittsburgh, Lincoln had recruited important allies and strengthened his presidency before it began. Once again, by appearing in the flesh, he had removed the sting of the insults that rained down constantly in the press. After seeing him, an opposition editor admitted that Lincoln was not quite as evil or as ugly as he had been led to believe: "He is by no means a handsome man, [but] his facial angles would not break a looking glass."[94]

The obstacles ahead were still formidable. On this same Valentine's Day, Congress wrapped up a hearing into the possibility of local plots against Lincoln, stating, not very persuasively, that it had found only a *modest* amount of evidence that assassins were actively seeking to kill him.[95] That same day, a congressman swore that Lincoln would never be inaugurated, in a conversation with Charles P. Stone, the army officer working to secure the Capitol.[96] Every day, Pinkerton's men and women were gathering evidence of new threats in Baltimore. There are indications that Lincoln and his advisers were worried enough that they contemplated going to Washington directly from Pittsburgh, by a much shorter distance. Yet they decided to press on.[97]

A thousand miles to the south, there was no rest as Jefferson Davis was a whirl of activity. His train trip was accelerating, as he started his long run from Jackson to Montgomery. Soon he was speaking as often as Lincoln; so often, in fact, that he slept in his suit. To the extent that we can hear Davis on the road—the paper trail is much thinner—his speeches bore little resemblance to Lincoln's modest expressions of hope. Instead, Davis was promising his trackside audiences that the border states would soon join the Confederacy, and England would recognize their newly formed nation.[98] He added the taunt that "grass will grow in the Northern cities where the pavements have been worn off by the tread of commerce."[99]

But judging from the crowds at Pittsburgh, it seemed unlikely that grass would be growing in these streets anytime soon. Given the amount of sunlight able to penetrate the smoke, it was not clear that grass even *could* grow there. The tread of commerce was so heavy that it was even taking people *below* the pavements, deep into the earth, where Pittsburgh's heavy metals rested, ready to be converted into energy. Over the next four years, the city's foundries would contribute three thousand cannon and ten million pounds of shot and shell to defend the Union. During the next decade, its population would increase at a rate of 75 percent.[100] In contrast, the population of the Alabama county where Davis spoke was 18,283; it would grow to 19,410 over the same period.

Davis needed to provoke. Like Lincoln, he was preparing his people for a huge contest. But as the day ended, it was clear that he had no idea what he was talking about. Two days later, Jefferson Davis gave a speech at Montgomery, where he predicted that Northerners would soon "feel Southern steel."[101] Unfortunately for him, most of that steel was made in Pennsylvania.

It had been the longest and hardest day of the journey, and many miles remained. But as usual, Lincoln pressed on, securing a tactical advantage as well as a vital outpost. George Washington had always understood the Forks of the Ohio to be critical to the defense of America. By adding Pittsburgh to his column, Lincoln had found a source of power that Jefferson Davis could only dream of.

Henry M. Flagler, circa 1850, Cleveland [1]

8

THE FOREST

Within the forest glades they found the house of Circe,
built of polished stone in a place of wide outlook,
and round about it were mountain wolves and lions . . .

—Homer, *The Odyssey*, book 10, lines 210–12[2]

PITTSBURGH TO CLEVELAND
FEBRUARY 15, 1861

AN OCEAN OF UMBRELLAS

Lincoln rose early, as usual. Friday morning brought more of the heavy rains that had cast a pall over his arrival. But he had promised a speech, and the weather did not intimidate the hearty souls of western Pennsylvania.[3] As Lincoln looked out from the Monongahela House, he could see five thousand people outside under "an ocean of umbrellas."[4] The *New York Times* said it was the largest crowd ever assembled in Pittsburgh.[5] They had slogged through the mud, eager to understand where the country was headed.[6]

At eight thirty, he began to speak. It was a strange speech, and left many confused. In the past three days, Lincoln had improvised brilliantly, giving an emotional farewell at Springfield, and then charming crowds with his humor, his modesty, and his homespun way of speaking, so free of rhodomontade. In subtle ways, he was rewriting the political playbook, using these intense encounters to remind Americans of all they still had in common.

This new politics was intuitive, as a natural actor took the stage with no script and interacted with his audience. It could be wordless; some of the trip's best moments had come when Lincoln simply stood before the people and allowed them to take him in.

But in the rain at Pittsburgh, he stepped back into politics as usual and delivered a dry policy speech—one of the addresses that he had written out by hand, so carefully, during his sitting sessions with his sculptor in Springfield. *Too* carefully, as it turned out: the formal speech sounded as if a sculptor had chiseled each letter, straining to avoid a mistake. It was a serious miscalculation. The rain-soaked audience wanted warmth and light; instead, Lincoln delivered a cold summary of his fiscal policy. Suddenly a conventional politician stood before them—and not a very interesting one.

Lincoln's topic was the tariff: the import duty that raised much of the federal budget and helped manufacturers. That was a matter of lively interest in Pennsylvania, where legislators bickered endlessly about which industries should be protected. But it was not necessary for him to address such a dense topic, and he did not do it well. By delving into economic matters that he did not entirely grasp, he reminded Americans that he was still a work in progress.

The tariff was popular around Pittsburgh, where the new extractive industries benefited from federal protection. Lincoln had supported tariffs since the beginning of his career, when they were a key part of the "American System" designed by his hero, Henry Clay, a pillar of the Whig party. The Whigs disintegrated in the fractiousness of the 1850s, but the Republicans revived many of their economic ideas, even as they reached out to moderate Democrats and Know-Nothings. The Republican platform had been devised with great care, and Lincoln's strategic silence on this topic had helped him to appeal to different audiences. They were all listed in the twelfth point of the platform, which explained how "the whole country" would benefit from a Republican economy, including workingmen, mechanics, manufacturers, and farmers. As the Republican Party coalesced in

Pennsylvania, it included both labor leaders and business owners, eager to bring in jobs.

All of this might have lent itself to a persuasive speech, including an economic appeal for Union, which would have appealed to the wavering border states. But it fell short of the mark.[7] The speech exposed gaps in Lincoln's understanding of the economy, which his long silence during the campaign had concealed. A little too honestly, he said, "I must confess that I do not understand this subject in all of its multiform bearings, but I promise you that I will give it my closest attention, and endeavor to comprehend it more fully."[8] That was not what five thousand people freezing in the rain wanted to hear. At one point, he actually asked John Nicolay to read aloud the official party plank dealing with the tariff. That tedious detour taxed their patience again.[9] A week later, in Harrisburg, Pennsylvania, Lincoln said that his remarks on the economy "were rather carefully worded. I took pains that they should be so."[10] But too much care, in this case, had produced a speech with almost nothing to say.

Lincoln also got into trouble by again saying that "there is really no crisis except an artificial one." By that, he meant simply that it was still possible to return to the *status quo ante* as soon as tempers cooled.[11] But tempers were *not* cooling, as anyone could plainly see. Jefferson Davis was moving quickly today, and a new government was organizing itself at Montgomery, well in advance of his own. No crisis in American history had ever been *less* artificial.

The Democratic newspapers were especially harsh. One lamented "an ignorance so gross that school-boys might laugh at him." The *Pittsburgh Post* ridiculed a geographic error in the speech: Lincoln's river eye momentarily failed him as he gazed across the Monongahela and identified "the troubles across the river," as if he were looking at the South.[12] That strategy had worked for him at Cincinnati and Steubenville, when he could look across the Ohio into Kentucky and Virginia. But here in Pittsburgh, the other side just meant more Pennsylvania.[13] Henry Villard was devastating: "What he said was nothing but crude, ignorant twaddle, without point or meaning." He added that it "strengthened my doubts as to his capacity for the high office he was to fill."[14]

Sourbeck House, Alliance, Ohio (Prints and Photographs Division, Library of Congress)

THE SEVEN RANGES

Lincoln had spoken longer than he intended—a half hour rather than fifteen minutes—and now he needed to rush back through Pittsburgh's crowded streets toward the station to resume his journey.[15] Yet another procession of politicians and marching bands formed to accompany him, but it was another hard passage, slowed by the bystanders who were trying desperately to grab Lincoln's hands.[16]

As his entourage boarded a train for Cleveland, a cynic might have commented that Lincoln was heading in precisely the wrong direction. The Special was now pointed northwest for a trip that was supposed to bring him southeast to Washington. But the zigzag of politics required him to avoid arriving too soon, and there were millions more to meet en route. The crowds around the depot were festive, animated by Lincoln's presence and the revelry that always accompanied a departure. A new locomotive was festooned with bunting, local militias fired salutes of farewell, and the people pressed ever closer, trying to touch him. There was a good deal of kissing as the crowd surged toward Lincoln, passing children over the heads of adults to reach him. A hilarious moment ensued when three attractive young women came near the president-elect and were kissed by him—but then recoiled as some of the younger members of Lincoln's entourage tried to claim the same privilege. Presumably, it was his son Bob and his usual partner in mischief, John Hay.[17]

An impressive new locomotive, *The Comet*, stood ready to carry them back toward Ohio.[18] At ten in the morning, it started.[19] For the first few miles, the irrepressible Bob Lincoln sat next to the engineer and drove the train.[20] At first, the train could only make its way slowly because it had to find its way through "masses of shouting humanity."[21] A few miles west, a "brief pause" was made, and "the rear car was surrounded by hundreds of workmen from the railroad and machine shops, who gave Mr. Lincoln a warm welcome in most unmistakable terms."[22]

Then they broke past Pittsburgh and followed the same Ohio riverbank that Lincoln had glided over a day earlier. An anonymous reporter for the *Chicago Tribune* offered a vivid postcard from the moving train:

"As we rattled on down along the river bank, crowds, about the little stations, dwellers in solitary residences, and farm houses, homes of industry, on land, and from the bosom of the Ohio, the steamers and hands on coal flats, all saluted the President's Train while it dashed by. Every village gave its demonstration."[23]

Just over the state line, in Wellsville, there was another locomotive change, as *The Comet* was replaced by *The Meteor*, built by the same Massachusetts firm.[24] Lincoln stood before a sizeable crowd and received a basket of apples from a stranger, at which point a little boy's high voice piped up, "Mr. Linkin, that man is running for postmaster!" The crowd erupted in "screams of laughter," while the would-be postmaster "collapsed."[25]

The train resumed its journey, bending toward Cleveland. Soon it began to slice through a large Vermont-shaped parcel of land called the Seven Ranges, dating back to the earliest days of the federal government, when this land was meted out to veterans and pioneers. Even before Ohio became a state, the parcel was an important test case for Congress, still uncertain how to manage the enormous challenge of administering the public lands of the West.

Throughout the Seven Ranges, the people came out to see the train fly past. But a twenty-minute stop at Alliance got a little too festive. Local committees were always straining to show off their hospitality, with parades of handsome young Zouaves and elderly veterans of the War of 1812.[26] Many had been brought in by special excursion trains. Inevitably, guns were fired off; but in Alliance there was a grotesque mishap. As the Special came in, a cannon discharged a blast much too close to the windows near where the Lincolns were sitting and showered glass on Mary Todd Lincoln. Even in the friendliest places, danger lurked around every corner.[27]

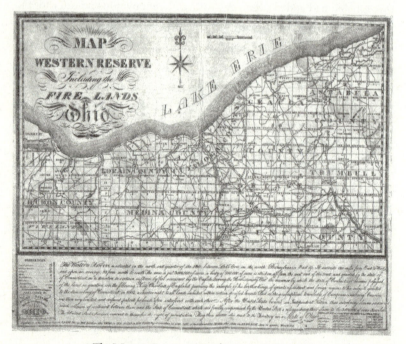

The Western Reserve, 1833 (Rumsey Collection)

THE WESTERN RESERVE

A few miles north of Alliance, the Special crossed from Stark County to Portage County; an uneventful crossing, to be sure, but redolent with meaning. Lincoln had just entered the Western Reserve, another statelet within a state. At the time of independence, this section of northern Ohio was still a part of Connecticut—nearly as large as the original, with 3.3 million acres of prime real estate. The parcel had been included in Connecticut's royal charter of 1662 and, as its name suggested, was considered a western extension of the state. But it became difficult to hold as Americans poured west to fill up the new lands after the war. In 1796 Connecticut sold its Ohio land to a group of Connecticut investors.

Still, Connecticut's strong influence remained, and many of the new settlers came from there, bringing their families and their New England values. Moses Cleaveland, whose last name would grace the metropolis of the Western Reserve, thought of it as "New Connecticut," a state unto itself.[28] Even after the Western Reserve was folded into Ohio, it continued to act like a sovereign realm. Local cartographers printed their own maps, as if the rest of Ohio was irrelevant, and the name of the Western Reserve was preserved in the colleges and academies that proliferated in these pretty towns. (Money for public education was written into the original purchase of the Reserve.)[29]

Certainly there was a physical resemblance between the two Connecticuts. With its trim farms, white churches, and village greens, New Connecticut seemed very much like the original.[30] William Dean Howells would later remember that "the population was almost purely New England in origin." James Garfield, the future president, claimed that in some ways it was "more thoroughly New England" than New England itself.[31]

Unsurprisingly, New-New-England was beside itself as Lincoln sped through its domain. It had been a long time since anyone could remember a president who was not, somehow, in the pocket of the South. They cheered wildly as the train passed, and gathered in town after town to hear his wry, self-deprecating remarks. He had done very well in these precincts.

Since leaving Springfield, Lincoln had gone east, south, and, this morning, even west, as he retraced his path out of Pittsburgh. Now the Special was heading due north toward Lake Erie. The weather was turning colder, but Lincoln's reception could not have been warmer, mile after mile, as the people streamed toward the train tracks and cheered the bearded apostle of change.

Despite the tranquil surfaces of these trim villages, emotions were running high in the final weeks of James Buchanan's presidency, as federal slave catchers combed the region for African-Americans who could not prove that they were free. Many Ohioans objected, hiding runaways in secret larders and doing whatever they could to resist. To many, it felt as if the Western Reserve had become a sanctuary, not just *within* the United States but also *from* the United States. For it was U.S. marshals who came after the runaways, and patience was running thin with a government that seemed to lack any moral compass.[32] Some were so angry that they had no patience for Lincoln, either—he was too moderate for their taste. An abolitionist newspaper caustically proposed that a "fugitive slave hunt" be created as an entertainment during his visit—an angry reference to Lincoln's support for the Fugitive Slave Act, one of the compromise measures of 1850.[33]

One prominent abduction had rattled the Western Reserve in September 1858, when an escaped eighteen-year-old named John Price was caught in Oberlin, then set free by a crowd of angry rescuers. A sensational trial followed. Although the Fugitive Slave Act was upheld, huge antislavery rallies were held in Cleveland (facilitated by railroads that were able to move people quickly, at discounted rates, to be there).[34] Ohio's own internal fissures were exposed by the ensuing controversy: the U.S. Marshal in question came from the state's southern district, and it was not clear that he was empowered to act in the state's northern district.[35] Locally, as well as nationally, democracy in America was fraying at the seams.

Lincoln's election suggested that new policies were coming, but in these final weeks of the old regime, there were intense flare-ups between Ohioans

Sara Lucy Bagby[36]

and U.S. marshals. Only a few weeks before the president-elect's trip, tensions exploded all over again when a young woman living in Cleveland found herself in the center of the national argument. Sara Lucy Bagby was a former slave, of mixed-race ancestry, working as a domestic servant. She had escaped from Virginia to Pittsburgh, and made her way to Cleveland, following the same route Lincoln was now on. On January 19, federal marshals broke down the door of the home where she worked, forcibly removed her, and successfully returned her to slavery—although it required 150 deputies to escort her through Cleveland's furious crowds. That she was pregnant meant that her unborn child would become a slave as well; a thing, not a person.[37]

To most Ohioans, this was an outrage against decency, and another proof that America had lost its way. The rawness of recent events was one of many reasons that so many people were responding deliriously as the Special passed by. Lincoln helped Americans to feel that they were taking back their country from a cabal that was destroying its very purpose. So the people of the Western Reserve came out from their farms and villages to cheer as the Special came through.[38]

It was over quickly, an exciting blur of a few seconds as the train raced by them, going "nearly a mile a minute," or sixty miles an hour, according to the papers. But that was enough to know that a new kind of president was on his way. The *Western Reserve Chronicle* described the day as "one continued ovation." Even a fleeting glimpse of Lincoln was enough for people of the small towns to come out and "have one look at a live president."[39] From "all classes," they found their way to the trackside, even as the rain turned to snow, and waited for "the object of interest" flew past.[40]

Unfortunately, the object was wearing down. Henry Villard noted that "Mr. Lincoln was less talkative today. He sat in the rear car mostly engaged in reading newspapers and silent reflections."[41] But the crowds had energy to spare, and they gave it to him. At Ravenna, they chanted "No compromise!"[42] Lincoln responded with a droll speech about his misadventures the day before.[43] At Hudson, he was met by five thousand people, a crowd bolstered by an excursion train from Akron full of ladies waving handkerchiefs.[44]

Enormous numbers of young men were in these crowds as well, aware that the train would change their lives forever. The small town of Poland was not quite on the train route, but close. Like Hudson, it boasted an academy, which it needed to justify its elaborate nickname, "the Athens of the Mahoning Valley." An Ohio family, the McKinleys, had moved there just so their son William could attend. After graduating in 1859, he tried college but withdrew, probably for financial reasons, and found a position teaching public school in Poland. Like so many young men from Ohio, he soon would be sent South to fight. If William was standing at trackside, he might have caught a glimpse of his future secretary of state, as a young John Hay sat inside his moving office, scribbling away.[45]

William McKinley, 1859[46]

Lincoln was now drawing near his destination. Outside the train windows, the farms were beginning to vanish, replaced by more crowded scenes. As Lincoln sped past a factory, 225 iron workers gave him a robust cheer.[47] For the last section, the locomotive was outfitted with a large decorative bowsprit, as if the train were amphibious and could plunge into Lake Erie like an iron narwhale, tusk first. A few years earlier, a traveling Englishwoman had confided to her journal that she was terrified her train would do just that, because American brakes were so unreliable.[48] But Lincoln was safe, protected not only by the protuberance but also by another enormous crowd, eager to keep the ship of state afloat for another day. He drew up, well short of danger, and prepared to say hello to Cleveland.

Cleveland, 1877[49]

CLEVELAND

Coming into Cleveland by train was a charming experience, as many writers had noted already. When Alexis de Tocqueville visited three decades earlier, he was shocked to find such a well-appointed city so far from the East Coast. Only moments before his arrival, he had been traveling through a "dark forest," expecting to lodge "at the foot of a tree." Then suddenly he emerged from a clearing and found himself in "a place where you will find everything." Within seconds, he went from "the most savage scenes to the most smiling pictures of civilized life."[50]

Europeans loved the surprise of seeing an actual forest pressing up closely against the Forest City. Isabella Bird described a haunting scene of gliding through the "primeval woods" on a train, passing near "gigantic" tree trunks more than a hundred feet high and covered by a canopy so dense that it barely admitted light even in the middle of the day. There was no sign of civilization except the tracks below and the telegraph lines above. But that was enough, she thought to herself, as she pondered the "three trembling electric wires, which will only cease to speak with the extinction of man himself." Excitingly, her reverie was interrupted by a forest fire, which nearly "roasted" her alive. But the train was able to avoid the falling tree branches and the flames, "leaping like serpents." Undaunted, the Iron Monster delivered her, shaken but intact, to her destination.[51]

Eventually the forest and its dangers receded, as Cleveland expanded and absorbed its neighboring woods. But the memory persisted, and the nickname Forest City stuck. In fact, there *was* something arboreal about these tastefully landscaped scenes. A local guide boasted that "its best streets are lined with lofty trees, giving it the rural and pleasant air which reminds us of a city in the forest."[52] One street, Euclid Avenue, was a triumph of well-placed shrubberies, elms, beeches, and maples, offering shade to Cleveland's elites. Fittingly, for a street named after the Greek mathematician, it ran in a straight line for most of its journey.[53]

The rain was turning into a driving snow as the Special came into Cleveland and met the cold air coming off Lake Erie.[54] Lincoln was feeling worse, with a bad cold, and he spoke even less than usual. Given the inclement weather, train officials arranged for him to disembark at a station two miles from the center of town and then come in by carriage. But the pressure never let up: thirty thousand rambunctious Clevelanders lined the streets, and a reporter noted that a "Vesuvian eruption of Stars and Stripes" had covered every visible surface with American flags.[55]

When Lincoln appeared, a huge sound was heard; Villard tried to describe the noise as "a universal, deafening shout." Lincoln responded with "deep gratitude and emotion." Despite the snow, he stood up in his carriage all the way to the hotel, acknowledging the cheers "in his unaffected, hearty manner." It was an open barouche, with four white horses, carrying him forward in the snow.[56] People ran up to hand him flowers or simply come near.[57] An elderly German lady was gratified when she approached, and he spoke a few words to her in her language. Villard added, "The expression of his face showed plainly that he meant much more than he could convey by bowing and waving his hat."[58]

It was the most triumphant entry into Cleveland that anyone could remember. Villard thought it was the loudest reaction to Lincoln since he left Springfield. The parade found its way to Euclid Avenue, where Lincoln was escorted by a local militia, the Cleveland Grays, and a medley of fire companies and marching bands. One reporter noticed a live eagle perched on a wreath over a sidewalk as the procession filed past.[59] True to Cleveland's nautical heritage, a fully rigged boat on wheels, full of sailors, formed part of the procession, heading toward the lake until they reached the city's grandest hotel.[60]

The Weddell House was a commanding structure, five stories tall, that occupied most of a city block.[61] There Lincoln found another enormous crowd, ten thousand strong. The hotel was not far from the spot that Tocqueville had recognized as Cleveland's reason for existence: the place where the Cuyahoga River flowed into Lake Erie. It was not a long river, but it had briefly served as the western boundary of the United States, according to a quickly forgotten 1795 treaty with Native Americans. Moses Cleaveland had wisely selected the location of the city that would bear his name. Even fish seemed to agree, as they spawned happily in the rich waters where the river met the lake. A century later, the river would have a different reputation, thanks to its tendency to catch fire; but in Cleveland's early years, the Cuyahoga deepened the feeling that this meeting place of waters was a natural paradise.[62]

By reaching Cleveland, Lincoln had arrived at another vital source of power. Like Pittsburgh, it was a cog in the new set of networks that were extracting fossil fuels from the earth and shipping them to the East. The Forest City had found a new destiny, one that had nothing to do with trees—at least not living ones. Instead, Cleveland was embracing the ancient vegetative matter that had turned into petroleum, over millions of years, and was now spurting out of wells in Pennsylvania. After it was extracted, the oil needed to be refined, a different line of business entirely. After the first wells came in, Cleveland claimed that role.

Lake Erie helped. In Cleveland's earliest years, it was dangerous to be so close to the lake, with the British prowling nearby. It had taken years of fighting to establish the right of the United States to exist in these parts, an argument that was not entirely resolved until the naval victories of Oliver Hazard Perry on Lake Erie during the War of 1812. Those heroics were still fresh in the minds of many Clevelanders; only a few months before Lincoln's arrival, an impressive statue of Perry was unveiled, with many veterans of the Battle of Lake Erie in attendance. A mock naval battle was staged, far removed from the real war clouds that were gathering.[63]

But since the completion of the Erie Canal in 1825, Cleveland had been able to ship goods by water to New York, and other canals helped to reach the interiors of Ohio and Pennsylvania. Then the arrival of the railroad transformed the city again. Between 1850 and 1860, its population more than doubled, from 17,034 to 43,417.[64] As New York and Chicago stretched toward each other, Cleveland was a natural beneficiary. But it also pursued its own opportunities, toward the oil wells of Pennsylvania, and the iron ranges of northern Minnesota, which could be reached via the Great Lakes.[65]

Soon the Forest City was sprouting forests of smokestacks. As the railroad economy surged, Cleveland churned out rails, locomotives, and huge quantities of iron and steel.[66] Cleveland's proximity to Pittsburgh helped each city. Only ninety-nine miles separated them, the route Lincoln had just traveled—and a massive commerce flowed along this line, linking the Ohio River and the Great Lakes. A century later, the Cleveland-Pittsburgh link would gird another revolution, connecting an early segment of the ARPANET, the precursor to the Internet. The original groove for all of that information had been dug in the rail bed that had just delivered Lincoln to the shores of Lake Erie.

ROCK OIL

A quiet young bookkeeper with a mind for figures was in Cleveland as Lincoln's noisy parade came through. He had voted for the Republican candidate, and in some ways he resembled him, with his abstemious habits and steady self-control. But John D. Rockefeller was seeking a destiny of his own, far removed from the untidiness of politics. Ironically, he found it in the mess of black goo gushing out of the earth in Pennsylvania.

John D. Rockefeller at 18, Cleveland, circa 1858[67]

After petroleum was discovered in 1859, Cleveland's entrepreneurs scrambled to take advantage of their nearness to the fields.[68] At first glance, John D. Rockefeller was not the most likely candidate to win the contest. He was slender and unassuming; early photographs reveal a wisp of a young man, gazing heavy-lidded from the frame. But those lids concealed a keen eye for opportunity. With supreme organization, he would convert "rock oil" into one of the greatest sources of energy the world had ever seen.

Rockefeller had arrived in Cleveland eight years earlier after growing up in upstate New York, where his father was a "botanical physicist" who sold quack medicines and cancer cures. At the same time, "Doctor" Rockefeller admired education, and migrated to the Western Reserve, in part, to enroll his sons in a decent school.

Cleveland was a pioneer in high school education—thanks to the shrewd Connecticut planners who had required public financing to pay for it. It offered one of the few places west of the Alleghenies where young men and women could continue their education into their teenage years, and its Central High School was a model of what a school could be. Any student could attend, "even the poorest, if possessed of talent and application," and receive an education that was free, first-rate, and coeducational. Rockefeller would marry a student he met there, Laura Spelman, who had boldly declared her own form of independence in a valedictory address titled "I Can Paddle My Own Canoe." Lincoln's parade went right past the school's cheering students.[69]

John D. Rockefeller was an intensely serious young man, unlikely to cheer anything, but watching all the same. He wrote with a careful hand and signed his name that way, with the middle initial, from a young age.[70] He did well in school, but on the eve of graduation, he dropped out to enroll in E.C. Folsom's Commercial College, where ambitious young men could learn the correct standards of financial reporting and bookkeeping.[71]

In 1855 Rockefeller found his first job, as a clerk, and commenced a detailed list of his personal expenditures, from his toothbrush (eighteen cents) to "five pare shoe strings" (twenty-five cents).[72] As he rose, he brought a similar scrutiny to the subtle ways in which the economy was changing. He was drawn to Cleveland's waterfront and the magical place where the Cuyahoga met Lake Erie. Where the earliest visitors had noticed spawning fish, his sharp eye detected a different kind of activity, as steamships, canal boats, and railroads gamboled as near to one another as they could.

Rockefeller absorbed everything he could about the flow of traffic in this busy interchange. "My eyes were opened to the business of transportation," he wrote with understatement. In a less guarded moment, the young bookkeeper confessed that he was so obsessed that he would run up and down the tops of freight cars when necessary to get the exact information he needed.[73] If cargoes could be unloaded with lightning speed, and wastefulness eliminated, then the West could be settled more quickly. That future would come even more quickly if new sources of power could be discovered, shipped easily along the rails.

After the frenzy following the discovery of oil, Rockefeller watched ever more closely. Despite what was obviously a dirty business—the Allegheny River caught fire in 1863, like the Cuyahoga in 1969—the priggish young man was pulled toward it, attracted by its moneymaking potential and the need for a strong managerial hand.[74] He opened a commission house, handled the complex transportation needs of clients, and kept edging closer to the problem of distribution.[75] It was one thing to get the oil out of the earth, but how to get it to the world's markets? Here was a worthy challenge for a transportation genius.

Eventually Rockefeller decided that his talents were better suited to the challenges of refining and shipping the oil rather than extracting it. Two years after Lincoln's visit, the young Clevelander would launch an oil refinery along a small creek that flowed into the Cuyahoga, called Kingsbury Run, adjacent to a rail line that was under construction.[76] This afterthought of a rivulet, hardly noticeable on a map, was the perfect place to refine the crude oil spilling out of Pennsylvania before sending it by rail and water to the rest of the world.

From this modest creek, the Standard Oil Company would reshape America's corporate order, much as Lincoln would reshape its politics. Standard Oil would go on to become the world's largest refiner, but it was much more than that. It also refined the very nature of business itself. There, along the grimy banks of the Cuyahoga, Rockefeller was inventing the modern corporate order. He ruthlessly eliminated inefficiencies wherever he found them: hiring carpenters to build his own barrels, then buying forests near the Forest City to supply his own wood. He found uses for petroleum by-products that no one had realized, and shipped and sold those products, too.

As Standard Oil grew into a vast global concern, it developed new practices never mentioned at E.C. Folsom's Commercial College.[77] As Rockefeller's tormentor, Ida Tarbell, explained in her muckraking history of Standard Oil, he demanded and received rebates from the railroads, effectively making it impossible for smaller organizations to compete. Standard Oil also learned to lubricate other wheels of machinery through lobbying and the emerging science of public relations. Another Clevelander who went to Central High School with Rockefeller was Mark Hanna, who would pioneer the new political strategies that large amounts of money made possible. When Hanna's protégé, William McKinley, was elected to the presidency in 1896, it marked another result that could be traced back to these earlier friendships along the Cuyahoga.[78]

Each year, Rockefeller extended his empire. Five years after Lincoln's visit, Cleveland had fifty refineries, second only to Pittsburgh.[79] In some ways, Cleveland had the upper hand: its train and water routes connected more easily to New York City and, by extension, to Europe. That giant gulp of energy would tilt power toward the North. As he had done in Pittsburgh the day before, Lincoln was harnessing resources for the struggle to come. As the Special wound its way through the new industrial landscapes, it had a way of finding what it needed.[80]

Another prominent supporter of Lincoln was a railroad man named Amasa Stone, who moved to Cleveland in 1850 to connect its trains with Columbus, Chicago, and the East. Stone made a fortune with his projects, which included early support for Rockefeller's ventures. Rockefeller's oil flowed along Stone's lines, at discounted rates, and they built houses near each other on Euclid Avenue.[81]

A different house on Euclid would play a large role in Lincoln's story, long after his parade had passed down it. Stone's daughter Clara would marry John Hay, and in 1875 they moved into a new home on the same street, where they lived for nearly ten years. During this time, Hay worked on the foundational ten-volume biography of Lincoln that he wrote with John Nicolay. From around the country, research findings were mailed to Euclid Avenue, supplying raw material for the literary edifice Hay was building. In other words, Lincoln's parade in Cleveland never really ended.[82]

WEDDELL HOUSE

After the parade, Lincoln prepared to speak to an enormous throng in downtown Cleveland, outside Weddell House. Ten thousand people had

Lincoln in Cleveland[83]

braved the elements, waiting to hear from him. He had an unusually good perch to speak from, thanks to a balcony, strewn with colored lanterns, that protruded from the second floor. At five thirty, he began.[84]

Fortunately, an artist was able to capture the moment, with near-photographic fidelity. In a sketch that appeared in *Frank Leslie's Illustrated Newspaper*, the entire scene is laid out.[85] Much of the drawing is occupied by the people of Cleveland, spread out below Lincoln as far as the eye can see. They are diverse: men and women, young and old, of all complexions.

When he first glimpsed Lincoln, in 1859, William Dean Howells described a tiny stick figure, in the distance, who seemed to be making the people jump up and down by the force of his words. The sketch creates the same impression: Lincoln is a mere set of lines, leaning over his balcony like a praying mantis. But he is *animated*, holding out his arm in a gesture of defiance, keeping his massive audience rapt, leaning so far over the railing that he appears to be in some danger of falling.

It was a short, graceful speech, which began by simply stating the obvious: the weather was terrible. "We have been marching about two miles through snow, rain, and deep mud," he reminded them, and thanked them

Lincoln in the open air (detail from previous image)

for their fortitude. Then, typically, Lincoln removed himself from the equation and reminded them that their proper concern was the Union—not him. He praised the Democrats who were there, along with the Republicans, and his good nature carried the speech to the end. Sensing the naval history around him, and the veterans of the old battles against the British on Lake Erie, he concluded with praise for the "good old ship of Union."[86]

Some of those veterans were presented immediately after the speech, at a reception in his honor. Once again, there was a "crushing pressure" from the crowd as it enclosed him. Lincoln was again in pain—Villard commented that his arms and hands had become so sore that he needed to stand at "a comfortable distance" from the crowd and merely let them get a look at him. He tried to stand at the foot of a stairway, to be seen in a more orderly way, but it did little to stem the tide of human traffic streaming toward him.[87]

Certainly some of the people jockeying for position in the hotel's crowded corridors were office seekers, or "orfus seekers," as America's best-known humorist, "Artemus Ward," spelled it. Ward was the pseudonym of Charles F. Browne, a young journalist from Maine who had found his way to Cleveland, like so many other New Englanders. Writing for the *Cleveland Plain Dealer*, he developed a wildly popular persona, a slangy salesman of wax figures, offering caustic commentary on the people he met while traveling. Even the mirthless John D. Rockefeller was said to delight in these newspaper sketches.[88] Browne wrote a parody of visiting Lincoln in Springfield, surrounded by exactly the same "orfus seekers" who were clogging the Weddell House.[89] In the sketch, the fictitious Ward advises Lincoln to fill his Cabinet with "Showmen," because they are simple entertainers, with no political background of any kind. ("They hain't got a darn principle!") Lincoln cherished these sallies.[90]

One of the guests who came to the Weddell House that night left a poignant description of Lincoln at the end of another bruising day. Albert Gallatin Riddle was a newly elected Ohio congressman, broadly sympathetic to the antislavery cause. A year earlier, he had defended the abolitionists who had freed a fugitive slave in the Oberlin case, and he was the kind of Wide Awake citizen who was waiting, intently, for Lincoln to arrive. When he came close, Riddle was powerfully impressed. Lincoln seemed an irresistible force, enormous in stature.[91] Riddle recalled that "he stood on the landing-place at the top of a broad stairway, and the crowd approached him from below." This exaggerated Lincoln's height and what Riddle called his "lathy form." Riddle was overwhelmed: "My heart sprang up to him—the coming man. Of the thousand times I afterward saw him, the first view remains the most distinct impression; and never again to me was he more imposing."[92]

Riddle also added interesting details about Lincoln's dialect, not so far from Artemus Ward's: "His manner was strongly western; his speech and pronunciation southwestern." Years later, Riddle still conveyed some amazement that the man upon whom all hopes rested acted so differently from a conventional politician. During a crowded reception with Cleveland's most distinguished leaders, Lincoln was easily distracted into yet another height-measuring contest, in a nearby room, with a tall, gangly youth named Ab McElrath.[93]

At last, beyond exhaustion, Lincoln was finally able to escape the crowd and find his suite.[94] But a telling piece of evidence suggests that Lincoln's night was far from restful. The next morning, Riddle saw the president-elect again—Lincoln invited him to spend a day on the next leg of the trip—and it was as if Lincoln had turned into a different person. When Riddle joined him at the station, as he recollected, "the vivacity of the night before had utterly vanished, and the rudely sculptured, cliffy face struck me as one of the saddest I had ever seen. The eyes especially had a depth of melancholy which I had never seen in human eyes before."[95]

Edward Everett[96]

ZIGZAG PROGRESS

Back east, others were having trouble reading Lincoln, too. His speeches had been read with great interest in the salons of Washington, New York, and Boston. The same twangy dialect that could delight a western audience, with Lincoln's flair for improvised humor, could sound tinny to sophisticated eastern readers. Edward Everett was a formidable arbiter of taste, as the former president of Harvard and an expert on Greek oratory. He wrote a withering assessment in his diary. "The president-elect is making a zigzag progress to Washington," Everett began, but he was disturbed by how "ordinary" the speeches were, destitute of "felicity and grace," even of pertinence.

Glumly, he concluded, "he is evidently a person of very inferior cast of character, wholly unequal to the crisis." They would meet two years later, when each honored the dead in his own way at Gettysburg. By that time, Everett knew that Lincoln was far from ordinary.[97]

As Lincoln was ending the day, many in the press were writing their own form of funeral oration. The *Plain Dealer*, reviewing his transit across the face of Cleveland, asserted bluntly that he was "not equal to the present emergency." It added the prediction that his "triumphal procession to the Capitol will prove a funeral procession to his reputation."[98]

That was still better than an *actual* funeral. In Lincoln's mail on February 15, there were new letters warning about the trouble expected at Baltimore. All day, Allan Pinkerton and his men had been picking up alarming signals there over casual conversation in saloons and oyster houses. One local businessman expressed bitter regret that Southerners had not yet taken over Washington, but he swore that they would, or "blow up" everything inside it before letting the North have a city they considered their own. Pinkerton himself met a Corsican barber, Cypriano Ferrandini, who claimed to be the mastermind of the plot to assassinate Lincoln on his way through Baltimore. His eyes "glistened" with rage, and he "quivered" with rage as he spoke. "Lincoln shall die in this city," he promised.[99]

There were many other troubling signs. In Washington, John Tyler's last-ditch peace conference was not going well. Thirteen states did not even send delegates, and the new states of the Confederacy were not represented. Many newspapers, Northern and Southern, excoriated this "fossil convention." But still, it was drawing headlines and revealed yet another president trying to take charge, in addition to the two would-be presidents racing eastward on their trains. Seven resolutions had been introduced earlier in the day, in a desperate attempt to stave off secession. They were dead on arrival, offering too little, too late.[100]

Farther South, however, government seemed to be working just fine. In Montgomery, the new Provisional Congress of the Confederate States had passed a resolution that President-elect Jefferson Davis should appoint a commission of three persons to be "sent to the government of the

United States of America, for the purpose of negotiating friendly relations between that government and the Confederate States of America, and for the settlement of all questions of disagreement between the two governments upon principles of right, justice, equity, and good faith." In the event that negotiations were not possible, the Confederate Congress also resolved to take Fort Sumter at Charleston and Fort Pickens in Pensacola, by force if necessary.

As these news flashes suggested, time was running out for a peaceful solution. Symbolically, Lincoln and Davis were now headed in opposite directions. Davis was still creaking along toward his inaugural, only three days away, but he had finally turned south after his long run to the east. Lincoln had turned decisively to the north, with his thrust into snow-covered Cleveland. Davis continued to give combative speeches. In Cartersville, Georgia, he blamed the North and its "hell born fanaticism" for forcing the Southern states to secede. The separation was "forever," he announced.[101]

In a few distant places, actual fighting was beginning. As Lincoln was ending his day in Cleveland, the authority of the United States was vanishing in Texas. Benjamin McCulloch, a newly minted colonel in the Confederate army, had organized a large group of volunteers to ride all night and demand the surrender of U.S. forts and arsenals in the morning.

Happily, the presidential party was unaware of these developments as they fell asleep in their treetop suite, high above the Forest City. Writing to his fiancée, John Nicolay observed that the journey had become less chaotic. "For the first time," he elaborated, the crowds were "tolerably well controlled by the police and military," and we "got through without any jam." The rooms were comfortable, the meal was satisfying, and, all in all, they were "about as well taken care of as was possible under the circumstances." Nicolay concluded, "The whole party has very pleasant recollections of Cleveland."[102]

But another hard day of travel loomed the next morning. To get to Buffalo would require a jag to the northeast; more "zigzag progress," to use Edward Everett's derisive phrase. With events spinning out of control in Washington, it struck many Americans that Lincoln was heading entirely in the wrong direction.

A daredevil, the Great Farini, hanging from a tightrope over Niagara Falls (1860)[1]

9

A LITTLE PATH

He became tan, and his cheeks filled out, and on his chin the beard grew dark.
—Homer, *The Odyssey*, book 16, lines 175–77[2]

CLEVELAND TO BUFFALO
FEBRUARY 16–17, 1861

LAKE SHORE

Saturday opened promisingly for the weary presidential entourage, waking up high above Cleveland. The weather had cleared, and they could look out over Lake Erie as dawn crept in. To those with a philosophical bent, these immense inland seas offered an "ocean-like expansiveness," as Herman Melville had commented in *Moby-Dick*. That view may have filled Lincoln's sails as he prepared for another long day.

Once again, a large crowd turned out for Lincoln's 9:00 departure from the lakefront station of the Cleveland, Painesville and Ashtabula Railroad. A sparkling new version of the Special was ready to whisk him on his way, including a car that was "beautifully carpeted, curtained, and upholstered for the occupancy of the president's party."[3]

To the strains of "Hail Columbia," the train eased away, but people kept straining to shake Lincoln's hand, even as the Special accelerated. That seemed innocent at first, like democracy in action, until it became clear that they were not letting go. Finally, Lincoln's entourage intervened, freeing him from the crowds trying to pull him toward them. Liberated, he stood on the back platform, performing his awkward bow to the people.[4]

After a relatively well-controlled event the night before, and a plush new car to ride in, Lincoln had every reason to believe the road ahead would be easier. It was a long, straight path to Buffalo, through reliably Republican districts, along the shore of Lake Erie.[5] It was the second-smallest of the Great Lakes but still so large that the earliest French explorers wondered if it ultimately led to China. They called it the Lac du Chat, or Lake of the Cat.[6] It was more temperamental than the other lakes: younger and shallower, with winds so strong that they could raise the water level in one place and expose bottom in another. Normally, these gusts blew in from the southwest, toward Buffalo. For most of the day, with this wind at his back, Lincoln would be able to gaze at the lake as he sped along one of America's prettiest stretches of railroad.[7] What could go wrong?

Plenty, as it turned out. Lincoln's voice was growing hoarser, and he was often reduced to whispering. Alarming messages from Baltimore were increasing, and hate mail never stopped coming in. To travel quickly was one way to protect him, and today's Special would oblige. But Lincoln would discover, upon reaching his destination, that his admirers could be nearly as lethal as his enemies. Just when it seemed he could not go any farther, he found a tiny passage, wide enough for a single person, that allowed his journey to continue.

After clearing Cleveland's limits, the Special picked up speed, blowing its whistle and thrilling onlookers. But every few miles, it would slow again to visit a town. In small communities, it would stop for a minute; in the bigger ones, it would stay for five. That could lead to confusion in a one-minute town with aspirations. For town leaders, it was the chance of a lifetime to say something memorable, with a president listening. In Geneva, Ohio, a local official identified as T. D. Leslie, Esq., gave a long welcoming speech, exhorting Lincoln to stand by the Constitution and offering a few of his own recommendations for solving the crisis. Before Lincoln could respond, the Special pulled away, with T. D. Leslie, Esq., still orating.[8]

Seated near Lincoln, John Hay was writing again, after a hiatus. Out the window, he could see endless lines of people, "ranged along platforms, swarming upon adjoining roofs, clinging upon posts and fences."[9] Sometimes they ranged a little too close, pulled in by all the excitement. Many displayed their enthusiasm in a time-honored way: by setting off explosive charges as the train went by. Just east of Cleveland, in Euclid, a spectator blew off his hand when a cannon fired prematurely.[10] Alarmingly, he was seen lying on the ground, receiving medical attention, as the train filed past. The telegraph briefly reported that he had died; a corrected account then brought him back to life, much to the relief of all.[11]

Just before eleven, the Special glided over the Ashtabula River without incident. Fifteen years later, in 1876, another train would not be as lucky: ninety-two people were killed when a passenger train plunged into the river after the bridge collapsed. It was the worst train disaster yet in the United States, and for John Hay, it was a personal trauma as well—his father-in-law, Amasa Stone, had built the bridge. Stone would later take his own life in the aftermath of the tragedy.

But in 1861 the bridge held, and the Special passed over into Ashtabula, well known for its enmity to slavery. A crowd of three thousand pressed up against the station, only to find that Lincoln's voice was "so husky as to be inaudible except to those immediately around him." That surely disappointed the locals, but then, suddenly, some of his western humor flashed out. When the crowd called for Mary to appear, Lincoln joked that he could not induce her to appear, as "he had always found it very difficult to make her do what she did not want to do." The crowd laughed at his candor, and no one laughed harder than he did, at his own joke.[12]

As he neared the border with Pennsylvania, Lincoln passed through one last Ohio village, Conneaut. There he whispered a speech so short and quiet that it is remarkable it was transcribed at all: "I have lost my voice and cannot make a speech, but my intentions are good." Then, in the silence that followed, a local citizen blurted out an instinctively patriotic sentiment for a Lakeman: "Don't give up the ship!" That phrase, immortalized when uttered by a dying naval commander, James Lawrence, during a dark moment of the War of 1812, had become even more celebrated when Oliver Hazard Perry adopted it for his personal flag before winning his great victories on Lake

Erie. Lincoln responded, "With your aid, I never will as long as life lasts."[13] It was another happy encounter; the right thing said, in the right place.

After that touching scene, a local reporter, seeing Lincoln for the first time, described his face with a keen eye. Once again, an audience member was impressed by his raw physicality, so different from the way most politicians looked. His hardened physiognomy complemented the serious argument he was making. There were "unmistakable lines of determination, tempered with humanity written upon his lineaments." Like so many other eyewitnesses of the journey, the writer complained that "the common portraits and caricatures do not express correctly his features," missing the subtleties of "the original." He, too, found his way back to the nautical image that many found comforting as Lincoln raced through the countryside:

"Anxiety and care are perceptible upon his face, but there is nevertheless, a calm, unassuming something about it which leads the beholder to hope that he may be the instrument in the hands of the people, of quieting the troubled waters, and the good old ship-of-state may be brought back to her former safe and quiet moorings."[14]

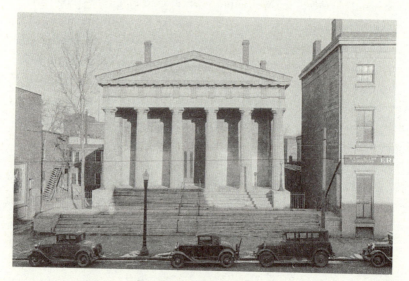

Erie Custom House (1935)[15]

THE ERIE TRIANGLE

The ship of state then sailed into Pennsylvania for the second time in three days. Yet this stretch of lakefront was a world away from Pittsburgh. The so-called Erie Triangle jutted up from the rest of the state to claim a short piece of shoreline between Ohio and New York. It was sometimes likened to a chimney atop a house—an apt metaphor for a state that was burning so many minerals. But this northern wedge also revealed a few of the fault lines underlying Lincoln's argument for the Union.

For earlier generations, this had been another sinkhole of geographical confusion, claimed by four states at the same time, to say nothing of Native Americans and the British. Massachusetts and Connecticut had old claims to the Erie shoreline from their original charters, while New York and Pennsylvania had pushed back and asserted their own claims. As usual, settlers swarmed in well before anyone knew the final outcome.

For a time, the founders declared the Triangle Lands a federal district, until they could resolve the mess—which they did by awarding it to Pennsylvania in 1792. A talented surveyor, Andrew Ellicott, came out to mark the boundaries of the Triangle, immediately before turning his attention to another federal district: the District of Columbia. It was as if this remote parcel was a test run for the new capital that would be squeezed between Maryland and Virginia.[16]

At Girard, shortly before noon, the Special took on a passenger, as if it were a normal train. It was anything but, and neither was this passenger, carrying a red-and-blue blanket as he signaled his desire to board. Horace Greeley, the editor of the *New-York Tribune*, may have been the most famous journalist in the country. His support had helped Lincoln win the election, and it surprised no one that he would want to be close to a big story. But he claimed, feebly, that he thought he was boarding a regular train, as if he had no knowledge that Lincoln was aboard. If so, he may have been the only person in the United States unaware of that fact.[17] Then, even more implausibly, Greeley got off at the next stop, as if embarrassed by the lameness of his story. The Special rumbled on, imperturbably.[18]

The train entered Erie at 12:22, where Lincoln found another huge crowd.[19] Pennsylvania did not have many ports, but it made the most of Erie. Because it faced international waters, it needed a Custom House, and an exquisite Greek temple served that purpose, doubling as a post office. For Lincoln, a triumphal arch had been built over the track.[20] As he drew near, a local band began "experimenting" upon patriotic songs, in Hay's wry phrase.

As the Special eased in, with the usual pandemonium, another terrifying mishap occurred when a building collapsed. Henry Villard recorded that "a large number of curious Republicans," boys and older men, had gathered on a roof to see the train, when the building gave way, and the people were left to "scramble among the ruins." Miraculously, no one was hurt. Lincoln gave a brief speech to a crowd that included "elderly women, with umbrellas and spectacles, mounted upon chairs," as well as "aged gentlemen, with crutches and benedictions," and parents clutching infants.[21] A reporter noted that the president-elect was "hoarse and fatigued," but nevertheless gripped the flag with "an unyielding determination to defend and uphold it."[22] The Special's departure was easier than its arrival, and a few miles east, it crossed another frontier, into New York.

Grace Bedell, age fourteen

WESTFIELD

Shortly after one in the afternoon, the Special slowed for its first stop in New York, Westfield. A large banner read, "Welcome Abraham Lincoln to the Empire State." The town might have been described as sleepy—in fact, George Pullman had formed the idea of a sleeping car precisely because of his frequent trips here to visit his mother.[23] But today Westfield was wide awake.

At a stage near the station, Lincoln began making his usual remarks. Suddenly, in midspeech, he departed from his script to ask if a young girl was present; specifically, a girl who had written to him, urging that he grow a beard. This was a thrilling departure from the norm.[24]

Grace Bedell was then twelve years old, living with four brothers of voting age in addition to her father. With the hardened instincts of a ward boss, she had written to the candidate in October, promising that she could deliver these five votes if Lincoln would oblige her by growing a beard. Remarkably, he did.[25]

In response to his question, a boy in the crowd yelled, "There she is, Mr. Lincoln!" and pointed to Grace, whose father thereupon brought her close to the train so that the president-elect could thank her.[26] Lincoln stooped to kiss her, and John Hay recounted, with a little too much detail, "the young girl's peachy cheek must have been tickled with a stiff whisker, for the growth of which she was herself responsible."[27]

The encounter with Grace Bedell had only taken a moment but would alter each of their lives. For Lincoln, it was another chance to improvise on the road, creating human interactions that were not in any known playbook for politicians. They came naturally to him; it is impossible to imagine Jefferson Davis embracing the public in quite the same way.

But the meeting with Grace Bedell was just the sort of anecdote that was sure to release a volley of angry criticism from Southern newspapers, furious at Lincoln, and withering toward his corny ways as he made steady progress eastward.[28] Some Northerners, too, expressed dismay: a Democratic newspaper injected race and sex into the story, writing, "Old Abe is cultivating his whiskers and kissing the girls along the route. The telegraph, however, does not inform us what Mrs. Lincoln thinks of this kissing business, or what color the girls are."[29] The kisses could quickly turn sinister if painted the wrong way, and Lincoln's enemies were happy to oblige.[30]

But his instincts were sound, and the short meeting with Grace Bedell became one of the more touching encounters of the train ride. Long before presidents had formal media strategies, Lincoln had found another way to break through to the vast newspaper-reading public—as irate Southern editors must have understood. Thanks to alert reporters in Philadelphia and Cleveland, a Lincoln legend was assembled quickly and distributed to a wide audience.[31]

For the girl who sailed innocently into the middle of this storm, it was the event of a lifetime; a brush with hirsute greatness. At first, Grace was overwhelmed, so mortified by the attention that she ran home and hid under a wagon.[32] None of it sounds well thought out; Lincoln mentioned her from the back of the train, then she was "half led, half carried to the platform." He stepped down, took her hand, and said, "You see, I let those whiskers grow for you, Grace." She was "much confused" and, in the tussle, crushed a bouquet of roses she had hoped to present to him.[33]

But then, with constant retelling, the story settled into its final shape. Grace never tired of remembering it. Three years later, she recalled the encounter as she wrote a second letter to Lincoln, asking him to arrange a job for her, as her family had fallen on hard times.[34] In 1878 she told her story again, to the *New York Times*, then again in 1908, and again in 1925.[35] A recurring theme in her accounts was her sense that Lincoln's eyes were "sadly pathetic" beneath the surface excitement of the event.[36]

The story will never die, although she finally did, long after moving out to the small town of Delphos, Kansas. She lived until November 2, 1936—the day the BBC pioneered the use of television, the instrument many future politicians, in Lincoln's long wake, would use to appear more human.[37]

Grace Bedell Billings in her sixties[38]

The next stop down the line was Dunkirk, where Lincoln spoke to a crowd of twelve thousand from neighboring villages, including Fredonia.[39] In Dunkirk, a bit of spontaneous political theater turned "electric," according to a witness.[40] A large flag was unfurled next to Lincoln, and he instinctively stood next to it, turned to the crowd, and said, "I ask you to stand by me so long as I stand by it." Hay wrote that it was "impossible to describe the applause and the acclamation with which this Jacksonian peroration was greeted." Men waved their hats, waved their handkerchiefs, and the crowd was so excited that they ran after the train as it pulled away.

Inside the Special, they were boisterous as well; Hay reported the presidential party singing "patriotic songs out of tune."[41] Soon the distant shore of Canada came into view, as the train came around the curve of the lake, toward Buffalo. If they were no longer singing, they would have heard a slowly growing roar from the unruliest crowd the Special had yet encountered.

Buffalo (1888)[42]

BUFFALO

A little past four, the Special crossed the Buffalo River, just south of the city, and wound its way toward the Exchange Street Station.[43] Out the window, Lincoln would have seen great hulks of buildings, where the ships unloaded their cargoes.

The train slowed in the final blocks, surrounded by a mass of humanity, estimated at 75,000. John Hay called it the largest crowd ever seen in that part of the country.[44] Ordinarily, that was a mark of praise. But something dangerous was beginning to happen. Despite an effort to close the doors to the station, the crowd kept increasing, as people found their way into the building's apertures. The situation quickly became "alarming," as a reporter described it.[45] With less and less room to get through, the presidential party was hemmed in on all sides.

Buffalo had been growing very quickly. According to the 1860 census, it was the tenth largest city in the country, with a population of 81,129, nearly all of whom seemed to be in the station. The population had nearly doubled since 1850. It was also a very *foreign* city: roughly 60 percent of its citizens were born abroad, mainly in Germany and Ireland.[46] Growth had been especially explosive in the last two years, as new factories began to crank out parts for the railroad economy such as like axles and piston rods—which would help Buffalo become an automotive leader a generation later.[47] With a favorable position on Lake Erie, and trains that never stopped coming, Buffalo had plenty of jobs to offer. Immigrants could find work here within days of landing in New York.

The Special pushed its way into the station with difficulty. A huge cheer erupted when Lincoln descended from the train. It was a kind of rolling thunder that followed the tracks, wavelike, gaining volume. For a few seconds, everything was normal. Lincoln was greeted by the thirteenth president of the United States, Millard Fillmore, who mumbled a few words of congratulations "upon the safety of his journey and the preservation of his health."[48] Almost as soon as he said those words, his journey became unsafe and his health endangered, as the crowd rushed toward him.

Niagara Falls in winter, circa 1850[49]

FOAM AND ROAR

The loud roar turned out to be ominous. For decades, travelers coming into Buffalo described a different kind of roar: the sound of Niagara Falls, nearby. To feel the spray was considered an essential immersive experience; European travel writers, especially, loved to get close and feel a rush of terror as they approached the cataract. Charles Dickens felt "the ground tremble" as he heard "the mighty rush of water."[50] Alexis de Tocqueville crawled onto a ledge and gasped for air, petrified, as the water rushed past him. Later, when he wrote *Democracy in America*, several passages suggested that he still felt some of that fear. He sometimes described democracy as a force of nature with a leveling power that could obliterate everything in its way. In terms that were not entirely complimentary, he compared it to a "strong current" propelling people, if they were not careful, toward an "abyss."[51]

In his own travels, Lincoln, too, had visited the falls, at least twice. In a fragment that he wrote out, he expressed his wonder before deep geological time and the untold millennia represented by the spectacle. Niagara seemed to be in perpetual motion ("never froze, never slept, never rested") through the ages. But he sensed the danger of the falls, too, and noted its deafening sound: "the water, thus plunging, will foam, and roar."[52]

"Foam and roar" described the train station, too, as people continued to pour in.[53] As soon as Fillmore finished his welcome, the crowd erupted. Thousands of people suddenly "made a rush" upon them, "overpowering the guard" and the presidential entourage "with a perfect furor."

The writers there took some time to describe what happened next. In the *New York Herald*, Henry Villard noted, "A scene of the wildest confusion ensued."[54] As the crowd pressed in on all sides, Lincoln was unable to move from the train into the station. More people kept coming into the station, where there was no room. This pressure began to build, until the heavy doors of the station snapped like toothpicks.[55] But the people inside were trapped and could not leave despite mounting panic. Soon they grew terrified, and "cries of distress were heard on all sides." Villard added, "It is really a wonder that many more were not crushed and trampled to death."[56]

Lincoln's fame had helped generate tremendous good will on the journey to this point, with large and boisterous crowds creating a festive air. But this wind could turn destructive at a moment's notice. The soldiers protecting him were quickly overmatched by a force that was "irresistible."[57]

At the center of the maelstrom were Lincoln and his guards. They had experienced difficult crowd conditions already on the trip, but nothing like this. The crowds just kept coming toward him until there was no room for anyone to move. During the worst of it, the papers reported that "the tall form of Mr. Lincoln and the venerable head of Mr. Fillmore were seen to sway to one side and the other as the crowd surged in upon them on either side, and the people acted more like a lot of savages than anything else."[58]

The most terrifying moment occurred when police lowered their bayonets in desperation, then could not move them out of the way. A man was nearly impaled as the crowd pushed him toward the bayonets, helplessly. According to an Ohio reporter, he was nearly murdered in full view ("the point of a bayonet, sharp as a stiletto, pressed against the breast of a man, and there seemed for a moment no mode of saving him from being pierced by it"). The reporter had seen "agitated multitudes" many times but never anything to compare with "the fearful rush of this crowd" after Lincoln. People were nearly fainting; many were injured. "It was awful," he concluded.[59]

If innocent civilians had been stabbed to death by soldiers wielding bayonets, in this moment of anxiety about America's future, it would have been a disaster. Perhaps two inches more, and the bayonet would have killed him, instead of pressing against his chest. That was the margin separating life and death for a nameless man, and perhaps for Lincoln's cause as well. John Hay also wrote about the experience and lost some of his glibness as he described a breakdown in crowd control. The military arrangements were "utterly inadequate," and as the train approached the depot, the crowd swept away the soldiers and police "like weeds before an angry current."[60]

Lincoln's bodyguards were badly shaken up. Major David Hunter was "crushed violently against the wall," and his shoulder was dislocated; he had to wear a sling for the rest of the trip. An elderly man who had the misfortune to be standing near Lincoln had three ribs broken, serious internal injuries, and copious amounts of blood streaming from his mouth and nose.[61] The papers were shocked that it had spun so quickly out of control, but relieved that the melee had not caused more damage. Many people escaped from the mob "with a feeling of gratitude for their lives."[62]

Lincoln may have been one of them. The person at the center of the madness was able to emerge unscathed, but it was a close call. Hay admitted that Lincoln "narrowly escaped unpleasant personal contact with the crowd."[63] His friends and a few police and soldiers had formed a protective phalanx around him, but they were essentially trapped. Then, through a "desperate" effort, they were able to create a tiny opening—Nicolay described it as "a little path." They rushed Lincoln through it and into a carriage waiting for him in front of the station. But the "little path" immediately closed up behind him as soon as he went through it, leaving the rest of his entourage stranded both from Lincoln and from each other, obligated to fight their way forward—as Nicolay put it, with "the most strenuous and persevering elbowing."[64] Some were furious afterward and demanded that Lincoln decline future public appearances—which of course he could not do.[65]

The *Buffalo Commercial Advertiser* went into chilling detail in a postmortem, describing men with broken bones limping out of the station, and unconscious women lying near fire hydrants, where they had been carried in hopes that the water would revive them.[66] Lincoln's visit to Buffalo, designed to tighten another clamp, had nearly sunk the ship of state.

From the depot, Lincoln and the crowds then moved through the streets of Buffalo, toward the American Hotel. Once again the crowd was unruly, and the presidential party was nearly repulsed before it could make it inside.[67] Nicolay wrote with contempt that "all was confusion."[68]

Buffalo's acting mayor greeted Lincoln with insipid congratulations

Lincoln in Buffalo (*Frank Leslie's Illustrated Newspaper*), March 2, 1861

that his progress "thus far toward the federal capital has been without accident or any circumstance to mar the pleasure of your journey." That seemed odd, so soon after a near disaster. Lincoln responded amiably, as usual, and spoke from the hotel balcony about "my rather circuitous route to the federal capital."[69]

After the speech, he met with local politicians, then rested with his family. Another levee for the public was held at 7:30, in which the now-familiar ritual of a long line filing past Lincoln was organized. When three ladies went by one of them exclaimed to another, "I'd like to kiss him!" Lincoln overheard the remark and responded, "Come on, then!"[70]

The levee ended at 9:30, then Lincoln endured a visit from a delegation of twenty-five local German-Americans. He responded briefly but eloquently, affirming that "they were no better than anyone else, and no worse."[71] This bland statement was reassuring in a city that was struggling with its diversity; its most prominent politician, Millard Fillmore, had run as a Know-Nothing four years earlier.

Lincoln was adept at uniting these strands. But once again, it was clear how narrow his path was—so narrow at the train station that it had opened only for a second, just for him. Presidents could not isolate themselves from the people; that would destroy the very democracy Lincoln was trying to save. But to let the people come as close as they had, without adequate safeguards, was a new danger that the founders had not anticipated. That dark truth would be revealed again, including the most tragic day in Buffalo's history, September 6, 1901. Forty years after Lincoln's visit, President William McKinley was shot and killed by an anarchist who was easily able to approach him, simply by joining a receiving line.

After witnessing the strain of Lincoln's journey, a Cleveland reporter ventured an opinion that would have been unfamiliar to most of the young people who had grown up reading *McGuffey's Readers* and the stories of great Americans:

"We do not wish to be President! Whatever our ambitions may have been heretofore, however our bosom may have swelled at the reflection that we should some day reach that exalted station, still we say that we no longer aspire to the office. We have seen enough of what it is to be President to effectually quench any ambition that we may have been inspired by prophetic words of the past. This reporter declines to run."[72]

But another person in Buffalo that day would reach a different conclusion. Stephen Grover Cleveland would run for president three times, and win twice, becoming both the twenty-second and the twenty-fourth president, by our complex system of counting. He had moved to Buffalo in 1855 to improve his prospects and felt a growing interest in politics as great events swirled around him. It is unimaginable that he would have missed a seismic event like Lincoln's visit. His office downtown was adjacent to Millard Fillmore's, and, as one of Cleveland's biographers wrote, "He hardly ever left Buffalo."[73] When he arrived in Washington in 1885 to begin his own presidency, it was the first time this president-elect had ever seen the nation's capital.[74]

In 1861 Cleveland was twenty-four years old and working as a law clerk,

Grover Cleveland (New Jersey State Archives)

while also helping his uncle, Lewis F. Allen, publish his annual survey of short-horn cattle. The 1861 edition of the survey mentioned Grover Cleveland in print for the first time, as Allen thanked his nephew for his work in assembling the publication. Their prodigious accounting of the nation's cattle included the fact that four bulls born in 1860 had already been named "Abe Lincoln."[75]

As the original of that name looked back on his day, in his hotel, he may have wondered if his train trip was helping or harming his cause. He was on a pilgrimage to restore calm, principled self-government, yet order was breaking down everywhere he went. Would democracy survive the attempt to save it? During the campaign, a cartoon had captured Lincoln as a tight-rope walker, trying to get accross Niagara Falls. He had survived his passage through Buffalo, but only by a whisker.

Grain elevators, Buffalo River, circa 1883[76]

THERMOPYLAE

The next day, as the *Buffalo Courier* described the melee, a writer reached back to ancient Greece to convey how slender Lincoln's "little path" had been the night before. "The Pass of Thermopylae was a memorable performance," he began, "but it was no such jam as the Pass of the Central Depot."[77] Thermopylae was a reference to a narrow pass where the Greeks made a heroic stand in 480 BC, against a larger Persian force that got wedged into a tight corridor of its own.

A narrow pass was an accurate way to describe Buffalo, too—and not just because of the little path Lincoln had found the night before. A huge commerce went through the small channel where the Erie Canal met the Great Lakes. Locals called it "the Great National Exchange."[78]

Buffalo had worked hard for that honor. A half century earlier, few would have predicted the rise of a busy city in this location. Buffalo's origins were so obscure that no one seemed to know where the city's name came from.[79] Although a Buffalo Creek flows nearby, not a single buffalo had ever been seen in the region. Millard Fillmore claimed feebly that "Buffalo" came from a misspelling of "Beaver" on an early treaty document. Another theory put forth was that French traders had tried to pass off horse meat as buffalo, nearby; hardly a creation myth to build a great city upon.[80]

A village grew nonetheless and refused to vanish, even after the British burned it to the ground in 1813. A decade later, Buffalonians improved their harbor, at exactly the moment when the backers of the Erie Canal began to look for a western terminus. The canal opened there in 1825 and changed everything.[81] Every year, the city grew, as a huge east-west traffic came through, connecting the Great Lakes with the Canal, and New York City. When a railroad was added in 1842, linking Buffalo to Albany, it grew some more.

It took time to move all of this freight through a congested port, but that same year, a local inventor pioneered a steam-powered device to load and unload boats. It was only a simple contraption of belts and pulleys moving buckets, at first.[82] But the grain elevator, as it came to be known, revolutionized shipping. Soon these immense, brightly colored structures were lining the Buffalo River, and the city's waterfronts grew even busier.[83]

With an immense storage capacity and a crucial location, Buffalo soon enjoyed a central role in a global food chain that stretched from Lincoln's prairie to Europe. By the time of the president-elect's visit, it had become the largest grain port in the world, with rivers of corn and wheat flowing through. With so many new Americans coming into the United States, it was natural that a sizeable number would follow the same deep furrow in the reverse direction, and they did, finding their way to Buffalo and beyond.[84]

Buffalo became so good at transportation that it pioneered a new kind of express service, sending goods around the country more quickly than the postal service. According to legend, a young freight agent named Henry Wells absorbed this lesson after making a tidy profit when he brought in a shipment of oysters, fresh from the Atlantic, to a group of hungry diners in Buffalo.[85] With a partner, William Fargo, he founded a shipping concern in 1850, called American Express.

It was an immediate success, and two years later they organized Wells Fargo, specifically to move information and money between the West and the Northeast, along the same routes so well known to Lincoln.[86] Soon train stations all along the line had Wells Fargo offices for sending telegrams and money. As it became easier to pay across long distances, credit expanded, and the West grew closer to the East. All of those exchanges made it easier for a frontier politician to rise.

The credit revolution has never ended. More than a century after Lincoln passed through, Wells Fargo created one of the first credit cards in 1966, to connect banks in New York and California. Five decades later, there are trillions of credit card transactions a year, each paying tribute to Buffalo's genius at connectivity.

Any harbor moving this much food and humanity was bound to be lively, and eyewitnesses described a bustling port, with steamers and scows of all sizes bumping up against one another.[87] The docks were crowded with swaggering sailors and canal men, who also bumped frequently—and policemen who felt it necessary to patrol in pairs.[88] Herman Melville cherished Buffalo's colorful characters; in *Moby-Dick*, he wrote, "the Canaller would make a fine dramatic hero, so abundantly and picturesquely wicked is he." The first chapter of *Moby-Dick* to appear in print, "The Town-Ho's Story," described an adventure in which a Buffalo rough named Steelkilt defended his honor (while warning his challengers never to "prick the Buffalo").[89] By coming through the narrow pass, barely, Lincoln had avoided that fate.[90]

But he still had very little room to maneuver and not much time. Far to the South, Jefferson Davis was making progress of his own. A New York newspaper described him on the train, "wrapped up in a blanket," but rousing himself from sleep to speak to small Georgia towns, with bonfires lighting his way. It is difficult to find transcripts; unlike Lincoln, Davis was far from the centers of publishing. But those that exist suggest that the Confederacy's president-elect was in an aggressive mood, threatening to "assassinate the

whole vandal Congress" in Washington, and to burn New York and Philadelphia to the ground if they did not give way to his demands.[91]

In Atlanta, he gave a fiery speech that laid bare his foreign policy, which
was about as far from George Washington's as it was possible to be. Specifically, he noted that the West Indies and northern Mexico were no longer
"forbidden fruit" and might easily be conquered for the Confederacy. The
same day, a secessionist from Texas, Louis Wigfall, wrote a letter to Davis
contending that they could find five or ten thousand recruits for the South
in New York City. Wigfall predicted that "force will be used in a few weeks."

Davis also celebrated the South's liberation from the United States,
which he likened to a "dead body" that was weighing down his own ship
of state, as if describing a whaler with a large, heavy carcass attached to the
side. Lincoln, exhausted, may have felt like that at times. But for the first
time in a week, he did not have to make a train the next morning.[92]

Millard Fillmore, 1849[93]

LEAPFROG

The seventh day of Lincoln's odyssey was, mercifully, a day of rest. The previous week had been one of unrelieved motion, noise, and chaos. Huge crowds had turned out in Indianapolis, Cincinnati, Pittsburgh, Columbus, Cleveland, and Buffalo. He had reached out to thousands already, at punishing cost. But the trip was making a difference. Even when the president-elect said nothing, the response was overwhelming, as at Ashtabula, when he could barely speak, and the crowd burst into "a state of din-bewildered enthusiasm," screaming simply because he was there. Or when Lincoln didn't leave the train at all, the spectators lining the tracks could look in and see him gliding past, and know that they had a leader on the move.

Lincoln could take solace as well in the fact that his family and entourage seemed happy. His friend Norman Judd paid a barbed compliment when he commented, "Mrs. L behaves quite well—and the children have been reasonably good considering what they are." He added ominously, "I have kept at a respectful distance from the lady, only paying my proper respects." Meanwhile, Lincoln's oldest son, Bob, was generally staying out of trouble, despite being surrounded by temptations.

But any realistic assessment of the trip to date would have to include anxiety over Lincoln's personal condition and the danger he faced constantly as he moved through enormous crowds with little protection. It was becoming harder for him to speak, thanks to "hoarseness of his voice and soreness of his chest."[94] He was constantly in pain—especially his hands, after the nightly ordeal of shaking hands with thousands of local well-wishers. On this Sunday morning, he was feeling more pain than usual. O. H. Dutton, a New York journalist, explained, "It is absolutely impossible for Mr. Lincoln to be a formalist in anything. If he makes a speech, he must say what he thinks; and when he shakes hands, he does it with a hearty will, in which his entire body joins. The consequence is that he is more weary after receiving a hundred people than some public men we could all name after being shaken by a thousand."[95]

The private fears that John Nicolay expressed in his letters to his fiancée revealed far more than any speech could about how grueling the trip was. Buffalo had been the most frightening experience to date, but all those receptions had taken their toll. Joseph Howard Jr., writing in the *New York Times*, noticed a listlessness in Lincoln that bordered on vacuity: "listening to a prosy address or shuddering at the brazen efforts of some country band, his eye is dull, his complexion dark, his mouth compressed, and his whole appearance indicates excessive weariness, listlessness, and indifference."[96]

If Lincoln occasionally lost interest in trying to please the media, that would not be difficult to understand. Despite his grueling progress, the press continued to withhold judgment, mixing snide commentary along with its reporting of the news. A typically asinine comment could be found in the *Buffalo Daily Republic*: "We were seriously disappointed in the physique of the president-elect, but we have neither the time nor the space to give the rationale of our dissatisfaction."[97] The *Springfield Republican* called him "a simple Susan."[98]

Many of the New York papers were noticeably severe. The *New-York World* called Lincoln's journey "in bad taste," "useless," "undignified," and "foolish."[99] The *New York Herald* was frequently caustic in the extreme, and excoriated Lincoln for his "little speeches" en route, which failed to display either the "disposition or the capacity to grapple manfully with the dangers of this crisis."[100] The *Herald* also ridiculed Lincoln's occasional tendency to become "jovial" and act like a "raconteur," with the "Union practically dissolved, the public treasury empty," and "a reign of terror existing over one-half of the country." Desperate for leadership, the *Herald* complained that Americans were getting "nonsense"—speeches that claimed "all this was nothing, only a bagatelle, a mere squall which would soon blow over."[101]

Norman Judd knew just how hard it had been. He had seen all of the trip's struggles up close, and he was in constant communication with Pinkerton's agents in Baltimore. But in spite of that danger, he wrote, "Whatever doubts may have existed as to the expediency of this kind of journey would be entirely dispelled if the doubters could see what I have seen." Judd felt that the trip had been "effective in the extreme." James Garfield, who had heard Lincoln at Columbus, thought that the "tour is having a very fine effect in strengthening the hopes of the Union men—and the back-bones of 'Emasculates.' " In Albany, a leading Republican paper paid Lincoln a backhanded compliment by admiring how little damage he had caused while speaking so often: It "is no easy matter to talk so much and to do so little harm in talking." The piece continued, "Very few men have the faculty to say nothing, and fewer still to speak at all under circumstances like those which surround Mr. Lincoln." [102] That was high praise from the political boss who controlled the paper, Thurlow Weed. But other Republican leaders were not sure; in Washington, Charles Francis Adams Sr. worried in his diary, "I am much afraid that in this lottery we may have drawn a blank," he wrote pessimistically before falling asleep. [103]

The news continued to be bad from the South. In Texas, the day had begun with exuberant militias parading near federal properties, demanding their surrender. The commander of U.S. forces, Major General David E. Twiggs, meekly complied, rendering his 2,700 troops useless. Just like that, more than a tenth of the army had evaporated. Twiggs also handed over a huge cache of weapons and ammunition stored in his forts. One of them was the Alamo, so evocative of an earlier generation's fighting spirit. This time, it fell without a shot. [104]

Twiggs would soon join the Confederacy, but for some of his officers, that was a bewildering prospect. In San Antonio, Lieutenant Colonel Robert E. Lee rode over to investigate and was shocked to see men with red insignias on their shirts, clearly part of some new fighting force. When they asked him to join them, he was indignant. Lee had been writing letters to his wife, expressing his reverence for the Union, and for her kinsman, George Washington. But sentiments like that were quickly becoming outdated in Texas, and Lee struck one observer as "a column of antique marble." Some of the Texas hotheads were later overheard planning to assassinate Lincoln, "either on his journey to the Capitol or during the ceremony of inauguration." They would have to join a long queue of others, well ahead in their preparations. [105]

Lincoln had no means to respond yet; he could only watch these developments from afar. But it would certainly do no harm to pray for guidance, and on this day of rest, Lincoln accepted an invitation from Millard Fillmore to attend church and dine with him afterward.

Fillmore was not a natural ally. The two former Whigs had some history together; chance encounters at political gatherings over the years.[106] But Fillmore's disappointing presidency had never quite lived down the way it started, after Zachary Taylor's death resulted in Fillmore's elevation from the vice presidency. (A historian once remarked that even to discuss Millard Fillmore is to overrate him.)[107] Across the 1850s, as Lincoln grew, Fillmore seemed to shrink, growing closer to the Know-Nothings.[108]

But Fillmore was still a formidable local figure full of charm and influence (Queen Victoria allegedly called him the handsomest American she ever met).[109] He was a loyal Buffalonian and loyal to his country as well—at least loyal enough to welcome Lincoln in a way that was meaningful in the dark days of February 1861. A year later, he would denounce Lincoln as a "tyrant" who "makes my blood boil."[110]

But on this Sunday, they were able to smooth over their differences. To be seen with a former president was helpful to Lincoln and added to his legitimacy. As a Buffalo newspaper wrote, "Mr. Lincoln's ground, most firmly taken, is that he is to be president of the American people and not of the Republican Party."[111]

Fillmore picked up Lincoln at 10:00 and brought him to the First Unitarian Church. One of the pastor's children later added to the memory of that day: "Mr. Fillmore stood in his usual place. . . . By his side stood a man, gaunt, sallow, who, with melancholy face, bent reverently at the sound of prayer." After the sermon, the pastor came down from the pulpit and "looked for a moment into the serious eyes of the visitor, while he pressed his hand." The child never forgot that brief glimpse of Abraham Lincoln "passing on to the fulfillment of his stormy destiny."[112]

Lincoln survived this somber church service without too much damage, to judge from an anecdote later the same day. He returned to his hotel at two o'clock to find his sons Tad and Willie playing leapfrog with the son of the hotel owner. That was an opportunity too good to resist for a man with the weight of the world on his shoulders. Decades later, the hotel owner's son remembered what happened next. "The two boys and I were playing leapfrog in a room of the hotel," he recalled, "when President Lincoln came in and joined in the game. He was a very friendly man," he added, pointing out, "he didn't act like a president." [113]

Fillmore had also foiled expectations. At 7:30, the former nominee of the Know-Nothing Party invited Lincoln to a meeting at which an expert on Native Americans, John Beeson, spoke about their mistreatment. A group of Native Americans were there, adding their own voices, with songs and speeches. Beeson was an Englishman who had taken their cause to heart. In 1857 he wrote *A Plea for the Indians*, a book that argued eloquently for their rights, tried to prevent future massacres, and expressed his belief that "the Indians have at least as good a system as we possess." [114] After the lecture, Lincoln spent a second night in the American Hotel and prepared for an early departure the next morning, refreshed.

Throughout the day, Jefferson Davis had made more progress. After his speech the day before in Atlanta, Davis resumed his train journey from Georgia to Alabama. He arrived at Montgomery late on the seventeenth, the eve of his inauguration, and gave a short speech to an enthusiastic crowd. [115] By any measure, he was winning the race against Lincoln, still two weeks away from his inaugural address.

To make matters worse, new alarms kept coming from Baltimore. On the same afternoon that Lincoln was playing leapfrog, Lucius Chittenden received an invitation to a remarkable meeting. The Vermonter was still attending the mystic séances of John Tyler's peace conference in hopes of some kind of magical agreement. Yet he was alarmed by the constant rumors that Lincoln would never make it to his inaugural. With several other young Republicans, he formed a committee of safety to protect the president-elect during his arrival. But on this Sunday, he learned just how real the dangers were, when a messenger summoned him to a secret meeting in Baltimore that evening.

Chittenden caught a northbound train from Washington. He was riding happily when a stranger stumbled into him on the car. Only afterward did he realize that he had been slipped a piece of paper with instructions on how to find the secret meeting in a private home. There he met with a group of Baltimore Republicans, who now possessed detailed knowledge of a plot to assassinate Lincoln. They told him that a large throng of "roughs and plug uglies," thousands strong, planned to surround him during his arrival and "tear him to pieces." [116] It was to be a kind of ritual assassination, with a long line of plotters going through his car, each stabbing him. But just in case, they also had hand grenades and other explosive devices.

In Baltimore taverns and sporting houses, gamblers were openly betting on Lincoln's chances of survival. The odds were lengthening every day. To Chittenden's amazement, one of the accomplices in the assassination plot was produced that Sunday afternoon, and brought in to tell his part of the story. He was an Italian immigrant who had lost his nerve, and repeated the simplistic thoughts that he had been ordered to think by the leaders of the conspiracy. "A bad president was coming in the cars to free the negroes and drive all the foreigners out of the country," and "the good Americans wanted him killed." [117]

All of these plotlines were now converging. On the same day, February 17, Allan Pinkerton became convinced of the extent of the Baltimore plot and "resolved upon prompt and decisive measures to discover the inward workings of the conspirators." But even if he could verify the rumors, it was far from certain that he could get a warning to the presidential party in time. As Chittenden had learned, the police were deeply implicated in the conspiracy, and any attempt to warn Lincoln would by itself risk danger. Nor was it certain that Pinkerton's agents could even find Lincoln, as he picked up speed. The day of rest had been welcome, but now he needed to make up for lost time, across the greatest distance yet. [118]

James F. Ryder, *Atlantic & Great Western Railway*, 1862[1]

10

THE STRAIGHT LINE

When rosy-fingered Dawn came bright and early,
They yoked the horses to the painted carriage,
And drove out from the gate and the echoing porch.
At a light touch of the whip, the horses flew.
Swiftly they drew towards their journey's end,
On through the fields of wheat, until the sun
Began to set and shadows filled the streets.

—Homer, *The Odyssey*, book 3, lines 491–97[2]

BUFFALO TO ALBANY
FEBRUARY 18, 1861

A HISSING DEMON

Monday began cruelly for the weary travelers, with a wake-up call at four in the morning. The weather was bitter, and so were the younger members of the party, dismayed to be starting so early. John Hay later remembered this "weird cluster of men, cloaked and muffled, who gathered gloomily in the dim corridors."[3] They had a long road ahead, their greatest distance yet, and they fell in line numbly, filing through a ghostly light.

The idea was to board the train quietly, to avoid the chaos that had greeted Lincoln when he came into Buffalo. But that memo failed to reach a local militia, which showed up at the American Hotel at four thirty in the morning, beating drums, only to find an even louder organization, the

Union Cornet Band, warming up. Together they jubilantly woke up everyone within earshot. At five thirty, they bugled through the streets of Buffalo, accompanying the dazed presidential party toward the station. It became even rowdier after a group of firemen, awake all night after fighting a fire, joined in the procession.[4]

But once they entered the depot, they found it deathly still, shrouded in a "grim, cavernous darkness." As they walked through the room where so many people had been trapped, it seemed unearthly. Past "winking lamps," they struggled toward the locomotive, which reminded Hay of a "hissing demon."[5] Nicolay, too, was affected by the strangeness of the scene; he called it "spectral," as if he sensed the presence of ghosts. As they shuffled through the "ominous shadows," listening to "the clanging and hissing sounds," they felt a strong sense of what Nicolay called "unreality."[6]

Reality was coming quickly, all the same. Later that day, Jefferson Davis would be inaugurated, a stark political fact that Lincoln's calm nostrums had done nothing to prevent. Secessionists were jubilant. From Alabama, William L. Yancey said, "The man and the hour have met." No one could say that of Lincoln; the man and the hour were still trying to find each other, and six hundred hard miles still lay ahead.

Upon closer inspection, the "hissing demon" was a locomotive named *Dean Richmond*. That amused the party, for Richmond was a prominent Democrat. But the train was quickly Republicanized with an image of Lincoln that covered a kerosene headlight. That cosmetic adjustment allowed the train to project his likeness into the darkness ahead. For the few stragglers who were up this early, along the tracks, they would see an illuminated transparency of the bearded face, followed by the genuine article a few seconds later.

At 5:48 a.m., it lurched forward, commencing a journey of 297 miles to the east. Each of those miles had been inspected carefully by train crews the day before.[8] After so many near disasters and a rising threat level, railroad officials were beginning to understand that special precautions would be necessary to deliver this package to its destination.[9] In a bluish

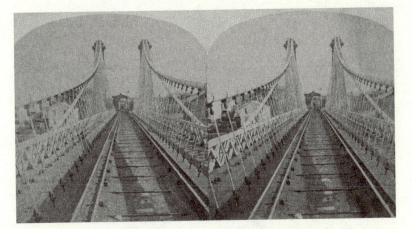

The Niagara Falls Suspension Bridge, near Buffalo, early 1860s[9]

light, the locomotive found the path cut into the forest and began hurtling toward the capital of the Empire State.[10] Rosy-fingered dawn crept in at 6:43, but she was too late to catch the early risers, who were already moving very fast.[11]

The New York Central was on the cutting edge of railroad thinking, shearing off delays wherever it could find them, and building longer and better express routes. Today the Lincolns could enjoy an ingenious new car that offered a place to lie down and ventilated air. Its chairs were so comfortable that a passenger might "sit, recline, or lie on its sumptuous velvet cushions."[12] That Ottoman splendor would be welcome on a long day of travel.

Lincoln knew the New York Central well. A year earlier, almost to the day, he had been offered a lucrative position by its president, Erastus Corning, who was impressed by his speech at the Cooper Union.[13] If Lincoln had accepted, he would have been a far wealthier man and close to New York's social whirl as he defended the great interests of the railroad with a thousand legal subtleties—a hair splitter instead of a Rail-Splitter.

But the fates were pulling him toward a different destination. As he settled into his well-cushioned car, he could prepare for his next ordeal and steel himself for the intrigues of Albany.

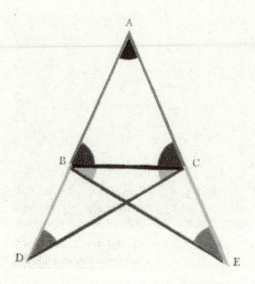

From *The First Six Books of the Elements of Euclid* (London: William Pickering, 1847)[14]

LINE AB

It would be a straight shot across New York, one that fit well with Lincoln's Euclidean course of reading. A year earlier, while riding on a train in Connecticut, Lincoln had praised the six books of the Greek mathematician's *Elements* as the foundation of his thinking. In the *Elements*, Euclid described the ideal properties of a straight line, which he placed between two imaginary points, A and B. "Let AB be the given finite straight line," he had written more than two thousand years earlier.[15]

Surprisingly, AB had become an *actual* line, between two cities, Albany and Buffalo, that stood at opposite ends of New York. Nor was it just *any* line; this was one of America's vital links, yoking East and West ever tighter. Every year, it straightened, as engineers eliminated curves, smoothed out gradients, and bypassed small towns to build the fastest link possible. Railroad officials along the route used a phrase, "the Straight Line," to describe the Euclidean idea that dominated their dreams.[16]

In his own way, Lincoln, too, was trying to straighten crooked lines. When he mused on America's imperfections, he often wrote in a Euclidean language, trying to reduce problems to their essentials. In 1854 he penned a note to himself: "If A. can prove, however conclusively, that he may, of right, enslave B.—why may not B. snatch the same argument, and prove equally, that he may enslave A?" Years later, the Gettysburg Address would owe something to Euclid's idea that a proposition was not true until proven.

But Lincoln had some distance to go yet. On this frigid day, the Special would travel almost the entire width of the Empire State as it bore down on Albany. New York's capital was already notorious for intrigue, and it would require tact to get through the next turnstile without paying too high a fare. Thurlow Weed, the old arachnid, had been spinning his webs there for decades. It would be difficult to say which of his three nicknames was the worst: "The Wizard of the Lobby," "The Dictator," or "My Lord Thurlow." [17]

But Albany was vital to Lincoln as the key to New York. This huge state had been critical to his election, and he needed the support of its people if he was going to stand any chance of success as president. New York was by far the largest state in the Union, with 3.88 million souls counted by the 1860 census, well ahead of Pennsylvania (2.9 million). In fact, it held more people than the free population of the *entire* Confederacy, as measured on its first day of existence—today.

Like most state capitals, Albany provided amply for itself through state expenditures. But it was also growing in other ways, because of its favorable location in the railroad economy. A natural crossroads, it sat near the confluence of the Mohawk River, flowing from the west, and the mighty Hudson, pulling everything toward New York City. Travelers had paused here since it was a place where Native American paths converged in the forest.[18] But a modern city was now coming into its own, as the New York Central kept whittling away at the Straight Line.

The route largely followed the Erie Canal along its flattened course, avoiding the mountain ranges to the south, called the Endless Mountains in the early maps. Beginning in 1842, "through" trains were running between Albany and Buffalo, with limited stops, allowing passengers to stay in their cars for the entire journey. To go "through" meant new kinds of tickets, new arrangements between railroads, and a new science of baggage management, tracking all of these moving parts. When the New York Central Railroad was formed in 1853 from a cluster of small local railroads poking into these villages, it brought concentration to these tasks.[19]

The new efficiencies required an exact knowledge of time, and the telegraph was indispensable in helping New Yorkers to synchronize with one another. Albany had been fifteen minutes ahead of Buffalo, but now every through train needed to be exquisitely timed, to avoid the local trains running along the same tracks. As speed increased, so did danger. But New Yorkers were becoming very precise and were making some of the best clocks in the country.[20] Throughout the day, as the Special raced eastward, Lincoln's progress was measured down to the second by telegraph operators conveying news of his exact whereabouts.[21]

He had come through these parts before, during earlier, less successful forays into politics. In September 1848 he visited Albany as a foot soldier in the cause of electing Zachary Taylor. On that journey, he met Thurlow Weed for the first time. Then, the presidency would have been an absurd daydream for a young legislator of no great distinction. Now, every mile was bringing it closer.

East of Buffalo, the Special was proceeding briskly, lapping up the miles in the early light of day, and leaving its signature, in smoke, against the sky. As the train raced across the flat farmland of Erie County, John Hay looked out the windows at the farmers feeding their cattle, chopping wood, and performing their never-ending tasks. Still smarting from the early departure, he ridiculed the "mouldy proverbs" that praised the value of rising early to work.

But he and western New York were now awake, and his writing improved as he described the huge crowds that he could see out the windows. There was a lot of noise in Hay's account, with people erupting in cheers and personal messages of support, "blessing Old Abe" as he spent a few seconds with them.[22]

Today's route would bring Lincoln through the backyard of his former rival, William H. Seward, the pride of Auburn, New York. They were allies now, and as Lincoln raced through Seward's homeland, New Yorkers received him with open arms. They were not daunted in the slightest by the weather. Hay wrote, "I have seen the snowflakes melt upon a million upturned faces today."[23] The papers reported that "in the grey twilight of the early day, crowds of country people had gathered at every little station along the first part of the route," where they bid "a cordial Godspeed to the rapidly flying train."

Godspeed was the perfect term, as the train pushed its limits. The *New York Times* reported that Lincoln covered his first thirty-seven miles in thirty minutes.[24] That may have been due to the fact that there was a new engineer at the throttle: Robert Lincoln, who rode in the cab for much of the day, exhilarated.[25]

But the pace was hard to sustain. West of Bergen, a little after seven in the morning, an acrid burning smell alarmed the engineer enough that he brought the Special to a halt. An axle box on a forward car had overheated from the high speed and needed ten minutes to cool down.[26] More moderately, the Special resumed its progress and began to approach the first significant city of the day.

Recently rediscovered full-plate daguerreotype of Frederick Douglass[27]

ROCHESTER

At 7:35 a.m., a huge crowd was waiting as the Special pulled into Rochester. Like all the cities along the Straight Line, it was growing rapidly, with a population that had doubled over twenty years to 48,204. Trains were helping Rochester to diversify its economy, and city leaders had recently upgraded Rochester's nickname from "the Flour City" to "the Flower City."[28]

Rochester was also well known as a sympathetic stop on the Underground Railroad, thanks to its most famous resident, Frederick Douglass, who had lived there since 1848. He and his family had already helped about five hundred slaves to find their freedom.[29] There were many reasons that Douglass found Rochester a congenial place to live. He was protected by a community that sympathized with his position, and he could lower his profile when necessary. But he could *raise* it, too. Thanks to Rochester's happy situation along the New York Central, it was easy to arrange lecture tours, publications, and the distribution of photographs.[30] Over the course of a long life, Douglass became the most widely photographed American of the nineteenth century.[31]

Rochester and photography would become nearly synonymous in the fullness of time.[32] George Eastman was only six years old in 1861, but when he grew older, he would find new ways to take pictures, simpler than the wet-plate processes in use. Other local tinkerers helped Americans to see better, with critical refinements in optics and glass.[33] The inventors along the corridor spurred each other on, inventing new substances when they ran out of natural materials. As he worked his way forward, Eastman used celluloid, a new chemical compound that stemmed from the experiments of an Albany inventor, John Wesley Hyatt, in the early 1860s. In response to a cash prize to design a new kind of billiard ball, Hyatt perfected a new kind of substance—plastic—that he could reshape into almost anything.[34]

Douglass also liked Rochester for the allies that he found there, seeking to deepen democracy in their own way. The Flower City was a bastion of women's rights, especially after the suffragist Susan B. Anthony moved there in 1845.[35] Trains allowed lecturers to move quickly from one awakened town to the next, along the so-called Lyceum circuit. Other women leaders lived in close range—the distinguished crusader, Elizabeth Cady Stanton, was in Seneca Falls—and as a women's movement began to cohere, it benefited from the *actual* movement made possible by a busy corridor.[36]

Throughout the 1850s, Douglass forged common cause with women leaders. The plight of women was often likened to slavery in an era when wives were legally defined as the property of their husbands, and when Douglass gave his famous address, "What to the Slave Is the Fourth of July?", it was before a women's organization. He signed his letters to Anthony, "Yours for the freedom of man and woman always."[37]

Many of the strategies developed by the Underground Railroad could be applied to the plight of women who needed special protection to escape abusive husbands. Only two months before Lincoln's arrival, Rochester citizens helped the wife of a politician, struggling to keep her thirteen-year-old daughter during a bitter divorce proceeding, by using some of the evasions they knew from their work with escaped slaves. These included disguises and carefully planned railroad journeys with friends distributed throughout the cars. That case had caused turmoil within the women's movement; not all felt that it was wise to challenge the system so openly, and they had debated all of these topics—women's rights and slavery—in heated public meetings held along the corridor in January. Lincoln was coming through a part of the country that was extremely wide awake.[38]

Presumably, Douglass was paying close attention as the Special came into Rochester, carrying this new president, so different from his predecessors. Like many in the vanguard of the antislavery movement, Douglass had doubts about Lincoln, who had never denounced slavery as forcefully as he would have liked. At the same time, Douglass surely felt the force of the wind blowing in from the West. It is not certain that he was there, jostling against the fifteen thousand who gathered downtown to greet Lincoln, but it is hard to imagine that he would have missed a moment so freighted with significance.[39]

As the Special eased into Rochester, local cannoneers fired a thirty-four-gun salute, and pandemonium reigned. For a moment, the train could not proceed through the crowd, until militias cleared a way. A large contingent was waiting for the president-elect outside the Waverley Hotel, where it had been announced that he would speak.[40] But a division superintendent decided it was too dangerous to move Lincoln from the train to the hotel and back. Instead, he spoke from the rear car. Many of those assembled never even knew that he had come and gone, and waited for him at the wrong location. Others were luckier, including a young boy who was standing so close to the train that he was able to clamber up onto the rear platform and greet Lincoln personally. Lincoln shook his hand, and said, "Good morning, little boy." Another eyewitness who stood very close was John Sylvester Wilson; interviewed in 1915, when he was a hundred years old, he still remembered Lincoln as "the homeliest man I ever saw."[41]

Daniel Waldo, from *The Last Men of the Revolution* (1864)[42]

SYRACUSE

An unforgiving schedule demanded that they press on, and the Special quickly resumed its progress. At 8:44, the train pulled into a small town,

Clyde. Although it only stayed until 8:49, the *New York Times* reported an event of significance. During the five minutes allotted, a local photographer stood on a woodpile and took pictures of Lincoln at the rear end of the car—photographs that have never surfaced.[43]

The Special "greatly accelerated" over the next section—Robert Lincoln may have been at the throttle again—then it eased up in the approach to Syracuse, the so-called Salt City. On the way in, the train's telegraph crackled with the news that another huge crowd was waiting.[44] At 9:52, when the train arrived, there were ten thousand people assembled, even though the snow was beginning to come down harder. A boy who threw a snowball at Lincoln was promptly arrested, as was "a cross-eyed rag picker" who was detained for "squinting at the president."[45] Nearby, a live eagle was on display, to inspire the crowd, but he failed in his assignment. Hay mockingly described this poor specimen as a "pusillanimous example" of the breed, which, "catching an accidental sight of the president-elect, turned away in terror and hid its head in the bosom of a sympathetic policeman."[46]

Fortunately, a more reliable national symbol was on the platform. The Reverend Daniel Waldo had fought in the American Revolution and was still going strong at age ninety-eight. He had slowed down—the *New York Times* wrote that he was "so infirm as to be scarcely able to totter"—but he would live three more years, long enough to appear in a book of photographs that included all known veterans of the Revolution. Lincoln was delighted to meet someone who had voted for both George Washington and him.[47]

Then the Special darted forward again, eager to win its own battle against time. Near Syracuse, a small village called Pompey, after the Roman general, had given the world Leonard Jerome, a prosperous investor in railroads.[48] During a long and sometimes lurid career, he made a great deal of money, lost nearly as much, and earned a reputation as a sportsman and a breeder of horses.

Breeding was of great interest to his children as well. Jerome's daughter, Jennie, married a son of the Duke of Marlborough, who sired her son, Sir Winston Churchill. To the end of his life, Churchill relished his relationship to American history, including his ironical descent from soldiers who had fought against the Crown in the Revolution, and from indigenous Americans as well.

In 1960 the arch defender of the British Empire told his doctor, "You may not know it, but I am descended from a Seneca Indian squaw."[49]

This was a curious stretch, as the ship of state sailed from one town to another, with names evoking the ancient Mediterranean. After Syracuse, the train passed through Rome, the hometown of Norman Judd, Lincoln's traveling companion, now actively communicating with Allan Pinkerton about the threat in Baltimore.[50] It pulled into Utica at 11:15, where the usual welcoming committees had gathered. The senior class of Hamilton College was there, along with a huge crowd, likened by a reporter to "a huge pythonic monster," writhing and twisting.[51]

Lincoln began to speak, but was interrupted by a "crazy man, with long moustache and beard, with a shepherd's crook for a cane."[52] The presidential entourage, constantly on the lookout for threats, may have formed fleeting thoughts of the Grim Reaper; but happily, it was a harmless local eccentric, overstimulated. In a tour designed to meet as many people as possible, it was inevitable that addled citizens would come out sometimes, drawn to the excitement. The chaos was fairly constant; in his reporting, Henry Villard noted that Lincoln's remarks were often accompanied by catcalls, hidden from official transcripts: "At all of the stops, impertinent individuals addressed Mr. Lincoln in a very familiar manner."[53] At the same time, there was something in the president-elect's calm manner that poured balm on an overheated nation.

Another eyewitness kept his tongue until 1915, when a letter-writer to the *New York Times*, John Seymour Wood wrote that he had seen Lincoln as a boy. He added a curious note: "I had the impression he was in mourning for someone." According to Wood, "His complexion was dark as an Indian," and his height was overwhelming to a child seeing him for the first time. Wood wrote, "He was so tall he had to lean forward and put his head out under the roof of the car."[54]

As the train continued eastward, Mary Todd Lincoln decided to upgrade her husband's appearance and asked their African-American attendant, William Johnson, to do something about it. He soon emerged from the baggage car with a new broadcloth overcoat and a hatbox. With an air of scientific detachment, the *New York Times* reported that Lincoln's appearance had improved "by fifty percent." It added that he had been wearing "a shocking bad hat and a very thin old overcoat."[55]

At 12:05 p.m., the Special rolled into the pretty village of Little Falls, alongside the frozen Erie Canal. On the hotel veranda, a group of women waved their kerchiefs to the strains of "Hail Columbia," and church bells "chimed sweetly."[56] This tranquil setting was about as far from the raging ideological battles of the twentieth century as could be imagined, but it was here, along this same stretch of track, that the author Ayn Rand began to conceive her theory of dominant movers and shakers. In 1947, during her research for *Atlas Shrugged*, she was permitted by the New York Central to drive one of its locomotives, an experience that thrilled her and supported her theory that society needs to be led by fast drivers who enjoy danger.[57]

Lincoln might have disagreed, given his experience just down the line at Schenectady. A few young movers and shakers, showing a little too much leadership, took it upon themselves to fire a celebratory cannon as Lincoln's train approached. The only problem was that they managed to fire it directly *into* his train, taking out a section of the forward car, shattering three windows "into atoms," covering passengers with broken glass, and terrifying everyone.[58] For the second time since the trip started, an errant artillery blast had caused windows to break near the Lincolns. He seemed shaken, according to an eyewitness.[59] It was an extraordinarily dangerous mistake that might have easily caused a tragedy.

By coincidence, Schenectady was a good place to repair a train. The Schenectady Locomotive Works was an important manufacturer, and it was spinning off other enterprises. In 1856 a local mechanic of farm machinery, George Westinghouse Sr., opened a small shop nearby. Here his son began to tinker, first with steam engines, then with other technologies related to train travel, including the air brake he would perfect in Pittsburgh—an idea that came to him after witnessing a derailment between Schenectady and Troy. By May 1860, at the age of thirteen, he was already an employee, the beginning of a brilliant career that would lead to a long roster of inventions, including breakthroughs in electricity and portable engines. They, in turn, inspired Henry Ford.[60]

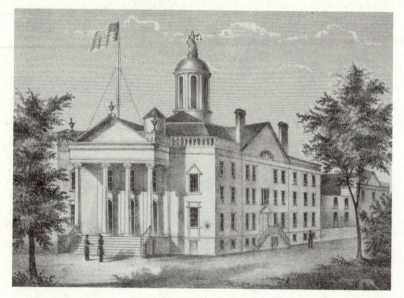

The New York Capitol, 1866[61]

ALBANY

Lincoln was nearing his destination now. The Special was entering the country of the Albanians, as they styled themselves.

With its Dutch memories and the natural venality that settles over a capital, Albany was more conservative than Rochester and Syracuse. The newer cities were more receptive to religious revivals and the social and cultural movements that seemed to go with them, including the antislavery crusade. When abolitionists came to Albany, as they had a month earlier, for a convention, they considered it "the heart of the enemy's country."[62] To make matters worse, a virulent spat between local political factions was in full boil, and they were fighting like "Kilkenny cats."[63] A Republican governor had been elected on Lincoln's coattails, but the historically Democratic city was unlikely to welcome Lincoln with open arms. Albany was, technically, a city on a hill; yet few would hold up Albanian democracy as a model for the world.

Yet there were also deep feelings for the Union, in a place where Americans had joined together before in dark times. Long before the United

States came into existence, the concept of a union had begun to take shape in 1754, when Benjamin Franklin urged the colonies to send representatives to a meeting here to discuss the French and Indian War beginning. He may have drawn inspiration from the effective alliances of the Iroquois Confederacy, well known in these parts. The Albany Congress was imperfect—no colony south of Maryland sent a delegate—but a new sense of collective purpose emerged from the talks. One idea, in particular, had endured: that a single person, called a "president-general," could somehow lead this nearly ungovernable people. Lincoln was doing his best to prove that it was possible.

The Special began to slow as it passed through the outskirts and started a gentle descent. The New York Central had built large workshops in the western part of town, and telegraph wires stretched in every direction, keeping Albany in a constant conversation with the outside world. At the top of a hill, the Dudley Observatory kept all of these movements aligned, thanks to a large collection of clocks, chronometers, and celestial measuring devices. It was deeply involved in the challenge of regulating time between the major hubs of the New York Central's network. As the Special passed through the machine shops of the New York Central, a signal was flashed to a militia at the Observatory, which fired a twenty-one-gun salute.[64] All within earshot knew that Lincoln was arriving.

Albany's ambitious politicians must have viewed Lincoln with wariness as he came into view; and doubtless the opposite was also true. Even then, New York's government was famous for its infighting, and he would have to step carefully, avoiding promises to job seekers and other encumbrances. As he continued to wear down from the trip, Lincoln needed to get through the evening with as little damage as possible.[65]

Once again, crowd control was a problem, with another tremendous surge greeting the train. But the militias that were supposed to protect Lincoln were late, and the situation broke down. People swarmed around the cars of the Special, and underneath as well, getting very close to Lincoln. As Henry Villard noted, with rising alarm, "Little boys and big men climbed under and over the train, only to be kicked and thrown back." The police did their best to afford a measure of protection, but they were outnumbered. Villard wrote, "All was confusion, hurry, disorder, mud, riot, and discomfort."[66]

For some time ("the wait was a very long one"), Lincoln was held captive, unable to leave the train and move through the crowd until soldiers arrived. Helplessly, the presidential party endured the sight of fights breaking out and the sound of people clambering onto the roof of the car. The crowd began to grow impatient, leading to tense shoving matches with the police and loud demands of "Show us the Rail-Splitter!" and "Trot out Old Abe!" Many of them were drunk. A newspaper described the crowd as "vulpine"—fox-like—but they were more dangerous than that.[67]

Eventually soldiers arrived and cleared a way to a platform, where the object of their interest stood before the people, with no hat. The *Chicago Tribune* wrote that he appeared "pale and worn."[68] This was not exactly the Rail-Splitter that they knew from countless woodcuts and crude prints; instead, there was an older-seeming man, "tired, sunburned, adorned with huge whiskers." According to Villard, the crowd that was so desperate to see him in the flesh did not recognize him at first because he looked so different from the "smooth-shaven, red-cheeked individual" they were expecting.[69]

As Lincoln rose up to his full height, they understood. Then, after a few seconds of stunned silence, they cheered. But their temporary confusion confirmed how much was in flux during Lincoln's journey. He made his way toward a carriage and stood up straight in it, passing through them unsteadily. Villard described him as "bowing and swaying like a tall cedar in a storm."[70]

Lincoln's haggard appearance troubled bystanders. A young observer thought that the man upon whom all hopes rested looked "much wearied & care worn."[71] A Democratic paper thought he "does not look as if he had the bodily vigor to stand the pressure upon him." It also blamed him for the behavior of the crowd, as "rude hands jostled him and his underlings commanded him; and all about him the struggle was who was to control him."[72] Some in the crowd vented darker feelings. One man said, audibly, "That Negro lover will never get to the executive mansion." Immediately, "a big burly fellow" nearby came over and punched him in the face.[73]

Finally, Lincoln arrived at the goal of his pilgrimage: the government palace that stood atop the hill. As the place where the most populous state in the Union was governed, it was an important shrine to democracy. Appropriately, it was surmounted by a statue of Themis, the Greek patroness of assemblies.[74]

As Lincoln arrived, another huge crowd greeted him, carrying banners that read, "No Compromise." Lincoln walked up the front steps, with soldiers firing another round of salutes, adding to the din. At the top of the steps, according to the *Chicago Tribune*, he turned to face the multitudes, who "greeted him with a perfect roar of applause." He gazed at the crowd, "in apparent amazement at its vastness," then entered the building.[75]

Inside, he encountered New York's governor, Edwin Morgan, and they exchanged brief remarks. Lincoln flattered Morgan by pointing out that his state held more people than the entire country at the time of independence. He then spoke before the legislature, ably expressing his "awe" before the example of the founders and hinting at a theme he would develop more fully: that the upcoming battle was a struggle on behalf of "civil and religious liberty for all time to come."[76]

Chester Alan Arthur, 1858[77]

HEART BURNINGS

The rest of the day was a blur of receptions, made worse by the severe jealousy existing between the governor and the legislature. Morgan arranged for some private time with Lincoln, but for a depressing reason: he wanted to find out if war was coming, and then, armed with that information, make some quick investments. The longer Lincoln stayed with Morgan, the more agitated the legislature became. Its members had established competing committees to welcome the president-elect, and now each side wanted to welcome him simultaneously.[78] The result was a standoff, with no one entirely satisfied. Lincoln and his friends found this quarreling "undignified and absurd." Albanian democracy was a work in progress.[79]

As Lincoln made his way through the maze of receptions, he found that Governor Morgan had an unusually large staff of personal retainers. For ceremonial occasions, he wanted a bigger retinue, and toward that end, he gave out ornamental titles to young men who had supported his election campaign. One of these young men was his "engineer in chief," a handsome lawyer, active in Republican politics, who had carefully grown a set of magnificent muttonchops that widened his face by several inches. The young Chester A. Arthur would become another successor to Lincoln, as the twenty-first president.[80]

In the evening, Lincoln and his party navigated the warring receptions as best they could, going from one to the other. Then he had to bear another cross: a long public reception at the Delavan House, where he and his family were staying. Here he shook hands with upward of a thousand people. Although Lincoln had survived many of these receptions on the journey, this one was harder, perhaps because he and his family had finally arrived in the East and were forced to suffer the judgments of those who looked down upon the West. Snide New Yorkers privately noted his wife's fashion lapses, including wearing rings outside her gloves, and a dress that revealed her bare arms.[81] Villard conveyed that it had been unpleasant: "The whole reception has been a sort of failure—a miserable botch, characterized with snobbery throughout." He predicted that it would lead to "heart burnings" and lingering ill will.[82]

The Lincolns finally escaped, with "gratitude for their safe deliverance," after a long night of being "leveed and receptioned by remorseless ladies and gentlemen." It would be uncharacteristic of Lincoln to dilate long on these snubs (and characteristic of Mary Todd Lincoln to do just that). Evidently, something had rubbed them the wrong way. Henry Villard recorded that they went to bed "too annoyed and angered to sleep," and resolved never to return to Albany.[83]

But despite these smoldering embers, the long day brought real achievements. Lincoln had survived a cannon blast into his train and had drawn nearly three hundred miles closer to his goal. He had encountered tens of thousands of loyal New Yorkers en route. Many were favorably impressed. One witness was relieved to find the new president not nearly as "ogre-like" as he had been led to believe, but "perfectly presentable." An Albany clergyman wrote, "I think ninety-five percent more of him than before I saw him. He will put his foot down pretty firmly in time."[84]

As the day was ending, John Hay wrote evocatively of the long ride that had started in the predawn darkness of Buffalo. It could be summed up in three words: "crowds, cannons, and cheers." All day long, New Yorkers had stood along the track, in the largest numbers yet, as the ship of state sailed through a sea of humanity. The people were intensely alive in Hay's account, "surging" toward the train, "swinging" their hats and banners, "cheering" loudly as the Special came through. They were everywhere he looked, "clinging along roofs and balconies and pillars, fringing long embankments, swarming upon adjacent trains of motionless cars, shouting, bellowing, shrieking, howling. All were boisterous," he wrote of the tens of thousands he had seen out the window, "bubbling" with feeling for their country. Thanks to Lincoln, they had been "transformed into patriots," ready to defend it. This was a genuine achievement, though it might never register as a newspaper headline. Yet it signaled a profound change in the air and brought hope to a people who had felt despair for a long time. Hay ended his account with a note of pride that he had witnessed one of the most memorable days in American history.[85]

But even if Hay was right, Lincoln was riding a tiger. Other observers resorted to the kinds of words a zookeeper might use as they tried to describe the same crowds that had thrilled Lincoln's young secretary. Even in

Hay's sympathetic account, there was something menacing about a crowd that looked "curiously wavy and undulating." Others had noticed it too, such as the reporter in Utica who called the crowd "a huge pythonic monster."[86]

In Albany, as at Buffalo, Lincoln had barely escaped the python's embrace, and the half hour in which he was trapped in his car, unable to move, did not augur well as he prepared to visit the largest city in the country. "He enters New York tomorrow afternoon," the Manhattan lawyer George Templeton Strong wrote into his diary late on February 18.[87]

Since the trip began, Lincoln had been promising anyone who would listen that everything would be fine if Americans simply remained calm. But if he could not control his own journey, how could he possibly restore order to a huge nation? Around the country, peace was already fraying as angry vigilantes roamed the countryside searching for targets to attack. Some were secessionists, allied with Jefferson Davis; other were simply acting on their own. During the lawlessness that prevailed in the listless final days of the Buchanan administration, it was often hard to tell the difference.

That same night, in Nebraska City, Nebraska, a pro-Southern group broke into an old government fort and flew South Carolina's Palmetto flag, before loyal Nebraskans took it down the next day.[88]

The situation was still restive in Texas, where large groups of armed vigilantes were roaming the streets, exhilarated by their easy acquisition of all American military assets. Robert E. Lee remained in an agony of indecision, still loyal to a country that barely seemed to exist anymore. All night, alone, he paced the floor and prayed.[89]

In Baltimore, the situation seemed to be disintegrating as the Special drew closer. Pro-Southern militias were training along the tracks; one recruit claimed, indiscreetly, that they had a thousand men ready to surround Lincoln's train during his passage through the city. During his meeting with New York's governor, Lincoln had been handed a letter from one of the few Republicans in Baltimore, reporting that it was "inadvisable" to hold any public events there. Baltimore's marshal of police had let it be known that he would not provide any protection for the presidential cortège.[90]

But Lincoln's friends were beginning to stir from slumber. At 5:16 that evening, as he was fighting his way through Albany's throngs, a young widow quietly boarded a train from Baltimore to New York. The redoubtable Kate Warne had learned a great deal about the threat to kill Lincoln during her undercover work in Baltimore over the past week. Using her aliases (Mrs. Cherry, Mrs. Barley) and an Alabama drawl, she had gathered information so vital that Pinkerton now asked her to intercept the presidential party, carrying letters that described the threat. She would ride all night, with strict instructions to put the letters into Lincoln's hands. But that would be a challenge, for she was unknown to Lincoln and his entourage, and she would be trying to penetrate his security cordon, in the center of America's largest city. It was entirely possible that his guardians, who had failed in so many ways to protect him, would succeed in blocking the delivery of this urgent message intended to save his life.[91]

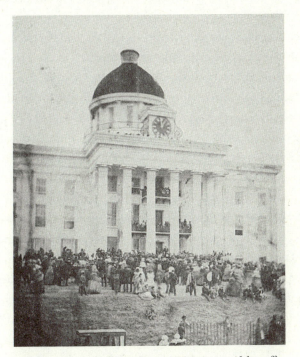

Inauguration of Jefferson Davis, Montgomery, Alabama[92]

INAUGURATION

Other bad news was coming in as well. Jefferson Davis had scored an important victory earlier in the day simply by reaching his destination. Tomorrow's papers would carry lavish details of the new presidency that had begun at Montgomery, before the columns of a different Capitol. While Lincoln was kissing children, Davis was issuing edicts and acting with the full authority of his new office.

The inauguration had come off without a hitch. In his address, Jefferson Davis projected defiance toward the United States, warning that "millions would suffer" if anyone sought to deter the Confederacy. But he also had shown some reverence for American history, citing the Declaration of Independence as a justification for launching a new government.[93] His reading was very different from Lincoln's: there was no mention of human rights, only the "rights" of a planter class that felt "entitled" to any rights it could identify for itself.[94]

Lincoln would need to act quickly to rescue the founding documents and reassert their unifying message. As he knew, there were inconsistencies within the Confederate argument; broken links that were immediately apparent to a careful reader. It was awkward to use the language of rights to defend a government based upon slavery. No one in Alabama was claiming to hold up the new regime as a model for the world to emulate, as Lincoln was consistently doing in his speeches. To even call the Confederacy a democracy was a stretch; Davis had been elected by a hastily convened gathering of political leaders, mostly wealthy planters, with little interest in asking the people for a vote. There was no other candidate, and already the new government was veering away from principles dear to Americans, such as the four-year presidential term. Lincoln was constantly reminding his audiences that they would have a chance to remove him; but Davis would never run for reelection. He simply stayed in office, ruinously, as if the Confederacy were an extension of himself. In New York, the diarist George Templeton Strong called him "Lord Davis."[95]

There were other paradoxes. The new Confederacy was still dependent upon the reliable delivery of the U.S. Mail, and instead of a national anthem, it played "The Marseillaise." Tellingly, its constitution would omit the words "We the People." Its flag was not yet a settled matter, with designs still coming in. One possibility was a flag that would be nearly identical to the Stars and Stripes, but with altered colors (a red field of stars, and blue stripes), as if these Southerners still longed to be a part of the country they were leaving. Other designs were more overtly religious, such as a Bible resting on a bale of cotton.[96] But even if some elements were still coming into focus, the Confederacy had declared itself to the world, and by beating Lincoln in their race, Davis scored an important tactical victory. The *Charleston Mercury* crowed, "The United States of America are dissolved forever! 'Alas, poor Yorick! I knew him well!' But what a sad rogue he was."[97]

The Shakespearean reference (from *Hamlet)* would have been instantly familiar to Lincoln. But he would have disputed the point that the republic had died. In his own inaugural address, kept carefully by his side at all times, Lincoln was carrying his answer to all of these insults to democracy.

John Wilkes Booth[98]

THE APOSTATE [98]

Another Shakespearean was nearby as the Lincolns fell asleep, restively. Just down the street from the Delavan House was Stanwix Hall, a domed hotel where a talented actor was staying during an engagement with the Gayety Theatre. Earlier in the day, Lincoln's parade had passed directly in front of the hotel, and the actor.[99]

John Wilkes Booth had enjoyed an explosive run in Albany, dazzling audiences with his raw physicality, and frightening them too, with glimpses of the violence that seemed to lie just below the surface of his powerful performances. Like Lincoln, he had been touring along a nearly identical route: he had come to Albany from Rochester, playing in *Othello*, *The Merchant of Venice*, *Macbeth*, and *Richard the Third*, among other works.[100] In Rochester, he performed before sold-out houses ten nights in a row and received rave reviews. One critic wrote of his *Richard the Third*, "nothing had ever excelled it." Lincoln loved the play and could cite long passages from memory.[101]

In Albany, Booth was thrilling audiences all over again, but the intensity of his performances had brought him close to an uncomfortable edge. At the Gayety, he was performing in *The Apostate*, a melodrama in which he played a Spaniard named Pescara. It was a macabre play in which the Spaniard, simmering with hatred for Islam, kills a number of Muslims, which required a great deal of swashbuckling swordplay onstage. Six nights earlier, on Lincoln's birthday, Booth had cut another actor with his sword, then later in the same play, he fell on his dagger, plunging the knife three inches into his own ribs. He continued the performance, bleeding profusely in full view of the crowd.[102] Booth was blurring the boundaries between art and life.

As he convalesced over the next few days, the actor warmly expressed his political sentiments in favor of the South, so freely that he was warned by his theater to tone them down. On February 18 he saw Lincoln go by and the people cheering him. The sight upset him; the people were clearly warming to the new president, and professional jealousy may have played a role, too. Lincoln was drawing bigger crowds.[103] Later, Booth asked a friend,

"Is this not a Democratic city?" By that he meant the upper-case *D*: a partisan city that ought to give a rough reception to the incoming Republican.

He suppressed his feelings, barely, and on the same night that Lincoln was feted in the capital, Booth returned to the stage in *The Apostate,* with his right arm tied to his side, "fencing with his left, like a demon," as if striking out at someone.[104] In the play, he asks, not that rhetorically, "What if I rush and with a blow strike life from his heart?"[105] Violence continued to follow him, and two months later, while still in Albany, Booth's blood flowed profusely again, as life continued to imitate art in his jumbled world. On April 26 a newspaper article titled "All for Love and Murder" described how an enraged actress, Henrietta Irving, stabbed Booth in the face and then tried, unsuccessfully, to take her own life.[106]

Booth was described as "the Great Tragedian" in the Albany papers, but no one, even with Lincoln's prophetic powers, could have known how much tragedy lay in the future. Once again, Albany was acting as a crossroads, briefly uniting these travelers for a night in their very different journeys. With a long day of travel behind him, Lincoln now prepared to head south.

John Bachmann, *New York and Environs*, fish-eye view, 1859[1]

11

THE FRONT DOOR

The wretched man is stranded on an island.

—Homer, *The Odyssey*, book 5, line 13[2]

FEBRUARY 19–20, 1861
ALBANY TO NEW YORK CITY

THE NORTH WIND

Even before the Lincolns awoke at seven o'clock, people were streaming toward New York City.[3] At four in the morning, Pinkerton's agent Kate Warne arrived from Baltimore with urgent information about the assassination plot she and her colleagues had uncovered.[4] She would not have been encouraged by the early-morning papers, full of information about Lincoln's travel plans. An article in the *New York Times*, titled "Preparations in New York," described exactly where his parade would go and where the police would be arrayed. In so doing, it offered a road map for anyone wishing to do him harm.[5]

Lincoln was not scheduled to arrive in New York until three in the afternoon. But as the sun was rising, crowds were already forming around the Hudson River Railroad terminus in Manhattan.[6] They knew that history was in the air. The day before, Jefferson Davis had thrown down a gauntlet, asserting the South's right to launch a new country. In Washington, James Buchanan was said to be wavering and might officially receive an envoy from the new government, a gesture that would make it that much easier for foreign governments to do so.[7] The fate of the republic seemed to rest with Lincoln's answer. So, the crowds stood there, waiting.[8]

Before he could begin the next leg, Lincoln had to extricate himself from Albany, legendary for its entanglements. The *New York Herald* called it a city in which "progress, like locomotion, is uphill work."[9] Getting out was not easy: Lincoln had to survive another blast of ordnance, as several gunners made "frantic" attempts to explode a cannon during the departure.[10] The same morning, the front page of the local newspaper included a rave review of John Wilkes Booth, "undoubtedly one of the finest actors this country ever produced."[11]

The Special had a relatively simple goal this morning. After crossing the Hudson, it would proceed along the river's eastern bank toward Manhattan. There were no hills to climb; it was a long, majestic route, at the water level. On a normal day, that would have been simple, but for days, the Hudson

Buchanan and Lincoln, *Vanity Fair,* May 9, 1861[12]

had been rising dangerously. A late-winter thaw, following a heavy snow, had released torrents of water and ice into the river's upper reaches, with a force that astonished river watchers.[13] It was almost as if the north wind— *Boreas*—was blowing in, to fill Lincoln's sails at the exact moment the ship of state turned toward the South.

In the hands of a versatile press agent, melting ice could be interpreted as good news—a political cartoon depicted the outgoing president, James Buchanan, as a rapidly shrinking iceberg, with Lincoln rising over the horizon, a warming sun.

But to a civil engineer, these speeding ice floes were a lethal threat. On the morning of Lincoln's departure, they were cascading downstream and slamming into Albany's waterfront. One iron bridge "was lifted off its foundations and thrown down," while another bridge was severely damaged and rendered impassable. Many downtown buildings were surrounded by water, and people were paddling through the streets in rowboats.[14]

It was clear that the Special could not use the damaged bridges. Yet everything depended on Lincoln getting across. The solution was

Ice floes in Albany[15]

counterintuitive. If the Special went north instead of south, it could try to find a better crossing. Walt Whitman would later write a poem, "To a Locomotive in Winter," celebrating the force of a train surging forward against the white snow, irresistible, a law unto itself. So the Special proved to be.

Turning directly into the wind, it headed upriver, toward the ice. At Cohoes, the Special glided through "solid phalanxes" of men and women, close to the track, who had come out of the factories to give him "tremendous cheers."[16] Near the place where the Mohawk River flowed into the Hudson, it was easier to bridge the great river. Still, this crossing had its own liabilities: the bridge would burn down a year later, and after it was replaced, the new bridge collapsed while a train was crossing.[17] Fortunately, on this day it held the weight, and the Special delivered Lincoln safely to his next destination.

Skaters on the Hudson[18]

TROY

On the other side lay Troy, a substantial community of nearly forty thousand, named after the ancient city besieged in *The Iliad*. Famously, the original Troy's walls had been breached by a wooden horse, but today the Iron Horse did the same work with less fuss. As the Special pulled in, Lincoln found a huge crowd, fifteen thousand strong.[19]

From Troy, Lincoln could finally begin his approach to New York, along one of the most dramatic routes in North America, parallel to the Hudson for 144 miles.[20] A splendid new train was summoned, pulled by a new locomotive named *Union*, which burned coal instead of wood. Lincoln would be traveling to Manhattan in style.

The new Special sparkled with pride, befitting a New York express. Its cars were painted an exuberant orange, with brown and black highlights. The interior was also sumptuous, as the press reported with awe.[21] The *New York Times* called Lincoln's car "one of the handsomest, perhaps, ever run in this country." The paper described a paradise of upholstery, with "rich sofas," "luxurious chairs," crimson plush, and a thick, blue silk, studded with thirty-four stars, for all of the states. Heaters warmed the car, light poured out of cut-glass globes, and the interior was draped with a "dark-blue cloth of fine texture, trimmed with tricolored gimp braid and tassels."[22] The Rail-Splitter had come a long way from his log cabin.

Lincoln took some time to inspect the locomotive, and expressed "much gratification and surprise" at its splendor.[23] But as the press inspected *him*, it found that he was sorely in need of an upgrade. "Towering above all," a reporter noted, "with his face and forehead furrowed by a thousand wrinkles, his hair unkempt, his new whiskers looking as if not yet naturalized, his clothing illy arranged, Mr. Lincoln sat toward the rear of the saloon car." As he drew closer to Manhattan, his fashion violations would earn growing ridicule.[24]

The great emporium was already palpable. More than five hundred employees of the Hudson River Railroad were spread out down the route, scouring the track, forming a human chain that allowed them to signal one another all the way to New York. A pilot locomotive, *Young America*, was in front of the Special, blowing its whistle to clear away bystanders.[25] The crackle of gunfire could be heard all day, as men fired off weapons to salute the passing train and signal others down the road it was coming.[26]

It was a spectacular ride along the water's edge, which local railroad guidebooks described in rich detail.[27] These were some of the most sublime landscapes North America had to offer, as so many painters had already discovered. All morning, Lincoln beheld a Hudson River School of his own, as the train sped through one gorgeous landscape after another. "Huge piles of ice" were floating down the river, in "all sorts of fantastic shapes," almost like ghost ships sailing alongside the Special. As he looked out over the wide river, he could see skaters frolicking on the ice, where it was frozen close to the shore. Every few miles, the train would pass through another village, and he would stand on the back platform, so the people could see him, silhouetted against the snow.[28]

A few miles south of Troy, the Special entered Columbia County, familiar to Lincoln as the home of a great chieftain. At Stuyvesant (10:36 a.m.), a road led a short distance to the tranquil village of Kinderhook, one of hundreds of inland communities where the old Dutch accents could still be heard.[29] There the eighth president of the United States, Martin Van Buren still breathed, dispatching letters to old colleagues, trying to make sense of the confusing new reality.

Lincoln and Van Buren had a great deal of shared history, most of it on opposite sides of the Whig-Democratic divide that dominated the early part of Lincoln's career. Their paths crossed memorably in 1842, when the former president was traveling in Illinois, desperately trying to build support for another run, and mud forced him to retire for the night in the small town of Rochester. To entertain Van Buren, a call went out to find the funniest storyteller in the area, and Lincoln was summoned. They swapped anecdotes until midnight, and Lincoln kept his guests "convulsed in laughter." Van Buren finally asked his guests to leave, because his sides were sore from laughing. He wrote later that he never "spent so agreeable a night in my life."[30]

The next stop was Hudson (10:56 a.m.), a whaling center, despite its distance from the ocean.[31] Nearby, the painter Frederic Church, a stalwart of the Hudson River School, was working on a large painting, *The Icebergs*, that bore some resemblance to Lincoln's travel experience on this day. The painter had

Frederic Church, *The Icebergs*, 1861[32]

spent much of his career exploring exotic southern locales in the Andes, but in early 1861 he too seemed to feel an energy coming from the north.

The sun was beginning to peek through, and the towns came in quick succession.[33] Next came Rhinebeck (12:00), where Lincoln could see more skaters.[34] Fifteen miles to the south, the Special passed through the small village of Hyde Park, where a local gentleman of means, James Roosevelt, had done well by investing in railroads, including the one Lincoln was riding along. His son Franklin would later take his own trains to the White House from this location.[35]

The Special reached Poughkeepsie at 12:25. An "immense throng" came out to hear Lincoln. The crowd, "mainly ladies," took a strong interest in Lincoln's son Tad, who refused to exhibit himself before the hordes. Instead, he preferred to lie concealed beneath a window of the Special, which, of course, increased their frenzy that he show himself. He would not. Instead, his father stood up and let the crowds take him in. Lincoln was disarmingly honest, saying that his main purpose in standing before them was "seeing you and being seen by you."

Here the Special changed locomotives, from the *Union* to the *Constitution*, and Lincoln paused in his remarks to admire the trains, draped with flags.[36]

George Armstrong Custer, class of 1861, U.S. Military Academy[37]

WEST POINT

After a brief stop at Fishkill (1:08), the Special snaked farther south along the Hudson, bending with the river.[38] Across the river, at Newburgh, the flag was flying from George Washington's old headquarters.[39] From his window, Lincoln could see a dramatic landscape, with the river narrowing between steep elevations on both sides. At Cold Spring, the Special slowed for another curve. Here Lincoln might have heard a sound described in the guidebooks of the time, the "deep breathing" of nearby furnaces, and the "sullen, monotonous pulsations of trip hammers," as a guidebook put it— emanating from the West Point Foundry, an important ironworks close to the station, where armaments and locomotives were forged.[40]

Appropriately, these furnaces of war lay just below the parapets of West Point, on the opposite side of the Hudson. There the cadets were already quarrelsome, as Northerners and Southerners began to self-separate. Even as the national anthem was played, there was audible hissing from the

Southern side.⁴¹ Dutifully, the academy continued to train all of its young men, despite the conundrum that they were about to go to war with each other. There would be two classes of 1861, because the army, in its haste to get officers into the field, rushed out a second class.⁴²

Peekskill, 1851⁴³

A few more bends brought the speeding train to Peekskill, where the delegation pulled in at 1:41 and departed at 1:44.⁴⁴ Those three minutes were never forgotten by those who were there. The *New York Herald* provided details: a local politician indulged in all the grandiloquent gestures of his time, stretching his arms out and gesticulating, as if to give a great Ciceronian oration. The crowd laughed at him, then booed. "Time's up! Scat! Git on!" The more they shouted ("We want to hear Lincoln, we don't want you!"), the more he "extended his arms oratorically," as if frozen in panic, a statue in the wrong place. The crowd was beginning to get abusive ("Get down!"), and the speaker "blushed and stammered," when Lincoln finally stood up and satisfied them with a quick, graceful message of thanks. He could not stop laughing at the other speaker, whose arms were still gesticulating frantically as he tried to finish, with the train's whistle signaling its impatience.⁴⁵ Everywhere the old idols were tumbling before the western wind.

South of Peekskill, the Hudson opened magnificently, becoming so wide that the Dutch had called it a sea: the *Tappan Zee*. As the Special continued to head south, Lincoln passed by a forbidding structure at the water's edge. He went onto the back platform of the train so that he could be seen by a large group of men, standing alongside the tracks, all wearing the same uniform, horizontally striped.

From *Ballou's Pictorial Drawing-Room Companion*, November 1855[46]

These were the inmates of Sing Sing, one of the prisons that had attracted Alexis de Tocqueville and Gustave de Beaumont when they came to the United States in 1831 to study penal reform. One of Sing Sing's innovations was a rigidly enforced silence—so that as Lincoln passed slowly through them, they looked at one another without saying a word.[47]

After this silent communion, Lincoln returned to the car. Soon they were at Tarrytown, where Washington Irving had made his home. (He claimed the town was named for the tendency of local men to tarry at the village tavern on market days.) His stories such as "Rip Van Winkle" had tapped into a profitable nostalgia for the preindustrial past, a nostalgia that may have been deepened by the fact that his house was too close to the tracks. He described the railroad sounds as "unearthly yells and howls and screams indulged in for a mile on a stretch and destructive of the quiet of whole neighborhoods."[48] The Special did not tarry, but as it pulled nearer, it did add one unscheduled stop. Near Dobbs Ferry, the train went by an orphanage, and Lincoln ordered a quick stop so that the children could gather around the train and see him.

Company of Wide Awakes, with Elisha Otis, celebrating Lincoln's election, at the Otis Elevator Works, Yonkers, New York[49]

At Yonkers, the Special passed a factory where a new device was being manufactured that would forever change New York. It was a kind of railroad that went straight up into the sky—an early version was called the "Vertical Screw Railway." But eventually it would be called by a simpler name: the elevator. Its inventor was a former toymaker from Vermont, Elisha Otis, who had filed his patent only a few weeks earlier. Otis had been trying to improve railroad brakes when he began to look into the problem of carrying weight upward, along grooved metal tracks, with power supplied by a steam engine.[50] At first, his device was intended to help factories move heavy equipment from one floor to another, but he was beginning to understand that it could move people as well, and New York's skyline was already changing as a result. After Lincoln's election, a small company of Wide Awakes, including

Otis himself, had stood to be photographed, with the Hudson in the background and the train track just out of view.

Bridge into Manhattan, 1861[51]

SPUYTEN DUYVIL

The only obstacle remaining was Spuyten Duyvil Creek, a rivulet that marked the northern boundary of Manhattan. Its Dutch name ("spouting devil") referred to the strong currents that flowed here between the Harlem and Hudson Rivers, but it was not as infernal as its name. In 1853 a small, sturdy bridge was built to carry trains across, and from that moment, it was possible to board a train in New York City and take it to Chicago and beyond.[52]

The Special chugged across the bridge, and Lincoln was on the island of Manhattan. The terrain appeared unexceptional at the northern fringe: a few forested hills, sparsely populated, which the Special glided past, hugging the shore of the Hudson. But this was a deceptive calm. For as the train continued along the river, Lincoln could see an ever-growing profusion of people, cheering, jeering, and making all the sounds Manhattanites used to welcome an outsider. Walt Whitman, an ornithologist of sorts, specializing in the city's noises, called it a barbaric yawp.

Soon Lincoln was passing the remnants of Fort Washington, named after the great general, despite the fact that it was the site of one of his grimmer defeats. After that loss, four months after the Declaration of Independence, more than two thousand subdued American soldiers had been paraded through the streets of New York, where the people cheered wildly for the victorious British and jeered the losers. New Yorkers could be fickle.

But they had welcomed Washington back in 1789, when he assumed the presidency. So crowded were the streets that day that the people resembled "Heads standing as thick as Ears of corn before the Harvest."[53] Some of those ears of corn were still alive seventy-two years later, as Lincoln approached. They could remember a time, before Washington, when there was no presidency at all. Perhaps Washington and Lincoln were the bookends to a quaint tradition that had run its course?

The Special snorted its way through a hardworking neighborhood far uptown. At 156th Street, the tracks passed rudely over the front lawn of John James Audubon, the late naturalist. He had located his house here to

1865 lithograph of Minniesland, the home of John James Audubon, with a railroad passing[54]

contemplate the broad panoramas of the Hudson and the charm of birdsong, before the intrusion of the railroad brought a new kind of whistle into his life.[55]

At Sixtieth Street, the Special deviated from its view of the Hudson and began to charge into the city, plunging down Eleventh Avenue, through a sooty landscape of coal storage tanks, car shops, and engine houses.[56] As Lincoln drew closer, the noise grew more deafening. A guidebook warned its readers that "the great characteristic of New York is din and excitement."

But there were other ways that passengers could tell they were entering a great city. The next day's papers commented, with some embarrassment, on the olfactory assault that New York City presented to the president-elect. The *New York Herald* sniffed that "some portions of the city west of Broadway" were "not particularly remarkable for their beauty, elegance, or odor."[57] The *New York Sun* called it a "strange and dirty locality."[58] A reporter for the *New-York Tribune* wrote, almost as if seeing the neighborhood for the first time, "it is low, lumbery, muddy, piggy, tenement-housey, noisy; in short, nasty."[59]

It was unusual to see a president-elect coming through these gritty streets. This part of town was known for its "disorderly houses," a euphemism for a brothel, an institution spreading rapidly with the city's unchecked growth.[60] A guidebook from 1855 estimated that there were twenty-five thousand prostitutes. As a New Yorker of the time said, speaking of houses of ill repute, "It would be more difficult to say where they are not than where they are."[61]

In the final minutes of his ride, the president-elect still had a bit of grooming to do before his appearance on New York's big stage. Thanks to alert reporting, the scene was captured, although not revealed until decades later, when a journalist published a remembrance of these final seconds. There was a brief conference as Lincoln gathered with his advisers to go over what he would say in his remarks. Lincoln settled the matter with a brief declaration: "I haven't any speech ready," he said. "I shall have to say just what comes into my head at the time."[62]

Then there was a different kind of consultation, with his closest adviser. The train had stopped, and "through the windows, immense crowds could be seen." Their clamor was so loud that it "drowned the blowing off steam of the locomotive." In that anxious moment, Lincoln huddled with his wife. Mary Lincoln opened her handbag and said, "Abraham, I must fix you up a bit for these city folks." Lincoln lifted her upon the seat before him, so that she might brush his unruly hair and fix his off-kilter tie. He asked her, "Do I look nice now, Mother?" To which she responded, "Well, you'll do, Abraham." [63]

Suitably improved, Lincoln was ready to face the hordes.

Lincoln arriving in New York [64]

NEW YORK CITY

At the station, an enormous crowd was waiting. The depot covered most of a block, between Ninth and Tenth Avenues at Thirtieth Street.

The crowd erupted as the Special came into view. At three o'clock exactly, the train slowed for a final curve by the Archimedes Iron Works, before entering Tenth Avenue, its whistle shrieking and its bell ringing as if to prove that it belonged in this very loud place, where guns were firing in welcome.[65] Finally, it turned east at Thirty-Second Street and slowly pulled into the Hudson Railroad terminus. When it entered the depot, the crowd surged, nearly beyond the ability of the huge police force to restrain it.[66]

New York's artists and engravers were out in force at the station, and they did their best to capture the jostle.[67] One of them was a twenty-year-old Thomas Nast, rapidly sketching his impressions as he saw Lincoln for the first time. His drawings revealed a beard that had grown in fully and a cartoonist who thrilled in the pleasure of drawing it.[68]

Thomas Nast, first sketches of Lincoln [69]

Even by New York standards, this was a huge crowd—the biggest most commentators had ever seen.[70] The artists did their best to depict all the people there. Their drawings captured New Yorkers of all stripes, black and white, male and female, young and old, straining for a peek at the tall man just getting into a handsome barouche pulled by six black horses, to begin his motorless motorcade. All around him, men doffed their hats and cheered, and street urchins gamboled freely, just out of reach of the authorities. A few people were knocked down as the crowd careened wildly.[71]

As soon as Lincoln left his private car, the crowds swarmed through it, asking where he had been seated. Uncertain, they sat everywhere they could, so that they could later brag that they had sat in the president-elect's chair.

Having survived his arrival, Lincoln was now ready to see a bit of the city. He was already familiar with New York, which had done so much to lift his presidential hopes a year earlier. It was not merely the Cooper Union address that catapulted him into national prominence. All year long, the tiny iron fingers of New York's printing establishments kept up a frantic pace, distributing rustic images of the Rail-Splitter from this very urban place.[72]

Hudson River Railroad Station (1902)[73]

Charles Dickens was amazed at how many handbills he saw with Lincoln's portrait as he walked New York's streets around the time of the election. Now the people could gaze upon the original.[74]

But there were still many snares in Lincoln's path. Once again, he had almost no protection as he exposed himself to the crowds lining the street. It was a formidable place, even for a hardy Westerner. When Davy Crockett came to New York, the famous frontier fighter had a rare attack of nerves, admitting, "I would rather risk myself in an Indian fight than venture among these creatures after night."[75]

New York was indisputably Northern, but the South was very close. The newspapers were always reporting the arrival of ships coming in from Charleston, Savannah, Mobile, and New Orleans, and careful harbor watchers believed that slave ships were still sailing from this free port on a regular basis.[76] In a harbor fluttering with flags on this festive day, Southern vessels refused to fly Old Glory. One captain hanged Lincoln in effigy from a yardarm.[77]

Nor could he expect many favors from local political leaders. Lincoln had only won 35 percent of New York City's voters, and the mayor was conspicuously absent during his arrival ceremony.[78] Fernando Wood had spent much of the previous year touting his friendship with Southerners—he had been mentioned as a possible running mate for Jefferson Davis earlier in the year.[79] A month before Lincoln's arrival, Wood publicly threatened that New York might declare itself a "Free City" and continue to do business with all sides, as if nothing had changed.[80] A little too openly, he revealed his utter self-absorption, arguing that if the country fell apart, "it behooves every distinct community as well as every individual to take care of themselves." To Lincoln, that was a recipe for no country at all.[81]

Southern sympathies were especially keen among business elites.[82] From their rolltop desks, they wrote notes of encouragement to the new president of the Confederacy and schemed about the commercial arrangements that would follow its launch.[83] These were old, comfortable relationships. New York vessels had been carrying Southern cotton around the world since before the Revolution.[84] When Southern planters needed credit, New York banks were happy to offer loans, which gave them a vested interest in slavery's success.[85] Creditors often became slave owners themselves, for they routinely stepped in to manage Southern plantations when a slave owner died intestate or allowed his debts to grow too large. Corporate ownership offered investors a way to maximize profits, while avoiding individual responsibility. Selling arms to slave owners was another way to deepen the relationship.[86] A rare Southerner who supported Lincoln wrote that New York was "virtually an annex of the South."[87]

Before Lincoln's election, it was uncertain which way New York would go. In late October the Secretary of the Treasury, Howell Cobb, had visited New York with the hope of bringing the city into the new country he and Jefferson Davis were planning.[88] In their private communications, Southern leaders thought that they could recruit between five and ten thousand New Yorkers to their cause.[89] Mayor Wood had even sent a delegation to Montgomery to witness the inaugural of Davis a day earlier.[90] It was fair to wonder which side he was on.

The way that markets had responded to Lincoln also worried his supporters. After he was elected, panicky rumors spread up and down Wall Street that the Republicans were radicals who wanted to punish the wealthy.[91] Many business leaders blamed Lincoln for the fact that Southern states were seceding. Throughout December and January, they were signing petitions, leading delegations to Washington, and demanding compromise with "our Southern brethren," in language nearly treasonous. One insider called the city "a seething caldron."[92]

But Lincoln knew that most New Yorkers did not want to see the country fall apart. There were an astonishing number of them. On the same day that he arrived, so did hundreds of others, carried by ships from Germany, England, Cuba, Colombia, and China. They never stopped coming. New York's population in 1860 was 813,669, and Brooklyn (266,661) was not even counted in that figure. More than half came from other countries.[93] In the twelve months since Lincoln's last visit, New York had added another 15,000 or so—more than his hometown of Springfield (population 9,360) or Montgomery (8,843). The new capital of the Confederacy did not rank among the hundred largest communities in the United States, the country it had just left.[94]

New York's preeminence was not obvious at the dawn of the republic, when it was smaller than Philadelphia and, in many ways, less sophisticated. No sidewalks were installed until 1790, and Benjamin Franklin joked that New Yorkers seemed unsure of themselves on Philadelphia's impeccable pavement, slipping and sliding like parrots on a mahogany table.[95]

But the Empire City had come up quickly, thanks to pluck, enterprise, and the spectacular gift of its location. Centuries earlier, the indigenous Lenape had called Manhattan "the moneymaking island," among other names, because the harbor's seashell beds were perfect for the manufacture of wampum.[96] After Europeans arrived, they too found it convenient for

moneymaking. A maritime economy naturally flourished on this perfect island, where fresh and salt water mingled, the harbor channels were deep, and
Long Island offered protection against the wrath of the Atlantic Ocean. It
almost had not turned out that way: in 1800 a new sandbar nearly closed off
the harbor, a development that would have changed the map of American
history forever. But the bar faded away, like so many of New York's rivals.[97]

Before the ink was dry on the documents ending the American Revolution, Manhattan merchants were sending ships around the world. The
Empress of China left New York on Washington's Birthday in 1784 and
a half year later became the first American vessel to trade with the Chi-
nese. They called these New Yorkers "New People." As ships grew faster,
the Atlantic seemed to shrink, especially after the first steamship crossed
from England in 1838. New York was closer to London than its rival cities to the South; and it also forged a faster connection to the West. After
the Erie Canal was finished, a New Yorker boasted that the city had become "so enriched that she may call Ohio her kitchen-garden, Michigan
her pastures, and Indiana, Illinois, and Iowa her harvest fields." The trains
brought those fields that much closer.[98]

If geography gave precious advantages to the city, its entrepreneurs
were quick to improve upon them, leveraging their position through new financial instruments, rapid communications, and a concentration of capital
in the investment houses of Lower Manhattan. Greek temples to the gods of
finance were thrown up and torn down with sufficient regularity that New
York was described as "a city of modern ruins."[99]

One of the prettier ones, the Custom House, stood on the site
of Washington's inauguration. A voluminous global commerce came
through its Doric columns, so much that this one building was able to
supply approximately two-thirds of the revenues of the United States
through duties on imports.[100] It also made the Custom House a well-
known center of graft, a far cry from the idealism that radiated from its
austere Greek lines.[101]

Lincoln would have his work cut out defending democracy in a place where corruption was rampant and poverty was deepening. As he knew from his visit a year earlier, there were hundreds of homeless children wandering the streets, at the same time that millionaires were proliferating. (An 1860 survey found 115.)[102]

But even with these blemishes, New York always offered a tantalizing vision of the future. In 1861 the city was beginning to aspire upward, with ever-taller buildings made of iron and glass, and foundations sunk deep into the Manhattan schist. Even higher, airships were exploring in New York's airspace; throughout the summer of 1860, a steam-powered balloon, the *City of New York*, circled above its namesake, dazzling earthbound mortals.

Despite the efforts of its mayor to secede, the Empire City was essential to any future of the United States. Lincoln sometimes called New York "the

City of New York[103]

front door," his phrase for the public face that America presented to the rest of the world. Standing in front of the door, he was ready to knock.[104]

Lincoln's parade (*New-York Illustrated News*, March, 2, 1861)

THE PARADE

Lincoln's parade was a glorious chaos from the start.[105] One observer wrote, "Such a crowd as greeted his arrival I have never seen. A distance of probably six miles, on the route from the Depot to the Hotel, the streets were positively jammed with human beings, of all sizes, sexes, and colors."[106]

The *New York Herald* noted that Lincoln's parade route, down Ninth Avenue, was in a neighborhood that "seldom" received dignitaries. Whether consciously or not, Lincoln had chosen the perfect way to enter this vainglorious city. To the people around the station, his arrival was a "godsend." They swarmed around the neighboring streets, which, the *Herald* observed, "are as clean as they usually are," and cheered madly from windows and rooftops.

Once again, the simple fact of Lincoln's physiognomy affected them. The *Tribune* wrote, "A glimpse of his plain, straightforward, honest face, so full of deep earnest honest thought . . . so won the multitude that they burst into such spontaneous, irrepressible cheers as gladdened the heart and moistened the eye." Just to see him built confidence in "the coming man" and raised hopes that he would deal with the "almost civil war now raging in the land."[107]

At Twenty-Third Street, the procession turned east toward Madison Square. At the corner of Twenty-Third Street and Fifth Avenue, a young woman named Lavinia Goodell, the daughter of an Ohio abolitionist, watched breathlessly from a balcony. "All the city was alive," she wrote to her sister, using all of his nicknames:

"I have seen 'Abe'—'Old Abe'—'Honest Old Abe' &c - &c !!!" . . .

Lincoln was riding hatless, and she found him "much better looking than is represented." She noticed his "long nose," adding that he was "thin, energetic looking, smiling and pleasant, frank and open." He looks young, she thought to herself, before concluding, "Altogether I was quite favorably struck with him, and feel deeply interested in his welfare."[108]

A few minutes later, two blocks to the south, a twelve-year-old boy saw him pass by fleetingly. For Augustus Saint-Gaudens, the impression was seared forever into his consciousness as he saw "the figure of a tall and very dark man" bowing to the crowds. Many years later, he would create one of the great Lincoln sculptures, based on this memory of a few seconds.[109]

Some noticed the sadness inside him, though, and were troubled by it. A preacher, Dr. S. Irenaeus Prime, remembered later that Lincoln seemed "weary, sad, feeble, and faint" during the parade—and not at all like "the man for the hour."[110] George William Curtis noticed, "He looked at the people with a weary, melancholy air, as if he felt already the heavy burden of his duty."[111]

But most were swept up in the day's excitement. The procession continued down Fifth Avenue toward Union Square, where another throng was waiting. Inside the presidential party, John Nicolay looked out and beheld "a continuous fringe of humanity" crowding "the side streets, doors, balconies, windows" and "even the roofs of buildings" in their desperation to get "a clear view of the president-elect."[112] It would have been natural to pause in a place named after the Union, but there were appointments ahead, so the parade turned onto New York's busiest street.

"Broadway on a Rainy Day," stereograph, 1859[113]

BROADWAY

From Union Square, they found Broadway and continued southward. A contemporary called the busy street "a perfect kaleidoscope."[114] The traffic never stopped—one person actually counted how many vehicles went by in an hour (1,200).[115] It was loud, too, thanks to a constant "omnibus thunder" that resembled Niagara's roar.[116] After cobblestones were introduced, Edgar Allan Poe complained that it would be impossible to invent "a more ingenious contrivance for driving men mad through sheer noise."[117]

More than any other street in the city, Broadway conveyed New York's flash. Even its layout showed swagger, defying the grid as it cut a broad diagonal swath through Manhattan. Already, New York's planners were trying to plan ways for new railroads to soar in the air, above Broadway's busy pedestrians, and to run underground as well.[118]

As Lincoln came down Broadway, block by block, everyone seemed to be talking at once. The street's merchants were already expert in devising catchy slogans and there were banners everywhere.[119] Some were wordy ("Fear Not, Abraham, I Am Thy Shield and Thy Exceeding Great Reward"), others got to the point with a more telegraphic efficiency ("Right

Makes Might").[120] A publishing house, Putnam's, edited its banner down to the bare essentials: "Welcome, Lincoln." In another location, a longer sign read, "Abraham Lincoln, President of the United States," but the *P* had faded, so it said *resident* instead.[121]

Farther downtown, another wordsmith was busy getting into position. The lawyer George Templeton Strong walked uptown from his office to meet the parade but noted that Broadway was crowded and became impassable above Canal Street. He got close to the parade as Lincoln crossed Houston Street and soon had material for his diary entry of the day: "The great rail-splitter's face was visible to me for an instant, and seemed a keen, clear, honest face, not so ugly as his portraits."[122] That was reassuring, but Strong also confided his fear that there was an "even" chance that assassins would try to take Lincoln's life before he could be inaugurated.[123]

At the northeast corner of Broome and Broadway, Lincoln might have noticed an unusual architectural specimen. The E. V. Haughwout Building held a store that offered expensive china, cut glass, and other fine goods. It was made of cast iron, like many of the new buildings on lower Broadway, and boasted the first elevator to be installed in a commercial building, with power supplied from a steam engine in the basement.[124] It was thrilling to visitors and a sign of life to come in a city that had nowhere to go but up.[125]

From here, it was a short distance to Lincoln's final destination: the Astor House, a hotel where he would stay two nights. After a long, clamorous ride through the dusty streets of New York, he must have been gratified by the serenity it seemed to offer, as he beheld yet another Greek temple, ready to take in a weary traveler.

PARALLAX

But in front of the Astor House, it was not serene at all, as Lincoln had to navigate another huge crush of traffic. A crowd had been waiting for

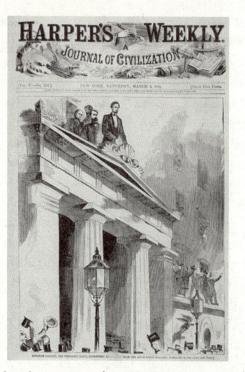

Lincoln at the Astor House (*Harper's Weekly*, March 2, 1861)

hours, amusing itself by watching a dog escape the attempts of the police to catch it, and shouting "He's coming!" even when Lincoln was nowhere to be seen.[126]

Finally, he came into range, although the crowd had now grown so large that it nearly prevented Lincoln's arrival. The *New York Herald* described it as "a jam from which egress was absolutely impossible." Some women fainted in place; acrobatic young men clambered up trees and lampposts to escape the crush.[127]

Even before he entered the hotel, two people were watching him closely, from different vantage points. It is possible to re-create this unusual parallax from their detailed notes afterward. Inside the Astor House, from a third-floor window, Kate Warne stared intently at the man whose life she had come to New York to save. She had traveled all night from Baltimore to warn

Lincoln of a plot against his life and had been waiting for him since four in the morning.[128] She described her first impression in a report she made to Allan Pinkerton: "Lincoln looked very pale and fatigued."[129] An image of the president-elect speaking from the Astor House portico reveals the faint outline of a female face watching over him from the window behind him. Could this be his protectress?

Across the throng, Lincoln was being scrutinized just as carefully by a curious-looking man seated in a horse-drawn omnibus, stuck in traffic. His graying beard made him look older than his age, forty-one.

Walt Whitman had been waiting for Lincoln for a long time. A former reporter, he was a keen observer, and as Lincoln made his way through the crowd, he had plenty of time to watch, thanks to the gridlock caused by the arrival. He was a bit stalled himself, having delivered a stunning work of poetry in 1855, which he then followed with a few "quicksand years," trying to keep afloat.[130] He had recently released a third edition of his poems, but

Detail from the previous image, revealing an observer in the window

he was restless, waiting for the next great chapter of his life to begin. On this day it would, as yet another bystander was swept up in the backdraft of Lincoln's journey.

To a degree, they knew each other already. After his election, Lincoln had begun to appear in Whitman's dreams.[131] There is a charming story, difficult to verify, that Lincoln knew Whitman, too. According to the memoir of a former clerk, Lincoln's law partner, William Herndon, brought *Leaves of Grass* to his attention in Springfield. After bringing it home, Lincoln returned the book the next day, joking that he "had barely saved it from being purified in fire by the women." Yet there were telltale signs that it had registered. "Every blade of grass is a study," Lincoln said to a group of Wisconsin farmers in 1859, constituting "a world of study within itself."[132]

Whitman's likely location, near the men climbing trees; detail from *New York Illustrated News*, March 2, 1861

Eighteen years later, in a lecture, Whitman remembered the scene as it unfolded, second by second. All in all, it could not have lasted longer than a minute. "I shall not easily forget the first time I ever saw Abraham Lincoln," he began. Suddenly he was back there, waiting in the crowd as the black carriages drew up to the Astor House:

A "tall figure" appeared from one of the carriages, but instead of acting officiously, he paused "leisurely on the sidewalk" and "look'd up at the granite walls and looming architecture of the grand old hotel." Whitman was instantly captivated, especially after the tall figure indulged in "a relieving stretch of arms and legs" before turning around, for more than a minute, "to slowly and good-humoredly scan the appearance of the vast and silent crowds."

Whitman brought a forensic attention to the next few seconds:

> From the top of an omnibus (driven up on side, close by, and blocked by the curbstone and the crowds), I had, I say, a capital view of it all and especially of Mr. Lincoln: his looks and gait; his perfect composure and coolness; his unusual and uncouth height; his dress of complete black, stovepipe hat pushed back on his head; dark-brown complexion; seamed and wrinkled yet canny-looking face; black, bushy head of hair; disproportionately long neck; and his hands held behind, as he stood observing the people. He look'd with curiosity upon that immense sea of faces, and the sea of faces return'd the look with similar curiosity. In both there was a dash of comedy, almost farce, such as Shakespeare puts in his blackest tragedies.[133]

As soon as Lincoln descended from his carriage, Whitman felt a vivid danger in the air. The newspaper accounts were more upbeat, but Whitman remembered "a sulky, unbroken silence," ominous to those who were accustomed to "the usual demonstrations of New York in wild, tumultuous hurrahs." Years later, he still felt the peril that enveloped Lincoln during his arrival:

There was much anxiety in certain quarters. Cautious persons had fear'd that there would be some outbreak, some mark'd indignity or insult to the president-elect on his passage though the city, for he possess'd no personal popularity in New York, and not much political. . . . The crowd that hemmed around consisted, I should think, of thirty to forty thousand men, not a single one his personal friend, while, I have no doubt (so frenzied were the ferments of the time) many an assassin's knife and pistol lurked in hip- or breast-pocket there—ready, soon as break and riot came.

For a few seconds, the tension continued, but then Lincoln performed another stretch, almost as if he were doing his calisthenics in full view of Manhattan:

"The tall figure gave another relieving stretch or two of arms and legs; then, with moderate pace, and accompanied by a few unknown-looking persons, ascended the portico steps of the Astor House, disappeared through its broad entrance—and the dumb-show ended." [134]

For the rest of his life, Whitman was entranced by the most unusual politician he had ever seen.

Astor House, 1899[135]

ASTOR HOUSE

It was more difficult for Lincoln to enter the hotel than Whitman's account suggested. The *New York Times* called the crowd "impenetrable," but with some help from the police, he found another little path.[136]

As he made his way through the door, Whitman's reverie ended, and New York resumed its frantic pace. The Astor House had far too much self-regard to allow poets to loiter in its busy lobby. Though it mimicked an ancient architectural form, it was a citadel of modernity, known for its well-appointed rooms.[137] An English traveler praised it as the "Niagara" of hotels.[138] That may have alluded to the most spectacular feature of the Astor House: its advanced plumbing, including flush toilets and bathtubs. These miniature Niagaras, one for each room, were made possible by a steam engine in the basement, which pumped the water, stored in a tank on the roof, throughout the building. The hotel also could offer climate control by circulating gusts of hot and cold air as needed.[139] Years later, the novelist Henry James recalled its "vast dark warm interiors." His older brother, William James, was born there.[140]

Lincoln had stayed in the hotel a year earlier when preparing to give his speech at Cooper Union. On that occasion, he struck his hosts as profoundly awkward, especially in contrast to the urbane whirl of the Astor House. According to his escort committee, "He felt uneasy in his clothes and a strange place. His form and manner were indeed odd, and we thought him the most unprepossessing man we had ever met."[141]

But from that visit, Lincoln's presidency had taken shape. Each time he walked through the columned portico of the Astor House, his destiny became clearer. As he knew very well, it was the political headquarters of Thurlow Weed, the kingpin. If these walls could talk, they would have much to say about the secret political history that had brought him this far. One especially critical decision had been made here, on December 21, 1859. When Republican bosses decided to let Chicago host the 1860 convention, they gave Lincoln a vital advantage over the front-runner, William H. Seward.[142]

Two months later, the Astor House rewarded him again, when his hosts took him a short distance up Broadway to the photographer Mathew Brady's studio, where they adjusted his clothes and hair to capture a suitably presidential likeness ready for mass distribution.[143] Much of his campaign had been run out of the Astor House by a "Sub-National Committee" that met regularly here throughout the fall of 1860, to distribute publicity and sort through the mysteries of how to pay the bills.[144] It was no wonder that the newspapers reported that he felt more "at home" in this hotel than any other.[145]

In other ways, too, the Astor House served the needs of a would-be president trying to reach the people. Close by was Printing House Square, where Lincoln could find the densest media cluster in the country. After eight days of hard travel, he had found his way to the white-hot center of an information economy that had its eye squarely on him. All wires led here; in fact, the plan to lay a submarine telegraph cable across the Atlantic had been hatched inside the Astor House.[146]

After making it through the crowd, Lincoln was quickly escorted to a four-room suite on the second floor, including rooms that Zachary Taylor and Franklin Pierce had once stayed in.[147] A *Times* reporter was able to peek in, and saw "the elect" sitting with a pile of dispatches, freshly delivered, and lozenges for his throat.[148]

Lincoln had not yet spoken to New York, so he clambered out a window on the second floor, and stepped onto a balcony to say a few words to the crowd still massed outside. From that elevation, just above the portico and pediment, he could have looked out over much of the city and seen what Whitman called "strangely oriental, V-shaped Manhattan."[149]

In essence, it was a speech about not speaking, another graceful offering from a president-elect who had become skilled at knowing how much to feed a voracious media and how much to hold back.

Astor House Rotunda, 1901[150]

A LADY SEATED AT A TABLE

As soon as his short speech was finished, Lincoln went back inside and braved his way to a reception, so crowded that guests "emerged like pressed figs." [151] A well-known boxer, nearly as tall as Lincoln, was among those waiting in line to shake hands. "There's Tom Hyer," someone said. Lincoln responded, "I don't care so long as he don't hit me," to uproarious laughter.[152] A lavish dinner followed in room 43. Over the mantel, there was a large print of Washington crossing the Delaware, reminding all that more rivers lay ahead.[153]

Outside, there was an intense scrum in the hotel's corridors, as office seekers sought out the presidential presence.[154] At 8:20, Lincoln went downstairs to a large room, where he gave another speech. In his remarks he confessed that he had often refrained from speaking because he didn't quite know what to say. That candor hit the mark, and the crowd applauded roundly. Then, another long round of handshaking. A reporter praised him: "It is a real shake, without any shame about it." [155]

As night settled upon Manhattan, the lights continued to blaze on Broadway and inside the hotel's well-appointed rooms. It had been another long day, and Lincoln had made his most dramatic thrust southward since the long trip began. He was now only 225 miles from Washington.

But before the day could end, one more set of meetings was required. They were sobering. Kate Warne, the spy working for Allan Pinkerton, had been waiting since four in the morning to present her findings to Lincoln's advisers. Late in the evening, she was finally given her chance. Every day had brought more conclusive information about the plot to kill Lincoln in Baltimore. Pinkerton had written out his alarm in a letter to Norman Judd and given it to Warne to transmit. She waited throughout the day for Judd to arrive—he had missed the morning departure from Albany. Finally, he came to her room in the evening, in response to her urgent note. He wrote later, "I followed the servant to one of the upper rooms of the hotel, where, upon entering, I found a lady seated at a table with some papers before her."

Those papers laid out the assassination plot in detail. Judd read them while smoking a cigar and realized immediately that he had underestimated the seriousness of the plot. He had kept Pinkerton's earlier messages to himself, to "avoid causing any anxiety on the part of Mr. Lincoln." But the news kept getting worse. Pinkerton now believed that a huge conspiracy existed, including hundreds or perhaps thousands ready to assassinate Lincoln. They hoped to trick him, by asking him to speak. Then, in this moment of democratic vulnerability, they would surround him and kill him.[156]

Now Judd realized that it was urgent to tell Lincoln everything. They were soon joined by Edward Sanford, an executive with deep knowledge of the rail and telegraph networks. They talked until late. Finally, after they left, a telegram was delivered to Warne's room, from Pinkerton in Baltimore. As if sensing their stupefaction, he wrote, "Tell Judd I meant all I said, and that today they offer ten for one, and twenty for two," an allusion to the betting odds against Lincoln's life in the gambling dens of Baltimore.[157] She summoned Judd one last time, who returned to take in this new taunt.

Judd may also have known that in Washington, Winfield Scott was leading an inquiry of his own, deploying undercover agents, with help from New York's superintendent of police, John Kennedy. They were rapidly coming to the same conclusion as Pinkerton.[158] All vectors were now converging. If Lincoln was told about the new threats that evening, he would have gone to bed with yet another heavy burden. But he simply could not falter, especially here in New York, with so many reporters watching his every step.

Fancy Ball scene (*Frank Leslie's Illustrated Newspaper*, March 9, 1861)

MILLIONAIRES

The next morning, February 20, crowds were milling around the Astor House, buzzing with excitement. But it was still difficult to know how to read this easily distracted city. The morning *Times* touted a "Fancy Ball" that would be held the next day, with guests dressing in interpretive outfits that parodied the national crisis. It would prove to be a grotesque affair, featuring freakish animal costumes that proclaimed no allegiance to any cause. Other New Yorkers were marketing new products around the national crisis, while doing precious little to avert it. It was hardly reassuring to read about a fattened forty-pound "Lincoln Turkey," enjoying his last days on earth in P. T. Barnum's museum. Barnum claimed that the bird would be eaten by his namesake on the day of the inauguration, in the feeding frenzy that followed the ceremony. But first, they would both have to get there.[159]

At 8:30, Lincoln left the hotel to attend a breakfast with leading financiers from Wall Street.[160] This was uncharted territory; he was not entirely comfortable discussing his economic plans, and it showed. His small talk, usually effortless, was leaden. An observer commented that nobody was "at his ease, and Mr. Lincoln the least of all." A different guest reported that "Lincoln made a bad impression." He may have been put off when his hosts began to brag about being millionaires. Lincoln floated an awkward attempt to claim that he too was a millionaire, because of his vote tally. It fell flat.[161]

City Hall, 1855[162]

CITY HALL

At eleven in the morning, Lincoln walked out of the Astor House for his next meeting, with Mayor Fernando Wood, in City Hall. It was just across a small park that had served as a kind of common ground for centuries, celebrating democracy's triumphs and failures.[163] A decade earlier, after the passage of the Fugitive Slave Act in 1850, the first former slave captured by federal marshals, James Hamlet, had been brought here in chains, to the shock of New Yorkers.

Mayor Wood received Lincoln in a ceremonial chamber that included George Washington's desk and a prominent statue of the first president.[164] Wood had campaigned against Lincoln throughout the fall, arguing that the election of "a broomstick" would be preferable to the man now standing before him. Since the election, he had looked the other way as weapons were sent to the South, and sent friendly "commissions" to the seceded states to arrange for their new relations.[165]

But his charisma was beginning to wear thin, especially after he secretly married a sixteen-year-old girl on Christmas. Although that fact was not widely known, Wood's public positions were increasingly delusional, including his hopes for an unaffiliated "Republic of New York."[166] During their meeting, Wood delivered a short speech asserting the importance of New York's commercial interests and came close to demanding that Lincoln give in.

The president-elect listened patiently to the self-absorbed politician before him, resplendent in his double-breasted frock coat. Lincoln had seen his type before. The papers noted that he had "a dreamy expression of the eye" while Wood was speaking. Then he smiled and gave a short, polite speech, adding this jab: "There is nothing that can ever bring me willingly to consent to the destruction of this Union, under which not only the commercial city of New York, but the whole country has acquired its greatness."[167] Something had happened in those few seconds; an eyewitness believed that it was another turning point, with Lincoln signaling his contempt for the selfish types who had run the country for so long.[168]

The speech was followed by the usual reception, including the unavoidable receiving line. As soon as the door opened, the crowd rushed in so fast that a reporter compared it to "tapping a new barrel of ale." Girding himself, Lincoln chose to stand next to the Washington statue and went to work.[169] Over the next two hours, he shook 2,000 hands and bowed 2,600 times.[170] His small talk was back in form. When told, somewhat pompously, "The flag of the country is looking at you," Lincoln quipped, "I hope it will not lose any of its eyes."[171] When a visitor from Canada shook his hand, he said, "I suppose I must shake hands with representatives of foreign nations." Then, to a gentleman from South Carolina, he said the same thing, sardonically.[172]

After the reception was finished, Lincoln climbed into a carriage for the quick ride back to the Astor House. Norman Judd rode with him, which suggests that they were discussing the information of the night before. During the ride, the crowd tried desperately to peer into the carriage and

Hannibal Hamlin [173]

"almost clogged the wheels" so that it could not go forward. After it got free, the *Times* wrote that people ran after it, "pell-mell like a flock of sheep."[174]

At 4:30, Hannibal Hamlin arrived on the New Haven Railroad.[175] Lincoln's running mate had been on a railroad journey of his own, covering much shorter distances in New England but greeting crowds nearly as rapturous. One in New Haven nearly pulled him off his train with their desperate handshaking; he replied that he wished he were Briareus, a minor Greek deity with a hundred arms, so that he had more to give them.[176]

The reunion of Hamlin and Lincoln sent reassuring signals around the nation, that the administration was beginning to cohere. They enjoyed a relaxed dinner that evening, including a New York delicacy: oysters on the half shell. According to Hamlin, Lincoln stared at the oysters on his plate "with a half-doubting, half-smiling look and said, as if he had never eaten

Assassination scene, from 1860 score of *A Masked Ball*[177]

such a dish before, "Well, I don't know that I can manage these things, but I guess I can learn."[178]

A NIGHT AT THE OPERA

The oysters were less dangerous than they looked, but other threats lurked nearby. Hamlin was aware of rumors that Lincoln was in danger, according to stories he told his son. Less than a day after Kate Warne's warnings about the Baltimore plot, Lincoln had to attend an opera about an assassination. In fact, the opera manager had taken out a large ad in the *New York Times*, boasting that the president-elect would be in attendance.[179]

Nine days earlier, on February 11, New York had witnessed the American premiere of a new work by Giuseppe Verdi, *Un ballo in Maschera*, or *A Masked Ball*. It was a politically charged work, describing the murder of a leader who is killed while attending a musical performance—based loosely on the slaying of King Gustav III of Sweden, killed during an opera in 1792. It was censored by Italian authorities as Verdi was writing it, not only because it treated the volatile topic of assassination but also because three Italians had tried to kill Napoléon III of France in 1858. Verdi responded by altering the names of characters and the title, then, implausibly, setting the scene in colonial Massachusetts.

Despite these dizzying plot twists, New Yorkers loved the opera.[180] When Lincoln went in, the atmosphere was electric. He entered with Mary after the performance had begun. A reporter spoke for many when he wrote, "We all glared at Lincoln, we mentally devoured him." When he came in, "one thousand opera glasses turned in one direction."[181]

But even if the audience members were dazzled by Lincoln's celebrity, they were ready to pounce on any lapse. As he entered the Academy of Music, he committed another fashion blunder. Instead of wearing white gloves, he wore black—the only man in the crowded theater to do so. A Southerner remarked scornfully, "I think we ought to send some flowers over the way to the Undertaker of the Union." To anyone who knew him, the idea of covering Lincoln's huge hands with gloves seemed absurd.

Andrew Carnegie noted that he once saw Lincoln holding up two "white-gloved hands," which looked like "two legs of mutton." But the faux pas had been noted and duly registered.[182]

Fortunately, there were others, more tolerant, in the audience, and the Lincolns were enthusiastically applauded during the performance. A rousing version of "The Star-Spangled Banner" was performed as well.[183] One columnist was amazed at his height—"we saw seven feet of president"—but added that Lincoln looked "calm and self-possessed," and "he gave one the idea of power, stern, rugged, and uncompromising, but still there was in the smile something gentle."[184] Another, writing in the *Herald*, wrote, "He seems tremendously rough, and tremendously honest and earnest."[185]

This roughness could work for him or against him, depending on the audience. To some, his rusticated airs and awkward body language argued against his presidency even before it began. The diarist George Templeton Strong likened him to a "yahoo" or "gorilla," while a visiting Frenchman, a cousin of Napoléon III, was repelled by his "large, hairy hands" and thought he resembled a boot maker.[186] Henry Ward Beecher, the Brooklyn minister, was an ally, but even he wrote, "It would be difficult for a man to be born lower than he was. He is an unshapely man. He is a man that bears evidence of not having been educated in schools or in circles of refinement."[187] One hotel guest did not mince words: in his opinion, Lincoln was "making an ass of himself." It was "disgusting, and exceedingly humiliating . . . that we have become so degenerate, as to forward an obscure ignoramus like the president-elect—to the highest position in the known world."[188]

Lincoln had long experience with these kinds of slurs, and he endured his mistake with the gloves. But the themes of *A Masqued Ball* struck uncomfortably close to home. Lincoln had been asked if he wanted to wear a mask to this performance, to shield himself from the crowd's scrutiny. He declined, answering, "The papers say I wear a mask already."[189]

Later that evening, twenty-two members of the German Quartette Club, from Hoboken, New Jersey, managed to penetrate the presidential suite at the Astor House, and they began to serenade the Lincolns, loudly, right outside the door to their room. After some time, Mary Todd Lincoln opened the door to listen politely. When asked about her husband, she replied that he had gone to bed early because of "excessive weariness." The singers finally departed, and at that precise moment, when sleep might have finally descended, a forty-piece band began to play outside the Astor House, accompanied by 150 Wide Awakes, the young men marching in Northern cities, resplendent in caps and capes. Finally, Hannibal Hamlin was roused to say a few words, and the Wide Awakes left contented, having lived up to their name by waking up most of the hotel.[190]

Around the country, many others were awake, too, fearing what would come next. Even among his friends, there were murmurs of unhappiness. A day earlier, Charles Francis Adams Jr. arrived in Washington, where he found his family members "blue as indigo." William Seward, Lincoln's ally, was upset that Lincoln was talking too much, "saying whatever came into his head," during a trip of "peripatetic oratory." As Adams noted, Seward felt that "the whole game" was in his hands ten days earlier; but he now felt that Lincoln had somehow taken it from him.[191]

Elsewhere in Washington, the lamps were burning late, as Southerners and Northerners tried to find new openings. They were quickly vanishing, as the stark reality set in of two governments, up and running, implacably hostile. In Montgomery, the Confederate Congress passed bills authorizing the creation of an executive branch, with Departments of State, Justice, Treasury, Navy, and War, just like those in Washington.[192] Most Southerners were exuberant, but in South Carolina, the diarist Mary Chesnut grew despondent. Presciently, she wondered, "What now? . . . We have risked all, and we must play our best, for the stake is life or death."

For Lincoln, the stakes were similar as he drew closer to the capital. The next morning, the presidential party would be leaving early to cross the Hudson and continue on toward Philadelphia. It would be another hard slog, nearly to the Mason-Dixon Line. But his whirlwind visit to Manhattan had improved his standing. Less than forty-eight hours after he arrived, he was departing a city far more solidly in the Union than when he arrived. Even *with* New York in the Union, he would have plenty of problems. But without it, he stood no chance at all.

As he prepared to push into the South, Lincoln knew how difficult the next few days would be. The warnings were coming more frequently, with more details each time. But he had made it this far, trusting his instincts.

Years later, when he published his memoir, Horace Greeley recounted a story about rivers that Lincoln told during his tumultuous passage through New York. At a time when everyone he met was asking him if there was to be a war, Lincoln reached into his vast repertoire and told an anecdote about traveling through a country that had been flooded by rain, creating an endless succession of swollen rivers to cross. One of them, Fox River, was rumored to be larger and more dangerous than all the others, and the travelers panicked just thinking about it. Finally, they found a Methodist preacher, who reassured them, "I know all about Fox River. I have crossed it often and understand it well, but I have one fixed rule with regard to Fox River: I never cross it till I reach it." [193]

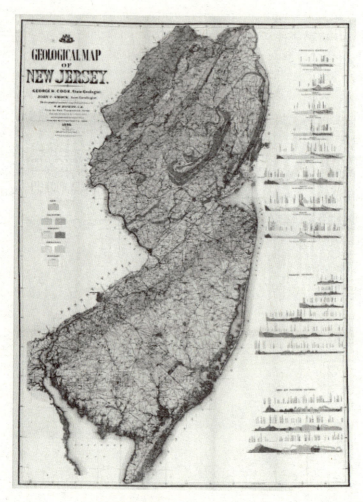

Geological Map of New Jersey (1868)[1]

12

THE GARDEN

With that, the noble hero crossed the threshold.

—Homer, *The Odyssey*, book 13, line 65[2]

NEW YORK, NEW JERSEY, AND PHILADELPHIA
FEBRUARY 21, 1861

ROOM 41

Lincoln had tarried in New York nearly two days—a long time for a president-elect racing against time. Every hour deepened the established fact of the Confederacy, now three days old and seemingly unassailable in its distant capital, more than a thousand miles away. There Jefferson Davis was free to act presidentially, issuing a never-ending stream of commands, telling everyone their place in his universe.

In room 41 of the Astor House, Lincoln wielded little authority except the power to keep going. Despite all the noise of the night before, he rose early, as always, and readied himself for the next stage of the journey. At this hour of the day, an army of commuters was already streaming into Manhattan's workplaces. Lincoln would sail against the human tide, taking a ferry to Jersey City, where he would find a train waiting. Today's Special would carry him to the west for a few deceptive miles before bending toward the south, and his true destination.

His goal today was Philadelphia, where the national experiment had begun in 1776. He was closing in on George Washington now. Lincoln had been talking about his predecessor since the trip began, but in recent days, Washington seemed to be listening. His image was everywhere Lincoln looked. When it came time to shake all of New York's hands, Lincoln positioned himself next to Washington's statue.[3] In his suite at the Astor House, over the mantel, there was a print of *Washington Crossing the Delaware* hanging over him.[4]

The painting was the work of a German immigrant, Emanuel Leutze, conscious that Germany had failed in its own attempt at democracy in 1848.[5] Lincoln often spoke about what America's example meant to the world; here was living proof. (Ironically, the original painting was destroyed when American bombers flattened the German museum where it was held, in 1942.) Near the end of his life, Henry James recalled the powerful impact of encountering the painting as a small boy, in the years before Lincoln's election. He marveled at the sense of purpose that Washington radiated, standing up "in such difficulties, and successfully balancing."[6]

Lincoln, too, would cross the Delaware today, albeit with both feet planted comfortably on the floor of his train car. Crossing rivers was turning into something of a specialty for the presidential party. After getting across the

Emanuel Leutze, *Washington Crossing the Delaware,* 1851 (Metropolitan Museum of Art)

Hudson, he would pick up Washington's trail and head toward Trenton. The general had come through New Jersey often: traveling at a stately pace on his way to his own inauguration in 1789, and a bit more quickly when fleeing the British during his ignominious escape from New York in 1776.

If all went well, Lincoln would arrive in Philadelphia just in time to celebrate Washington's Birthday the next morning, with a flag raising at Independence Hall. That backdrop offered the perfect chance to say something meaningful about the republic, in its holiest sanctuary. If Lincoln could not stop the Confederacy from growing, he could still fight back in his own way, by reminding Americans where they came from.

To the naked eye, his winding journey had not been very direct, especially in the early going, as he trailed between state capitals, going hundreds of miles out of the way. But now his strides were surer. A friend of Lincoln's had once described him as "giraffe-like" as he loped toward the lectern to make a speech.[7] It was not just the length of his legs or his awkward posture; it was the deceptive way in which he could suddenly go very fast toward a destination after a slow, spavined start. His rise from obscurity to the nomination had followed a similar logic. Suddenly he was bearing down upon the capital, whether it was ready for him or not.

But that meant the danger was increasing as well, and his friends felt a rising anxiety. Horace Greeley believed that "substantial cash rewards" had been offered to anyone who would kill the president-elect, and predicted that the only way he could make it to Washington was "disguised like a fugitive felon or spy."[8] In Trenton, where Lincoln would be in a few hours, "villainous posters" had been seen around town, calling for demonstrations against him.[9]

Despite these distractions, Lincoln needed to concentrate. To speak in Independence Hall would require serious thought about the American Revolution and the meandering course of the country since then. Throughout the journey, creaky veterans of the war had been propped up for a handshake, a bit of political theater that still held currency in a country that was obsessed by the drama of its founding. But Lincoln would need more than that. Reflexive patriotism was not enough; he needed to find his way into the heart of the story and retrieve the moral arc that made it so compelling.

Only two years earlier, Lincoln had described his education as "defective" in a questionnaire.[10] But few Americans had read about American history with more purpose. He had begun to disenthrall himself with his long walks to find books, most of which described long pilgrimages or journeys into American history. Now these themes were merging, as he drove toward the beginning.

Every mile seemed to bring Lincoln closer to George Washington. But there was also something in Washington's Olympian detachment that kept his chasers at bay. In a chapter of *Moby-Dick* titled "The Spirit Spout," Herman Melville described an apparition, a "silvery jet," far off in the distance, that the whalers of the *Pequod* could never quite catch up to. "Lit up by the moon," Melville wrote, "it looked celestial; seemed some plumed and glittering god uprising from the sea."

That is roughly how Washington appeared to New Yorkers in 1789, ready to become the country's first president. As he crossed the Hudson,

Southworth and Hawes, *Young Girl with Portrait of George Washington*, circa 1850[11]

he seemed to rise out of the water, a god, mid-apotheosis, with actual por-
poises leaping before the prow of his boat. A New Jersey congressman,
Elias Boudinot, accompanied Washington across the Hudson, and wrote
to his wife of the armada of small craft that came close to their boat, offering "shouts of Joy" as he approached. They made so much noise that sea
creatures rose out of the water to "know what was the Cause of this Joy." [12]

It was unlikely any sea creatures would throw themselves at Lincoln on
this day, although he had been exposed to quite a few of the bottom-feeders
who trolled the murkier depths of New York's politics. Even as he was preparing to leave the Astor House, the office seekers and lobbyists were in
their favorite place—the lobby—waiting for him to pass through.

At eight sharp, Lincoln and his entourage appeared there to make their
good-byes. An Episcopalian minister, George C. Shepard, saw him and gave
an unvarnished opinion. "He is no great beauty," Shepard recorded for posterity, but he added a note that Lincoln was "not so bad looking as they
say." [13] Every vote counted.

Outside the hotel, newsboys were hawking the news. Most of it was depressing. With hostilities imminent, Congress had tried to find some emergency funding to prop up the tiny American military, but that had led to a
bitter backlash from Southern members, and Virginians were threatening to
secede if it passed. Another bill, to build new sloops for the navy, was likely
to be vetoed by James Buchanan, still president of the United States. If a divided Congress took even the mildest steps to assert its authority, it elicited
howls of outrage from Southern sympathizers.

Meanwhile, from Alabama, Jefferson Davis fulminated against the
North, threatening mayhem to any who dared challenge his authority. In
Charleston, federal troops braced themselves for the attack they knew was
coming. [14] Many noted a feeling of rising violence in the air. On the same
day that Lincoln was waking up in the Astor House, Henry David Thoreau
wrote a long entry in his journal about the instinct to kill, so universal that
he observed it in a small kitten. [15]

From the Astor House, it was a short distance to the foot of Cortlandt
Street, which housed the slips for the New Jersey ferries. At the pier, he was

obliged to wait a few minutes; the ferry was late. During the brief interval, Lincoln could surely see all the ships flying the Stars and Stripes in his honor. Doubtless, he also saw the Southern vessels, which refused to.

The ferry landing was a well-tread place where thousands of commuters alighted every morning. It would remain important to New Yorkers even as the maps changed and developers poured landfill here, reclaiming every inch of the river that they could. A busy underground train station would later be built, and towering structures above. In fact, Lincoln was waiting for his ferry on the exact site where the World Trade Center would later stand.[16]

Near Bedloe's Island, July 18, 1860[17]

FERRY CROSSING

Soon a handsome side-wheel steamboat arrived, the *John P. Jackson*, ready to ferry Lincoln to the other side.[18] New Jersey's elected officials had crammed themselves onto the *Jackson* and now began to all speak at once. From the moment his carriage was wheeled onto the boat, the "high dignitaries of Jersey," as the *Times* called them, began to warble their song of welcome.

Fortunately, the passage across the Hudson was brief, thanks to the *Jackson's* churning side-wheel.[19]

Throughout the train trip, Lincoln had imagined himself to be sailing on the ship of state, as if his land barge was somehow waterborne. At long last, he was, as the *Jackson* freed her lines and began to head into a gentle western wind.[20] The Hudson was a mile wide as it emptied into one of the great natural harbors of the world, in the place that Henry James would call "the Beautiful Gate."[21]

Beyond lay the blue Atlantic. Lincoln's quick river eye would have grasped the powerful tidal currents where the Hudson met the harbor, but there were strong currents of history as well. These were the waters that Washington had glided over, thrilling the sea creatures. But the waters separating two states could also be treacherous. New York and New Jersey had often clashed over their boundaries and the rules of commerce in the early years of the republic.[22] Those differences had subsided, but they still flared up from time to time, in the same harbor where so many immigrants were arriving every day with the highest hopes for democracy.

A large steamship, the *Kangaroo*, was coming in at this very moment, bringing in a new load of 108 immigrants from Liverpool.[23] Its passengers were heading toward an old sandstone fort that jutted out from lower Manhattan, not far from where Lincoln boarded. It had been built to repel invaders, but now welcomed them, as the country's first immigration facility. The so-called Castle Garden was neither a castle nor a garden; its name was merely a rebranding effort for a versatile structure that already served many roles, including as a venue for outdoor concerts. A different kind of music could now be heard there, as families speaking in hundreds of languages came through. Yiddish speakers would later invent a new word—a *kesselgarten*—to describe a loud, chaotic situation.[24] At almost exactly the same place where the Hudson flowed out into the Atlantic, so forcefully that it carved a deep submarine canyon stretching hundreds of miles, a river of humanity was flowing in.

The ferry took a long route so that Lincoln could see a bit of the harbor.

To the south, there were a few shapes rising out of the river. Some were islands; others, shoals, rising above the waterline only at low tide and particularly dangerous to passing boats, as Lincoln would have known. All were adjacent to New York's legendary oyster beds, so richly endowed that New York claimed to hold half of the world's oyster population. In fact, the two nearest islands had been called Great Oyster and Little Oyster, among many other names, earlier in their history.[25]

With time, the identity of these indistinct places would become clearer. The more northern one, renamed Ellis Island, would serve as the great entry station for more than twelve million immigrants entering the United States between 1892 and 1954.[26] The southern island, Great Oyster, would become Bedloe's, then Liberty Island, the foundation for the statue of *Liberty Enlightening the World*, a gift from France to the United States, as a gesture of respect from one republic to another.[27] This was the nearest Lincoln would approach to either island, barely noticeable in 1861. But his transit past them was relevant, for the words he was searching for that day would help a better country come into existence; one that would be proud of this great harbor, bravely open to the world.

Nineteenth-century stereograph, Castle Garden Immigrant Depot[28]

THE JERSEYS

By the time Lincoln's party made it to the other side, a raucous reception was already under way. At Jersey City, the ferry docked in a dazzling new rail-and-ferry terminal, where twenty thousand people had already gathered. As the ferry approached, the crowd experienced "a prolonged popular patriotic spasm." John Hay, tongue in cheek, called it "the most picturesque" crowd yet.[29] To the New York press, these "primitive Jerseymen" seemed like "an entirely distinct species." Men, women, and children were out of control as Lincoln came near: "pushing, crushing, yelling, hooting."[30] The *Times* reported that "it was like being in a hydraulic press, or going through a rolling-mill, or being run over by the cars, or pinched between the ferry-boat and the bridge, or suffering *hara kari.*"[31]

So great was the pressure that Lincoln could not, at first, reach his train. He improvised a few droll remarks, but conditions remained chaotic. Mickey Free, a pint-sized Irishman, four feet tall, jumped out of the crowd to grab Lincoln's hand, but was clubbed by a policeman, "to the amusement of the crowd."[32] After much shoving, the presidential party reached the train, but it was a close call. The local police, confused, actually impeded their efforts, blocking Lincoln and his friends with their batons and letting just about anyone else pass through toward the cars.

Finally, the presidential party boarded the train and began the journey across New Jersey, with a "terrific whoop" from the Iron Horse and a speed that startled the local cattle grazing near the right of way. The Special was festive today, sporting a red, white, and blue smokestack with a "Union" on either side and a "1776" in front. That seemed appropriate as Lincoln resumed his pursuit of George Washington.[33]

Like many commuters before and since, Lincoln settled in as the Special began to race across the terrain that separated New York and Philadelphia, a great natural in-between that seemed built for rapid transit.[34] A month earlier, the diarist George Templeton Strong had come through these marshy meadows—not yet Meadowlands—and disdained them as a "primeval chaotic bog."[35] But the flat land was well suited to railroads, and *primeval* was the right word to describe a region that had seen the movement of peoples, back and forth, as far back as history remembered. Tens of thousands of years earlier, glaciers had glided across, leaving furrows in the earth as a signature of their early commute.[36] Indigenous peoples developed elaborate pathways across these same furrows as they shuttled back and forth between the Atlantic, the Hudson, and the Delaware.[37] When Europeans began to settle here in the seventeenth century, they too built paths, often on top of the older ones.[38] Countless American families, including Lincoln's ancestors, had come across these trails in their migrations to the West.[39]

But it took some time before New Jersey's identity was fully established. In the early years, it was occasionally lumped into a greater New York; the Dutch aired out their idea of a New Netherland that went all the way from the Connecticut River (or as they called it, the *Versche*) to the Delaware (the *Zuydt*).[40] New Englanders, too, cast their eyes longingly at this attractive land—many would settle in northern New Jersey towns and build puritanical villages that would not have been out of place in Connecticut. Farther south, closer to Philadelphia, small settlements of Swedes, Finns, Walloons, and Flemings gave it the feeling of a hodgepodge. New Jersey was a bit of a New Everything.

That feeling continued with the passage of time, as both Southerners and Northerners settled in a place they called "the Garden of North America."[41] The Garden was big enough for all of them, although it was divided by a long diagonal line in 1676, separating "East Jersey" from "West Jersey."[42] Together they were often called the Jerseys, as if this were an unruly family instead of a single place.

But the division was temporary, and New Jersey grew into a happy equipoise. A great portion of the state drooped toward Delaware and Maryland, some of it even lower than the Mason-Dixon Line. To the north, New Jersey was a very different place, more urban, yet tugged both east and west by the two largest cities in the country. Local wits called it "a cask tapped at both ends."[43] It could be startlingly progressive—New Jersey granted women the right to vote with its first constitution of 1776.[44] Yet it could also resist change stubbornly, as Lincoln knew firsthand.

Despite the inconsistencies, New Jersey had carved out an increasingly central role for itself as it joined all of these places to one another. It was critically important in the American Revolution and then again in the early years of the new government, especially as the capital moved from New York to Philadelphia. If the huge country had any center at all, it was somewhere in here, between the first two cities.

Accordingly, new roads began to sprout around the state, and the travel time shrank between New York and Philadelphia, from three days in the middle of the eighteenth century, to the half-day trip Lincoln was making today.[45] Trains were a key to the transformation, and New Jerseyites built new lines everywhere they could, including brand-new places (Atlantic City) that they invented simply because the train could deliver vacationers there.[46] Paterson grew into a major hub of locomotive manufacturing, and the Garden State became a fertile seedbed of innovation.[47] For an inventor such as Thomas Edison, always working near the railroad, it would prove to be the perfect place to bring new products to market, a Garden of Earthly Delights. Because of its lenient tax codes, New Jersey also became, in the words of one historian, a "green pasture for foaling corporations."[48]

A year earlier, the Garden State had been a challenge for Lincoln as he pondered his difficult road to victory. New Jersey delegates played an important role in Lincoln's nomination and helped him move past Seward; the state's habitual dislike of New York had been helpful to him.[49] But it was also a more Southern state, and strongly Democratic.[50] Lincoln failed to carry it in November, when Stephen Douglas won the popular vote. (He and Lincoln split the electoral vote.)[51] New Jersey's Democratic newspapers were thrilled that their state had resisted the Northern tide and what they called the "fatal black vomit" of Lincoln's Republicanism. Predictably, Republicans looked askance at New Jersey's stubbornness; the New York Times dismissed New Jersey as "the South Carolina of the North."[52]

As in New York, some local voices had flirted with secession in the aftermath of Lincoln's victory.[53] They were defeated, but there was an older longing to work with the South that went back far in New Jersey's history. After the Revolution, New Jersey had nearly become the national capital, when the newly united states were trying to fix an acceptable midpoint. (Trenton was a candidate for this honor and became the seat of Congress briefly, in 1783.) Princeton University's nearness to the South had always made it a favorite among the sons of the planter elite, and it would serve as a springboard for a Southerner's presidential ambitions when Woodrow Wilson left to become the governor of New Jersey.

New Jersey could feel Southern in other ways as well. Dueling was tolerated; just north of Lincoln's landing spot, a sitting vice president, Aaron Burr, had murdered Alexander Hamilton in 1804.[54] Slavery had been more entrenched in New Jersey than in most Northern states, and had not entirely disappeared. Laws restricting slavery had been dutifully passed, but forms of long-term servitude for African-Americans endured, and the 1860 census revealed pockets still in existence. Only five years before Lincoln's arrival, in February 1856, an elderly African-American woman was sold as a "slave for life" in New Jersey, despite the fact that slavery had nominally been eliminated. She was born in 1789, the year the presidency began, and despite a great deal of well-intended verbiage since then, her status was essentially unchanged.[55]

As the presidential party went deeper into New Jersey, they were delighted to find huge crowds everywhere they went. Hay would write later that night, "The journey through New Jersey today was unexpectedly brilliant." After a quick ride from Jersey City, Lincoln reached Newark at nine thirty. An open carriage with four white horses was ready to parade him before a crowd estimated at seventy-five thousand.[56] They were full of "wild, crazy excitement"—the *Times* wrote that they "swarmed like bees, who seemed touched with electricity, and who must have had throats lined with brass."[57] But again, there was a hint of danger as the swarm came too close to the president-elect. The *Times* added, "The Jersey police were utterly incapable of protecting the president from the pressure of the crowd." [58]

At 10:17, they were back on the Special, greeting large crowds in Elizabeth (15,000), Rahway (7,000), and New Brunswick (5,000). Lincoln spoke sparingly but effectively. Writing in the *New York Times*, Joseph Howard Jr. suggested that Lincoln's vocal inflections were unusually compelling: "There certainly is a peculiar charm about the voice of Mr. Lincoln, which fascinates the hearer, and constitutes one of the elements which go to the forming of a character so almost universally popular." [59]

At Princeton, the train slowed down just long enough for him to hear a few college songs before resuming his progress south. Despite their harmonies, Princeton students were more deeply divided over the war than any other college in the North. Many students would soon leave for the South, to join the Confederacy; by one account, as many as two hundred left their bucolic campus to join the Lost Cause. Before leaving, one of them, a young Marylander, inscribed a photograph to a classmate on the other side, "Your true friend and enemy." [60]

New Jersey State House, ca. 1846[61]

TRENTON

At 11:50, the Special pulled into Trenton, New Jersey's capital since 1790.[62] Since then, this city at the falls of the Delaware had grown as both an administrative center and a place of industry. Crossing the Delaware was a daily fact of life: ferries performed the task at first, but in 1839 a bridge was built, sturdy enough to carry railroads, allowing through trains to go all the way from Jersey City to Philadelphia.[63] Not long after that triumph, Trenton became known for its bridge-building prowess. In 1848 John Roebling moved his cable-spinning factory here from Pennsylvania, and over the next century, many of the most magnificent spans in the country would be built from elements forged at the Roebling plant.[64]

New Jersey's legislature was housed in an attractive structure that, like most of them, did its best to project the grandeur of Greece. That grandeur had been elusive in Trenton's early years; to save money, the first version of the state capital used stucco painted to resemble granite.[65] But if Lincoln was looking for George Washington, Trenton was a good place to find him. No state saw more revolutionary battles fought than New Jersey, and it was in Trenton that the tide had turned when he crossed the Delaware in December 1776, in the scene captured so dramatically by the famous painting. Washington had secured an unexpected victory with his tactical action, surprising an encampment of Hessians, who surrendered.

But it was also something more than that, as Lincoln understood. It was a moral victory as well as a military victory. By taking action, Washington had altered the story of a war that was going badly and given his fellow Americans a new reason to believe in their country. The general had also taken care to treat his Hessian prisoners with humanity. Trenton had shown the world that a new kind of country was coming into existence, determined to earn a decent respect from the world for its ideals as well as its determination to defend itself. It was only *after* the victory that Congress sent out copies of the Declaration to the states.[66]

When Washington approached from the south, in 1789, during his inaugural journey, Trenton was a memorable stop. He came through a "triumphal arch" made of laurel and evergreen, supported by thirteen columns. A large artificial sunflower was placed near him, as if he were the sun. Other flowers were strewn in his path by a small army of "little girls, dressed in snow-white robes," and "long rows of young virgins," trilling a song to the new president as he passed through this surreal scene.[67]

Lincoln's approach from the north was less regal. Another large crowd had gathered, and inside, the legislators were not behaving well.[68] John Hay described the chaos and crowding inside the New Jersey State House, where "there was rather more tumult than would generally be considered consistent with the owl-like gravity of a legislative assembly." Hay gave the exact words these would-be owls screeched at one another: "Down in front!" and "Hats off!"[69] They were also passing inane resolutions: after Republicans proposed a bill asserting that Abraham Lincoln was "a man six foot four inches in height," Democrats responded with one declaring the official policy that "when this House shall have seen Abraham Lincoln, they will have seen the ugliest man in the country."[70]

Lincoln could appreciate a joke with the best of them. In hundreds of earlier appearances on the political stage, humor had been crucial to his rise, offsetting his awkwardness. But as he drew nearer to the presidency, a cloak of gravity descended over him. He paid no attention to the sophomoric high jinks of the legislators and the jokes that were flying around the chamber. He had come to Trenton with a higher purpose: to strengthen the sinews of Union. It was a request that carried the implicit demand for young men to fight, and presumably die, in order to make their country whole again.

The president-elect, dressed again in funereal black, seemed to understand the nature of sacrifice better than the others in the room. Something inside him was expanding on this day, as if anticipating Washington's Birthday. He had already given more than fifty speeches on his journey. In a few of them, he had misspoken. In a great many others, he had said very little. But on this day, Lincoln would soar.

Upon arrival, he gave two speeches in quick succession, first to the state senate; then, across the hall, to the assembly. Both chambers were overflowing. Lincoln might easily have spoken a few platitudes and been done with it. Instead, he found fresh words about the predicament they faced. Each speech said something genuinely new, as he reached to find meaningful words in a setting that mattered.

Before the senate, he began by addressing "Old New Jersey"—a nice phrasing. Lincoln naturally went into the story of George Washington, but as he vented his feelings, he spoke about himself as well and allowed more light to shine into the dark spaces of childhood than was the norm. He told the suddenly hushed room that in "the earliest days of being able to read," he had found "a small book": the famous biography of Washington by Mason Weems. At the dawn of his literacy, this book had registered deeply. He remembered all of the stories Weems told, but Washington's heroism "here at Trenton" stood out in particular:

"The crossing of the river; the contest with the Hessians; the great hardships endured at that time, all fixed themselves on my memory, more than any single revolutionary event, and you all know, for you have all been boys, how these early impressions last longer than any others. I recollect thinking then, boy even though I was, that there must have been something more than common that these men struggled for." [71]

The legislators remained rapt as Lincoln continued his surprisingly personal foray into his memories. An important thought was struggling to come out—it would emerge fully formed at Gettysburg. The cause of democracy mattered to *all* people on earth. Something *more than common* had united Americans when they threw off the yoke of British rule. Their yearning for self-determination had given courage to other peoples. A remarkable catalogue of rights had been woven into the country's founding document, suggesting that human beings were capable of governing themselves, humanely. Winning the war was important; but it was even more important that they had articulated "something that held out a great promise to all the people of the world to all time to come." [72] This "great promise" had made a difference. If the Confederacy succeeded in starting a new country, based on slavery, it would destroy the special hope that the world's millions had vested in America.

Lincoln then made a promise of his own: that the Union would be "perpetuated" in accordance with "the original idea" of the Revolution. In other words, he would *not* consent to its dismemberment, the way that so many were urging him to. He would *not* become the president of a half country, or even worse, a country with a half-baked understanding of its history. On the contrary, he would insist that the original idea be *remembered*. He would do all that he could to uphold the principles of republican self-government and the Declaration's thundering chorus of equality. Lyrically, he added, "I shall be most happy indeed if I shall be an humble instrument in the hands of the Almighty; and of this, his almost chosen people."[73] *Almost* chosen—a carefully chosen phrase, spoken by a craftsman who did little by accident.

Grant Wood, *Parson Weems' Fable* (1939)[74]

CABINET OF FORTITUDE

Where did this surge of inspiration come from? Who knows where any writer finds an inner reserve? Lincoln had gone quite a bit past Parson Weems, who was never a very reliable historian. To the parson's way of thinking, a story that was "enliven'd" was more likely to sell well, and profit was important to him. (He once wrote his publisher, "You have a great deal of money lying in the bones of old George, if you will but exert yourself to extract it.") Weems also "enliven'd" his own relationship to the story by claiming to be "formerly Rector of Mount-Vernon Parish"—no such parish existed.

But readers enjoyed the fairy tales that he spun, draping a mist of magical realism over American history. Cabbages miraculously grew in the Washington family garden, spelling out Washington's name as they floriated . . . Indian legends claimed that Washington could not be killed by a bullet because of his special destiny . . . Divine interventions routinely saved the day. During the account of the Delaware crossing, Weems described a supernatural deity, "the Genius of Liberty," hovering in the air near Washington and protecting him from harm. He often saw angels flying in the skies—in his imaginary universe, that is where the founders went after they died, transfigured into celestial beings, wearing "robes like morning clouds streaked with gold."[75]

Lincoln did not write like that; he would have been laughed out of Illinois if he did. But he understood the power of America's story, viscerally. He, too, saw angels—in two weeks, he would end his first inaugural address with a stirring meditation on "better angels," after receiving a note from William H. Seward that urged him to appeal to the "guardian angel of the nation."[76]

He may also have been thinking of another writer linked to Trenton. Lincoln had been reading Thomas Paine since he was a young man, impressed by the force of Paine's cantankerous faith in democracy.[77] Paine was not quite a founder, but pamphlets like *Common Sense* deeply

affected the American people as they girded themselves for war. One of
Paine's classic essays, his first issue of *The American Crisis,* had come out
just before Washington crossed the Delaware. In fact, Washington and his
troops read the pamphlet just before they crossed, according to lore.[78] In
that essay, Paine expressed ideas that tracked closely with the themes Lincoln was working out as he drew closer: that even a peace-loving people
may be forced to go to war to defend a principle . . . that the depths of
winter often call out these higher qualities . . . that "the spirit of the Jerseys" could be called upon in such a dark hour. Paine had written about
Washington: "There is a natural firmness in some minds which cannot
be unlocked by trifles, but which, when unlocked, discovers a cabinet of
fortitude."

As he prepared to cross the Delaware in his own way, Lincoln was dis-
covering his own cabinet of fortitude. His voice was ragged; he looked exhausted, but as he remembered the spirit of the Jerseys, something seemed
to bolster him.

THE FOOT COMES DOWN

Having delivered a stunning speech to the state senate, Lincoln crossed over
to the assembly and did it again. He began slowly, explaining his long strategy of silence over the previous year, and the need to gather information
while seeking "the best and safest ground." He swore "no malice toward any
section," using a word that he would repeat four long years later, in his second inaugural, when he promised "malice to none."[79] He insisted that he
loved peace as much as any man alive. But then came a simple gesture that
revealed how different he was from James Buchanan. It was a small gesture,
yet there was force in it.

As John Hay recounted, Lincoln was speaking quietly, with a voice as
"soft and sympathetic as a girl's." Still, it could be heard throughout the
entire chamber. Then, suddenly, after proclaiming his desire for reconcili-
ation, Lincoln said, "I fear we shall have to put the foot down firmly." He

spoke those words "with great deliberation, and with a subdued intensity of tone." Then, he acted them out, unforgettably, by lifting his foot up, then pressing it down, "with a quick, but not violent gesture, upon the floor."

The room exploded. As Hay wrote, "He evidently meant it. The hall rang long and loud with acclamations. It was some minutes before Mr. Lincoln was able to proceed." Then, when they grew quiet again, "he asked them to stand by him so long as he did right." With these words, Hay explained, Lincoln captured the room. There was something in his soft speech that transfixed these seasoned politicians. Hay elaborated, "There was a peculiar naivete in his manner and voice, which produced a strange effect upon the audience. It was hushed for a moment to silence which was like that of the dead. I have never seen an assemblage more thoroughly captivated and entranced by a speaker than were his listeners yesterday by the grim and stalwart Illinoisan."[80]

Others caught the electricity in Lincoln's voice as well. In the *New York Times*, Joseph Howard Jr. noted something similar to Hay's observation, and caught a feminine quality: "His voice was singularly melodious, having all the sympathetic winsomeness of a woman's combined with the nervous vigor of a man's."[81] It is curious to hear Lincoln's voice described that way; yet there was nothing indeterminate about the message to the South, as his foot came down.[82]

This was the clear statement everyone had been waiting for. Lincoln was crossing a Rubicon of his own, very near to where Washington had crossed the Delaware. Prior to Trenton, there had been some temporizing in Lincoln's remarks on the journey, suggesting that the crisis might go away. At Trenton, he did not say that. The entire country noticed and knew what lay ahead. He had found his footing, in every sense.

John Nicolay later reflected on this moment as a crucial turning point. Lincoln was growing each day, and that growth included his exposure to the people themselves, seething, restless, desperate to hear the words that would light the way forward. At Trenton, he found exactly the right tone.

Nicolay observed "the loud and continued cheering" that followed that moment and concluded that "he had struck the keynote of the popular will
of the North." [83] Another young man in Washington expressed the same
thought. With "one stamp of his foot," Henry Adams wrote, "the President
called the whole nation to arms." [84]

It was not merely what he offered, but also what he held back. Lincoln's
modesty appealed to listeners as much as his originality. After years of pos-
turing by leaders, this was a clarifying wind. A writer, Mary Livermore, later
recalled standing at the edge of "an effervescing crowd" during Lincoln's
trip, hoping that she might look upon "the rugged, homely face of our future President." His "simple, unaffected, but almost solemn words" thrilled
through his listeners.

She also offered, verbatim, the responses of others in the audience
as they shouted out their thoughts while Lincoln was speaking. "He
seems like an honest man! . . . He is probably not much of a statesman,
nor even a politician . . . but . . . he is honest and loyal. . . . There is no
spread-eagle nonsense about him—that is one consolation." An acute
listener, George Templeton Strong, had used the same words: "the absence of fine writing and spread-eagle-ism is a good sign." [85] The time
for flowery speeches had passed. Lincoln's homely turns of speech, his
soft voice, his black suit, and his melancholy air all pointed to a new
realism, long overdue after all the years of swollen, narcissistic oratory.
Mary Livermore concluded, "All were feeling their way to an anchorage
in him." [86]

But even at anchorage, the ship of state was in great danger, as he understood better than his audience. In the final lines of his speech to the assembly, Lincoln seemed to allude to the multiplying threats. He asked for their
help guiding the ship through a voyage "surrounded by perils," and added a
haunting final line: "If it should suffer attack now, there will be no pilot ever
needed for another voyage." [87]

After leaving the capital, with his keynote still ringing in the air; Lincoln
was accosted by another crowd. A witness wrote, he was "set upon as if by

a pack of good-natured bears, pawed, caressed, punched, jostled, crushed, cheered, and placed in imminent danger of leaving the chamber of the assembly in his shirtsleeves, and unceremoniously at that." He survived, and was escorted to a lunch described as a cold collation. (One legislator dismissed it as a "cold collision." [88]) Again, there were too many people. A nice detail, captured by Hay, described Lincoln walking through the kitchen, "where a number of men in paper caps, and smelling of burnt pie, saluted him gravely and made gestures with ladles." [89] But when they finally sat down to eat, a caterer's nightmare was unfolding. According to Hay, half the room had forks but no food; the other half had food but no forks. Eventually they worked it out.

Thomas Nast, "Country people" cheering Lincoln on the way to Philadelphia (*New-York Illustrated News*, March 9, 1861)

THE ROAD TO PHILADELPHIA [90]

Having done his duty, Lincoln returned to the Special. There were so many people that it required an effort simply to board the train, but he finally succeeded, and his party left Trenton at 2:30.[91] Trailing smoke and cinders, the Special eased onto the railroad bridge, and in his own way, Abraham Lincoln crossed the Delaware.

On the other side was Pennsylvania, a state Lincoln had visited twice already on this journey. As he pressed forward, there were thousands of men, women, and children lining the tracks. A remarkable image, drawn somewhere on "the road to Philadelphia," captured one of the most indelible impressions of the trip. The young sketch artist Thomas Nast had the inspired idea to look out the window as the Special sped through the landscape. His drawing, which appeared in the *New York Illustrated News*, revealed a scene that would have been very familiar to Lincoln after ten days on the road: A gaggle of Americans stood outside the window, waving to the train as it flashed by. Young and old, male and female, black and white; these were the almost chosen people, in all their glory.

The Special hugged the Delaware for most of its short journey, before it began to enter the northern suburbs of Philadelphia to the usual sounds of cannonry.[92] A little before four o'clock, the train stopped at Kensington. Lincoln dismounted and was escorted to an open carriage pulled by four white horses. Unfortunately, he had to spend the next half hour shivering there while his inept hosts tried to get people into the other carriages.[93]

Finally, the parade started. Despite snow, America's second largest city was determined to welcome Lincoln in style.[94] A crowd estimated at a hundred thousand turned out. They were packed so densely that some storefront windows were smashed as the procession passed. The usual chaos ensued when a salute of one hundred guns was discharged, startling the horses and more than a few people. (A high constable landed in the mud.[95]) It was only with the greatest difficulty that Lincoln's bodyguards were able to protect him from the "wild mass of human beings" who were constantly pressing up against him during the four-mile parade route.

Ironically, Lincoln's guards were so effective that they nearly prevented one young man from approaching with a desperately important message designed to save his life. George H. Burns was an assistant to Allan Pinkerton, who had asked him to get an urgent encoded note to Norman Judd. But Judd was seated next to Lincoln, and every time Burns came close, he was rebuffed. Finally, after a tremendous effort, he was able to get the note into Judd's hands as the parade passed the corner of Broad and Chestnut. That small act set in motion many others.[96]

At five o'clock, the delegation arrived at the Continental Hotel, where another large crowd had gathered to hear him.[97] From the balcony, the president-elect gave his third memorable speech of the day, explaining that Philadelphia was far from a random stop on a railroad timetable. For Lincoln, this was the most sacred shrine yet. Each of the state houses had been important; but Independence Hall was the place where the founders had signed the Declaration. Inside this building, the United States had come into existence.

As he began to speak, he sensed its nearness. In one of the more remarkable speeches of his journey, Lincoln went into a kind of rapture as he contemplated the building he would visit the next morning. He promised that he would bring "a sincere heart" to the great task that lay ahead—all evangelicals since the Great Awakening had understood "heart religion" to be preferable to "head religion."

Then he turned to the building itself, almost as if Independence Hall were alive. He promised that he would do nothing that was inconsistent with the teaching of its "holy and most sacred walls." Inside those walls, Lincoln imagined some living, breathing power; an oracle to be consulted, as if he could see the "Genius of Liberty" that he had read about, all those years ago, in the stories of the Revolution that thrilled him as a young reader. He asked the crowd to "listen to those breathings" and stated, "I have never asked anything that does not breathe from those walls."

Then, as if channeling a long-forgotten sermon heard on the Indiana frontier when he was a boy, Lincoln ended his brief remarks with a startling promise given in a very old language: "May my right hand forget its cunning and my tongue cleave to the roof of my mouth if ever I prove false to those teachings."[98] That was straight out of the King James Bible, and Psalm 137: "If I forget thee, O Jerusalem, let my right hand forget her cunning. If I do not remember thee, let my tongue cleave to the roof of my mouth." That Psalm described the Hebrew people's lament for a holy city that had been lost. It was not a great leap to think of Washington, D.C., the city that had nearly been lost over the Great Secession winter.[99]

There was still hope, if he could make it there safely. But as Lincoln was speaking, another messenger was speeding toward him on a desperate train journey of his own, to bring a new warning of the danger Lincoln faced in the final approach.

The interior of Independence Hall, from a nineteenth-century stereograph[100]

FIREWORKS

After another long receiving line, with huge crowds spilling out into the streets of Philadelphia, Lincoln was treated to a lavish fireworks display. It built in intensity, then culminated in an apparition that seemed like something out of the Book of Revelation. Next to a giant shield of red and blue, words written in silver fire appeared in the sky: "Welcome, Abraham Lincoln. The Whole Union."[101]

It was the exuberant finish to another long day. With three powerful speeches, Lincoln had sharpened his argument that democracy was worth the supreme effort needed to save it. For much of the day, he had been inside a train pulled by a locomotive with "1776" emblazoned on its smokestack. Now, at long last, he had made his way to Independence Hall. On the eve of Washington's Birthday, he had found the perfect setting to say something for the ages. The platform was already prepared: a stage had been built next to Independence Hall, where Lincoln was expected to speak at sunrise.

He might have retired for the night, confident that everything was ready for the next morning. It had been thirteen straight hours of grueling activity since he left the Astor House. But just after ten, his peace was disturbed by a series of visitors bearing the darkest news imaginable. The combined effect of these visitors upended all of his carefully laid plans for the rest of the journey, for they confirmed Kate Warne's warnings the night before that a well-organized plot had been organized to murder him during his passage through Baltimore. After eleven days of celebrating democracy in the most public way, Lincoln would now have to use subterfuge to make it through the final snares of his odyssey. That would compromise his message and expose him to bitter ridicule as he closed in on his destination. But the alternative was unthinkable.

The tension between two starkly different realities had been growing all day. In his speeches, he continued to paint mesmerizing word pictures about democracy. But ahead, the shadows were lengthening as more information came in about Baltimore. As Lincoln knew from Kate Warne, Allan Pinkerton had penetrated a determined network of killers. Simultaneously, a different group of detectives, working for the New York Metropolitan Police, had uncovered similar information. Their findings were beginning to circulate to the highest levels of the U.S. government—or what passed for it—in Washington. As Lincoln was coming into Philadelphia, these officials understood how urgent it was to warn him. But communicating the intelligence was no easy matter, because Lincoln was moving so quickly, and the crush of people around him made it difficult to get a message through.

A breakthrough came when Norman Judd received the encrypted message handed to him during the tumult of the parade. The note invited him to meet "J. H. Hutchinson" in a nearby hotel, the St. Louis. "Hutchinson" was an alias for Allan Pinkerton, who had come up from Baltimore to explain what he knew. Judd found his way there, and they began to speak at 6:45. Pinkerton had a sobering tale to tell.[102] Only moments after Lincoln described his faith in the founders, Pinkerton poured out new details of the plot to murder the president-elect in cold blood as he came through Baltimore. They were joined by Samuel Felton, the president of the Philadelphia, Wilmington and Baltimore Railroad, who had hired Pinkerton in the first place, after Dorothea Dix came to him with her first whisper of a conspiracy.

Judd now understood the scope of the threat and determined to arrange a meeting between Pinkerton and Lincoln. But that was easier said than done; there were hundreds of hands to shake, and fireworks to watch. When they finally ended at 10:15, the president-elect was brought through the crowded corridors of the hotel to Judd's room. Pinkerton recalled later that throughout this highly confidential meeting, a large crowd stood outside the hotel room, simply because Lincoln was inside.[103]

At last, Pinkerton and Lincoln were face-to-face, and the detective went through the details of the plot. The plan was for a mob to surround him after he pulled into Baltimore's Calvert Street Station and got into a carriage. There, in a vulnerable choke point, he would be stabbed or shot to death after a diversionary brawl was created nearby to draw the police. The police might even be in on it: Pinkerton had found evidence that they would offer little help as Lincoln came through the seething city. The prevailing feeling among the plotters was "This G-d d-d Lincoln shall never pass through there alive."[104]

The president-elect listened carefully, without dramatic emotion. But according to Pinkerton, a "shade of sadness" fell over his face as he heard this tawdry story, so antithetical to the democratic reverie he had just been crafting in his remarks.[105] "I could not believe there was a plot to murder me," Lincoln recalled a few years later to an interviewer.[106]

Baltimore had been worrying Lincoln's entourage since well before the trip started. Four years earlier, James Buchanan had been jostled during his own presidential progress through the city.[107] In recent weeks, a steady tide of new warnings had come in Lincoln's mail, in addition to Pinkerton's reports.[108]

Now there was a torrent of new questions. Every detail relating to the final thrust into Washington was critically important. As they talked, Pinkerton asked hard questions: for example, did Lincoln really know William Wood, his trip planner? He had to confess that he did not. In a sense, Lincoln's protectors had to guard Lincoln from himself, for his "confiding and innocent nature" was a danger to "the man upon whom the nation's destiny rested."[109]

Pinkerton strongly urged Lincoln to leave for Washington that very evening and foil the plotters. Norman Judd, however, counseled caution: to appear afraid would be catastrophic at a time when confidence was so tenuous. Lincoln reassured Judd that he was not afraid of embarrassment; he could take "anything that was necessary."[110] But he decided to reject Pinkerton's advice, and stay. He had important appearances to make the next morning in Philadelphia and then in Harrisburg. Still, he promised the detective that he would consider an alternative route to the capital after his public schedule was finished the next day. Pinkerton wrote, "I never saw him more cool, collected, and firm."[111]

Frederick Seward[112]

A LATE-NIGHT VISIT

With that unpleasant business settled, Lincoln went back to his room at about eleven. Now, at last, his exhausting day could end—or so he thought. But there he found *another* visitor, who had been sitting silently in the presidential suite, waiting. Frederick Seward was the thirty-year-old son of William Henry Seward, and at noon, he had been in the senate gallery of the Capitol when his father summoned him. The elder Seward had just been approached by Winfield Scott and his able officer, Charles P. Stone. Earlier in the day, Stone had learned of a similar plot from the operatives working for the New York police. Stone and Scott rushed the alarming news to Seward, the de facto leader of the incoming government until Lincoln's arrival.[113]

Seward quickly saw the danger and sent his son out of the Capitol, with urgent instructions: "I want you to go by the first train. Find Mr. Lincoln wherever he is." [114] The younger Seward carried a note written by Stone, scrawled so quickly that it had words crossed out. [115] He raced north through Baltimore and, when he got out at Philadelphia, went straight to Chestnut Street, "crowded with people, gay with lights, and echoing with music and cheering" from Lincoln's presence in the Continental Hotel. After finding Robert Lincoln at the head of the stairway in the lobby, the younger Lincoln escorted him directly to his father's bedroom. He sat there waiting for more than an hour, "in the quiet room that was in such contrast to the bustle outside." When Lincoln finally came in, Seward recognized him immediately from his portraits, but noticed that the images failed to capture "his pleasant, kindly smile" and the "careworn look" that had settled over his features. [116]

Presented with this new, disturbing information, Lincoln became a lawyer, and cross-examined Seward. It soon became clear that neither he nor his father knew anything of Allan Pinkerton, which proved to Lincoln that they had arrived at their conclusions independently and that they must therefore be true. Matters were quickly coming to a head. It is doubtful anyone within the presidential party slept much that night.

Pinkerton did not know of Frederick Seward's visit, but he was already a whirlwind of activity. All night long, he crisscrossed Philadelphia, waking up railroad and telegraph officials, to plan a secret route for Lincoln, to begin the next evening. [117] His work ended just before sunrise, when Lincoln's next public event was scheduled, at Independence Hall. [118] Through his relentless activity, Pinkerton had brought a measure of railway exactitude into what remained a very uncertain situation. But even still, a great deal was unknown, and could not be known, until the secret trip to Washington began.

In the capital, the situation remained volatile. Small signs were disturbing: in the War Department, a fire started inside the office of the secretary of war after a spark from a chimney blew in a window and landed on some papers on his desk. Tempers were rising after Georgians seized three New York vessels in Savannah. [119] At 11:30, a New York congressman, Charles Van Wyck, was walking home past the Capitol when he was brutally attacked and nearly killed by knife-wielding assailants. Although wounded, he survived, after shooting one of his assailants.[120] Earlier in the day, Van Wyck had given an incendiary speech against slavery.[121] It seemed like things were falling apart, even before Lincoln could get there.

As the day ended, Charles Francis Adams Sr. was still writing his doubts about Lincoln into his diary: "I confess I am gloomy about him. His beginning is inauspicious. It indicates the absence of the heroic qualities which he most needs."[122] Little did he know of the adversity Lincoln faced as they both retired.

The grueling trip was nearly over. The president-elect was less than two hundred miles from the capital, and expressing himself in new ways, as his breakthrough speeches kept proving. Tomorrow promised to be even better, as he prepared to address the nation about its founding principles. But after that, the dangers would cascade, as Lincoln's flurry of late-night visitors had warned. Was the Special carrying Lincoln to his destiny or his doom? With Washington's Birthday dawning, that remained an open question.

Lincoln at Independence Hall, February 22, 1861[1]

13

THE FOUNTAIN

He is more sensible than other humans,
And makes more sacrifices to the gods.

—Homer, *The Odyssey*, book 1, lines 67–68[2]

PHILADELPHIA TO HARRISBURG
FEBRUARY 22, 1861

DAYBREAK

The last day of the journey began early, in the darkness. The sun rose on schedule—6:44 a.m.—as did the president-elect, hours earlier.[3] Around the country, newspapers noted the beauty of the sunrise.[4] Lincoln may have wondered if he would ever see another.

The grim revelations of the night before made it clear that hundreds and perhaps thousands of men had stockpiled weapons and were ready to kill him as he came through Baltimore. Now he faced two terrible options: to ignore the threats would be suicidal, but to alter his well-laid plans and sneak into Washington was nearly as lethal, in a political sense. A rain of scorn would fall upon him at the worst possible moment. He wanted to enter the capital like a colossus, the people's champion. The new plan would have him skulking in like a bandit.

Still, the decision had been made. Almost no one in his party knew it yet, but Lincoln would deviate from course, following a Z-like zag in order to evade the death trap that had been set for him. Thanks to Allan

Pinkerton's long night, the railroads were wide awake and ready to deliver their secret cargo. Pinkerton was going to bed just as Lincoln was getting up; ships passing in the night.[5]

If all went well, Lincoln would arrive in Washington twenty-four hours later, just in time for the next sunrise. But he would have to run a gantlet around his own advisers as well as his would-be assassins. For much of the trip, he would be exposed, in a common sleeping compartment, with ordinary passengers. To make matters worse, he had a full day of difficult events, including some wrangling with Pennsylvania politicians and a challenging speech to give at Independence Hall.

But if he delivered it well, the incoming president might give himself some breathing room. He needed help; why not ask the founders? Lincoln had once described the Declaration as a fountain. As he drew closer to Washington, he could drink from it and draw nourishment for the final thrust.[6]

Around the country, many others found themselves at a fork in the road as George Washington's birthday dawned. Even the smallest gestures were pregnant with symbolism as Americans tried, awkwardly, to celebrate their history as a single people.[7] Eleven days earlier, on the same day that Lincoln's journey began, Congress had voted to call February 22 a national holiday; but in the same vote, Northerners and Southerners disagreed about whether to invite a Massachusetts orator, Edward Everett, to address them. To celebrate George Washington was one matter, but to explore the principles the country was founded upon, as Everett was likely to do—that was simply too controversial.[8]

As Lincoln was beginning his day, many others were readying themselves for patriotic observances. Seven hundred miles to the South, Charleston remained the nation's flash point, where nerves were fraying as a long stalemate continued between the soldiers facing each other across the harbor. Just after dawn, the morning stillness was shattered by the sound of cannon fire.

Was this the dreaded attack on Fort Sumter?

Curiously, it was something close to the opposite: a patriotic round of thirteen volleys by South Carolinian artillery, in honor of the original colonies. The salute must have created mixed emotions for the federal troops living day to day under the mouth of the cannons inside Fort Sumter. Still, they felt obliged to reply, and did, with a riposte of their own: thirty-four blasts, one for each of the states, including those that had seceded.[9] Even as they menaced each other, these Americans recognized their shared bond.

That ambivalence was also felt in New Orleans, where a massive military parade was held. Louisianans profited from the occasion to eat and drink handsomely. (A local paper commented on the "vast array of meat bones, scraps, and broken bottles" left behind by an army of paradegoers.) Portraits of Washington lined the route, but the flag he'd fought for had suddenly become toxic. There were a few "star-spangled banners," but they were just that: banners with stars on them, merely decorative, not flags at all. Instead, ships and buildings flew jury-rigged flags, with pelicans, a state symbol. When an actual U.S. flag was unveiled by a brave Unionist near the Mississippi levee, it nearly caused a riot.

Still, the reporter could not help betraying a sigh of regret as he contemplated the "noble banner" and reflected on the "strong, powerful love of the old republic" that many Southerners felt as they lurched forward, unsteadily.[10] Others felt it too: when an Ohioan, living in Louisiana, happened across this scene, he was sickened to see the flag disrespected. In his diary, William Tecumseh Sherman confessed his anguish at seeing Americans indulging in a "glorious rejoicing at the downfall of our own country."[11]

In the city that bore Washington's name, it would have been logical to expect a sparkling display of birthday pageantry. But the challenge of arranging the annual celebration proved too difficult for the Buchanan administration, entering its death agonies. As federal troops were forming for their traditional birthday parade down Pennsylvania Avenue, they received urgent orders from the White House to disband—President Buchanan was fearful that this display of militarism might offend Southerners. Later the same day, after hearing complaints that the military parade had been canceled, he overruled himself and tried to get replacements to walk along the original parade route long after the moment had passed. Then he wrote a note to former president John Tyler, apologizing for having done that.[12]

Jefferson Davis suffered no such indecision; he was already scheming about how to expand his empire, and on February 22 he mailed secret orders urging preparation for the seizure of Fort Pickens, on Florida's Gulf Coast.[13] A former governor of Virginia, Henry Wise, wrote him the same day to assure him that Virginia would soon join the cause.[14]

Throughout the South, others were acting boldly, sensing that history favored their cause. Many saw Lincoln as a mere pretender and expected him to meet a grisly fate, sooner rather than later. Newspapers encouraged such speculation. In Macon, Georgia, a private in a militia company, B. Pope Freeman, won a shooting contest and boasted to his local paper that his aim would have been even better if he had "Honest Old Abe" in his sights.[15]

Even Northerners were sending messages of support to the new Confederate government, growing stronger by the hour. On the same day that Lincoln would speak at Independence Hall, a Philadelphia widow named Ann G. Wight was mailing a letter to Jefferson Davis, enclosing a design for the Confederate flag.[16]

Mercifully, designing a new flag was not on the list of problems that Lincoln had to face. The old one had served honorably since it, too, was designed by a Philadelphia widow, Betsy Ross, back in the days of the Second Continental Congress. Another star had just been added, for Kansas, and today Lincoln was expected to hoist an enormous version of the enlarged Stars and Stripes over Independence Hall at daybreak.

Despite the hour, the city was abuzz. Even before sunup, a "vast concourse" had gathered in front of Independence Hall.[17] All knew that this would be a special day. Lincoln had been invoking George Washington from the moment his journey began. To hear him in the flesh, on Washington's Birthday, within the sacred precincts of Independence Hall—that was political theater too good to miss. So, they came out in droves to hear him greet the sunrise.

This was not Lincoln's first visit to the shrine. He had seen its exterior in 1848, when he attended the Whig Convention that nominated Zachary Taylor for the presidency. At that time, Lincoln was enjoying his one and only term as a congressman and had joined a club of Taylor supporters, the Young Indians. They were organized by Alexander Stephens, a Georgian who became friendly with the awkward Illinois representative. Since then, Stephens had risen nearly as high: he was the newly elected vice president of the Confederate States of America.[18]

Stephens and Lincoln had been writing to each other in hopes of reducing the tensions. But there were fundamental differences in the way that they looked at American history. Lincoln believed the Declaration of Independence applied to *all* Americans. A month later, on March 21, Stephens would attack the Declaration of Independence as a lie. In a speech delivered in Savannah, he proposed that the Confederacy was based upon the "cornerstone" of racial inequality and the specific belief that "the negro is not equal to the white man." Equality, according to Stephens, was a "sandy foundation." Instead, they would build upon the "great physical, philosophical, and moral truth" of white supremacy. Historians remain indebted to him for saying more clearly than most of his fellow Confederates what their government stood for.[19]

Lincoln would pursue a different tack. To arrive at Independence Hall on Washington's Birthday was a master stroke, even before any speech was given. It was the right place to reflect on the feelings that still held Americans together. Eighty-five years earlier, as Betsy Ross was sewing the new flag, Thomas Jefferson had stitched together a document claiming a higher purpose for the new country. It would stand for ideas much larger than itself, including a core belief that human beings were born equal and that they were entitled to basic freedoms, protected by legal rights. There was nothing sandy about this foundation.[20]

Freedom was an uncomfortable topic for the Confederacy. In his inaugural address, four days earlier, Jefferson Davis had asserted the "right" to abolish a government, but he said little about the higher purpose of his government, except to remove trade restrictions on cotton. For that matter, freedom was not much discussed in the White House; it had been many years since *any* president of the United States had uttered a memorable thought about what, exactly, America stood for. Certainly James Buchanan had not; his inaugural address had inanely hoped for a time when the public would lose interest in debating the injustice of slavery, and would instead "be diverted from this question to others of more pressing and practical importance."[21]

Presidents had once been expected to speak of America's moral purpose. In his first inaugural, Washington had suggested that Americans had been entrusted with a responsibility to safeguard the republican form of government. In his notes for that speech, he warned against "a false kind of patriotism" that mindlessly trumpeted America's size and strength, without understanding the seriousness of the mission to prove that people could govern themselves. In his farewell address, he used the word *Union* over and over again, urging Americans to resist the demagogues who would try to divide them.[22]

Lincoln had been reading the farewell in advance of his journey. He knew that the urgency of the hour, the symbolism of the setting, and his own strong feelings demanded something better, in the spirit of the founders themselves.

Nineteenth-century stereograph of a side of Independence Hall, with a statue of George Washington[23]

THE STAGE

In the days before Lincoln's arrival, a six-foot wooden platform had been built next to Independence Hall. A more suitable backdrop could hardly be imagined. The founders had created a series of masterpieces here, but the site had an even older history. Long before Philadelphia was founded, Native Americans held their own councils on this spot.[24] Then, in 1732, a building was begun, so early that there were anxieties that Philadelphia belonged to Maryland and not Pennsylvania (because of overlapping charters given to the Calvert and Penn families). That would have been a problem for a building designed to house Pennsylvania's government.

But those doubts had been removed with the exact work of two British surveyors, Charles Mason and Jeremiah Dixon. In 1763 Mason and Dixon set out from Philadelphia—indeed, from this very building—to demarcate the line that separated the two provinces. Gazing into the heavens night after night, charting their position by the stars, they plotted one mile after another, bringing cartographic order to the chaos of a huge wilderness. But even as they solved one argument, they opened up another one, far more worrisome. For as slavery began to disappear on one side of the line, the Mason-Dixon Line became the symbol of the divide between North and South.[25]

Philadelphia was very close to the edge of that debate. It was only fifteen miles away from Delaware, where slavery was protected, and every tremor of the national argument was felt along the boundary. Local Quakers had been resisting slavery for some time, and in 1780 Pennsylvania passed a gradual emancipation act, another proud moment for Independence Hall.[26]

That only deepened the desire of enslaved Americans to make their way north, and Philadelphia became one of "the great central stations" of the Underground Railroad."[27] A slave who escaped successfully, Henry "Box" Brown, earned his nickname by mailing himself in a three-foot long crate to an address in Philadelphia.[28] For Frederick Douglass, it was a critical stop in his flight north. But as his own writing confirmed, African-Americans often felt ambivalent about Independence Hall, which felt like a monument to broken promises.

Nor did it help that so many entrepreneurs tried to exploit the building for their own purposes. In 1802 its second floor was leased to the painter Charles Willson Peale.[29] To entice visitors, he created an immersive museum experience that included art, ventriloquism, and moving pictures. (Peale pioneered an ancestor of cinema called the magic lantern.[30]) His museum also gathered a menagerie of stuffed animals, including exotic creatures sent back from the West by the explorers Meriwether Lewis and William Clark. Daringly, Peale once asked an elderly Benjamin Franklin if he would consider lending his body to taxidermy.

Franklin declined to respond, but Peale was right to sense that Americans want to commune with the founders. A steady stream of visitors came to the shrine, eager to sit in John Hancock's wooden chair, or to cast an eye on Washington, whose stony reserve was realistically captured by a large statue in the corner. The room in which these artifacts were gathered was called the Hall of Independence, and eventually that phrase, reordered, was applied to the building itself.[31]

The living and the dead were not so far apart in these rooms. Lincoln had imagined a "midway world" in his youthful verse, where they could mingle across the divide. Independence Hall was a natural place to speak to the immortals, especially after it began to exhibit the remains of statesmen. When John Quincy Adams died in 1848, his body was carried by train to Independence Hall. Four years later, Lincoln's hero, Henry Clay, was brought here after he died.[32] For many Americans, these rooms held far more history than the half-finished buildings of Washington.

But local African-Americans remained resistant to the cult of the founders. "What a mockery they all seemed," a young African-American woman named Charlotte L. Forten wrote as she gazed at the paintings of revolutionary heroes in Independence Hall.[33] To local black families, the building told a different story. Slaves had been sold across the street in the eighteenth century, and in recent years, a dark new chapter began for the proud old structure.[34]

Since the 1830s, the building's second floor had been rented to a U.S. Marshal, who added a district court and a jail. But with the passage of the Fugitive Slave Act in 1850, the marshal was obligated to capture suspected runaways. As a result, Independence Hall saw a new function: as a holding pen for African-Americans about to be returned to slavery, after having built lives of freedom.

A bitter dispute raged as activists protested against this odious intrusion into one of the country's most sacred spaces. An African-American newspaper in Washington, the *National Era*, was incredulous that human beings were being jailed and enslaved on the very spot where Jefferson had written his "immortal words" about equal rights.

In 1851 local emotions were raised to a fever pitch when a forty-year-old washerwoman, Hannah Dellam, was arrested in an advanced state of pregnancy, along with her nine-year-old son. There was a tense standoff with police, but eventually she was forced back to bondage, with her son and her unborn child.[35] If Lincoln heard the building "breathing" the night before, it could well have been his intuitive understanding that there had once been human beings trapped inside, powerless to escape.

In other ways, as well, America's broken promises resonated through these chambers. Many came to this emotionally charged site to express grievances of their own: nativists who wished to exclude immigrants; and their polar opposites, recent immigrants who wanted to embrace American history. Rallies were held to express solidarity with those fighting for their own form of democracy in Europe, or in defense of labor, or simply to protest the South's actions during the secession crisis.[36] Whenever something seemed deeply wrong with the country, crowds would come here to renew their faith.[37] So the stage was set for Lincoln when he arrived in the early morning of February 22. It would have been difficult to find a building that more accurately captured the contradictions of the American people.

The stage

APPLE OF GOLD

At dawn, Lincoln left his hotel in a carriage, accompanied by a group of Mexican War veterans and his son Tad. They arrived at Independence Hall to find a crowd packed in around the outdoor stage, ready for the holiday observance. The ceremony required only a few words, but for Lincoln, it was a chance to say much more. If he could compose a compelling narrative about American history, he could begin the work of reuniting a people who, despite their differences, shared a powerful set of memories.

In Montgomery, Jefferson Davis was doing all he could to cloak the Confederacy with legitimacy as its fourth day began. There were plenty of ways he might have claimed Washington's Birthday for the South. His wife's grandfather had fought under Washington in New Jersey.[39] Yet Davis was silent on February 22. Lincoln was not. Historians looking for causes of the North's victory in 1865 could do worse than to study this morning in 1861, when one president articulated a vision for his country, and the other said nothing.

Among the many ways in which Lincoln had been insulted over the past year was a pervasive scorn for his lack of learning. He was criticized in the North as well as the South for his thin credentials, and his reputation for telling funny stories often was held against him, as if he were incapable of more serious reflection. But it would have been difficult to find anyone in the country, including far better-educated statesmen, with a deeper commitment to the founders and their words.

In his first major speech, in 1838, a young Lincoln nearly ran out of adjectives as he approached "a once hardy, brave, and patriotic but now lamented and departed race of ancestors." They never stopped crowding into the midway world of his imagination, where the dead roamed at will, dispensing oracular wisdom.[40] That was especially true on a day honoring "the mightiest name of Earth," as Lincoln had called Washington in 1842.[41]

But he needed to approach the old landmark carefully. The founding documents were full of trap doors, like the building itself. Jefferson Davis might easily have argued, from the same stage, that slavery had been written into those documents from the moment the ink was dry. Yet Lincoln knew what an impoverished reading that was. He could find his way into a much richer document.

The crowd may have expected some boilerplate about Washington on his birthday, but Lincoln mentioned no founder at all. Instead, he talked humbly about the way he understood the Declaration, and the hope it inspired, particularly in the soaring cadences of its second paragraph—the one that celebrated the equal rights that inhere in all people. These words were not added randomly; the purpose of the new country was, precisely, to affirm the rights. It was the mortar that held the bricks together. Indeed, he often thought of these words as a kind of building, a "temple of liberty" that anyone could walk into. So he had described the document in one of his debates against Stephen Douglas.[42]

For some time, Lincoln had been arguing that the people and their better angels were not so far apart. The "people," of course, were a diverse lot; there had never been a country as variegated as this one. Every year brought more of them. For some, self-government was difficult, as Dorothea Dix knew from her extensive work treating the mentally ill. For others, self-government was illegal, as millions of enslaved African-Americans knew, despite the longing to be citizens. But inside each person, Lincoln argued, a fundamental worth could be found. Not a financial value, to be calculated on the auction block, but something deeper, which included an unfettered potential to make the most of one's ability.

No piece of parchment did more to express this worth than the Declaration of Independence, and it was that document, above all others, that he came into Independence Hall to defend. To him, it was far more than a piece of paper in a musty archive. It was *alive*. His secretary, John Nicolay, called it "his political chart and inspiration." By arguing simply that Americans needed to live up to their founding ideals, Lincoln conveyed an urgent message to a people desperate to remember a less corrupt time, when America spoke to the world.[43]

He had been pondering the Declaration's words for a long time, after finding them inside a book about Indiana statutes. From a young age, it served as a scripture that naturally fit his leveling instincts.[44] His stepmother once explained that he could not rest until he grasped the nub of an argument. To get there, Lincoln would repeat key phrases until he had completely mastered them: "Self-evident" . . . "All men are created equal" . . . "Creator" . . . "unalienable rights" . . . "life, liberty and the pursuit of happiness."

His mind moved slowly at first, but then irresistibly. He sought "the inwardness of the thing," as he once phrased it to a visiting gun maker.[45] Throughout the 1850s, Lincoln hammered away at the Declaration, like a blacksmith seeking what is valuable in an ingot and discarding the rest. The key word is *all*. "All men are created equal." It permits no equivocation. On that small anvil, Lincoln had forged his career.

After he returned to politics in 1854, indignant over the spread of slavery, the Declaration was always close at hand. In the speech that announced his return, it was vividly there as he urged a cheering crowd, "Let us readopt the Declaration of Independence."[46] Four years later, as he readied himself to debate Stephen Douglas, Lincoln pasted a copy of the Declaration's second paragraph inside a notebook that he carried with him to record his thoughts.[47] Sometimes it seemed as if the words filled him up with oxygen. He grew en-larged as he spoke them, immensely tall. An eyewitness to a speech described the climactic moment when Lincoln would "eulogize" the Declaration: "Then he extended out his arms, palms of his hands upward, . . . as if appealing to some superior power for assistance and support."[48]

Others detected that "superior power" as well. Alexander Stephens, whose interpretation of the Declaration was so different, perceived a "reli-gious mysticism" beneath Lincoln's attachment.[49] In Washington, William H. Seward told the Adams brothers that he had noticed the same quality, a "vein of sentiment" running through Lincoln's mind that invested the arti-facts of American history with a sacred significance. Unlike so many cynical politicians, who recycled the old platitudes without pausing to digest them, Lincoln seemed to actually *believe* that the Declaration's promises were true. That made him dangerous to a system that had grown quite comfortable with its moral rot.[50]

In the years leading up to Lincoln's election, the Declaration had lost some of its luster, as Southern politicians chiseled away at it. To them, the idea that African-Americans had rights was anathema—especially after African-American leaders began to claim the Declaration for themselves.[51] Three years earlier, Chief Justice Roger Taney of the Supreme Court con-cluded that "the enslaved African race were not intended to be included" and possessed "no rights which the white man was bound to respect."[52] An Indiana senator, John Pettit, called the Declaration of Independence "a self-evident lie."[53]

To Lincoln, that was a grotesque misreading. Rejecting Pettit's claim, Lincoln said, with some heat, "If it had been said in old Independence Hall, seventy-eight years ago, the very door-keeper would have throttled the man and thrust him into the street." The tendency to pick and choose which ideals were convenient violated both his ethics and his mathematics—as Euclid knew, thousands of years earlier, equal meant *equal*.

The document applied to all, and America's moral influence in the world depended on that fact. It did not parcel out its rights to the highest bidder. If the experiment succeeded, it would give hope to *all* people, in *all* places, for *all* time.

Only a few weeks earlier, Lincoln had written out the word *all* four times on a small fragment of paper. On December 30 he received a letter from Alexander Stephens asking that he say something to calm the waters. The Georgian used a beautiful expression, from the book of Proverbs, to ask Lincoln in a way that was sure to engage him: "a word fitly spoken by you now would be as 'apples of gold in pictures of silver.' "[54]

Here was a kind of chess game, over the meaning of America, between two old friends who were now on the opposite side of a widening divide. Lincoln argued to himself, on that scrap of paper, that the "apple of gold" was the sentence about equality in the Declaration.

"That something is the principle of 'Liberty to all'—the principle that clears the *path* for all—gives *hope* to all—and, by consequence, *enterprize*, and *industry* to all."[55]

By denying equality, slavery did the opposite. It exalted the rich over the poor, it created a permanent racial caste system, and it made a mockery of life, liberty, and the pursuit of happiness. In 1858, during his debate with Stephen Douglas, Lincoln predicted a future crisis over "the tendency of prosperity to breed tyrants." But he also saw hope for a solution, right in front of all Americans: "When in the distant future some man, some faction, some interest, should set up the doctrine that none but rich men, or none but white men, were entitled to life, liberty, and the pursuit of happiness, their posterity might look up again to the Declaration of Independence and take courage to renew the battle which their fathers began."[56]

In other words, Lincoln came to Independence Hall with as clear a purpose as Thomas Jefferson had in 1776. He had spent his entire life approaching this stage.

Hoisting the flag[57]

WORDS TO LIVE BY

Lincoln was ushered inside Independence Hall, where he was welcomed by yet another city council, then asked to speak. It was his first time inside the shrine. Instead of going on at great length, he spoke with the precision of a surgeon and the feeling of a poet. The day before, in Trenton, Lincoln had appeared to go into a kind of reverie as he remembered reading about the Revolution as a child.

Now he took those thoughts and sharpened them. He acknowledged where he was, gracefully, expressing "deep emotion" at standing in the place where the country came into existence. According to one source, he was speaking in "a low tone, hardly audible." But his feelings were written all over his face, which clearly showed "the emotion with which he stood in the historic room." [58]

Then, a bold, personal statement: "I have never had a feeling politically that did not spring from the sentiments embodied in the Declaration of Independence." It brought the house down. His next few sentences remembered the dangers that the founders exposed themselves to—in a way that suggests he was mentally girding himself for the next twenty-four hours. But Lincoln kept returning to the "great principle or idea that kept this Confederacy so long together"—reappropriating the word for the United States of America.

Then he explained the great idea, more succinctly than the day before. It was not the "mere" matter of separation from England, but the creation of something more rarefied: a nation devoted to liberty for all. "Something" in the Declaration gave "hope to the world for all future time." The transcript recorded "great applause." He hammered some more on the ingot, finding the word *all* again, twice: "the weights should be lifted from the shoulders of all men . . . all should have an equal chance."

The speech had already done everything that anyone might have asked. But then Lincoln offered a stunning conclusion. He declared that he would be "one of the happiest men in the world" if the country could be saved with its great idea intact—but added that he would "rather be assassinated on this spot than to surrender it." It was not the first time Lincoln had visualized his own death. [59] But it was powerfully real, given what he had learned the night before, concerning the threats against his life. He then hesitated briefly, wondering if he had said too much, but returned to the point that he was willing to live by his words and, if necessary, die by them. An eyewitness described his manner as "very intense," and added that he slapped his knee "violently" as he said these words. [60]

Some speeches are more moving than their transcripts can convey. Lincoln may have been speaking softly, but what he said was unforgettable to those who were in the room. With this electrifying performance, condensed into a minute or two, Lincoln had reset America's moral compass. After all his stumbles earlier in his journey, he had found the right words at the best possible moment. Spoken early in the day, they would easily make the next day's papers. Like a mechanic looking for the hidden spring that operates a mechanism, he had found his way to the source of his country's greatness. It had always been hiding in plain view, inside one of the Declaration's smallest words.

The next day, a perceptive writer in the *New York Herald* grasped the significance of what had just happened. In the course of a simple visit to a patriotic shrine, Lincoln had restored the radical promise inherent in the Declaration. He had often praised the "electric cord" inside it, the promise of equal rights for all.[61] Now he had celebrated that equality in the most public way. The reporter predicted that Lincoln's short speech "means nothing more or less than the progressive steps of African emancipation to the full consummation of the work."[62] In other words, freedom and citizenship. If his enemies came to the same conclusion, it would make the next twenty-four hours even more dangerous.

But Lincoln's work was not done. Immediately afterward, he was escorted outside to the platform, where he was expected to raise an enormous new flag. The sunlight was streaming in as the president-elect came through the crowd and mounted the stage.

A local daguerreotypist named Frederick DeBourg Richards was standing in the right place at the right time and quickly took four photographs. They are the only photographs that remain from Lincoln's long journey, as if he were moving too quickly to be captured. Appropriately, he is a blur. But he is clearly in action, leaning forward, a hand thrust forward. The trees were full of men who had climbed up to find better seats and were hanging on every word Lincoln said. Drawings of the same scene revealed many people lifting their hats or raising their arms in excitement. Kate Warne was there too, ever vigilant. A Philadelphia reporter compared the crowd to "a huge field of grain undulating to the wind," as if the new president had brought the prairie with him.[63]

Lincoln spoke again, briefly, but with power, predicting that more stars would be added to the flag in due time, and that five hundred million Americans would someday live together in broad fraternity. Then he

Detail of Lincoln at Independence Hall[64]

turned to the agreeable duty of hoisting the flag. There was something in the physical act that captured the crowd's fancy. Once again, Lincoln was utterly unlike the inert occupant of the White House. He threw off his coat "in an offhand, easy manner," with a "backwoodian" style. Then, like a sailor half his age, he pulled vigorously on the halyard, raising the flag higher with vigorous tugs until it caught a gust of wind at the perfect moment.[65] *Harper's* described the shouts of the people there, "like the roar of waves which do not cease to break." For three full minutes, they cheered, in a crescendo that went from "fearful" to "maniacal." Many cried "tears of joy."[66] Lincoln hardly ever spoke about the intense experiences of his trip, but later that day, he admitted how powerful it had been to visit Independence Hall. To speak about the Declaration, in the room where it was signed, gave voice "to the feelings that had been really the feelings of my whole life." In effect, he had repeated the act of the signers, swearing to give his life to defend his principles.[67]

Once again, Lincoln had intuitively adapted to the moment. A day before, he had been losing his voice; now he had found it. His words were eloquent, but it went beyond that, as the country saw the images of a new leader, hale and hearty, raising Old Glory with the strength of his own labor. With the help of the photographers and draftsmen in the audience, including Thomas Nast, he created an immersive visual experience against a perfect backdrop. When the illustrated weeklies came out, millions of Americans could feel that they, too, had been at Independence Hall on Washington's Birthday. They did not need to climb trees; they could simply look on from their armchairs.

As the sun rose higher, a better future seemed possible for the old republic. Lincoln thought the sight of the flag, flaunting "gloriously" in the early-morning light, had offered "an omen of what is to come."[68] With a few gestures and a speech of deep meaning, he had restored integrity to Independence Hall.[69]

Pennsylvania Capitol[70]

HARRISBURG

After his triumph, Lincoln was given another parade through the streets of Philadelphia, then boarded an elegant train that had been used by the Prince of Wales during his visit a few months earlier. Here was a predicament that must have appealed to Lincoln's wry sense of humor. Only minutes after his celebration of the Declaration, he now found himself in a splendid royal compartment, recently occupied by the heir to England's King George III. Adding to the disorientation, the Special was now moving west, after having gone to so much trouble to bring him east. It was almost as if he were closing a circle and heading home after completing his spiritual pilgrimage to Independence Hall.

But the journey was far from finished, and Lincoln still had worldly matters to think about. Ahead lay Harrisburg, the next capital, where he needed to sort through Byzantine rivalries relating to Cabinet appointments.[71] The Special moved briskly, thundering over the tracks at a rate even faster than the maximum speed.[72]

Soon it arrived in Lancaster, another early capital of the United States. There Lincoln encountered unresponsive crowds, different from the throngs who had just cheered him at Philadelphia. He was feeling ill—"so unwell he could hardly be persuaded to show himself"—but he was roused briefly to peer out the window as the train sped past Wheatland, the home of James Buchanan. That graveyard of presidential ambitions was hardly a sight calculated to improve his spirits. To make matters worse, Lincoln had to keep planning his secret trip through Baltimore. The rest of the presidential party was beginning to sense that a great drama was hatching.[73]

The Special pulled into Harrisburg at two, and the president-elect went to meet the governor, Andrew Curtin.[74] Despite the multitude of problems crashing down upon him, Lincoln had serious business to transact. Pennsylvania had been critical to his nomination and election.[75] He needed to thank a local boss, Simon Cameron (who would join his cabinet as secretary of war), while placating Governor Curtin, who detested Cameron.[76] Lincoln also had to give another serious speech, to Pennsylvania's legislature, which represented almost a tenth of the country. He did, but he was running out of time, as every hour brought him closer to his night flight. Tensions were rising within Lincoln's entourage, all too aware that the most dangerous miles lay ahead.[77]

It was finally time to break the news, and Lincoln summoned them inside a Harrisburg hotel, the Jones House. There Norman Judd explained the assassination threat and the new plan to travel all night to Washington.[78] Predictably, there was an outpouring of emotion. Two military officers, Edwin Sumner and George Hazzard, deplored the plan. Sumner nearly "wept with anger" and called it "a damned bit of cowardice." Instead, he demanded a squad of cavalry so that he could "cut his way" to Washington; but the prospect of slaughtering Marylanders en route to Washington failed to win over the room. Hazzard proposed that they find fifty thousand soldiers to accompany them; that was not going to happen either. The entire U.S. Army held a third of that, most of whom were in the West.[79] Finally, the group turned to Lincoln, who had been silent while Judd confided the details.

"Unless there are some other reasons besides ridicule," he said, "I am disposed to carry out Judd's plan."[80]

But who would go? A consensus sharpened around Allan Pinkerton, who was in Philadelphia, organizing the secret trip, and Ward Hill Lamon, Lincoln's banjo-playing friend from Illinois. Lamon was physically imposing, and Mary Todd Lincoln wished for him to be there, close to her husband, ready to defend him at any cost.[81] Others in the party were apprehensive. John Hay betrayed palpable fear in a letter to a friend, writing, "Tomorrow we enter slave territory. There may be trouble in Baltimore. If so, we will not go to Washington, unless in long, narrow boxes."[82]

Around five, the group sat down for a final supper together, before the ordeal of the long night was to begin. They had come a long way, but this was hardly a celebration. Mary Todd Lincoln was "much disturbed" by the dangerous plan.[83] Later, she would have to be locked into her room, according to one account, because she was sobbing violently and "very un-manageable."[84] Another witness, Alexander McClure, wrote that Lincoln was silent. He wondered, "What would the nation think of its president stealing into the capital like a thief in the night?"[85] Unfortunately, he had run out of options.

Outside, events were already in motion, as the railroad men, alerted by Judd and Pinkerton, began to act. Thomas Scott, the whirlwind of the Pennsylvania Railroad, had been organizing the trains all day and person-ally supervised the cutting of the telegraph wires from Harrisburg, so that the media would remain uninformed of Lincoln's whereabouts after he had left.[86] For the next twelve hours, Pennsylvania's capital would be cut off from the world.

Around a quarter to six, Lincoln said good-bye to Governor Curtin by the back door of the Jones House.[87] Curtin remembered later a few telling details. Lincoln "neither in his conversation or manner exhibited alarm or fear," but "seemed pained and surprised that a design to take his life existed," almost as if he were apologizing for the fact that men hated him. Just before leaving, he made a few quick adjustments to his wardrobe, donning "a soft wool hat" he had never worn before and the same old coat he had worn to see his stepmother a few weeks earlier. He went out the back door, bare-headed, then put on the hat. The transformation was remarkable. As Lin-coln recalled it: "I put on the soft hat and joined my friends without being recognized by strangers, for I was not the same man."[88]

A carriage was waiting, and Lincoln climbed in as anonymously as pos-sible. Lamon was inside already, along with a telegraph operator and two Pennsylvania Railroad officials.[89] The carriage sped off toward the depot, where Lincoln found a small train waiting for him. This humble train—now, unexpectedly, the Presidential Special—started toward Philadelphia as if it were the most ordinary commuter railroad in the world. It was simply an engine, a tender, and a passenger car.[90] As they made their way east under great secrecy, the crew began to understand its mission. When the fireman caught a glimpse of his famous passenger, facing backward, he cried out to the engineer that the Rail-Splitter was on the train. The engineer replied, "Just keep the engine hot." [91]

One of Pinkerton's men sent a telegraph to him in Philadelphia, using Lincoln's new code name: "Nuts left at six—Everything as you directed—all is right." [92] Others devised their own ways of referring to the unnameable passenger. After the telegraph office closed, it began to be whispered in Harrisburg: "The bird has flown." [93] As darkness settled over the Pennsylvania hills, the small train kept chugging to the east, its lamps extinguished. Its engineer wrote later, "I have often wondered what the people thought of that short train whizzing through the night. A case of life and death, perhaps, and so it was." [94]

A few weeks earlier, Lincoln had written out his feelings for the Declaration on a scrap of paper, readying himself for this day. At the end of his private reflection, he wrote an extra note to himself: "that we may so act, we must study, and understand the points of danger." Now he was heading straight for them, with the fate of the republic riding on his survival, and a long night beginning.

From *Philadelphia, Wilmington and Baltimore Railroad Guide*, 1856[1]

14

THE RIVER OF NIGHT

*With a taut sail she [the ship] forged ahead all day, till the sun went down
and left her to pick her way through the darkness.*
                                        —Homer, *The Odyssey*, book 11, lines 11–12[2]

HARRISBURG TO WASHINGTON
FEBRUARY 22–23, 1861

ARLINGTON HOUSE

In Washington, as the day was ending, tensions were rising among the city's
factions, anxious as Lincoln drew closer. The capital's more acute observers
understood already that the train speeding toward them signaled a death
knell for the old ways.

The courtly protocols of a Southern city had done nothing to avert
the crisis, and, in fact, had deepened it. Now, as the Special began its final
run, the charging train seemed to symbolize the nation's impatience with
a capital that had done so little for so long. But as night crept over the
Federal City, the ancient rituals would be observed one last time, unforgettably.

At Arlington House, the home of the Lee family, the servants were preparing the magnificent old mansion for a special dinner in honor of Washington's Birthday. Despite all of the terrible news, there was a holiday to celebrate,
and it was important to honor George Washington inside this home, where
his adopted son had built a shrine, with the general's personal effects lovingly

Stereograph of Arlington House, 1867–1871[3]

on display. A remarkable meeting of old dynasties was planned, almost as if the Plantagenets and Angevins were holding court again.

The guests were members of the Adams family, old friends and college classmates of the Lees. They were Northerners, of course, but on this evening, all were united in their reverence for George Washington. Lees and Adamses had been together before: when a Lee cousin, Richard Henry Lee, proposed independence for the thirteen colonies in June 1776, John Adams was there to second it. It was often said, not entirely in jest, that the American Revolution was the result of a temporary alliance between these two proud lines.[4]

No one had a stronger claim to George Washington's legacy than the evening's hostess. Mary Anna Custis Lee was the daughter of Martha Washington's grandson, George Washington Parke Custis, who had been raised by the great man after his father died. Arlington House was well known for her priceless collection of artifacts. All around the grand home were the heirlooms that her father had preserved through a lifetime of devotion. Visitors to Arlington House felt the general was almost in the room as they gazed reverently at a punchbowl inscribed *G.W.*, or saw his old tea service, or his field tent from the war days, or the bed he slept in.[5]

In a sense, this was the original Washington monument, more satisfying

than the half-finished obelisk marring the view. The house was a living
shrine to George Washington's memory, all the more so because of its vantage point, high on a hill overlooking the city that bore the general's name.
With six massive Doric columns, modeled after the Greek ruins at Paestum,
it was the first Greek Revival residence in the new country.[6] Unlike Roman
Washington, dominated by the Capitol, this was a Greek temple, set atop a
hill, to honor a specific deity.

As it turned out, the view that was so lovely would also condemn the
property, for the hilltop offered a perfect location to plan an attack on Washington. For that reason, the Lees would soon be asked to evacuate their magnificent home. But those unpleasant realities were not yet discernible in the
final hours before the Special arrived. Until Lincoln presented himself—*if*
he presented himself—it was possible to believe that the old ways would
endure just a little longer. Accordingly, Arlington House was filled with the
sounds of laughter and tinkling glasses, quickly refilled by the servants, as
Northerners and Southerners broke bread together for one last sumptuous
evening.

Unfortunately, some family members could not attend the grand celebration. Far to the south, Mary's husband, Lieutenant Colonel Robert E.
Lee, was on his way back from Texas, after the surrender of the United States
Army a few days earlier, and the expulsion of officers who remained loyal to
the flag George Washington had done so much to defend. As he made his
way back toward his wife and children, on a Homeric odyssey of his own, he
must have felt like a man without a country.[7]

Many years later, Henry Adams, one of the guests that evening, would
write in amazement about how unready the old families were for the cataclysm that was speeding toward them. Of Roony Lee, the son of Robert E.,
he wrote, he "was as little fit to succeed in the struggle of modern life as
though he were still a maker of stone-axes, living in caves." Nor did he spare
himself, wondering if he stood nearer to the year 1 than to the twentieth
century. Adams remembered the feeling just before Lincoln arrived: "Like
all the rest, he could only wait for he knew not what, to send him he knew
not where."[8] The long wait was almost over.

Stereograph of a Pennsylvania Railroad scene, circa 1875[9]

WHERE IS NUTS?

While the ghosts were gliding from room to room behind the massive columns of Arlington House, a very different drama was unfolding a little more than a hundred miles away. To the east of Harrisburg, Lincoln's unmarked train was making rapid progress. Its fireman remembered later, "If ever I got a fast ride, I did that night." In one tiny hamlet, Downingtown, the Iron Horse stopped for water, and Lincoln was able to get tea and a roll. Then it resumed its way, toward Philadelphia and points south.[10]

Back in Harrisburg, the suddenness of Lincoln's departure had led to rumors. To maintain secrecy, some reporters were locked in their rooms, but the news was leaking in spite of that precaution.[11] At a crowded reception, the excitable townspeople repeated one false story after another.[12] "There were sharpshooters along the tracks, shooting at the passengers!" "The bridges were burning!" "Roadside explosives were going off as the train went by!"[13] None of that was true. Still, Lincoln was about as vulnerable as he could be as he barreled along in the tiny train, through darkening vales.

But Pinkerton and Scott had planned the trip well, and as Lincoln drew closer to Philadelphia, the rail network closed ranks around him. All other trains had been cleared from the route, and the telegraph operators were speaking to one another in code. Pinkerton, waiting anxiously for him to arrive, telegraphed back to Harrisburg, "Where is Nuts?"[14]

At 10:03, Nuts arrived at the same West Philadelphia depot where he had departed from the city earlier the same day. Pinkerton was waiting with a carriage. He later described Lincoln with his coat "thrown loosely over his shoulders without his arms being in the sleeves." He added, he was as "calm and collected as I ever have seen him."[15]

But they had plenty to worry about, including how to sort out fiction from fact in the rumors that were reaching them. Lincoln had heard that Seward now believed that fifteen thousand men intended "to blow up the railroad tracks" or "fire the train" to keep him from getting through.[16] As they were discussing the danger, Lamon opened his personal arms cache and offered Lincoln a revolver and a Bowie knife. The president-elect declined, saying that he had "no fears."[17] Ahead of schedule, they drove around Philadelphia, pretending to be "in search of some imaginary person."[18] Pinkerton later wrote that they drove to the north. Not far in that direction, there was a large, landscaped mental hospital, where the residents might have taken pity at the sight of a carriage that seemed to be lost.

THE PACKAGE

In the main station of the Philadelphia, Wilmington and Baltimore Railroad, the last southbound train was preparing for departure. The passengers were boarding, and the crew members were going about their business. All was ready, with one exception: the train conductor had been told to wait for an important package, which would be delivered just before departure.[20] Only a tiny number of people knew that Lincoln *was* the package.

Near the back of the train, next to a sleeping car, a young woman was waiting calmly, as if expecting a relative. Once again, Kate Warne was exactly where she needed to be. She had just bribed a conductor with a half dollar, explaining that she would need four berths cordoned off so that her invalid brother could rest in peace. All night long, her sharp wits would improve

Lincoln's chances. She was also armed if more forceful measures were necessary.[21]

Nearby, another Pinkerton agent, George Dunn, had purchased tickets for a night passage to Washington. But after buying them, he noticed "a small party of men, who from their quiet talk, vigilant appearance, and watchfulness, seemed to be on the alert, for Somebody or Something."[22] Getting around these men was suddenly an urgent new challenge. But the two agents were superbly ready. With "considerable trouble," Dunn secured a key to the back door of the sleeper car, where Kate Warne had cordoned off the four berths.

It was nearly time for the train to leave, but the final few steps from Lincoln's carriage were some of the most dangerous of all. At the last minute, just before midnight, a fake package was delivered to the conductor, to distract him, while the real package—Abraham Lincoln—slipped quietly into the sleeper through the back door and was ushered into his berth. Pinkerton and Lamon followed close behind. Within seconds after boarding, the train was moving. The final journey to Washington had begun.[23]

After the night was over, Kate Warne wrote up a report for Pinkerton. With understatement, she noted, "Nothing of importance happened through the night." Lincoln must have known how much she had done for him, for she remarked that "he talked very friendly for some time." When the conductor needed their tickets, Pinkerton handed them out, so that Lincoln would not be seen. Then he lay down in his berth. Mrs. Warne's final comment in her report was as follows: "Mr. Lincoln is very homely, and so very tall that he could not lay straight in his berth." With her penchant for nondescript prose, it was unlike her to use a word as evocative as *homely*.[24]

But despite her aversion to detail, she conveyed one of the more arresting images of the trip, as the incoming president, upon whom so many hopes rested, tried to contort his body to fit into a small compartment. A passage in *Moby-Dick* describes another bad sleep, in the course of a fiery sermon concerning Jonah as a fugitive, confined to a berth so tiny that the ceiling is "almost resting on his forehead." [25] All Americans knew that slavery, somehow, had propelled Abraham Lincoln into the presidency. Now, to a striking degree, he was experiencing what it felt like to be a runaway slave, traveling at night, changing clothes, avoiding the looks of conductors, walking onto the train at the last possible second (as Frederick Douglass had in Baltimore). It would be a long seven hours before daylight, in these cramped conditions, where every appearance—to use a washroom, for example—exposed him to danger.

Later the same day, a New York newspaper would complain about Lincoln's luxurious travel arrangements, which it likened to the "pomp of royalty." The article also wondered why he could not be more like Jefferson Davis, "a plain man, of simple manners," who traveled on "ordinary" trains. [26]

As the train lurched southward, a mere handful of people knew that the pedestrian night train had suddenly become the Presidential Special. Acutely aware, Allan Pinkerton stood out on the rear platform, reading the landscape for danger signs, looking for his men. By prior arrangement, they were standing along the track in the darkness, making secret gestures to him—two lights flashing—as the train sped by. Inside the compartment, the passengers could not sleep. As Kate Warne wrote, "The excitement seemed to keep us all awake." But Pinkerton added, Lincoln "could not have shown more calmness." [27]

They were soon in Delaware, the first slave state of the journey, but they did not stay long, as the train kept rumbling forward. Soon the Special approached the Maryland boundary, marked out in the earth by old crownstones bearing the armorial crests of the Calvert and Penn families. This was the line that Mason and Dixon had calculated, taking their bearings each night by consulting the stars. Back in the fall, before Lincoln was even elected, a well-meaning citizen had written to the candidate and warned, "when you cross Masons & Dix. Line keep you eyes OPEN and look out for you enimeys." Doubtless, most of the passengers in his compartment were following that advice. [28]

On the other side of the line, the South began, according to most reckonings.[29] Lincoln was now on the eastern shore of Maryland, racing toward Chesapeake Bay, the theater for so much of America's early history. Soon the night train was approaching the spectacular natural opening where the Susquehanna River meets the bay's headwaters. Lincoln said, "We are at Havre de Grace, we are getting along very well. I think we are on time."[30]

Lincoln had reason to feel satisfied at the train's progress. To cross the Susquehanna was another sign of how far he had come. The founders had nearly placed the capital here in 1789. But then Jefferson and Madison had intervened and struck the famous deal with Hamilton, locating the government on the Potomac. Because of their negotiating skill, Lincoln had many hours still to go.[31]

Trains could not yet get across the wide Susquehanna, so the cars were carried across by a steamboat. In the dead of night, Lincoln was entering one of the most dangerous stretches of the journey. This was the place that the president of the railroad, Samuel Felton, had worried about. Maryland had countless small streams requiring wooden bridges, which were vulnerable to sabotage.[32] As he stared into the darkness, Pinkerton was reassured to see a light go on and off, twice."[33]

Only seven miles away, Pinkerton's men had discovered a nest of terror in what is now the town of Perryman, where a militia of Southern sympathizers was drilling with the intent to kill Lincoln.[34] Although near to Pennsylvania, this section of Maryland was well known for its Southern sympathies. For Frederick Douglass, escaping north along the same train route in 1838, the river passage at Havre de Grace marked the place of greatest terror; he was nearly caught here.[35]

As Lincoln raced in the opposite direction, the danger was increasing with every mile, especially as the train began to approach Baltimore, the city that Pinkerton had been calling "the seat of danger" since his earliest letters to Samuel Felton.[36]

As if to stress the point, the author of a local railroad guide added a few descriptive details about the landscape they were entering. With all the waterways that flowed beneath the train trestles, the guide boasted that it was a paradise for duck hunters, one of America's great "shooting grounds." Fortunately, Maryland's hunters believed in fair play and felt that it was sporting to "give every bird one chance for its life."[37] That would have brought small comfort to the quiet party. But as they approached each bridge, Pinkerton saw the reassuring lights winking on and off.[38]

A few years earlier, Walt Whitman had written a strange work that he called "Night Poem"—later, he would change its title to "The Sleepers." It described the way that sleeping Americans looked, in all of their poses, as the poet peered down on them during a nocturnal flight of his own. Whitman saw them all: the voter, the politician, the fugitive, the slave, and a shrouded body lying in a coffin.[39] Lincoln was all of those things at once as the train rumbled south.

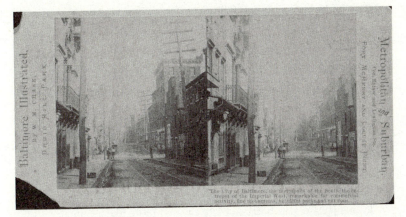

A dark alley in Baltimore, "the metropolis of the South."[40]

MOBTOWN

The night train eased into Baltimore around 3:30 in the morning, snaking along the harbor's edge, through the coaling stations and blacksmith shops that crowded near the station. Burning kilns cast a yellow light over the surroundings; according to the guide, they were fired constantly in the ceaseless quest for energy.[41] Through the darkness, it might have just been possible to make out the dim outline of Fort McHenry and its famous ramparts, just across the harbor. Given the political climate within the city, one can imagine that the sight of the flag flying over the fort was as reassuring to Lincoln as it had been to Francis Scott Key, when he composed "The Star-Spangled Banner" here during the War of 1812.

All trains from the northeast came into an immense barn, the President Street Station of the Philadelphia, Wilmington and Baltimore Railroad. It was here that a young man dressed as a sailor walked onto a moving train in 1838, a precarious first step for Frederick Douglass on his way to freedom.[42] As soon as they arrived in Baltimore, Kate Warne left to go to a hotel after her brave night's work. Another operative briefly whispered to them that "all was right."[43]

City guidebooks called Baltimore "the Monument City" for its statuary—in particular, a Washington Monument of its own, taller than the unfinished obelisk struggling upward near the White House. Once again, Baltimore had outperformed the nation's disappointing capital. A mere thirty-eight miles separated the two, and yet all evidence indicated that one city was superbly located, and fully engaged with the world, while the other had almost no trade of any kind. In Washington, there were barely any ships; its only traffic was its eternal gossip about itself.[44] But Baltimore's busy harbor was filled with vessels, from North and South. In 1860 it was America's fourth largest city, with 212,418 people.

In many ways, this bustling place seemed more like a capital, pulsing with Northern and Southern energy at the same time. Presidential nominating conventions routinely met here to anoint their candidates, and it was far more cosmopolitan than Washington, with glittering theatricals and literary salons. Its railroads converged from all directions, while Washington lagged behind, with only a single line built—to Baltimore. Nearly a quarter of Baltimore's population was foreign born, and new immigrants arrived constantly.[45] As Pinkerton and his agents fanned out across the city in search of assassination threats, they had been surprised to learn that one of the leading plotters was a Corsican barber, Cypriano Ferrandini, who fancied himself a freedom fighter.[46]

But if Baltimore was exciting, it was also dangerous. As Frederick Douglass had discovered, the city seethed with racial tensions. A large African-American population gave it a darker complexion than any Northern city; for many, this was a point of pride. Douglass called it a "paradise" compared with plantation living.[47] But even if most African-Americans (25,680) were free, a significant number (2,218) were enslaved, and local politicians were trying to enslave more through arrests of questionable legality and a growing culture of intimidation.[48] Baltimore's leaders were proud of its status as the largest metropolis of the slaveholding South.[49]

In other ways, too, it was a roiled place. Baltimore wharves may have welcomed thousands of immigrants, but Maryland was a Know-Nothing stronghold, where anti-immigrant gangs roamed the streets at will, sowing terror. On Election Days, God-fearing citizens would do all they could to avoid street thugs such as the Plug Uglies, the Butt Enders, the American Rattlers, and the Blood Tubs, so famous for intimidating voters that Baltimore earned a new nickname: Mobtown.[50] Democracy could quickly turn into a blood sport: in the 1856 election, 30 people were killed and 350 injured as voters went to the polls.[51] Baltimore's toughs were famous for using a sharp tool, the awl, as a means of persuasion. Henry Adams once saw a Know-Nothing parade featuring "a huge wooden awl." One would-be voter was punctured twenty-four times.[52] It was a long distance from "awl" to "all," the word Lincoln kept coming back to as he read the Declaration.

His friends had always known that this would be the hardest part of his journey. On Election Day, he had come in a dismal fourth in Maryland, with just 2.5 percent of the vote.[53] When a group of local Republicans tried to hold a procession, they were assaulted in the presence of the local police chief.[55] Every city that Lincoln had come through offered him a reception or a parade; but Baltimore officials never indicated the slightest desire to welcome the president-elect, nor did they offer any guarantees of protection. The chief of police, a Southern sympathizer, claimed that he had no extra men available that day.[56]

Baltimore's geography was also challenging for anyone who wanted to pass through inconspicuously. Its leaders had placed limits on the rights of locomotives to enter the city, for fear of noise and fire. As a result, passengers continuing south were pulled by horses, in their cars, through the downtown streets to the Camden Street Station, where they were reattached to trains leaving for Washington.[57] As Pinkerton had learned, it was precisely in this situation, when Lincoln was most vulnerable, that assassins hoped to strike, aided by the chaos of the huge crowd that would be watching his movements.[58]

Because of the hour, the streets were deathly quiet as the horses pulled Lincoln's car, hearse-like, through the dark streets. They were led by two teamsters, "Daddy" Smith and Tim Murphy, who guided the horses carefully, keeping their distance from some crowds milling around.[59] Pinkerton wrote that "Mr. Lincoln did not get up," suggesting a very quiet passage as the president-elect lay still in his berth, the car moving at a stately clip-clop. Lamon remembered the other passengers sleeping "as peacefully as if Mr. Lincoln had never been born."

When they arrived at the Camden Street Station, the noise suddenly increased. A night watchman, likely drunk, was trying to wake up a ticket agent, asleep in a wooden shed very close to Lincoln's car. The watchman kept pounding on the side of the shed with his club, shouting, "Captain, it's four o'clock!" Up and down the lines, the precise knowledge of railroad time, down to the second, was crucial to the smooth operation of the trains. But that memo had failed to reach this employee. Over and over he repeated the phrase "four o'clock"—for twenty minutes, without adjustment—much to Lincoln's amusement. He "appeared to enjoy it very much" and "made several witty remarks showing that he was as full of fun as ever."[60] In the distance, they could hear passengers inside the depot, singing "Dixie."[61]

Telling jokes in the dead of night was a good way to chase away the ghosts of Baltimore. The Camden Street Station was about five blocks south of the churchyard where one of Lincoln's favorite poets, Edgar Allan Poe, lay buried. According to a friend, Lincoln "read and loved 'The Raven'—repeated it over & over." The friend elaborated that he liked it "because it was gloomy." [62]

The poem describes a night scene, after midnight, in which the author peers into the darkness, wondering what is out there. In many ways, the night is a character itself—Poe compares it to a river, specifically, the "Plutonian" river one must pass over, toward the underworld, where the dead live. With dawn only a couple hours away, Lincoln was nearly across the river of night. But he still needed to make one last push. A new locomotive, Engine 236, was being hitched to the cars, to speed the sleepers to Washington. [63]

Benjamin Latrobe, early design for the tomb of George Washington, never built [64]

KEEPER OF THE TOMB

Around 4:30, the train eased out of Baltimore toward the District of Columbia. The seat of danger was now behind him, but the road ahead was perilous in its own way. This slender ribbon of track was all that connected the capital to the North. Samuel F. B. Morse had laid out his original telegraph along these lines, and an immense amount of information flowed to and from Washington through this narrow corridor. Accordingly, it was vital to the defense of the United States. Every night, it was being watched closely by Southern sympathizers.[65]

Lincoln had not seen Washington for twelve years, since the ignominious close of his single term in Congress. The city was full of rumors of plots and counterplots, swirling like the dust that blinded pedestrians on Pennsylvania Avenue. During her brief stay there in December, Dorothea Dix had called it "the city of the dead," and, like Baltimore, it had its ghosts. George Washington died in 1799, just before the government could move to the spot he had approved, but his death lingered in the minds of the city's designers, who hoped to turn the Capitol into a necropolis of sorts. They originally intended to inter Washington's body inside a basement crypt, but his family had chosen to bury him at Mount Vernon. Still, the crypt was there, empty, below the rotunda, in the same building where so many people had threatened to kill Lincoln There was still a job on the Capitol payroll, Keeper of the Tomb. His assignment was to keep a star-shaped light illuminated in case the room was ever needed.[66]

Then there were the living ghosts: the arthritic politicians who had crept up to but not yet crossed the Plutonian river. Even as a new era was struggling to be born, they clutched at the levers of power with their bony fingers. Inside the Willard Hotel, the tenth president, John Tyler could be seen working the famous lobby every day. He had been trying to broker a last-minute deal that would surrender all of the principles Lincoln was elected to defend.

Tyler was the antithesis of Lincoln: well bred, supercilious, and deeply wedded to the old way of doing things. As the owner of forty-three slaves, he had a strong interest in preserving the status quo and would soon prove that with his wholehearted loyalty to the Confederacy. Henry Adams spoke witheringly of him as an old man who had reappeared from "the cerements of his forgotten grave" to add one last obstacle.[67] Night after night, rivers of alcohol flowed through the rooms of the Willard as the lobby dwellers conspired to extend the life of slavery, and of their own careers, feeding at the public trough. Southern spies were known to operate there as well.[68]

The night train sped toward all of these specters, closing the distance as it raced through Maryland's lush farmland. The Baltimore and Ohio had laid these tracks in 1835, in an early burst of railroad enthusiasm, and they remained the only way a train could enter the capital of the United States.[69] No trains could approach from the south or the west; the Potomac managed to be too wide for railroad bridges and too shallow for big ships, simultaneously. By blocking so much commerce, it was the perfect symbol for the city that it lazily irrigated with its brackish waters.[70]

Lincoln had crossed hundreds of rivers on his long journey from Springfield. As he raced to the South, he still had a few more in front of him. Three Maryland rivers had presented challenges to the Baltimore and Ohio as it built tracks into the capital. The Patapsco River was the hardest to cross, cutting a deep ravine between two hills. To address that problem, Latrobe designed a viaduct worthy of the Romans, stretching seven hundred feet in a long curve, sixty-five feet above the river. The challenge was considered impossible at first, with critics denouncing it as "Latrobe's Folly." When it was dedicated, on July 4, 1835, it was the largest bridge in the country. It carries railroad traffic to this day.[71]

Thomas Viaduct, 1858[72]

South of the viaduct, the night train veered toward Annapolis Junction, a small crossing where another line came in from Annapolis. This was an important relay, sending signals all day long between Washington and the rest of the country. In the earliest days of the telegraph, its inventors, Samuel Morse and Alfred Vail, had naturally followed the train tracks, and Annapolis Junction was an important way station as they labored to string the first copper wires between Washington and Baltimore. It has never ceased to be a place where currents of information course; today it lies adjacent to the National Security Agency.

If Pinkerton was out on the platform from time to time, checking for the blinking lights that his men were signaling, then it is plausible to believe that the incoming president seized a few moments to stand outside, uncovered, in the onrushing air. At night, in a car full of sleepers, the risk would have been acceptable. Kate Warne had observed that his bed was too small, and the temptation would have been great to stretch his legs. Weather reports indicate that the skies were mostly clear that night; it is possible that he interrupted a fitful sleep to look toward the heavens.[73] At Independence Hall, he had hoisted a new flag aloft and mentioned the appearance of a new star as a harbinger of good fortune.[74]

It is not difficult to imagine Lincoln blinking at the stars, and the stars blinking back. Five years earlier, his friends had described the way he stared at the heavens with the wonder of a child along the banks of Lake Michigan. That night, in his "mild, pleasant voice," he spoke of the "poetry and beauty which was seen and felt by seers of old" as they contemplated the constellations wheeling around the Earth in their nightly course. On that earlier occasion, he had astonished his friends with his celestial knowledge. But he acknowledged happily that even more knowledge would come in the future. With better "computations," the universe would open its secrets to human beings, and they would fly only "a little lower than the angels."[75]

But first, these not-quite-angels would need to prove that they were capable of governing themselves. Looking up at the same stars, Mason and Dixon had charted a line dividing the country into two zones, free and unfree. An

African-American surveyor, Benjamin Banneker had also looked toward the heavens as he sought to establish the boundaries for a capital in which he could never enjoy anything like equal rights. A few weeks earlier, gazing at the stars on the flag, James Russell Lowell had wondered if they made any sense at all, or if it was all just a formless chaos. But Lincoln had always found it comforting to gaze heavenward and to find the old familiar constellations, still there, "fixed and true in their places."[76]

The stars were winking out as the train crept closer. It had been nearly twenty-four hours since this long day had started in Philadelphia. Washington's Birthday was over, and the night was surrendering to a new dawn. The shapes of the Maryland landscape were becoming more distinct in the bluish light of early morning. The ship of state had changed its shape many times, from a royal compartment, to a horse-drawn carriage, to the humble night train he was now riding. But he had crossed the river of night.

These were the ragged landscapes that Henry Adams had seen as a child on a train, coming to see his grandmother, with unfenced animals coming close to the track, and the unspoken menace of slavery heavy in the air.[77] But there was beauty in a Southern landscape, too. Adams loved the "heavy smells" of the catalpa trees, so unfamiliar to a Northerner, and the delicate interplay of sunshine and shadow beneath their limbs. Surely Lincoln was alert to all of the ways that nature was alive in these final miles. The birds must have been singing, especially on a warming February day—the temperature would reach sixty-seven degrees today.[78] The light brightened further as the train passed through the village of Bladensburg, where the British had humbled the Americans in battle thirty-six years earlier, before setting fire to the grubby capital. Lincoln was now invading along the exact same route.

BOUNDARY STONES

Around five thirty, the Special swerved to the southwest and officially crossed into the District of Columbia when it darted between two old stones standing vertically in the ground. These markers were the oldest federal monuments of them all: two of forty stones that had been arranged in a square, seventy years earlier, to demarcate the federal district when it was laid out in 1790 and 1791. Letters carved into the face read "Jurisdiction of the United States." It was reassuring to find a capital, still here, part of a country of that name.[79]

Other presidents, even Southerners, had expressed their own reservations about entering this pugilistic place, squared like a boxing ring. Just before his own inauguration, Thomas Jefferson wrote to his daughter that going to Washington was like being "in an enemy's country."[81] Still, he faced none of the danger that Lincoln now confronted as he braced himself for the home stretch.[80]

Augustus Kollner, "Tiber Creek Northeast of the Capitol," 1839[81]

Slowly, the first signs of the Federal City came into view, including the giant unfinished dome of the Capitol.[83] Off the Bladensburg Road, the Special passed near the bronze foundry of a sculptor, Clark Mills. Inside, a bronze goddess, nearly twenty feet tall, stood with her sword, as if defending the city. The statue, titled *Freedom*, had been designed in Italy and was being re-assembled for placement atop the dome, whenever it would be completed. But it had been a difficult process, as Americans wrestled over yet another incomplete symbol of their disjointed nation. Deeply interested, Jefferson Davis had carefully removed any symbols that might be interpreted as an-tislavery, including a liberty cap. The resulting design seemed to promise plenty of freedom to those who already had it; quite a bit less to those who did not. One of the foundry's most talented workers was a slave named Philip Reid; he had saved the project with his ingenuity after an Italian ar-tisan walked off the job. Perhaps he was awake, firing up the foundry for a new day, as the small train rolled past.[84]

In these outer precincts, settlement was patchy at best, but it thickened as the Special kept chugging toward its destination. Soon it found the Tiber, the small stream that flowed toward the Capitol. Together, the train and the river meandered through the District, through stables and humble dwell-ings crowded closely together. These outermost neighborhoods were far from Washington's corridors of power, but Lincoln would have appreciated how much work was done here. Already, with daylight, men and women were up, taking care of their families: lighting fires, washing clothes, feed-ing and grooming horses, nodding to the train as it slowed for its final push into the city. They would have been the first Americans to greet their new president as he entered his capital. In his own way, he too was getting ready to clean out a stable.

Many African-Americans lived out here, in the alleyways that ran be-hind the streets, with colorful names like Goat Alley and Tin Cup Alley, barely on the map.[85] Most were not slaves; 84 percent of the city's African-Americans were free people of color. Three in four worked in transporta-tion. It is safe to assume that as Lincoln's train rumbled slowly through these streets, there were African-Americans out along the tracks, helping the train to find its way forward in the early morning light, holding lanterns, removing obstacles, guiding the Special to its final rest.[86] By the law of the restrictive Black Codes, African-Americans were not allowed out after ten at night. But it was early morning now, and the work of bringing in the night train took precedence. The City of the Dead was waking up.[87]

The Special skirted Mount Olivet Cemetery and the Trinidad neighborhood, and began to penetrate a more densely populated part of town, including an unmarked patch of marshy terrain called Swampoodle (a contraction of *swamp* and *puddle*), where a cluster of recent immigrants lived.[88] The city had changed a lot since Lincoln's last day here in 1849. Between 1850 and 1860, Washington's population grew from 51,687 to 75,080, a rate of 45 percent.

But in certain ways, it had not changed at all. It still clung stubbornly to its old slave pens—the holding facilities for African-Americans who were not free. Even as slavery was tearing apart the country, Southern politicians prevented the removal of the slave pens from the capital. In 1842 a Northern abolitionist observed that maintaining slavery was a "point of honor" for the South, "a sort of symbol and proof of its control over the government of the country." So the pens endured, despite a decline in slavery, relative to Washington's free black population, which grew threefold between 1830 and 1860.[89] Slavery would remain unassailable in the district as long as Southern senators, Supreme Court justices, and presidents maintained their long habit of control over the government.

Many had fought against this national shame—including Congressman Abraham Lincoln, who introduced a bill to end slavery in Washington in January 1849, near the end of his forgettable term. He proposed a form of compensated emancipation, but then withdrew it for lack of support.[90] The memory of the slave pens still rankled five years later, when he began to speak out again. In Peoria, Illinois, in 1854, Lincoln described the view out the windows of the Capitol, over "a sort of negro-livery stable, where droves of negroes were collected, temporarily kept, and finally taken to Southern markets, precisely like droves of horses."[91] The human stables were still there in 1861. Even in the weeks preceding Lincoln's inauguration, Washington's newspapers ran advertisements for upcoming slave auctions.[92]

But a long night was ending, and the train was closing in. A few final curves, and the Special was bearing down on the Capitol. The line straightened out at the end, pointing toward the incomplete dome. Indeed, the station was so close—two blocks away—that it almost appeared as if the train would go right into the building, as underground trains would do in the twentieth century, hurrying senators to their votes. There was a gradient shift, as the train began to chug up this final hill. At long last, Lincoln was approaching the end of the line.

Washington Depot, 1872[93]

WASHINGTON DEPOT

At six in the morning, the unassuming train pulled into the depot of the Baltimore and Ohio Railroad. Lincoln was in the back compartment, ready to disembark, but it was still dangerous. A few more steps were required. An extraordinary effort had brought him this far; now he needed to get through the depot and then over to the Willard Hotel.

As the three passengers prepared to exit the sleeping car, Pinkerton hoped that they could avoid observation by acting like the other passengers disembarking. They waited a short interval, then came down the steps, and began to walk. For a few moments, the plan seemed to work. The most famous man in America was on the platform, only blocks from the Capitol, and no one seemed to know.

Lincoln kept ambling down the platform, unrecognized in his unfamiliar soft hat and pea jacket. The city was still sleeping off the excitement of the evening's entertainments, when it had tried, and failed, to celebrate Washington's Birthday. The local militias that had been parading so ostentatiously, threatening to stop Lincoln, were all in their beds, dreaming of glory. Lincoln kept walking, undetected.

But there were eyes everywhere. At trackside, a man was standing behind a pillar, watching very closely, waiting. Even after all the passengers seemed to have left the train, he remained, focused. Finally, he saw three more passengers step off the back car, unobtrusively, and begin to walk toward the front of the station. One of them was unusually tall and had a "long, lank form." [94]

As they passed by, he looked "very sharp" at them, then reached out forcefully, and grabbed the tall man in the center, saying, "Abe, you can't play that on me." This was the moment Allan Pinkerton had been dreading. He jabbed the stranger hard with his elbow, then was ready to strike him again when Lincoln forcibly intervened, grabbing Pinkerton's arm. Lincoln said quickly, "Don't strike him, Allan, don't strike him! That is my friend Washburne—don't you know him?" [95]

Elihu Washburne, an Illinois congressman, had been alerted to the secret plan by Frederick Seward and arrived early at the depot to add his strength to the tiny security phalanx around the president-elect. Washburne had also been consulting Winfield Scott about the dangers that still faced Lincoln; he knew that these final steps were among the most perilous of the entire journey.

By coincidence, the first man to welcome Lincoln to the capital had been the last one to see him, twelve years earlier, as he left Washington, all but certain that his political career was finished. On the night that Zachary Taylor was inaugurated, in 1849, the two friends stayed up very late, marveling at the festivities. Typically, Lincoln could not find his hat as they departed at four in the morning, and Washburne's last memory was of a "tall and slim man," disjointed and uncovered, starting out on a long walk toward his rooming house on Capitol Hill.[96] Even decades later, when he told this story, there was a trace of incredulity in Washburne's account that this awkward young man had grown into the president of the United States.

Washburne's account is crucial for details of Lincoln's appearance in the final moments of his journey. He described him as wearing a "low-crowned hat, a muffler around his neck, and a short bob-tailed overcoat." Washburne observed that there was still a great deal of Illinois in his appearance; he looked more like a "well-to-do farmer" from the Midwest, ready to take out a land warrant, than a distinguished statesman like James Buchanan.[97] But there was no doubt about it, the president-elect had arrived.

Pinkerton apologized to Washburne for the roughness of his greeting, and the party continued to make its way through the station. Fortunately, no one in the crowds milling around the station took note of them. Outside, they found a carriage that Washburne had arranged for, and took it a short distance through the Serbonian Bog of Pennsylvania Avenue. Soon they were at Willard's Hotel, in the very heart of the lobbying culture that had done so much to preserve the status quo. It survived a few minutes more, as Lincoln came in undetected by the other guests. Then William H. Seward arrived.[98] He and the incoming president had a great deal to talk about, but Lincoln expressed himself "rather tired" and went to a room, alone at last. Once again, he had leveled every obstacle.

Pinkerton had a bath and breakfast, and sent out telegrams to all of the railroad officials who were waiting to hear from him. Using his colorful code language, Pinkerton assured them that Nuts (Lincoln) had arrived at Barley (Washington). The package had been delivered. When he heard the news, Samuel Felton, the railroad president who first heard the warning from Dorothea Dix, shouted for joy.[99]

The day after: president-elect Abraham Lincoln,
Washington, February 24, 1861[100]

STOMACH BITTERS

In a city where little stayed secret, it did not take long for the news to spread, which it did, explosively. Washington awoke slowly to the news of his arrival, then did what it does best. Wild rumors spread around town, most of which were incorrect, and all day a crowd milled in the lobby of the Willard, speculating inconclusively. John Hay wrote sarcastically, "The number of conjectures which have been hazarded would, if they were dollars, pay the national debt."

Along Pennsylvania Avenue, one store did a thriving business in a new remedy for indigestion, Lincoln Stomach Bitters.[101] That might have come in handy, as heartburn deepened among the sycophants of the Buchanan regime, indignant that their days of easy access were coming to an end. Southerners, especially, were overheard expressing their amazement that he had survived his journey—suggesting that fears of assassination were well founded. By avoiding that result, Lincoln not only frustrated his enemies, but also weakened them. They had promised to prevent a Lincoln presidency. His refusal to acquiesce made them look foolish. He had walked right into a hotel known for its Southern sympathies, and asked for a room.[102]

Lincoln would be excoriated for sneaking through Baltimore, and ridiculed by the media, some of whom were angry at being left out of the secret. One egregious bit of reporting appeared in the *New York Times,* a paper that traditionally supported Lincoln. Joseph Howard Jr. concocted an absurd story that Lincoln had worn a Scotch cap to disguise himself, and that was all it took for cartoonists, songwriters, and tellers of tall tales to begin issuing demeaning caricatures of Lincoln, with his bony knees protruding from a kilt.

The new day would bring other forms of bad news as well. The papers were full of rumors—the *New York Herald* feared a new Haitian Revolution was beginning, and was scathing toward Lincoln's "pointless speeches," particularly his "misty allegory" about the ship of state. Later on February 23, Texas voters would vote decisively to ratify secession, 46,129 to 14,697.[103] In the evening, more visitors came to see Lincoln, including the peace conference delegates, led by former president John Tyler. It was a final exhalation of hot air, as if the swamp still had a few undrained air pockets. From the lobby of the Willard, they slinked in, demanding yet another compromise.

Lincoln listened patiently, then responded with an apt phrase for someone who had come a long way and was tired of detours. So many long-winded answers; so many exceptions carved out of what were thought to be binding agreements; so many hidden protections for the Slave Power—all carefully built into the system like secret drawers inside a piece of cabinetry. He had survived countless twists and turns in his own journey just to be there, and he did not want to be distracted from the purpose of his odyssey. To restore the people's government, it was time for a new approach, more honest, a straight line between Euclidean points. Lincoln answered, "I cannot agree to that. My course is as plain as a turnpike road."

Later in the day, the rest of Lincoln's entourage would come in, having survived their own passage through Baltimore. The crowds there were wild, expecting Lincoln. With each train that came through, they acted like "a hive of bees," swarming the train and running on top of the cars for a glimpse. (They did not believe reports that he was already in Washington.) So high was the level of excitement that a riot nearly erupted when Lincoln's luggage was seen being removed from one train and transferred to another, with the telltale *A.L.* written on the side of a large traveling case. Some speculated that he might be hiding inside, a ruse to ensure his survival for another day. It had worked for Henry "Box" Brown.

That prompted more confusion for a mob that was so divided that it could not decide whether to attack the luggage or defend it. Eventually a courageous committee of citizens mustered to escort the presidential bags through the streets of Baltimore, just in case he was hiding inside. The luggage survived the ordeal. But angry young men were still swarming, furious that Lincoln had made it through. In another part of town, a group of them pulled an African-American carriage driver off his horse and wrote "Abe Lincoln" in chalk letters upon his back. They might have done worse, but the police intervened in the nick of time.[104]

Other problems were coming in fast and furious. But Lincoln had arrived, intact, to assume the office to which the people had elected him. The next day, Charles Francis Adams Sr. recorded an unusual weather observation in his diary. He noticed "a wind that sweeps over this city with mighty power."[105] A great leveling blast was blowing in from the west, sweeping away the mephitic air of a city that had been isolated from the rest of the country for too long. With a final, feeble wheeze, the Buchanan administration was giving up the ghost.

No one knew yet what a Lincoln presidency would mean, but the fact that he had survived the ordeal meant that his presidency would actually begin. All the earth-shaking events of the next four years would emanate from that fact. Maryland was still in the Union; so was Virginia, for a while longer. Washington was safe. Lincoln had won an immense tactical victory, even before the war began. His odyssey was complete.

Crowds gathering at the Capitol, March 4, 1861[106]

ELECTRICAL COMMUNION

The *New York Herald* sensed that something very important had just happened. When it reported Lincoln's safe arrival, it predicted that future generations of children would barely believe it, and compared Lincoln's journey to that of Sinbad the Sailor.[107] Over the previous twelve days, he had traveled 1,904 miles, along eighteen different railroad lines, through eight states. He had given at least 101 speeches. By his words, and his physical presence, he had shored up America's flagging belief in her institutions. Millions of Americans had glimpsed a top hat parting a sea of humanity, or seen a bearded man wave from the back of a speeding train, or bow from a hotel balcony, and felt a connection to their government. Most had never seen a president, and never would again.[108]

Despite exhaustion, Lincoln had grown throughout the ordeal. After a few missteps, his speeches became masterful, especially near the end, when he began to discover the mystical power that would lift his oratory to the heights he achieved at Gettysburg and the Second Inaugural. No president has ever climbed to a higher altitude. He restored a sense that America's words mean something.

Even with the threat of assassination dogging every step, he deepened as he neared Philadelphia and drew nourishment from its wellsprings. Independence Hall strengthened him. It was his peculiar genius to see in one moral crisis (1861) a chance to revisit another (1776) and reassert the leveling power of the Declaration of Independence. By emphasizing its promise of dignity for all, Lincoln dealt a powerful blow to the Confederacy, at precisely the moment it needed international recognition. Several of his speeches achieved greatness and could not have come at a better time for a beleaguered president-elect. With a more sophisticated grasp of American history, he outmaneuvered Jefferson Davis at a time when "President Davis," as the press was calling him, had far more power to lead a government than he did. By winning the race, Lincoln restored America's claim to be a country founded upon a moral principle.

Lincoln grappled his way toward these breakthroughs under the most difficult conditions, getting sicker as the train kept going, losing his voice, enduring the crush of countless receptions. His admirers were nearly as dangerous as his enemies, and it was a small miracle he survived some of the unrulier receptions or the moments when cannons were accidentally fired into his train by overeager welcoming committees. His speeches were routinely distorted by political rivals and the press, to convey thoughts he did not mean. That made speaking a great burden. And yet he understood that he needed to talk constantly and shake thousands of hands to win back a country that had lost its way. Each touch made a difference. It was a physical agony, as his intimates knew. But he had worked hard all his life, and did not shirk his duty.

Lincoln never wrote about what it must have been like to be at the center of attention in a way that no American had ever been. But his secretary John Nicolay conveyed some of the ups and downs of a harrowing journey, arguing that it would be hard for anyone to ever understand "the mingled excitement and apprehension, elation and fatigue" that Lincoln endured every day of the journey. The downs were impressive. Lincoln was criticized relentlessly and, even on the verge of assuming office, struck many sophisticated commentators as unpresidential. Reporters ridiculed his appearance; jaded political operatives read his speeches aloud "amidst irresistible bursts of laughter." [109]

But perhaps that is precisely what made this trip so memorable. Lincoln was not trying to impress Washington's callow insiders. He was speaking above and beyond them, to the people themselves. Never has any president needed to, more urgently. As the country disintegrated, he had to persuade them that he was fighting for them, just as they would fight for him. He literally reached out to them, shaking hands by the tens of thousands. Henry Villard sometimes wrote caustically of Lincoln's "clodhopper" appearance, but he had to admit, "He never refused to respond to a call for his appearance whenever the train stopped."

John Nicolay continued, "As Mr. Lincoln's journey progressed, his wisdom in making it one of public oration became apparent." It was not just the words he came to say, day in and day out, to immense throngs and to tiny clusters of rural families waving mutely as the train sped past. There was something about the awkward man himself. They saw him and heard his earnest voice, and felt reassured. By an alchemy that we cannot perceive through any photograph, the physical experience of seeing and hearing Lincoln inspired people. Nicolay wrote, "His whole bearing, manner, and utterance carried conviction to all beholders that the man was of them as well as for them."

Then he added an observation worthy of Tocqueville. Nicolay believed that Americans, so used to hearing speakers at large rallies, could tell the difference between a fraud and a genuine leader. With their "fine discrimination," they could judge the moral fiber of a man. It was almost as if "a current of electrical communion" connected the people to Lincoln, an invisible telegraph that fused his thoughts with theirs. Nicolay knew that cynics would doubt his claim that Lincoln inspired this kind of electricity. But he added that anyone "who stood near him throughout this memorable journey can give earnest testimony to its presence from Lincoln to the people."[110]

The "electrical communion" between Lincoln and his people would never wane. Forged over a grueling train trip, it was a political achievement of the highest importance. It worked in both directions, sustaining him as well. Lincoln's electric communion saved the republic. Remembering the extraordinary journey, Nicolay sighed in amazement. "A proper description," he wrote, "would fill a volume."[111]

Lincoln inaugurated[112]

CRAZYDOM

Nine days after arriving, Lincoln walked out of Willard's Hotel with the draft of the speech that he had guarded so jealously and nearly lost among a sea of black valises in the baggage hold of an Indianapolis hotel. The day had dawned inauspiciously, with rain, "leaden skies," and "tornadoes of dust." But then it improved appreciably, and the sun came out "in all its brilliancy." [113]

When a carriage arrived with the outgoing president, James Buchanan, Lincoln faced one of the first decisions of his administration. Should they enclose the carriage or ride uncovered? Lincoln chose an open barouche, so that "all could see him." When they arrived at the Capitol, they found a throng of thirty thousand people waiting, far bigger than any inaugural crowd to date. [114] It was the largest crowd that the capital had ever seen.

From great distances, the people had streamed in to witness the peaceful transfer of power. To be sure, there were threatening elements in addition to the morning rain. The newspapers noticed a sizeable contingent of "roughs and plugs" from Baltimore, and many representatives of "crazydom," the disturbed people who always surface upon grand public occasions. Dorothea Dix would not have been surprised; no mental institution seemed large enough to contain all of America's malcontents, especially in the final minutes of the Great Secession Winter. [115]

One visitor, a "little man in large, red whiskers," decided to give an inaugural address of his own in front of the Capitol, near where Lincoln was about to speak. The police did their best to seize him, but he eluded capture by climbing a tree near the East Portico, just in front of the two presidents, and selecting "a strong and convenient branch." From that well-chosen site, roughly at the same height as Lincoln's podium, he pulled out a wad of manuscripts and began to read a homily on "the vices of the times," complete with "oratorical flourishes." These "gyrations" began to attract attention from the huge crowd below. Several policemen climbed up after him, but he evaded them by scaling higher, into the "topmost branches," where they were unwilling to go. Still, the officers had performed a public service: he was now so high in the tree that he was mostly out of earshot. After concluding his speech, he let go of all of the pages with a final flourish. It would be difficult for Lincoln to top that performance. [116]

As the weather improved, so did the mood. There was a burst of laughter when an old lady, frustrated in her attempt to get near Lincoln, demanded that the crowd "secede," or she would be forced to use "coercion." [117] Huge crowds of good-natured westerners were there, ready to fortify their new president, and soldiers mingled with the crowd, quietly preserving order. There were also many African-Americans, despite local laws against their presence on the grounds of the Capitol.[118] They too wanted to protect him. Sharpshooters could be seen along the parade route, poised atop Washington's rooftops, and arrayed along the Capitol's windows. Below the wooden platform where Lincoln would stand, Winfield Scott had deployed his artillery, a last answer to the death threats that had never stopped coming in since November 6. The final seconds were ticking on the most difficult presidential transition in American history.[119]

To stand at the East Front of the Capitol would place Lincoln in the most public position, helplessly exposed. Since the dark days of November and December, many of the death threats had centered upon this time and place. If, as so many Southerners believed, Lincoln did not deserve this office, then it was tempting to prove it on the very steps of a building that had been so hospitable to Southern interests for so long. To those who loved Shakespeare, as many of these dramatic plotters did, the Capitol was the right place to eliminate a Caesar. Even the sharpshooters could do little to stop a Southern sympathizer from getting very close. A newspaper that day acknowledged "reports that an attempt would be made to shoot Mr. Lincoln while delivering his inaugural." [120]

But democracy required a firm declaration of principles from a leader to his people. Lincoln responded as he always did, by standing up to his full height and doing his job. In front of his fellow Americans, he took the oath of office with "much solemnity." At that moment, democracy was vindicated. Government of the people would endure.[121]

Quietly, he reached into his pocket and put on his steel-rimmed spectacles. This was the moment of peak vulnerability. With the glasses, Lincoln looked older. A wag in the audience yelled, "Look at old goggles!" Heart-beats raced, and the police rushed over, but all was safe. Then the new president launched into his speech in a clear, high-pitched voice, with something of the prairie in it. "Fellow citizens of the United States," he began, emphasizing the word *United*.[122]

Alexander Gardner, Photograph of Abraham Lincoln, February 5, 1865[1]

EPILOGUE

HOME

I want to go back home,
and every day I hope that day will come.
If some god strikes me on the wine-dark sea,
I will endure it. By now I am used
to suffering—I have gone through so much,
at sea and in the war. Let this come too.

—Homer, *The Odyssey*, book 5, lines 219–242[2]

Toward the end of his presidency, Lincoln began to dream of home. As the weather softened in the spring of 1865, he longed to see Springfield again, now that his journey was nearly completed.

The Civil War had been "fundamental and astounding," as he phrased it at his second inaugural. The cataclysm, when it came, was total. Nearly eight hundred thousand brave young men gave their lives in service to their conflicting ideas of the nation. No American was untouched by it; it touches us still.

Yet the republic survived, sustained by the same perseverance Lincoln had shown throughout his journey. From the moment he arrived, things improved. Democracy not only refused to die, it *deepened*. Soldiers paused to vote while fighting; women played an essential role on the home front; African-Americans made steady strides toward freedom and citizenship.

The Civil War tested Americans like no crisis before or since. But in the long run, it forged a stronger nation.

Lincoln continued to move as president, visiting troops by water and by rail, and occasionally taking longer trips to charitable events in Baltimore and Philadelphia. One journey in particular summoned memories of the earlier one. When he went to Gettysburg in November 1863 for the dedication of a cemetery, he brought along a few friends. Hay and Nicolay were there, as usual, and Lincoln also invited William Johnson, the young African-American who had been aboard the Special in 1861. Since then, Johnson had worked briefly in the White House but, with Lincoln's help, he moved to the Treasury Department, where he found work as a porter. Still, he came back to see the president and to shave him—the slender evidence suggests something of a friendship.

To get to Gettysburg, the train needed to go through Baltimore. Once again, there were difficulties, precisely at the choke point, as he transferred from one station to another. Years after the fact, a member of his military escort remembered the "gang of roughs" that had clambered aboard the platform, trying to come "into his car" as it was being tugged by horses through the streets. It required some vigorous bayonet work to dislodge them; they refused to give up until "severely pricked." Then Lincoln rumbled forward, imperturbable, to deliver his paean to democracy.[3]

In other ways, too, the journey took a toll. Lincoln came down with a fever in Gettysburg that exposed him to a different kind of danger. Most accounts labeled it a "varioloid," a mild form of smallpox, but it may have been the genuine article. He recovered, but William Johnson contracted a case of his own, possibly from Lincoln, and died in January 1864. His demise added to the president's woes and suggested that Lincoln, too, had been standing on death's doorstep, even as he delivered his most famous speech. Afterward, he personally handled the administration of Johnson's tiny estate and paid for his coffin.[4]

The *River Queen*[5]

FREE AS AIR

In the final weeks of the war, Lincoln continued to travel, almost recklessly, as if he might end the trauma by going straight into it. These new journeys seemed like extensions of his earlier ones. He was drawn to the water—to "your element," as he remarked to his secretary of the navy, Gideon Welles, while describing a vivid dream on the last day of his life. In that dream, he was on a vessel, moving rapidly, toward an "indeterminate shore."

Indeterminate shores were easy to find that spring, as the Confederacy began to collapse. Huge challenges were coming in quickly, relating not only to Reconstruction and the integration of the seceded states, but also to the settlement of the West and the imminent return of the United States to a global community that had not exactly missed the awkward colossus. These were uncharted waters, full of new obstacles.

Some of the shores were literal, as Lincoln went deeper into Virginia, seeking the war's end. In March 1865 he began a long trip by boat.[6] As Ulysses Grant was closing in on Richmond, he invited Lincoln to his headquarters at City Point, where the Appomattox and James Rivers converge.[7] To get there, Lincoln sailed down the Potomac and out into the open waters of Chesapeake Bay, then up the James River toward the Confederate capital.

He took a big side-wheeler, the *River Queen*. Once again, he was moving, on an improvised ship of state.

It was a curious journey, and the longest time that Lincoln was ever away from the White House. The president came closer to the fighting than was prudent, tempting fate at many moments. He lived modestly, close to the water, in a small cabin on the flagship of an admiral, David D. Porter.

He seemed happy in these straitened circumstances, reminiscent in some ways of his earliest work as a pilot, on the rivers that all flowed south. His childhood still could surface unexpectedly. One day he surprised a group of visitors with his intense appreciation of a single tree, tall and well proportioned, like the great oaks he had grown up among.[8]

On the morning of April 4, there were black plumes of smoke over Richmond, and the news came in that the city had fallen. Lincoln exclaimed to Admiral Porter, "Thank God that I have lived to see this! It seems to me that I have been dreaming a horrid dream these past four years, and now the nightmare is gone."[9]

But the nightmare had not disappeared entirely. Lincoln decided to get as close as he could. To do so, he needed to clamber into ever-smaller vessels in order to get through waters that had become dangerously clogged with dead horses, wrecked boats, and floating torpedoes close enough to touch.[10] Lincoln was a specialist in getting boats over obstacles, but these were difficulties on a different order. From his naval vessel, the USS *Malvern*, he switched to a barge pulled by a tugboat. Then, for the final push, he was carried in a simple rowboat—a captain's gig—manned by twelve sailors, pulling at their oars as if they were ancient Phoenicians. When they arrived, just below Richmond, Lincoln simply walked out of the boat and onto the riverbank.[11] Parts of the city were still on fire from the battles of the day before, and explosions could be heard nearby.

This was an indeterminate shore if there ever was one—a kind of no-man's-land, controlled by Grant's troops, but still dangerous. There was no reception committee in this forbidding landscape, but one soon formed. A group of African-Americans working nearby understood who had landed. As Lincoln made his way forward, they gathered around him in significant numbers. Moved, Lincoln made a spontaneous speech—an important one, in which he laid out his hopes for their freedom. It is not listed in the official collection of Lincoln's speeches, perhaps because it was not recorded at the time and only set down twenty years later, from memory, by a witness. But it rings true. There, along the same river that had seen the first African slaves brought to Virginia, Lincoln tried to set matters right:

> My poor friends, you are free—free as air. You can cast off the name of slave and trample upon it; it will come to you no more. Liberty is your birthright. God gave it to you as he gave it to others, and it is a sin that you have been deprived of it for so many years. But you must try to deserve this priceless boon. Let the world see that you merit it and are able to maintain it by your good works. Don't let your joy carry you into excesses. Learn the laws and obey them; obey God's commandments and thank him for giving you liberty, for him you owe all things. There, now, let me pass on; I have but little time to spare. I want to see the capital and must return at once to Washington to secure to you that liberty which you seem to prize so highly.[12]

The naval officer who recorded these words added that Lincoln seemed transported as he welcomed these new citizens. His face was illuminated from within, and he "really seemed of another world." Lincoln added a personal promise to one of them: "As long as I live, you shall have all the rights which God has given to every other free citizen of this republic."[13]

There was a touching scene as an elderly man came over to address the president of the United States. Raising his crownless straw hat, he said, "May the good Lord bless you and keep you safe." With tears in his eyes, Lincoln lifted his own hat and bowed to him, one citizen acknowledging another.[14]

It could be argued that this muddy riverbank was the true destination of the long journey he had set out on, four years earlier. But these happy scenes were marred by a dread that also seemed to follow Lincoln, as if he had tempted fate too many times. He had seen the carnage of the war up close, and a few days earlier had walked past corpses killed in the final fighting over

Petersburg. In early March his wife did a strange thing: for no apparent reason, Mary Todd Lincoln ordered an extensive wardrobe of black mourning clothes.[15] A drawer in his desk held a thick folder of what he called, simply, "Assassination Letters."[16] He was losing weight, and his hands often turned cold. One night, he startled his bodyguard, William Crook, looking "tall and white and ghostly." Sometimes, as Crook passed outside the room Lincoln slept in, he could hear him moaning in his sleep.[17]

Those fears understandably deepened as they entered the Confederate capital. William Crook saw him recoil when "the thunder of the cannon told him that men were being cut down like grass." Within the smoldering city, they encountered a sullen white population seething with resentment.

Ruins of Richmond, with Virginia Capitol, 1865[19]

Crook believed that he saw a man in gray pointing a gun at Lincoln from a second-story window, only to pull away as the bodyguard stepped in front of the president. A journalist witnessing these scenes wrote that the people had "daggers in their eyes."[18]

For years, it had been fashionable to claim that America was less lovely than Europe because it lacked picturesque ruins.[19] Now the South was littered with them, its Greek Revival banks and courthouses shattered, like the temples of old, as if two thousand years had elapsed, rather than four. In Richmond, the State Capitol had survived the bombardment, but from its hilltop, it now surveyed a landscape of utter desolation.

TALKING WITH THE DEAD

Lincoln also seemed to be approaching another kind of shore. Mary Todd Lincoln later recounted he was struck by the beauty of a country graveyard during his visit to Richmond. Noticing the flowers bursting forth from every grave, he said to her, "Mary, you are younger than I. You will survive me. When I am gone, lay my remains in some quiet place like this."[21]

Finally, it was time to return to Washington, and surely the bodyguards were relieved when he came back from the front. A young French diplomat accompanied him and kept meticulous notes of their conversations. The talk turned literary, and Lincoln read aloud from *Macbeth*. He was especially struck by the lines in Act 3, when Macbeth expresses envy for Duncan, the king he has killed. Lincoln seemed to appreciate the calm that had come to the dead leader, to whom "Treason has done its worst: nor steel, nor poison / Malice domestic, foreign levy, nothing, / Can touch him further."[22] But he may also have felt some empathy for the tormented Macbeth, suffering from "the affliction of these terrible dreams / that shake us nightly." Macbeth was one of the roles that John Wilkes Booth was best known for.

It was natural that Lincoln should think of mortality, after what he had seen in Richmond. Yet he surprised the Frenchman with the vividness of what he was seeing in his private midway world.[23] "Do you ever find yourself talking with the dead?" he once asked a startled army officer.[24]

As the *River Queen* continued up the Potomac, the river narrowed, and at one particularly lovely bend, they passed the seat of George Washington. Noticing Mount Vernon, Lincoln's French guest, the Marquis de Chambrun, predicted that Americans would someday revere Springfield as well. The word *Springfield* seemed to awaken Lincoln as if "from a trance." He turned to Chambrun and expressed how happy he would be to finally make it home.[25]

Even after returning to a capital city that was exultant in the final days of the war, Lincoln continued to wander in an underworld that no one else could see.[26] His African-American seamstress, Elizabeth Keckley, thought he was beginning to live in another place even while on this earth. When he gave his last speech, on the night of April 11, she thought he resembled a "demi-god" more than a man.[27]

Official ceremony to return the U.S. flag to Fort Sumter, April 14, 1865[28]

CLOUDS

As the sun rose on April 14, all felt it was likely to be a day for the history books. In his diary, Benjamin Brown French wrote, "the day was one of the most perfect imaginable." In Charleston, the original flag that Major Robert Anderson had brought with him when he evacuated Fort Sumter was to be raised again over the same fort.[29] That would be a moment for the ages, bringing even more finality than Lee's surrender at Appomattox five days earlier.[30] As the day continued, Lincoln brought Ulysses Grant to a meeting of the Cabinet. Neither could have known that Grant would be living in the White House in less than four years.

It was during this meeting that Lincoln told the story of the indefinite shore he had glimpsed in his dream the night before. The reliable diary of Gideon Welles, the secretary of the navy, offers the most immediate version of the president's words. As Lincoln described it for the rapt Cabinet, it was a recurring dream that always preceded "great news." In the dream, Lincoln "seemed to be in some singular, indescribable vessel."[31] "We shall, judging from the past, have great news again very soon," Lincoln surmised.

Walt Whitman was also anticipating great news as the spring rushed in. The Brooklyn poet had moved to Washington, and was noticing strange portents in the skies. As he put it, "The heavens, the elements, all the meteorological influences, have run riot for weeks past." During Lincoln's second inaugural, Whitman was struck by the way "a curious little white cloud, the only one in that part of the sky, appeared like a hovering bird, right over him."

As soon as Lincoln spoke, the weather changed. In the morning, the skies had been dark, "with slanting rain, full of rage." Then, when he appeared, they were bathed in sunshine, with an "atmosphere of sweetness" so clear that it showed the stars and planets in the middle of the day. Whitman noticed one in particular: the evening star, Venus, was shining brilliantly against the western sky. "It seems as if it told something," he wrote in a note to himself.

The birds were acting oddly as well. Whitman's young friend, the naturalist John Burroughs, had seen large flocks of blackbirds sitting in the trees around the White House. As soon as the inaugural address was finished, Burroughs noticed that "the wind roared like a lion over the woods."[32]

By some accounts, Lincoln was happy, almost giddy, on April 14. During a ride with his wife, she commented, "Dear husband, you almost startle me by your great cheerfulness."[33] But Lincoln's bodyguard, William Crook, painted a different picture. He wrote, "The president was more depressed than I had ever seen him and his step unusually slow."[34] Again, a cloud seemed to hover over him. As they walked between the White House and the War Department, Lincoln noticed some drunken men nearby. That was enough to prompt him to turn to Crook and say that he believed there were men who wanted to take his life, adding, "I have no doubt they will do it." That night, as he headed to the theater, he said "good-bye" to Crook instead of the usual "good night."[35]

Crossing over: A locomotive near Niagara Falls, circa 1856[36]

BLACK, BLACK, BLACK

Despite these premonitions, the American people were unready for the tidal wave of grief that crashed over them after Lincoln crossed his final river. Henry James, waking up in Boston, noticed a deep blackness before dawn and felt his pulse racing, along with a general restlessness, without yet knowing why. Then, when the news came, "a huge general gasp" filled the streets "with a great earth shudder."[37] Ralph Waldo Emerson said that as the news traveled, swiftly, it felt as if an eclipse were spreading its shadow across the planet.[38] In New York, Whitman also felt a supernatural energy, as if the heavens were speaking. Shattered, he wrote in a disjointed way, unable to make a sentence: "Lincoln's death—black, black, black—as you look toward the sky—long broad black like great serpents slowly undulating in every direction."[39]

For many, like Whitman, the bond had been personal, ever since the poet first glimpsed Lincoln during his train journey. "I never see that man without feeling he is one to become personally attached to," Whitman wrote after watching him go by in his plain two-horse carriage after the stupendous second inaugural.[40]

Thousands who saw him on his train trip in 1861 felt the same way. At a time when the federal government was an abstract entity, at best, under James Buchanan, he became the living embodiment of a better idea. All felt the danger as he stood before enormous numbers of people, friendly and unfriendly alike. But the moment demanded that he stand up, and he did. He had survived the journey, and the war, and the Union was intact.

But in the dark days that followed the assassination, few saw any silver linings. A pall settled over Washington. A year earlier, at a sanitary fair in Philadelphia, Lincoln had quoted the opening lines of Shakespeare's *Henry VI*: "Hung be the heavens with black, yield day to night!" Now that prophecy was enacted, as mourning crepe decorated every storefront in the capital and in every other Northern city as well.[41]

Even before the long night of April 14 was over, it was obvious how much the country had changed in the four years since Lincoln arrived in the Federal City. The same networks that had done so much to protect him during his journey greatly expanded under his presidency. Trains and telegraphs quickly became indispensable as the North organized for total war. Southerners were amazed by how quickly Northerners could rebuild tracks that had been torn up or restring the telegraph wires that kept up the incessant Yankee chatter. During the war, the U.S. Military Telegraph Corps built eight to twelve miles of telegraph line a day; and the military alone sent six and a half million messages. In March 1861 it took seven days and seventeen hours for a Pony Express rider to get Lincoln's first inaugural to the West Coast; four years later, the transmission of his second inaugural was instantaneous.[42] The country changed forever as tens of thousands of miles of wire stretched across the vast continent, tightening the sinews of Union. Later, telephone and fiber-optic lines would be laid along the same routes.[43]

Ever since Lincoln's arrival, Washington had been a different kind of city, as if he'd brought the Lightning with him. By 1865, massive amounts of information were flowing in and out, and the city would never again return to its sleepy isolation. Throughout the long night of April 14, the telegraph lines were lit up, bringing the news from this once-isolated capital to the rest of the country. From Lincoln's bedside, Secretary of War Edwin Stanton was sending out bulletins that instantly "flashed over the wires."[44] When Lincoln's struggle ended, all knew, with railroad precision, that it was 7:22 a.m.[45]

In the South, on the contrary, the news came more slowly. Mary Chesnut wrote that the only means of communication they had in South Carolina were the chimneys that were left standing after their homes were burned. Bitterly, she called them "little telegraph poles to carry the news of Sherman's army backward."[46]

But even in death, Lincoln united his people. From around the country, they began to stream into Washington. It had become much easier to reach since Lincoln's clandestine arrival in 1861. Four years as the headquarters of a titanic war effort had transformed the half-finished capital into a busy hub, far less Southern than it had been. A proliferation of train lines and telegraph lines now snaked their way into the District of Columbia and Alexandria.

By Tuesday, April 18, a hundred thousand people had arrived, doubling the city's population.[47] They could not possibly all fit into the funeral service, to be held in the East Room of the White House at noon the next day, but a huge number pressed their way in. Near the end of the service, the Reverend Phineas D. Gurley, the Lincoln family pastor, walked over to the star-studded coffin and put his hand on it. Spontaneously, the audience stood up as Dr. Gurley intoned, "you, our honored friend and head . . . will survive yourself and triumph over the injustice of time."[48]

The injustice of time was not a problem that day. At precisely noon, as the service was taking place in the White House, bells were tolling around the nation, inviting Americans into thousands of houses of worship, all remembering Lincoln in their own way, simultaneously. That, too, was an act of union.[49] The writer Edward Everett Hale called it "the most impressive religious service ever held in this country."[50]

The services were wordy and lachrymose—in other words, they barely resembled their subject. But Americans, prostrate with grief, needed consolation, and so the floodgates opened. Their preachers sensed the national mood for sentimentality and held nothing back. Suddenly a politician who had barely survived the 1864 election was being recast as the incarnate of his people, a figure whose humble birth and gentle wisdom might have been lifted straight from the New Testament.

Hundreds of these sermons were published by a people desperate to understand what had happened, including one by an Episcopalian minister in Orange, New Jersey. In the fullness of time, James S. Bush would become the grandfather of one president and the great-grandfather of another. In April 1865 he added his voice to a loud chorus and regretted the passing of "a life no mortal could bear."[51]

In Washington, a large procession formed to escort Lincoln from the White House to the Capitol, and to begin his homeward journey. It included railroad workers, government employees, firemen, schoolchildren, wounded veterans, recent immigrants, and Native Americans. One group was especially conspicuous. Four thousand African-Americans marched at the back of the procession, while another group of African-Americans, a Union regiment freshly returned from the war, accidentally found itself in the front, after intercepting the parade. It was if the book of Matthew was being enacted—in the words of the Savior, "many that are first shall be last; and the last shall be first."[52]

Washington had changed in so many ways during the war that it was difficult to enumerate them all. What had been a disjointed place became more whole, the slave pens were shut down, the swampy terrain was improved, and the Capitol dome was completed. The latter task was made easier by a steam engine, another sign that the railroad economy had arrived. To feed the engine's appetite, old wood was salvaged from the older dome, as if the new building needed to destroy the old, to start again, with a clean slate.

One profound difference was that this city, so indifferent to the plight of African-Americans before 1861, became a major destination for former slaves fleeing the South. At least twenty thousand so-called contrabands found their way to Washington during the war, and other African-Americans came from other directions to lend support to the war effort. Over the decade, the African-American population rose by 223 percent.[53]

As a result, a capital that had been founded to perpetuate the influence of slavery now found itself, ironically, as one of the blackest cities in the United States. It has never lost that distinction, and, to this day, a city swollen with transient government employees and smug lobbyists derives much of its coherence—its soul—from this more settled population. That may have been an accident of war, but even if unplanned, it made Washington a worthier capital of a great nation. It remains an enduring legacy of Lincoln's ride.

Near the end of the procession, as the catafalque approached the rise in Capitol Hill, it followed the railroad tracks that Lincoln had come in along four years earlier.[54] Then, unerringly, it found its way to the ark of the republic, the Capitol Rotunda. Lincoln's coffin was placed on an elevated bier, below the dome he had seen through to completion. The stars lining the coffin's exterior seemed appropriate for the night of mourning that had begun. All the paintings and statuary were shrouded with one exception: a statue of Washington wearing a black military sash.[55] Lincoln had been following him ever since the morning his train left Springfield, and he might

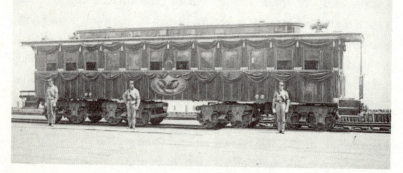

The *United States*[57]

have occupied the empty crypt that had been built for Washington two levels below the rotunda. In the end, his widow preferred Springfield. So, another journey was planned, to bring him home.[56]

A LANE TO LET HIM PASS

But first the people needed to say farewell. The next day, the president's open coffin rested in the middle of the room while thousands of mourners filed by. A young friend of Lincoln's, Noah Brooks, had the inspiration to climb up to the top of the huge dome, to better witness this democratic ritual. He described the people, looking "like black atoms moving over a gray paper" as they filed patiently past the bier.[58]

Lincoln once described a dream to Hay and Nicolay in which he was transported to "some great assembly" where "the people made a lane to let him pass." One of the people said, "He is a common-looking fellow." Even while dreaming, Lincoln's agile mind was alert to a joke opportunity, and he came back with the perfect retort: "Friend, the Lord prefers common-looking people: that is why he made so many of them."[59]

Something like this imaginary scene began to unfold, as a lane opened up through which Lincoln could pass. He would follow almost the exact same route that he had taken four years earlier. The train had brought him to Washington; now it would bring him back.

In 1862 Congress had passed a war measure that gave the War Department the authority to operate any American railroad in an emergency. That authority was now invoked to prepare Lincoln's final journey.[60] Near the Capitol, inside the same depot Lincoln had come into, a special train was waiting. It consisted of nine cars in all: six for passengers, two for baggage, and two cars that were unusual. The first was a luxury car built for senior officials by the Philadelphia, Wilmington and Baltimore Railroad—the same line that had done so much to protect Lincoln in 1861. It would carry the friends and family of the Lincolns. The second car would carry Lincoln himself, in his mahogany casket, and a second casket holding his son Willie, who died in February 1862, a year after he and his brother did so much to enliven the train trip. Most passenger cars did not have names—only locomotives did. But this car was so important that it had been given one: the *United States*.

The long car was magnificent, and drew immediate attention for its size and grandeur.[61] It had been intended for Lincoln's personal travel, although never in this particular way. Its designers wanted a car that conveyed the might of the nation, beginning a tradition that would stretch to "U.S. Car No. 1" (the name for Franklin Roosevelt's private train car) and Air Force One.[62] The work had been completed just weeks earlier.[63]

The long journey began with the familiar lurch forward, carefully, through the large crowd. Retracing the route Lincoln took in 1861, the funeral train sped north toward Baltimore, the scene of so much anxiety on the way in. There was no trouble this time. On the contrary, the *New-York Tribune* wrote, "White and black stood side by side in the rain and the mud, with eyes strained upon that coffin, with eyes running over, and with clasped hands."[64]

Many of the same personnel were aboard, and as they retraced their route, they stayed in the same hotels and met the same dignitaries.[65] Pittsburgh was deleted, and Chicago added, but otherwise there was an eerie symmetry between the two trips. It had only been four years since his earlier passage, and many of the same teams of horses and drivers were still available. But instead of pulling his carriage, they were now leading his catafalque through oceans of humanity.[66]

Once again, millions encountered Lincoln and came away profoundly affected. It was a grim yet redemptive passage, as millions of Americans gazed upon the mortal remains of their fallen leader.[67] Some communities improvised religious services as the train went by; others simply absorbed the sight of the passing coffin, slowing down as it went through the heart of a town. No one knew more intimately the nature of sacrifice than the people who had given so many young men to save the republic. Seeing him again required them to confront the unavoidable evidence of death one more time. But it also honored their own sacrifices and fulfilled Lincoln's promise to them, that he would never abandon the ship. Democracy was a great cause, worthy of a great sacrifice.

Even away from the cities, it was crowded at trackside. Farms and small towns emptied as the train approached, so that grievers could stand near as the

Lincoln's funeral procession, New York, April 25, 1865[68]

train whooshed by. In many places, communities improvised mourning rituals, with young women draped in black.[69] A locomotive engineer remembered later that it could be difficult to move the train forward, because the tracks became slippery from all the flowers that were left on them or simply thrown at the train as it went by.[70] It often seemed like entire villages had come out to pay their respects. Mothers held infants over their heads to better see the passing coffin, visible through the windows. The elderly were carried down in their chairs.[71] People of all ages wept openly. In Lancaster, Pennsylvania, an old man watched from his carriage: James Buchanan, who had been so eager to escape the White House at the same time that Lincoln was risking his life to get there.[72]

The time of day did not matter; they came out at all hours. At night, the train's two lights could be seen from far off, shining forward, far down the track. The townsfolk added to that illumination with their torches. So many lined the tracks in upstate New York that a witness likened it to a "pillar of fire."

In his own agony, Walt Whitman poured out four poems relating to Lincoln's death, one of which described an immense funeral procession moving from city to city. He used a striking image in "When Lilacs Last in the Dooryard Bloom'd": a coffin advancing through the land, as if under its own motive power. It proceeded from one community to the next, like a raft floating downstream, uniting them in a universal lamentation. All were included as the coffin went through the crowded downtowns of surging cities, and past tiny trackside hamlets, little more than dots along a line when they were first drawn into the railroad maps.

In Philadelphia, Independence Hall was bathed in an eerie luminescence of red, white, and blue, with more than a hundred candles flickering. At least a hundred thousand people came through the old building.[73] In New York, the crush was even greater. The coffin was taken across the Hudson on a barge while all the sailors of New York's busy harbor stood silently on their ships, watching it pass. Then it made its way up Broadway, block by block, through huge crowds, passing the same buildings Lincoln had visited: the Astor House and City Hall.[74] One witness estimated that a hundred thousand were already lined up at two in the morning and that a million and a half watched the procession.[75] Among them were two small boys looking out from a window near Union Square: a six-year-old Theodore Roosevelt and his brother Elliott. In Madison Square, an eleven-year-old girl, Jennie Jerome, was also watching and never forgot the sight of the vast catafalque, as she would tell her son, Winston Churchill. Shopkeepers could not keep enough mourning crepe in stock. A witness compared the city to "an immense black and white flower."[76]

North of New York, Lincoln was pulled by the same two locomotives as four years earlier: the *Constitution* leading the *Union*, and both of them leading the *United States*.[77] The cannonry of West Point issued a loud salute as the fallen commander passed by. Then the train glided through Hyde Park, where another funeral train would arrive in 1945, from Georgia. On that long journey, Elliott Roosevelt's daughter, Eleanor, lay in her berth with the shade up, looked out at the grieving faces of thousands of Americans, and thought of Lincoln.[78]

Everywhere it was the same: in Albany, Buffalo, Cleveland, Columbus, and Indianapolis, throngs came out to say farewell to the man they called "the People's President."[79] In Chicago, the train passed by the tomb of Stephen Douglas, then carried Lincoln back into the city where he had been nominated only five years earlier. The line of people waiting to pay their respects stretched five miles.

Finally, the train curved south, toward Springfield, along the route Lincoln took so many times as a younger man.[80] Southwest of Chicago, it went through Lockport, where a banner draped at the depot spoke with Lincolnesque brevity: "Come Home."[81] He finally did, on May 3, when the long black train steamed into Springfield.[82] During his long ride in 1861, he had often joked about a hearse that was so slow it would not make it to the cemetery before resurrection day. Now, at last, he had arrived at his final destination. The long journey, a round trip of sorts, was over.[83]

The next day, May 4, Springfield's church bells chimed again, as they had on the morning of his departure, four years earlier.[84] "Rise up and hear the bells," Whitman intoned in one of his eulogies, and if Lincoln did not, just about everyone else in Springfield did. Even Lincoln's horse, Bob, was dressed in mourning attire.

In his poem, Whitman offered a sprig of lilac to the passing coffin to ease its passage. In fact, something like that happened on the day that Lincoln was laid to rest. When the undertakers were going through their final preparations, they found a tiny rosebud, attached to a geranium leaf, that had settled in his clothing, near his heart. It had likely fallen from a flower left by one of the millions of mourners who had filed past.[85] The small tribute seemed all the more fitting for its anonymity. Americans had grieved deeply during his long journey home, and they had grieved together, as a single people. To the end, he served a higher cause.

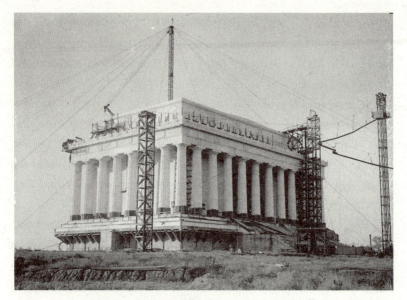

The Lincoln Memorial under construction, 1915[86]

REST

Would Lincoln at last be able to rest in peace?

At first, the answer seemed to be no, as the local authorities continued to move him—fourteen times—to better satisfy their notions of what a proper shrine should look like.[87] But Lincoln settled into place and began to occupy his unique role in the American psyche. With time, the politician who barely survived the journey to his own inauguration became the central figure in our pantheon. Well before the funeral ride was over, his apotheosis was under way, as a thousand sermons lifted him high above the earth, in a flight path all his own, just below the better angels.

Some of the early eulogies caught the essence of what Lincoln would become. In 1861, leading Easterners had dismissed Lincoln's country-cloddish ways as unbecoming to his office. Now they came around. In his eulogy, on April 19, 1865, Ralph Waldo Emerson spoke of the train trip, when he marveled at the way "the new pilot" arrived, "hurried to the helm in a tornado." Emerson understood how important it had been for Americans to see and hear their new president in the flesh. "The president stood before us as a man of the people," Emerson remembered, for "he had a face and a manner which disarmed suspicion, which inspired confidence, which confirmed good will."[89] The trip had exposed that face, and Americans, seeing him, responded. He left Springfield as the head of a party that was barely in control of the mechanics of governance; he arrived in Washington as a genuine president-elect.

When he came home, and they saw his face again, it confirmed for millions of Americans that an era had ended—not just the war itself but also a long and bitter struggle over what kind of country the United States should be. They knew that an unutterable tragedy had taken place, but they also understood that the country had become more honest with itself. They trusted Lincoln's vision of an America that aspired to keep the promises of the Declaration of Independence. Even if they had lost him, they knew that "the Union is not assassinated," as Whitman put it.[90] They were not naïve; they knew that the Declaration set a difficult standard, one that they would often fail to reach. But to pretend it did not exist was to slowly become a different kind of country, with no moral standards at all.

For the young, Lincoln's death was a scar they would carry for the rest of their lives. But as Henry James wrote, the tragedy also educated them, and they learned to move forward as a more realistic people after surviving "this perfection of a classic woe."[91]

Jane Addams, the urban reformer, was only four years old at the time, but for her, the news was a seminal moment in her life. She came home to find two white gateposts decorated with "American flags companioned with black" in front of her house. Asking why they were there, her father, in tears, told her that the greatest man in the world had died. The two flags, along with her father's tears, created what she called her "baptism" into "the thrilling and solemn interests of a world lying quite outside the two white gateposts."[92]

Remembering Lincoln helped these younger Americans as they grappled with problems of their own. Millions had seen Lincoln go by on his way to Washington and never forgot the look of his careworn face. Keeping that face in front of the public became, for some, a new kind of calling, closely related to the preservation of democracy. A young sculptor, Augustus Saint-Gaudens, was deeply affected by the sight of Lincoln passing through New York's throngs in 1861. More than a half century later, his fleeting glimpse was still seared in his memory: "What remains in my mind is seeing in the procession the figure of a tall and very dark man, seeming entirely out of proportion in his height with the carriage in which he was driven, bowing to the crowds on each side."[93]

Four years later, when Lincoln's remains were brought back to New York, Saint-Gaudens twice braved long lines to pay his respects in city hall. There he studied Lincoln's face carefully, until "this completed my vision of the big man." He then realized his vision in the monumental sculpture of Lincoln, thinking deeply, that now stands in Chicago's Lincoln Park. Jane Addams often would walk by the statue to find the strength for her own labors on behalf of the poor.[94]

The leaders who succeeded him did not rise up to the same level, as anyone could tell within weeks.[95] But Lincoln's words did not disappear easily and confirmed that his ideals could not be rescinded as long as people were willing to remember them. His speeches were widely reprinted and reread and continued to do good work for generations to come, puncturing the bombast of politicians and stating core truths with minimal adornment. Hay and Nicolay did prodigious work over their lifetimes, bearing witness into the twentieth century. In 1905, just before he died, Hay had a dream of seeing Lincoln in the White House. Lincoln handed him two letters to answer, as if there were still unfinished business between him and the American people.[96]

Many of Lincoln's words were still moving at a high rate of speed around the country decades after his death. His papers were held by his son Robert Todd Lincoln. Perhaps remembering the near disaster of losing his father's inaugural address, the younger Lincoln carried them with him everywhere he went. That included travel on Pullman cars, as he went between his homes in Chicago, Washington, and Vermont. The speeches—which would not be deposited in the Library of Congress until 1947—stayed close to him, comfortable at railroad speed. It was as if the journey had never ended.[97]

Robert Lincoln's close identification with the Pullman Car Company—he became its president in 1897—suggests that for him, too, the railroad exercised a powerful pull, long after the 1861 excitement was over. During the journey, he had been exhilarated by a chance to drive the Iron Horse. But two years later, he was nearly crushed when he slipped and fell as he was boarding a train in Jersey City. At the last minute, he was pulled to safety by the strong arm of a stranger. As it turned out, that arm belonged to Edwin Booth, the celebrated tragedian—and the brother of John Wilkes Booth.[98]

In other ways, too, Lincoln's train rolled on. Between 1865 and 1873, more than thirty-five thousand miles of tracks were laid, greater than the entire domestic rail network in 1860. Freed from the war, bridge builders turned their attention to new challenges and spanned the Ohio and the Mississippi. Track gauges became more uniform, and time zones would be standardized in 1883.[99]

To careful observers, it was obvious that a grand consolidation had taken place. Americans were now living in a new economy, their every need supplied by the massive systems that had organized so efficiently during the war. Trains brought supplies to the front, and soldiers sometimes even negotiated the shipment of their own bodies as they lay dying. When the war ended, American Express, once a small delivery service in Buffalo, had nine hundred offices.[100]

It ended in different places for different people. One of the most poignant endings came many months after Appomattox and the assassination, as a Confederate naval vessel, the CSS *Shenandoah*, limped into the port of Liverpool, England, uncaptured. It surrendered the next day, November 6, 1865—five years to the day since the Lightning had spread the news of Lincoln's election. As these last Confederates were brought back to the United States, they must have blinked their eyes in amazement at the utter transformation. Millions of new Americans would follow them across the Atlantic, on ships of their own, relieved to arrive in a nation that stood more clearly for freedom than it had. So many immigrants came between 1860 and 1870 that the population grew 22.6 percent, to 38.5 million, despite the massive loss of war dead. By 1870, when a new census was compiled, it was difficult to tell that any war had happened at all.

During his train trip, Lincoln had seen the way his country was changing quickly, through sidelong glances out the window. The discovery of petroleum on the eve of the war had delivered a remarkably useful substance to the North, just when it needed, urgently, to lubricate the machinery of production. During a celebration of Lincoln's second inaugural in New York, a banner bragged "Oil Is King Now, Not Cotton." [101] It seemed to ooze out of every surface. On the fateful day of April 14, 1865, a large fire burned out of control at a Pennsylvania well, leading many to fear the well was lost. Instead, the fire just increased its capacity. [102]

The abundance of fossil fuels, in tandem with the internal combustion engine, took Americans to many new places. A generation later, when automobiles were introduced, their inventors derived crucial insights from the railroad, in every category, from suspension to hydraulics to gears. [102] When an automobile pioneer, Carl Fisher, began to dream of a national highway that would link the two coasts, he named it, even before it existed, the Lincoln Highway. It was dedicated in 1913, fifty years after Gettysburg, and ran more than three thousand miles, from Times Square in New York to Lincoln Park in San Francisco. Small statues of Lincoln were erected at landmarks along the way as highway markers, in the same way that the Greeks built shrines to their deities, so that weary travelers would not lose their way. A Jefferson Davis Highway was also created, beginning in Arlington, Virginia, across the street from the Lincoln Memorial, and running all the way to California. Even in death, their race continued. [103]

Not all welcomed the economic forces unleashed by the Civil War as a victory for Lincoln's homespun Republicanism. Henry Adams was troubled by the new fiefdoms he saw rising around him, and the corruption that slinked back easily into Washington's gilded chambers. To Ida Tarbell, it was perfectly consistent to admire Lincoln in one book and attack John D. Rockefeller in another. She never forgot the day of the assassination or the intensity of her father's grief. The hard questions she asked remain valid, long after Lincoln's train did so much to change the country. Eugene V. Debs, who grew up in Indiana, working in train yards, claimed that Lincoln would have been a Socialist—even while he fought epic labor battles against the

Pullman Car Corporation, led by Robert Lincoln.[104] With the passage of time, it became more difficult to align Lincoln with current events, which never prevented anyone from seeking to do just that.

People ice skating in front of the Lincoln Memorial, early twentieth century[105]

THE RACE OF LIFE

Lincoln would be amused by our tendency to seek him through elaborate Greek portals, such as the Lincoln Memorial, a lovely Doric temple that would have been unrecognizable in the isolated settlements of his childhood, except to the "wizzards" who periodically drifted in, speaking in ancient tongues.[106] But he would appreciate that it has become a monument to something larger than him: a place where Americans can talk to one another about the kind of country they would like to live in, a more perfect Union than the one we know. Indeed, it perfectly embodies Lincoln's idea that all of us who believe in the Declaration of Independence can step inside a "temple of liberty," open to all. In that sense, the

Greek shrine works perfectly, remembering the candor of the Ancients as they grappled their way toward something better, all those centuries ago.

That was the kind of conversation he hoped to have, out in the open air, in February 1861. There were moments it seemed sure to fail. But as Walt Whitman said, in an offhand comment about Lincoln, people can discover their greatest qualities in "the moment of their greatest need." [107] There was something epic about the scale of his achievement; a lonely figure, silhouetted against an enormous canvas, finding his way forward. As Whitman wrote, he had "everything against him—wind, tide, current, terrible odds, untried seas." Yet he brought the ship of state into a safe harbor.

His triumph leveled the way for later generations. By the fall of 1865, Victor Hugo was writing that "America has become the guide among the nations," and hopes for democracy were revived around the world. Lincoln would surely admire the way that Americans came together for the difficult challenges of the next century. All of our greatest national achievements have drawn strength from the South, West, and North, working together. All races, all religions: *e pluribus unum*. Without the Civil War, and its tempering of the national character, could the United States have mounted a global campaign against Fascism and prevailed in the Second World War? Surely the military effort would have been feebler, without the coordinated manufacture of war matériel across the regions, or the rhetoric of freedom Franklin D. Roosevelt used to inspire the world. He, too, used the word *all* when speaking of the world's peoples and their rights, as Nelson Mandela and many others noticed in struggles of their own. [108]

In all of these ways, Lincoln tilled the ground for those who came later. Near the end of the war, he spoke of "our children's children" to a group of Ohio soldiers, and expressed his hope that they would have an equal chance "in the race of life." [109] By winning the race of his life, he helped to make that possible.

"Human nature will not change," Lincoln said in response to a serenade in 1864. "In any future great national trial," he predicted, Americans would find people who were exactly "as weak and as strong, as silly and as wise, as bad and as good" as those who lived in his day. The point of history, he mused, was not so much to blame people for their shortcomings as it was to gain wisdom for the struggles yet to come. "I believe in sticking to it," he said in one of his many unscripted speeches along the way. He understood that the cause of democracy was larger than he was. Whenever possible, he directed attention away from himself and toward the people, who must be the ultimate sentinels of their fate in any democracy worthy of the name.[110]

On the day of Lincoln's second inaugural, a New York photographer, Lewis Rutherfurd, captured a striking image of the moon. It looked close enough to touch, much as Lincoln had wanted to during his stargazing conversations with friends. On the day that an American did, in 1969, it was another triumph for southerners, westerners, and northerners working together. It goes without saying that we have had failures too—we see them on a daily basis. But the refusal to fall apart in 1861 made a difference.

Lewis M. Rutherfurd, *Moon*, March 4, 1865[111]

ALICE MAYHEW

(1932–2020)

It is said an Eastern monarch once charged his wise men to invent him a sentence, to be ever in view, and which should be true and appropriate in all times and situations. They presented him the words: "And this, too, shall pass away." How much it expresses! How chastening in the hour of pride! How consoling in the depths of affliction! "And this, too, shall pass away." And yet, let us hope, it is not quite true. Let us hope, rather, that by the best cultivation of the physical world, beneath and around us, and the intellectual and moral world within us, we shall secure an individual, social, and political prosperity and happiness, whose course shall be onward and upward, and which, while the earth endures, shall not pass away.

—Abraham Lincoln, Address before the
Wisconsin State Agricultural Society,
September 30, 1859

ACKNOWLEDGMENTS

It would be a cliché to compare the writing of this book to a journey. But it did originate in earlier travel. Around the age of ten, I went on an overnight train trip to Washington, and never quite got over the excitement of pulling into Union Station at dawn, with the dome of the Capitol visible just beyond, reflecting the sunrise.

Many years later, I had a very different travel experience. On September 11, 2001, I was flying from Philadelphia to Seattle. It was a beautiful cloudless morning, and I remember a feeling of awe at the sight of the Allegheny and the Monongahela, coming together at Pittsburgh to form the Ohio. Not long after that, I was jolted from my reverie as the plane began to descend, too fast, and the pilot announced that we had been directed to the nearest airport because of a terrorist threat. In the confusion of the moment, many passengers assumed that the threat was to our plane.

We were directed to an airstrip that felt too small, with cornstalks pressing up to the tarmac. The passengers exhaled, then rushed for the exits. We quickly learned that there was no danger, but in the next few moments, the full horror of that morning's events became clear. After considerable chaos, it became clear that no more planes would be flying that day, and the only option was to rent a car. So deep was my geographical ignorance that I did not know whether I should try to continue my journey toward Seattle, where I had a meeting later that day, or return to Philadelphia. I chose the latter course, worried, like so many Americans that day, about loved ones.

What followed was a strange day of driving back toward my point of origin, slowly, while trying to take in the news. By the time I had reached southern Indiana, I wanted to take a break, and began to drive on small roads, through the centers of towns, instead of around them. That did not quicken the trip, or lessen the impact of the news, but it was cathartic to go through one real place after another. Each was a shrine to democracy, the ideal that felt so vulnerable that day. I stayed off the highways for a long spell, reassured to see people gathered in town squares, talking to each other. This older

America was alive and well, despite the horror of the attacks. Eventually, I made it back to the Philadelphia airport at four in the morning, where I retrieved my car, and drove back to the eastern shore of Maryland.

All of that is a long way from 1861, but when I came across the story of Lincoln's train trip, I was drawn to it. In a very different crisis, Lincoln's odyssey through the heartland reassured Americans that they possessed a great strength if they trusted each other. Lincoln had been to Champaign, or as it was called then, West Urbana. A lawyer named Henry C. Whitney recalled a remarkable moment when Lincoln stopped in his office and pulled Byron's "Childe Harold" down from his bookshelf, then read aloud from a passage that described the "host of hatred" that could be expected by anyone who dared to climb up to the "mountain tops" of political summitry, and survey his enemies with "a sedate and all-enduring eye." [1]

The story first beckoned in the winter of 2010–2011, when I was reading about the months that preceded the Civil War. At the request of two talented editors, George Kalogerakis and Clay Risen, I was helping to curate of a series of history essays in the *New York Times*, titled "Disunion," that probed the ways in which the country was falling apart, 150 years earlier. It was a joy to work with George and Clay, first as an editor, and then as a writer. At their urging, I found the story of Lincoln's train trip, and began to write it out in February 2011. I wrote quickly, like a journalist, covering Lincoln's journey in real time. After thirteen days, I had written thirteen essays in the *Times*, providing a detailed outline of the book to come.

Little did I know that finishing the book would require the better part of eight years. As it turned out, the act of writing it took longer than the entire Lincoln administration. But there was a great deal of research to be done in order to complete the story of these thirteen days. I was inspired by other books that looked closely at a narrow moment: *A Nervous Splendor*, by Frederic Morton; *Five Days in London*, by John Lukacs; and *Big Trouble*, by J. Anthony Lukas, to name only a few. I also enjoyed Graham Robb's *The Discovery of France*, and its exploration of all of the different places that can co-exist inside a country.

Following the research trail was another journey. In fact, I wrote long stretches of the book while riding trains to and from the libraries I needed to visit. For their heroic work, I'm grateful to the librarians of Harvard, Brown, Columbia, the New-York Historical Society, the New York Public Library, the Library of Congress and the National Archives. Michael Brewer of NOAA was always helpful when I needed information about the weather or the skies. At the Metropolitan Museum of Art, Quincy Houghton and Jeff Rosenheim were learned sources for questions about art and photography. Sara Georgini was always ready to answer questions about the Adams papers at the Massachusetts Historical Society. I particularly want to thank Harvard's Center for Hellenic Studies and Gregory Nagy for a research fellowship in the early phase.

During these eight years, it became much easier to do detailed research online, and that helped to fill out the story. I was eager to read the local newspapers that described Lincoln's train as he went through all of the small towns. Thanks to enlightened local historical societies, and the foundations who support them, many of those newspapers can now be read from a laptop, for free. I would like to acknowledge the late James Billington for his visionary work putting these newspapers online, especially through the Chronicling America site (supported by the National Endowment for the Humanities). I also want to thank my friend David Rumsey for all that he has done to make maps available to all. I relied heavily on Google Maps and nineteenth-century railroad maps as I retraced every mile of the journey. I wanted to follow each curve, and imagine what Lincoln was seeing out the window. Over time, the land and water almost became characters in the book. It felt important that Lincoln was seeing so much of the country, as it was seeing him.

I can never thank friends and family members enough. My father offered a close reading that helped me catch many—though I fear not all—of the infelicities that can attach to a long piece of writing. All of my other family members helped, including my mother and brother, and the Rhinelander family, unfailingly supportive. I remember other bits of conversation with grandparents, long ago, that nudged me along, including a grandmother who grew up with a sturdy faith in Lincoln's Republicanism; a grandfather who assigned bits of Homer to read; and another set of grandparents who radiated the quiet virtues of Lincoln's Midwest. Lincoln once called older relatives "a living history . . . to be found in every family." That was certainly my experience.

There were many conversations along the way. Marc Mazzarelli and I have been talking about trains since we were teenagers. David Michaelis was a constant source of camaraderie, and historical knowledge. Karenna Gore was another contributor to the "Disunion" series, and her deep, empathetic understanding of American history enlightened me on all of the broader democratic questions underlying the book. Her reading greatly improved the manuscript. The writer whose prodigious work launched "Disunion," Adam Goodheart, dazzled me with the book that came out of those essays, *1861: The Civil War Awakening*, and his gift for friendship encouraged me when the journey slowed down. I feel fortunate that I was able to teach at Washington College, with Adam and many other friends, including Clayton Black and Donald McColl, and I am proud of how much the C.V. Starr Center for the Study of the American Experience has accomplished since its founding.

I also want to say a word of thanks to the undergraduates who inspired me along the way, particularly a remarkable group of Brown students, including Sam Gilman, Jason Ginsberg, and Mathias Heller, who wanted to think about Lincoln, in their parlance, 24-7. In addition, I am grateful to the Brown Department of Classics, and to

Johanna Hanink, who helped with some Greek translations. I also appreciated the exquisite recent translation of *The Odyssey* by Emily Wilson.

Lincoln distrusted biography as a genre, because the biographer "describes the success of his hero in glowing terms, never once hinting at his failures and blunders." Lincoln experienced many of the failures that make life more interesting, and I certainly did as well. But I always had the support of friends and fellow travelers, which softened those setbacks. They include Marie Arana, Anthony Bevilacqua, Clara Bingham, Emily Bingham, Polly Carpenter, Hillary Chute, Miranda Cowley, Lara Heimert, Quincy Houghton, Stow and Rhonda Kelner, Max Kennedy, Mike McLaughlin, Susan Morrison, George Perkins, Mary Rhinelander, Tim Rhodes, Will Thorndike, and Julie Warburg.

There was not a day that I did not appreciate the broad community of Lincoln scholars. I could not have written this book without their immense erudition. Douglas L. Wilson, the codirector of the Lincoln Studies Center at Knox College, was unfailingly generous. I learned a great deal from his work, as well as the contributions of Michael Burlingame, Doris Kearns Goodwin, Harold Holzer, James McPherson, Joshua Wolf Shenk, Frank Williams, and Garry Wills, among others. Needless to add, we are all indebted to the great Lincoln scholars of earlier generations. Going back to the beginning, I savored everything ever written by Lincoln's secretaries, John Nicolay and John Hay. Robert Hoffman kindly allowed me to consult Hay's scrapbook from the 1861 trip.

The Lincoln community is lucky to have the Gilder Lehrman Institute for American History, which does so much to promote the study of the Civil War. Any discussion of teaching reminds me to acknowledge my own teachers, long ago. Alan Heimert stimulated an interest in Lincoln in graduate school, and encouraged me to read in his extensive library, now reconstituted as a reading room at Columbia University. In other ways, I benefited from proximity to great historians like Daniel Aaron, Bernard Bailyn, Alan Brinkley, Andrew Delbanco, David Donald, Donald Fleming, Henry Louis Gates, Jr., Pauline Maier, Leo Marx, Werner Sollors, and Gordon Wood.

New friends in New York were unstintingly generous as well. I admire the Carnegie Corporation of New York for all the good that it does, and I want to thank Vartan Gregorian and Jeanne D'Onofrio for their support. I am proud to be a Senior Fellow at a different Carnegie institution, the Carnegie Council for Ethics in International Affairs. In the summer of 2019, the Morgan Library asked me to curate an exhibition about Walt Whitman—that experience deepened the writing of this book. Teaching at the Macaulay Honors College of the City University of New York has been thrilling, thanks to brilliant students, and the dedication of Dean Mary Pearl.

I felt lucky to work alongside the talented professionals who guided the manuscript to completion. It was an honor to work with Alice Mayhew, whose immense knowledge of Lincoln illuminated every step of the way. Her passion for history left a deep impression on me, and our lunches were a great highlight of this time. I also appreciated her precision. I was tempted to quote Lincoln to justify my expansive early drafts ("All creation is a mine, and every man, a miner"). But in the end, I thought better of it and made the necessary cuts. I hope it serves as a worthy memorial to a great lady and a good friend. I'm also grateful to Maria Mendez, Amar Deol, Jonathan Karp, Phil Metcalf, and Thomas LeBien, who originally signed the book. Connie Brown of Redstone Studios drew a beautiful map for the endpapers. I could not have asked for a better friend in the process than my extraordinary agent, Tina Bennett, who read every word, repeatedly, and always made it better.

Near the end of the writing, I wandered in the Congressional Cemetery in Washington, where Lincoln was originally going to be interred. There I accidentally stumbled upon the headstone of Hannibal Hamlin, a government clerk from Maine. The stone conveyed little information beyond the fact that he was born thirteen days before Lincoln, in 1809, and died in November 1862. His name was vaguely familiar, not only because he was the cousin of Lincoln's vice-president, of the same name, but because, as I learned later, his brother was my grandmother's grandfather.

I wondered why he was buried so far from home, and learned that he had volunteered in the early months of the war, when African-Americans began to stream into Washington from the South, liberating themselves. That created a kind of refugee crisis for a city that was not well set up to receive them. When a Freedman's Relief Association was organized, he became its president, working daily to welcome these incoming families, before he contracted consumption and died. With these short lines, I wanted to offer a slightly longer epitaph for a forgotten American, eager to help his country act more like the "great family" that Lincoln had promised it could be.

On that subject, the book is dedicated to my son Freddy, whose work among the mentally impaired has been a source of "sweet light in darkness," as it is written in *The Odyssey*. Mental health was the key to this story; the clearest warning of the danger Lincoln faced came from another light-bearer, Dorothea Dix, who worked in the same community. Lincoln's survival in February 1861 stemmed in no small part from her conviction that citizens in a democracy should feel some responsibility for each other. That belief persists, undiminished, even in the gathering twilight.

NOTES

FRONTISPIECE

1. Abraham Lincoln Papers, Manuscripts Division, Library of Congress, www.loc
   .gov/exhibits/lincoln/interactives/journey-of-the-president-elect/feb11/arti
   fact1_524_html.

PROLOGUE: THE HOLY TOWN OF TROY

1. Homer, *The Odyssey*, trans. Emily Wilson (New York: W. W. Norton, 2018), 105.
2. Richard F. Burton, *The City of the Saints and Across the Rocky Mountains to California* (New York: Alfred A. Knopf, 1963), 14.
3. Fred W. Brinkerhoff, "The Kansas Tour of Lincoln the Candidate," *Kansas Historical Quarterly* 13 (1944): 294–307.
4. Henry Villard, *Memoirs of Henry Villard, Journalist and Financier, 1835–1900*, vol. 1 (Boston: Houghton Mifflin, 1904), 134–35; Herman Melville, *Selected Poems of Herman Melville*, ed. Hennig Cohen (New York: Fordham University Press, 1991), 99. The meteorological observations are on the website A Lincoln Guide K. T. 1959, accessed February 25, 2017, https://alincolnguide.com.
5. Burton, *City of the Saints*, 22–23.
6. Joel K. Bourne Jr., "Last American Slave Ship Is Discovered in Alabama," *National Geographic*, May 22, 2019; Sylviane A. Diouf, *Dreams of Africa in Alabama: The Slave Ship Clotilda and the Story of the Last Africans Brought to America* (New York: Oxford University Press, 2007).
7. Brinkerhoff, "Kansas Tour of Lincoln, 300.
8. Albert D. Richardson, "Lincoln in Kansas," *Transactions of the Kansas State Historical Society, 1901–1902*, vol. 7, ed. George W. Martin (Topeka, KS: W. Y. Morgan, 1902), 538–39.

9. William O. Tidwell, *Come Retribution; The Confederate Secret Service and the Assassination of Abraham Lincoln* (Jackson: University of Mississippi Press, 1988), 225.

10. Walt Whitman claimed to be there as well, standing "very near" as the old man mounted the scaffold; Walt Whitman, *Complete Poetry and Collected Prose*, ed. Justin Kaplan (New York: Library of America, 1982), 380.

11. Abraham Lincoln, speech at Leavenworth, Kansas, December 3, 1859, in *The Collected Works of Abraham Lincoln*, vol. 3, ed. Roy E. Basler (New Brunswick, NJ: Rutgers University Press, 1953), 502.

12. "Important from Washington," *New York Herald*, December 2, 1859, 4. The proposed headquarters of the Southern confederacy was Richmond, a prediction that proved true.

13. Ibid. The next day, the governor of South Carolina threatened to secede if a Republican was elected. *Washington (D.C.) Evening Star*, December 3, 1859, 2.

14. Allen Thorndike Rice, ed. *Reminiscences of Abraham Lincoln by Distinguished Men of His Time* (New York: Harper and Brothers, 1909), 26.

15. Gary Ecelbarger, *The Great Comeback: How Abraham Lincoln Beat the Odds to Win the 1860 Republican Nomination* (New York: St. Martin's Press, 2008), 98.

16. Lincoln also visited Elwood, Doniphan, Atchison, and Leavenworth on this trip; Atchison is slightly west of Troy.

17. Lincoln, *Collected Works*, vol. 3, 511; Lincoln ended his short autobiography with a terse phrase, "no other marks or brands recollected," as if describing a runaway slave.

18. Douglas L. Wilson and Rodney O. Davis, eds., *Herndon's Informants: Letters, Interviews and Statements About Abraham Lincoln* (Urbana: University of Illinois Press, 1998), 31, 420.

19. Ibid., 457; William Henry Herndon, *Herndon's Life of Lincoln: The History and Personal Recollections of Abraham Lincoln, as Originally Written by William H. Herndon and Jesse W. Weik* (Cleveland: The World Publishing Company, 1949), 63–64.

20. "Across the Continent on the Kansas Pacific Railroad" (Route of the 35th Parallel); Digital Commonwealth, Boston Public Library https://www.flickr.com/photos/boston_public_library/sets/72157625323048991.

21. See Mary Bilder, *Madison's Hand: Revising the Constitution* (Cambridge, MA: Harvard University Press, 2015).

22. *New York Herald*, December 2, 1859, 1.

23. Joyce Mendelsohn, letter to the editor, *New York Times*, September 19, 1992; "New York City," Thomas Jefferson Foundation online, accessed May 2, 2017, https://www.monticello.org/site/research-and-collections/new-york-city. Jefferson had been trying for years to get rice from Vietnam, rumored to be the best in the world. "Rice," Thomas Jefferson Foundation online, accessed April 7, 2017, https://www.monticello.org/site/house-and-gardens/rice.

24. Joel Achenbach, *The Grand Idea: George Washington's Potomac and the Race to the West* (New York: Simon & Schuster, 2004), 34–35.

25. John C. Reed, Jr., Robert S. Sigafoos, and George W. Fisher, *The River and the Rocks: The Story of Great Falls and the Potomac River Gorge* (Washington, U.S. Government Printing Office, 1980).

26. Ted Widmer, "Draining the Swamp," *New Yorker,* January 19, 2017.

27. Achenbach, *Grand Idea*, 36n.

28. Kenneth R. Bowling, *Creating the Federal City, 1774–1800: Potomac Fever* (Washington, D.C.: American Institute of Architects Press, 1988), 56, 59–60; John O'Connor, *Political Opinions Particularly Respecting the Seat of Federal Empire: being an attempt to demonstrate the utility, justice, and convenience of erecting the great city in the centre of the states, or in the centre of their power, most humbly inscribed to His Excellency the president, by a citizen of America* (Georgetown, 1789), 10, 12–13.

29. Ibid.

30. Ainsworth R. Spofford, "The Coming of the White Man, and the Founding of the National Capital," *Journal of the Washington Academy of Sciences* 1 (January 18, 1900): 248–249. North Carolina's accession in the summer of 1790 gave the necessary votes to the proposal for a southern location—especially since Rhode Island had not yet come into the Union.

31. Freeman Cleaves, *Old Tippecanoe: William Henry Harrison and His Time* (New York: Charles Scribner's Sons, 1939), 331–32.

32. K. Jack Bauer, *Zachary Taylor: Soldier, Planter, Statesman of the Old Southwest* (Baton Rouge: Louisiana State University Press, 1985), 251–53; Holman Hamilton, *Zachary Taylor: Soldier in the White House* (Indianapolis: Bobbs-Merrill, 1951), 144–46.

33. *The Federalist* (NY: The Modern Library; ed. Edward Mead Earle), 80–81.

34. Ibid., 83. Even before independence, in 1775, Congress ordered the colonies "to put their Roads in good Repair, and particularly the great Roads that lead from Colony to Colony." But that was more of an aspiration than a reality; see Pauline Maier, *American Scripture: Making the Declaration of Independence* (New York: Knopf, 1997), 13–14.

35. John Adams to John Taylor, December 17, 1814; Founders Online, National Archive; https://founders.archives.gov/documents/Adams/99-02-02-6371.

36. John Hay, *Lincoln's Journalist: John Hay's Anonymous Writings for the Press, 1860–1864* (Carbondale: Southern Illinois University Press, 1998), 23; Lincoln to George C. Latham, July 22, 1860, in Lincoln, *Collected Works*, vol. 4, 87. Latham would accompany Lincoln on his journey.

37. John Hay, *At Lincoln's Side: John Hay's Civil War Correspondence and Selected Writings*, ed. Michael Burlingame (Carbondale: Southern Illinois University

Press, 2000), 115; Walt Whitman also compared the Civil War to the *Iliad*; in his book *Memoranda During the War: Civil War Journals, 1863–1865* (Mineola, NY: Dover, 2010), he called it a story for "centuries to come," comparable to "Homer's siege of Troy."

38. Photograph of Abraham Lincoln by Samuel M. Fassett, October 4, 1859; Brown University Library; https://repository.library.brown.edu/studio/item/bdr:311329/.

CHAPTER 1: THE LIGHTNING

1. Photograph of Abraham Lincoln by William Marsh, May 20, 1860; Metropolitan Museum of Art, https://www.metmuseum.org/art/collection/search/283191.

2. Homer, *The Odyssey* (trans. Emily Wilson), 188.

3. Harold Holzer, *Lincoln, President-Elect: Abraham Lincoln and the Great Secession Winter 1860–1861* (New York: Simon & Schuster, 2008), 33; Harold Holzer, "Election Day 1860," *Smithsonian* (November 2008).

4. William E. Baringer, *A House Dividing: Lincoln as President-Elect* (Springfield, IL: Abraham Lincoln Association, 1945), 4–5.

5. Hay, *Lincoln's Journalist*, 14.

6. See George B. Prescott, *History, Theory and Practice of the Electric Telegraph* (Boston: Ticknor and Fields, 1860), 356; Tom Standage, *The Victorian Internet: The Remarkable Story of the Telegraph and the Nineteenth Century's On-Line Pioneers* (New York: Walker, 1998), 58, 182.

7. John Nicolay remembered the sound of the "clicking instruments" afterward; John G. Nicolay, *An Oral History of Abraham Lincoln: John G. Nicolay's Interviews and Essays,* ed. Michael Burlingame (Carbondale: Southern Illinois University Press, 1996), 106. Lincoln had been invited by the telegraph office to spend the evening "where you can receive the good news without delay." John G. Nicolay Papers, Manuscript Division, Library of Congress.

8. John G. Nicolay Papers, Manuscript Division, Library of Congress.

9. Holzer, *Lincoln, President-Elect,* 37, 39.

10. Adam Goodheart, *1861: The Civil War Awakening* (New York: Alfred A. Knopf, 2011), 97.

11. Melvin L. Hayes, *Mr. Lincoln Runs for President* (New York: Citadel, 1960), 221; Maury Klein, *Days of Defiance: Sumter, Secession and the Coming of the Civil War* (New York: Alfred A. Knopf, 1997), 22.

12. Philip Van Doren Stern, *Prologue to Sumter: The Beginnings of the Civil War from the John Brown Raid to the Surrender of Fort Sumter* (Greenwich, CT: Fawcett, 1961), 133–34. Edmund Morris, *Edison* (New York: Random House, 2019), 538–84.

13. Newspaper clipping, *New Haven (CT) Daily Palladium*; John G. Nicolay Papers, Manuscript Division, Library of Congress; Holzer, *Lincoln, President-Elect*, 41, 45; *Cincinnati Daily Press*, November 7, 1860.

14. Standage, *Victorian Internet*, 9; Burton, *City of the Saints*, 33.

15. Robert Luther Thompson, *Wiring a Continent: The History of the Telegraph Industry in the United States, 1832–1866* (Princeton, NJ: Princeton University Press, 1947), 29; Hayes, *Lincoln Runs for President*, 214.

16. Robert Luther Thompson, *Wiring a Continent*, 248. Many accounts of the "Carrington Event" are given in James L. Green, "Eyewitness Reports of the Great Auroral Storm of 1859," *Advances in Space Research* 38, no. 2 (2006): 145–54. They include predictions made in both the North and the South that a disaster would soon follow the event. See also M. A. Shea and D. F. Smart, "A Compendium of Eight Articles on the 'Carrington Event' Attributed to or Written by Elias Loomis in the *American Journal of Science*, 1859–1861," *Advances in Space Research* 38, no. 2 (2006): 313–85.

17. Daniel Boorstin, *The Image: A Guide to Pseudo-Events in America* (New York: Vintage, 1962, 1992), 57; see also William B. Sprague, *Visits to European Celebrities* (Boston: Gould and Lincoln, 1855).

18. Adrienne LaFrance, "In 1858, People Said the Telegraph Was 'Too Fast for the Truth'—Sound Familiar?," *Atlantic*, July 28, 2014, https://www.theatlantic.com/technology/archive/2014/07/in-1858-people-said-the-telegraph-was-too-fast-for-the-truth/375171/; *New York Times*, August 19, 1858.

19. On the weather, see Goodheart, *1861*, 49.

20. Benjamin Brown French, *Witness to the Young Republic: A Yankee's Journal, 1828–1870*, ed. Donald B. Cole and John J. McDonough (Hanover, NH: University Press of New England, 1989), 338.

21. Huge slave auctions were held in the year before Lincoln's election; Diouf, *Dreams of Africa in Alabama*; Daniel P. Mannix, *Black Cargoes: A History of the Atlantic Slave Trade* (New York: Viking, 1962), 271–75; Anne C. Bailey, *The Weeping Time: Memory and the Largest Slave Auction in American History* (New York: Cambridge University Press, 2017), 3, 11; Frederic Bancroft, *Slave Trading in the Old South* (New York: Ungar, 1931, 1959), 354; Charlene Mires, *Independence Hall in American Memory* (Philadelphia: University of Pennsylvania Press, 2002), 94–96.

22. The *New-York Illustrated News*, January 19, 1861, 161–62, described a northern school teacher in Alabama who was stripped, tarred, and feathered for her sympathy for slaves.

23. "Secession on Trial," *New York Times*, February 16, 1861. See also William C. Cochran, *The Western Reserve and the Fugitive Slave Law: A Prelude to the Civil War*

(Cleveland: Western Reserve Historical Society, 1920), 167; Matthew Karp, *This Vast Southern Empire: Slaveholders at the Helm of American Foreign Policy* (Cambridge, MA: Harvard University Press, 2016). Henry Adams, *The Great Secession Winter of 1860–61 and Other Essays*, ed., George E. Hochfield (New York: A. S. Barnes, 1958), 4–7. Many Southerners wished to carve new slave states out of Mexico; see Burlingame, *Lincoln: A Life*, vol. 1 (Baltimore: Johns Hopkins University Press, 2008), 697.

24. George Bickley called on Mexico to accept its inevitable "Americanization;" *New York Times,* July 23, 1860, 3.

25. On corruption, see Michael F. Holt, *The Election of 1860: "A Campaign Fraught with Consequences"* (Lawrence: Kansas University Press, 2017), 29–33; George Templeton Strong, *The Diary of George Templeton Strong*, vol. 3, ed. Allan Nevins and Milton Halsey Thomas (New York: Macmillan, 1952), 103.

26. Whitman, *Complete Poetry and Prose*, 1314.

27. Ibid., 1313–14.

28. Ibid., 1310–11.

29. Ibid., 281, 1308–9.

30. Ibid., 1325.

31. *New York Times,* July 23, 1860; July 24, 1860; *New York Daily Tribune*, July 23, 1860; *Burlington (VT) Free Press,* July 27, 1860; *Harper's Weekly*, August 4, 1860. The phenomenon was described in detail, years after the fact, by a variety of witnesses from New England to Washington; see James H. Coffin, "The Orbit and Phenomena of a Meteoric Fireball, Seen July 20, 1860," *Smithsonian Contributions to Knowledge*, vol. 16 (Washington, D.C.: Smithsonian Institution, 1870). Another meteor was seen over Cincinnati on August 2; see *New York Times,* August 7, 1860. See also Sarah Zielinksy, "Rare Meteor Event Inspired Walt Whitman," Smithsonian.com, last modified June 7, 2010, https://www.smithsonianmag.com/science-nature/rare-meteor-event-inspired-walt-whitman-29643165.

32. Holzer, *Lincoln, President-Elect,* 37–38.

33. Ibid.

34. Ibid., 45

35. Ibid., 58; Burlingame, *Lincoln: A Life*, vol. 1, 692; Donald R. Kennon, ed., *A Republic for the Ages: The United States Capitol and the Political Culture of the Early Republic* (Charlottesville: University of Virginia Press, 1999), 273.

36. Strong, *Diary of George Templeton Strong*, vol. 3, 64.

37. The State Capitol, Sangamon County Court House and Marine and Fire Insurance Building were Greek Revival; Baringer, *A House Dividing*, 9.

38. Prints and Photographs Divison, Library of Congress.

39. Damon Wells, *Stephen Douglas: The Last Years, 1857–1861* (Austin: University of Texas Press, 1971), 254–55; Robert W. Johansen, *Stephen A. Douglas* (New York: Oxford University Press, 1973), 800–803; *Yorkville (SC) Enquirer,* November 8, 1860.

40. Hayes, *Lincoln Runs for President,* 214. Hayes noted that the news took longer to reach California and Oregon, and that it was not until December 1 that Washington, D.C., received the news that Lincoln had "apparently" won those states (215).

41. Dwight Lowell Dumond, ed., *Southern Editorials on Secession* (New York: Century, 1931), 221.

42. Donald E. Reynolds, *Editors Make War: Southern Newspapers in the Secession Crisis* (Nashville: Vanderbilt University Press, 1966), 217.

43. Charles Eugene Hamlin, *The Life and Times of Hannibal Hamlin,* (Cambridge, MA: Riverside Press, 1899), 354; James M. McPherson, *Battle Cry of Freedom: The Civil War Era* (New York: Ballantine, 1988), 224; Adam Goodheart, "The Happiest Man in the South," *New York Times,* December 17, 2010; Ted Widmer, "Lincoln Speaks," *New York Times,* November 22, 2010; Michael Davis, *The Image of Lincoln in the South* (Knoxville: University of Tennessee Press, 1971), 13–14; Jörg Nagler, "Abraham Lincoln's Attitudes on Slavery and Race," *American Studies Journal,* no. 53 (2009), http://www.asjournal.org/53-2009/abraham-lincolns-attitudes-on-slavery-and-race.

44. Roy Franklin Nichols, *The Disruption of American Democracy* (New York Macmillan, 1948), 347, 352, 364; Steven Hahn, "What Lincoln Meant to the Slaves," *New York Times,* February 12, 2011.

45. Waddy Thompson to Thomas Corwin, October 16, 1860, Abraham Lincoln Papers, Manuscript Division, Library of Congress. A writer in Albany noted an upsurge in fugitive slaves escaping north, December 17, 1860; see Eric Foner, *Gateway to Freedom* (New York: W. W. Norton, 2015), 221.

46. Andrew Ward, *The Slaves' War: The Civil War in the Words of Former Slaves* (Boston: Houghton-Mifflin Harcourt, 2008), 10, 46.

47. Nichols, *Disruption of American Democracy,* 345, 351, 361; Davis, *Image of Lincoln,* 13; *New York Herald,* February 9, 1861; David C. Mearns, *The Lincoln Papers,* vol. 2 (Garden City, NY: Doubleday, 1948), 413.

48. A. Scott Berg, *Wilson* (New York: G. P. Putnam's Sons, 2013), 31–32.

49. Mary Boykin Chesnut, *A Diary from Dixie,* ed. Ban Ames Williams (Cambridge, MA: Harvard University Press, 1980), 1. Different variations of the diary give different versions.

50. Hayes, *Lincoln Runs for President*, 219–20; *The Diary of Edmund Ruffin* (ed. William Kauffman Scarborough; Baton Rouge: Louisiana State University Press, 1972), I, 483, 551.

51. Nichols, *Disruption of American Democracy*, 361–62; David C. Keehn, *Knights of the Golden Circle: Secret Empire, Southern Secession, Civil War* (Baton Rouge: Louisiana State University Press, 2013), 78. For a statement of the group's beliefs, see a letter from George Bickley, *New York Times*, July 23, 1860.

52. Keehn, *Knights of the Golden Circle*, 17.

53. In July 1864 Jefferson Davis said, "We seceded to rid ourselves of the rule of the majority." See John William Draper, *A History of the Civil War*, vol. 3 (New York: Harper and Brothers, 1867), 474.

54. Hayes, *Lincoln Runs for President*, 220; Dumond, *Southern Editorials on Secession*, 229, 261.

55. Nathaniel Hawthorne quoted in Carl Sandburg, "The Face of Lincoln," in Frederick Hill Meserve, *The Photographs of Abraham Lincoln* (New York: Harcourt, Brace, 1944). Hawthorne's lines were deleted by the *Atlantic Monthly* before publication.

56. "Star of the North, or the Comet of 1861," detail from decorated envelope, Brown University Library.

57. David E. Meerse, "Buchanan, Corruption and the Election of 1860," *Civil War History* 12, no. 2 (June 1966): 117, 130.

58. Leonard L. Richards, *The Slave Power: The Free North and Southern Domination, 1780–1860* (Baton Rouge: Louisiana State University Press, 2000), 8–9.

59. Draper, *History of the Civil War*, vol. 1, 479–81.

60. Charles F. Adams believed that "the question is one of power" rather than an emotional feeling about slavery itself. See Burlingame, *Lincoln: A Life*, vol. 1, 690.

61. Carl F. Krummel, "Henry J. Raymond and the *New York Times* in the Secession Crisis," *New York History* 32 (October 1951): 381.

62. Nathaniel Hawthorne, "Chiefly About War Matters," The Atlantic (July 1862), https://www.theatlantic.com/magazine/archive/1862/07/chiefly-about-war-matters/306159.

63. Texas voters ratified secession in a referendum on February 23.

64. A list of all of the seizures of federal forts is provided in the *New York Illustrated News*, February 2, 1861, 201. See also Strong, *Diary of George Templeton Strong*, vol. 3, 115–16; Draper, *History of the Civil War*, vol. 1, 558–59.

65. Burton J. Hendrick, *Statesmen of the Lost Cause* (Boston: Little, Brown, 1939), 79.

66. James Russell Lowell, "E Pluribus Unum," *Atlantic Monthly*, February 1861; Edward Weeks and Emily Flint, *Jubilee: One Hundred Years of the Atlantic* (Boston: Little, Brown, 1957), 9.

67. Carl Schurz, *The Reminiscences of Carl Schurz*, vol. 2 (New York: McClure, 1908), 219.

68. National Museum of American History, Smithsonian Institution, www.american history.si.edu/lincoln/railsplitter; see also Rufus Rockwell Wilson, *Lincoln in Caricature: A Historical Collection, with Descriptive and Biographical Commentaries by Rufus Rockwell Wilson*, intro., R. Gerald McMurtry (New York: Horizon Press, 1953), 14–15.

69. Strong, *Diary of George Templeton Strong*, vol. 3, 74.

70. Harold Holzer, "Election Day 1860," *Smithsonian*, November 2008; http://www.smithsonian.com/history/election-day-1860-84266675/?page=7.

71. Holzer, *Lincoln, President-Elect*, 42, 44; only three of Springfield's twenty-three ministers voted for him; Ward H. Lamon, *The Life of Abraham Lincoln* (Boston: James R. Osgood, 1872), 499.

72. The 1860 Republican platform is given in *The Works of William H. Seward*, vol. 4, ed. George E. Baker (Boston: Houghton, Mifflin, 1889), 679–80.

73. Fragment dated November 15, 1860, John G. Nicolay Papers, Manuscript Division, Library of Congress; cited in Burlingame, *Lincoln: A Life*, vol. 1, 700; Michael Burlingame, ed., *With Lincoln in the White House: Letters, Memoranda and Other Writings of John G. Nicolay, 1860–1865* (Carbondale: Southern Illinois University Press, 2000), 10.

74. Alexis de Tocqueville, *Democracy in America*, vol. 1, ed. Phillips Bradley (New York: Alfred A. Knopf, 1997), 136.

75. Lincoln to Martin Morris, March 26, 1843, *Collected Works of Abraham Lincoln* (ed. Roy P. Basler, New Brunswick: Rutgers University Press, 1953), vol. 1, 320.

76. Wilson and Davis, *Herndon's Informants*, 87.

77. Lamon, *Life of Abraham Lincoln*, 504.

78. Andrew A. Freeman, *Abraham Lincoln Goes to New York* (New York: Coward-McCann, 1960), 76–77. In Philadelphia, a similar list, of thirty-four, was prepared, and again Lincoln was missing.

79. Ecelbarger, *Great Comeback*, 12–15.

80. Abraham Lincoln, "Autobiography Written for John L. Scripps," June 1860, *Collected Works of Abraham Lincoln*, vol. 4, 62.

81. Edmund Wilson, *Patriotic Gore: Studies in the Literature of the Civil War* (New York: Oxford University Press), 122. In his original manuscript Lincoln spelled it "mid-way," but most have deleted the hyphen since then.

82. Reinhard H. Luthin, *The First Lincoln Campaign* (Cambridge, MA: Harvard University Press, 1944), 21.

83. Hayes, *Lincoln Runs for President*, 17–18; Mark A. Plummer, *Lincoln's Rail-Splitter: Governor Richard J. Oglesby* (Champaign: University of Illinois Press, 2001), 41–42.

84. Joseph Cannon, *Abraham Lincoln: Speech of Joseph G. Cannon of Illinois* (Washington, D.C.: Government Printing Office, 1910), 8.

85. Wayne C. Temple, "Lincoln's Fence Rails," *Journal of the Illinois State Historical Society* 47, no. 1 (Spring 1954): 23.

86. Hayes, *Lincoln Runs for President*, 134; Goodheart, *1861*, 35–36, 41.

87. Allan Gurganus wrote that he "looks hand-carved the hard way," and called his face "a private pocket worn inside out." See Allan Gurganus, "The Ramada Inn at Shiloh," *Granta* 35 (April 1, 1991), available at Allan Gurganus online, accessed August 6, 2017, http://www.allangurganus.com/essays/first-essay-title.

88. Henry Villard, *Lincoln on the Eve of '61: A Journalist's Story* (New York, Alfred A. Knopf, 1941), 3–4; also Villard, *Memoirs*, vol. 1, 93.

89. Joseph Medill, describing a speech of May 29, 1856. Cited from Rufus Rockwell Wilson, *Intimate Memories of Lincoln* (Elmira, NY: Primavera Press, 1945), 156; see "The Journalists: Joseph Medill (1823–1899)," Mr. Lincoln & Friends, accessed September 5, 2017, http://www.mrlincolnandfriends.org/the-journalists/joseph-medill.

90. Stern, *Prologue to Sumter*, 83.

91. Hayes, *Lincoln Runs for President*, 27–28.

92. Paul M. Angle, *"Here I Have Lived": A History of Lincoln's Springfield, 1821–1865* (Chicago: Abraham Lincoln Book Shop, 1971), 165, 176, 178, 244; Plummer, *Lincoln's Rail-Splitter*, 35.

93. Hayes, *Lincoln Runs for President*, 36.

94. Ibid., 54.

95. Ibid., 61.

96. Stern, *Prologue to Sumter*, 113.

97. Hayes, *Lincoln Runs for President*, 65.

98. Ibid., 164.

99. Ibid., 109.

100. Ibid., 119–20.

101. Ibid., 246.

102. Ibid., 160–61.

103. Charles Dickens, "Election Time in America," *All the Year Round*, April 13, 1861, 68–72. Dickens also described a group of Lincoln haters from the South in the lobby of an elegant hotel on Broadway; as they bite their cigars, "they cherish an angry hatred of Lincoln, for most of them are Cuban sugar-planters, or gentlemen of property from Louisiana, and wear sumptuous watch-chains at their fobs three inches broad."

104. Hay, *Lincoln's Journalist*, 14–15.

105. John Hay, *Memorial Address on the Life and Character of William McKinley* (Washington, D.C.: Government Printing Office, 1903), 15–16.

106. Horace Greeley warned, "It is not yet certain that the Federal District will not be in the hands of a proslavery rebel array before the 4th of March"; Horace Greeley to Abraham Lincoln, December 22, 1860, David C. Mearns, *Lincoln Papers*, vol. 2, 349–50.

CHAPTER 2: WAITING FOR LINCOLN

1. Mathew Brady, *James Buchanan, head-and-shoulders portrait, facing front*, Library of Congress https://www.loc.gov/item/2004663892; a similar portrait is also held by the Library of Congress; https://www.loc.gov/item/2004663891.

2. Homer, *The Odyssey*, trans. Robert Fitzgerald (Garden City, New York: Anchor Books), 1963.

3. John G. Nicolay and John Hay, *Abraham Lincoln: A History*, vol. 3 (New York: Century Company, 1890), x, 246, 347.

4. Villard, *Lincoln on the Eve*, 15.

5. *The Papers of Jefferson Davis*, vol. 6, *1856–1860*, ed. Lynda L. Crist and Mary S. Dix (Baton Rouge: Louisiana University Press, 1989), 366, 668.

6. Davis, *Image of Lincoln*, 12–13.

7. Burlingame, *Lincoln: A Life*, vol. 1, 688.

8. Ted Widmer, "Lincoln Speaks."

9. Lincoln, *Collected Works*, vol. 4, 143–44.

10. Ibid., 144.

11. Hay, *Lincoln's Journalist*, 17.

12. Lincoln, *Collected Works*, vol. 2, 115–16; Donald S. Spencer, *Louis Kossuth and Young America: A Study of Sectionalism and Foreign Policy* (Columbia: University of Missouri Press, 1977), 24.

13. Walt Whitman, *Manly Health and Training: To Teach the Science of a Sound and Beautiful Body*, ed. Zachary Turpin (New York: Simon & Schuster, 2017). Henry Thoreau slyly suggested that beards were a form of environmental activism, offering men a chance to "make a sylvan appearance" and protest the disappearance of forests; Henry D. Thoreau, *The Maine Woods* (Princeton: Princeton University Press, 1972), 320.

14. Adam Goodheart, "Lincoln: A Beard Is Born," *New York Times*, November 24, 2010.

15. Most scholars follow William Herndon's claim that Lincoln began to write the inaugural address "late in January"; see Douglas L. Wilson, *Lincoln's Sword: The Presidency and the Power of Words* (New York: Alfred A. Knopf, 2006), 45–46.

16. Thomas Corwin to Abraham Lincoln, December 11, 1860; William Seward to Abraham Lincoln, December 28, 1860; Joseph Medill to Abraham Lincoln, December 31, 1860; Abraham Lincoln Papers, Manuscript Division, Library of Congress.

17. Prints and Photographs Divison, Library of Congress; see also Widmer, "Draining the Swamp."

18. Corwin to Lincoln, December 11, 1860, Abraham Lincoln Papers, Manuscript Division, Library of Congress.

19. Elaine C. Everly and Howard H. Wehmann, "Then Let Us to the Woods Repair: Moving the Federal Government and Its Records to Washington in 1800," in Kenneth R. Bowling and Donald R. Kennon, *Establishing Congress: The Removal to Washington, D.C., and the Election of 1800* (Athens: Ohio University Press, 2005), 68.

20. Henry Adams, *The Education of Henry Adams,* ed. Edward Chalfant and Conrad Edick Wright (Boston: Massachusetts Historical Society, 2007), 33–34.

21. One of his cousins was Robert Barnwell Rhett, a leading Southern fire-eater.

22. Henry Adams, *Education of Henry Adams,* 70–71.

23. Edward Gibbon, *The History of the Decline and Fall of the Roman Empire* (London: Macmillan Company, 1914), vol. 4, 58–61.

24. Samuel Eliot Morison, *Three Centuries of Harvard* (Cambridge, MA: Harvard University Press, 1936), 263, 300–301; Charles Francis Adams, *Charles Francis Adams, 1835–1915: An Autobiography* (Boston: Houghton Mifflin, 1916), 26.

25. Henry Thoreau, *The Annotated Walden,* ed. Philip Van Doren Stern (New York: Bramhall, 1970), 231–32; Richard Higgins, "The Harvard in Thoreau," *Harvard Gazette,* June 29, 2017; Thoreau wrote lyrically in *Walden,* "I would fain be a track-repairer somewhere in the orbit of the earth." Cyrus Felton, *A Genealogical History of the Felton Family* (Marlborough, MA: Pratt Brothers, 1886), 221–23.

26. "Washington City," *Atlantic Monthly* 7, January 1861, 8; Ernest B. Furgurson, *Freedom Rising: Washington in the Civil War Era* (New York: Alfred A. Knopf, 2004), 15.

27. Charles Francis Adams, *Autobiography,* 43–44.

28. *New York Illustrated News,* December 15, 1860, 81. There were different types; "grievance-mongers" and "tricky wire pullers"; those with "silver tongues" could do well in Washington.

29. Henry Adams, *Education of Henry Adams,* 84.

30. John Calhoun considered Washington the "Thermopylae" of the coming battle over slavery; to the Slave Power; it was critical to slavery's defenders. Chris Myers Asch and George Derek Musgrove, *Chocolate City: A History of Race and*

Democracy in the Nation's Capital (Chapel Hill: University of North Carolina Press, 2017), 49.

31. "Reminiscences of Washington," *Atlantic Monthly*, January 1880, 57.

32. Henry Adams, *Education of Henry Adams*, 34, 41, 77. Anthony Trollope wrote that Washington resembled Palmyra in Syria; Nick Yablon, *Untimely Ruins: An Archeology of American Urban Modernity, 1819–1919* (Chicago: University of Chicago Press, 2009), 81.

33. Prints and Photographs Division, Library of Congress; see also "Washington, D.C.: The Early Years," in "Picture This," Library of Congress blog, https://blogs.loc.gov/picturethis/2013/06/washington-d-c-the-early-years-2.

34. Achenbach, *Grand Idea*, 262–63; Charles Dickens, *American Notes* (New York: St. Martin's Press, 1985), 102.

35. Account of George Combe, Clement Eaton, *The Leaven of Democracy* (New York: George Braziller, 1963), 67.

36. "Reminiscences of Washington," *Atlantic Monthly* (January 1880), 55–56.

37. A Massachusetts congressman, Theodore Sedgwick, wrote, "The climate of the Patowmack is not only unhealthy, but destructive to northern constitutions." See Widmer, "Draining the Swamp."

38. Klein, *Days of Defiance*, 48–49.

39. Whitman, *Complete Poetry and Collected Prose*, 1310.

40. "Reminiscences of Washington," *Atlantic Monthly*, January 1880, 57–58; Margaret Leech, *Reveille in Washington: 1860–1865* (New York: Harper and Brothers, 1941), 5–6; Margaret Brent Downing, "The Earliest Proprietors of Capitol Hill," *Records of the Columbia Historical Society*, vol. 21 (1918) 1–23.

41. Roy Franklin Nichols, *The Disruption of American Democracy*, 188.

42. Ibid., 329–30.

43. Prints and Photographs Division, Library of Congress; see also Adam Goodheart, "A Lincoln Photograph—and a Mystery," *New York Times*, November 5, 2010; the photograph, titled "The Lincoln Column," may be consulted at http://www.loc.gov/pictures/resource/cph.3b32800.

44. Charles Francis Adams, *Autobiography*, 44.

45. Ernest Samuels, *Henry Adams: Selected Letters* (Cambridge, MA: Harvard University Press, 1992), 32.

46. L. E. Chittenden, *Recollections of President Lincoln and His Administration* (New York: Harper and Brothers, 1901), 36.

47. Henry Adams, *Great Secession Winter*, 7.

48. Henry Adams, *Henry Adams and the Secession Crisis: Dispatches to the Boston Daily Advertiser*, December 1860–March 1861, ed. Mark J. Stegmaier (Baton Rouge: Louisiana State University Press, 2012), 1.

49. Henry Adams, *The Letters of Henry Adams*, vol. 1, eds. J. C. Levenson, Ernest Samuels, Charles Vandersee, and Viola Hopkins Winner (Cambridge, MA: Harvard University Press, 1982), 216; Charles Francis Adams, *An Address on the Life, Character and Services of William Henry Seward* (Albany, NY: Weed, Parsons, 1873), 45.

50. Adams called it "a battle after the Homeric style." Henry Adams, *Great Secession Winter*, 6.

51. Strong, *Diary of George Templeton Strong*, vol. 3, 89.

52. Meerse, "Buchanan, Corruption and Election of 1860," 116.

53. Holt, *Election of 1860*, 29–31; Meerse, "Buchanan, Corruption and Election of 1860," 116–31.

54. Ben Perley Poore, *Perley's Reminiscences of Sixty Years in the National Metropolis* (Philadelphia: Hubbard Brothers, 1886), vol. 2, 43–46.

55. Meerse, "Buchanan, Corruption and Election of 1860," 131. An Iowa senator said that Lincoln had won more for his honesty and the "known corruption" of the Democrats than because of "the negro question."

56. A search through the U.S. Library of Congress's Chronicling America newspaper database produced evidence of two speeches, to the University of North Carolina (June 1859) and from the balcony of the White House (July 9, 1860); I am grateful to Zachary Turpin for help researching this question.

57. Henry L. Dawes, "Washington in the Winter Before the War," *Atlantic Monthly*, August 1893, 160–61; Furgurson, *Freedom Rising*, 26.

58. Nicolay and Hay, *Lincoln: A History*, vol. 3, 327.

59. Russell McClintock, "Rethinking the Old Public Functionary," *New York Times*, December 30, 2010. Thompson was later accused of complicity in Lincoln's assassination.

60. A report issued on January 16, 1861, revealed that Floyd had shipped 115,000 guns to the South; Henry J. Raymond, *History of the Administration of President Lincoln* (New York: J. C. Derby and N. C. Miller, 1864), 56; Keehn, *Knights of the Golden Circle*, 90; Strong, *Diary of George Templeton Strong*, vol. 3, 115.

61. Keehn, *Knights of the Golden Circle*, 93; McClintock, "Rethinking the Old Public Functionary."

62. Meerse, "Buchanan, Corruption and Election of 1860," 117; Holt, *Election of 1860*, 30.

63. *Chicago Tribune*, February 15, 1861; it was denounced as "the great national robbery," Strong, *Diary of George Templeton Strong*, vol. 3, 100; *Chicago Tribune*, February 16, 1861; *New York Times*, February 15, 1861, 1; Nicolay and Hay, *Lincoln: A History*, vol. 3, 74.

64. Frederick Seward, *Reminiscences of a War-Time Statesman and Diplomat* (New York: G. P. Putnam's Sons, 1916), 143.

65. *Washington (D.C.) Evening Star*, March 5, 1861.

66. Nicolay and Hay, *Lincoln: A History*, vol. 3, 77–78; Dawes, "Winter Before the War," 163; Fred Nicklasan, "The Secession Winter and the Committee of Five," *Pennsylvania History* 38, no. 4 (1971): 373–74.

67. *New York Times*, January 1, 1861. A document was found in the Senate, near the chair of the vice president, exposing a plan to divert arms to the South, and suggested that Buchanan was being administered "powerful doses"—as if he were medicated—but its authenticity could not be confirmed. *New York Herald*, February 9, 1861, 3.

68. Thomas Cadwallerder to Abraham Lincoln, December 31, 1860, Abraham Lincoln Papers, Manuscript Division, Library of Congress.

69. Joseph Medill to Abraham Lincoln, December 31, 1860, Abraham Lincoln Papers, Manuscript Division, Library of Congress.

70. Adams, *Henry Adams and the Secession Crisis*, 64.

71. John Plumbe Jr., *White House*, ca. 1846, Prints and Photographs Division, Library of Congress.

72. Leonard Swett, "The Conspiracies of the Rebellion," *North American Review* (February 1887); Lamon, *Life of Abraham Lincoln*, 264; Wigfall was later implicated in the Baltimore plot; see Norma Cuthbert, *Lincoln and the Baltimore Plot*, 141 (San Marino: Huntington Library, 1949); Furgurson, *Freedom Rising*, 22.

73. Thurlow Weed cited a letter from Judah Benjamin, asking if the South might return to the British empire, in *Autobiography of Thurlow Weed*, vol. 2, ed. Harriet A. Weed (Boston: Houghton Mifflin, 1884), 313–15; Benjamin claimed later, "The letter is a fiction, but to some extent founded on fact." Robert Doutat Meade, *Judah P. Benjamin: Confederate Statesman* (New York: Oxford University Press, 1943), 140–41.

74. *Diary of George Templeton Strong*, vol. 3, 87, 89, 95.

75. Charles Pomeroy Stone, "Washington on the Eve of the War," *Century Illustrated* 26, July 1883, 9.

76. Furgurson, *Freedom Rising*, 29; Nicklasan, "Secession Winter and the Committee of Five," 379; *New York Times*, February 8, 1861, 4.

77. Nicklasan, "Secession Winter and the Committee of Five," 379; George L. P. Radcliffe, *Governor Thomas H. Hicks of Maryland and the Civil War* (Baltimore: Johns Hopkins Press, 1902), 43–44.

78. Charles Lockwood and John Lockwood, "Confederates at the Gate," *New York Times*, April 7, 2011; Keehn, *Knights of the Golden Circle*, 95–96, 102–3.

79. Nicklasan, "Secession Winter and the Committee of Five," 379–80.

80. Weed, *Autobiography of Thurlow Weed*, vol. 2, 331. A senator from Massachusetts, Henry Dawes, later described a plot that would have seized the Capitol, the

Treasury, and the national archives; Furgurson, *Freedom Rising*, 28; Nicklasan, "Secession Winter and the Party of Five," 372–88. The *Chicago Tribune* warned that a "secret society" had formed, and that "it is the purpose of the South to seize the Capitol at some time prior to, or on the 4th of March." *Chicago Tribune*, January 15, 1861.

81. John Nicolay to Therena Bates, January 6, 1861, in Burlingame, *With Lincoln*, 23.

82. Cuthbert, *Lincoln and the Baltimore Plot*, 33, 39; Adams, *Henry Adams and the Secession Crisis*, 65; Adams's source was likely Seward. Klein, *Days of Defiance*, 226; Mearns, *Lincoln Papers*, vol. 2, 355–57, 378, 398, 435.

83. The handsome Greek Revival Treasury building was attractive to Southerners as well; its redesign was the work of a South Carolinian, Robert Mills; see Stone, "Washington on the Eve," 17; Dawes, "Winter Before the War," 162.

84. Ledger K, Manuscripts Division, Library of Congress; many Southern members of Congress had books out from the Library of Congress during the Civil War; see *New York Times*, February 13, 1861.

85. Lockwood and Lockwood, "Confederates at the Gate"; George Templeton Strong used the sobriquet "Lord Davis." *Diary of George Templeton Strong*, vol. 3, 113.

86. *Scientific American*, March 2, 1861, 137–38; Blaine Lamb, *The Extraordinary Life of Charles Pomeroy Stone: Solder, Surveyor, Pasha, Engineer* (Yardley, PA: West-hoome, 2016), 84.

87. Nicklasan, "Secession Winter and the Committee of Five," 376; Henry S. Free, cited in, *Lincoln in Peekskill* (Peekskill, NY: Lincoln Society, 1926), 8.

88. Furgurson, *Freedom Rising*, 29; Nicklasan gives the total as 654; "Seccession Winter and the Committee of Five," 387.

89. Stone, "Washington on the Eve," 15, 18.

90. Taylor Peck, *Round-Shot to Rockets: A History of the Washington Naval Yard and U.S. Naval Gun Factory* (Annapolis: Naval Institute, 1949), 115.

91. Edward Everett claimed that the South had always coveted Washington in his long speech at Gettysburg; see Garry Wills, *Lincoln at Gettysburg: The Words That Remade America* (New York: Simon & Schuster, 1992), 218–20. Henry Adams thought the South wanted to invite New York City and California, but not New England and upstate New York, into its new government. See Henry Adams, *Henry Adams and the Secession Crisis*, 65, 69–70.

92. The Declaration of Independence was on display in the Patent Office; see "The Declaration of Independence: A History," https://www.archives.gov /founding-docs/declaration-history.

93. Cuthbert, *Lincoln and the Baltimore Plot*, 33, 39; Henry Adams believed the plan had nearly come to pass, but was compromised by South Carolina's hasty secession and Floyd's corruption; see *Henry Adams and the Secession Crisis*, 65;

Chittenden, *Recollections of President Lincoln*, 28; Strong, *Diary of George Templeton Strong*, vol. 3, 100, 115.

94. Dawes wrote that the two boxes were "in the sole custody of the vice president"; Dawes, "Winter Before the War," 164; Furgurson, *Freedom Rising*, 39. The man delivering Maryland's electoral certificates, William Byrne, would later be implicated in the plot to assassinate Lincoln in Baltimore; see Cuthbert, *Lincoln and the Baltimore Plot*, 141.

95. Keehn, *Knights of the Golden Circle*, 87; George Templeton Strong mentioned this fear in his *Diary of George Templeton Strong*, vol. 3, 99; Chittenden, *Recollections of President Lincoln*, 28, 36–46.

96. Chittenden, *Recollections of President Lincoln*, 63; Cuthbert, *Lincoln and the Baltimore Plot*, 6.

97. David Hunter to Abraham Lincoln, October 20, 1860, Abraham Lincoln Papers, Manuscript Division, Library of Congress. In Maryland, Governor Hicks also heard about "forcible opposition"; Lockwood and Lockwood, "Confederates at the Gate"; Keehn, *Knights of the Golden Circle*, 95–96, 102–3.

98. Tidwell, *Come Retribution*, 225, 239.

99. Chittenden, *Recollections of President Lincoln*, 60.

100. Prints and Photographs Division, Library of Congress; see also Lockwood and Lockwood, "Confederates at the Gate."

101. Nicolay and Hay, *Lincoln: A History*, vol. 3, 83.

102. Margaret Leech, *Reveille in Washington, 1860–1865* (New York: Harper and Brothers, 1941), 1–4; Lockwood and Lockwood, "Confederates at the Gate"; Nicklasan, "Secession Winter and the Committee of Five," 386; Stone, "Washington on the Eve," 13.

103. Cuthbert, *Lincoln and the Baltimore Plot*, 140–41.

104. Stone, "Washington on the Eve," 11–12.

105. Ibid., 7–25; Nicklasan, "Secession Winter and the Committee of Five," 381; Furgurson, *Freedom Rising*, 29.

106. Stone, "Washington on the Eve," 13, 20.

107. Ibid., 13, 20.

108. Nicklasan, "Secession Winter and the Committee of Five," 373; Weed, *Autobiography of Thurlow Weed*, vol. 2, 332. Stanton wrote to Salmon P. Chase that the South wanted to make Washington its capital; see John Niven, *Salmon P. Chase: A Biography* (New York: Oxford University Press, 1995), 231–32. Klein, *Days of Defiance*, 226.

109. Henry Adams, *Henry Adams and the Secession Crisis*, 182. George Templeton Strong wrote almost the same phrase; *Diary of George Templeton Strong*, vol. 3, 85.

110. Raymond, *History of the Administration of President Lincoln,* 58; Chittenden, *Recollections of President Lincoln,* 27–30.

111. Elihu Washburne to Abraham Lincoln, February 3, 1861, Mearns, *Lincoln Papers,* vol. 2, 435.

112. Henry Adams, *Henry Adams and the Secession Crisis,* 182.

113. Unidentified photographer, "Dorothea Dix," National Portrait Gallery; http://www.npg.si.edu/exh/1846/images/7700500c.jpg.

114. Frances Tiffany, *Life of Dorothea Lynde Dix* (Boston: Houghton Mifflin, 1890), 130; Helen E. Marshall, *Dorothea Dix: Forgotten Samaritan* (Chapel Hill: University of North Carolina, 1937), 197–98. A South Carolinian, James L. Petigru, had borrowed from the language of mental health to describe his state: "too small for a republic and too large for an insane asylum."

115. Cornelius Felton, "Notes on Lecturing Tour, January 16, 1856, to February 21, 1856; Papers of Cornelius Conway Felton, University Archives, Harvard University Library.

116. Tiffany, *Dorothea Lynde Dix,* 333–34; William Schouler, *A History of Massachusetts in the Civil War* (Boston: E. P. Dutton, 1868), 59–65; Samuel Felton to Dorothea Dix, August 1, 1861, Harvard University Library; Cuthbert, *Lincoln and the Baltimore Plot,* 125n. Samuel Felton, "Extract from an Autobiography Written by Samuel Morse Felton for His Children in 1866," Historical Society of Pennsylvania.

117. John W. Forney, *Anecdotes of Public Men* (New York: Harper and Brothers, 1873), 248, 257; Cuthbert, *Lincoln and the Baltimore Plot,* 4, 23, 28, 125–26.

118. Courtesy of Chicago History Museum, https://images.chicagohistory.org/detail/en/34453/1/EN34453-portrait-of-kate-warne.htm.

119. Allan Pinkerton, *The Spy of the Rebellion: Being a True History of the Spy System of the United States Army During the Late Rebellion* (New York: G. W. Carleton, 1883).

120. Cuthbert, *Lincoln and the Baltimore Plot,* 23, 28; Forney, *Anecdotes,* 251; Allan Pinkerton, *History and Evidence of the Passage of Abraham Lincoln from Harrisburg, Pa., to Washington, D.C., on the 22d and 23d of February, 1861,* 8–9; Schouler, *Massachusetts in the Civil War,* 62.

121. Stone, "Washington on the Eve," 21; Cuthbert, *Lincoln and the Baltimore* Plot, 130–31.

122. Anonymous, "G.A. A Wide Awake" to Abraham Lincoln, Tuesday, December 11, 1860, Abraham Lincoln Papers, Manuscript Division, Library of Congress.

123. A. H. Flanders to John G. Nicolay, January 12, 1861, John G. Nicolay Papers, Manuscript Division, Library of Congress.

124. Carl Sandburg, *Lincoln Collector: The Story of Oliver R. Barrett's Great Private Collection* (New York: Bonanza, 1960), 45, 60–65. Lincoln received so much mail

that Henry Villard recommended he add a mail car to his train; see Mearns, *Lincoln Papers*, vol. 1, 36–37, 287, 315.

125. Anonymous, "A Lady" to Abraham Lincoln, February 1861, Abraham Lincoln Papers, Manuscript Division, Library of Congress.

126. George W. Hazzard to Abraham Lincoln, January 1861, Abraham Lincoln Papers, Manuscript Division, Library of Congress.

127. William J. Evitts, *A Matter of Allegiances: Maryland from 1850 to 1861* (Baltimore: Johns Hopkins University Press, 1974), 157, 166.

128. Christopher S. German, photograph of Abraham Lincoln, February 9, 1861; sixteenth plate tintype copy from lost negative, https://commons.wikimedia.org/wiki/File:Abraham_Lincoln_O-44,_1861.jpg.

129. Abraham Lincoln to Joseph Gillespie; cited in Burlingame, *Lincoln: A Life*, vol. 1, 758.

130. Douglas L. Wilson, *Lincoln's Sword*, 55; Harold Holzer, *Lincoln, President-Elect*, 262–71.

131. Abraham Lincoln to Samuel Haycraft, June 4, 1860, John G. Nicolay Papers, Manuscript Division, Library of Congress. Lincoln wrote, "Would it be safe? Would not the people lynch me?" Printed in Lincoln, *Collected Works*, vol. 4, 69–70.

132. Lamon, *Life of Abraham Lincoln*, 464–65, 476. Four years earlier, gunshots had been fired near James Buchanan during his own inauguration; Tidwell, *Come Retribution*, 9.

133. Helen Nicolay, *Lincoln's Secretary: A Biography of John G. Nicolay* (New York: Longmans, Green, 1949), 56.

134. Lincoln, *Collected Works*, vol. 4., 175–76; Burlingame, *Lincoln: A Life*, vol. 1, 703.

135. Walt Whitman, *Poetry and Prose*, 463.

136. Lincoln, *Collected Works*, vol. 4, 172.

137. Scott sent his "Views Suggested by the Imminent Danger of a Disruption of the Union . . ." on October 29, 1860; Roy E. Basler, ed., *Collected Works of Abraham Lincoln*, vol. 4, 137n.

138. *The Federalist*, 84.

139. Marc Bloch, *The Royal Touch: Sacred Monarchy and Scrofula in England and France* (London: Routledge and K. Paul, 1973).

140. Elizabeth F. Ellet to Abraham Lincoln, December 31, 1860; Mearns, *Lincoln Papers*, vol. 2, 362.

141. Nicolay and Hay, *Lincoln: A History*, vol. 3, 289.

142. Henry Adams, *Great Secession Winter*, 26.

143. Charles F. Adams, *Autobiography*, 75.

144. Charles Gould to Henry C. Bowen, February 5, 1861; Henry Bowen to Abraham

Lincoln, February 5, 1861; Abraham Lincoln Papers, Library of Congress. This letter gives considerable information about the plot forming, and Samuel Felton's role in exposing it; Burlingame, *Lincoln: A Life,* vol. 1, 745.

145. Abraham Lincoln to William Seward, January 3, 1861, Lincoln, *Collected Works,* vol. 4, 170.

146. Wood was likely recommended by a combination of Thurlow Weed (who visited Lincoln on December 20), William Seward, and Erastus Corning; see Villard, *Memoirs,* vol. 1, 147–48; *Letters of Henry Adams,* 76; Cuthbert, *Lincoln and the Baltimore Plot,* 61, 68, 134; John G. Nicolay and John Hay, *Complete Works of Abraham Lincoln* (New York: Lamb Company, 1905–1906, vol. 6, 101; Hay, *At Lincoln's Side,* 190; Burlingame, *Lincoln: A Life,* vol. 2, 2; Holzer, *Lincoln, President-Elect,* 277–79. Wood gave himself an impressive title, "Superintendent of Arrangements;" John G. Nicolay Papers, Box 1, Manuscript Division, Library of Congress.

147. The planning likely began with Thurlow Weed's visit on December 20, 1860. On January 22 Lincoln mentioned that the planning was not yet finished (Roy Basler, ed., *Collected Works of Abraham Lincoln,* vol. 4, 179), but on January 27 John Nicolay wrote to his fiancée to say Lincoln had decided the previous day on the basic outline of the route; see John Nicolay to Therena Bates, January 27, 1861, John G. Nicolay Papers, Manuscript Division, Library of Congress; Nicolay and Hay, *Complete Works of Abraham Lincoln,* vol. 6, 101.

148. George Washington to Henry Knox April 1, 1789, Founders Online, National Archive; https://founders.archives.gov/documents/Washington/05-02-02-0003.

CHAPTER 3: THE IRON MONSTER

1. "Early Photograph of the *Tioga,*" Courtesy of the Railroad Museum of Pennsylvania, Operated by the Pennsylvania Historical and Museum Commission http://explorepahistory.com/displayimage.php?imgId=1-2-5B4.

2. Homer, *The Odyssey,* trans. A. T. Murray, Cambridge: Harvard University Press, 1919; http://www.perseus.tufts.edu/hopper/text?doc=Perseus%3Atext%3A1999.01.0136%3Abook%3D8%3Acard%3D469.

3. Villard, *Lincoln on the Eve,* 54.

4. Adam Goodheart, "The South Rises Again and Again and Again," *New York Times,* January 28, 2011.

5. Burlingame, *Lincoln: A Life,* vol. 1, 757.

6. John W. Starr, *Lincoln and the Railroads* (New York: Dodd, Mead, 1927), 169–70.

7. Ibid., 165. A witness, Henry C. Whitney, said that this coat was the same one Lincoln wore during his secret passage through Baltimore.

8. Lamon, *Life of Abraham Lincoln*, 472–73.

9. Herndon, *Life of Lincoln*, 389; Charles H. Coleman, *Lincoln and Coles County, Illinois* (New Brunswick, NJ: Scarecrow, 1955), 203–9.

10. Burlingame, *Lincoln: A Life*, vol. 1, 26; Wilson and Davis, *Herndon's Informants*, 106.

11. Wilson and Davis, *Herndon's Informants*, 107–8.

12. Another version of the farewell gives her words as "Abe, I'll never see you alive again. They will kill you." Coleman, *Lincoln and Coles County*, 203–9.

13. Holzer, *Lincoln, President-Elect*, 291.

14. Roger Chapin, *Ten Ministers: A History of the First Presbyterian Church of Springfield, Illinois, 1828–1953* (Springfield, IL: 1953), 24.

15. Ralph Waldo Emerson, *Journals and Miscellaneous Notebooks*, vol. 11 (Cambridge, MA: Harvard University Press, 1975), 530.

16. *Cleveland Herald*, February 11, 1861.

17. William K. Ackerman, *Historical Sketch of the Illinois Central Railroad* (Chicago Fergus Company, 1890), 25–26.

18. John Tyndall, *Contributions to Molecular Physics in the Domain of Radiant Heat* (London: Longmans, 1872), 38, 40.

19. Burlingame, *Lincoln: A Life*, vol. 2, 1.

20. Remembering a flatboat trip to New Orleans when he was 22, Lincoln recalled, "I acted both as the engineer and engine;" ibid., vol. 1, 56.

21. Angle, *"Here I Have Lived,"* 152, 160, 163–66, 178.

22. *The Collected Works of Abraham Lincoln*, vol. 4, 204.

23. Hayes, *Lincoln Runs for President*, 123; Rufus Rockwell Wilson, *Lincoln in Caricature*, 24–25.

24. Edward Hungerford, *The Story of the Baltimore and Ohio Railroad, 1827–1927* (New York: G. P. Putnam's Sons, 1928), 89–90.

25. Marvin Fisher, *Workshops in the Wilderness: The European Response to American Industrialization* (New York: Oxford University Press, 1967), 73.

26. Thaddeus Hyatt, "A Word from Mr. Hyatt About that Flying Machine," *Scientific American*, November 24, 1860, 342, "Steam Carriages for Streets and Roads," 345.

27. James A. Ward, *Railroads and the Character of America, 1820–1887* (Nashville: University of Tennessee, 1986), 34; at least one locomotive was called the *Monster*; see John H. White Jr., *American Locomotives: An Engineering History* (Baltimore: Johns Hopkins University Press, 1968), 66–77.

28. Wolfgang Schivelbusch, *The Railway Journey* (New York: Urizen, 1979), 119–20.

29. Nicholas Clapton, *Moreschi: The Last Castrato* (London: Haus, 2004), 28; *Frank Leslie's Illustrated Newspaper*, February 12, 1859.

30. Schivelbusch, *Railway Journey,* 75; Fisher, *Workshops in the Wilderness,* 54.

31. Dickens, *American Notes,* 58; Fisher, *Workshops in the Wilderness,* 157.

32. Domingo Sarmiento Faustino, *Sarmiento's Travels in the United States in 1847* (Princeton, NJ: Princeton University Press, 1970), 157–58, 161.

33. John Stauffer, *Giants: The Parallel Lives of Frederick Douglass and Abraham Lincoln* (New York: Twelve, 2008), 44–46.

34. Wilbur H. Siebert, *The Underground Railroad for the Liberation of Fugitive Slaves,"* *American Historical Association Annual Report,* 1895, 398; Aaron Marrs helpfully explains the ways in which African-Americans were sometimes allowed to ride on integrated cars in the South in *Railroads in the Old South: Pursuing Progress in a Slave Society* (Baltimore: Johns Hopkins University Press, 2009; William G. Thomas, *The Iron Way: Railroads, the Civil War, and the Making of Modern America* (New Haven, CT: Yale University Press, 2011), 36.

35. One of the most popular antislavery songs was "Get Off the Track!," about a train bringing people to freedom; see Chapter 7.

36. White Jr., *American Locomotives,* 72–73, 86–87, 114, 468–76. White gave the number of components for a typical locomotive as 6270.

37. Fisher, *Workshops in the Wilderness,* 72.

38. Alfred D. Chandler Jr., *The Railroads: The Nation's First Big Business, Sources and Readings* (New York: Harcourt, Brace and World, 1965), 13.

39. George Wilson Pierson, *Tocqueville and Beaumont in America* (New York: Oxford University Press, 1938), 590.

40. Of the roughly twenty-two thousand miles of track built in the 1850s, nearly half was in the upper Midwest; Chandler Jr., *The Railroads,* 3, 21; *The United States on the Eve of the Civil War As Described in the 1860 Census* (Washington, D.C.: U.S. Civil War Centennial Commission, 1963), 73.

41. Carl R. Fish, "The Northern Railroads, April, 1861," *American Historical Review* (July 1917): 778–93; Hamilton Schuyler, *The Roeblings: A Century of Engineers, Bridge-Builders and Industrialists* (Princeton, NJ: Princeton University Press, 1931), 33; Gene D. Lewis, *Charles Ellet Jr.: The Engineer as Individualist, 1810–1862* (Urbana: University of Illinois Press, 1968); David Plowden, *Bridges: The Spans of North America* (New York: Viking Press, 1974).

42. Chandler Jr., *The Railroads,* 7, 9.

43. Eviatar Zerubauel, "The Standardization of Time: A Sociological Perspective," *American Journal of Sociology* 88, no. 1 (July 1982): 8.

44. William Cronon, *Nature's Metropolis: Chicago and the Great West* (New York: W. W. Norton, 1991), 74–81; David S. Landes, *Revolution in Time: Clocks and the Making of the Modern World* (Cambridge, MA: Harvard University Press, 1983), 285–287, 317.

45. In 1849 Alexander MacKay wrote that to go into Virginia was a transition "as great as is the change from the activity of Lancashire to the languor and inertness of Bavaria," cited in C. Malcolm Watkins, "Artificial Lighting in America, 1830–1860," *Annual Report of the Smithsonian Institution* (1951): 386. On literacy and mail, see Ronald Zboray, *A Fictive People: Antebellum Economic Development and the American Reading Public*, 72, 196.

46. The *List of Patents for Inventions and Designs, Issued by the United States, from 1790 to 1847* (Washington, D.C.: J. and G. S. Gideon, 1847) indicates that roughly 5 percent of U.S. patent applications came from the future states of the Confederacy. The annual reports of the commissioner of patents suggest similar figures; see also *Subject Matter Index of Patents for Inventions Issued by the U.S. Patent Office from 1790 to 1873, Inclusive* (Washington, D.C.: General Printing Office, 1874). Hinton Rowan Helper also provided information on patents in *The Impending Crisis of the South and How to Meet It* (ed. George M. Fredrickson, Cambridge: Harvard University Press, 1968), 294.

47. Helen Nicolay, *Lincoln's Secretary*, 17. In December 1860 many feared that Southern militias would take over the Patent Office if they invaded Washington; see *Scientific American*, December 15, 1860, 393, and February 2, 1861, 74.

48. Robert Luther Thompson, *Wiring a Continent*, 240; Standage, *Victorian Internet*, 57-58; Menaham Blondheim, *News Over the Wires: The Telegraph and the Flow of Public Information in America, 1844–1897* (Cambridge: Harvard University Press, 1994), 190; Carleton Mabee, *The American Leonardo: A Life of Samuel F. B. Morse* (New York: Alfred A. Knopf, 1944), 294; James D. Reid, *The Telegraph in America* (New York: Derby Brothers, 1879), 116–28; Oliver Gramling, *AP: The Story of News* (New York: Farrar and Rinehart, 1940), 24; Joshua D. Wolff, *Western Union and the Creation of the American Corporate Order, 1845–1893* (New York: Cambridge University Press, 2013), 2, 31.

49. Jacob Abbott, *The Harper Establishment: How Books Are Made*, repr. (New Castle, DE: Oak Knoll Press, 2001), 121, 127.

50. Thomas A. Horrocks, *Lincoln's Campaign Biographies* (Carbondale: Southern Illinois University Press, 2014), 21, 104; Wolff, *Western Union*, 25. Wolff estimates that there were forty-six thousand miles of telegraph wires in 1860. Susan Schulten, "News of the Wired," *New York Times*, January 13, 2012; Hayes, *Lincoln Runs for President*, 55–56; Luthin, *First Lincoln Campaign*, 6–10.

51. New York grew from 515,547 (1850) to 813,669 (1860); South Carolina's white population was 291,300; see also Adam Goodheart, "The Census of Doom," *New York Times*, April 1, 2011.

52. *Manufactures of the United States in 1860* (Washington, D.C.: Government Printing Office, 1865), vi.

53. *United States on the Eve of the Civil War*, iii, 22–23, 27–34, 53.

54. Susan Schulten, *Mapping the Nation: History and Cartography in Nineteenth-Century America* (Chicago: University of Chicago Press, 2012), 24.

55. Carlton J. Corliss, *Main Line of Mid-America: The Story of the Illinois Central* (New York: Creative Age Press, 1950), 88; Edwin S. S. Sunderland, *Abraham Lincoln and the Illinois Central Railroad: Main Line of Mid-America* (New York: privately printed,1955), 30. Chicago had one railroad in 1850; ten years later, there were fifteen, with more than a hundred trains arriving daily; Maury Klein, *Unfinished Business: The Railroad in American Life* (Hanover, NH: University Press of New England, 1994), 10.

56. Cronon, *Nature's Metropolis.*

57. After the Crimean War disrupted the shipment of Russian wheat, Illinois farmers were all too happy to supply the shortfall, thanks to trains that could carry foodstuffs quickly to the east; Chandler Jr., *The Railroads*, 22; Paul W. Gates, *The Farmer's Age: Agriculture, 1815–1860* (New York: Holt, Rinehart and Winston, 1960), 166.

58. Chandler Jr., *The Railroads*, 22.

59. Another early claimant to that record was in North Carolina; see White Jr., *American Locomotives*, 13; H. Roger Grant, *The Louisville, Cincinnati and Charleston Rail Road: Dreams of Linking North and South* (Bloomington: Indiana University Press, 2014), 30–31, 35–36, 43. Robert Riegel, *The Story of the Western Railroads* (New York: Macmillan, 1926), 3; Michel Chevalier, *Society, Manners and Politics in the United States: Letters on North America* (ed. John William Ward, Garden City, New York: Doubleday, 1961) , 75.

60. John M. Bryan, ed., *Robert Mills* (Washington, D.C.: American Institute of Architects Press, 1989), 93–95; John M. Bryan, *Robert Mills: America's First Architect* (New York: Princeton Architectural Press, 2001), 173, 248; Blanche Marsh, *Robert Mills: Architect in South Carolina* (Columbia, SC: R. L. Bryan, 1970), 12.

61. Grant, *Louisville, Cincinnati and Charleston Rail Road*, 53–54, 78–85, 163.

62. Ulrich Bonnell Phillips, *A History of Transportation in the Eastern Cotton Belt to 1860* (New York: Octagon Books, 1908, 1968), 14.

63. Grant, *Louisville, Cincinnati and Charleston Rail Road*, 84.

64. Klein, *Unfinished Business*, 11; George Rogers Taylor and Irene D. Neu, *The American Railroad Network, 1861–1890* (Cambridge: Harvard University Press, 1956), 13, 24, 28, 33, 42–44, 46.

65. Taylor and Neu, *American Railroad Network,* 30.

66. It was at Baltimore, between stations, that Massachusetts troops were vulnerable to attack in April 1861.

67. Theodore Kornweibel Jr., *Railroads in the African American Experience: A*

Photographic Journey (Baltimore: Johns Hopkins University Press, 2010), 11, 18, 23.

68. Susan O'Donovan, "William Webb's World," *New York Times*, February 18, 2011.

69. Ulrich Bonnell Phillips, *History of Transportation in the Eastern Cotton Belt*, 385, 396.

70. See Helper, *Impending Crisis of the South*, 291, 405, 407; Elias Loomis, "Astronomical Observatories in the United States," *Harper's Magazine* 13, June 1856, 51; see also Lynne Kirby, *Parallel Tracks: The Railroad and Silent Cinema* (Durham, NC: Duke University Press, 1997), 51.

71. Marrs, *Railroads in the Old South*, 3.

72. The Wide Awakes organized themselves along railroads. See Jon Grinspan, " 'Young Men for War': The Wide Awakes and Lincoln's 1860 Presidential Campaign," *Journal of American History* 96, no. 2 (September 2009): 367–78.

73. 1860 and 1850 census tables in *United States on the Eve of the Civil War*, 73; see also the helpful website created by William Thomas, http://railroads.unl.edu/views/item/slavery_rr.

74. Fish, "Northern Railroads," 778–93.

75. Ulrich Bonnell Phillips, *History of Transportation in the Eastern Cotton Belt*, 9, 18–20, 388, 390.

76. Burlingame, *Lincoln: A Life*, vol. 1, 691.

77. Jefferson Davis to the Congress of the Confederate States, November 18, 1861, *The Papers of Jefferson Davis*, Rice University; https://jeffersondavis.rice.edu/archives/documents/jefferson-davis-congress-confederate-states.

78. *Papers of Jefferson Davis*, vol. 6, 359.

79. The phrase was used in William Smith, ed., *The Book of the Great Railway Celebrations of 1857* (New York: D. Appleton, 1858) 79.

80. These were at Alexandria, Virginia; Cincinnati, Ohio; Louisville, Kentucky; and Cairo, Illinois; see Thomas, *Iron Way*, 71. The point is also explored in Fish, "Northern Railroads," 778–93; and in Taylor and Neu, *American Railroad Network*, 48.

81 Raleigh & Gaston Railroad locomotive *Romulus Saunders*, North Carolina Museum of History, https://www.ncpedia.org/biography/wilder-gaston-hillary.

82. Richard Campanella, *Lincoln in New Orleans: The 1828–1831 Flatboat Voyages and Their Place in History* (Lafayette: University of Louisiana at Lafayette Press, 2010), 14; Wilson and Davis, *Herndon's Informants*, 257.

83. Campanella, *Lincoln in New Orleans*, 15.

84. Burlingame, *Lincoln: A Life*, vol. 1, 17–18.

85. Herndon, *Life of Lincoln*, 18.

86. Lincoln, *Collected Works of Lincoln*, 4:63.

87. Burlingame, *Lincoln: A Life*, vol. 1, 7.

88. Ibid., 20. A. H. Chapman testimony in Wilson and Davis, *Herndon's Informants*, 97.

89. Burlingame, *Lincoln: A Life*, vol. 1, 7–8, 20, 23.

90. Wilson and Davis, *Herndon's Informants*, 98.

91. Francis Marion Van Natter, *Lincoln's Boyhood: A Chronicle of His Indiana Years* (Washington, D.C.: Public Affairs, 1963), 34; Herndon, *Life of Lincoln*, 32–33.

92. Wilson and Davis, *Herndon's Informants*, 12

93. William A. Meese, *Abraham Lincoln: Incidents in his Life Relating to Waterways* (Moline, IL: Desaulniers, 1908), 7.

94. Wilson and Davis, *Herndon's Informants*, 17.

95. Burlingame, *Lincoln: A Life*, vol 1., 25, 35, 43. On the different versions of this story, see Campanella, *Lincoln in New Orleans*, 27–29. Regarding an early legal case involving Lincoln's ferrying passengers, see William H. Townsend, "Commonwealth of Kentucky Vs. Abraham Lincoln," *American Bar Association Journal* 14, no. 2 (February 1928): 80–82.

96. Auguste Levasseur, *Lafayette in America in 1824 and 1825; or, Journals of Travels in the United States*, vol. 2 (New York: White, Gallaher and White, 1829), 158–64; J. Bennett Nolan, *Lafayette in America Day by Day* (Baltimore: Johns Hopkins University Press, 1934), 286.

97. Burlingame, *Lincoln: A Life*, vol. 1, 43–44; Campanella, *Lincoln in New Orleans*, 76–82, 117; Van Natter, *Lincoln's Boyhood*, 146.

98. Herndon, *Life of Lincoln*, 63.

99. Burlingame, *Lincoln: A Life*, vol. 1, 56; Campanella, *Lincoln in New Orleans*, 149, 168–75, 208; Starr, *Lincoln and the Railroads*, 10; Carleton B. Case, *Wit and Humor of Abraham Lincoln* (Chicago: Shrewesbury Publishing, 1916), 136.

100. Herndon, *Life of Lincoln*, 64. According to a persistent legend, Lincoln saw a voudou priestess who predicted that he would someday become president; Campanella, *Lincoln in New Orleans*, 209.

101. Robert Gudmestad, *Steamboats and the Rise of the Cotton Kingdom* (Baton Rouge: Louisiana State University Press, 2011), 177; Harry P. Owens, *Steamboats in the Cotton Economy: River Trade in the Yazoo-Mississippi Delta* (Jackson: University Press of Mississippi, 1990), 10.

102. Harry E. Pratt, "Lincoln Pilots the *Talisman*," *Abraham Lincoln Quarterly* 2, no. 7 (September 1943): 321, 323; Herndon, *Life of Lincoln*, 72–73; Rufus Rockwell Wilson, Lincoln, *Uncollected Works*, vol. 1, 47.

103. Lincoln, *Collected Works*, vol. 1, 5–6, 8–9; Starr, *Lincoln and the Railroads*, 13; Campanella, *Lincoln in New Orleans*, 222.

104. Burlingame, *Lincoln: A Life*, vol. 1, 80–82, 95, 96, 102; Rufus Rockwell Wilson, *Uncollected Works*, vol. 1, 81, 101, vol. 2, 35, 42–43, 53; Herndon, *Life of Lincoln*, 87; Paul Simon, *Lincoln's Preparation for Greatness: The Illinois Legislative Years* (Urbana: University of Illinois Press, 1965), 26–29, 39, 261; James William Putnam, *The Illinois and Michigan Canal: A Study in Economic History* (Chicago: University of Chicago Press, 1918), 10.

105. Starr, *Lincoln and the Railroads*, 25, 28, 34; Sunderland, *Lincoln and the Illinois Central*, 6; Corliss, *Main Line of Mid-America*, 8–9; Burlingame, *Lincoln: A Life*, vol. 1, 121; Simon, *Lincoln's Preparation for Greatness*, 76–105; Herndon, *Life of Lincoln*, 130, 140; Isaac Kuhn, ed., *Abraham Lincoln: A Vast Future* (Champaign, IL: self-pub., 1946), 25–27; Angle, *"Here I Have Lived,"* 144.

106. Burlingame, *Lincoln: A Life*, vol. 1, 129.

107. Joshua A. T. Salzmann, *"Safe Harbor: Chicago's Waterfront and the Political Economy of the Built Environment, 1847–1918"* (PhD diss., University of Illinois at Chicago, 2008), 35; Burlingame, *Lincoln: A Life*, vol. 1, 248; Mentor L. Williams, "The Chicago River and Harbor Convention, 1847," *Mississippi Valley Historical Review* 35 (March 1949): 607–26; Starr, *Lincoln and the Railroads*, 95.

108. Mentor L. Williams, "Chicago River and Harbor Convention, 1847," 610, 625; Burlingame, *Lincoln: A Life*, vol. 1, 277.

109. Francis Fisher Browne, *The Everyday Life of Abraham Lincoln* (Chicago: Browne and Howell, 1913), 276.

110. Christopher Derose, *Congressman Lincoln* (New York: Threshold, 2013, 182–83; Burlingame, *Lincoln: A Life*, vol. 1, 263.

111. *Report of the Commissioner of Patents for the Year 1849*, pt. 1 (Washington, D.C.: Office of Printers to the House of Representatives), 262.

112. Jason Emerson, *Lincoln the Inventor* (Carbondale: Southern Illinois University Press, 2009), 4–6.

113. Herndon, *Life of Lincoln*, 239; Emerson, *Lincoln the Inventor*, 14–17.

114. Jason Emerson, *Lincoln the Inventor*, 32.

115. Thorndike Rice, ed., *Reminiscences of Abraham Lincoln*, 19–20.

116. Prints and Photographs Division, Library of Congress; see also Curtis C. Roseman, "A Pictorial History of the First Railroad Bridge Across the Mississippi River and Its Three Successors," *Riveraction*; http://www.riveraction.org/bridgehistory.

117. Jason Emerson, *Lincoln the Inventor*, 19, 21.

118. Brian Dirck, *Lincoln the Lawyer* (Urbana: University of Illinois Press, 2007), 92.

119. Burlingame, *Lincoln: A Life*, vol. 1, 334, 435–38; Starr, Lincoln and the Railroads,

58–59; Kuhn, *Lincoln: A Vast Future*, 33; John P. Frank, *Lincoln as a Lawyer* (Urbana: University of Illinois Press, 1961), 25, 92–94.

120. Allen Spiegel, *Abraham Lincoln, Esq.: A Shrewd, Sophisticated Lawyer in His Time*, 98; Kuhn, *Lincoln: A Vast Future*, 30; Starr, *Lincoln and the Railroads*, 81–82; Charles Moores, *Abraham Lincoln, Lawyer*, vol. 7, no. 10 (Greenfield: Indiana Historical Society Publications, 1922), 499.

121. Starr, *Lincoln and the Railroads*, 117–18; Moores, *Abraham Lincoln, Lawyer*, 519.

122. Starr, *Lincoln and the Railroads*, 82–84.

123. Ibid., 62-63; Sunderland, *Lincoln and the Illinois Central*, 18; Burlingame, *Lincoln: A Life*, vol. 1, 336.

124. Brian McGinty, *Lincoln's Greatest Case: The River, the Bridge, and the Making of America* (New York: Liveright, 2015).

125. It was also the birthplace of Lincoln's old adversary, Black Hawk. *Black Hawk: An Autobiography* (ed. Donald Jackson, Urbana: University of Illinois Press, 1955), 47.

126. Burlingame, *Lincoln: A Life*, vol. 1, 337; Starr, *Lincoln and the Railroads*, 92–94; George R. Taylor and Irene D. Neu, *The American Railway Network, 1861–1890*, 40.

127. David A. Pfeiffer, "Bridging the Mississippi: The Railroads and Steamboats Clash at the Rock Island Bridge," *Prologue* 32 (Summer 2004).

128. Starr, *Lincoln and the Railroads*, 106.

129. Burlingame, *Lincoln: A Life*, vol. 1, 337–38.

130. Dirck, *Lincoln the Lawyer*, 97; Starr, *Lincoln and the Railroads*, 113, 116; Wilson and Davis, *Herndon's Informants*, 87.

131. By coincidence, these were the stars by which Odysseus guided his raft. Homer, *The Odyssey*, book 5, line 272.

132. Starr, *Lincoln and the Railroads*, 100-103; Susan O'Connor Davis, "Lincoln's Hyde Park," *Hyde Park (IL) Herald*, May 6, 2015.

133. Eric Foner, *Free Soil, Free Labor, Free Men: The Ideology of the Republicans Before the Civil War* (New York: Oxford University Press, 1971), 38; Starr, *Lincoln and the Railroads*, 68, 155.

134. Don E. Fehrenbacher, *Prelude to Greatness: Lincoln in the 1850s* (Palo Alto, CA: Stanford University Press, 1962), 8; Burlingame, *Lincoln: A Life*, vol. 1, 487–88.

135. Robert W. Johannsen, *Stephen A. Douglas* (Urbana: University of Illinois Press, 1973, 1997), 304–21; Burlingame, *Lincoln: A Life*, vol. 1, 364.

136. Kuhn, *Lincoln: A Vast Future*, 44–45; Starr, *Lincoln and the Railroads*, 135–36; Burlingame, *Lincoln: A Life*, vol. 1 475, 545.

137. Villard, *Memoirs of Henry Villard*, vol. 1, 96.

138. Starr, *Lincoln and the Railroads*, 136; Kuhn, *Lincoln: A Vast Future*, 45; Michael Burlingame, *Lincoln: A Life*, vol. 1, 473; Johannsen, *Stephen A. Douglas*, 658–59.

139. Starr, *Lincoln and the Railroads*, 143–44.

140. Ibid., 144–45.

141. Lincoln argued that the federal government must be "put on a new track"; Burlingame, *Lincoln: A Life*, vol. 1, 429; earlier he had used the same expression, to describe his instability, after the death of Ann Rutledge in 1835 ("I run off the track"); ibid., 101.

142. Richard W. Fox, *Lincoln's Body: A Cultural History* (New York: W.W. Norton, 2015), 141.

143. Wilson and Davis, *Herndon's Informants*, 499.

144. Herndon, *Life of Lincoln*, 273.

145. Starr, *Lincoln and the Railroads*, 147.

146. Fehrenbacher, *Prelude to Greatness*, 8.

147. Schurz, *Reminiscences*, 89–91; Starr, *Lincoln and the Railroads*, 137–39; Rufus Rockwell Wilson, *Lincoln in Caricature*, 74; Burlingame, *Lincoln: A Life*, vol. 1, 473.

148. James MacKay, *Allen Pinkerton: The First Private Eye* (New York: John Wiley, 1996), 69, 77–86; Sunderland, *Lincoln and the Illinois Central*, 29.

149. Starr, *Lincoln and the Railroads*, 126, 160; Freeman, *Lincoln Goes to New York*, 55; Sunderland, *Lincoln and the Illinois Central*, 39.

150. *Chicago Press and Tribune*, August 8, 1860; H. Preston James, "Political Pageantry in the Campaign of 1860 in Illinois," *Abraham Lincoln Quarterly* 4, no. 7 (September 1947): 313–64; William E. Baringer, "The Presidential Candidate Attends a Rally," *Abraham Lincoln Quarterly* 4, no. 3 (September 1946), 129–31; Goodheart, *1861*, 25–55; Ian Hunt, "Iconic Political Symbols Stand the Test of Time," Abraham Lincoln Presidential Library Foundation online, accessed January 16, 2017, http://www.alplm.org/NewsEvents/News/IconicPoliticalSym bolsStandtheTestofTime.aspx.

151 Burlingame, *Lincoln: A Life*, vol. 1, 656.

152. Christopher S. German, photograph of Abraham Lincoln, February 9, 1861; Prints and Photographs Division, Library of Congress, https://commons.wiki media.org/wiki/File:Abraham_Lincoln_O-43_by_German,_1861.jpg.

153. Burlingame, *With Lincoln*, 25.

154. Hudson Strode, *Jefferson Davis: American Patriot, 1808–1861* (New York: Harcourt Brace, 1955), 401; Felicity Allen, *Jefferson Davis: Unconquerable Heart* (Columbia: University of Missouri Press, 1999), 267; *The Papers of Jefferson Davis*, vol. 7, ed. Lynda Lasswell Crist and Mary Seaton Dix (Baton Rouge: Louisiana State University Press, 1992), 37.

155. Lincoln, *Collected Works*, vol. 4, 188–89.

156. Schivelbusch, *Railway Journey*, 59.

157. Nathaniel Hawthorne, *The House of the Seven Gables* (New York: Henry Holt, 1917), 275–76.

158. Villard, *Lincoln on the Eve*, 64.

159. John Washington, *They Knew Lincoln* (New York: E.P. Dutton, 1942), 200–201.

160. *Memphis Daily Appeal*, February 9, 1861.

161. Scott D. Trostel, *The Lincoln Inaugural Train: The 1861 Journey of President-Elect Abraham Lincoln to Washington, D.C.* (Fletcher, OH: Cam-Tech, 2011), 9, 12.

162. Douglas L. Wilson, *Lincoln's Sword*, 58.

163. *New York Herald*, February 10, 1861, 4. The word is given incorrectly as *reflective* in Villard, *Lincoln on the Eve*, 64.

164. Villard, *Lincoln on the Eve*, 64.

165. Cuthbert, *Lincoln and the Baltimore Plot*, 5. Elsewhere, Pinkerton suggests the information came February 10; Pinkerton, *Spy of the Rebellion*, 54; *Discoveries and Inventions: A Lecture Delivered by Abraham Lincoln in 1860* (San Francisco: John Howell, 1915); the witness, Dr. Samuel Houston Melvin, thought that Lincoln's mail was affecting him.

166. Douglas L. Wilson, ed., *Lincoln Before Washington: New Perspectives on the Illinois Years* (Urbana: University of Illinois Press, 1997), 141.

167. Herndon, *Life of Lincoln*, 390; Holzer, *Lincoln, President-Elect*, 294. In Herndon's correspondence, there are other hints that Lincoln did not feel that he would survive his own presidency; see Wilson and Davis, *Herndon's Informants*, 185.

168. Henry B. Rankin, *Personal Recollections of Abraham Lincoln* (New York: G. P. Putnam's Sons, 1916), 226–27.

CHAPTER 4: FAREWELL

1. "Old State Capitol circa 1858," Abraham Lincoln Presidential Library and Museum; https://www.nps.gov/liho/learn/historyculture/springfield2.htm.

2. Homer, *The Odyssey*, trans. Wilson, 225–26.

3. Ward Hill Lamon, *Recollections of Abraham Lincoln* (Washington, D.C.: Dorothy Lamon Teillard, 1911), 30.

4. Harold K. Sage, "Jesse W. Fell and the Lincoln Autobiography," *Journal of the Abraham Lincoln Association* 3, no. 1 (1981).

5. Charles Francis Adams, *Autobiography*, 75; Harry J. Sievers, *Benjamin Harrison: Hoosier Warrior* (Chicago: Henry Regnery, 1952), 158.

6. Jesse Weik, *The Real Lincoln: A Portrait*, ed. Michael Burlingame (Lincoln: University of Nebraska Press, 2002), 313.

7. Thomas D. Jones, *Memories of Lincoln*, ed. Rufus Rockwell Wilson (New York:

Press of the Pioneers, 1934), 8. The bust is in the Indiana State House, although copies exist elsewhere.

8. "Lincoln's Springfield," March 16, 2007; http://lincolnsspringfield.blogspot .com/2007_03_16_archive.html.

9. Kreismann and Villard may have come together to the United States. See Wilson and Davis, *Herndon's Informants*, 700–701.

10. Villard, *Lincoln on the Eve*, 70–71. Some scholars believe that this incident happened earlier; see Hay, *At Lincoln's Side*, 189; Holzer, *Lincoln, President-Elect*, 238, 548; Wilson and Davis, *Herndon's Informants*, 700–701. Ruth Painter Randall believed that Kreismann was in Washington on February 9; see *Mary Lincoln: Biography of a Marriage* (Boston: Little, Brown, 1953), 196.

11. Weik, *Real Lincoln*, 330.

12. Ibid., 307. William E. Barton wrote it slightly differently in *The Life of Abraham Lincoln*, vol. 1 (Indianapolis: Bobbs-Merrill, 1925), 465.

13. Weik, *Real Lincoln*, 307.

14. Richard E. Hart, "Lincoln's Springfield: The Underground Railroad, Part 2," *For the People, A Newsletter of the Abraham Lincoln Association* 8, no. 2 (Summer 2006): 2; Richard E. Hart, "Springfield's African Americans as a Part of the Lincoln Community," *Journal of the Abraham Lincoln Association* 20 (Winter 1999): 35–54.

15. John G. Nicolay and John Hay, *Abraham Lincoln; A History*, vol. 3 (New York: Century, 1890), 290.

16. Nicolay and Hay called it "a throng of a least a thousand of his neighbors who had come to bid him good-bye;" *Lincoln; A History*, 290; Ward Hill Lamon remembered it as "a great mass of people," Lamon, *Recollections of Lincoln*, 30; Springfield's population was 9,320.

17. Villard, *Memoirs*, vol. 1, 149; Weik, *Real Lincoln*, 387.

18. John W. Washington, *They Knew Lincoln* (New York: E.P. Dutton, 1942), 184; a cartoon image of the farewell revealed a mixed-race audience, see Seba Smith, *The Letters of Major Jack Downing*.

19. Wilson, *Lincoln's Sword*, 10; Weik, *Real Lincoln*, 388.

20. John Nicolay, in Helen Nicolay, *Personal Traits of Abraham Lincoln*, 162.

21. On March 7, 1861, three days into the Lincoln administration, the *New York Times* ran a front-page story of a gift of two black horses from Wood to the new president's wife. She lobbied for his advancement throughout the spring, before changing her mind and deciding that he was "a very bad man." See Hay, "Mary Todd Lincoln's Unethical Conduct as First Lady," in *At Lincoln's Side*, 190, 273n27; *At Lincoln's Side: John Hay's Civil War Correspondence and Selected Writings*, 186, 191–92, 273–74.

22. Lamon, *Recollections of Lincoln*, 30–31.

23. Nicolay and Hay, *Lincoln: A History*, vol. 3, 290.

24. Villard, *Lincoln on the Eve*, 71.

25. Jones, *Memories of Lincoln*, 16.

26. Nicolay and Hay, *Lincoln: A History*, vol. 3, 290; Thomas D. Jones remembered that the train "thundered in," but other sources indicate it was already there; *Memories of Lincoln*, 16.

27. Wilson, *Lincoln's Sword*, 10.

28. Jones, *Memories of Lincoln*, 16. One reporter wrote that Lincoln said good-bye to his wife just before he spoke; *Harper's Weekly* (February 23, 1861). Another source suggested that Mary had accompanied him from the hotel; *Chicago Tribune*, February 12, 1861.

29. Lamon, *Recollections of Lincoln*, 30–31.

30. Nicolay and Hay, *Lincoln: A History*, vol. 3, 291.

31. Ibid.

32. Image 1 of Abraham Lincoln papers: Series 1. General Correspondence. 1833–1916: Abraham Lincoln, Monday, February 11, 1861 (Farewell Address), Library of Congress, Manuscripts Division; https://www.loc.gov/resource/mal.0728000/?sp=1.

33. Holzer, *Lincoln, President-Elect*, 299; Weik, *Real Lincoln*, 311.

34. A supporter in Cleveland urged Lincoln to read Washington's address; Holzer, *Lincoln, President-Elect*, 264.

35. According to *The Aeneid*, Odysseus stole the palladium to gain legitimacy for the Greeks.

36. Goodheart, "War for (George) Washington." In his farewell address to the Senate, Davis cited Calhoun but mentioned no founder by name. Lincoln cited Washington's farewell address in a speech at New Haven, March 6, 1860.

37. Wilson, *Lincoln's Sword*, 10–18, offered a superb explanation of the textual variants.

38. Lincoln had experimented with these literary strategies before. A manuscript fragment from 1858, at the time of the debates against Douglas, records a similar phrasing: "In this age, and this country, public sentiment is everything—with it, nothing can fail; against it, nothing can succeed." Abraham Lincoln, *Complete Works* (ed. Hay) I, 422.

39. Holzer, *Lincoln, President-Elect*, 304; Robert Browne, *Abraham Lincoln and the Men of his Time* (Chicago: Blakely-Oswald, 1901, 1907), 408–9.

40. Nicolay and Hay, *Lincoln: A History*, vol. 3, 291n.

41. Wilson, *Lincoln's Sword*, 298n12; Lincoln, *Collected Works*, vol. 4, 190–91.

42. "Three Versions of Lincoln's Farewell Address," http://www.abrahamlincolnon line.org/lincoln/speeches/farewell3.htm; Wilson, *Lincoln's Sword*, 13.

43. "Three Versions of Lincoln's Farewell Address," http://www.abrahamlincolnon line.org/lincoln/speeches/farewell3.htm.

44. Ibid.

45. Wilson, *Lincoln's Sword*, 11.

46. Hay, *At Lincoln's Side*, 116–17.

47. Nicolay and Hay, *Lincoln: A History*, vol. 3, 291; John Nicolay wrote elsewhere, "there was in it a sadness and a pathos almost prophetic;" see John Nicolay, "The Journey to Washington," in Helen Nicolay, *Personal Traits of Abraham Lincoln*, 156–57; Lamon also wrote that Lincoln did not expect to return alive; *Recollections of Lincoln*, 32

48. Hay, *At Lincoln's Side*, 137;

49. Lamon, *Recollections of Lincoln*, 32.

50. John Hay Scrapbook, Collection of Robert Hoffman; Hay, *Lincoln's Journalist*, 24.

51. Weik, *Real Lincoln*, 307; Villard, *Memoirs*, vol. 1, 150; Lamon, *Recollections of Lincoln*, 30.

52. Francis Springer to Abraham Lincoln, February 11, 1861, Abraham Lincoln Papers, Manuscript Division, Library of Congress.

53. Hay, *Lincoln's Journalist*, 25.

54. Villard, *Lincoln on the Eve*, 73; *Memoirs*, vol. 1, 148–49.

55. Harold Holzer, *Lincoln and the Power of the Press* (New York: Simon & Schuster, 2014), 282; Wilson, *Lincoln's Sword*, 15.

56. One of Robert's friends was George Latham, to whom Lincoln had written a letter about perseverance on July 22, 1860.

57. Hay, *Lincoln's Journalist*, 353; for more on Johnson, see Magness and Page, "Lincoln and Johnson." Johnson was listed as a member of the travelling party in the *New York Herald*, February 20, 1861.

58. Hay, *At Lincoln's Side*, 143–48; Goodheart, *1861*, 188–208; Ruth Painter Randall, *Colonel Elmer Ellsworth* (Boston: Little, Brown, 1960), 204–16.

59. Hay, *At Lincoln's Side*, 147.

60. A similar device is described in Helen Nicolay, *Lincoln's Secretary*, 65. There was also a gaggle of railroad officials. For passenger lists, see Hay, *Lincoln's Journalist*, 352–53; Holzer, *Lincoln, President-Elect*, 297-298; Nicolay and Hay, *Lincoln: A History*, vol. 3, 290n; Villard, *Memoirs*, vol. 1, 150; *New York Times*, February 12, 1861; *New York Herald*, February 20, 1861; Victor Searcher, *Lincoln's Journey to Greatness: A Factual Account of the Twelve-Day Inaugural Trip* (Philadephia:

Winston, 1960), 9; Stephen Fiske, "How Lincoln Was First Inaugurated," *Ladies' Home Journal*, March 1897. Searcher, *Lincoln's Journey to Greatness*, 8, gives the train crew as F. W. Bowen (superintendent of the road), Walter Whitney (conductor), Edward H. Fralick (engineer), Benjamin A. Gordon (fireman), Thomas Rose (brakeman), and Platt Williamson (baggage master).

61. Hay, *Lincoln's Journalist*, 353; Searcher, *Lincoln's Journey to Greatness*, 4; Fiske, "How Lincoln Was First Inaugurated"; Holzer, *Lincoln and the Power of the Press* (New York: Simon & Schuster, 2014), 281–82.

62. Holzer, *Lincoln, President-Elect*, 298.

63. *Frank Leslie's Illustrated Newspaper*, March 2, 1861, 232–233. The technique of artistic reproduction was explained in *Frank Leslie's Illustrated Newspaper*, December 15, 1861, 53.

64. *New York Times*, February 12, 1861.

65. *Chicago Tribune*, February 12, 1861.

66. Villard, *Memoirs*, vol. 1, 150; Searcher, *Lincoln's Journey to Greatness*, 19.

67. Paul Fatout, "Mr. Lincoln Goes to Washington," *Indiana Magazine of History* 47 (December 1951), 321. The fence had evidently been placed on the tracks by local boys, hoping to see Lincoln.

68. Ibid.

69. *The Diary of Orville Hickman Browning*, ed. Theodore Calvin Pease and James G. Randall (Springfield: Illinois State Historical Library, 1925), 454.

70. *Chicago Tribune*, February 12, 1861.

71. John Nicolay, "The Journey to Washington," in Helen Nicolay, *Personal Traits of Abraham Lincoln*, 158.

72. Waldo W. Braden, *Abraham Lincoln, Public Speaker*, 39; other commentators have given slightly different estimates.

73. John Nicolay, "The Journey to Washington," in Helen Nicolay, *Personal Traits of Abraham Lincoln*, 158.

74. Starr, *Lincoln and the Railroads*, 180.

75. John Nicolay, "Some Incidents in Lincoln's Journey from Springfield to Washington," in *Oral History of Lincoln*, 110.

76. Edwin Davis, "Lincoln and Macon County, Illinois, 1830–1831," *Journal of the Illinois State Historical Society* 25 (April–July, 1932): 63–107; Lincoln's passage into Illinois was difficult, and Lincoln was frostbitten after falling through ice; according to a cousin, John Hanks, he gave an early speech calling for better river navigation.

77. Villard, *Memoirs*, vol. 1, 150–51; Hay, *Lincoln's Journalist*, 25.

78. Searcher, *Lincoln's Journey to Greatness*, 12; Starr, *Lincoln and the Railroads*, 180.

79. *Chicago Tribune*, February 12, 1861; Searcher, *Lincoln's Journey to Greatness*, 13; Holzer, *Lincoln, President-Elect*, 306.

80. Villard, *Lincoln on the Eve*, 73–74.

81. *Chicago Tribune*, February 12, 1861.

82. John Gilmary Shea, *The Lincoln Memorial: A Record of the Life, Assassination and Obsequies of the Martyred President* (New York: Bunce and Huntington, 1865), 27; Tidwell, *Come Retribution*, 227; Henry J. Raymond, *The Life and Public Services of Abraham Lincoln* (New York: Derby and Miller, 1865), 158.

84. *Chicago Tribune*, February 12, 1861.

85. Courtesy of National Postal Museum; see also Priya Ganapati, "August 17, 1859: U.S. Air Mail Carried by Balloon," *Wired*, August 17, 2010; https://www.wired .com/2010/08/0817us-airmail-balloon.

86. Villard, *Memoirs*, vol. 1, 151. Colfax's grandfather served in the Life Guard that protected George Washington during the Revolution; Willard M. Smith, *Schuyler Colfax: The Changing Fortunes of a Political Idol* (Indianapolis: Indiana Historical Bureau, 1952), 138; G. J. Hollister, *Life of Schuyler Colfax* (New York: Funk and Wagnalls, 1886), 169, 175; Burlingame, *Lincoln: A Life*, vol. 1, 608–11. On Caleb Smith, see Vincent Tegeder, "Lincoln and the Territorial Patronage," *Mississippi Valley Historical Review* 35 (June 1948): 78.

87. Henry Villard Papers, Ms Am 1322 (637a), 87, Houghton Library, Harvard University.

88. Ibid.

89. "Poetry Written by Abraham Lincoln," http://www.abrahamlincolnonline.org /lincoln/speeches/poetry.htm.

90. Villard Papers, Ms Am 1322 (637a), 87, Houghton Library, Harvard University; Villard, *Memoirs*, vol. 1, 151; *Chicago Tribune*, February 12, 1861.

91. Searcher, *Lincoln's Journey to Greatness*, 23.

92. *Collected Works of Abraham Lincoln*, vol. 4, 192.

93. Ibid., 192–93; Stefan Lorant, introduction, in John Mason Potter, *Thirteen Desperate Days* (New York: Ivan Obolensky, 1964), xv. Variants of this story appear elsewhere, including Fiske, "How Lincoln Was First Inaugurated."

94. Sievers, *Benjamin Harrison*, 159–60; Fatout, "Lincoln Goes to Washington," 326.

95. Nicolay to Bates, February 11, 1861, John G. Nicolay Papers, Manuscript Division, Library of Congress. Orville Browning estimated it more conservatively, at twenty thousand; see *Diary of Orville Hickman Browning*, 454.

96. James R. Hetherington, "The History of Union Station," http://www.indiana history.org/our-services/books-publications/railroad-symposia-essays-1/The %20History%20of%20Union%20Station.pdf; *Indiana: A Guide to the Hoosier State* (New York: Oxford University Press, 1941), 210; Indianapolis called itself Railroad City.

97. Even before he turned twenty-five, Edison had lived in six of the towns Lincoln

would pass through on the Special; another Indiana boy drawn to the rails was Eugene V. Debs, whose long career as a labor leader began with his earliest work, at age fourteen, cleaning the grease from engines.

98. Charles W. Calhoun, *Benjamin Harrison* (New York: Times Books, 2005), 20; Benjamin Harrison to Abraham Lincoln, February 2, 1861; Abraham Lincoln Papers, Library of Congress. The recording of Harrison can be heard at "U.S. Presidential Audio Recordings," Vincent Voice Library, Michigan State University; http://www.lib.msu.edu/cs/branches/vvl/presidents/harrison.html.

99. John Nicolay, in Helen Nicolay, *Personal Traits of Abraham Lincoln*, 163; Helen Nicolay, *Lincoln's Secretary*, 64.

100. Norman Gasbarro, "Lincoln's Birthday 1861," *Civil War Blog*, http://civilwar.gratzpa.org/2011/02/lincolns-birthday-1861; Hay, *Lincoln's Journalist*, 25–26.

101. Villard, *Lincoln on the Eve*, 78.

102. Lincoln, *Collected Works*, vol. 3, 463–70.

103. Sievers, *Benjamin Harrison*, 158; Fatout, "Lincoln Goes to Washington," 322.

104. John Hay, writing occasional commentary on the trip, assumed that his readers would already have seen Lincoln's speeches, which "the telegraph will have given you." Hay, *Lincoln's Journalist*, 26, 352.

105. William Dudley Foulke, *Life of Oliver P. Morton* (Indianapolis: Bobbs Merrill, 1899), 107.

106. Lincoln, *Collected Works*, vol. 4, 193–94.

107. John Nicolay, "Journey to Washington," in Helen Nicolay, *Personal Traits of Abraham Lincoln*, 160; there are minor discrepancies in accounts of the sequence of speeches. See Cottman, "Lincoln in Indianapolis," 7.

108. Weik, *Real Lincoln*, 312–13.

109. Villard, *Memoirs*, vol. 1, 151.

110. On divorce as a metaphor for the tensions between North and South, see Adam Goodheart, "Divorce, Antebellum Style," *New York Times*, March 18, 2011.

111. Hay, *Lincoln's Journalist*, 26.

112. George S. Cottman, "Lincoln in Indianapolis," *Indiana Magazine of History* 24, March 1928, 9.

113. Poore, *Perley's Reminiscences*, vol. 2, 66; see also http://www.mrlincolnandnewyork.org/new-york-politics/lincoln-and-the-grip-sack.

114. *Diary of Orville Hickman Browning*, 454.

115. Hay, *Lincoln's Journalist*, 27.

116. Nicolay to Bates, February 11, 1861; John G. Nicolay Papers, Manuscript Division, Library of Congress; Helen Nicolay, *Personal Traits of Abraham Lincoln*, 161–62; Helen Nicolay, *Lincoln's Secretary*, 63.

117. Jay Leyda, *The Melville Log: A Documentary Life of Herman Melville, 1819–1891*, vol. 2 (New York: Harcourt Brace, 1951), 637; see also Nicolay, *Oral History of Lincoln*, 111–112.

118. Fatout, "Lincoln Goes to Washington," 328.

119. Hay, *Lincoln's Journalist*, 26.

120. Sievers, *Benjamin Harrison*, 160.

121. Hay, *Lincoln's Journalist*, 27.

122. Ibid., 26.

123. John G. Nicolay, "Some Incidents in Lincoln's Journey from Springfield to Washington," in *Oral History of Lincoln*, 108; Wilson, *Lincoln's Sword*, 53; Searcher, *Lincoln's Journey to Greatness*, 30.

124. John Nicolay, in Helen Nicolay, *Personal Traits of Abraham Lincoln*, 162.

125. Ibid., 164–65; Wilson, *Lincoln's Sword*, 57.

126. Lamon, *Life of Abraham Lincoln*, 473; Lamon remembered the incident taking place in Harrisburg.

127. Lamon, *Recollections of Lincoln*, 36; Lamon also added valuable information about the search process in the hotel office: "On going there, we found a great pile of all kinds of baggage in promiscuous confusion. Mr. Lincoln's keen eye soon discovered a satchel which he thought his own; taking it in his hand eagerly. he tried his key; it fitted the lock—the bag opened, and to our astonishment it contained nothing but a soiled shirt, several paper collars, a pack of cards, and a bottle of whiskey nearly full. In spite of his perplexity, the ludicrous mistake overcame Mr. Lincoln's gravity, and we both laughed heartily, much to the amusement of the bystanders." The story was reported in the February 23 *Baltimore Daily Exchange*, with an added barb that the inaugural was "yet missing."

128. Villard, *Memoirs*, vol. 1, 151–52.

129. Cuthbert, *Lincoln and the Baltimore Plot*, 25.

130. Lamon, *Recollections of Lincoln*, 32–33.

131. *Papers of Jefferson Davis*, vol. 7 (Baton Rouge: Louisiana State University Press, 1992), 37.

132. *Memphis Daily Appeal*, February 14, 1861, 2; William C. Davis, *Jefferson Davis: The Man and His Hour* (New York: Harper Collins, 1991), 303–7; *Papers of Jefferson Davis*, vol. 7, 37–42; Jefferson Davis, *The Rise and Fall of the Confederate Government*, vol. 1 (New York: D. Appleton, 1881), 231; "Jefferson Davis's Long Journey to Inauguration Is Recounted," *Gadsden (AL) Times*, February 6, 1961.

133. William J. Cooper Jr., *Jefferson Davis, American* (New York: Alfred A. Knopf, 2000), 328; *Papers of Jefferson Davis*, vol. 7, 41n; "Jefferson Davis's Long Journey to Inauguration."

134. Lorant, intro., in Potter, *Thirteen Desperate Days*, xiii.

135. Nichols, *Disruption of American Democracy*, 480.

136. Diary of Charles Francis Adams, February 11, 1861; Massachusetts Historical Society.

CHAPTER 5: PORKOPOLIS

1. Courtesy of the Public Library of Cincinnati and Hamilton County; this flag was retrieved by a five-year-old boy, Charles Hanselman, during Lincoln's procession through Cincinnati; and donated in 1933. See Heintz, "Cincinnati Reminiscences," 119.

2. Homer, *The Odyssey*, trans. Wilson, 266.

3. Villard, *Lincoln on the Eve*, 79.

4. These accounts were staggered over the next few days; see Holzer, *Lincoln, President-Elect*, 310; Searcher, *Lincoln's Journey to Greatness*, 35; *Richmond Dispatch*, February 16, 1861 (citing the *Charleston Mercury*).

5. In one rural enclave, Delphi, farmers were amazed to hear the cannonade as the Special raced down the track, twenty-four miles away; Fatout, "Lincoln Goes to Washington," 323.

6. Hay, *Lincoln's Journalist*, 28–29.

7. Ibid., 28. Orville Browning also commented on the crowds; *Diary of Orville Hickman Browning*, 454.

8. Cuthbert, *Lincoln and the Baltimore Plot*, 25; Judd later remembered this exchange taking place in Cincinnati, but Pinkerton's own records suggest that it was Indianapolis; see Cuthbert, *Lincoln and the Baltimore Plot*, 109.

9. Villard, *Lincoln on the Eve*, 79.

10. Hay, *Lincoln's Journalist*, 29; Villard, *Lincoln on the Eve*, 79.

11. Maurice G. Baxter, *Orville H. Browning: Abraham Lincoln's Friend and Critic* (Bloomington: Indiana University Press, 1957), 108–9.

12. *Diary of Orville Hickman Browning*, 455.

13. Baxter, *Orville H. Browning*, 109–10.

14. Hay, *Lincoln's Journalist*, 29; William T. Coggeshall, *Lincoln Memorial. The Journeys of Abraham Lincoln: From Springfield to Washington, 1861, as President-Elect; and from Washington to Springfield, 1865, as President Martyred* (Columbus: *Ohio State Journal*, 1865), 29.

15. Ibid., 29; Searcher, *Lincoln's Journey to Greatness*, 41.

16. Searcher, *Lincoln's Journey to Greatness*, 41–42.

17. Stephen Fiske, "A Message That Made History," in *Lincoln Among His Friends: A Sheaf of Intimate Memories*, ed. Rufus Rockwell Wilson (Caldwell, ID: Caxton, 1942), 303.

18. Ruth Painter Randall, *Mary Lincoln*, 200; her cousin Lockwood Todd also accompanied her.

19. Coggeshall, *Lincoln Memorial*, 29; Robert J. Gunderson, "Lincoln in Cincinnati," *Bulletin of the Historical and Philosophical Society of Ohio* 8 (October 1950): 258–66.

20. *Diary and Letters of Rutherford B. Hayes, Nineteenth President of the United States*, vol. 2, ed. Charles Richard William (Columbus: Ohio State Archeological and Historical Society, 1920), 5–6; Ari Hoogenboom, *Rutherford B. Hayes; Warrior and President* (Lawrence: University Press of Kansas, 1995), 108.

21. Henry Villard Papers, typescript manuscript (88) of *Lincoln on the Eve of '61*, Series V, (637a 2), Houghton Library, Harvard University.

22. Henry Villard papers, 89; MS Am 1322 (637a 2), Houghton Library, Harvard University.

23. *Chicago Tribune*, February 13, 1861.

24. *Cincinnati Daily Press*, November 7, 1860, 3.

25. William E. Gienapp, "Abraham Lincoln and the Border States," *Journal of the Abraham Lincoln Association* 13, no. 1 (1992): 13; Lincoln to Orville Browning, September 22, 1861; Lincoln, *Collected Works*, vol. 4, 532.

26. *Cape Ann (MA) Light and Gloucester Telegraph*, February 16, 1861.

27. Lincoln, *Collected Works*, vol. 4, 197.

28. Ibid., 200–201.

29. Burlingame, *Lincoln: A Life*, vol. 1, 150–51.

30. Mearns, *Lincoln Papers*, vol. 1, 280–82; Helen Nicolay, *Lincoln's Secretary*, 41.

31. *Chicago Tribune*, February 13, 1861.

32. Lithograph of Abraham Lincoln's Speech in Cincinnati, September 17, 1859; Ohio History Connection; http://library.cincymuseum.org/lincoln/items/litho1859.htm.

33. Gunderson, "Lincoln in Cincinnati," 259.

34. Barbara Allen, *Tocqueville, Covenant and the Democratic Revolution*, 323n20; Jon Butler, *Awash in a Sea of Faith: Christianizing the American People* (Cambridge, MA: Harvard University Press, 1990), 271–72.

35. Jonathan D. Sarna, "A Sort of Paradise for the Hebrews: The Lofty Vision of Cincinnati Jews," in Henry C. Shapiro and Jonathan D. Sarna, *Ethnic Diversity and Civic Identity: Patterns of Conflict and Cohesion in Cincinnati Since 1820* (Champaign: University of Illinois Press, 1992), 131–64.

36. Many leaders of the 1848 revolution ended up in Cincinnati; see Wittke, "Germans of Cincinnati," 11.

37. Melvin I. Urofsky, *Louis D. Brandeis: A Life* (New York: Pantheon, 2009), 8. A novel written in German in 1854, *Cincinnati*, described all manner of prostitutes,

swindlers, and petty thieves swarming in neighborhoods called Rat Town and the Bratwurst Quarter.

38. Charles Cist, *Sketches and Statistics of Cincinnati in 1851* (Cincinnati: William H. Moore, 1851), 74–77.

39. Arnold Schrier, "A Russian Observer's Visit to 'Porkopolis,' 1857," *Cincinnati Historical Society Bulletin* 29, no. 1 (Spring 1971): 43, 46; Emil Klauprecht, *Cincinnati, or The Mysteries of the West* (New York: Peter Lang, 1996), xv.

40. Albert Bernhardt Faust, *The German Element in the United States* (Boston: Houghton Mifflin, 1909), vol. 2, 131–32.

41. *Eclectic* was the term for a medical school in Cincinnati that pursued unusual lines of research into herbal and indigenous health practices; see John S. Haller, *A Profile in Alternative Medicine: The Eclectic Medical College of Cincinnati, 1845–1942* (Kent, OH: Kent State University Press, 1999).

42. Catherine Gilbertson, *Harriet Beecher Stowe* (New York: Appleton, 1937), 56.

43. In the winter of 1840–41, Lincoln wrote to a physician in Cincinnati, Dr. Daniel Drake, seeking advice, which may have related to a physical ailment of some kind or his despondency. That letter has never been found, despite much curiosity. See Joshua Wolf Shenk, *Lincoln's Melancholy: How Depression Challenged a President and Fueled His Greatness* (Boston: Houghton Mifflin, 2005), 59; Burlingame, *Lincoln: A Life*, vol. 1, 183.

44. Burlingame, *Lincoln: A Life*, vol. 1, 340.

45. Herndon, *Herndon's Lincoln*, 220; Michael G. Heintz, "Cincinnati Reminiscences of Lincoln," *Bulletin of the Historical and Philosophical Society of Ohio* 9 (April 1951): 113–20.

46. Raymond, *Life and Public Services of Lincoln*, 81–84; Rutherford B. Hayes showed Lincoln to his hotel room.

47. Gary Ecelbarger, "Before Cooper Union: Lincoln's 1859 Cincinnati Speech and Its Impact on His Nomination," *Journal of the Abraham Lincoln Association* 30, no. 1 (Winter 2009): 1–17.

48. Lincoln, *Collected Works*, vol. 3, 443, 453-454; Heintz, "Cincinnati Reminiscences," 119.

49. Cist, *Sketches and Statistics of Cincinnati*, 320.

50. Vernon David Keeler, *The Commercial Development of Cincinnati to the Year 1860* (Chicago: University of Chicago, 1938), 38–39.

51. Crist, *Sketches and Statistics of Cincinnati*, 46; Schrier, "Visit to 'Porkopolis,' " 37.

52. Cist, *Sketches and Statistics of Cincinnati in 1851*, 24.

53. Pierson, *Tocqueville and Beaumont in America*, 552.

54. Frances Trollope, *Domestic Manners of the Americans* (ed. Donald Smalley, New York: Alfred A. Knopf, 1949), 427.

55. They could be seen in a panoramic photograph, capturing most of Cincinnati in a single instant, poised for greatness, at 1:55 p.m. on September 24, 1848; Julie Rehmeyer, "1848 Daguerreotypes Bring Middle America's Past Back to Life," *Wired*, July 9, 2010, https://www.wired.com/2010/07/ff_daguerrotype_pan orama. See also "Panorama of Progress: Building a City in the Photographic Age," Public Library of Cincinnati and Hamilton County; http://1848.cincinnati library.org; at the precise moment of the photograph, Lincoln was speeding on a railroad (in Massachusetts).

56. John Quincy Adams, "An Oration Delivered Before the Cincinnati Astronomical Society," in I. Bernard Cohen, ed., *Aspects of Astronomy in America in the Nineteenth Century* (New York: Arno, 1980), 13.

57. Cist, *Sketches and Statistics of Cincinnati*, 108.

58. Ibid., 109.

59. Isabella Bird, *The Englishwoman in America* (London: J. Murray, 1856), 118.

60. Longworth's son-in-law, Larz Anderson, was the brother of Major Robert Anderson, in command of Fort Sumter.

61. Abby S. Schwartz, "Nicholas Longworth: Art Patron of Cincinnati," *Queen City Bulletin* (Spring 1988), 17.

62. Chase wrote to Norman Judd (January 20, 1861) and to Lincoln (January 28, 1861), urging a public journey; he wrote, "it is important to allow full scope to the enthusiasm of the people just now;" John Niven, ed., *The Salmon P. Chase Papers* (Kent. OH: Kent State University Press, 1996), vol. 3, 51–52.

63. Salmon P. Chase was also a member; Gilbertson, *Harriet Beecher Stowe*, 63–64.

64. Cist, *Sketches and Statistics of Cincinnati*, 74–77.

65. Joseph Stern, "The Team that Couldn't Be Beat," *Cincinnati Historical Society Bulletin* (Spring 1969): 28–29.

66. Trollope, *Domestic Manners of Americans*, 73.

67. Clara Longworth de Chambrun, *Cincinnati: Story of the Queen City* (New York: Scribner, 1939), 149.

68. Stanley Harrold, *Border War: Fighting over Slavery Before the Civil War* (Chapel Hill: University of North Carolina Press, 2010), 4; Keehn, *Knights of the Golden Circle*, 110; a founder of the Knights, George Bickley, lived in Cincinnati in the 1850s.

69. Harrold, *Border War*, 4.

70. Trollope, *Domestic Manners of Americans*, lvii.

71. Charles Crist, *Sketches and Statistics of Cincinnati in 1851*, 34.

72. *Uncollected Works of Abraham Lincoln*, vol. 2, 397; see also Levi Coffin's story of "Rose, the White Slave," in *Reminiscences of Levi Coffin, the Reputed President of the Underground Railroad* (Cincinnati: R. Clarke, 1880), 407.

73. Harrold, *Border War*, 67.

74. Levi Coffin, *Reminiscences of Levi Coffin, the Reputed President of the Underground Railroad*, 337, 471; another gripping account of anti-slavery activities in Cincinnati is William Birney, *James G. Birney and His Time* (New York: Appleton, 1889).

75. Harrold, *Border War*, 57–58, 156. The tragedy of Margaret Garner also influenced Toni Morrison's *Beloved*. For more on the ways in which slavery was tacitly supported in Ohio, see Matthew Salafia, *Slavery's Borderland*. See also Niven, *Salmon P. Chase*, 50-60; William E. Baringer, "The Politics of Abolition: Salmon P. Chase in Cincinnati," *Cincinnati Historical Society Bulletin* 29 (1971): 79–98.

76. Grant, *Louisville, Cincinnati and Charleston Rail Road*, 33, 48, 138, 164. In 1860 an important link in this chain was completed: a ninty-nine-mile railway between the Ohio and Lexington, Kentucky.

77. Joseph S. Stern Jr., "The Suspension Bridge: They Said It Couldn't Be Built," *Cincinnati Historical Society Bulletin* 23, no. 4 (October 1965): 218–19; Schrier, "Visit to 'Porkopolis,' " 46. An 1859 print shows an imaginary view of the span crossing the river, before it was built; see "Cincinnati," 1859; Martin F. Schmidt Collection, Kentucky Historical Society http://kyhistory.pastperfectonline .com/webobject/A52DF6D2-E60C-4DF2-BB2F-332756141273. The bridge would finally be completed in 1867.

78. *New York Times*, February 14, 1861. There were later reports that the Confederacy wanted to "recover" Cincinnati. Tidwell, *Come Retribution*, 176.

79. "Journey to the Slaughterhouse," illustration in "The Hog Trade of Cincinnati," *Harper's Weekly*, February 4, 1860.

80. Margaret Walsh, *The Rise of the Midwestern Meat Packing Industry* (Lexington: University Press of Kentucky, 1982), 34; Steve C. Gordon, "From Slaughterhouse to Soap-Boiler: Cincinnati's Meat Packing Industry, Changing Technologies and the Rise of Mass Production, 1825–1870," *IA*, vol. 16 (1990), 55–67; R. Douglas Hurt, "Pork and Porkopolis," *Cincinnati Historical Society Bulletin* 40 (1982): 197.

81. Hurt, "Pork and Porkopolis," 193.

82. Edward Deering Mansfield, *The Ohio Railroad Guide, Illustrated* (Columbus: Ohio State Journal, 1854), 6; Schrier, "Russian Observer's Visit to 'Porkopolis,' " 37.

83. Trollope, *Domestic Manners of Americans*, 88–89.

84. Cist, *Sketches and Statistics of Cincinnati*, 280.

85. Hay, *Lincoln's Journalist*, 27.

86. Chicago overtook Cincinnati as the leading city for packing meat in 1860; see Keeler, *Commercial Development of Cincinnati*, 36; Walsh, *Rise of the Midwestern Meat Packing Industry*, 20.

87. Some 475,000 hogs were packed in 1848, the peak antebellum year; Keeler, *Commercial Development of Cincinnati*, 13; Cist, *Sketches and Statistics of Cincinnati*,

228. In 1861, almost a half million hogs were packed at Cincinnati; Walsh, *Rise of the Midwestern Meat Packing Industry*, 20.

88. Walsh, *Rise of the Midwestern Meat Packing Industry*, 36; Cist, *Sketches and Statistics of Cincinnati*, 282.

89. Cincinnati was so linked to lard oil that it began to acquire a new nickname: "Lardoilopolis"; Steve C. Gordon, "From Slaughterhouse to Soap-Boiler: Cincinnati's Meat Packing Industry, Changing Technologies and the Rise of Mass Production, 1825–1870," *IA*, vol. 16 (1990), 57–58.

90. Cist, *Sketches and Statistics of Cincinnati*, 284–85; Isaac Lippincott, *A History of Manufactures in the Ohio Valley to the Year 1860* (New York: Knickerbocker Press, 1914), 179.

91. Keeler, *Commercial Development of Cincinnati*, 17, 22; James R. Beniger, *The Control Revolution*, 251; John H. White, *Cincinnati Locomotive Builders, 1845–1868* (Washington, D.C.: Smithsonian Institution, 1965), 5, 8, 131, 151; John H. White, *A History of the American Locomotive: Its Development, 1830–1880* (New York: Dover, 1979), 15. Better telegraph lines tied Cincinnati to the North as well. An 1851 guidebook, marveling at the new connectedness, wrote that Cincinnatians were closer to Boston than they had been to Columbus a decade earlier; Cist, *Sketches and Statistics of Cincinnati*, 310–11.

92. Bird, *Englishwoman in America*, 126; she noted that a similar piece of real estate was worth ten times more on the Ohio side.

93. Harrold, *Border War*, 8–9.

94. Lincoln, *Collected Works*, vol. 3, 446.

95. Longworth de Chambrun, *Cincinnati*, 213.

96. Prints and Photographs Division, Library of Congress.

97. Trollope, *Domestic Manners of Americans*, 145.

98. *New York Times*, February 18, 1861.

99. Hay, *Lincoln's Journalist*, 29.

100. *Chicago Tribune*, February 13, 1861; Gunderson, "Lincoln in Cincinnati," 258–66.

101. Gunderson, "Lincoln in Cincinnati," 261.

102. *New York Times*, February 18, 1861.

103. Burlingame, *Lincoln: A Life*, vol. 2, 8.

104. Hay, *Lincoln's Journalist*, 29–30.

105. Gunderson, "Lincoln in Cincinnati," 261; Trostel, *Lincoln Inaugural Train*, 37–39.

106. Burlingame, *Lincoln: A Life*, vol. 2, 8.

107. Henry F. Pringle, *The Life and Times of William Howard Taft*, vol. 1 (New York: Farrar and Rinehart, 1959), 3, 6.

108. Gunderson, "Lincoln in Cincinnati," 263–64.

109. *Diary and Letters of Rutherford B. Hayes, Nineteenth President of the United States,* vol. 2, 5.

110. Hoogenboom, *Rutherford B. Hayes,* 113.

111. *Diary and Letters of Rutherford B. Hayes, Nineteenth President of the United States,* vol. 2, 4.

112. Villard Papers, 89; Harvard University Library; *New York Times,* February 13, 1861.

113. Villard Papers, 89; Harvard University Library.

114. Ibid., 89–90.

115. *New York Times,* February 18, 1861.

116. Burlingame, *Lincoln: A Life,* vol. 1, 413, 432, 511, 541, 609, 613, 696.

117. Lincoln, *Collected Works,* vol. 4, 202; Burlingame, *Lincoln: A Life,* vol. 2, 9; Carl Wittke, "The Germans of Cincinnati," *Bulletin of the Historical and Philosophical Society of Ohio* 29 (January 1962): 4.

118. Villard Papers, 90, Harvard University Library; the furniture from Lincoln's room was preserved; Weldon Petz, *In the Presence of Abraham Lincoln* (Harrogate, TN: Lincoln Memorial University, 1973).

119. Hay, *Lincoln's Journalist,* 27–28.

121. *Cincinnati Daily Press,* February 13, 1861.

122 Villard, *Lincoln on the Eve,* 80.

123. *New York Times,* February 18, 1861.

124. Hay, *Lincoln's Journalist,* 30–31.

125. Daniel Stashower, *The Hour of Peril: The Secret Plot to Murder Lincoln Before the Civil War* (New York: Minotaur, 2013), 162.

126. Cuthbert, *Lincoln and the Baltimore Plot,* 27-31.

127 Ibid., 25, 31; John Mason Potter, *Thirteen Desperate Days* (New York: Ivan Obolensky, 1964), 34–42.

128. *New York Times,* February 13, 1861; William C. Davis, *Jefferson Davis,* 305.

129. *Richmond (VA) Times Dispatch,* February 16, 1861; *New Orleans Daily Crescent,* February 13, 1861.

130. *Letters of Henry Adams,* 88–89; Adam Goodheart, "The Ashen Ruin," *New York Times,* February 15, 2011.

131. *New York Times,* February 13, 1861.

132. Ibid.

133. Lamon, *Recollections of Lincoln,* 33–34.

CHAPTER 6: THE CHEESE BOX

1. Prints and Photographs Division, Library of Congress.

2. Homer, *The Odyssey,* trans. Wilson, 191.

3. Searcher, *Lincoln's Journey to Greatness*, 59.

4. Stashower, *Hour of Peril*, 163–64.

5. Ibid., 163–66; Potter, *Thirteen Desperate Days*, 42-43; Cuthbert, *Lincoln and the Baltimore Plot*, 31–32.

6. Lincoln, *Collected Works*, vol. 4, 170-71; Searcher, *Lincoln's Journey to Greatness*, 69; Potter, *Thirteen Desperate Days*, 44–46.

7. The peace conference that had begun to deliberate in Washington on February 4 was relevant to this point. Historians have often scorned it as ineffectual, but it kept the border states at the table during the crucial days when Lincoln was on his way to Washington.

8. Villard, *Lincoln on the Eve*, 81. One source has Captain John Pope joining the train here; Coggeshall, *Lincoln Memorial*, 41; Gunderson, "Lincoln in Cincinnati," 265.

9. Gunderson, "Lincoln in Cincinnati," 265.

10. *New York Times*, February 18, 1861.

11. Raymond, *Life and Public Services of Lincoln*, 158; Stashower, *Hour of Peril*, 162; Tidwell, *Come Retribution*, 227. The source of this account was the *Syracuse Journal* of February 23, 1861.

12. Henry J. Raymond, the editor of the *New York Times*, confirmed the story when he wrote, "an attempt was made on the Toledo and Western Railroad, on the 11th of February, to throw from the track the train on which he was journeying, and just as he was leaving Cincinnati a hand grenade was found to have been secreted on board the cars." *Life and Public Services of Lincoln*, 158.

13. *New York Times*, February 18, 1861.

14. Villard, *Lincoln on the Eve*, 81.

15. Xenia Depot; http://west2k.com/ohpix.xeniaprr.jpg.

16. Edward Deering Mansfield, *The Ohio Railroad Guide, Illustrated* (Columbus: Ohio State Journal, 1854), 4–5.

17. Ibid., 10.

18. Ibid., 13.

19. Ibid., 17, 20.

20. Ibid., between 32 and 33; Caleb Atwater, "A Description of the Antiquities Discovered in the Western Country; Originally Communicated to the American Antiquarian Society," in *Writings of Caleb Atwater* (Columbus: Scott and Wright, 1833). Atwater wondered if the Greeks had wandered thousands of miles off course to build these mounds; he claimed, "Homer frequently mentions them." See also Robert Silverberg, *Mound Builders of Ancient America* (New York: New York Graphic Society, 1968), 60.

21. Gunderson, "Lincoln in Cincinnati," 265.

22. These remarks came from a speech at London, Ohio; see Lincoln, *Collected Works*, vol. 4, 203-4.

23. Arthur M. Schlesinger Jr., *A Life in the Twentieth Century: Innocent Beginnings, 1917–1950* (Boston: Houghton Mifflin), 2000, 1.

24. *New York Times,* February 18, 1861.

25. Gunderson, "Lincoln in Cincinnati," 265.

26. *New York Times,* February 18, 1861.

27. *New York Times,* February 18, 1861; Villard, *Lincoln on the Eve*, 82. Xenia would welcome another presidential aspirant when William Jennings Bryan came to visit in 1896; see Arthur M. Schlesinger Jr., *A Life*, vol. 1, 4; Arthur M. Schlesinger Sr. *In Retrospect: The History of a Historian* (New York: Harcourt Brace and World, 1963), 16.

28. "Building Stones of the Ohio Capitols," https://geosurvey.ohiodnr.gov/portals /geosurvey/PDFs/Education/el19.pdf.

29. Holzer, *Lincoln, President-Elect*, 319.

30. Villard, *Lincoln on the Eve*, 82.

31. Coggeshall, *Lincoln Memorial,* 44

32. *New York Times,* February 18, 1861; Coggeshall, *Lincoln Memorial,* 43.

33. Coggeshall, *Lincoln Memorial,* 43–44.

34. *Cincinnati Daily Press,* November 7, 1860.

35. Prints and Photographs Division, Library of Congress.

36. Schulten, *Mapping the Nation*, 186. Two Virginians who moved to Ohio were Thomas Jefferson's two sons by Sally Hemings, Madison and Eston; Annette Gordon-Reed, *Thomas Jefferson and Sally Hemings: An American Controversy* (Charlottesville: University Press of Virginia, 1997), 15, 247–48.

37. Nicolay and Hay, *Lincoln: A History*, vol. 3, 280.

38. A nearby town, Circleville, was originally built around a series of concentric circles.

39. Daniel Kilham Dodge, *Abraham Lincoln: The Evolution of His Literary Style* (Champaign: University of Illinois Press, 1900, 2000), 5; Donald E. and Virginia Fehrenbacher, *Recollected Words of Abraham Lincoln* (Stanford, CA: Stanford University Press, 1996), 190; David Hirsch and Dan Van Haften, *Abraham Lincoln and the Structure of Reason* (Savas Beatie eBook; 2011), 43; http://the -american-catholic.com/2012/08/16/lincoln-and-euclid/.

40. For more on Lincoln and Euclid, see Drew R. McCoy, "An Old-Fashioned Nationalism: Lincoln, Jefferson and the Classical Tradition," *Journal of the Abraham Lincoln Association* 23, no. 1 (Winter 2002): 55–67.

41. Mechanics in Columbus were experimenting with early models of self-propelled

steam-powered vehicles. John H. White Jr., *The American Railroad Passenger Car* (Baltimore: Johns Hopkins University Press, 1978), 583.

42. Edward Deering Mansfield, *The Ohio Railroad Guide*, 59; Talbot Hamlin, *Greek Revival Architecture in America* (New York: Oxford University Press, 1944), 288.

43. Henry-Russell Hitchcock and William Seale, *Temples of Democracy: The State Capitols of the USA* (New York: Harcourt Brace Jovanovich, 1976), 110–13.

44. Talbot Hamlin, *Greek Revival Architecture*, 288; Thomas E. O'Donnell, "The Greek Revival Capitol at Columbus, Ohio," *The Architectural Forum* XLII (January 1925), 5–8

45. The State House was built with Ohio limestone hauled from nearby quarries west of Columbus, using a railroad built for that purpose in 1849.

46. Courtesy of the Ohio Geological Survey.

47. Horrocks, *Lincoln's Campaign Biographies*, 20.

48. Coggeshall was also secretary to Ohio's governor, William Dennison.

49. W. D. Howells, *Years of My Youth and Three Essays*, ed. David J. Nordloh (Bloomington: Indiana University Press, 1975), 58, 201; Freda Postle Koch, *Colonel Coggeshall: The Man Who Saved Lincoln* (Columbus: PoKo, 1985).

50. David Donald, *Lincoln Reconsidered: Essays on the Civil War Era* (New York: Vintage, 1947, 1961), 174. In addition to his history of Lincoln's journey, Coggeshall published an epic survey, *The Poets and Poetry of the West*, with Follett and Foster, in 1860.

51. William Dean Howells, *Literary Friends and Acquaintances* (New York: Harper and Brothers, 1900), 2; W. D. Howells, *Years of My Youth*, 59, 78.

52. W. D. Howells, *Years of My Youth*, 58

53. "The Pilot's Story" recounted the plight of a young mulatto mother who threw herself onto the paddle-wheel of a steamboat rather than be sold back into slavery; Mildred Howells, *Life in Letters of William Dean Howells*, vol. 1 (New York: Russell and Russell, 1928, 1968), 26; Kenneth Lynn, *William Dean Howells: An American Life* (New York: Harcourt Brace Jovanovich, 1970), 62, 81, 91–92.

54. W. D. Howells, *Life of Abraham Lincoln* (Springfield, IL: Abraham Lincoln Association, 1938), v; Lynn, *William Dean Howells*, 86; Mildred Howells, *Letters of William Dean Howells*, vol. 1, 3, 7.

55. Mildred Howells, *Letters of William Dean Howells*, vol. 1, 36; Horrocks, *Lincoln's Campaign Biographies*, 51–52; W. D. Howells, *Life of Lincoln*, ix.

56. Mildred Howells, *Letters of William Dean Howells*, vol. 1, 36; W. D. Howells, *Life of Lincoln*, 30–31.

57. William Dean Howells, *Literary Friends and Acquaintances*, 2. The publisher was satisfied with the quick profile, and apparently Lincoln was as well. Curiously,

Lincoln borrowed the book twice from the Library of Congress as president, long after it had served its purpose of electing him. It was still in the White House, checked out, on the night that he went to Ford's Theater; Ledger M, Manuscripts Division, Library of Congress; W. D. Howells, *Life of Lincoln*, xvii; a copy of the book with Lincoln's emendations was republished in 1938.

58. W. D. Howells, *Years of My Youth*, 117.

59. Lynn, *William Dean Howells*, 89.

60. William Dean Howells, *Literary Friends and Acquaintances*, 9, 405; Howells praised Lincoln above all other presidents for his literary appointments.

61. Union Station, Columbus, ca. 1864; https://en.wikipedia.org/wiki/Union _Station_(Columbus, OH).

62. Smith Stimmel, *Personal Reminiscences of Abraham Lincoln* (Minneapolis: H. M. Adams, 1928), 8.

63. W. D. Howells, *Years of My Youth*, 166–67.

64. Some of Lincoln's most eloquent speeches about the war effort were to Ohio soldiers; see "Speeches to Ohio Regiments," http://www.abrahamlincolnonline .org/lincoln/speeches/ohio.htm.

65. Coggeshall, *Lincoln Memorial*, 44.

66. *New York Times*, February 18, 1861.

67. Raymond, *Life and Public Services of Lincoln*, 78–81. The same book contained a letter from John Wilkes Booth contesting this claim ("This country was formed for the *white*, not for the black man"), 794.

68. J. G. Holland, *The Life of Abraham Lincoln* (Springfield, MA: G. Bill, 1866), 261.

69. Villard, *Lincoln on the Eve*, 83.

70. Coggeshall, *Lincoln Memorial*, 47; *New York Times*, February 18, 1861.

71. Goodheart, *1861*, 101.

72. Holzer, *Lincoln, President-Elect*, 319–20.

73. Goodheart, *1861*, 101. Many newspapers commented negatively on Lincoln's speech, especially in the South; Larry Tagg, *The Unpopular Mr. Lincoln: The Story of America's Most Reviled President* (New York: Savas Beattie, 2009), 108–12.

74. *New York Times*, February 18, 1861.

75. Coggeshall, *Lincoln Memorial*, 49–50.

76. Holland, *Life of Lincoln*, 263; Coggeshall, *Lincoln Memorial*, 50.

77. *Chicago Tribune*, February 16, 1861.

78. T. S. McFarland, quoted in Trostel, *Lincoln Inaugural Train*, 59.

79. Nicolay, *Oral History of Lincoln*, 113–14.

80. *Chicago Tribune*, February 16, 1861.

81. Nicolay, *Oral History of Lincoln*, 113–14.

82. *Chicago Tribune*, February 16, 1861.

83. Nicolay, *Oral History of Lincoln*, 111, 113.

84. Ibid., 110.

85. John G. Nicolay to Therena Bates, February 15, 1861, Papers of John G. Nicolay, Library of Congress.

86. Michael Burlingame, ed., *Oral History of Lincoln*, 112.

87. Stimmel, *Reminiscences of Lincoln*, 8.

88. Stimmel later served Lincoln as a bodyguard in the White House. His memoir, published in 1928, offered a wealth of personal detail about Lincoln's everyday life, including his clothes (his hat had several dents in it), and the way he looked on a horse ("interesting"). He noted that Lincoln's eyes, blueish-gray, were naturally sad most of the time; but would light up with "a special brilliancy" when animated by something "of special interest." Ibid., 10–11, 15, 20–21, 28, 30.

89. W. D. Howells, *Years of My Youth*, 175–76, remembered how Garfield would drop by his office to read Tennyson. Another future presidential aspirant, Victoria Woodhull, was often in Columbus; she grew up in Homer, Ohio; Lois Beachy Underhill, *The Woman Who Ran for President: The Many Lives of Victoria Woodhull* (Bridgehampton, NY: Bridgeworks, 1995), 31.

90. Theodore Clarke Smith, ed., *The Life and Letters of James Abram Garfield* (Archon Books, 1968; reprint of 1927 Yale University Press edition), I, 155. Garfield wrote these letters on February 17, 1861. The encounter is also described in Goodheart, *1861*, 91–103. On April 14, 1866, the first anniversary of Lincoln's assassination, Garfield would echo many of these thoughts in moving eulogy, delivered before Congress.

91. William T. Coggeshall to Abraham Lincoln, February 23, 1861, Abraham Lincoln Papers, Library of Congress.

92. Freda Postle Koch, *Colonel Coggeshall: The Man Who Saved Lincoln* (Columbus: PoKo Press, 1985), 3–5, 9–10; Mary Coggeshall's letter to her daughter, Emancipation Proclamation Coggeshall Busbey, February 25, 1908, reproduced in facsimile, 39–49. She alleged that William Coggeshall saved Lincoln's life from a grenade on the train, in Harrisburg. But this claim is repeated nowhere else, and Coggeshall did not appear in any of the lists of passengers that were published in newspapers.

93. W. D. Howells, *Years of My Youth*, 166.

94. Ibid., 166–67; Coggeshall noted that he "escaped" at four thirty and took refuge in the governor's mansion; Coggeshall, *Lincoln Memorial*, 50.

95. Holland, *Life of Abraham Lincoln*, 263.

96. *The Congressional Globe* wrote that the counting inside the House began at 12:20 pm; *Congressional Globe*, 36th Congress, 2nd Session (1860–1861), 893–894.

97. *Baltimore Sun*, February 14, 1861, 2.

98. Chittenden, *Recollections of President Lincoln*, 28, 40–41. According to Chittenden, citing a conversation with Adam Gurowski, a Polish immigrant and journalist, there was a well-organized plot, dating back to Lincoln's election, to cause a riot during the counting of the votes in the House, during which the Capitol would be seized and Jefferson Davis declared the president—of the United States of America.

99. *Chicago Tribune*, February 16, 1861.

100. Chittenden, *Recollections of President Lincoln*, 40–41; see also the diary of Horatio Nelson Taft (February 13, 1861), Library of Congress.

101. Senator Louis Wigfall of Texas, dismayed by Scott's riposte, asked if he would dare to arrest a senator for treason. Scott's answer: "No! I will blow him to h-ll!"; Chittenden, *Recollections of President Lincoln*, 46; Furgurson, *Freedom Rising*, 39.

102. Stashower, *Hour of Peril*, 168.

103. *Chicago Tribune*, February 14, 1861.

104. Worthington Chauncey Ford, ed., *Letters of Henry Adams* (1858–1891), 88.

105. Diary of Charles Francis Adams, February 13, 1861, Massachusetts Historical Society.

106. Chittenden, *Recollections of President Lincoln*, 41.

107. *Baltimore Sun*, February 14, 1861, 4.

108. *New York Times*, February 15, 1861.

109. Dawes, "Winter Before the War," 164.

110. *Congressional Globe*, 36th Congress, 2nd Session (1860–1861), 894; Dawes, "Winter Before the War," 164.

111. Diary of Charles Francis Adams, February 13, 1861; Massachusetts Historical Society.

112. Stashower, *Hour of Peril*, 168.

113. *Chicago Tribune*, February 14, 1861; *Cape Ann (MA) Light and Gloucester Telegraph*, February 16, 1861.

114. Holzer, *Lincoln, President-Elect*, 323–24.

115. *New York Times*, February 18, 1861.

116. Searcher, *Lincoln's Journey to Greatness*, 72.

117. W. D. Howells, *Years of My Youth*, 166.

118. Mildred Howells, *Letters of William Dean Howells*, vol. 1, 37–8; W. D. Howells,

Years of My Youth, 182; W. D. Howells, *Selected Letters,* vol. 1, 74–75 (letter of March 15, 1861); William Dean Howells, *Literary Friends and Acquaintances,* 80.

119. In book form it was issued as *Years of My Youth.*

120. William Dean Howells, *Literary Friends and Acquaintances,* 81–82.

121. *Papers of Jefferson Davis,* vol. 7, 40.

122. *Baltimore Sun,* February 15, 1861, 2.

123. William Dennison, Jr., to Francis P. Blair, February 19, 1861, Library of Congress

124. *New York Times,* February 18, 1861.

CHAPTER 7: HEART OF DARKNESS

1. Photograph of J. Milligan, Detre Library and Archives, Heinz History Center.

2. Homer, *The Odyssey,* trans. Wilson, 252.

3. *Chicago Tribune,* February 15, 1861.

4. Harold Holzer, *Dear Mr. Lincoln: Letters to the President* (Reading, MA: Addison-Wesley, 1993), 341.

5. Trostel, *Lincoln Inaugural Train,* 61.

6. Villard, *Lincoln on the Eve,* 83.

7. *Chicago Tribune,* February 14, 1861.

8. Ibid.

9. "Get Off the Track!", Lester S. Levy Sheet Music Collection, Johns Hopkins University, https://levysheetmusic.mse.jhu.edu/collection/012/156.

10. Villard, *Lincoln on the Eve,* 84.

11. Searcher, *Lincoln's Journey to Greatness,* 73–74; Villard, *Lincoln on the Eve,* 84.

12. They also sang "Lorena," "Bonny Eloise, the Belle of Mohawk Vale," "Sparkin' on a Sunday," and "De Gospel Train Am a-Coming," a spiritual with railroad references; Victor Searcher, *Lincoln's Journey to Greatness,* 73–74; Christian McWhorter, "The Birth of Dixie," *New York Times,* March 31, 2012.

13. Lincoln, *Collected Works,* vol. 8, 393.

14. Villard, *Lincoln on the Eve,* 84.

15. Lincoln, *Collected Works,* vol. 7, 206.

16. The mounds wind through the Moundbuilders Country Club; Christopher Maag, "Ohio Indian Mounds: Hallowed Ground and a Nice Par 3," *New York Times,* November 28, 2005.

17. Lincoln, *Collected Works,* vol. 7, 206; *New York Times,* February 15, 1861; *Chicago Tribune,* February 15, 1861.

18. Barnet Schecter, *George Washington's America: A Biography Through his Maps* (New York: Walker, 2010); Lawrence Martin, ed., *The George Washington*

Atlas (Washington, D.C.: U.S. George Washington Bicentennial Commission, 1932); John R. Van Atta, *Securing the West: Politics, Public Lands and the Fate of the Old Republic, 1785–1850* (Baltimore: Johns Hopkins University Press, 2014), 15.

19. Another Steubenville native was David Homer Bates, a young telegrapher of talent who would soon join Lincoln in the White House. See David Homer Bates, *Lincoln in the Telegraph Service: Recollections of the United States Military Telegraph Corps During the Civil War* (New York: Century, 1907).

20. Photograph of Point of Beginning Dedication, September 30, 1960, courtesy of East Liverpool Historical Society; http://www.eastliverpoolhistoricalsociety .org/addpob.htm.

21. *Chicago Tribune*, February 15, 1861; Lincoln, *Collected Works*, vol. 4, 207–8, identifies this incident as taking place at Wellsville, Ohio, a few miles away.

22. Stefan Lorant, *Pittsburgh: The Story of an American City* (Garden City, NY: Doubleday, 1964), 42; Andro Linklater, *Measuring America: How an Untamed Wilderness Shaped the United States and Fulfilled the Promise of Democracy* (New York: Walker, 2002), 1–6, 74–84.

23. Stanford W. Higginbotham, *The Keystone in the Federal Arch: Pennsylvania Politics, 1800–1816* (Harrisburg; Pennsylvania Historical and Museum Commission, 1952), 337n1. The phrase was first used in 1802 and 1803. See also *A History of the Appellation Keystone State, as Applied to the Commonwealth of Pennsylvania* . . . (Philadelphia: Claxton, Remsen and Haffelfinger, 1874).

24. *Chicago Tribune*, February 15, 1861.

25. Ironically, this narrow passageway was later expanded to become the widest railyard in the world, the Conway Yard, between 1956 and 1980.

26. Dickens, *American Notes*, 140.

27. Frank Crane, *George Westinghouse: His Life and Achievements* (New York: William H. Wise, 1925), 10–17; *George Westinghouse Commemoration* (New York: American Society of Mechanical Engineers, 1927). Pittsburgh was the site of the first commercial radio station, KDKA, founded in 1920; Frank C. Harper, *Pittsburgh: Forge of the Universe* (New York: Comet, 1957), 227.

28. For other smoky images of Pittsburgh, see Lorant, *Pittsburgh*, 120, 125.

29. J. H. Cramer, "A President-Elect in Western Pennsylvania," *Pennsylvania Magazine of History and Biography* 71, no. 3 (July 1947): 207.

30. *Lorant, Pittsburgh*, 81; Dickens, *American Notes*, 140; Chevalier, *Society, Manners and Politics in the United States*, 166; Barbara Freese, *Coal: A Human History* (New York: Basic Books, 2016), 108–9 .

31. *Pennsylvania: A Guide*, 299.

32. "Lancaster at War," October 16, 2011; http://www.lancasteratwar.com/2011/10/continuous-smoke-and-unpleasant.html.

33. James Parton, "Pittsburg," *Atlantic Monthly,* January 1868, 18, 21.

34. Photograph of railroad station at Allegheny City; http://www.west2k.com/pastations/allegheny.shtml.

35. *Pittsburgh Gazette,* February 15, 1861.

36. The Special came into the Allegheny City station; *New York Times,* February 15, 1861. In 1860 Pittsburgh had 49,221, and Allegheny City (not yet a part of Pittsburgh) had 28,702.

37. *Pittsburgh Gazette*, February 15, 1861.

38. Searcher, *Lincoln's Journey to Greatness,* 86.

39. Scott Trossel, *The Lincoln Inaugural Train* (Fletcher, OH: Cam-Tech, 2011) 67.

40. Burlingame, *Lincoln: A Life*, vol. 2, 13.

41. Prints and Photographs Division, Library of Congress.

42. Lorant, *Pittsburgh*, 12.

43. Cassandra Britt Farrell, "Fry-Jefferson Map of Virginia," *Encyclopedia Virginia*, Virginia Humanities; https://www.encyclopediavirginia.org/Fry-Jefferson_Map_of_Virginia; Henry Taliaferro, "Jefferson and Fry Revisited," *Journal of Early Southern Decorative Arts*; http://www.mesdajournal.org/2013/fry-jefferson-revisited.

44. Lorant, *Pittsburgh*, 44–46; for a survey of the tensions over the boundary, see "Virginia-Pennsylvania Boundary," http://www.virginiaplaces.org/boundaries/paboundary.html.

45. *New York Times*, February 15, 1861.

46. George Wilson Pierson, *Tocqueville in America* (Garden City, NY: Anchor, 1959), 347.

47. Seven out of Pittsburgh's nine representatives opposed it. *Pennsylvania: A Guide*, 297.

48. Lorant, *Pittsburgh*, 71.

49. Pittsburgh was already an important arms manufacturer, and even before the Civil War, was supplying weapons overseas. Michel Chevalier noted that Pittsburgh's cannons could be bought by "the Sultan Mahmoud, or the Emperor of Morocco . . . whoever will pay for them"; *Society, Manners and Politics in the United States*, 166.

50. On December 29 Floyd resigned in protest when Buchanan hesitated to let the order go forward; on January 3, with Floyd gone, the order was rescinded; Nichols,

Disruption of American Democracy, 426; Len Barcousky, "Pittsburgh Wins a Peaceful Victory," *Pittsburgh Post-Gazette*, April 1, 2011; Lorant, *Pittsburgh*, 133; http://digital.library.pitt.edu/cgi-bin/chronology/chronology_driver.pl?search type=dbrowse&year=1860&year2=1869.

51. Chevalier, *Society, Manners and Politics in the United States*, 166.

52. *Pennsylvania: A Guide*, 8–11.

53. Howard N. Eavenson, "The Early History of the Pittsburgh Coal Bed," *Western Pennsylvania Historical Magazine* 22, no. 3 (September 1939): 165–76.

54. David A. Waples, *The Natural Gas Industry in Appalachia* (Jefferson, NC: McFarland, 2005), 7.

55. Paul H. Giddens, *Early Days of Oil: A Pictorial History of the Beginning of the Industry* (Gloucester, MA: P. Smith, 1964), 1. A zoomable version of the 1755 map may be seen on the website of the Geography and Maps Division of the Library of Congress; https://www.loc.gov/resource/g3710.ar071000/. Evans also wrote "petroleum" near the future site of Steubenville.

56. Barbara Freese, *Coal*, 107.

57. Ibid., 105–6.

58. *Manufactures of the United States in 1860; Computed from the Original Returns of the Eighth Census* (Washington, D.C.: Government Printing Office, 1860), clxiii, clxxvii, cxc.

59. Barbara Freese, *Coal*, 122–23.

60. By 1865, half of America's steel came from Pittsburgh as well. *Pennsylvania: A Guide*, 300; A. Michael Sulman, "The Short Happy Life of Petroleum in Pittsburgh," *Pennsylvania History: A Journal of Mid-Atlantic Studies* 33 (1966): 52; Lorant, *Pittsburgh*, 96, 145, 162.

61. Coal consumption would double every decade to 1890; Barbara Freese, *Coal*, 137.

62. Lorant, *Pittsburgh*, 145, 161; James Parton, "Pittsburg," *Atlantic Monthly*, January 1868, 22.

63. Lorant, *Pittsburgh*, 197; *Pennsylvania: A Guide*, 299.

64. Sulman, "Short Happy Life of Petroleum," 56–59.

65. Abraham Lincoln to E.B. Washburne, December 13, 1860; Lincoln, *Collected Works*, vol. 4, 151.

66. Andrew Carnegie, *The Autobiography of Andrew Carnegie* (Boston: Northeastern University Press, 1986), 133.

67. Brian Black, *Petrolia: The Landscape of America's First Oil Boom* (Baltimore: Johns Hopkins University Press, 2000), 18, 52

68. Giddens, *Early Days of Oil*, 1; "A Map of the Middle British Colonies in North

America" (1755), by Lewis Evans, https://www.loc.gov/resource/g3710 .ar071000.

69. Giddens, *Early Days of Oil*, 1, 3.

70. Thomas A. Gale, *The Wonder of the Nineteenth Century!: Rock Oil in Pennsylvania* (Erie: Sloan and Griffeth, 1860), 42–43

71. Carnegie, *Autobiography*, 132. Andrew Carnegie called it "a vast picnic."

72. Sulman, "Short Happy Life of Petroleum," 53.

73. *Chicago Tribune*, February 15, 1861.

74. By the end of 1861, there were thirty-five refineries in Pittsburgh; Sulman, "Short Happy Life of Petroleum," 51; *Chicago Tribune*, February 15, 1861; Ernest C. Miller, "Pennsylvania's Petroleum Industry," *Pennsylvania History: A Journal of Mid-Atlantic Studies* 49 (July 1982): 203–5.

75. The news of the explosion was heard on the same day as the news that fighting had begun at Fort Sumter; Ida Tarbell, *All in the Day's Work: An Autobiography* (New York: Macmillan, 1939), 8.

76. Harold F. Williamson and Arnold Daum, *The American Petroleum Industry*, 112.

77. Sulman, "Short Happy Life of Petroleum," 53.

78. Thomas A. Gale, *The Wonder of the Nineteenth Century!: Rock Oil in Pennsylvania*, 13.

79. Booth came to Pennsylvania in 1864 to try his luck, after his voice had begun to fail onstage. In some desperation, he arrived in the oil regions, hoping to make enough money to support his expensive tastes. He staked a claim, then ruined it by detonating an explosive charge. See Ernest C. Miller, *John Wilkes Booth in the Pennsylvania Oil Region* (Meadville: Crawford County Historical Society, 1987); Ernest C. Miller, *John Wilkes Booth—Oilman* (New York: Exposition Press, 1947); "Dramatic Oil Company," American Oil and Gas Historical Society; https://aoghs.org/editors-picks/the-dramatic-oil-company.

80. Ida Tarbell, *All in the Day's Work*, 9; Miller, "Pennsylvania's Petroleum Industry," 202.

81. Scott was busy in February 1861, lobbying for a tax break; his ally was Senator Simon Cameron, whose support for Lincoln had been decisive in securing the Republican nomination. Cameron's oily dealings would cause problems for Lincoln, but he would serve as secretary of war, with Scott as assistant secretary of war; Samuel Richey Kamm, *The Civil War Career of Thomas A. Scott*, 1, 5–7, 17–45.

82. Carnegie, *Autobiography*, 88.

83. Ibid., 39, 59–60; Carnegie wrote that "young women operators were more to be relied upon than men." Lorant, *Pittsburgh*, 123; Carnegie, *Autobiography*, 67.

84. Carnegie, *Autobiography*, 65, 97–98.

85. Parton, "Pittsburg," 17.

86. Detre Library, Heinz History Center, see also "Abraham Lincoln's Valentine to Pittsburgh," *Historical Dilettante*, February 14, 2013; http://historicaldilettante .blogspot.com/2013/02/abraham-lincolns-valentine-to-pittsburgh_14.html.

87. *Pittsburgh Gazette*, February 15, 1861.

88. *Chicago Tribune*, February 15, 1861; Cramer, "President-Elect in Western Pennsylvania," 208. The detail of standing on a chair is from the *Pittsburgh Evening Chronicle*, February 15, 1861.

89. *Pittsburgh Gazette*, February 15, 1861; *Chicago Tribune*, February 15, 1861; Cramer, "President-Elect in Western Pennsylvania," 208.

90. Cramer, "President-Elect in Western Pennsylvania," 208; Burlingame, *Lincoln: A Life*, vol. 2, 14.

91. *Pittsburgh Evening Chronicle*, February 15, 1861.

92. Nicolay to Bates, February 15, 1861, John G. Nicolay Papers, Manuscript Division, Library of Congress.

93. Lincoln's hotel furniture was rediscovered in a maintenance building in 2006; "Abraham Lincoln's Valentine to Pittsburgh," *Historical Dilettante*, February 14, 2013; http://historicaldilettante.blogspot.com/2013/02/abraham-lincolns-valentine-to-pittsburgh_14.html.

94. *Pittsburgh Post*, February 17, 1861; cited in Len Barcousky, "Recounting Abraham Lincoln's Only Trip to Pittsburgh, 150 Years Ago," *Pittsburgh Post-Gazette*, February 13, 2011.

95. Diary of Charles Francis Adams, February 14, 1861, Massachusetts Historical Society; Tidwell, *Come Retribution*, 227.

96. Stone, "Washington on the Eve of the War," *The Century*, vol. 26 (July 1883), 458–466.

97. *New York Herald*, February 24, 27, 1861.

98. *Papers of Jefferson Davis*, vol. 7, 42–45. There is some inconsistency about the dates of the speeches Davis gave on his train trip: an Alabama newspaper claimed that he was in Stevenson, Alabama, on February 14, but as he wrote to his wife, he was just leaving Jackson that day.

99. Ibid., 42.

100. Lorant, *Pittsburgh*, 132, 137, 139.

101. *Papers of Jefferson Davis*, VII, 45

CHAPTER 8: THE FOREST

1. Courtesy of the Henry Morrison Flagler Museum; see also Ron Chernow, *Titan: The Life of John D. Rockefeller Sr.* (New York: Random House, 1998), 96. Flagler was a business partner of John D. Rockefeller's and helped him to launch

Standard Oil in Cleveland; Kate Bradley, archivist of the Flagler Museum, believes this daguerreotype was likely taken in Cleveland.

2. Homer, *The Odyssey*, trans. A. T. Murray (Cambridge, MA: Harvard University Press, 1919), http://www.perseus.tufts.edu/hopper/text?doc=Perseus%3Atext%3A1999.01.0136%3Abook%3D10%3Acard%3D208.

3. Cramer, "President-Elect in Western Pennsylvania," 210; *Cincinnati Daily Press*, February 16, 1861.

4. *Chicago Tribune*, February 16, 1861.

5. *New York Times*, February 16, 1861. In fact, the crowds who participated in the Whiskey Rebellion in 1794 were larger.

6. *Chicago Tribune*, February 16, 1861.

7. Lincoln, *Collected Works*, vol. 4, 211, 214.

8. Ibid., 211.

9. Burlingame, *Lincoln: A Life*, vol. 2, 15.

10. Lincoln, *Collected Works*, vol. 4, 245.

11. Ibid., 211.

12. Ibid.; Cramer, "President-Elect in Western Pennsylvania," 213–15.

13. Burlingame, *Lincoln: A Life*, vol. 2, 15.

14. Villard, *Memoirs*, vol. 1, 152; Cramer, "President-Elect in Western Pennsylvania," 215.

15. Cramer, "President-Elect in Western Pennsylvania," 216.

16. *Cincinnati Daily Press*, February 16, 1861.

17. Searcher, *Lincoln's Journey to Greatness*, 95.

18. *The Comet*, designed by the Mason Machine Works of Taunton, Massachusetts, later became the symbol of a Connecticut steam boiler company; see "Trains on US Advertising Covers and Patriotic Covers," http://alphabetilately.org/adv-trains-3.html.

19. *Chicago Tribune*, February 16, 1861.

20. Searcher, *Lincoln's Journey to Greatness*, 95.

21. Villard, *Lincoln on the Eve*, 86.

22. *Chicago Tribune*, February 16, 1861.

23. Ibid.

24. *Cincinnati Commercial*, February 16, 1861.

25. *Cleveland Daily Herald*, February 16, 1861; *Chicago Tribune*, February 16, 1861.

26. *Western Reserve Chronicle* (Warren, OH), February 20, 1861; Henry Villard quipped that the local Zouaves, who had brought hearty appetites, were there to keep the presidential party from overeating; Henry Villard papers (Ms Am 1322), Harvard University Library.

27. *Cincinnati Commercial,* February 16, 1861. Various sources have located this incident in different places. All agreed that a glass had shattered near the Lincolns, but some accounts placed it in a hotel in Alliance (Sourbeck House), not on the train, and others in nearby Ravenna. The *Cincinnati Daily Press* and the *New York Times* (February 16, 1861) reported that a blast had been fired in Alliance that smashed the hotel windows; William T. Coggeshall supported that view in his *Lincoln Memorial* (55). Others identified the train itself, or placed the explosion in nearby Ravenna (Henry Villard Papers, Ms Am 1322, Harvard University Library; *Western Reserve Chronicle* (Warren, OH); (February 20, 1861); *Cleveland Daily Herald* (February 16, 1861).

28. Moses Cleaveland referred to it as a state, "New Connecticut," on July 4, 1796; Harry F. Lupold and Gladys Haddad, *Ohio's Western Reserve: A Regional Reader* (Kent, OH: Kent State University Press, 1988), 251.

29. Linklater, *Measuring America,* 143–44.

30. Richard N. Campen, *The Architecture of the Western Reserve, 1800–1900* (Cleveland: Case Western Reserve University Press, 1971).

31. Lupold and Haddad, *Ohio's Western Reserve,* 250.

32. Ibid., 137.

33. *Anti-Slavery Bugle,* February 23, 1861.

34. Lupold and Haddad, *Ohio's Western Reserve,* 137, 141.

35. Jacob R. Shipherd, *History of the Oberlin-Wellington Rescue* (Boston: John P. Jewett, 1859), 2.

36. Courtesy of Cleveland State University; see also Michelle A. Day and Joseph Wickens, "The Arrest of Trial of Lucy Bagby," Cleveland Historical; https://clevelandhistorical.org/items/show/517#&gid=1&pid=1.

37. John Stauffer argues that many abolitionists were disappointed that the incoming Republican administration had not done more to prevent Sarah (or Sara Lucy) Bagby's reenslavement. See "Fear and Doubt in Cleveland," *New York Times,* December 22, 2010; Lupold and Haddad, *Ohio's Western Reserve,* 151; John E. Vacha, "A Late Gesture: The Case of Sara Lucy Bagby," *Ohio History* 76 (Autumn 1967): 220–31.

38. Lupold and Haddad, *Ohio's Western Reserve,* 137–41, 150–51; Cochran, *The Western Reserve and the Fugitive Slave Law,* 178–80; James Harrison Kennedy, *A History of the City of Cleveland* (Cleveland: Imperial, 1896), 382–83, 387.

39. *Western Reserve Chronicle* (Warren, OH), February 20, 1861.

40. *Chicago Tribune,* February 16, 1861.

41. Henry Villard papers (Ms Am 1322), Harvard University Library.

42. *Chicago Tribune,* February 16, 1861.

43. *Western Reserve Chronicle* (Warren, OH), February 20, 1861.

44. *Chicago Tribune,* February 16, 1861; *Cleveland Daily Herald,* February 16, 1861; *Western Reserve Chronicle* (Warren, OH), February 20, 1861.

45. William McKinley, ca. 1858; from Oscar K. Davis and John K. Mumford, *The Life of William McKinley* (New York: P.F. Collier and Son, 1901); https://com mons.wikimedia.org/wiki/File:McKinley_boy.png.

46. William H. Armstrong, *Major McKinley: William McKinley and the Civil War* (Kent, OH: Kent State University Press, 2000); H. Wayne Morgan, *William McKinley and His America* (Kent, OH: Kent State University Press, 2003), 11; Ida Tarbell was the Preceptress of Poland Seminary (as Poland Academy was renamed) from 1880 to 1882.

47. *Cleveland Daily Herald,* February 16, 1861; *Chicago Tribune,* February 16, 1861; *Western Reserve Chronicle* (Warren, OH), February 20, 1861.

48. *Cleveland Daily Herald,* February 16, 1861; *Chicago Tribune,* February 16, 1861. The English travel writer Isabella Bird feared that her train would enter the lake; Bird, *Englishwoman in America,* 112–14.

49. "Birds Eye View of Cleveland Ohio 1877," Geography and Maps Division, Library of Congress; https://www.loc.gov/item/73694507.

50. Alexis de Tocqueville, *Journey to America* (London: Faber and Faber, 1959), 133–34.

51. Bird, *Englishwoman in America,* 112.

52. *The Ohio Railroad Guide,* 125.

53. Euclid Avenue eventually reaches Euclid, Ohio, named after Euclid.

54. John Nicolay wrote to his fiancée that they had arrived "in pretty good time but in a snowstorm." Burlingame, *With Lincoln,* 28.

55. *Cleveland Daily Herald,* February 16, 1861; Burlingame, *Lincoln: A Life,* vol. 2, 16; James Harrison Kennedy, *History of Cleveland,* 388; Henry Villard Papers (Ms Am 1322), Harvard University Library

56. Henry Villard Papers (Ms Am 1322), Harvard University Library

57. *Cleveland Daily Herald;* February 16, 1861.

58. Villard, *Lincoln on the Eve,* 86–87.

59. *Cleveland Daily Herald,* February 16, 1861.

60. *Chicago Tribune,* February 16, 1861.

61. "Weddell House," Encyclopedia of Cleveland History; https://ech.case.edu /cgi/article.pl?id=WH2; "Lincoln Slept Here ... the Weddell House of Cleveland;" http://www.waymarking.com/waymarks/WM5MFX_Lincoln_Slept_ HereThe_Weddell_House_of_Cleveland; http://clevelandhistorical.org/items /show/247#.V1ap2FLrv_U.

62. A Moravian missionary, John Heckewelder, commented that the site where the Cuyahoga met Lake Erie was "a place to which the White Fish of the Lake

resort in the spring in order to Spawn"; Andro Linklater, *Measuring America,* 146. In 1969 the Cuyahoga River garnered national attention when it caught fire, after embers from a passing train ignited oil slicks and debris floating on the surface. That fire helped to give rise to the modern environmental movement. The river also caught fire in 1952; see "Cuyahoga River Fire," Ohio History Connection; http://www.ohiohistorycentral.org/w/Cuyahoga_River_Fire?rec=1642.

63. James Harrison Kennedy, *History of Cleveland,* 383–86.

64. *The Ohio Railroad Guide,* 86–87; "Population of 100 Largest Urban Places: 1850," U.S. Bureau of the Census; https://www.census.gov/population/www/documentation/twps0027/tab08.txt; James Harrison Kennedy, *History of Cleveland,* 379.

65. Fremont P. Wirth, *The Discovery and Exploitation of the Minnesota Iron Lands* (Cedar Rapids, IA: Torch Press, 1937), 4.

66. James Harrison Kennedy, *History of Cleveland* (Cleveland: Imperial, 1896), 370–371; Angus Sinclair, *Development of the Locomotive Engine* (New York: A. Sinclair, 1907), 358–360.

67. Courtesy of Stephan Loewenthiel; see also "Dawn's Early Light: The First Fifty Years of American Photography," Cornell University Library; http://rmc.library.cornell.edu/DawnsEarlyLight/exhibition/massproduction/index.html; Ambrotype Portrait of John D. Rockefeller, Cleveland, circa 1858.

68. Allan Nevins, *Study in Power: John D. Rockefeller, Industrialist and Philanthropist,* vol. 1 (New York: Charles Scribner's Sons, 1953), 24.

69. Grace Goulder, *John D. Rockefeller: The Cleveland Years* (Cleveland: Western Reserve Historical Society, 1972), 1, 9–10, 14; Andrew Freese, *Early History of the Cleveland Public Schools* (Cleveland: Robinson, Savage, 1876), 32, 36, 41; Chernow, *Titan,* 91

70. Goulder, *John D. Rockefeller,* 11.

71. Ibid., 14. In Cleveland, Platt Rogers Spencer developed an easily legible form of handwriting that he considered essential to business success. Spencerian script later would later become familiar around the world, in the logos of Coca-Cola and Ford.

72. Goulder, *John D. Rockefeller,* 4, 14, 32–34; Chernow, *Titan,* 46, 50.

73. Nevins, *John D. Rockefeller,* vol. 1, 11; Chernow, *Titan,* 101.

74. Ron Chernow, *Titan,* 81.

75. Ibid., 47.

76. Ibid., 78; Goulder, *John D. Rockefeller,* 61.

77. Miller, "Pennsylvania's Petroleum Industry," 207; Goulder, *John D. Rockefeller,* 53, 55, 59, 61; Ron Chernow, *Titan,* 69

78. Chernow, *Titan*, 79, 100, 113. Hanna's daughter married the grandson of Joseph Medill, the editor of the *Chicago Tribune*, and a major supporter of Lincoln in 1860. Medill had also edited a newspaper in Cleveland.

79. Ibid., 102, 111.

80. Nevins, *John D. Rockefeller*, vol. 1, 24.

81. Grace Goulder, *John D. Rockefeller*, 82; Chernow, *Titan*, 119.

82. John Taliaferro, *All the Great Prizes: The Life of John Hay, from Lincoln to Roosevelt* (New York: Simon & Schuster, 2013), 155–69.

83. *Frank Leslie's Illustrated Newspaper*, vol. 11, number 275 (March 2, 1861), 232, Periodicals Division, Library of Congress; https://www.loc.gov/item/99614052.

84. *Western Reserve Chronicle* (Warren. OH), February 20, 1861.

85. *Frank Leslie's Illustrated Newspaper*, March 2, 1861.

86. *Chicago Tribune*, February 16, 1861. Curiously, one transcript of the speech records "laughter" following Lincoln's assurances that the crisis will pass; see *Cleveland Daily Herald*, February 16, 1861.

87. Henry Villard Papers (Ms Am 1322), Harvard University Library; *Western Reserve Chronicle* (Warren, OH), February 20, 1861.

88. Grace Goulder, *John D. Rockefeller*, 39.

89. Constance Rourke, *American Humor: A Study of the National Character* (New York: Harcourt, Brace, 1931, 1959), 224.

90. Harold Holzer, ed., *The Lincoln Anthology: Great Writers on His Life and Legacy from 1860 to Now* (New York: Library of America, 2009), 24–28; Walter Blair, *Native American Humor* (San Francisco: Chandler, 1937, 1960), 404. In 1862 Lincoln read an Artemus Ward sketch entitled "A High-Handed Outrage at Utiky" to his Cabinet members as he was preparing to show them the first draft of his Emancipation Proclamation. In addition to his writing, Browne was a pioneer of what would now be called stand-up comedy.

91. Lupold and Haddad, *Ohio's Western Reserve*, 150; Burlingame, *Lincoln: A Life*, vol. 2, 16.

92. Francis Fisher Browne, *Everyday Life of Abraham Lincoln*, 274–75.

93. Ibid.

94. Later, Lincoln's suite would become a shrine of its own and maintained inviolate for a century, before the hotel was finally torn down in 1961; "The Weddell House Room in Which Lincoln Slept," Cleveland Historical; http://cleveland historical.org/files/show/2998#.V0jrOFLrv3g.

95. Francis Fisher Browne, *Everyday Life of Abraham Lincoln*, 274–75.

96. Metropolitan Musem of Art; see also Photograph of Edward Everett; Ben Mattison, "The Social Construction of the American Daguerreotype Portrait; http://www.americandaguerreotypes.com/FIG25.JPG.

97. Edward Everett Diary, February 15, 1861; Massachusetts Historical Society; for more on the negative reactions to Lincoln's speeches, see Tagg, *The Unpopular Mr. Lincoln*, 105–12; Burlingame, *Lincoln: A Life*, vol. 2, 19-23; Ted Widmer, "The Other Gettysburg Address," *New York Times*, November 19, 2013.

98. Burlingame, *Lincoln: A Life*, vol. 2, 17.

99. Worthington G. Snethen to Lincoln, February 15, 1861; see "House Divided," Dickinson College; http://hd.housedivided.dickinson.edu/node/35084; Cuthbert, *Lincoln and the Baltimore Plot*, 32-38, 40.

100. Raymond, *Life and Public Services of Lincoln*, 123–28; *New York Herald*, February 23, 1861.

101. *Papers of Jefferson Davis*, vol. 7, 42.

102. Burlingame, *With Lincoln*, 28.

CHAPTER 9: A LITTLE PATH

1. Platt D. Babbitt, "The Great Farini Hanging Upside Down from a Tight Rope Across the Niagara River Gorge," Thomas Fisher Library, University of Toronto.

2. Homer, *The Odyssey*, trans. Emily Wilson (New York: W. W. Norton, 2018), 375.

3. J. H. Cramer, "Abraham Lincoln Visits with His People," *Ohio Archaeological and Historical Quarterly* 57, no. 1, January 1948), 68; also available at the Ohio History Connection; https://resources.ohiohistory.org/ohj/browse/displaypages .php?display[]=0057&display[]=66&display[]=78; John Fagant, *The Best of the Bargain: Lincoln in Western New York* (Bloomington, IN: AuthorHouse, 2010), xi; Hay, *Lincoln's Journalist*, 31.

4. *Cleveland Daily Herald*, February 16, 1861; *Ashtabula (OH) Weekly Telegraph*, February 23, 1861; Fagant, *Best of the Bargain*, xii.

5. Along the same route, the Lake Shore Limited would become one of the New York Central's most celebrated trains in the twentieth century.

6. Russell McKee, *Great Lakes Country* (New York: Thomas Y. Crowell, 1974), 3.

7. Harlan Hatcher, *Lake Erie* (Indianapolis: Bobbs-Merrill, 1945), 18.

8. *Ashtabula (OH) Weekly Telegraph*, February 23, 1861; J. H. Cramer, "Lincoln Visits with His People," 66–78.

9. Hay, *Lincoln's Journalist*, 31.

10. Cramer, "Lincoln Visits with His People," 17.

11. Hay, *Lincoln's Journalist*, 31; another source says the incident happened at Willoughby, Ohio; see David Dirck Van Tassel and John Vacha, *Beyond Bayonets: The Civil War in Northern Ohio* (Kent, OH: Kent State University Press, 2006), 35.

12. *Ashtabula (OH) Weekly Telegraph*, February 23, 1861.

13. Cramer, "Lincoln Visits with His People," 75.

14. Ibid.

15. "Old Customs House, Erie, Pa.," 1935, Historic American Buildings Survey, Prints and Photographs Division, Library of Congress; http://www.loc.gov /pictures/item/pa0449.photos.133887p/resource.

16. *Pennsylvania: A Guide to the Keystone State* (New York: Oxford University Press, 1940), 42–43; "Boundary Stones of the District of Columbia," http://www .boundarystones.org.

17. Burlingame, *Lincoln: A Life*, vol. 2, 17.

18. Villard, *Lincoln on the Eve*, 87; Harlan Hott Horner, *Lincoln and Greeley* (Champaign: University of Illinois Press, 1953), 205; ibid., 205; one wag called Greeley "a self-made man who worships his creator;" Roy Morris, Jr, *The Better Angel: Walt Whitman in the Civil War* (New York: Oxford University Press, 2000), 19.

19. *Ashtabula (OH) Weekly Telegraph*, February 23, 1861; Searcher, *Lincoln's Journey to Greatness*, 114

20. The Custom House had been a bank; see the "Old Customs House" materials, Historic American Buildings Survey, Prints and Photographs Division, Library of Congress; Historic American Buildings Survey; https://www.loc.gov/pic tures/item/pa0449. Erie had endured a difficult struggle over railroad gauge; see Harlan Hatcher, *The Western Reserve: The Story of New Connecticut in Ohio* (Indianapolis: Bobbs-Merrill, 1949), 148; Fish, "Northern Railroads," 784.

21. Hay, ed., *Lincoln's Journalist*, 32–33.

22. Cramer, "President-Elect in Western Pennsylvania," 217.

23. Liston Edgington Leyendecker, *Palace Car Prince: A Biography of George Pullman* (Niwot: University of Colorado Press, 1992), 37.

24. Burlingame, *Lincoln: A Life*, vol. 2, 17. According to Burlingame, Lincoln's friend Gordon Hubbard had also urged that he grow a beard.

25. "Putting on Hairs: A Political Print and Lincoln's Beard," http://antiqueprints blog.blogspot.com/2010/02/putting-on-hairs-political-print-and.html. See letter from Grace Bedell Billings to William E. Barton, March 1, 1923, in Barton, *Life of Lincoln*, vol. 1, 515–17.

26. Burlingame, *Lincoln: A Life*, vol. 2, 18.

27. Michael Burlingame argues that John Hay wrote a series of articles covering the trip in the *New York World,* based on the fact that these articles were pasted into his scrapbook. See Hay, *Lincoln's Journalist*, 32.

28. Davis, *Image of Lincoln*, 30.

29. Holzer, *Lincoln, President-Elect*, 334.

30. Cramer, "Lincoln Visits with His People," 76–77; Searcher, *Lincoln's Journey to Greatness*, 116; http://www.buffalohistoryworks.com/lincoln/reception.htm.

31. Cramer, "Lincoln Visits with His People," 76–77.

32. Holzer, *Lincoln, President-Elect,* 334.

33. Grace Bedell Billings to William E. Barton, *Life of Lincoln,* vol. 1, 515–17.

34. Letter of January 14, 1864; http://cjonline.com/stories/110307/lif_214 584253.shtml#.V2Bhy1Lrv3h.

35. "Abraham Lincoln's Beard," *New York Times,* November 5, 1878; "Lincoln Once Beardless," *New York Times,* April 22, 1908; "Woman Says Lincoln Grew Beard for Her," *New York Times,* February 13, 1925.

36. "Abraham Lincoln's Beard," *New York Times,* November 5, 1878, 8; Holzer, *Lincoln, President-Elect,* 334.

37. Inevitably, the headline for her obituary in the *New York Times* read, "Suggester of Beard for Lincoln Dies, 88," *New York Times,* November 3, 1936.

38. "Abraham Lincoln's Beard: The Idea of an Eleven-Year Old Girl," http://rogerj norton.com/Lincoln50.html.

39. The name Fredonia, intended to give a Latinate sound to the word *freedom,* was coined by a prominent New Yorker, Samuel Latham Mitchill, who hoped that it would become the new name for the United States. That effort failed, but a century later, Fredonia would be the name of a mythical country invented by the Marx Brothers for the 1933 film *Duck Soup.*

40. *Ashtabula (OH) Weekly Telegraph,* February 23, 1861.

41. Hay, *Lincoln's Journalist,* 33; Burlingame, *Lincoln: A Life,* vol. 2, 18

42. Geography and Maps Division, Library of Congress.

43. http://www.buffalohistoryworks.com/terminal/history/history.html; link broken; "Buffalo, New York," The Great American Stations; http://www.greatamer icanstations.com/Stations/BFX.

44. Hay, *Lincoln's Journalist,* 33.

45. http://www.buffalohistoryworks.com/lincoln/reception.htm.

46. Mark Goldman, *High Hopes: The Rise and Decline of Buffalo, New York* (Albany: State University of New York Press, 1983), 72; data suggest that Buffalo had the highest percentage of foreign-born in the U.S. in 1860; see "Nativity of the Population for the 25 Largest Urban Places and for Selected Counties: 1860," U.S. Bureau of the Census; https://www.census.gov/population/www/documen tation/twps0029/tab20.html; http://www.buffalohistoryworks.com/lincoln /reception.htm.

47. Ibid., 63–67; *The City of Buffalo, Its History and Institutions* (Buffalo: Matthews, Northrup and Co., 1888), 13, 15, 19. George N. Pierce arrived in Buffalo in 1863 and enjoyed a long career that took him from making ornamental bird cages, to bicycles, to early automobiles. Presidents Taft, Wilson and Harding all drove Pierce-Arrows. See Hillary Mannion, "Motor Cars Come to the White

House;" https://www.whitehousehistory.org/motor-cars-come-to-the-white
-house; http://www.buffaloah.com/h/pierce/pierce.

48. Nicolay, *Oral History of Lincoln*, 115.

49. "Niagara Falls from the Canadian Side," ca. 1850, Metropolitan Museum of Art;
     https://www.metmuseum.org/art/collection/search/268360.

50. Dickens, *American Notes*, 182.

51. Pierson, *Tocqueville in America*, 298; Tocqueville, *Democracy in America*, vol. 1, 7.

52. Lincoln, *Collected Works*, vol. 2, 10-11; probably circa 1848.

53. Nicolay, *Oral History of Lincoln*, 115.

54. Villard, *Lincoln on the Eve*, 89.

55. Searcher, *Lincoln's Journey to Greatness*, 121.

56. Villard, *Lincoln on the Eve*, 89.

57. Burlingame, *Lincoln: A Life*, vol. 2, 18; Nicolay, *Oral History of Lincoln*, 115–16.

58. Ibid., 18.

59. *Ashtabula (OH) Weekly Telegraph*, February 23, 1861.

60. Hay, *Lincoln's Journalist*, 33.

61. In local reporting, Hunter's injury was also described as a broken collarbone and
     a dislocated shoulder.

62. *Ashtabula (OH) Weekly Telegraph*, February 23, 1861.

63. Hay, *Lincoln's Journalist*, 34.

64. Burlingame, *With Lincoln*, 28. Nicolay called it a "terrible struggle;" Nicolay, *Oral
     History of Lincoln*, 114.

65. Henry Villard papers, Ms Am 1322, Harvard University Library

66. http://www.buffalohistoryworks.com/lincoln/reception.htm.

67. Hay, *Lincoln's Journalist*, 34.

68. Burlingame, *Lincoln: A Life*, vol. 2, 19; Burlingame, *With Lincoln*, 28.

69. Holzer, *Lincoln, President-Elect*, 337.

70. Searcher, *Lincoln's Journey to Greatness*, 125; http://www.buffalohistoryworks
     .com/lincoln/reception.htm.

71. Searcher, *Lincoln's Journey to Greatness*, 126.

72. Ibid., 119.

73. Charles H. Armitage, *Grover Cleveland as Buffalo Knew Him* (Buffalo: *Buffalo
     Evening News*, 1926), 16–17; William E. Leuchtenburg, *The American President:
     From Teddy Roosevelt to Bill Clinton* (New York: Oxford University Press, 2016),
     6. A Buffalo historian, John Fagant, places Cleveland in the audience; see John
     Fagant, "Abraham Lincoln in Western New York" (May 2006); http://buffaloah
     .com/h/fagant/linc.html.

74. Leuchtenburg, *The American President*, 6.

75. Lewis F. Allen, ed., *The American Herd Book, Containing Pedigrees of Short-Horn*

Cattle, vol. V (Buffalo: R. Wheeler, 1861), 13–4; George F. Parker, *Recollections of Grover Cleveland* (New York: Century, 1909), 28.

76. Photograph by George Barker, Prints and Photographs Division, Library of Congress, https://www.loc.gov/resource/ppmsca.15765.

77. Searcher, *Lincoln's Journey to Greatness*, 121.

78. Goldman, *High Hopes*, 50.

79. Robert W. Bingham, *The Cradle of the Queen City: A History of Buffalo to the Incorporation of the City* (Buffalo: Buffalo Historical Society, 1931), 167.

80. John Fagant, "Buffalo's Name," http://buffaloah.com/h/fagant/bfloname.pdf.

81. Goldman, *High Hopes*, 50.

82. Ibid., 57–58; Allan Nevins, *Grover Cleveland: A Study in Courage* (New York, Dodd Mead, 1962), 31.

83. Nevins, *Grover Cleveland*, 29. "The First Grain Elevator/Early Grain Elevators," Historical Marker Project; http://www.historicalmarkerproject.com/markers /HM1LV3_the-first-grain-elevator-early-grain-elevators_Buffalo-NY.html; "Joseph Dart," http://www.buffaloah.com/h/dart/; http://www.buffalohistory works.com/grain/history/history.htm.

84. Goldman, *High Hopes*, 58–60. Peter Z. Grossman, *American Express: The Unofficial History of the People Who Built the Great Financial Empire* (New York: Crown, 1987), 44. In the early 1850s, the various railroads that came into Buffalo were united into the New York Central system; Goldman, *High Hopes*, 62. I am grateful to the Buffalo History Museum for help researching Buffalo's early history.

85. Lucius Beebe and Charles Clegg, *U.S. West: The Saga of Wells Fargo* (New York: E.P. Dutton, 1949), 23.

86. Grossman, *American Express*, 41–43, 65; Noel M. Loomis, *Wells Fargo* (New York: Clarkson N. Potter, 1968), 8–9; Nevins, *Grover Cleveland*, 31; Goldman, *High Hopes*, 60; Lucius Beebe and Charles Clegg, *U.S. West: The Saga of Wells Fargo*, 25–26; Noel M. Loomis, *Wells Fargo*, 15–16

87. Nevins, *Grover Cleveland*, 29.

88. Ibid., 50.

89. Herman Melville, *Moby-Dick*, 251

90. Express companies would play a significant role in the Civil War to come, helping soldiers send mail home, and organizing vast numbers of financial transactions needed to equip the fighting men at the front; Grossman, *American Express*, 70.

91. William C. Davis, *Jefferson Davis*, 305.

92. *Papers of Jefferson Davis*, vol. 7, 43–44. Using the language of whaling, Davis said, "We had cut loose from that 'dead body,' " *New York Herald*, February 23, 1861, 2.

93. Mathew B. Brady, photograph of Millard Fillmore, Prints and Photographs

Division, Library of Congress; https://en.wikipedia.org/wiki/Millard_Fillmore# /media/File:Millard_Fillmore_daguerreotype_by_Mathew_Brady_1849.jpg.

94. Holzer, *Lincoln, President-Elect*, 332.

95. Burlingame, *Lincoln: A Life*, vol. 2, 23.

96. Holzer, *Lincoln, President-Elect*, 332–33.

97. Fagant, *Best of the Bargain*, 57–58.

98. Harlan Hott Horner, *Lincoln and Greeley*, 204; this comment, from Samuel Bowles, originated in the *Springfield Republican*.

99. Burlingame, *Lincoln: A Life*, vol. 2, 21.

100. William E. Barton, *The Life of Abraham Lincoln*, vol. 1, 470.

101. Holzer, *Lincoln, President-Elect*, 332–33.

102. Burlingame, *Lincoln: A Life*, vol. 2, 22.

103. Charles Francis Adams, diary entry, February 16, 1861, Massachusetts Historical Society.

104. "Secession! Texas Makes its Choice," Texas State Library and Archives Commission; https://www.tsl.texas.gov/exhibits/civilwar/secession.html; Ralph A. Wooster, "The Civil War," Texas State Historical Association; https://tshaon line.org/handbook/online/articles/qdc02; *Harper's Weekly*, March 23, 1861; Dunn, "Knights of the Golden Circle," 567–69.

105. Roy Sylvan Dunn, "The Knights of the Golden Circle in Texas, 1860–1861," *Southwestern Historical Quarterly* 70, no. 4 (April 1967): 569.

106. Fagant, *Best of the Bargain*, 64.

107. Robert J. Scarry, *Millard Fillmore*, 343; *American Heritage*, July/August 1988, 63

108. Lincoln's described the Know-Nothings eloquently in a letter to Joshua Speed in 1855; Lincoln, *Collected Works*, vol. 2, 323.

109. Nevins, *Grover Cleveland*, 38.

110. Holzer, *Lincoln, President-Elect*, 337; Fillmore wished to be appointed as a military leader to defend Buffalo from a Canadian invasion; Mark Goldman, *High Hopes*, 122.

111. Fagant, *Best of the Bargain*, 70.

112. Ibid., 61–62. Another church member got to the point more quickly: "Mr. Lincoln is not a handsome man. But he looks sound."

113. http://www.buffalo.edu/ubreporter/archive/2009_01_21/flashback; Fagant, *Best of the Bargain*, 68; *Buffalo Evening News*, October 24, 1951. I am grateful to William Offhaus in the University Archives of the University of Buffalo for help with this research.

114. John Beeson, preface, in *A Plea for the Indians* (New York: John Beeson, 1858).

115. *Papers of Jefferson Davis*, vol. 7, 43.

116. Chittenden, *Recollections of President Lincoln*, 58–63.

117. The Italian informer also confirmed that Shakespeare was quoted by the conspirators; Chittenden, *Recollections of President Lincoln*, 61–63.

118. Stashower, *Hour of Peril*, 186–87.

CHAPTER 10: THE STRAIGHT LINE

1. Collection of William L. Schaeffer; see also Diane Waggoner, *East of the Mississippi: Nineteenth Century American Landscape Photography* (Washington, D.C.: National Gallery, 2017), 174.

2. Homer, *The Odyssey*, trans. Wilson, 151.

3. Hay, *Lincoln's Journalist*, 36–37.

4. Searcher, *Lincoln's Journey to Greatness*, 143.

5. Hay, *Lincoln's Journalist*, 37.

6. John Nicolay, "Some Incidents in Lincoln's Journey from Springfield to Washington," in *Oral History of Lincoln*, 117.

7. Searcher, *Lincoln's Journey to Greatness*, 146.

8. Ibid., 143, 146.

9. Prints and Photographs Division, Library of Congress.

10. I am grateful to Michael Brewer of NOAA for weather data and star positions.

11. *New York Herald*, February 18, 1861.

12. *Syracuse (NY) Standard*, February 16, 1861; see "Three Rivers," http://three rivershms.com/lincolntrains.htm.

13. Edward Hungerford, *Men and Iron: The History of New York Central* (New York: Thomas Y. Crowell, 1938), 178.

14. https://publicdomainreview.org/collection/the-first-six-books-of-the-ele ments-of-euclid-1847.

15. "Euclid, Elements" (Thomas L. Heath, ed.); http://www.perseus.tufts.edu /hopper/text?doc=Euc.+1.

16. Hungerford, *Men and Iron*, 68. It was also called the "Direct Line."

17. "Notable Visitors: Thurlow Weed (1797-1882)" Mr. Lincoln's White House, http://www.mrlincolnswhitehouse.org/residents-visitors/notable-visitors /notable-visitors-thurlow-weed-1797-1882.

18. *New York: A Guide to the Empire State* (New York: Oxford University Press, 1940), 182; Hungerford, *Men and Iron*, 10.

19. Hungerford, *Men and Iron*, 81, 96. See also Frank Walker Stevens, *The Beginnings of the New York Central Railroad: A History* (New York: G.P. Putnam's Sons, 1926), 317–30.

20. Blake McKelvey, *Rochester on the Genesee: The Growth of a City* (Syracuse, NY: Syracuse University Press, 1973), 64; Robert Luther Thompson, *Wiring a Continent*, 201–202, 271; Joshua D. Wolff, *Western Union and the Creation of*

the *American Corporate Order, 1845–1893* (Cambridge: Cambridge University Press, 2013), 2; G. Russell Oechsle and Helen Boyce, *An Empire in Time: Clocks and Clock Makers of Upstate New York* (Vestal, NY: National Association of Watch and Clock Collectors, 2003), 66–67, 132–133.

21. Edward Hungerford, *Men and Iron*, 82; Searcher, *Lincoln's Journey to Greatness*, 146.

22. Hay, *Lincoln's Journalist*, 37–38.

23. Ibid., 36.

24. *New York Times*, February 19, 1861; Searcher, *Lincoln's Journey to Greatness*, 170n.

25. Jason Emerson, *Giant in the Shadows: The Life of Robert T. Lincoln* (Carbondale: Southern Illinois University Press, 2012), 58.

26. *Chicago Tribune*, February 19, 1861; *New York Times*, February 19, 1861.

27. Rick Moriarty, "Frederick Douglass Mystery: How Did Rare Photo of Famed Abolitionist End Up in Syracuse?"; http://www.syracuse.com/empire/index.ssf/2016/04/frederick_douglass_mystery_how_did_rare_photo_of_famed_abolitionist_end_up_in_sy.html; John Stauffer, Zoe Trodd, and Celeste-Marie Bernier, *Picturing Frederick Douglass: An Illustrated Biography of the Nineteenth Century's Most Photographed American* (New York: Liveright, 2015), 3. Photograph courtesy of Onondaga Historical Association.

28. McKelvey, *Rochester on the Genesee*, 73–75; Alvin F. Harlow, *The Road of the Century: The Story of the New York Central* (New York: Creative Age Press, 1947), 109.

29. Rose O'Keefe, *Frederick and Anna Douglass in Rochester New York* (Charleston: History Press, 2013), 33, 71, 73

30. Douglass cited the New York Central as a reason he liked Rochester; *The Frederick Douglass Papers* (ed. John R. McKivigan; New Haven: Yale University Press, 2012), Series 2, Volume 3, Book 1, 211.

31. Stauffer, Trodd, and Bernier, *Picturing Frederick Douglass*, ix–x, xiv, xvii; Douglass gave four lectures on photography, and saw the medium as inherently democratic. Photographers helped him in other ways, too—in 1859, a photographer in Philadelphia aided his escape from U.S. marshals.

32. Two German immigrants, John Jacob Bausch and Henry Lomb, started a firm to manufacture eye-glasses in Rochester in 1853; E. E. Arrington, *History of Optometry* (Chicago: White, 1929), 97–98, 103; these optical advances would focus gun sights in the war; Rudolf Kingslake, *A History of the Rochester Camera and Lens Companies* (Rochester, NY: Photographic Historical Society, 1974).

33. Eastman's inventions included the roll of film (1884) and the Kodak camera (1888); see Stauffer, Trodd, and Bernier, *Picturing Frederick Douglass*, 30;

Elizabeth Brayer, *George Eastman: A Biography* (Baltimore: Johns Hopkins University Press, 1996), 16, 19; James W. Cortada, *Before the Computer: IBM, NCR, Burroughs and Remington Rand and the Industry They Created, 1865–1956* (Princeton: Princeton University Press, 1993), 15.

34. Robert Friedel, *The Making and Selling of Plastic* (Madison: University of Wisconsin Press, 1983), 13, 92–96; Robert Friedel, *Pioneer Plastic: The Making and Selling of Celluloid* (Madison: University of Wisconsin Press, 1983), 13, 93; Jeffrey Meikle, *American Plastic: A Cultural History* (New Brunswick, NJ: Rutgers University Press, 1995), 10–11.

35. Katharine Anthony, *Susan B. Anthony: Her Personal History and Her Era* (Garden City, NY: Doubleday, 1954), 74–77.

36. The railroad had significantly decreased the time needed to get from Seneca Falls (where Elizabeth Cady Stanton lived) to Rochester; Elisabeth Griffith, *In Her Own Right: The Life of Elizabeth Cady Stanton* (New York: Oxford University Press), 74.

37. Ida Husted Harper, *Life and Work of Susan B. Anthony* (Salem, NH: Ayer, 1983, repr. of 1898 edition), I, 215; a women's rights convention had just been held in Albany, February 7–8, 1861; I, 212.

38. Ibid., 200–205, 208; Griffith, *In Her Own Right*, 106.

39. John Stauffer suggests that Douglass was there; *Giants: The Parallel Lives of Frederick Douglass and Abraham Lincoln* (New York: Twelve, 2008), 219–220. Douglass was in the crowd at Lincoln's second inaugural address in 1865, and can be seen in a crowd photograph; see Paul Kendrick, "Lincoln and Douglass's Last Encounter," *New York Times*, March 5, 2015; David W. Blight, "The Dim Light of Hope," *New York Times*, March 1, 2011; Stauffer, Trodd, and Bernier, *Picturing Frederick Douglass*, xxi.

40. Searcher, *Lincoln's Journey to Greatness*, 147; Hungerford, *Men and Iron*, 80; Fagant, *Best of the Bargain*, 76–77.

41. Samuel C. Pierce, "Three Famous Visitors to Rochester," *Rochester Historical Society Publications*, vol. 3, 233n; Wilson interview in *Rochester Historical Society Publications*, XX, 22.

42. Prints and Photographs Division, Library of Congress; see also Ronald S. Coddington, "Father Waldo's America," *New York Times*, September 7, 2012.

43. *New York Times*, February 19, 1861; Fagant, *Best of the Bargain*, 84. The *Times* reported, "An enterprising artist had placed upon a convenient wood-pile a camera with which he secured pictures of the rear end of the car, of Mr. Lincoln, Mr. Wood, a brakeman, and an unlucky reporter."

44. *New York Times*, February 19, 1861; Fagant, *Best of the Bargain*, 85.

45. John Fagant, *The Best of the Bargain*, 89.

46. Hay, *Lincoln's Journalist*, 36; Holzer, *Lincoln, President-Elect*, 347; *Chicago Tribune*, February 19, 1861.

47. *New York Times*, February 19, 1861; Coddington, "Father Waldo's America."

48. Harlow, *Road of the Century*, 108–109; Leslie, *Remarkable Mr. Jerome*, 16–17.

49. Martin Gilbert, *Churchill and America* (New York: Free Press, 2005), 3; Jeffrey Richmond, "Jerome Park," http://antiquephotographics.com/jerome-park.

50. Arthur Edwards, *Sketch of the Life of Norman B. Judd*, 3, 12; a second note from Pinkerton reached Judd at Buffalo.

51. Fagant, *Best of the Bargain*, 90.

52. Holzer, *Lincoln, President-Elect*, 347; Fagant, *Best of the Bargain*, 92.

53. Villard, *Lincoln on the Eve*, 91.

54. *New York Times*, January 15, 1915.

55. *New York Times*, February 19, 1861; Searcher, *Lincoln's Journey to Greatness*, 150; Holzer, *Lincoln, President-Elect*, 347–48; Burlingame, *Lincoln: A Life*, vol. 2, 24.

56. Fagant, *Best of the Bargain*, 92.

57. Kevin Baker, "Ayn Rand's Rapture of the Rails," *Harper's*, June 6, 2014; http://harpers.org/blog/2014/06/ayn-rands-rapture-of-the-rails.; Ayn Rand, *The Letters of Ayn Rand*, ed. Michael S. Berliner (New York: Dutton, 1995), 188–93.

58. *Chicago Tribune*, February 19, 1861; *New York Times*, February 19, 1861; Fagant, *Best of the Bargain*, 93.

59. Abraham Lansing to Henry Gansevoort, February 20, 1861, Gansevoort-Lansing Papers, New York Public Library.

60. Frank Cross, *George Westinghouse: His Life and Achievements* (New York: William H. Wise Co., 1925), 13; Harry G. Prout, *A Life of George Westinghouse* (New York: Charles Scribner's Sons, 1922), 6–7.

61. Digital Collections, New York Public Library.

62. Ida Husted Harper, *Life and Work of Susan B. Anthony*, I, 211.

63. *Frank Leslie's Illustrated Newspaper*, March 2, 1861, 227; *New York Herald*, February 23, 1861.

64. William Kennedy, *O Albany! Improbable City of Political Wizards, Fearless Ethnics, Spectacular Aristocrats, Splendid Nobodies, and Underrated Scoundrels* (New York: Viking, 1983), 68; Peter Hess, "Lincoln and John Wilkes Booth in Albany," *The New York History Blog*; http://newyorkhistoryblog.org/2015/06/17/1861-lincoln-and-john-wilkes-booth-in-albany/; "Running on Albany Time," All Over Albany; http://alloveralbany.com/archive/2010/09/01/albany-time; J. Munsell, *Annals of Albany*, vol. 7, 303–309; "Early Railroads of New York," http://www.hoxsie.org/albany/

65. For a spirited history, see William Kennedy, *O Albany!*

66. Villard, *Lincoln on the Eve*, 92.

67. William Kennedy, *O Albany!*, 69; Holzer, *Lincoln, President-Elect*, 348; Searcher, *Lincoln's Journey to Greatness*, 153; Stashower, *Hour of Peril*, 200.

68. *Chicago Tribune*, February 19, 1861.

69. Villard, *Lincoln on the Eve*, 93.

70. Ibid., 94.

71. Holzer, *Lincoln, President-Elect*, 349.

72. Burlingame, *Lincoln: A Life*, vol. 2, 24.

73. William Kennedy, *O Albany!*, 68.

74. Hitchcock and Seale, *Temples of Democracy*, 54.

75. *Chicago Tribune*, February 19, 1861; Harry E. Pratt, *Concerning Mr. Lincoln: In Which Abraham Lincoln Is Pictured as He Appeared to Letter Writers of His Time* (Springfield, IL: Abraham Lincoln Association, 1944), 53.

76. Lincoln, *Collected Works*, vol. 4, 225–26.

77. Photograph of Chester Alan Arthur, ca. 1858, National Portrait Gallery; http://npg.si.edu/object/npg_NPG.80.19.

78. Searcher, *Lincoln's Journey to Greatness*, 154–55.

79. Burlingame, *Lincoln: A Life*, vol. 2, 23. Lincoln would have additional trouble with Morgan after assuming the presidency; see William E. Barton, *The Life of Abraham Lincoln*, I, 471.

80. George Frederick Howe, *Chester A. Arthur: A Quarter-Century of Machine Politics* (New York: Dodd, Mead, 1934), 7, 11, 19.

81. Burlingame, *Lincoln: A Life*, vol. 2, 23–25.

82. Villard, *Lincoln on the Eve*, 95.

83. Ibid., 96.

84. Burlingame, *Lincoln: A Life*, vol. 2, 25.

85. Hay, *Lincoln's Journalist*, 37–38.

86. Fagant, *Best of the Bargain*, 90; Hay, *Lincoln's Journalist*, 38.

87. Strong, *The Diary of George Templeton Strong*, vol. 3, 100.

88. "Secessionists Occupy a Disused Fort in Nebraska Overnight But Lose it to Unionists in the Morning;" http://hd.housedivided.dickinson.edu/node/35629.

89. Dunn, "Knights of the Golden Circle," 567–69; Walter L. Buenger, *Secession and the Union in Texas* (Austin: University of Texas Press, 1984), 154–158; Carl Coke Rister, *Robert E. Lee in Texas* (Norman: University of Oklahoma Press, 1946), 158–159.

90. Worthington G. Snethen to Abraham Lincoln, February 15, 1861; Abraham Lincoln Papers, Library of Congress; Cuthbert, *Lincoln and the Baltimore Plot*, 142; Stashower, *Hour of Peril*, 197.

91. Stashower, *Hour of Peril*, 201; Potter, *Thirteen Desperate Days*, 83–84.

92. Archibald Crossland McIntyre, photograph of the inauguration of Jefferson Davis, Montgomery, Alabama, Boston Athenaeum, February 18, 1861; https://commons.wikimedia.org/wiki/File:1861_Davis_Inaugural.jpg.

93. *Papers of Jefferson Davis*, vol. 7, 46–50.

94. *New York Herald*, February 23, 1861, 2.

95. Strong, *Diary of George Templeton Strong*, vol. 3, 113; South Carolina did not permit the popular election of presidential electors; see Baringer, *A House Dividing*, 46; Nichols, *Disruption of American Democracy*, 354, 359–60, 405.

96. *New York Herald*, February 23, 1861, 2.

97. Searcher, *Lincoln's Journey to Greatness*, 167.

98. John Wilkes Booth, date unknown; Hampden-Booth Theatre Collection, The Players Club; the Players Foundation for Theatre Education.

99. Peter Hess, "Lincoln and John Wilkes Booth in Albany," *The New York History Blog*, June 17, 2015; http://newyorkhistoryblog.org/2015/06/17/1861-lincoln-and-john-wilkes-booth-in-albany.

100. Terry Alford, *Fortune's Fool: The Life of John Wilkes Booth* (New York: Oxford University Press, 2015), 103.

101. Douglas L. Wilson, "His Hour upon the Stage," *American Scholar* (Winter 2012).

102. Alford, *Fortune's Fool*, 104; H. N. Phelps, *Players of a Century: A Record of the Albany Stage* (Albany, NY: Joseph McDonough, 1880), 325.

103. On April 15, 1861, after Fort Sumter was fired upon, the diarist George Templeton Strong met a young volunteer from Rochester, who said "he had voted for Abe Lincoln, and as there was going to be trouble, he might as well fight for Abe Lincoln. *Diary of George Templeton Strong*, vol. 3, 121.

104. Phelps, *Players of a Century*, 325.

105. Daniel Mark Epstein, *Lincoln and Whitman: Parallel Lives in Civil War Washington* (New York: Ballantine, 2004), 267.

106. Terry Alford, *Fortune's Fool*, 105, 107; Phelps, *Players of a Century*, 326–27. Four years later, tragedy would again connect Booth to Albany. The same night that he assassinated Lincoln, he nearly killed Lincoln's guest in the presidential box at Ford's Theater. Henry Rathbone was there with his fiancée, Clara Harris; they both came from Albany (her father had been mayor). See William Kennedy, *O Albany!*, 69–70.

CHAPTER 11: THE FRONT DOOR

1. Miriam and Ira D. Wallach Division of Art, Prints and Photographs, New York Public Library; see also Hannah Wirta Kinney, "John Bachmann's New York," *Visualizing 19th-Century New York*; http://visualizingnyc.org/essays/john-bachmanns-new-york.

2. Homer, *The Odyssey*, trans. Wilson, 180.

3. *New York Times*, February 20, 1861.

4. Potter, *Thirteen Desperate Days*, 95.

5. *New York Times*, February 19, 1861; Freeman, *Lincoln Goes to New York*, 107.

6. Freeman, *Lincoln Goes to New York*, 105.

7. Louis Wigfall to Jefferson Davis, February 18, 1861, *Papers of Jefferson Davis*, vol. 7, 51.

8. *New York Times*, February 19, 1861.

9. *New York Herald*, February 20, 1861.

10. Ibid.; *New York Times*, February 20, 1861.

11. William Kennedy, *O Albany!*, 69.

12. "James Buchanan Our Great Iceberg Melting Away," *Vanity Fair*, May 9, 1861; New York Public Library, http://digitalcollections.nypl.org/items/510d47dd -f6a3-a3d9-e040-e00a18064a99.

13. *Baltimore Sun*, February 15, 1861.

14. *New York Herald*, February 20, 1861.

15. *New York Illustrated News*, March 2, 1861, 268–69.

16. *New York Herald*, February 20, 1861.

17. Richard Sanders Allen, *Covered Bridges of the Northeast* (Brattleboro, VT: Stephen Greene Press, 1957), 97.

18. Benson J. Lossing, *The Hudson, from the Wilderness to the Sea* (Troy, NY: H. B. Nims, 1866).

19. *New York Times*, February 20, 1861; Searcher, *Lincoln's Journey to Greatness*, 169; *New York Herald*, February 20, 1860.

20. Alvin F. Harlow, *Road of the Century*, 106.

21. Searcher, *Lincoln's Journey to Greatness*, 170.

22. *New York Times*, February 20, 1861.

23. Ibid.; Searcher, *Lincoln's Journey to Greatness*, 173. The *New York Herald* noted Lincoln inspecting a locomotive (February 20, 1861).

24. William E. Barton, *The Life of Abraham Lincoln*, vol. 1, 470–71; Villard, *Lincoln on the Eve*, 96–97.

25. *New York Times*, February 20, 1861; Freeman, *Lincoln Goes to New York*, 16.

26. *New York Herald*, February 20, 1861.

27. The route of the Hudson River Railroad was completed in 1851; later it was consolidated into the New York Central; T. J. Stiles, *The First Tycoon: The Epic Life of Cornelius Vanderbilt* (New York: Alfred A. Knopf, 2009), 383–84; Winston Churchill's grandfather Leonard Jerome was a director; see Anita Leslie, *The Remarkable Mr. Jerome* (New York: Henry Holt, 1954), 65. For an example of a touristic account,

see *Hudson River and the Hudson River Railroad* (Boston: Bradbury and Guild, 1851); see Catskill Archive; http://www.catskillarchive.com/rrextra/abnyh.Html.

28 *New York Herald*, February 20, 1861.

29. Russell Shorto notes the persistence of Dutch speaking into the nineteenth century; *The Island at the Center of the World* (New York: Doubleday, 2004), 310.

30. "Martin Van Buren Meets Abraham Lincoln," April 13, 2013; http://sangamoncountyhistory.org/wp/?p=520; Ted Widmer, *Martin Van Buren* (New York: Times Books, 2005), 146–47. In the winter of 1860–61, Van Buren refused to join an initiative led by Franklin Pierce and the other former presidents to hold a Peace Convention; instead he promised "earnest and vigorous support to the Lincoln Administration;" see John Niven, *Martin Van Buren: The Romantic Age of American Politics* (New York: Oxford University Press, 1983), 610–611.

31. *New York Times*, February 20, 1861.

32. Dallas Museum of Art, Gift of Norma and Lamar Hunt; see also http://www.vanishing-ice.org/in-search-of-icebergs.

33. *New York Herald*, February 20, 1861.

34. Searcher, *Lincoln's Journey to Greatness*, 172; *New York Herald*, February 20, 1861.

35. Geoffrey Ward, *Before the Trumpet* (New York: Harper and Row, 1985), 3, 14, 33, 35; James Roosevelt was in Paris in early 1861; he was an investor in the line.

36. *New York Illustrated News*, March 2, 1861, 234; *New York Herald*, February 20, 1861.

37. National Portrait Gallery, Smithsonian Institution.

38. *New York Herald*, February 20, 1861.

39. *New York Herald*, February 20, 1861.

40. This noisy place had built America's earliest locomotives, including the *Best Friend of Charleston* and the *DeWitt Clinton*; on armaments, see Ron Sodalter, "The Guns of the Hudson," *New York Times*, January 24, 2014.

41. Stern, *Prologue to Sumter*, 170–71.

42. Ralph Kirshner, *The Class of 1861: Custer, Ames and Their Classmates After West Point* (Carbondale: Southern Illinois University Press), 1999.

43. *Hudson River and the Hudson River Railroad*; http://www.catskillarchive.com/rrextra/abnyh.Html.

44. Searcher, *Lincoln's Journey to Greatness*, 171.

45. Lincoln's three minutes in Peekskill were relived in a ceremony far longer than Lincoln's original visit, sixty-four years later, when a monument was dedicated. One young man who stood at Lincoln's feet in 1861 was Chauncy M. DePew, who would become a U.S. senator and railroad director; *Lincoln in Peekskill: Exercises at the Dedication of the Lincoln Memorial in Peekskill, October 6, 1925, in*

Commemoration of the Visit of Abraham Lincoln to Peekskill, February 19, 1861 (Peekskill, NY: Lincoln Association, 1926), 8–9.

46. "State Prison at Sing Sing," from November 1855 *Ballou's Pictorial Drawing-Room Companion.*

47. *New York Times,* February 20, 1861; *New York Herald,* February 20, 1861.

48. Edward K. Spann, *The New Metropolis: New York City, 1840–1857* (New York: Columbia University Press, 1981), 198.

49. Henry Collins Brown, *Old Yonkers,1646–1922, A Page of History* (New York: Valentine's Manual Press, 1922); https://archive.org/details/ldpd_11290305_000 /page/n55. Also see Jason Goodwin, *Otis: Giving Rise to the Modern City* (Chicago: Ivan R. Dee, 2001).

50. *New York Herald,* February 20, 1861; Jason Goodwin, *Otis: Giving Rise to the Modern City,* 12–14, 25–26.

51. "Harlem Bridge, 1861;" New York Public Library Digital Collections; The Miriam and Ira D. Wallach Division of Art, Prints and Photographs: Picture Collection, The New York Public Library. Accessed November 24, 2019. http://digitalcollections.nypl.org/items/510d47e2-eba1-a3d9-e040-e00a18064a99.

52. Carl W. Condit, *The Port of New York: A History of the Rail and Terminal System from the Beginnings to Pennsylvania Station* (Chicago: University of Chicago Press, 1980), 33.

53. T.H. Breen, *George Washington's Journey: The President Forges a New Nation* (New York: Simon & Schuster, 2016), 39–40.

54. David W. Dunlap, "Audubon's Last 'Dear Home' on West 155th," *New York Times,* May 3, 2011.

55. Ibid.

56. *New York Herald,* February 20, 1861; detail from *Plan of New York City from the Battery to Spuyten Duyvil Creek,* 1867, Geography and Maps Division, Library of Congress; https://www.loc.gov/resource/g3804nm.gct00085/?sp=9.

57. Searcher, *Lincoln's Journey to Greatness,* 184.

58. *New York Sun,* February 20, 1861.

59. Freeman, *Lincoln Goes to New York,* 105.

60. Christine Stansell, *City of Women: Sex and Class in New York,* 1789–1860 (Urbana: University of Illinois Press, 1987), 173. Timothy Gilfoyle wrote that houses of prostitution were concentrated on the West Side, especially near hotels; see *City of Eros: New York City, Prostitution, and the Commercialization of Sex, 1790–1920* (New York: W. W. Norton, 1992), 47.

61. Gilfoyle, *City of Eros,* 53.

62. Stephen Fiske, "When Lincoln Was First Inaugurated," in *Lincoln Among His Friends,* 304.

63. Fiske, "When Lincoln Was First Inaugurated," *Lincoln Among His Friends*, 304–5; *New York Herald*, February 20, 1861.

64. *Frank Leslie's Illustrated Newspaper*, March 2, 1861; see also Annik Lafarge, "President Lincoln on a Dangerous Day in Manhattan," Livin' the High Line, June 19, 2019; https://www.livinthehighline.com/2019/06/19/president-lincoln-on-a-dangerous-day-in-manhattan/.

65. *New York Herald*, February 20, 1861; Freeman, *Lincoln Goes to New York*, 18.

66. *New York Herald*, February 20, 1861; 1,300 of New York's 1,500 police were mobilized; *New York Times*, February 19, 1861; Freeman, *Lincoln Goes to New York*, 107.

67. Annik Lafarge, "High Line Architecture: Morgan General Mail Facility," Livin' the High Line, December 15, 2013; http://www.livinthehighline.com/2013/12/15/high-line-architecture-morgan-geneneral-mail-facility/.

68. Thomas Nast, Civil War Scrapbook, Brown University Library; Albert Bigelow Paine, *Thomas Nast: His Period and Pictures* (Princeton, NJ: Pyne Press, 1904, 1974), 70–71

69. Brown University Library, see also Adam Gopnik, "Uncovering Thomas Nast's First Drawings of Abraham Lincoln," *New Yorker*, March 5, 2018.

70. One estimate was 100,000; *Harper's Weekly*, March 2, 1861, 130.

71. *New York Times*, February 20, 1861.

72. Harold Holzer, Gabor S. Boritt, and Mark E. Neely, Jr., *The Lincoln Image: Abraham Lincoln and the Popular Print* (New York: Charles Scribner's Sons, 1984), 27; Gary L. Bunker, *From Rail-Splitter to Icon: Lincoln's Image in Illustrated Periodicals, 1860-1865* (Kent: Kent State University Press, 2001). Of the nineteen illustrated periodicals listed, thirteen were based in New York; see 374–377

73. Courtesy of New-York Historical Society.

74. Harold Holzer, *Lincoln at Cooper Union: The Speech That Made Abraham Lincoln President* (New York: Simon & Schuster, 2004), 96.

75. Luc Sante, *Low Life: Lures and Snares of Old New York* (New York: Farrar Straus Giroux, 1991), 292.

76. Walt Whitman, "The Slave Trade," *Life Illustrated*, August 2, 1856; Robert Greenhalgh Albion, *The Rise of New York Port, 1815–1860* (New York: Charles Scribner's Sons, 1939, 1970), chap. 6.

77. *New York Times*, February 20, 1861.

78. Hayes, *Lincoln Runs for President*, 208; Jerome Mushkat, *Fernando Wood: A Political Biography* (Kent, OH: Kent State University Press, 1990), 110; David S. Reynolds, *Walt Whitman's America*, 405.

79. Samuel Augustus Pleasants, *Fernando Wood of New York* (New York: Columbia University Press, 1948), 109.

80. Sante, *Low Life*, 263; Kenneth Jackson and David S. Dunbar, *Empire City: New York Through the Centuries* (New York: Columbia University Press, 2005), 363; Philip S. Foner, *Business and Slavery: The New York Merchants and the Irrepressible Conflict* (Chapel Hill: University of North Carolina Press, 1941), 285–296; John Lockwood and Charles Lockwood, "First South Carolina. Then New York?," *New York Times*, January 6, 2011; Wood's address was printed in the *New York Herald*, January 8, 1861.

81. *New York Herald*, January 8, 1861.

82. Mushkat, *Fernando Wood*, 100–101.

83. *Papers of Jefferson Davis*, vol. 7, 43. On the same day, a leading New York merchant, Alexander Hamilton Jr., wrote a note of congratulations to Davis.

84. Hom.Od. IX, 89-97.

85. Nichols, *Disruption of American Democracy*, 418, 472.

86. Only a month earlier, January 23, New York police seized a vessel, the *Monticello*, bound for Savannah with thirty-eight crates of guns and ammunition; Mushkat, *Fernando Wood*, 38; Benson J. Lossing, *History of New York City* (New York: George Perrine, 1884), 716.

87. Philip S. Foner, *Business and Slavery: The New York Merchants and the Irrepressible Conflict*, 1–14; Abram J. Dittenhoefer, *How We Elected Lincoln* (Philadelphia: University of Pennsylvania Press, 1916, 2005), 1.

88. Cobb came in late October 1860; Strong, *Diary of George Templeton Strong*, vol. 3, 54.

89. Louis Wigfall to Jefferson Davis, February 16, 1861, *Papers of Jefferson Davis*, vol. 7, 43.

90. I.N.P. Stokes, *The Iconography of Manhattan Island, 1498-1909*, vol. 3 (New York: Arno Press, 1967), 729–30; V, 1894; Nichols, *Disruption of American Democracy*, 466.

91. Nichols, *Disruption of American Democracy*, 364.

92. Lossing, *History of New York City*, 716; *New York Times*, December 17, 1860; Samuel Augustus Pleasants, *Fernando Wood of New York* (New York: Columbia University Press, 1948), 112; the loss to Northern investments was estimated at $478 million.

93. Edwin G. Burrows and Mike Wallace, *Gotham*, 737.

94. http://www.nyc.gov/html/nyc100/html/imm_stories/museum.; Spann, *New Metropolis*, 24. Between 1840 and 1855, 68 percent of all immigrants to the United States came through New York.

95. Stephen Jenkins, *The Greatest Street in the World* (New York: G. P. Putnam's Sons, 1911), 34.

96. Henry Christman, ed., *Walt Whitman's New York: From Manhattan to Montauk* (New York: New Amsterdam, 1963), 26. Ives Goddard, "The Origin and Meaning of the Name 'Manhattan,'" *New York History*, vol. 91, no. 4 (fall 2010), 277–293.

97. Albion, *Rise of New York Port*, 25–26.

98. Spann, *New Metropolis*, 5, 15. New York's share of U.S. steam tonnage rose from 38 percent to 75 percent between 1840 and 1860.

99. Frederick Trevor Hill, *The Story of a Street: A Narrative History of Wall Street from 1644 to 1908* (New York: Harper and Brothers, 1908), 155.

100. Fernando Wood, speech to the Common Council, January 7, 1861; *New York Herald*, January 8, 1861.

101. In 1868, 68 percent of all imports to the United States came through the port of New York. Spann, *New Metropolis*, 438n24, 95.

102. Ibid., 205.

103. *Frank Leslie's Illustrated Newspaper*, November 19, 1859.

104. Freeman, *Lincoln Goes to New York*, 109.

105. Ibid., 107. The *New York Sun* (February 20, 1861) reported "about 30" carriages in the procession.

106. Burlingame, *Lincoln: A Life*, vol. 2, 27.

107. Freeman, *Lincoln Goes to New York*, 108.

108. Elisabeth S. Peck, "Abraham Lincoln in New York," *Lincoln Herald* 60, no. 4 (Winter 1958): 129.

109. *The Reminiscences of Augustus Saint-Gaudens*, vol. 1, ed. Homer Saint-Gaudens (New York: Century, 1913), 41–42.

110. Francis Fisher Browne, *Everyday Life of Abraham Lincoln*, 276.

111. Burlingame, *Lincoln: A Life*, vol. 2, 27.

112. John Nicolay, in *Oral History of Lincoln*, 118.

113. New York Public Library; see also Edward Anthony and Henry T. Anthony, "Broadway on a Rainy Day," 1859, Visualizing 19th-Century New York; http://visualizingnyc.org/objects/ny-003-image-shows-333-broadway.

114. Mary Panzer, *Mathew Brady and the Image of History* (Washington, D.C.; Smithsonian Institution Press, 1997), 30.

115. Spann, *New Metropolis*, 3.

116. Ibid., 95.

117. Sante, *Low Life*, 47.

118. Spann, *New Metropolis*, 289; Bogdan Horbal, "Early Proposed Railways for New York, Part 1" January 16, 2015; New York Public Library, https://www.nypl.org/blog/2015/01/16/early-proposed-railways-nyc-1.

119. Sante, *Low Life*, 59.

120. *New York Times*, February 20, 1861; Freeman, *Lincoln Goes to New York*, 107; Holzer, *Lincoln, President-Elect*, 355.

121. *New York Herald*, February 20, 1861.

122. Strong, *Diary of George Templeton Strong*, vol. 3, 101.

123. Ibid., 102.

124. Jason Goodwin, Otis: *Giving Rise to the Modern City*, 17, 21.

125. Andreas Bogardus, *Lifted: A Cultural History of the Elevator*, 4–5; Lincoln would soon know the building for another reason as well. A few months later, Mary Todd Lincoln would return to the Haughwout Building on one of her New York shopping sprees, to buy expensive mauve china for the White House. On the last night of his life, Lincoln would drink from one of these cups—it would be found on a window ledge in the White House, where he had left it.

126. *New York Sun*, February 20, 1861.

127. *New York Herald*, February 20, 1861.

128. John Mason Potter, *Thirteen Desperate Days*, 96.

129. Stashower, *Hour of Peril*, 204; Cuthbert, *Lincoln and the Baltimore Plot*, 41.

130. David S. Reynolds, *Walt Whitman's America*, 405–6.

131. Epstein, *Lincoln and Whitman*, 66.

132. Ibid., 11, 46; an argument against the anecdote is made in Robert Bray, "What Abraham Lincoln Read—An Evaluative and Annotated List," *Journal of the Abraham Lincoln Association* 28, no. 2 (2007): 80.

133. Whitman, *Complete Poetry and Prose*, 1038.

134. Ibid.

135. Astor House, New York City, 1899; Robert L. Bracklow Photograph Collection. New-York Historical Society; Digital Culture of Metropolitan New York; http://dcmny.org/islandora/object/nyhs%3A32.

136. *New York Times*, February 20, 1861.

137. Jenkins, *Greatest Street in the World*, 139.

138. I.N.P. Stokes, *The Iconography of New York*, VI, 55.

139. Spann, *New Metropolis*, 98; Talbot Hamlin called it "almost twentieth century in conception"; Hamlin, *Greek Revival Architecture*, 152.

140. Henry James, *A Small Boy and Others*, ed. Peter Collister (Charlottesville: University of Virginia Press, 2011), 1011. According to family tradition, Ralph Waldo Emerson was staying at the same time and met the infant William James shortly after his birth.

141. Holzer, *Lincoln at Cooper Union*, 84–85.

142. Jenkins, *Greatest Street in the World*, 139; the campaigns of Henry Clay, Zachary Taylor, and Winfield Scott were organized in the Astor House; "The Passing of

the Astor House," *Literary Digest*, May 31, 1913, 1239; Luthin, *First Lincoln Campaign*, 20.

143. Robert Wilson, *Mathew Brady: Portraits of a Nation* (New York: Bloomsbury, 2013), 65.

144. Luthin, *First Lincoln Campaign*, 171.

145. *New York Times*, February 19, 1861.

146. Robert Luther Thompson, *Wiring a Continent*, 81, 219; Gillian Cookson, *The Cable: The Wire That Changed the World* (Stroud, UK: Tempus, 2003), 22.

147. The Lincoln party was given rooms 37, 39, 41 and 43; *New York Times*, February 19, and February 20, 1861. The furnishings are described in detail in the *New York Sun*, February 20, 1861.

148. *New York Times*, February 20, 1861.

149. Walt Whitman, *Specimen Days* (Boston: David R. Godine, 1971), 78.

150. Astor House File, George B. Corsa Hotel Collection, New-York Historical Society; see also Bernard D'Orazio, "The Astor House, New York's First Great—Yet Forgotten—Hotel," *The Tribeca Trib*, March 22, 2016; http://www.tribeca trib.com/content/astor-house-new-york's-first-great—yet-forgotten—hotel.

151. *New York Times*, February 20, 1861.

152. *Western Reserve Chronicle* (OH), February 27, 1861.

153. Ibid.; *New York Sun*, February 20, 1861.

154. *New York Herald*, February 20, 1861.

155. *Lincoln, Collected Works*, vol. 4, 230–31; *New York Herald*, February 20, 1861.

156. Cuthbert, *Lincoln and the Baltimore Plot*, 45.

157. Stashower, *Hour of Peril*, 206–8. On February 19, the same day, another operative would report an argument over the chances of Lincoln's survival among a group of conspirators bowling tenpins in Baltimore; ibid., 197.

158. Ibid., 214–17.

159. *New York Times*, February 19, 1861.

160. Andrew A. Freeman, *Abraham Lincoln Goes to New York* (New York: Coward-McCann, 1960), 108–9; Holzer, *Lincoln, President-Elect*, 361.

161. Holzer, *Lincoln, President-Elect*, 361–62.

162. Prints and Photographs Division, Library of Congress; http://www.loc.gov /pictures/resource/cph.3a23120.

163. Jenkins, *Greatest Street in the World*, 84–90.

164. *New York Times*, February 21, 1861.

165. Holzer, *Lincoln, President-Elect*, 362.

166. Mushkat, *Fernando Wood*, 109, 111.

167. *New York Times*, February 21, 1861.

168. Abram J. Dittenhoefer, *How We Elected Lincoln: Personal Recollections* (ed.

Kathleen Hall Jamieson; Philadelphia: University of Pennsylvania Press), 1916, 2005, 47. Dittenhoefer later thought this brief exchanged marked the beginning of emancipation.

169. *New York Times*, February 21, 1861.

170. Burlingame, *Lincoln: A Life*, vol. 2, 29; the *New York Times* (February 21, 1861) gave an even higher estimate.

171. *New York Times*, February 21, 1861.

172. Searcher, *Lincoln's Journey to Greatness*, 201.

173. Daguerreotype of Hannibal Hamlin; Prints and Photographs Division, Library of Congress; https://commons.wikimedia.org/wiki/File:Younger_Hannibal _Hamlin.jpg.

174. *New York Times*, February 21, 1861, 8.

175. *New York Times*, February 21, 1861.

176. Hamlin, *Life and Times of Hannibal Hamlin*, 383–87.

177. Frontispiece to the 1860 score of Giuseppe Verdi's *A Masked Ball*; Harvard University Library; https://en.wikipedia.org/wiki/Un_ballo_in_maschera# /media/File:Giuseppe_Verdi,_Un_Ballo_in_maschera,_Vocal_score_frontis piece_-_restoration.jpg.

178. Ibid., 387–388.

179. *New York Times*, February 21, 1861.

180. Hamlin, *Life and Times of Hannibal Hamlin*, 389.

180. On the night the Civil War began, Walt Whitman was attending this opera; David S. Reynolds, *Walt Whitman's America*, 406.

181. *New York Times*, February 21, 1861; Holzer, *Lincoln, President-Elect*, 365.

182. Andrew Carnegie, *Autobiography of Andrew Carnegie* (Boston: Houghton Mifflin, 1920), 105; Henry Adams noticed Lincoln having trouble with his gloves at his inaugural ball; see Edmund Wilson, *Patriotic Gore*, 118.

183. *New York Times*, February 21, 1861.

184. *Frank Leslie's Illustrated Newspaper*, March 2, 1861.

185. *New York Herald*, February 20, 1861.

186. Adam Goodheart, "A Peevish Prince, a Hairy-Handed President, a Disastrous Dinner Party," *New York Times*, August 2, 2011.

187. Freeman, *Lincoln Goes to New York*, 149.

188. Burlingame, *Lincoln: A Life*, vol. 2, 30.

189. Ibid., 29.

190. *New York Times*, February 21, 1861.

191. Charles Francis Adams (Jr.), *An Autobiography* (New York: Russell and Russell, 1968), 76–77. In his diary Charles Francis Adams Sr. noted that Lincoln seemed

"frivolous and uncertain" (entry for February 19, 1861); Massachusetts Historical Society.

192. *Papers of Jefferson Davis*, vol. 7, 55.

193. Horace Greeley, *The Autobiography of Horace Greeley; or, Recollections of a Busy Life* (New York: E.B. Treat, 1872), 405.

CHAPTER 12: THE GARDEN

1. "Nova Caesarea: A Cartographic Record of the Garden States, 1666–1888," Princeton University Library; https://library.princeton.edu/njmaps/state_of _nj.html"

2. Homer, *The Odyssey*, trans. Wilson, 318.

3. *New York Times*, February 21, 1861, 1.

4. *New York Herald*, February 20, 1861, 8; *New York Sun*, February 20, 1861. Lincoln was later painted standing before this print; see Photo of Travers Oil Painting of Lincoln, Rare Books and Special Collections Division, Library of Congress; https://www.loc.gov/resource/lprbscsm.scsm0646.

5. Natalie Spassky, ed., *American Paintings in the Metropolitan Museum of Art: A Catalogue of Works by Artists Born between 1816 and 1845*, vol. 2, 18, 22.

6. Ibid., vol. 2, 20. Other presidents also crowded into the scene; James Monroe is believed to be the young officer holding the flag

7. Joseph Medill quoted in "A Talk with Lincoln's Friend," *Chicago Daily Tribune*, February 6, 1944.

8. Holzer, *Lincoln, President-Elect*, 382.

9. *New York Times*, February 21, 1861, 1–2, 8.

10. *New York Times*, May 7, 1865.

11. Josiah Johnson Hawes, Girl with Portrait of George Washington, ca. 1850, Metropolitan Museum of Art; https://www.metmuseum.org/art/collection /search/268354.

12. Breen, *George Washington's Journey*, 39–40.

13. Pratt, *Concerning Mr. Lincoln*, 56; *New York Times*, February 22, 1861.

14. *New York Times*, February 21, 1861.

15. "The Writings of Henry D. Thoreau, University of California, Santa Barbara; http://thoreau.library.ucsb.edu/writings_journals_pdfs/J16f7.pdf.

16. I am grateful to David Rumsey for his help georectifying maps.

17. "Execution on Bedloe's Island, New York Bay, July 18, 1860, of Albert W. Hicks, the Notorious Pirate, for the Murder of Captain Burr and the Brothers Hicks;" published in *Frank Leslie's Illustrated Newspaper*, July 21, 1860.

18. The USS *John P. Jackson*, built a year earlier in Brooklyn, would soon be

repurposed by the U.S. Navy and put into service as part of the fleet in David Farragut's campaign to take New Orleans and the Mississippi.

19. *New York Times*, February 22, 1861, 1; *Philadelphia Inquirer*, February 22, 1861; Albion, *The of New York Port*, 146–47.

20. *New York Times*, February 22, 1861, 8; the wind was described as "W.N.W., blowing fresh."

21. Henry James, *The American Scene* (New York: Harper and Brothers, 1907), 139. James would wonder why "the Beautiful Gate" was condemned by fate to sit next to a "sordid city."

22. An 1834 compact gave New York the land above the water, and New Jersey the land below; see Michael J. Birkner, "The New York-New Jersey Boundary Controversy, John Marshall and the Nullification Crisis," *Journal of the Early Republic* (Summer 1992): 195–212.

23. *New York Times*, February 22, 1861, 8. The ship "arrived off the Battery at 7¼ A.M.," or 7:15; the passenger manifest listed a mixture of farmers, mechanics, bakers and butchers, many with wives and children.

24. Ted Widmer, "An Immigrant Named Trump," *New Yorker*, October 1, 2016.

25. *New York Herald*, February 22, 1; Mark Kurlansky, *The Big Oyster: History on the Half Shell* (New York: Random House, 2006), 35.

26. It was also called Kioshk, or Gull Island, by the Lenape Indians; see Mark Kurlansky, *The Big Oyster*, 39.

27. Other names included Kennedy's Island and Love Island.

28. Prints and Photographs Division, Library of Congress.

29. The terminal was described as "a vast dépôt;" *New York Times*, February 22, 1861, 1, 4; see Condit, *Port of New York*, 50; Hay, *Lincoln's Journalist*, 39.

30. *New York Herald*, February 22, 1861, 1.

31. Ibid.; *Philadelphia Inquirer*, February 22, 1861.

32. *Philadelphia Inquirer*, February 22, 1861.

33. William Gillette, *Jersey Blue: Politics in New Jersey, 1854–1865* (New Brunswick, NJ: Rutgers University Press, 1995), 127; Henry Villard was no longer in the traveling party, having stayed in New York; Hannibal Hamlin was a new addition; *Philadelphia Inquirer*, February 22, 1861.

34. *New York Times*, February 22, 1861, 1.

35. Strong, *Diary of George Templeton Strong*, vol. 3, 85.

36. Kenneth Chang, "Behind a Shopping Center in New Jersey, Signs of a Mass Extinction," *New York Times*, January 4, 2016; see also Robert Sullivan, *The Meadowlands: Wilderness Adventures at the Edge of a City* (New York: Scribner, 1998).

37. Peter O. Wacker, *Land and People: A Cultural Geography of Preindustrial New Jersey* (New Brunswick, NJ: Rutgers University Press, 1975), 63.

38. John P. Snyder, *The Mapping of New Jersey: The Men and the Art* (New Brunswick, NJ: Rutgers University Press, 1973), 37; Wacker, *Land and People*, 59.

39. A member of Lincoln's traveling party, David Hunter, was the grandson of Richard Stockton, one of New Jersey's signers of the Declaration; Varina Davis, the wife of Jefferson Davis, was a granddaughter of an early New Jersey governor, Richard Howell.

40. Snyder, *Mapping of New Jersey*, 14.

41. Andrew Burnaby, cited in John E. Pomfret, *Colonial New Jersey: A History* (New York: Charles Scribner's Sons, 1973), xv.

42. Snyder, *Mapping of New Jersey*, 23; John P. Snyder, *The Story of New Jersey's Civil Boundaries, 1606–1968* (Trenton, NJ: Bureau of Geology and Topography, 1969), 9; East and West Jersey were reunited in 1702.

43. Albion, *Rise of New York Port*, 77.

44. The right was stripped away in 1807; see "Stories from the Revolution," National Park Service; https://www.nps.gov/revwar/about_the_revolution/voting_rights.html.

45. *New Jersey: A Guide to Its Present and Past* (New York: Hastings House, 1946), 98; *Bergen County Panorama* (Hackensack: Bergen County, 1941), 121; Condit, *Port of New York*, 49; on early railroads in New Jersey, see *New Jersey: A Guide*, 100; Pomfret, *Colonial New Jersey*, 198; Albion, *Rise of New York Port*, 70; Condit, *Port of New York*, 45; White Jr., *American Locomotives*, 87, 105; Wheaton J. Lane, *From Indian Trail to Iron Horse: Travel and Transportation in New Jersey* (Princeton, NJ: Princeton University Press, 1939), 146; Snyder, *Story of New Jersey's Civil Boundaries*, 23. For an important early map showing New Jersey's centrality, see Christopher Colles, *A Survey of the Roads of the United States of America, 1789*, ed. Walter W. Rostow (Cambridge, MA: Harvard University Press, 1961).

46. *New Jersey: A Guide*, 294; "All Aboard! Railroads and New Jersey, 1812–1930," Rutgers Universities Libraries; https://www.libraries.rutgers.edu/rul/exhibits/nj_railroads/njrr.php#case:3. The Camden and Amboy was the line that Frederick Douglass used to reach New York; Foner, *Gateway to Freedom*, 2.

47. White Jr., *American Locomotives*, 14; *Manufactures of the United States in 1860, Compiled from the Original Returns of the Eighth Census.* (Washington: U.S. Census Office, 1865), clxxxviii.

48. *New Jersey: A Guide*, 49.

49. Thomas H. Dudley, "New Jersey's Part in Seward's Defeat," in *Lincoln Among His Friends*, 210–14.

50. *New Jersey: A Guide*, 320.

51. In 1864 New Jersey would enthusiastically back Lincoln's rival, George

McClellan, one of only three states to do so; "Lincoln and New Jersey," New Jersey State Archives; http://www.nj.gov/state/archives/lincoln.html.

52. William Gillette, *Jersey Blue*, 93, 105.

53. Ibid., 115.

54. Alexander Hamilton Jr. traveled out to Illinois in 1835, and wandered into a grocery store, where he encountered its proprietor, Abraham Lincoln, "lying upon the counter in midday telling stories;" William H. Macbean, *Biographical Register of St. Andrew's Society of the State of New York*, vol. 2 (New York: St. Andrew's Society, 1925), 18.

55. James J. Gigontino II, *The Ragged Road to Abolition: Slavery and Freedom in New Jersey, 1775–1865* (Philadelphia: University of Pennsylvania Press, 2015), 1, 8–9, 240.

56. *Philadelphia Inquirer*, February 22, 1861.

57. *New York Times*, February 22, 1861, 1.

58. Holzer, *Lincoln, President-Elect*, 370; *New York Times*, February 22, 1861, 4.

59. *New York Times*, February 22, 1861, 1; *Philadelphia Inquirer*, February 22, 1861.

60. W. Barksdale Maynard, "Princeton in the Confederacy's Service," Princeton Alumni Weekly, https://paw.princeton.edu/article/princeton-confederacys-service; April C. Armstrong, ""The Present Unsettled State of Our Country:" Princeton and the Civil War," https://blogs.princeton.edu/mudd/2015/04/the-present-unsettled-state-of-our-country-princeton-and-the-civil-war.

61. Prints and Photographs Division, Library of Congress.

62. *New Jersey: A Guide*, 45; between 1702 and 1790, the government operated from Perth Amboy and Burlington; see Snyder, *Mapping of New Jersey*, 38.

63. Condit, *Port of New York*, 48–49.

64. Pomfret, *Colonial New Jersey*, 196; *New Jersey: A Guide*, 403; Albion, *Rise of New York Port*, 70.

65. Hitchcock and Seale, *Temples of Democracy*, 51.

66. Maier, *American Scripture*, 153; David Hackett Fischer, *Washington's Crossing* (New York: Oxford University Press, 2004), 378.

67. Breen, *George Washington's Journey*, 38–39; Mason L. Weems, *The Life of Washington*, ed. Marcus Cunliffe (Cambridge, MA: Harvard University Press, 1962), 133.

68. *New York Times*, February 22, 1861, 1.

69. Hay, *Lincoln's Journalist*, 40.

70. Holzer, *Lincoln, President-Elect*, 371.

71. Lincoln, *Collected Works*, vol. 4, 235–36; also *New York Times*, February 22, 1861.

72. Lincoln, *Collected Works*, vol. 4, 236.

73. Ibid.

74. Grant Wood, *Parson Weems' Fable*, 1939, Amon Carter Museum of American Art.

75. Weems, *Life of Washington*, xviii–xix, xv, 42, lxi, 83, 169. For more on Weems, see Francois Furstenberg, *In the Name of the Father: Washington's Legacy, Slavery and the Making of a Nation* (New York: Penguin, 2006).

76. Lincoln's 1862 message to Congress and the Gettysburg Address both echo a phrase written by Weems about ensuring that "the last, best, trial of free government . . . [shall not] fai[l] upon the earth; Furstenberg, *In the Name of the Father*, 118.

77. Douglas L. Wilson and Rodney O. Davis, eds., *Herndon on Lincoln: Letters* (Urbana: University of Illinois Press, 2016), 134; Douglas L. Wilson, *Honor's Voice: The Transformation of Abraham Lincoln* (New York: Vintage Books, 1998), 77.

78. Jett Conner, "The American Crisis Before Crossing the Delaware?," *Journal of the American Revolution*, February 25, 2015; https://allthingsliberty.com/2015/02 /american-crisis-before-crossing-the-delaware.

79. Lincoln, *Collected Works*, vol. 4, 237.

80. Hay, *Lincoln's Journalist*, 40.

81. *New York Times*, February 22, 1861, 1.

82. Richard Duane, a Trenton minister, was six feet away when Lincoln's foot came down, and he called it "a very decided and appropriate gesture"; see William Gillette, *Jersey Blue*, 128. The weight of Lincoln's foot can still be felt in Maryland, where the state song includes a reference to "the despot's heel."

83. Nicolay, *Oral History of Lincoln*, 120.

84. Henry Adams, *Great Secession Winter*, 31.

85. Mary Livermore, *My Story of the War: A Woman's Narrative of Four Years' Personal Experience in the Union Army* . . . (Hartford, CT: A. D. Worthington, 1896), 553–54; Strong, *The Diary of George Templeton Strong*, vol. 3, 106.

86. Ibid., 55.

87. Lincoln, *Collected Works*, vol. 4, 237.

88. Burlingame, *Lincoln: A Life*, vol. 2, 31.

89. Hay, *Lincoln's Journalist*, 41.

90. Thomas Nast drawing of "Country People," *New York Illustrated News*, March 9, 1861; the original drawing is in the Brown University Library.

91. Ibid.; "Papers Read Before Lancaster County Historical Society," March 5, 1909, 59–60.

92. Joseph Howard Jr. gave a vivid account of the sounds of the arrival at Philadelphia; *New York Times*, February 22, 1861, 1.

93. Burlingame, *Lincoln: A Life*, vol. 2, 31.

94. James Bergquist, "Immigration (1790–1860)", Encylopedia of Greater Philadel-phia; http://philadelphiaencyclopedia.org/archive/immigration-1790-1860.

95. Trossel, *Lincoln Inaugural Train*, 145, 146.

96. Stashower, *The Hour of Peril*, 229.

97. The evening before, a Lincoln impersonator had spoken from the same balcony.

98. Lincoln, *Collected Works*, vol. 4, 239.

99. Frederick Douglass also referred to Psalm 137 in his speech, "What to the Slave is the Fourth of July?," delivered at Rochester in 1852. See "Frederick Douglass Project Fifth of July Speech," University of Rochester; http://rbscp.lib.rochester .edu/2945.

100. Prints and Photographs Division, Library of Congress.

101. *Philadelphia Inquirer*, February 22, 1861.

102. The meeting was scheduled for seven thirty but began around a quarter to seven; Cuthbert, *Lincoln and the Baltimore Plot*, 58; Stashower, *Hour of Peril*, 228.

103. Cuthbert, *Lincoln and the Baltimore Plot*, 64.

104. Ibid., 5; Pinkerton, *Spy of the Rebellion*, 66

105. Pinkerton, *Spy of the Rebellion*, 84; Holzer, *Lincoln, President-Elect*, 377–78. There were other rumors as well, of attempts to assassinate Lincoln with an air gun, or a revolver, or a train derailment; see Cuthbert, *Lincoln and the Baltimore Plot*, xiii.

106. Cuthbert, *Lincoln and the Baltimore Plot*, xv.

107. Burlingame, *Lincoln: A Life*, vol. 2, 32; George W. Hazzard was aboard the Spe-cial because of a warning he had written to Lincoln, urging him to go incognito through Baltimore: George W. Hazzard to Abraham Lincoln, January 1861; Abraham Lincoln Papers, Library of Congress.

108. "A Lady" to Abraham Lincoln, February 1861; Lincoln Papers, Library of Congress; Holzer, *Lincoln, President-Elect*, 382; Henry Bowen to Abraham Lin-coln, February 5, 1861; Charles Gould to Henry C. Bowen, February 5, 1861, Abraham Lincoln Papers, Library of Congress. Holzer, *Lincoln, President-Elect*, 382; Henry Bowen to Abraham Lincoln, February 5, 1861; Charles Gould to Henry C. Bowen, February 5, 1861, Abraham Lincoln Papers, Library of Con-gress.

109. Cuthbert, *Lincoln and the Baltimore Plot*, 8.

110. Holzer, *Lincoln, President-Elect*, 378 .

111. Pinkerton, *Spy of the Rebellion*, 85; Cuthbert, *Lincoln and the Baltimore Plot*, 11.

112. Mathew Brady, photograph of Frederick W. Seward; https://commons.wikime dia.org/wiki/File:Frederick_W._Seward_-_Brady-Handy.jpg.

113. Stone was the liaison to the New York police chief, John A. Kennedy; accord-ing to one source, they were also trying to reach Robert E. Lee; see Searcher,

Lincoln's Journey to Greatness, 258; Stone's note is in Cuthbert, *Lincoln and the Baltimore Plot*, 131–32.

114. Seward, *Reminiscences*, 135.
115. Lamb, *Extraordinary Life of Charles Pomeroy Stone*, 92–93.
116. Seward, *Reminiscences*, 135–36.
117. Pinkerton, *Spy of the Rebellion*, 85–87. Cuthbert explains the different sources of information and the rivalries between Lincoln's protectors, *Lincoln and the Baltimore Plot*, xi–xxii; Pinkerton's activities are described, 69–71.
118. Cuthbert, *Lincoln and the Baltimore Plot*, 70.
119. *New York Herald*, February 23, 1861, 6, 7.
120. *New York Times*, February 23, 1861; Adam Goodheart, "Guns, Blood and Congress," *New York Times*, March 16, 2011.
121. *New York Herald*, February 23, 1861, 7.
122. Diary of Charles Francis Adams (Sr.), Massachusetts Historical Society.

CHAPTER 13: THE FOUNTAIN

1. Abraham Lincoln raising a flag at Independence Hall, Philadelphia, February 22, 1861; Prints and Photographs Division, Library of Congress; https://www.loc.gov/item/2006683455/.
2. Homer, *The Odyssey*, trans. Wilson, 107.
3. I am grateful to Michael Brewer of NOAA for help with weather, stars, and sunrise information.
4. *New York Herald*, February 23, 1861, 3.
5. Pinkerton, *Spy of the Rebellion*, 87; Cuthbert, *Lincoln and the Baltimore Plot, 1861*, 61.
6. Lincoln described the Declaration as a "fountain" in a speech at Lewistown, Illinois, August 17, 1858; Lincoln, *Collected Works*, vol. 2, 547.
7. Henry Adams, *Education of Henry Adams*, 37.
8. Goodheart, "War for (George) Washington"; Norman Gasbarro, "Lincoln's Birthday 1861," Civil War Blog; http://civilwar.gratzpa.org/2011/02/lincolns-birthday-1861.
9. Ibid. Kansas joined the Union on January 29.
10. *New Orleans Daily True Delta*, February 23, 1861. I am grateful to Mary Lou Eichorn and Alfred Lemmon of the Historic New Orleans Collection for this information.
11. James Lee McDonough, *William Tecumseh Sherman, In the Service of My Country: A Life* (New York: W. W. Norton, 2016), 236; William T. Sherman, *Memoirs of General W. T. Sherman* (New York: Library of America, 1990), 182.
12. *Philadelphia Inquirer*, February 23, 1861, 1; Goodheart, "War for (George)

Washington"; Leech, *Reveille in Washington*, 34–35; Nicolay, *Oral History of Lincoln*, 7–76; *New York Herald*, February 23, 1861.

13. *Papers of Jefferson Davis*, vol. 7, 57.

14. Henry Wise to Jefferson Davis, February 22, 1861, ibid., 59.

15. Goodheart, "War for (George) Washington."

16. *Papers of Jefferson Davis*, vol. 7, 59.

17. *Philadelphia Inquirer*, February 23, 1861, 2; Pinkerton, *Spy of the Rebellion*, 87.

18. Bradley R. Hoch, *The Lincoln Trail in Pennsylvania: A History and Guide* (University Park: Pennsylvania State University Press, 2001), 43–44.

19. Instead of denying slavery's role in bringing the conflict, Stephens confirmed it as "the immediate cause of the late rupture and present revolution."

20. In September 1789 George Washington sent a message to the Pennsylvania legislature that included his hope that America's example would be "coextensive with the world"; Breen, *George Washington's Journey*, 107.

21. http://www.presidency.ucsb.edu/ws/?pid=25817.

22. George Washington, *Writings* (New York: Library of America, 1997), 714, 733.

23. Prints and Photographs Division, Library of Congress.

24. Mires, *Independence Hall*, 6.

25. Sally M. Walker, *Boundaries: How the Mason-Dixon Line Settled a Family Feud and Divided a Nation* (Somerville, MA: Candlewick Press, 2014), 63.

26. "Pennsylvania Abolition Society;" http://explorepahistory.com/hmarker .php?markerId=1-A-273 [CK].

27. Foner, *Gateway to Freedom*, 151; William Still, *The Underground Rail Road* (Philadelphia: Porter and Coates, 1872).

28. Foner, *Gateway to Freedom*, 103–4. The crate was described as "even too small for a coffin."

29. Edgar P. Richardson, Brooke Hindle, Lillian B. Miller, *Charles Willson Peale and His World* (New York: Harry Abrams, 1982), 80.

30. Charles Coleman Sellers, *Charles Willson Peale: A Biography* (New York: Charles Scribner's Sons, 1969), 406–7.

31. Mires, *Independence Hall*, 42, 65, 71, 102–3. Earlier, the building was known as the Old State House.

32. Ibid., 87.

33. Erica Armstrong Dunbar, *A Fragile Freedom: African American Women and Emancipation in the Antebellum City* (New Haven, CT: Yale University Press, 2008), 148–49.

34. On Philadelphia's Southern sympathies, see Judith Giesberg, "The Most Northern of Southern Cities," *New York Times*, May 22, 2011; Mires, *Independence Hall*, 14, 44.

35. Mires, *Independence Hall*, 94–96; Milt Diggins, *Stealing Freedom Along the Mason-Dixon Line: Thomas Macreary, the Notorious Slave Catcher from Maryland* (Baltimore: Johns Hopkins University Press, 2015), 62

36. There were rallies for the Union on December 18, 1860, and January 26, 1861.

37. In the 1960s, Independence Hall became linked to a new kind of freedom as some of the first demonstrations for gay rights were held there; see Adam Goodheart, "Lincoln's Funeral Train," *National Geographic*, April 2015.

38. *Frank Leslie's Illustrated Newspaper*, March 9, 1861.

39. "Samuel Emory Davis," https://jeffersondavis.rice.edu/people/samuel-emory-davis-0.

40. *Lincoln: Selected Speeches and Writings*, ed. Gore Vidal (New York: Library of America, 1992), 21, 54; Wills, *Lincoln at Gettysburg*, 249.

41. On February 22, 1842, Lincoln spoke to a group of temperance advocates who called themselves Washingtonians; Charles T. White, *Lincoln and Prohibition* (New York: Abingdon, 1921), 53–54; Lincoln, *Collected Works*, vol. 1, 279; six years later, he and Stephen Douglas helped to plan a "National Birth-Night Ball" for Washington in the capital.

42. Lincoln, *Collected Works*, vol. 2, 547.

43. Douglas L. Wilson, *Lincoln Before Washington*, 166.

44. Louis Warren, *Lincoln's Youth: Indiana Years*, 109, 169; there is fragmentary evidence that Lincoln was affected by the deaths of Adams and Jefferson.

45. Jed Morrison, "Target Practice with Mr. Lincoln," *New York Times*, August 19, 2013.

46. Edwin D. Freed, *Lincoln's Political Ambitions, Slavery and the Bible* (Eugene: Pickwick, 2012), 72; Andrew Delbanco, "Lincoln's Sacramental Language," in Eric Foner, ed., *Our Lincoln: New Perspectives on Lincoln and His World* (New York: W.W. Norton, 2013), 213; Drew R. McCoy, "An Old-Fashioned Nationalism: Lincoln, Jefferson and the Classical Tradition," *Journal of the Abraham Lincoln Association* 23, no. 1 (Winter 2002), 58. See also W. Caleb McDaniel, "New Light on a Lincoln Quote," posted April 2, 2011; https://wcm1.web.rice.edu/new-light-on-lincoln-quote.html; Lincoln, *Collected Works*, vol. 2, 276; Edwin D. Freed, *Lincoln's Political Ambitions, Slavery and the Bible*, 72–73.

47. The Declaration was included in the *The Revised Statutes of Indiana*, a book Lincoln read as a youth; Merrill D. Peterson, "This Grand Pertinacity," 2; Emanuel Hertz, *The Hidden Lincoln: From the Letters and Papers of William H. Herndon* (Garden City, NY: Blue Ribbon Books, 1940), 20; he would walk to read the book at his friend David Turnham's; see Townsend, "Commonwealth of Kentucky Vs. Abraham Lincoln," 82.

48. Hertz, *Hidden Lincoln*, 192.

49. McCoy, "An Old-Fashioned Nationalism, 55.

50. Charles F. Adams, remarks delivered in *Proceedings of the Massachusetts Historical Society*, vol. 42 (1909), 148.

51. New York and New Jersey passed gradual emancipation acts on July 4 (in 1799 and 1804, respectively), and Nat Turner originally planned his rebellion for July 4, 1831; Maier, *American Scripture*, 198.

52. https://www.law.cornell.edu/supremecourt/text/60/393.

53. Douglas L. Wilson, *Lincoln Before Washington*, 167; Merrill D. Peterson, *"This Grand Pertinacity:" Abraham Lincoln and the Declaration of Independence* (Fort Wayne: Lincoln Museum, 1991), 7; see also Lincoln's speech at Chicago, October 27, 1854; Lincoln, *Collected Works*, vol. 2, 283–84.

54. Proverbs 25:11 reads: "A word fitly spoken is like apples of gold in pictures of silver."

55. Abraham Lincoln, "Fragment on the Constitution and Union," circa January 1861; *Collected Works*, vol. 4, 168–69.

56. Lincoln, *Collected Works*, vol. 2, 546; Lincoln expressed a similar thought in his speech on the Dred Scott decision, June 26, 1857; ibid., 406. As he put it then, the Declaration was "one hard nut to crack." In 1863 Lincoln would describe the Civil War as "an effort to overthrow the principle that all men were created equal." Douglas L. Wilson, *Lincoln Before Washington*, 178.

57. *Harper's Weekly*, March 9, 1861; see also Steve Currall, "When Lincoln Came to Independence Hall," Hidden City, February 25, 2013; http://hiddencityphila .org/2013/02/when-president-elect-lincoln-came-to-independence-hall.

58. *Philadelphia Inquirer*, February 23, 1861, 2.

59. On August 17, 1858, at Beardstown, Illinois, Lincoln said, "You may do anything with me you choose, if you will but heed these sacred principles. You may not only defeat me for the Senate, but you may take me and put me to death." Lincoln, *Collected Works*, vol. 2, 547; see also Burlingame, *Lincoln: A Life*, vol. 1, 146; and a manuscript fragment, circa July 1858, in Lincoln, *Collected Works of Abraham Lincoln*, vol. 2, between 482 and 483.

60. *Papers Read Before the Lancaster County Historical Society, March 5, 1909*, vol. 12, no. 3 (Lancaster, PA: 1909), 65.

61. Lincoln used "electric cord" in his speech of July 10, 1858, at Chicago, while discussing his belief that the Declaration was available to all people of all ethnic groups; see Lincoln, *Collected Works*, vol. 2, 500.

62. *New York Herald*, February 23, 1861, 6.

63. Richards had been photographing old Philadelphia buildings in the years before Lincoln's visit; see Frederick De Bourg Richards Photograph Collection, Library

Company of Philadelphia; https://www.philadelphiabuildings.org/pab/app/co_display_images.cfm/1163768.

64. http://imagesearchnew.library.illinois.edu/cdm/singleitem/collection/lincoln/id/24/rec/6.

65. *New York Herald*, February 23, 1861, 5.

66. *Philadelphia Inquirer*, February 23, 1861, 3.

67. Lincoln, *Collected Works*, vol. 4, 244–45.

68. Ibid.

69. When Lincoln lost his inaugural address briefly in Indianapolis, he worried that he lost his "certificate of moral character"; Lamon, *Recollections of Lincoln*, 36.

70. "Hills Capitol" in Harrisburg; https://commons.wikimedia.org/wiki/File:Hills_Capitol.jpg.

71. Holzer, *Lincoln, President-Elect*, 387.

72. *Papers Read Before the Lancaster County Historical Society, March 5, 1909*, vol. 12, no. 3, 62.

73. Ibid., 74.

74. Norman Gasbarro, "Abraham Lincoln in Dauphin County," Civil War Blog; http://civilwar.gratzpa.org/2011/03/lincoln-in-dauphin-county

75. Colonel A. K. McClure, "How We Make Presidents: Recollections of Lincoln's Two Campaigns," *Saturday Evening Post* 172, no. 33, February 10, 1900, 710–71.

76. Colonel A. K. McClure, "The Night at Harrisburg," *McClure's*, vol. 5, June 1895, 91–96.

77. Hay, *Lincoln's Journalist*, 42.

78. Burlingame, *Lincoln: A Life*, vol. 2, 36–37; Swett, "Conspiracies of the Rebellion."

79. Clayton R. Newell, *The Regular Army Before the Civil War, 1845–1860* (Washington, D.C.: Center of Military History, United States Army, 2014), 50; Burlingame, *Lincoln: A Life*, vol. 2, 36–37.

80. Lamon, *Life of Abraham Lincoln*, 522; Holzer, *Lincoln, President-Elect*, 390–92; Burlingame, *Lincoln: A Life*, vol. 2, 34; Judd's account is given in Wilson and Davis, *Herndon's Informants*, 432–435.

81. Norma B. Cuthbert, *Lincoln and the Baltimore Plot*, 78

82. Nicolay and Hay, *Lincoln: A History*, vol. 3, 314–15; John Hay to Annie Johnston, February 22, 1861; Brown University Library. One member of the party prepared a will; *New York Herald*, February 24, 1861.

83. McClure, "Night at Harrisburg," 92.

84. Burlingame, *Lincoln: A Life*, vol. 2, 36.

85. McClure, "Night at Harrisburg," 92–93.

86. Pinkerton, *Spy of the Rebellion*, 93; the wires were cut by Andrew Wynne, a lineman, who climbed poles two miles outside the city; Lamon, *Life of Abraham Lincoln*, 521

87. Holzer, *Lincoln, President-Elect*, 392.

88. Cuthbert, *Lincoln and the Baltimore Plot*, xvi; some accounts also have Lincoln wearing a shawl; Holzer, *Lincoln, President-Elect*, 394.

89. Pinkerton, *Spy of the Rebellion*, 86; Pinkerton, *History and Evidence of the Passage of Abraham Lincoln*, 21–22, 29–33. The officials were G. C. Franciscus and Enoch Lewis, the telegraph operator was John Pitcairn Jr. Franciscus had arranged the train; Cuthbert, *Lincoln and the Baltimore Plot*, 12–15.

90. Andrew Curtin, "Why Seward Was Put Aside for Lincoln," in *Lincoln Among His Friends*, 195–200.

91. Claude R. Flory, "Garman, Black and the 'Baltimore Plot'," *Pennsylvania Magazine of History and Biography* 94, no. 1, January 1970, 101–3.

92. Holzer, *Lincoln, President-Elect*, 393.

93. Norman Gasbarro, "Abraham Lincoln in Dauphin County," Civil War Blog; http://civilwar.gratzpa.org/2011/03/lincoln-in-dauphin-county.

94. Pinkerton, *History and Evidence of the Passage of Abraham Lincoln*, 33; Flory, "Garman, Black and the 'Baltimore Plot'," 101–3. The engineer was Ed Black; the fireman was Daniel E. Garman.

CHAPTER 14: THE RIVER OF NIGHT

1. Charles P. Dare, *Philadelphia, Wilmington and Baltimore Railroad Guide; Containing a Description of the Scenery, Rivers, Towns, Villages, and Objects of Interest along the Line of Road* (Philadelphia: Fitzgibbon and Van Ness, 1856), 142.

2. Homer, *The Odyssey*, trans. E. V. Rieu (London: Penguin Books, 1946), https://archive.org/stream/TheOdyssey/TXT/00000166.txt.

3. *Arlington House, VA* (1867–1871), Prints and Photographs Division, Library of Congress.

4. See *Adams Family Correspondence*, vol. 4, 155n; More recently, Henry Adams and William "Roony" Lee (both present at the dinner) had been Harvard classmates together; Adams wrote about Roony Lee in *The Education of Henry Adams*, and created a major Lee character (Madeleine Lee) in his 1880 novel *Democracy*. Earlier the same day, Charles Francis Adams Jr. noted in his diary that Seward complained of waiting for Lincoln, "kissing girls and growing his whiskers," while the crisis grew in Washington; diary of Charles Francis Adams, Jr., February 22, 1861; I am grateful to Sara Georgini of the Massachusetts Historical Society for her transcription.

5. See George Washington Parke Custis, *Recollections and Private Memoirs of Washington* (New York: Derby and Jackson, 1860), 57. See also Murray H. Nelligan,

Custis-Lee Mansion: The Robert E. Lee Memorial (Washington: National Park Service, 1966), B. J. Lossing, "A House," *Harper's Monthly Magazine* (September 1853).

6. William George Rudy, "Interpreting America's First Grecian Style House: The Architectural Legacy of George Washington Parke Custis and George Hadfield" (Master's Thesis, University of Maryland, 2010), 21; another source claims that the inspiration for Arlington House was the Temple of Theseus (now known as the Temple of Hephaestus) at Athens; *Harper's Monthly Magazine* 7, no. 40 (September 1853), 436.

7. On February 22, Lee was at Indianola, Texas, awaiting a steamer to New Orleans; see Douglas Southall Freeman, *R.E. Lee: A Biography* (New York: Charles Scribner's Sons, 1936), I, 428–429; as Union soldiers tore down Lee's orchards, they repurposed the wood for telegraph poles; see Jamie Stiehm, "The War Comes Home for Lee", New York Times, July 30, 2011.

8. Henry Adams, *Education of Henry Adams*, 41, 45, 84.

9. Frederick Gutekunst, Pennsylvania Railroad Stereograph Collection, Library Company of Philadelphia.

10. Pinkerton, *Spy of the Rebellion*, 86; Pinkerton, *History and Evidence of the Passage of Abraham Lincoln*; 21–22, 29–33; Stashower, *Hour of Peril*, 273.

11. Stephen Fiske, "When Lincoln Was First Inaugurated," in *Lincoln Among His Friends*, 305.

12. *Philadelphia Inquirer*, February 23, 1861, 8

13. *Philadelphia Inquirer*, cited in Norman Gasbarro, "Abraham Lincoln in Dauphin County," Civil War Blog, http://civilwar.gratzpa.org/2011/03/lincoln-in-dauphin-county.

14. Cuthbert, *Lincoln and the Baltimore Plot*, 76.

15. Ibid., 77, 132; Pinkerton described Lincoln's hat as brown in one account and black in another (Cuthbert, 15); Cleveland Moffatt, "How Allan Pinkerton Thwarted the First Plot to Assassinate Lincoln," *McClure's* (November 1894), 529.

16. Holzer, *Lincoln, President-Elect*, 394; in his 1864 comments to Lossing, Lincoln did not mention this threat.

17. Cuthbert, *Lincoln and the Baltimore Plot*, 79.

18. In his own reminiscence of these events, given to Benson J. Lossing in 1864, Lincoln remembered some of these details inaccurately; he thought that Pinkerton had gone ahead to Baltimore without him, and he added Norman Judd to the entourage; Cuthbert, *Lincoln and the Baltimore Plot*, xv–xvi.

19. Dare, *Philadelphia, Wilmington and Baltimore Railroad Guide*, 41.

20. Cuthbert, *Lincoln and the Baltimore Plot*, 14–16; 75, 77; Pinkerton, *History and*

Evidence of the Passage of Abraham Lincoln, 27–28. Pinkerton gives the departure time as 10:55 p.m. in one place (*History and Evidence*) and as 11:50 in another (Cuthbert, 77).

21. Pinkerton, *History and Evidence of the Passage of Abraham Lincoln*, 35–36; Cuthbert, *Lincoln and the Baltimore Plot*, 80, 144; Pinkerton, *Spy of the Rebellion*, 95.

22. Cuthbert, *Lincoln and the Baltimore Plot*, 144.

23. Cuthbert, *Lincoln and the Baltimore Plot*, 16, 77, 79. The Philadelphia, Wilmington and Baltimore was a pioneer in sleeping cars; see John H. White, Jr., *The American Railroad Passenger Car*, 209

24. Cuthbert, *Lincoln and the Baltimore Plot*, 79, 81.

25. Lincoln would meet Melville at the White House exactly a month later, on March 22, 1861; Leyda, *Melville Log*, vol. 2, 637.

26. *New York Herald*, February 23, 1861, 2.

27. Cuthbert, *Lincoln and the Baltimore Plot*, 15, 79, 81.

28. F. R. Shoemaker to Abraham Lincoln, October 17, 1860; Abraham Lincoln papers, Library of Congress; the Mason-Dixon line is also a North-South line between Maryland and Delaware.

29. Lincoln crossed the Mason-Dixon line near Elkton, Maryland.

30. *Harper's Weekly*, February 23, 1861, 124; Cuthbert, *Lincoln and the Baltimore Plot*, 16.

31. Dare, *Philadelphia, Wilmington and Baltimore Railroad Guide*, 54.

32. The Susquehanna was too wide to bridge, and trains took a steamship across the Bay at Havre de Grace; see Cuthbert, *Lincoln and the Baltimore Plot*, 4, 126; Villard, *Memoirs*, vol. 1, 163.

33. Pinkerton, *Spy of the Rebellion*, 96.

34. Cuthbert, *Lincoln and the Baltimore Plot*, 21.

35. Frederick Douglass, *Life and Times of Frederick Douglass* (Hartford, CT: Park, 1882), vol. 2, 247–49.

36. Cuthbert, *Lincoln and the Baltimore Plot*, 23.

37. Dare, *Philadelphia, Wilmington and Baltimore Railroad Guide*, 31–33, 38–39.

38. Pinkerton, *Spy of the Rebellion*, 96.

39. The poem had no title in the 1855 edition of *Leaves of Grass*; then it was titled "Night Poem" in the 1856 edition; finally Whitman called it "The Sleepers" in 1871; see Ed Folsom's notes, "Background of 'The Sleepers;'" http://www.classroomelectric.org/volume3/folsom/background.html.

40. Prints and Photographs Division, Library of Congress.

41. Dare, *Philadelphia, Wilmington and Baltimore Railroad Guide*, 28–29.

42. The President Street depot was not yet built in 1838, but the train Douglass took, toward Philadelphia, left from the same location.

43. Cuthbert, *Lincoln and the Baltimore Plot*, 81.

44. *The Daily Exchange* (Baltimore), February 23, 1861, lists Baltimore's shipping news.

45. Martin Ford, "Gangs of Baltimore," *Humanities* vol. 29, number 3 (May/June 2008) https://www.neh.gov/humanities/2008/mayjune/feature/gangs-balti more.

46. Ferrandini (there are variant spellings) was inspired by the efforts of an Italian nationalist, Felice Orsini, to assassinate Napoleon III in 1858; Cuthbert, *Lincoln and the Baltimore Plot*, 7, 35–37.

47. Leroy Graham, *Baltimore: The Nineteenth Century Black Metropolis* (Lanham, MD: University Press of America, 1982), 252; Christopher Phillips, *Freedom's Port: The African American Community of Baltimore, 1790–1860* (Urbana: University of Illinois Press, 1997), 57, 89, 184, 195, 204–5.

48. See "Black Marylanders 1860," part of "Legacy of Slavery in Maryland," a website created by the Maryland State Archives, http://slavery.msa.maryland.gov /html/research/census1860.html.

49. Christopher Phillips, *Freedom's Port*.

50. Evitts, *A Matter of Allegiances*, 109.

51. Martin Ford, "The Gangs of Baltimore," *Humanities* vol. 29, number 3 (May/June 2008) https://www.neh.gov/humanities/2008/mayjune/feature/gangs -baltimore.

52. J. Thomas Scharf, *The Chronicles of Baltimore* (Baltimore: Turnbull Brothers, 1874), 574; Henry Adams, *Great Secession Winter*, 19.

53. In Maryland, Lincoln received 2,294 votes, as opposed to 42,482 for Breckenridge, 41,760 for Bell, and 5,966 for Douglas; see http://www.presidency.ucsb .edu/showelection.php?year=1860; He received 1,082 votes in Baltimore; *Cincinnati Daily Press*, November 7, 1860.

54. Three days after Lincoln won the presidency, Maryland's governor, Thomas H. Hicks, wrote to a Southern friend, wondering if they were sending people to kill the president-elect; see Scharf, *Chronicles of Baltimore*, 584; letter from Governor Thomas H. Hicks to E. H. Webster, November 9, 1860.

55. Burlingame, *Lincoln: A Life*, vol. 2, 33.

56. Cuthbert, *Lincoln and the Baltimore Plot*, 6–7.

57. H. M. Flint, *Railroads of the United States, Their History and Statistics* (Philadelphia: John E. Potter, 1868), 231.

58. The assassins believed that Lincoln was coming from Harrisburg into Baltimore's Calvert Street Station and intended to attack him there, in a narrow vestibule; Cuthbert, *Lincoln and the Baltimore Plot*, 5–7, 27; see also Dawes, "Winter Before the War," 105–6.

59. "Mr. Lincoln Passes Through But Does Not Stop in Baltimore," *Baltimore and Ohio Magazine* 9, February 1922, 9–11.

60. Cuthbert, *Lincoln and the Baltimore Plot*, 16, 81; Lamon, *Life of Abraham Lincoln*, 525

61. Allan Pinkerton, *Spy of the Rebellion*, 97.

62. Wilson and Davis, *Herndon's Informants*, 519; I am grateful to Douglas L. Wilson for help with this point.

63. "Mr. Lincoln Passes Through But Does Not Stop in Baltimore," *Baltimore and Ohio Magazine* 9 (February 1922), 9–11.

64. Benjamin Henry Latrobe, "Washington Monument," Prints and Photographs Division, Library of Congress; http://www.loc.gov/pictures/item/200169 8065.

65. Morse laid out his original telegraph from the old Supreme Court chamber of the Capitol to the Pratt Street railroad depot in Baltimore; Robert Luther Thompson, *Wiring a Continent*, 24. In April 1861 the telegraph lines were cut, increasing the danger to Washington; Henry Villard described it as "an island in midocean in a state of entire isolation;" Villard, *Memoirs*, vol. 1, 167.

66. Karal Ann Marling, "The United States Capitol as Mausoleum: or, Who's Buried in Washington's Tomb?," in Kennon, *Republic for the Ages*, 448.

67. Goodheart, "Ashen Ruin."

68. George W. Walling, *Recollections of a New York Chief of Police* (New York: Caxton, 1887), 72–73.

69. Hungerford, *Baltimore and Ohio Railroad*, 164, 172.

70. The northern terminal of the Richmond, Fredericksburg and Potomac Railroad was at Quantico, about thirty miles south of Washington; ibid., 157.

71. Hungerford, *Baltimore and Ohio Railroad*, 166–67.

72. Thomas Viaduct, ca. 1858, engraving from *The United States Illustrated*; https://en.wikipedia.org/wiki/Thomas_Viaduct#/media/File:Thomas_Viaduct_wide_angle_shot.jpg.

73. I am grateful to Michael Brewer of NOAA for these weather calculations.

74. Lincoln, *Collected Works*, vol. 4, 241.

75. Starr, *Lincoln and the Railroads*, 101–2.

76. *Lincoln's Own Stories*, ed. Anthony Gross (Garden City, NY: Garden City Publishing, 1912), 184.

77. Henry Adams, *Education of Henry Adams*, 33–34.

78. Weather information courtesy of Michael Brewer of NOAA.

79. "Boundary Stones of the District of Columbia," http://www.boundarystones.org.; Fred E. Woodward, "A Ramble Along the Boundary Stones of the District of Columbia with a Camera," *Records of the Columbia Historical Society* 10 (1907):

63–87. The African-American scientist Benjamin Banneker assisted with the placement of the stones; "Benjamin Banneker and the Boundary Stones of the District of Columbia," National Park Service; https://www.nps.gov/places/sw-9 -intermediate-boundary-stone-of-the-district-of-columbia.htm. I am grateful to Stephen Powers for his research.

80. Thomas Jefferson to Martha Jefferson Randolph, January 26, 1801; Massachusetts Historical Society.

81. Augustus Kollner, "Tiber Creek Northeast of the Capitol," 1839, Prints and Photographs Division, Library of Congress; https://www.loc.gov/item/2004 662005.

82. Three out of four new arrivals in Washington came from the South. Asch and Musgrove, *Chocolate City*, 105.

83. Lamon, *Life of Abraham Lincoln*, 525.

84. "Philip Reid and the Statue of Freedom," Architect of the Capitol; https://www .aoc.gov/philip-reid-and-statue-freedom; https://www.aoc.gov/art/other-stat ues/statue-freedom; Carol Morello, "Slave Who Helped Build Capitol's Statue of Freedom Honored with Historical Marker," *Washington Post*, April 16, 2014; Maggie Esteves, "Building Freedom: The Story of an Enslaved Man and a Statue," U.S. Capitol Historical Society; https://uschs.wordpress.com/tag/clark-mills.

85. James Borchert, "The Rise and Fall of Washington's Inhabited Alleys: 1852–1972," *Records of the Columbia Historical Society* 71–72 (1971–1972): 267–88; Dorothy Provine, "The Economic Position of the Free Blacks in the District of Columbia, 1800–1860," *Journal of Negro History* 58, no. 1 (January 1973): 61–72.

86. Howard Gillette Jr., ed., *Southern City, National Ambition: The Growth of Early Washington*, 1800–1860 (Washington, D.C.: George Washington University, 1995), 9, 86.

87. An act of 1827 prohibited free African-Americans from going out after ten. See Letitia Woods Brown, *Free Negroes in the District of Columbia* (New York: Oxford University Press, 1972), 140.

88. Asch and Musgrove, *Chocolate City*, 100.

89. Georgia's legislature threatened to secede if slavery was ever removed from the District. Ibid., 97; http://civilwardc.org/interpretations/narrative/emancipa tion.php.

90. Michael Burlingame, *The Inner Lincoln* (Urbana: University of Illinois Press, 1994), 25–26; Kenneth J. Winkle, "Emancipation in the District of Columbia," Civil War Washington; http://civilwardc.org/interpretations/narrative/eman cipation.php; see also http://www.lincolninwashington.com/2012/10/31 /lincoln-and-the-abolitionists-at-the-sprigg-house.

91. Abraham Lincoln, Speech at Peoria, October 16, 1854; *Complete Works*, vol. 2,

253; Robert S. Pohl, "The Slave Market on East Capitol: A Capitol Hill Urban Legend," http://www.capitalcommunitynews.com/content/slave-market-east -capitol-0.

92. Adam Goodheart, "A Capital Under Slavery's Shadow," *New York Times*, February 25, 2011; Damani Davis, "Slavery and Emancipation in the Nation's Capital," Prologue (Spring 2010), https://www.archives.gov/publications /prologue/2010/spring/dcslavery.html. See also the "Slave Market of America," broadside, 1836, Prints and Photographs Division, Library of Congress; http://www.loc.gov/pictures/item/2008661294.

93. "Washington Depot with U.S. Capitol in the Distance," from *Photographic Views of the Baltimore and Ohio Railroad and Its Branches from Lake Erie to the Sea* (1872) Prints and Photographs Division, Library of Congress.

94. Elihu B. Washburne, in Allen Thorndike Rice, *Reminiscences of Abraham Lincoln*, 37–38.

95. Cuthbert, *Lincoln and the Baltimore Plot*, 82; Allan Pinkerton claimed that they descended "among the first" to disembark, but Washburne's detailed account insists that they were the final passengers to leave the train.

96. Thorndike Rice, *Reminiscences of Abraham Lincoln*, 19–20.

97. Ibid., 37–38.

98. Several accounts claim that Seward was there at the station to greet Lincoln. Pinkerton claimed so in 1866 (see Cuthbert, *Lincoln and the Baltimore Plot*, 16), as did the *Philadelphia Inquirer*, February 25, 1861. Washington papers also supported the claim. Charles Francis Adams Sr. wrote that Seward was there, in his diary entry, February 23, 1861; Massachusetts Historical Society. But Pinkerton claimed otherwise in the account he composed in 1861, immediately after the trip, and Washburne remembered that Seward met them at Willard's Hotel (Allen Thorndike Rice, *Reminiscences of Abraham Lincoln*, 39). Lamon also remembered Seward arriving at Willard's; *Life of Abraham Lincoln*, 526.

99. Forney, *Anecdotes*, 255.

100. Alexander Gardner photograph of Abraham Lincoln, February 24, 1861; Prints and Photographs Division, Library of Congress.

101. *National Republican* (Washington, D.C.), February 25, 1861.

102. A Texas senator, Louis Wigfall, still in Washington, was overheard saying that he was "disgusted" at his Southern friends for failing to kill Lincoln; to his mind, it was a test of the South's credibility. He added, "he was tempted to say he would have nothing more to do with such a d-d set of humbugs." Strong, diary entry from March 7, 1861, *Diary of George Templeton Strong*, vol. 3, 107. See also Poore, *Reminiscences*, vol. 2, 62.

103. *New York Herald*, February 23, 1861; Dunn, "Knights of the Golden Circle," 561.

104. *Baltimore Sun,* February 25, 1861. The crowd rushed into Hamlin's car and nearly removed him; Hamlin, *Life and Times of Hannibal Hamlin,* 390.

105. Diary of Charles Francis Adams, Sr., February 24, 1861; Massachusetts Historical Society; I am grateful to Sara Georgini for help relating to the Adams family; Adams recorded a long entry for February 25 that included Lincoln's explanation of the decision to go through Baltimore in secrecy.

106. Prints and Photographs Division, Library of Congress; see also Ted Widmer, "Better Angels," *New York Times,* March 3, 2011; https://opinionator.blogs.ny times.com/2011/03/03/lincoln-addresses-the-nation/#ftnWidmer.

107. *New York Herald,* February 24, 1861, 4.

108. Robert H. Browne, *Abraham Lincoln and the Men of His Time,* vol. 2. (Cincinnati: Jennings and Pye, 1901), 506; Holzer, *Lincoln, President-Elect,* 389.

109. Burlingame, *Lincoln: A Life,* vol. 2, 19, 21.

110. John G. Nicolay, "Some Incidents in Lincoln's Journey from Springfield to Washington," in *Oral History of Lincoln,* 110. Nicolay wrote evocatively of the journey in several places, including "The Journey to Washington," a chapter in Helen Nicolay, ed., *Personal Traits of Abraham Lincoln* (New York: Century, 1912), and an unpublished manuscript, "Lincoln's Speeches on the Journey to Washington," in John G. Nicolay Papers, Manuscript Division, Library of Congress.

111. Nicolay and Hay, *Lincoln: A History,* excerpted in *Century Illustrated Monthly* 35, December 1887, 266.

112. Prints and Photographs Division, Library of Congress.

113. *Washington (D.C.) Evening Star,* March 4, 1861; *National Republican* (Washington, D.C.), March 5, 1861.

114. *Washington (D.C.) Evening Star,* March 4, 1861.

115. Ibid.

116. Ibid.

117. *National Republican* , March 5, 1861.

118. Constance Green, *The Secret City: A History of Race Relations in the Nation's Capital* (Princeton, NJ: Princeton University Press, 1967), 56.

119. Helen Nicolay, *Personal Traits of Abraham Lincoln,* 168–169.

120. *Washington (D.C.) Evening Star,* March 4, 1861.

121. *Evening Star,* March 4, 1861. The *National Republican* (March 5) has the oath following the address; the *Evening Star* has the address following the oath; the *Evening Star* has more detail and better reporting.

122. Holzer, *Lincoln, President-Elect,* 453; Ted Widmer, "Better Angels," *New York Times,* March 3, 2011. Later that night, Charles Francis Adams Sr. wrote in his journal, "Thus ends this most trying period of our history;" Journal of Charles Francis Adams Sr., Massachusetts Historical Society.

EPILOGUE: HOME

1. Abraham Lincoln, photographed by Alexander Gardner, February 5, 1865; Prints and Photographs Division, Library of Congress, https://www.loc.gov /resource/cph.3a52094/; see also Errol Morris, "The Interminable, Everlasting Lincolns," *New York Times*, December 1, 2013.

2. Homer, *The Odyssey*, trans. Wilson, 187.

3. Martin P. Johnson, *Writing the Gettysburg Address* (Lawrence: University Press of Kansas, 2013), 71.

4. Phillip W. Magness and Sebastian Page, "Mr. Lincoln and Mr. Johnson," *New York Times*, February 1, 2012; "Employees and Staff: William Johnson," Mr. Lincoln's White House; http://www.mrlincolnswhitehouse.org/residents-visitors /employees-and-staff/employees-staff-william-johnson-1864. Johnson may have been buried at Arlington National Cemetery; a simple headstone there honors a "William H. Johnson" with the word *Citizen*. But the records were not very detailed for a young African-American. See also John E. Washington, *They Knew Lincoln*, ed. Kate Masur (New York: Oxford University Press, 2018), 127–34.

5. The *River Queen* had a history of its own, as the setting for the Hampton Roads Conference in February 1865, when Alexander Stephens and Lincoln met one last time. It would endure as a ferryboat in New England for decades until it returned to the Potomac and burned in a fire in 1911. In its final years, it was "an excursion boat for negroes."

6. "Abraham Lincoln in Virginia;" https://www.virginia.org/lincolninvirginia.

7. David D. Porter, *Incidents and Anecdotes of the Civil War* (New York: D. Appleton, 1885), 281.

8. Marquis Adolphe de Chambrun, *Impressions of Lincoln and the Civil War*, trans. Adelbert de Chambrun (New York: Random House, 1952), 31.

9. Porter, *Incidents and Anecdotes of the Civil War*, 294.

10. William H. Crook, *Through Five Administrations: Reminiscences of William H. Crook, Body-guard to President Lincoln*, ed. by Margarita Spalding Garry (New York: Harper and Brothers, 1910), 52; Porter, *Incidents and Anecdotes of the Civil War*, 284, 291–92.

11. Charles Carleton Coffin, "Late Scenes in Richmond," *Atlantic* (June 1865); Kevin Morrow, "Lincoln's Triumphant Visit to Richmond," *New York Times*, April 7, 2015.

12. Porter, *Incidents and Anecdotes of the Civil War*, 297–98.

13. Ibid., 296–98; while Porter did not offer this story until his book was published in 1885, Adolphe de Chambrun recorded, on the same day, that Lincoln would soon be acting decisively and would perhaps give a speech on the situation of African-Americans; this statement is clearer in the original French version than it

is in translation; see René de Chambrun, ed., *Un Francais Chez les Lincoln* (Paris: Librairie Academique Perrin, 1957), 88.

14. Andrew Ward, *The Slaves' War*, 245.

15. Ruth Painter Randall, *Mary Lincoln*, 371.

16. Marquis Adolphe de Chambrun, "Personal Recollections of Mr. Lincoln," *Scribner's*, January 1893, 26–38.

17. Crook, *Through Five Administrations*, 13, 57.

18. Ibid., 54, 59. Crook also believed John Wilkes Booth and his accomplices were trying to harm Lincoln while he was staying on the river; see ibid., 46, and Porter, *Incidents and Anecdotes*, 303. Coffin described Lincoln's visit in "Late Scenes in Richmond."

19. Marvin Fisher, *Workshops in the Wilderness*, 160.

20. *Richmond Custom House and Capitol, April 1865*; Prints and Photographs Division, Library of Congress; https://www.loc.gov/item/2018666787.

21. Isaac Arnold, *The Life of Abraham Lincoln* (Chicago: A. C. McClurg, 1906), 435; Ida M. Tarbell, "The Death of Abraham Lincoln," *McClure's* 13, August 1899, 375.

22. *Malice* was a word he had chosen for one of his most resonant lines in the second inaugural, near the end.

23. *Lincoln: Selected Speeches and Writings*, 53.

24. Lincoln added, "Since Willie's death, I catch myself every day involuntarily talking with him as if he were with me"; Waldo W. Braden, ed., *Building the Myth: Selected Speeches. Memorializing Abraham Lincoln* (Urbana: University of Illinois Press, 1990), 83.

25. Marquis Adolphe de Chambrun, *Impressions of Lincoln and the Civil War*, 83–84.

26. Ward Lamon told a famous but not entirely reliable story, about a vivid dream in which Lincoln encountered his own coffin in the East Room of the White House; Ruth Painter Randall, *Mary Lincoln*, 379.

27. Elizabeth Keckley, *Behind the Scenes with Lincoln in the White House: Memoirs of an African-American Seamstress* (Mineola, NY: Dover, 2006), 73, 75. She added her fear: "what an easy matter would it be to kill the President."

28. Blain Roberts and Ethan J. Kytle, "When Old Glory Returned to Fort Sumter," *New York Times*, April 16. 2015.

29. E. D. Townsend, *Anecdotes of the Civil War in the United States* (New York: D. Appleton, 1884), 210–20.

30. Roberts and Kytle, "When Old Glory Returned."

31. Welles probably wrote out his account on April 18; see *The Civil War Diary of Gideon Welles* (Urbana: Knox College Lincoln Studies Center and University of Illinois Press, 2014), 623–24. Don E. and Virginia Fehrenbacher suggest that

Welles later added the words "towards an indefinite shore," see *Recollected Words of Abraham Lincoln*, 547. The dream was also described in Frederick Seward, *Reminiscences*, 255; Seward was attending the cabinet meeting in place of his injured father.

32. Whitman, *Specimen Days*, 40; *New York Times*, March 12, 1865; John Burroughs, *Wake-Robin* (Boston: Houghton-Mifflin, 1904), 149–50.

33. Ruth Painter Randall, *Mary Todd Lincoln*, 380.

34. Crook, *Through Five Administrations*, 65. Crook surmised this was evidence of "his sudden changes of mood."

35. Ibid., 66–68.

36. Frederick and William Langenheim, *Niagara Falls, Summer View, Suspension Bridge, and Falls in Distance*, ca. 1856, Getty Center Open Content Program; https://commons.wikimedia.org/wiki/File:Langenheim_Brothers_(Frederick _and_William_Langenheim)_-_Niagara_Falls,_Summer_View,_Suspen sion_Bridge,_and_Falls_in_the_Distance_-_Google_Art_Project.jpg.

37. Henry James, *Notes of a Son and Brother* (New York: Charles Scribner's Sons, 1914), 430.

38. Braden, *Building the Myth*, 30.

39. Charles I. Glicksberg, *Walt Whitman and the Civil War* (Philadelphia: 1933), 174–175

40. *New York Times*, March 12, 1865.

41. Hoch, *Lincoln Trail in Pennsylvania*, 140. In his speech of June 16, 1864, Lincoln paraphrased the line, saying of the war, "it has carried mourning to almost every home, until it can almost be said that the 'heavens are hung with black;' " Lincoln, *Collected Works*, vol. 7, 364.

42. Arthur King Peters, *Seven Trails West* (New York: Abbeville, 1996), 166, 173, 190; Ted Widmer, "And the End Came," *New York Times*, March 3, 2015; David Homer Bates, *Lincoln in the Telegraph Office* (New York: The Century Co., 1907), 22, 174–182

43. When the name "Sprint" was selected for a new provider of long-distance telephone service in 1972, its name came from an acronym for Southern Pacific Railroad Internal Network Telecommunications; Tung-Hui Hu, *A Prehistory of the Cloud* (Cambridge, MA: MIT Press, 2015), 1, 5; Melissa Block, "Sprint Born from Railroad, Telephone Businesses," October 15, 2012, National Public Radio; http://www.npr.org/2012/10/15/162963607/sprint-born-from-railroad -telephone-businesses; Jane Tanner, "New Life for Old Railroads," *New York Times*, May 6, 2000, http://www.nytimes.com/2000/05/06/business/new -life-for-old-railroads-what-better-place-to-lay-miles-of-fiber-optic-cable.html.

44. David Homer Bates, *Lincoln in the Telegraph Office*, 371–72.

45. Arthur King Peters, *Seven Trails West*, 173; Peters mistakes Benjamin Harrison for his grandfather; San Francisco even got out a newspaper with the news on April 15; http://www.sfchronicle.com/news/article/Chronicle-Covers-How-Lincoln-s-death-helped-7247305.php; Martha Hodes points out that stretches of the West without telegraph service heard the news much later; see Hodes, *Mourning Lincoln*, 54–55.

46. Mary A. DeCredico, *Mary Boykin Chesnut*, 126; see also diary entry of Mary 2, 1865.

47. Victor Searcher, *The Farewell to Lincoln* (New York: Abingdon Press, 1965), 66; many came by special train; see Martha Hodes, *Mourning Lincoln*, 143.

48. Searcher, *Farewell to Lincoln*, 77.

49. Ibid., 65–66.

50. Ibid., 268.

51. James S. Bush, *The Death of President Lincoln: A Sermon Preached in Grace Church, Orange, New Jersey, April 16, 1865* (Orange, NJ: E. Gardner, 1865), 4

52. Searcher, *Farewell to Lincoln*, 80–81.

53. Allan Johnston, *Surviving Freedom: The Black Community of Washington, D.C., 1860–1880* (New York: Garland, 1993), 75, 107. Other sources give the number of incoming African-Americans as even higher; see "Washington, the Strategic Capital," Civil War Washington; http://civilwardc.org/interpretations/narrative/essay.php.

54. Searcher, *Farewell to Lincoln*, 83.

55. Ibid., 85.

56. Rubil Morales-Vazquez, "Redeeming a Sacred Pledge: The Plans to Bury George Washington in the Nation's Capital," in *Establishing Congress: The Removal to Washington, D.C., and the Election of 1800*, ed. Kenneth R. Bowling and Donald R. Kennon (Washington, D.C.: U.S. Capitol Historical Society, 2005).

57. S. M. Fassett, *President Abraham Lincoln's Railroad Funeral Car*, 1865, Prints and Photographs Division, Library of Congress; http://www.loc.gov/pictures/item/91732552/; "Lincoln Funeral Train Commemorative," WVNC Rails; http://wvncrails.weebly.com/lincoln-funeral-train-commemorative.html.

58. "Abraham Lincoln and the U.S. Capitol," Abraham Lincoln Online; http://www.abrahamlincolnonline.org/lincoln/sites/uscapitol.htm.

59. Nicolay and Hay, *Lincoln: A History*, x, 347.

60. Searcher, *Farewell to Lincoln*, 63, 267.

61. Hoch, *Lincoln Trail in Pennsylvania*, 123.

62. An elaborate private car designed for Franklin Roosevelt, the *Ferdinand Magellan*, or U.S. Car No. 1, is described in Robert Klara, *FDR's Funeral Train: A Betrayed Widow, a Soviet Spy, and a Presidency in the Balance* (New York: Palgrave

Macmillan, 2010), xvi; Edward G. Lengel, "Franklin D. Roosevelt's Train Ferdinand Magellan; White House Historical Association; https://www.whitehouse history.org/franklin-d-roosevelt-rsquo-s-train-ferdinand-magellan.

63. Searcher, *Farewell to Lincoln*, 87–89, 271. The car burned in a prairie grass fire, March 18, 1911; see Stephen J. Taylor, "The Fall of the House of Ford," Hoosier State Chronicles, April 14, 2015; also http://blog.newspapers.library.in.gov /tag/lincoln-funeral-train; George B. Abdill, *Civil War Railroads* (Seattle: Superior, 1961), 186; Scott D. Trostel, *The Lincoln Funeral Train: The Final Journey and National Funeral for Abraham Lincoln* (Fletcher, OH: Cam-Tech, 2002), 28–29.

64. *New York Tribune*, April 25, 1861, "With Malice Toward None," The Library of Congress Bicentennial Exhibition; https://www.loc.gov/exhibits/lincoln/in teractives/long-journey-home/apr_21/article_3_602a1_highlight_1.html.

65. Hay and Nicolay stayed aboard until Baltimore. Ward Lamon would go all the way. David Hunter guarded the coffin, as he had once guarded the president-elect. Elihu Washburne, who greeted Lincoln when he arrived, rode with him this time. Up ahead, in the pilot train, sat some of the railroad executives who had helped usher Lincoln in through Baltimore.

66. Searcher, *Farewell to Lincoln*, 71, 81, 90–91; Hoch, *Lincoln Trail in Pennsylvania*, 125; Abdill, *Civil War Railroads*, 187; William Coyle, *The Poet and the President: Whitman's Lincoln Poems*, 112.

67. General Edward Townsend wrote, "more people looked upon the remains of the late Commander- in-chief during this period than had ever before viewed the form of man from whom life had departed;" Searcher, *Farewell to Lincoln*, 249.

68. *The Funeral of President Lincoln, New York, April 25, 1865*, Prints and Photographs Division, Library of Congress; http://www.loc.gov/pictures/re source/stereo.1s01778.

69. Some diary entries described these rituals; see the diary of Alice Strickler Keyes, http://rememberinglincoln.fords.org/sites/default/files/AliceStricklerKeyes Diary.pdf.

70. Trostel, *Lincoln Funeral Train*, 65.

71. Searcher, *Farewell to Lincoln*, 288–89; Townsend, *Anecdotes of the Civil War*, 226, 230; Hoch, *Lincoln Trail in Pennsylvania*, 127–28.

72. Dorothy Meserve Kunhardt and Philip B. Kunhardt Jr., *Twenty Days* (New York: Harper and Row, 1965), 144.

73. Townsend, *Anecdotes of the Civil War*, 230. As many as three hundred thousand came to Philadelphia during the visit of the funeral train; see Kunhardt and Kunhardt Jr., *Twenty Days*, 147, 150.

74. Trostel, *Lincoln Funeral Train*, 83.

75. Martha Hodes, *Mourning Lincoln*, 152. Looking at New York's crowds, a writer, E. C. Stedman, wrote that a vulgar woman "is never so elegant as when in black."

76. Lewis Mumford, *The Brown Decades*, 3; Jay Winik, *April 1865*, 358.

77. Searcher, *Farewell to Lincoln*, 154.

78. William Pedersen and Michael R. Williams, *Franklin D. Roosevelt and Abraham Lincoln: Competing Perspectives on Two Great Presidencies* (New York: Routledge, 2016), 51. A radio dramatization of Lincoln's funeral train, *The Lonesome Train*, became popular in 1945; William Coyle, *The Poet and the President: Whitman's Lincoln Poems*, 116.

79. Trostel, *Lincoln Funeral Train*, 113.

80. Some accounts claim that George Pullman added his prototype sleeping car, the *Pioneer*, to the funeral train; John H. White Jr., *The American Railway Passenger Car* (Baltimore: Johns Hopkins University Press, 1978), 248–49; see also Joseph Husband, *The Story of the Pullman Car* (Chicago: A. C. McClurg, 1917), 28–35.

81. Searcher, *Farewell to Lincoln*, 240.

82. Ibid., 291.

83. Villard, *Lincoln on the Eve*, 99–100.

84. Jeremy Prichard, " 'Home is the Martyr': The Burial of Abraham Lincoln and the Fate of Illinois' Capital," *Journal of the Abraham Lincoln Association* 38, no. 1 (Winter 2017).

85. Townsend, *Anecdotes of the Civil War*, 241.

86. Prints and Photographs Division, Library of Congress; see also Elliot Carter, "Behind the Scenes at the Lincoln Memorial," Architect of the Capital: Hidden History in Washington D.C.; https://architectofthecapital.org/posts/2016/7/30/underneath-the-lincoln-memorial.

87. "Lincoln Memorial and 'I Have a Dream,' " Ghosts of D.C., https://ghostsofdc.org/2013/09/11/lincoln-memorial-dream/

88. Goodheart, "Lincoln's Funeral Train."

89. Braden, *Building the Myth*, 30–31.

90. Whitman, *Specimen Days*, 41.

91. Henry James, *Notes of a Son and Brother*, 430.

92. Jane Addams, "The Influence of Lincoln," chap. 2 in *Twenty Years at Hull-House* (New York: Macmillan, 1912), 23–42.

93. *Reminiscences of Augustus Saint-Gaudens*, vol. 1, 41–42; Saint-Gaudens saw Lincoln pass "on the corner of Twentieth or Twenty-First Street and Fifth Avenue."

94. Ibid., 51; Addams, "Influence of Lincoln."

95. Richard White, *Railroaded: The Transcontinentals and the Making of Modern America* (New York: W. W. Norton, 2011), passim.

96. Joshua Zeitz, *Lincoln's Boys: John Hay, John Nicolay, and the War for Lincoln's Image* (New York: Viking, 2014), 2.

97. Jason Emerson, *Lincoln the Inventor*, 46.

98. The date of this incident is given as 1863 or 1864; see Robert Todd Lincoln letter of May 6, 1919, in Paul M. Angle, ed., *A Portrait of Abraham Lincoln in Letters by his Oldest Son* (Chicago: Chicago Historical Society, 1968), 37–38.

99. Ted Widmer, "Did the American Civil War Ever End?," *New York Times*, June 4, 2015; Eric Foner, *Reconstruction*, 465–67.

100. Peter Z. Grossman, *American Express: The Unofficial History of the People Who Built the Great Financial Empire*, 70; the Sears empire would be built by Julius Rosenwald, who grew up near Lincoln's home in Springfield.

101. Brooks McNamara, *Day of Jubilee*, 109.

102. Paul H. Giddens, *Birth of the Oil Industry*, 128. The well had once included John Wilkes Booth among its investors. In Pennsylvania, which supplied 80 percent of the North's coal needs, production nearly doubled over the course of the war, from twelve million to twenty million tons a year; Barbara Freese, *Coal*, 127; "Coal and Iron," Pennsylvania Civil War 150; http://pacivilwar150.com/ThenNow /IndustryCommerce/CoalIron.html.

103. The portion of the Jefferson Davis highway in Alexandria was renamed in 2018.

104. Kathleen Brady, *Ida Tarbell: Portrait of a Muckraker* (New York: Seaview, 1984), 14. Ray Ginger, *The Bending Cross: A Biography of Eugene Victor Debs* (New Brunswick, NJ: Rutgers University Press, 1949), 230.

105. Prints and Photographs Division, Library of Congress; image created between 1909 and 1932.

106. Widmer, "The Other Gettysburg Address."

107. Whitman in conversation with Horace Traubel, September 26, 1888; cited in William Coyle, *The Poet and the President: Whitman's Lincoln Poems* (New York: Odyssey Press, 1962), 49.

108. Elizabeth Borgwardt, *A New Deal for the World: America's Vision for Human Rights* (Cambridge, MA: Harvard University Press, 2005), 29. Charles P. Stone, who aided Winfield Scott in the weeks preceding Lincoln's trip, helped to build the pedestal for the Statue of Liberty. The son of Samuel Felton was also a railroad executive, and led the U.S. Army's railroad operations in France during World War One.

109. Lincoln, *Collected Speeches*, VII, 512.

110. Abraham Lincoln, "Response to Serenade," November 10, 1864; Lincoln, *Collected Works*, vol. 8, 100–101; "Remarks at Poughkeepsie," February 19, 1861; ibid., vol. 4, 228.

111. Stephanie Miles, "Dark Side of the Moon: Forensic Analysis of Lewis M.

Rutherfurd's 'Moon,'" National Gallery of Canada, August 21, 2018; https://www
.gallery.ca/magazine/in-the-spotlight/dark-side-of-the-moon-forensic-analysis
-of-lewis-m-rutherfurds-moon; http://americanhistory.si.edu/collections
/search/object/nmah_1187790; Rutherfurd was the father of Lucy Mercer
Rutherfurd's husband, Winthrop Rutherfurd.

ACKNOWLEDGMENTS

1. Henry C. Whitney, cited in Daniel Kilham Dodge, *Abraham Lincoln: The Evolution of His Literary Style* (Urbana: University of Illinois Press, 2000), 11.

INDEX

Page numbers in *italics* refer to illustrations. Page numbers beginning with 475 refer to notes.

ABOUT THE AUTHOR

TED WIDMER is a Distinguished Lecturer at the Macaulay Honors College of the City University of New York. In addition to his teaching, he writes actively about American history in the *Washington Post*, the *New Yorker*, and the *New York Times*, where he helped to create the *Disunion* feature about the Civil War. He is a Senior Fellow at the Carnegie Council for Ethics in International Affairs.